GLOBALIZATION

Also by Jan Aart Scholte

ENCYCLOPEDIA OF GLOBALIZATION (*co-editor, forthcoming*)
CIVIL SOCIETY AND GLOBAL DEMOCRACY (*forthcoming*)
CIVIL SOCIETY AND GLOBAL FINANCE (*editor*)
CIVIL SOCIETY VOICES AND THE INTERNATIONAL MONETARY FUND
CONTESTING GLOBAL GOVERNANCE: Multilateral Economic Institutions and Global Social Movements (*co-author*)
INTERNATIONAL RELATIONS OF SOCIAL CHANGE

Globalization

A Critical Introduction

Second Edition

Jan Aart Scholte

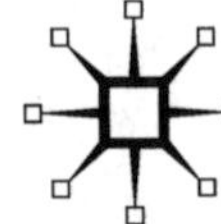

First edition 2000
Second edition 2005

Published by
PALGRAVE MACMILLAN
Houndmills, Basingstoke, Hampshire RG21 6XS and
175 Fifth Avenue, New York, N.Y. 10010
Companies and representatives throughout the world

PALGRAVE MACMILLAN is the global academic imprint of the Palgrave Macmillan division of St. Martin's Press, LLC and of Palgrave Macmillan Ltd. Macmillan® is a registered trademark in the United States, United Kingdom and other countries. Palgrave is a registered trademark in the European Union and other countries.

ISBN-13: 978–1–4039–0448–5 hardback
ISBN 10: 1–4039–0448–0 hardback
ISBN-13: 978–0–333–97702–6 paperback
ISBN 10: 0–333–97702–5 paperback

This book is printed on paper suitable for recycling and made from fully managed and sustained forest sources.

A catalogue record for this book is available from the British Library.

A catalog record for this book is available from the Library of Congress

10 9 8 7 6 5 4 3 2 1
14 13 12 11 10 09 08 07 06 05

Printed in China

Summary of Contents

List of Boxes xi

Preface to the Second Edition xiii

Preface to the First Edition xvii

Acknowledgements xix

List of Abbreviations xx

Introduction 1

PART I FRAMEWORK OF ANALYSIS

1 Globalization Debates 13

2 Defining Globalization 49

3 Globalization in History 85

4 Explaining Globalization 121

PART II CHANGE AND CONTINUITY

5 Globalization and Production: From Capitalism to Hypercapitalism 159

6 Globalization and Governance: From Statism to Polycentrism 185

7 Globalization and Identity: From Nationalism to Hybridization 224

8 Globalization and Knowledge: From Rationalism to Reflexivity 256

PART III NORMATIVE AND POLICY ISSUES

9 Globalization and (In)Security 279

10 Globalization and (In)Equality 316

11 Globalization and (Un)Democracy 348

12 (Re)constructing Future Globalizations 382

Conclusion 424

Bibliography 426

Index 477

Contents

List of Boxes xi

Preface to the Second Edition xiii

Preface to the First Edition xvii

Acknowledgements xix

List of Abbreviations xx

Introduction 1

Framework of analysis 2
Change and continuity 4
Normative and policy issues 6

PART I FRAMEWORK OF ANALYSIS

1 Globalization Debates 13

Main points of this chapter 13
Where to start? 15
Continuity or change? 22
Liberation or shackles? 29
What to do? 37
Conclusion 47

2 Defining Globalization 49

Main points of this chapter 49
Rise of the g-word 50
Starting premises for definition 52
Redundant concepts of globalization 54
A way forward 59
Qualifications 75
Conclusion 84

3 Globalization in History 85

Main points of this chapter 85
Intimations of globality: to the nineteenth century 87
Incipient globalization: to the mid-twentieth century 91

Contemporary accelerated globalization 101
Conclusion 117

4 Explaining Globalization 121

Main points of this chapter 121
Contending theories 123
An eclectic synthesis 135
Conclusion 152

PART II CHANGE AND CONTINUITY

5 Globalization and Production: From Capitalism to Hypercapitalism 159

Main points of this chapter 159
Expanded commodification 161
Altered organization 177
Conclusion 183

6 Globalization and Governance: From Statism to Polycentrism 185

Main points of this chapter 185
The obsolescence of statism 188
The reconstructed state 192
Multi-scalar public governance 202
Privatized governance 214
(Global) civil society 218
Conclusion 221

7 Globalization and Identity: From Nationalism to Hybridization 224

Main points of this chapter 224
Globalization and the nationality principle 227
Plural national identities 231
Nonterritorial identities 239
Hybridization 252
Conclusion 254

8 Globalization and Knowledge: From Rationalism to Reflexivity 256

Main points of this chapter 256
Epistemology 258
Ontology 267

Methodology 269
Aesthetics 273
Conclusion 274

PART III NORMATIVE AND POLICY ISSUES

9 **Globalization and (In)Security** **279**

Main points of this chapter 279
Peace 281
Crime 284
Ecological integrity 285
Health 288
Poverty 289
Financial stability 294
Employment 296
Working conditions 300
Identity 304
Knowledge 306
Social cohesion 308
Conclusion 311

10 **Globalization and (In)Equality** **316**

Main points of this chapter 316
Class inequalities 320
Country inequalities 325
Gender inequalities 334
Other inequalities 340
Conclusion 344

11 **Globalization and (Un)Democracy** **348**

Main points of this chapter 348
The limits of statist liberal democracy 351
Citizen ignorance 355
Institutional process failures 361
Structural inequalities 371
Conclusion 380

12 **(Re)constructing Future Globalizations** **382**

Main points of this chapter 382
General policy strategy 383
Enhancing human security 396

Enhancing social equality 404
Enhancing democracy 410
Towards implementation 417
Conclusion 421

Conclusion **424**

Bibliography 426

Index 477

List of Boxes

Core theses on globalization 8
Globalization debates in summary 47
Manifestations of globality in summary 74
Summary chronology of incipient globalization, 1850s–1950s 100
Summary indicators of accelerated globalization in contemporary history 117
Contending social explanations of globalization 135
Principal dynamics of globalization 153
Implications of globalization for production in summary 184
Implications of globalization for governance in summary 222
Implications of globalization for identity in summary 254
Implications of globalization for knowledge in summary 274
Globalization and (in)security in summary 312
Globalization and (in)equality in summary 345
Globalization and (un)democracy in summary 380
Towards more humane globalization 422

Preface to the Second Edition

Books on globalization date quickly in the early twenty-first century. It is only five years since the publication of the first edition, but rapid developments in the practice and research of globalization, as well as in my own thoughts and experiences of globality, have already necessitated a large-scale revision.

In terms of concrete actions and trends, the first edition was completed only a few months after the anti-WTO protests in Seattle and before the subsequent upsurge of high-profile resistance against prevailing policy approaches to globalization. It was written before the striking militarization of globalization fuelled by the attacks of 9/11, wars in Afghanistan and Iraq, heightened disputes over nuclear proliferation, and intensified state surveillance of citizens. Moreover, it predated the Bush Administration's retreat from multilateralism, the introduction of the euro, and the WTO impasse at Cancún. The intervening years have in addition brought further so-called 'Post-Washington Consensus' reforms of policies towards economic globalization. Hence the book has required considerable updating to catch up with current events.

Of course it is easy to overestimate the significance of the short-term beat of history. The immediacy of recent occurrences, crammed into our consciousness by 24/7 media saturation, can easily distract us from deeper, more pervasive, and more persistent features of social relations. Globalization is largely a matter of what the historian Fernand Braudel called the *longue durée*, the extended time frame of generations and centuries where the principal features and forces of societal development tend to reside (Braudel, 1958). Hence, although events of five years may put some aspects of globalization into sharper relief or a different light, it is unlikely that core attributes of the process would change in such a short period. Surface appearances of globality like the SARS health scare of 2003 come and go; the deeper trend of growing transplanetary social connectedness persists.

Globalization still matters very much in 2005. Yes, certain calculations of a few types of global movements have of late shown a year-on-year deceleration. For example, foreign exchange turnover declined between 1998 and 2001 owing to developments such as the introduction of the euro, although these transactions had increased substantially again by 2004. The rate of foreign direct investment (FDI) inflows slowed for three years in 2001–3, although FDI too has since rebounded. In fact, almost all empirical indicators of globality have persisted and often risen further in significance since 2000. Daily life continues to be increasingly suffused with issues of global health, global ecology, global travel, global communications, global military activities, global production processes, global markets, global meanings, global regulations, and global social movements. In the light of this continued significance it is hardly surprising that the number of references to 'globalization' in the Library of Congress catalogue has multiplied more than sevenfold in the five years since the first edition (LoC, 1999, 2005).

Thus several recent proclamations of a purported end of globalization are unsustainable (Gray, 2001; James, 2001; Rugman, 2001; Ralston Saul, 2004; Rosenberg, 2005). To be sure, many exuberant claims of an earlier generation of writings (including some by the present author) about the scale, scope, intensity and impact of globalization need to be qualified or abandoned. For example, the growth of transplanetary connections between people is clearly not prompting the end of geography, the demise of the state, the disappearance of the nation, or the dissolution of modernity. However, a scaling down of previous exaggerations about globality should not be confused with a decline in actual globality. Obituaries for globalization are highly premature.

Indeed, the better literature on globalization has become progressively more sophisticated over the 20 years since the concept entered academic circulation. Such writings offer tighter conceptualization, more evidence, and greater nuance. Nevertheless, significant challenges remain for future research on globalization. For one thing, global (as distinct from international) data continue to be in short supply. Most statistics are still calculated in relation to state-country units. In addition, little tightly consolidated and systematically elaborated theorization of globalization is available. The literature to date has been much richer in description and prescription than in explanation. Meanwhile, interdisciplinarity generally remains more aspiration than actuality in globalization studies. Many scholars have proclaimed the necessity of transcending narrow disciplinary divisions in order more fully to understand globalization, but few studies have successfully done so. Likewise, the widely recognized need for more intercultural approaches to the subject has gone largely unanswered. Most writings remain heavily west-centric – and many are more narrowly Anglo-centric or US-centric to boot.

The second edition of this book aims to make advances on the first in each of these respects. Five years of further research have allowed a greater accumulation and interpretation of more distinctly global data. Five years of further reflection have permitted greater consolidation of theory. Regarding interdisciplinarity, the second edition draws more widely from – and hopefully better integrates – work in the fields of Anthropology, Business Studies, Economics, Geography, History, Humanities, Law, Politics and Sociology. With respect to interculturality, I hope the second edition shows positive effects of my firsthand exposure in ten countries across Africa, Asia, Eastern

Europe, the Middle East and Latin America, as well as my involvement in the coordination of half a dozen global research projects since 2000.

The broad chapter structure of this edition remains the same as the first, but the contents of the chapters are markedly different. Chapter 1 now synthesizes a greatly expanded literature on globalization, with more than double the number of sources consulted in its preparation. Chapter 2, now twice its previous length, substantially reconsiders the definition of globalization, with significant implications for the book as a whole. Chapter 3 redrafts the history of globalization in the light of the more carefully specified definition. Chapter 4 more fully, explicitly and systematically delineates the theoretical premises that inform contending analyses of globalization as well as the account in this book. While Chapter 8 has been lightly revised, Chapter 5 (on production) has been more fully updated with recent data, trends and literature. Chapters 6 (on governance) and 7 (on identity) have in addition been considerably reconceived. Likewise, the consequences of contemporary globalization for human security (Chapter 9), social equality (Chapter 10), and democracy (Chapter 11) have been more thoroughly researched, substantially reconceptualized, and more carefully weighed. As a result, it may be hoped that the reflections for future policy offered in Chapter 12 are more firmly grounded.

The ten objectives set out in the preface to the first edition of *Globalization: A Critical Introduction* remain the same, but I hope the second edition moves a bit closer to achieving these aims and leaves readers more empowered to shape an increasingly global world in their preferred directions. Nevertheless, remaining shortfalls in my own thinking, coupled with ongoing deluges of events and publications around globalization, no doubt guarantee the need for a third edition in due course.

JAN AART SCHOLTE

Note: all $ figures refer to United States dollars; all dates are by Christian chronology (BC/AD).

Preface to the First Edition

Not another book on globalization! No doubt many a prospective reader will at first despair that a further title has squeezed onto already overcrowded shelves. Has this hype-propelled bandwagon not already slaughtered too many trees?

In some respects critics have grounds to complain that recent years have seen too much written about globalization. Aspiring academics, consultants, journalists and politicians have all rushed to have their say on 'the big G'. Publishers have been only too happy to flog wares that sell. Some have even slipped the term 'globalization' into titles of works that actually say nothing on the subject.

Yet despite this feverish output of words, we arguably still have far to go in consolidating concepts, methods and evidence with which to identify and measure globalization. Likewise, the literature to date has produced few tightly focused full-length assessments of the causes and consequences of globalization. In these circumstances, ideas of globalization have readily become so diverse, so broad, so loose, so changeable – in a word, so elusive – that one can pronounce virtually anything on the subject.

This situation is worrying. More is at stake in the analysis of globalization than publishers' revenues and the careers of would-be gurus. A clear, precise, explicit and consistently used concept of globalization can reveal a great deal about continuity and change in contemporary social life. Such a notion can also provide a basis for careful, critical and creative assessments of efficiency, security, justice, democracy and ecological integrity in today's world. Globalization is too important to be handled casually and opportunistically.

With these concerns to the fore, my objectives in writing this book have been:

(a) to develop a specific and distinct concept of globalization. Most existing formulations are steeped in ambiguity and inconsistency, or merely use 'globalization' as a synonym for other, older terms;

(b) to offer a multidimensional understanding of globalization. Most existing examinations are more narrowly focused, for example, in political economy, cultural studies, law, or social ecology;

(c) to address – squarely and systematically – questions concerning causation and consequence. Existing studies of globalization tend to offer only rather scattered observations on causation and limited coverage of consequences;

(d) to nurture a historical perspective that places contemporary developments in a long-term context. Many existing accounts of globalization have a shortsighted 'presentist' character;

(e) to appreciate the intricate interplay of continuity and change in globalization. Far too often, debate has become mired in polarized exchanges between smug 'realists' who deny change and exuberant 'globalists' who deny continuity;

(f) to ground the argument in a breadth and depth of both quantitative and qualitative evidence. Past treatments of globalization frequently rely too heavily on incidental illustration and anecdote;

(g) to acknowledge the diversity of experiences of globalization. Much of the existing literature remains silent on issues of context, overlooking different impacts and appreciations of globalization in relation to, for example, age, class, country, gender, nationality, race, religion, sexual proclivity, urban/rural location, and so on;

(h) to explore, carefully and systematically, a range of normative questions, particularly in relation to security, equity and democracy. Much past work on globalization involves facile celebration or unmeasured critique;

(i) to reflect on the implications of the knowledge developed through (a)–(h) for political action. Most existing academic works on globalization go little beyond general exhortations, if they consider policy responses at all;

(j) to avoid oversimplification yet remain accessible and engaging for a general reader. Too much public discussion of globalization has become soundbite, while too much academic treatment of the subject has slipped into unnecessary jargon and disempowering obfuscation.

In sum, I have aimed in this book to provide definition, description, periodization, explanation, judgement and – on the basis of this understanding – cautious prescription. I have tried to be explicit with theory and careful with evidence. The account is intended to be transdisciplinary and also sensitive to social and historical context. The argument is meant to retain focus, clarity, consistency and accessibility.

The book of course falls short of these aspirations at various points, but I hope that the pursuit of foolhardy ambitions has nevertheless yielded a provocative argument. The book will achieve its purpose if others are inspired to refine, extend, critique or overthrow the knowledge presented here. In the process readers will, I hope, take globalization that much more seriously: in further research, in policy, and in the choices of everyday life.

JAN AART SCHOLTE

Acknowledgements

If anything, my debts in writing this book have accumulated even faster than the literature on globalization over the past five years. An already dense list of acknowledgements in the first edition would need to be expanded much further still in order to name what are by now hundreds of individuals and institutions who have given me insights, inspirations and other supports for this book. Only a very abbreviated list can follow.

To begin with, heartfelt thanks are due to the many academic colleagues, students and policy practitioners who have generously published reviews of the first edition or given me private feedback. I accumulated a thick pile of much-valued comments that have stimulated many changes for this new version of the book. The revised argument does not come close to answering all the criticisms, but I hope the analysis is improved for having heard them.

Even more than the first edition, my work of the past five years has benefited from affiliation with the Centre for the Study of Globalisation and Regionalisation, based at the University of Warwick with a generous core grant from the Economic and Social Research Council. A foremost acknowledgement is due to CSGR's founding director, Richard Higgott, and the other staff, associates and visitors who have created such a positive professional base for my studies.

During the interval between editions I have also had the privilege to work on several policy-related projects that have significantly shaped my conceptualization of globalization. CSGR and the United Nations University supported a study of civil society and global finance. Projects with the North–South Institute and the International Monetary Fund exposed me to the heart of IMF relations with citizen groups. The Ford Foundation backed a major wider examination of civil society and democracy in global affairs. The latter undertaking could never have succeeded without the expertise of ten dedicated country coordinators and the generosity of nearly 400 contributing civil society practitioners.

Throughout, the preparation of the second edition has had exceptional support from my publisher, Steven Kennedy. Much appreciation is also due to the expertise and patience of the production team coordinated by Keith Povey and to Eliza Gaffney for help with the index.

Finally, with global research placing heavy demands on the most local sphere, my deepest appreciation once more goes to Masha and Polly for living this book with me.

JAN AART SCHOLTE

List of Abbreviations

ABM	anti-ballistic missile
ACP	African, Caribbean and Pacific
ADR	American Depository Receipt
AIDS	acquired immunodeficiency syndrome
AMF	Asian Monetary Fund
ANC	African National Congress
APEC	Asia-Pacific Economic Cooperation
ARPANET	Advanced Research Projects Agency Network
ASEAN	Association of South East Asian Nations
ASEM	Asia-Europe Meetings
AT&T	American Telephone and Telegraph Company
ATM	automated teller machine/Asynchronous Transfer Mode
BBC	British Broadcasting Corporation
BIS	Bank for International Settlements
BIT	bilateral investment treaty
BJP	*Bharatiya Janata Party*
BP	British Petroleum
BRICS	Brazil, Russia, India, China and South Africa
BSE	bovine spongiform encephalitis
CDF	Comprehensive Development Framework (of the World Bank)
CEDAW	Convention on the Elimination of All Forms of Discrimination Against Women
CEO	Chief Executive Officer
CERD	Committee on the Elimination of Racial Discrimination
CFC	chlorofluorocarbon
CFSP	Common Foreign and Security Policy (of the EU)
CHIPS	Clearing House Interbank Payment System
CIETAC	China International Economic Trade Arbitration Commission
CITES	Convention on International Trade in Endangered Species of Wild Fauna and Flora
CJD	Creutzfeldt-Jakob disease
CLS	Continuous Linked Settlement
CNN	Cable News Network
COIAB	Coordination of Indigenous Peoples Organizations of Brazil

COSATU	Confederation of South African Trade Unions
CSGR	Centre for the Study of Globalisation and Regionalisation
CSO	civil society organization
CSR	corporate social responsibility
CUT	Central Workers' Union (of Brazil)
DBS	direct broadcast satellite
DOT	Digital Opportunity Task Force (of the G8)
DSB	Dispute Settlement Body (of the WTO)
EAC	East African Community
Easdaq	European Association of Securities Dealers Automated Quotation
ECU	European Currency Unit
EDS	Electronic Data Services
EPZ	export processing zone
ERM	(European) exchange-rate mechanism
ESF	European Social Forum
EU	European Union
FAO	(United Nations) Food and Agriculture Organization
FATF	Financial Action Task Force
FDI	foreign direct investment
FfD	Financing for Development
FLAG	Fibreoptic Link Around the Globe
FPZ	free production zone
FSC	Forest Stewardship Council
FT	*Financial Times*
FTA	free trade area
FTAA	Free Trade Area of the Americas
G7	Group of Seven
G8	Group of Eight
G10	Group of Ten
G20	Group of Twenty
G24	Group of Twenty-Four
G77	Group of Seventy-Seven
GATT	General Agreement on Tariffs and Trade
GCC	Gulf Cooperation Council
GDI	gender-related development index
GDP	gross domestic product
GDR	Global Depository Receipt
GEF	Global Environment Facility
GEO	Global Environmental Organization
GLOBE	Global Legislators Organization for a Balanced Environment
GM	genetically modified

GRI	Global Reporting Initiative
GSP	Generalized System of Preferences
HAI	Health Action International
HDI	Human Development Index
hinwi	high net worth individual
HIPC	Highly Indebted Poor Countries Initiative
HIV	human immunodeficiency virus
IAEA	International Atomic Energy Agency
IAIS	International Association of Insurance Supervisors
IASB	International Accounting Standards Board
IATA	International Air Transport Association
IB	International Baccalaureate
ICANN	Internet Corporation for Assigned Names and Numbers
ICAO	International Civil Aviation Organization
ICBM	intercontinental ballistic missile
ICC	International Criminal Court/Inuit Circumpolar Conference
ICFTU	International Confederation of Free Trade Unions
ICJ	International Court of Justice
ICT	information and communications technologies
IEC	International Electrotechnical Commission
IFAC	International Federation of Accountants
IIF	Institute of International Finance
ILGA	International Lesbian and Gay Association
ILO	International Labour Organization
IMF	International Monetary Fund/International Metalworkers Federation
INTELSAT	International Telecommunications Satellite Organization
Interpol	International Criminal Police Organization
IOE	International Organization of Employers
IOSCO	International Organization of Securities Commissions
IPR	intellectual property right
IPU	Inter-Parliamentary Union
IRA	Irish Republican Army
ISDN	Integrated Services Digital Network
ISMA	International Securities Market Association
ISO	International Organization for Standardization
IT	information technology
ITT	International Telephone & Telegraph Corporation
ITU	International Telecommunication Union
IUCN	International Union for the Conservation of Nature/World Conservation Union

IUF	International Union of Food, Agricultural, Hotel, Restaurant, Catering, Tobacco and Allied Workers' Associations
IULA	International Union of Local Authorities
LCA	London Court of Arbitration
lgbt	lesbian, gay, bisexual and transgender
LIBOR	London Inter-Bank Offered Rate
LME	London Metal Exchange
LTCM	Long Term Capital Management
M&A	merger(s) and acquisition(s)
MAI	Multilateral Agreement on Investment
MDGs	Millennium Development Goals
MERCOSUR	*Mercado Común del Sur* (Southern Common Market)
MFA	Multi-Fibre Arrangement
MOU	memorandum of understanding
MSF	*Médecins sans frontières* (Doctors Without Borders)
NAFTA	North American Free Trade Agreement
Nasdaq	National Association of Securities Dealers Automated Quotation
NATO	North Atlantic Treaty Organization
NEPAD	New Partnership for Africa's Development
NGO	nongovernmental organization
NIC	newly industrializing country
NIEO	New International Economic Order
NPT	Treaty on the Non-Proliferation of Nuclear Weapons
NWICO	New World Information and Communications Order
NYSE	New York Stock Exchange
OAS	Organization of American States
OAU	Organization of African Unity (now African Union)
ODA	overseas development assistance
OECD	Organisation for Economic Cooperation and Development
OIC	Organization of the Islamic Conference
OPCW	Organization for the Prohibition of Chemical Weapons
OPEC	Organization of Petroleum Exporting Countries
OPM	*Organisasi Papua Merdeka* (Free Papua Organization)
OSCE	Organization for Security and Cooperation in Europe
OSSREA	Organization for Social Science Research in Eastern and Southern Africa
PANA	Pan African News Agency
PC	personal computer
PGA	Peoples' Global Action against 'Free' Trade and the World Trade Organization
PRSP	Poverty Reduction Strategy Paper

PSI	Public Services International
RITIMO	*Réseau d'Information Tiers Monde* (Third World Information Network)
RSS	*Rashtriya Swayamsevak Sangh*
S&P	Standard and Poor's
SADC	Southern African Development Community
SARS	severe acute respiratory syndrome
SDI	Strategic Defense Initiative
SDR	Special Drawing Right
SDRM	Sovereign Debt Restructuring Mechanism
SEZ	special economic zone
SWIFT	Society for Worldwide Interbank Financial Telecommunications
TB	tuberculosis
TINA	there is no alternative
TOEFL	Teaching of English as a Foreign Language
TRIPS	Trade-Related Aspects of Intellectual Property Rights (WTO Agreement on)
UN	United Nations
UNCTAD	United Nations Conference on Trade and Development
UNDP	United Nations Development Programme
UNEP	United Nations Environment Programme
UNESCO	United Nations Educational, Scientific and Cultural Organization
UNFPA	United Nations Fund for Population Activities
UNHCR	United Nations High Commissioner for Refugees
UNI	Union Network International
UNICEF	United Nations Children's Fund
UNIFEM	United Nations Development Fund for Women
UNPO	Unrepresented Nations and Peoples Organization
UTC	universal time coordination
UTO	World Federation of United Towns
VAT	value-added tax
VHP	*Vishwa Hindu Parishad*
WACLAC	World Associations of Cities and Local Authorities Coordination
WCL	World Confederation of Labour
WEF	World Economic Forum
WHO	World Health Organization
WIN	World Insurance Network
WIPO	World Intellectual Property Organization
WMCASPM	White Middle-Class Anglo-Saxon Protestant Male
WMD	weapons of mass destruction

WRI	World Resources Institute
WSF	World Social Forum
WSIS	World Summit on the Information Society
WSJ	*Wall Street Journal*
WSJ-E	*Wall Street Journal* (Europe edition)
WTO	World Trade Organization/World Tourism Organization
WWF	World Wildlife Federation/World Wide Fund for Nature
Y2K	year 2000 (millennium bug for computers)

Introduction

Framework of analysis
Change and continuity
Normative and policy issues

'We don't know what globalization is, but we have to act!' So spoke a peasant activist in Thailand recently (Sopa, 2002). His exclamation – where conviction meets uncertainly to yield frustration – well epitomizes current knowledge and politics of globalization. It is impossible to avoid the issue, but difficult to specify what it involves. Concerned citizens feel a need to respond, but most are unclear how. Globalization is regularly characterized as one of the greatest challenges before humankind today, but what is to be done about it?

What is globalization? When has globalization emerged and spread? Why has globalization occurred? How, if at all, has globalization generated social change? What benefits and harms have flowed from globalization? Inasmuch as globalization can bring good, how can the positive outcomes be maximized? Insofar as globalization can have ill effects, how might they be avoided? These questions, which grip much contemporary political debate, form the core concerns of this book.

'Globalization' stands out for a large public, spread across the world, as one of the defining terms of contemporary society. The former Prime Minister of Malaysia, Mahathir Mohamad, is one of many who have proclaimed the twenty-first to be a 'global century' (Nederveen Pieterse, 2000: 4). The first Director-General of the World Trade Organization (WTO), Renato Ruggiero, described globalization as a reality 'which overwhelms all others' (WTO-2, 1996b). Although such pronouncements may slip into hyperbole, it is clear that substantial parts of humanity have staked significant parts of their policies, their fortunes, their careers, their identities and their convictions on the premise that the present is an increasingly global world.

Yet, if asked to specify what they understand by 'globalization', most people reply with considerable hesitation, vagueness, and inconsistency. Moreover, much discussion of globalization is steeped in oversimplification, exaggeration and wishful thinking. In spite of a deluge of publications on the subject, analyses of globalization tend on the whole to remain conceptually inexact, empirically thin, historically ill-informed, economically and/or culturally illiterate, normatively shallow, and politically naïve. Although globalization is widely assumed to be crucially important, people generally have scant idea what, more precisely, it entails and how they should respond to it. As media magnate Ted Turner has put it, 'globalization is in fast-forward, and the world's ability to understand and react to it is in slow motion' (HDR, 1999: 100).

This highly unsatisfactory situation – one that has often also afflicted my own thinking on globalization – is what prompted me to write this book. While inevitably it does not come close to resolving the problems, my hope is that the text will help readers to engage with – and advance – what are often muddled and deadlocked debates.

As its title indicates, the book offers a *critical* introduction. It is critical of the widespread loose use of the term 'globalization'. It is critical of many (often wild) claims that have been made about globalization. It is critical of many consequences of globalization to date, and it is critical of inadequate policy responses to those negative effects. In the course of critique, however, the book also aims to offer positive ways forward for knowledge and politics of globalization.

The argument develops in three main steps. The first phase (Part I: Chapters 1–4) establishes a framework of analysis. The second phase (Part II: Chapters 5–8) examines impacts on social order. The third phase (Part III: Chapters 9–12) explores normative and policy issues. The rest of this introduction summarizes the argument that is developed through this three-part structure of the book.

Framework of analysis

The four chapters in Part I elaborate, in turn: the key issues in debates surrounding globalization; a general definition of the process; a chronology of the trend; and an account of the causal dynamics involved in globalization. These chapters both specify the approach adopted in this book and compare that perspective with the main competing viewpoints taken elsewhere in the literature on globalization.

Chapter 1, on globalization debates, surveys the wide array of claims and counterclaims that have been made in connection with globalization. Regarding definition, for example, some people equate 'global' relations with 'international' relations, while others emphasize a difference between the two notions. In respect of scale, some analysts see globalization as a pervasive and overriding fact of contemporary society, while others dismiss globalization as a fantasy. Concerning chronology, some say that globalization is a recent development, while others date its beginnings far back in history. As regards explanation, some account for globalization in materialist terms of capitalism and technology, while others emphasize ideational forces connected with identity and knowledge. On the question of social change, some assessments affirm that globalization is fundamentally reconfiguring contemporary society, while others assert that old social structures persist unaffected. In normative terms, some evaluations champion globalization, while others denounce its consequences. With regard to policy, different people have promoted competing neoliberalist, rejectionist, reformist, and transformist courses of action. In short, the first chapter summarizes what is at issue in current deliberations about globalization.

Chapter 2 focuses in more detail on the vexed issue of defining globalization. Five general conceptions are distinguished: globalization as internationalization; globalization as liberalization; globalization as universalization; globalization as westernization; and globalization as respatialization with the spread of transplanetary social connections. It is argued that the first four definitions are largely redundant. Only the last notion gives 'globalization' a distinctive meaning – and at the same time identifies a key contemporary historical development. In the remainder of the book, therefore, globalization refers to the advent and spread of what are alternately called 'global', 'transplanetary', 'transworld' and in certain respects also 'supraterritorial' social spaces. That said – as Chapter 2 also stresses – the contemporary rise of transplanetary and supraterritorial connectivity has by no means brought an end to territorial geography and associated economies, governments and identities. Global and territorial spaces coexist and interrelate in complex fashions.

Chapter 3 situates globalization in history, addressing the hotly contested questions of chronology and periodization. Here it is argued that, if globalization is understood as the spread of transplanetary and supraterritorial relations, then the trend has mainly unfolded in the past half-century. True, harbingers of globality can be traced back hundreds of years, and notable transworld connectedness existed from the middle of the nineteenth century. However, as evidence presented in Chapter 3 indicates, the greatest expansion of transplanetary relations – including the main emergence of supraterritoriality – has transpired since the middle of the twentieth century. Moreover, at the moment the trend shows little sign of stopping, let alone reversing.

Chapter 4 explores explanations of globalization. This issue is key, since explanation forms a basis for prediction, prescription and action. Assessments of the consequences of, and workable policy responses to, globalization depend largely on interpretations of the forces that have generated the trend. The first half of the chapter reviews a number of contending theories of globalization, including liberalism with its emphasis on market economics, political realism with its emphasis on power politics, Marxism with its emphasis on capitalist dynamics, constructivism with its emphasis on inter-subjective communication, poststructuralism with its emphasis on knowledge power, and feminism with its emphasis on gender relations. The second half of the chapter then elaborates the eclectic historical-sociological approach that is adopted in this book. Taking that perspective, the rise of transplanetary connectivity is argued to result mainly from a combination of: (a) certain turns in capitalist development; (b) an enabling regulatory apparatus provided through a host of state, suprastate and private governance mechanisms; (c) several circumstances in the construction of identities; and (d) important aspects of modern rationalist knowledge.

In sum, Part I establishes that globalization is a distinctive and significant feature of recent world history that involves several of the core forces of modern social relations. True, much talk of globalization is muddled, redundant, unsubstantiated and hyped. However, the concept can be constructed in ways that it brings to light important circumstances of contemporary society that other vocabulary and analysis does not reveal.

Change and continuity

Drawing on the general framework of analysis developed in Part I, the second set of four chapters assesses in what ways and to what extent globalization has affected the social order. Globalization is simultaneously an effect and a cause. It is both an explanandum (something to be explained) and an explanans (something that – partly – explains). Whereas Chapter 4 examines the social forces that have prompted the growth of transplanetary and supraterritorial connectivity (that is, globalization as outcome), Chapters 5–8 consider how this reconfiguration of geography has in turn affected other aspects of social structure (that is, globalization as causal force). In a word, has globalization while reorganizing social space also encouraged wider social transformations?

Chapter 5, on the subject of globalization and production, argues that, at the same time that transplanetary connections have arisen partly out of capitalism, they have also reverberated back to help reshape and extend capitalism. Contemporary accelerated globalization has done little thus far to challenge the predominance of capitalism, that is, an economy centred on surplus accumulation. On the contrary, the growth of transworld spaces has encouraged major extensions of capitalist production, including in areas of information, communications, finance, mass consumerism, and biotechnology. The spread of global relations has also brought some notable shifts in the ways that processes of surplus accumulation operate. Examples include offshore arrangements and transworld corporate alliances. However, globalization has not put the structure of capitalism itself under threat. If anything, the current more global situation has become one of hypercapitalism.

Chapter 6, regarding globalization and governance, suggests that greater transplanetary connectivity has promoted a shift from a statist to a polycentric mode of regulation. This chapter first dismisses frequently heard claims that heightened globalization is prompting a general retreat or even demise of the territorial state. National governments have remained a major locus of regulation and have shown no sign of moving towards dissolution. However, globalization has encouraged changes in several significant features of the state, for instance, in terms of the constituencies that it serves and the policy tools that it uses. Moreover, the old statist focus on centralized country governments as the sole site of governance is not viable in a more global world. The spread of transplanetary relations has stimulated a growing role in regulation for substate, suprastate and nonstate agencies. In this way large-scale globalization during contemporary history has helped to open an era of polycentrism, with multiscalar and diffuse governance.

Chapter 7, on globalization and identity, maintains that the recent unprecedented expansion of transworld relations has tended to attenuate nationality, particularly as this sense of self and community is connected with established states. State-nations remain important, but they have lost the near-monopoly on constructions of collective identity that they held in the early and mid-twentieth century. In addition, globalization has encouraged a dissociation of many notions of nationhood from existing states. The spread of transplanetary relations has thereby furthered a growth of micro-nations on a substate scale, region-nations on a suprastate scale, and transworld national diasporas. At the same time, globalization has advanced a number of other, nonterritorial constructions of identity, for instance, connected to faith, class, gender, or humankind as a whole. Overall, then, globalization has stimulated a pluralization of identities, with a host of different national and nonterritorial frameworks of being and belonging. Often this pluralization has converged on individual persons, who then experience a hybrid sense of self that encompasses a melange of several nationalities and nonterritorial affiliations.

Chapter 8 completes this book's assessment of change and continuity in social structures by examining the consequences of globalization for knowledge. At the same time as arising partly out of modern rationalism, the spread of transplanetary connections has also had repercussions for that structure of knowledge. On the one hand, expanding globality has often promoted an extension of modern rationality: that is, secular, anthropocentric, instrumental, techno-scientific thinking. On the other hand, globalization has also encouraged some anti-rationalist reactions, in forms such as religious revivalism and postmodernism. In addition, the spread of transworld relations has furthered some shifts in ontologies, in methodologies, and in aesthetics. In general, contemporary globalization has promoted a move from unquestioning rational*ism* to more reflexive rational*ity*.

In sum, Part II suggests that the past half-century of intense globalization, as a major reconfiguration of social geography, has unfolded in conjunction with several important shifts in other primary social structures. The growth of transplanetary and supraterritorial spaces has both encouraged, and been encouraged by, the emergence of: (a) new forms of capitalist production; (b) multilayered and more diffuse governance; (c) multidimensional and more hybrid identities; and (d) greater questioning of rationalist knowledge. At the same time, the spread of transworld connections has thus far shown few signs of bringing an end to capital, state, nation, and modern rationality. As ever in history, then, globalization has involved an intricate interplay of change and continuity.

Normative and policy issues

As Part III of the book indicates, the changes and continuities associated with globalization can have both positive and negative impacts on the quality of life. The normative evaluation of globalization undertaken in the third set of chapters highlights themes of human security, social equality, and democracy. Some readers might expect issues of economic efficiency also to be highlighted as a principal policy concern. For example, mainstream economists would tend to judge globalization largely in terms of the gains or losses that it brings to the productive deployment of scarce world resources. However, the perspective taken in this book regards economic efficiency and growth as secondary to – and in the service of – security, equality and democracy. Productivity is therefore not treated as a primary normative question in its own right.

Chapter 9, on the subject of 'Globalization and (In)Security', investigates how the rise of transplanetary and supraterritorial connections between people has affected conditions of confidence and danger in society. The discussion examines human security in a multifaceted fashion, covering peace, crime, ecological integrity, health, poverty, financial stability, employment, working conditions, identity, knowledge and social cohesion. Across these various aspects of risk the evidence is mixed. In some respects globalization has promoted increased human security, for example, with certain disincentives to war, improved means of humanitarian relief, new job opportunities, and greater cultural pluralism. However, in other ways globalization has helped to perpetuate or even deepen armed conflict, environmental degradation, epidemics, poverty, financial crises, unemployment, exploitation of workers, cultural destruction, and social disintegration. Yet none of these positive or negative consequences for human security has been intrinsic to increased globality per se. In each case, the outcome has resulted from the policies adopted towards the reconfigured social geography. Political choice is the key.

Chapter 10 considers the hotly contested question of 'Globalization and (In)Equality'. This issue is examined in terms of the distribution of life chances on lines of class, country, gender, race, urban/rural divides, age, and (dis)ability. Again the evidence turns up mixed. On the positive side, the intense globalization of recent decades has in certain cases improved possibilities for young people, poor countries, women and other subordinated social circles to realize their potentials. More negatively, however, globalization has in other cases reinforced or increased various arbitrary hierarchies in contemporary society. Again, however, the important variable in the relationship between globalization and (in)equality has generally not been globalization as such, but rather the policy approach to that trend. A more global world can be more equal if people choose to make it so.

Chapter 11 addresses the problem of 'Globalization and (Un)Democracy'. Here claims that a more global world offers people greater opportunities for collective self-determination are assessed against arguments that globalization has deepened democratic deficits. On the one hand, the contemporary period of increased transplanetary connectivity has paralleled a spread of liberal democratic institutions to an unprecedented number of states. However, citizens have far from adequate involvement and control in current governance of global relations. Much of these democratic shortfalls result from ignorance, as schools, the mass media, civil society associations and governance agencies themselves fail to educate the public sufficiently about globalization. Other democratic shortcomings lie in institutional arrangements, as elections, parliaments and courts fail to provide adequate mechanisms for public participation and public accountability in the regulation of global relations. In addition, the various deep social inequalities discussed in Chapter 10 have severely detrimental effects on democracy in the contemporary globalizing world. Once more, however, the problem is not globalization itself, but the ways that it has been approached to date. Other, more democratic, globalizations are possible.

Thus circumstances in each of the main areas of normative concern – human security, social equality, and democracy – have developed mainly as a result of policy choices in respect of globalization. To the extent that outcomes have been unhappy so far, different policies could improve matters. Under the title of '(Re)constructing Future Globalizations', Chapter 12 considers various strategies and measures that might steer growing transplanetary connectivity in more positive directions. After critically reviewing neoliberalist, rejectionist, reformist and transformist approaches to shaping globalization, this book opts to advocate a mix of 'ambitious reformism' and 'cautious transformism' as the most practicable progressive course available at the present time. A number of measures are suggested that could bring substantially greater human security, social equality and democracy within an overall social order that is increasingly structured by hypercapitalism, polycentric governance, hybrid identities, and reflexive rationality. The opportunities for, and the obstacles to, achieving these alternative globalizations are also evaluated.

Core theses on globalization

(1) globalization is best understood as a reconfiguration of social geography marked by the growth of transplanetary and supraterritorial connections between people

(2) although globalization so defined made earlier appearances, the trend has unfolded at greatest speeds, on greatest scales, to greatest extents, and with greatest impacts since the middle of the twentieth century

(3) with regard to causality, globalization as a development in the structure of geography is closely interrelated with concurrent developments in structures of production, governance, identity and knowledge

(4a) contemporary intense globalization is marked by continuity inasmuch as the trend has not erased primary pre-existent social structures such as territorialist geography, capitalist production, state governance, national identity and rationalist knowledge

but

(4b) globalization has also prompted notable changes in certain attributes of territoriality, capital, state, nation and modern rationality

and

(4c) globalization has encouraged the growth of additional areas and forms of accumulation, non-state loci of governance, non-national forms of identity, and non-rationalist types of knowledge

(5a) contemporary intense globalization has had some important positive consequences with respect to human security, social equality, and democracy

but

(5b) the recent unprecedented growth of transplanetary and supraterritorial connectivity has also been associated with various heightened insecurities, exacerbated inequalities and deepened democratic deficits

(6a) these positive and negative outcomes have not flowed from globalization as such, but from policy choices that can be debated and changed

and

(6b) contemporary globalization could yield much better results in terms of human security, social equality, and democracy with a change of policy course from neoliberalism to a blend of ambitious reformism and cautious transformism, although the political challenges of achieving this reorientation must not be underestimated.

In sum, Part III advances an indictment of neoliberalist globalization, not a condemnation of globalization as such. (The distinguishing features of neoliberalism are detailed in Chapter 1.) Insofar as globalization to date has often increased insecurity, inequality and democratic deficits, these negative outcomes can be largely attributed to the neoliberalist policy frameworks that have dominated the (mis)management of transplanetary and supraterritorial spaces since the 1980s. Alternative, better approaches are available for the future.

In a word, then, this book aims to advance understandings of globalization that can help to shape the process in positive directions. For convenient reference, the core points of the overall argument are reviewed in the box on page 8. Readers will also find boxes elsewhere in the book that summarize the contents of the respective chapters.

Part I

Framework of Analysis

Since everything concerning globalization is deeply contested, nothing about it can be taken for granted. Each account of the issue has to make its starting points explicit and clear. A lengthy first part of this book must therefore carefully establish a general framework for analysing globalization.

To this end Chapter 1 sets the scene of debate with a survey of the many points of disagreement about globalization. Chapter 2 examines various notions of globalization and particularly specifies the definition that guides the analysis in this book. Chapter 3 elaborates a chronology of globalization that corresponds to this conception. Chapter 4 then considers different explanations of globalization and presents the account that informs the present book. With the framework of analysis thus developed in hand, the consequences of globalization can be systematically explored in Parts II and III.

Chaper 1

Globalization Debates

Main points of this chapter
Where to start?
Continuity or change?
Liberation or shackles?
What to do?
Conclusion

Main points of this chapter

- globalization is a thoroughly contested subject
- many of the disputes relate to starting premises regarding the definition, measurement, chronology and explanation of globalization
- other debates concern the ways and extents that globalization has or has not changed society, including its primary structures of production, governance, identity and knowledge
- additional arguments centre on normative evaluations of globalization, namely, whether it enhances or undermines human security, social equality and democracy
- further disagreements revolve around policy responses to globalization, in particular between neoliberalist, rejectionist, reformist and transformist strategies

Along the road between Iganga and Mbale, a crew heaves pickaxes to lay fibre-optic cable that will connect peripheral districts of eastern Uganda into global telecommunications networks. In New Delhi, taxi chauffeurs ask their foreign passengers how many hours' flying away they live. To mark post-Soviet times, a billboard in Moscow directs consumers to a 'Super Shop' called 'Global USA', located down the street from Lenin's tomb. Another sign, rising above the *favelas* of São Paulo, urges passing drivers to 'Globalize Jesus!', while an Islamist in Tehran celebrates global governance as the coming of the Mahdi, the twelfth Imam. In the Nile Delta a transborder company's local buyer of potatoes for the fryers of Europe adorns life with mobile phone, fashion spectacles, satellite television and sports utility vehicle, all the while dressed in traditional *galabeyya*. A boutique in Portland, Oregon, sells 'global clothing', while a restaurant on London's Brompton Road peddles 'global food'. From Beijing to Johannesburg, from Davos to Porto Alegre, a stream of world summits and world forums discuss the implications of globalization for human security, social equality and democracy.

These snapshots relate just a few of the countless occasions – across continents, age groups, classes, cultures, races, sexes, and urban and rural settings – when the present author has encountered 'global-ness' while writing (and now rewriting) this book. No doubt all readers can assemble their own collection of such incidents, if perhaps not as scattered as the above examples. It is today pretty well impossible to avoid the issue of globalization. 'Globalspeak' has become standard fare among journalists, politicians, managers, advertisers, bankers, entertainers, officials, computer experts, activists and researchers across the planet. The vocabulary of 'globalization' has entered almost all of the world's major languages. Daily life now brings continual references to global communications, global finance, global health problems, global markets, global migration, and global justice.

'Globalization' has also become a heavily loaded word. People have linked the notion to pretty well every purported contemporary social change, with arguments about an emergent information age, a retreat of the state, the demise of traditional cultures, and the advent of a postmodern epoch. In normative terms, some people have associated globalization with progress, prosperity and peace. For others, however, the word has conjured up deprivation, disaster and doom. No one is indifferent. Most are confused.

To begin to bring some order to this analytical disarray, the present opening chapter maps the many claims and counterclaims that have been made about globalization. At the same time the following pages locate the arguments advanced in this book within those debates. From this discussion readers can obtain both a survey of existing globalization research and a preview of the particular perspective taken between these covers.

The first section notes the highly diverse starting points that people have adopted when they examine globalization. In other words, these paragraphs foreshadow the issues that are addressed in detail in the rest of Part I. The second section of the chapter surveys various affirmations and denials of social change that analysts have connected with globalization. These paragraphs thus introduce the questions treated more fully in Part II. The third section assembles multiple plaudits and denunciations of globalization, while the fourth section lays out the broad spectrum of policy lines that can be advocated in respect of globalization. These last two sections thereby review the matters that are handled at length in Part III.

Of course the diversity of published arguments about globalization must not be exaggerated. After all, most research on the subject has emanated from countries of the North and is published in English. Moreover, most studies of globalization have come from a limited social base of urban-based, white, professional, Judaeo-Christian, middle-aged men. Given these biases, the existing literature – however wide-ranging it may be – does not adequately cover many experiences of globalization.

Where to start?

Many debates about globalization never get past disputes over starting premises regarding definition, scale, chronology and explanatory framework. On definition, people have often conceived of globalization in radically different terms, thereby talking past each other from the outset. On scale, people have made widely varying assessments of the extent of globalization. At one end of the spectrum certain observers claim that today's world is fully globalized; at the opposite pole ultra-sceptics deny that any globalization whatsoever has occurred. On questions of chronology, some accounts trace globalization back to ancient history, while others date its origins back only several decades. Regarding explanations, analysts have identified widely differing cultural, economic, political and/or technological dynamics of globalization. With such contrasting starting points, many globalization debates have been foredoomed to deadlock.

What's in a word?

Disputes and confusions about globalization often begin around issues of definition. Indeed, many people invoke notions of globalization without indicating explicitly what they mean by the term. For example, various commentators have described globalization as 'a stage of capitalism' or 'late modernity' without specifying the content of such phrases. Or authors have made unfocused remarks that globalization is 'a new way of thinking'. Circular definitions are not much help either, with statements like 'globalization is the present process of becoming global' (Archer, 1990: 1). In these and other ways, 'globalization' has frequently become a label to cover whatever strikes the fancy. Little wonder, then, that critics have decried the emptiness of 'global babble'. As early as 1943 a US congresswoman complained that it was all 'globaloney' (Luce, 1943).

Yet such wholesale rejections are unfair. After all, many key notions in social analysis can be used loosely and vaguely. How often does one find airtight conceptualizations of 'class', 'culture', 'money', 'law', 'development', 'international', etc.? Moreover, some usages of 'globalization' are considerably more illuminating than loose globe talk. A serious academic literature on the subject has developed over the past two decades.

All the same, confusion persists because the more specific ideas of globalization are often highly diverse. At least five broad conceptions can be distinguished. These definitions are in some ways related and to some extent overlapping, but their emphases are substantially different.

One common notion has conceived of globalization in terms of *internationalization*. From this perspective, 'global' is simply another adjective to describe cross-border relations between countries, and 'globalization' designates a growth of international exchange and interdependence. In this vein Paul Hirst and Grahame Thompson have identified globalization in terms of 'large and growing flows of trade and capital investment between countries' (1996: 48). Evidence of such 'globalization' is purportedly also to be found in enlarged movements between countries of people, diseases, messages and ideas.

A second usage has viewed globalization as *liberalization*. Here 'globalization' refers to a process of removing state-imposed restrictions on movements between countries in order to create an 'open', 'borderless' world economy. On these lines one analyst suggests that 'globalization has become a prominent catchword for describing the process of international economic integration' (Sander, 1996: 27). Evidence for such 'globalization' in recent decades can be found in the widespread reduction or even abolition of regulatory trade barriers, foreign-exchange restrictions, capital controls, and (for citizens of certain states) visas.

A third conception has equated globalization with *universalization*. Indeed, when Oliver Reiser and Blodwen Davies coined the verb 'globalize' in the 1940s, they took it to mean 'universalize' and foresaw 'a planetary synthesis of cultures' in a 'global humanism' (1944: 39, 201, 205, 219, 225). In this usage, 'global' means 'worldwide', and 'globalization' is the process of spreading various objects and experiences to people at all corners of the earth. We could in this sense have a 'globalization' of automobiles, Chinese restaurants, decolonization, cattle farming, and much more.

A fourth definition has treated globalization as *westernization* or *modernization*, especially in an 'Americanized' form (Spybey, 1996; Taylor, 2000). Following this idea, globalization is a dynamic whereby the social structures of modernity (capitalism, rationalism, industrialism, bureaucratism, individualism, and so on) are spread the world over, normally destroying pre-existent cultures and local self-determination in the process. 'Globalization' in this sense is sometimes described as an imperialism of McDonald's, Hollywood and CNN (Schiller, 1991; Barber, 1996; Ritzer, 1996; Gowan, 1999). Martin Khor has similarly declared that 'globalization is what we in the Third World have for several centuries called colonization' (Khor, 1995; see also Biel, 2000; Ling, 2000).

A fifth approach – one that is developed in this book – has identified globalization as *respatialization*. Following this interpretation, globalization entails a reconfiguration of social geography with increased transplanetary connections between people. On these lines, for example, David Held and

Anthony McGrew have defined globalization as 'a process (or set of processes) which embodies a transformation in the spatial organization of social relations and transactions' (Held *et al.*, 1999: 16; also Massey, 1994; Short, 2001; Rosenau, 2003). In particular, some authors have associated contemporary globalization with a tendency towards deterritorialization, so that social space can no longer be wholly mapped in terms of territorial places, territorial distances and territorial borders (Ó Tuathail, 2000). In this vein the present book highlights the rise of supraterritoriality in contemporary globalization.

Each of these five conceptions can generate an elaborate and in one or another way revealing account of contemporary history. However, in spite of some overlap between these various notions, their respective foci are significantly different. Thus, for example, people who identify globalization as internationalization and people who approach it as respatialization develop very different understandings of the problem.

Fact or fantasy?

Both when they agree and when they disagree on the general definition of globalization, people have often held widely differing assessments regarding the extent of the development. On the one hand, analysts who might be characterized as 'globalists' claim that contemporary social relations have become thoroughly globalized. Globalists also tend to regard globalization as the single most important fact of contemporary history. In contrast, ultra-sceptics have dismissed any notion of globalization as myth. Between these extremes, other analysts have treated globalization as a significant trend, but one that coexists with other important developments and is far from finished. These more measured accounts have often also stressed the uneven incidence of globalization among countries, classes, and other social groupings.

Globalist pronouncements about the ubiquity and all-importance of globalization have issued both from gung-ho supporters of the trend and from its implacable opponents. The promoters have included a number of corporate consultants and champions of new technologies. For example, management gurus like Kenichi Ohmae and John Naisbitt have created bestsellers with their praises of a 'borderless world' (Ohmae, 1990; Naisbitt, 1994). Much of the business press has heralded 'the stateless enterprise' that maximizes efficiency and profits by operating freely across a global field (Holstein *et al.*, 1990). Similarly, many Internet enthusiasts have regularly overstated the number of online connections and the scale of electronic commerce. Many advertisers, journalists, politicians and others prone to hyperbole have also celebrated the present as a thoroughly globalized world.

Some critics of current directions of globalization have also made strong claims about the scale of the process. For instance, a number of civil society activists and dissident academics have suggested that global corporations now rule the world (Barnet and Cavanagh, 1994; Brecher and Costello, 1994; Korten, 1995; Berger *et al.*, 1998–9; Barlow and Clarke, 2001). On similar lines many of the same circles have denounced global governance agencies like the International Monetary Fund (IMF), the World Bank and the WTO for usurping power from states and local governments (Barker and Mander, n.d.; George and Sabelli, 1994; Burbach and Danaher, 2000). Meanwhile a number of religious revivalists and reactionary nationalists have protested that a deluge of globalization is erasing traditional cultures. In this vein the National Front leader in France, Jean-Marie Le Pen, has railed against his country being sent to the 'abattoirs of Euro-globalization' (*Globe and Mail*, 3 May 2002: A7).

Whether as supporters or as critics of globalization, globalists have regarded the trend as holding foremost and overriding importance in contemporary history. In this vein several writers have taken the current growth of global communications to be as significant as the spread of printing presses 500 years ago, the invention of writing 5,000 years ago, or the development of human speech 40,000 years ago (Ploman, 1984: 37; Gates, 1995: 8–9). For his part the former President of Brazil, Fernando Henrique Cardoso, has affirmed that the implications of global consciousness are as great for the present day as was the Copernican revelation, five centuries ago, that the earth revolved about the sun rather than vice versa (Cardoso, 1996).

At an opposite extreme to globalist pronouncements, ultra-sceptics have denied the existence of any such thing as globalization. For these analysts, all globe-talk is empty jargon, fad, hype, myth and rhetoric. Claims concerning globalization are greatly exaggerated, if not utter fantasy. Doubters have dismissed talk of 'globalization' as new-fangled vocabulary for age-old conditions of world politics. Studies of this phantom subject are therefore a waste of time. Shut this book!

From the sceptics' standpoint, much that is said about the so-called 'global' economy is mythical (Zysman, 1996; Hirst and Thompson 1999: 2, 6; Helliwell, 2000). Purportedly 'global' companies are in fact deeply embedded in their respective home countries, and their actions are thoroughly enmeshed in the logic of interstate relations (Kapstein, 1991–2; Ruigrok and Van Tulder, 1995; Doremus *et al.*, 1998). Indeed, for these analysts alleged 'globalization' has done and will do nothing to alter the basic fact of world politics, namely, the sovereign state (Krasner, 1994; Nicholson, 1999). So-called 'global' governance institutions have not exercised any power separately from their state members. Talk of 'global' civil society and 'global' culture is similarly nonsense.

Others like the present author have fallen between the globalist and ultra-sceptical extremes. From such a perspective globalization is indeed a distinctive and important development in contemporary world history. However, its scale and consequences need to be carefully measured and qualified. Nor is globalization the only, or in all situations the most significant, trend in society today. Rather, it unfolds alongside – and is closely interlinked with – other major social trends, like the shifts in structures of production, governance, identity and knowledge that are considered in Part II.

In addition, more measured assessments of the scale of globalization have often emphasized the uneven spread of the process. On such an account, some countries (like the USA) and regions (like Western Europe) have generally experienced more globalization than others (like Mongolia or Sub-Saharan Africa). Likewise, urban centres have on the whole accumulated more global connections than rural areas. Global relations have also tended to fall unevenly across different age groups, classes, cultures, genders and races. In a word, measurements of globalization are far more complex than either the globalists or the ultra-sceptics make out.

Old or new?

Along with definition and scale, another issue of starting principles in debates about globalization concerns chronology. Is the spread of global relations new to contemporary history? Or did the trend start several generations, centuries or even millennia ago? Or is globalization a cyclical phenomenon that comes and goes from time to time? As might be expected, the chronology that one describes varies with the definition that one adopts.

For example, analysts who define globalization in terms of internationalization or liberalization often regard the process as a recurrent trend that has appeared at several previous junctures in the history of the modern states-system. In this vein Ian Clark has distinguished alternating phases of 'globalization' and 'fragmentation' in international history (Clark, 1997). A number of studies have emphasized that, in proportional terms, levels of trade, permanent migration and investment between countries were as high (if not higher) in the late nineteenth century as they were in the run-up to 2000 (cf. Zevin, 1992; Wade, 1996; Hirst and Thompson, 1999; O'Rourke and Williamson, 1999). On the grounds of such evidence many commentators have declared that there is nothing new in contemporary globalization.

Other accounts also give globalization a long history, but view it in linear rather than cyclical terms. These authors generally hold that globalization started on a small scale anywhere from 100 to 500 years ago and reached unprecedented rates in recent decades. In this fashion, Roland Robertson has spoken of a 'germination phase' of globalization between the early fifteenth and the mid-eighteenth centuries and a 'take-off' period from the middle of the nineteenth century (1992: 58–9). For their part, the business analyst Michael Porter and the world-systems theorist Christopher Chase-Dunn have located the start of globalization in the late nineteenth century (Porter,

1986: 42; Chase-Dunn, 1989: 2). On the other hand, this perspective on the history of globalization sees important quantitative and qualitative differences between the nineteenth century and the present day (Baldwin and Martin, 1999; Bordo *et al.*, 1999; Keohane and Nye, 2000).

Meanwhile, other arguments suggest that globalization has been entirely novel to present times. On these accounts global relations only dawned with the jet aeroplane and the computer network. From such a perspective, current history is experiencing a 'first global revolution' and a sudden leap to 'new realities' (Drucker, 1989; King and Schneider, 1991).

By adopting a conception of globalization as the growth of transplanetary and more particularly supraterritorial social relations, the present book draws mostly from the second of the three general chronological frameworks just summarized. Global connections have certain antecedents in earlier centuries, but they have figured as a pervasive, major aspect of social life mainly since the middle of the twentieth century. Various indicators are presented in Chapter 3 to demonstrate exponential increases of globality in recent decades. That said, exact measurement of global relations remains difficult, inasmuch as most social data (trade and investment flows, political participation, recreational activities, and so on) are collected in relation to country and other territorial units. We lack sufficient global statistics.

Further debates concerning the historical trajectory of globalization relate to its future course. According to some accounts the twenty-first century will experience a continuation – if not a further acceleration – of current high rates of globalization. A second perspective suggests that globalization will slow or stop once it reaches a certain plateau. A third forecast regards globalization as a cyclical trend, so that the recent phase of rising global relations is transient and will be succeeded by another phase of decline (Rugman, 2001; James, 2001). A fourth prediction anticipates a future of de-globalization as a consequence of nationalist and localist opposition. The analysis presented in this book expects further globalization for the foreseeable future, although policy choices will substantially affect the rates and directions of that expansion.

What drives globalization?

As with questions of definition, scale and chronology, no consensus exists in respect of the forces that propel globalization. In fact, most studies of the subject have largely ducked questions of explanation. Their descriptions, measurements, evaluations and prescriptions regarding globalization have not been rooted in an explicit theory. The present book attempts to avoid this shortcoming by laying out an explanatory framework in its fourth chapter.

Even though most explorations of globalization have left their theoretical perspective implicit, a broad distinction can be discerned between idealist and materialist approaches. Methodologically idealist accounts have regarded globalization as a product of mental forces such as imagination, invention, metaphor, identity and ideology. Examples of theories that tend towards idealism include social constructivism, postmodernism and postcolonialism.  In contrast, methodological materialists have treated globalization as a result of concrete forces such as nature, production, technology, laws and institutions. Examples of theories that tend towards materialism include liberalism, political realism, Marxism, and social ecology. In contrast to both idealism and materialism, the eclectic approach adopted in this book treats both concrete and mental circumstances as important drivers and shapers of globalization. Hence, as elaborated in Chapter 4, and as reflected in the chapter themes of Part II, the analysis assigns causal significance to matters of identity and knowledge as well as to matters of production and governance. Indeed, the ideational and material aspects of globalization are held to be co-determining, such that each significantly moulds the other.

Cutting across the idealist–materialist divide, another key point of theoretical debate pits individualist against structuralist understandings of globalization. Methodologically individualist arguments regard globalization as an outcome of decisions made by social actors (such as businesspeople, citizens, officials and politicians). In contrast, methodologically structuralist perspectives treat globalization as a product of forces embedded in the social order (like capitalism, the states system, nationalism, rationalism, and so on). Thus theoretical debates about globalization replay age-old disputes in social enquiry between voluntarists and determinists over the degree to which agency (read, people's choices) shapes history. On this core methodological point the present account takes what some have called a 'structurationist' position, where structure and agency are mutually causative (Giddens, 1984; Scholte, 1993: ch 7). Hence the book is filled with references both to actor decisions (especially in Part III) and to deeper social forces (especially in Part II), as well as to the links between them.

A third broad methodological problem for globalization studies concerns the relationship between the analyst and the analysed. On the one hand, following the presumptions of 'social science', many authors take a positivist position that academic investigations stand apart from, and need not have impact upon, the social reality that they study. From this methodologically objectivist position, researchers on globalization can treat the knowledge that they produce as politically neutral. On the other hand, methodological subjectivists (like some radical postmodernists) argue that knowledge emanates entirely from the experience of the person who constructs it. These ultra-relativists may also maintain that all opinions have equal merits, with no scope for moral judgements between the contending positions. On the objectivist–subjectivist spectrum, as in the idealist–materialist and the agent–structure debates, the present book takes a middle perspective, with a supposition that knowledge and other aspects of reality form a duality of reciprocal causation. In other words, an understanding of globalization reflects the social conditions that surround its construction; and at the same time that understanding reverberates back into and helps to shape those wider concrete circumstances. Thus academic knowledge of globalization not only has intellectual significance, but political consequence as well. Adopting this assumption of a mutual determination between theory and practice, the book makes no effort to skirt normative issues and policy challenges. On the contrary, explicit attention is given throughout to thinking through the political implications of the arguments presented.

Needless to say, the questions of theory just addressed – like those of definition, measurement and periodization – require far more elaboration than is given above. All of these matters are therefore treated at greater length in later chapters of Part I. The purpose in this opening chapter is merely to identify crucial issues of starting points that any account of globalization needs to address.

Continuity or change?

Along with arguments over definition, scale, periodization and explanation, discussions of globalization have tended in good part to be debates about change in contemporary society. Many people have shared the intuition, articulated here by the sociologist Anthony Giddens, that 'the emergence of globalized orders means that the world we live "in" is different from that of previous ages' (1991: 225; also Burbach and Robinson, 1999; Giddens, 2002). Accepting Philadelphia's Liberty Medal in 1994, Prague's playwright-politician Václav Havel suggested that, whereas previously war provided the chief stimulus to social transformation, now forces of change emanate mainly from globalization. Countless other social commentators have also been tempted at one or the other moment to issue a similar sweeping pronouncement about the world-historical significance of contemporary globalization.

Yet what, more specifically, is the character of social change in the context of current globalization? Indeed, has increased global-ness in contemporary life significantly reshaped the primary structures of social relations? Is there anything veritably new in this purported 'new world order'? Or has globalization merely generated superficial shifts (that is, at the level of objects, institutions, perceptions, etc.) while leaving the underlying social framework intact?

As intimated above, the approach adopted in this book regards social organization as having five interrelated primary aspects: that is, related to geography, production, governance, identity and knowledge. From this perspective, globalization would bring about social transformation to the extent that this trend in geography has provoked changes in the prevailing modes of economy, regulation, social psychology and culture. As the following paragraphs indicate, analysts have developed widely varying assessments of the type and extent of social change in each of these four areas.

Production

In respect of economy, some research has linked globalization to a full-scale transformation of the mode of production, while other accounts have only seen continuity. On the 'all-change' side of this argument, many writers in business studies have claimed that global markets, global competition and global management have fundamentally reshaped the visions, organization and behaviour of firms (Porter, 1990; Pucik *et al.*, 1992; Bleeke and Ernst, 1993; Taylor and Weber, 1996; Bartlett and Ghoshal, 1998). Countless authors have also stressed the relationship between globalization and technological revolutions in transport, communications and data processing. These developments have changed what is produced and how it is produced. Many observers have in this light characterized the global economy as an information, knowledge, postindustrial, network or service economy (Bell, 1973; Katz, 1988; Carnoy *et al.*, 1993; Castells, 1989, 1996–7; Bryson and Daniels, 1998; Neef, 1998; Shapiro and Varian, 1999). With a grand sweep, Alvin and Heidi Toffler have affirmed that human history has entered a 'third wave' of knowledge society after the 'first wave' of peasant life and the 'second wave' of industrial civilization (Toffler, 1980; Toffler and Toffler, 1994). Certain commentators have furthermore associated expanding global relations with a decline or even demise of capitalism. Thus some accounts have linked globalization with 'late capitalism' (intimating that this mode of production is nearing termination) or a 'postcapitalist society' (suggesting that the world has already moved beyond capitalism) (Jameson, 1991; Drucker, 1993).

These affirmations of structural change in the economy have provoked equally strong counterclaims of continuity in the general mode of production. For example, some analysts have insisted on the persistent centrality of manufacturing industry in a global economy (Cohen and Zysman, 1987). More broadly, Marxists and others have highlighted the underlying persistence of capitalism in contemporary globalization (Magdoff, 1992; Chesnaid, 1994; S. Amin, 1996, 1997; Marshall, 1996; Went, 1996, 2000; Burbach *et al.*, 1997; McChesney *et al.*, 1998; Berger *et al.*, 1998–9).

A third general line of argument has regarded the relationship between globalization and capitalism as one of change-within-continuity. Such accounts argue that the spread of global relations has provoked shifts (or, to invoke the jargon, a 'restructuring') in the ways that surplus accumulation occurs. For example, globalization may have brought a new world division of labour, a rise of regionalism, greater concentration of production in giant corporations, more accumulation through consumerism and finance capital, and a move from so-called 'Fordist' to 'post-Fordist' regimes for the control of labour. However, behind these changes capitalism remains firmly in place as the underlying mode of production.

As is elaborated in Chapter 5, the present account follows the third broad approach. Accelerated large-scale globalization in contemporary history has been closely associated with several important turns in the development of capitalism, but globalization has by no means been the midwife of a post-capitalist society. On the contrary, thus far globalization has left capitalism as entrenched as ever, if not more so, to the point that one could even speak of an onset of 'hypercapitalism'.

Governance

Along with questions of economy, much discussion of globalization and social change has focused on issues of governance (Prakash and Hart, 1999; Nye and Donahue, 2000; Keohane, 2001; Held and McGrew, 2002; Kahler and Lake, 2003). Has the development of a more global world brought fundamental changes in the ways that social life is regulated? Is contemporary society acquiring a new mode of governance because of globalization?

Many debates on globalization and governance have concerned the nature and fate of the state. For example, various commentators have affirmed that contemporary globalization has deprived the state of sovereignty (Camilleri and Falk, 1992; Wriston, 1992; Sassen, 1997). More broadly, a number of analysts have linked the growth of global relations to 'the diminished nation-state', 'the decline of the nation-state', and 'the retreat of the state' (Cable, 1995; Schmidt, 1995; Strange, 1996). Other writers have gone still further to connect globalization with 'a crisis of the nation-state', 'the obsolescence of the state', and 'the extinction of nation-states' (Horsman and Marshall, 1994; Dunn, 1995; Ohmae, 1995; Khan, 1996; Bauman, 1998: ch 4; Hudson, 1999; Bamyeh, 2000). On these accounts, states are helpless victims of globalization.

Such assertions have triggered a host of rebuttals. For example, certain authors insist that globalization has done nothing to undermine sovereign statehood (Thomson and Krasner, 1989; Krasner, 1993). According to this view a state could, if it wished, extricate itself from global relations that would otherwise limit its autonomy. Similar arguments have affirmed that global flows (in communications, ecology, etc.) do not necessarily undermine the state and indeed may in some cases strengthen it (Mann, 1997). Likewise, these perspectives maintain that the state retains substantial capacities to govern global economic activities (Boyer and Drache, 1996; Weiss, 1998; Hirst and Thompson, 1999). Indeed, say the continuity theorists, states (especially the major states) remain the prime regulatory force even in that purportedly most globalized of economic sectors, namely finance (Kapstein, 1994; Pauly, 1997; Helleiner, 1998, 1999).

A third general strand in debates about globalization and governance – an approach that is also developed in Chapter 6 of this book – focuses less on the viability of the state per se and more on shifts in its character. These arguments hold that, while contemporary globalization has not threatened the existence of the state, the process has involved changes in its forms and functions (Jessop, 1994; Camilleri *et al.*, 1995; Panitch, 1996; Evans, 1997; Scholte, 1997; Shaw, 1997). For example, say such authors, sovereignty has acquired substantially different meanings and dynamics in a globalizing world (Lapidoth, 1992; Spruyt, 1994; Gelber, 1997; Schrijver, 1997; Clark, 1999: ch 4). For his part, Bob Jessop has discerned a shift under the pressures of global capital from a Keynesian welfare state to what he calls a 'Schumpeterian workfare state' that subordinates social policy to the demands of labour market flexibility and the constraints of international competition (1993: 9). Meanwhile Philip Cerny has described a 'competition state' that takes measures (in exchange-rate, fiscal, monetary, regulatory and trade policies) to attract and retain footloose global capital (1990: ch 8; 1997; also Bratton *et al.*, 1996).

Various accounts of the mode of governance in a globalizing world – including the present book – have also described a more general structural shift away from the statist so-called 'Westphalian system' that held sway prior to the late twentieth century (Rosenau and Czempiel, 1992; Rosenau, 1997; Herod *et al.*, 1998; Held *et al.*, 1999; Scholte, 2001; Keane, 2003). For these analysts, governance under conditions of large-scale globalization has come to involve more than states. Authority has become increasingly 'multi-level' or 'multi-scalar' across substate (municipal and provincial) bodies and suprastate (macro-regional and transworld) agencies as well as state organs. In addition, various private sector and civil society actors have taken on regulatory roles. On this line of argument states survive under globalization, but they are no longer the sole – and in some cases not even the principal – site of governance.

Identity

Another issue of globalization and social change that has provoked considerable controversy relates to identity and associated constructions of social bonds. In academic circles, these debates have unfolded mainly in anthropological and sociological writings (Featherstone, 1990; King, 1991; Mlinar, 1992; Robertson, 1992; Friedman, 1994; Appadurai, 1996; Cvetkovich and Kellner, 1997; Jameson and Miyoshi, 1998; Meyer and Geschiere, 1998; Tomlinson, 1999). However, much popular speculation has also enquired whether globalization makes people more similar or more different. Does globalization encourage homogenization or heterogenization of identities?

On the one hand, many commentators (particularly those who conceive of globalization in terms of liberalization or westernization) have argued that the process brings about a worldwide 'cultural synchronization' (Hamelink, 1983: 3; also Tomlinson, 1995; Norberg-Hodge, 1999b; Warnier, 2003). In the words of Theodore Levitt, an early champion of global markets, 'everywhere everything gets more and more like everything else as the world's preference structure is relentlessly homogenized' (1983: 93). For these analysts, globalization has harmonized and unified, often crushing traditional ways of life when they have deviated from the dominant western pattern. As a result, cultural diversity has had its day. Globalization is diffusing a single world culture centred on consumerism, mass media, Americana, and the English language. Depending on one's perspective, this homogenization entails either progressive universalism or oppressive imperialism.

In contrast, other diagnoses – including the analysis elaborated in Chapter 7 of this book – have linked globalization with enduring or even increased cultural diversity (Appadurai, 1990; Hannerz, 1992: ch 7; Cable, 1994). For one thing, such accounts emphasize, global communications, markets, etc. are often adapted to fit diverse local contexts. Through so-called 'glocalization', global news reports, global products, global social movements and the like take different forms and make different impacts depending on local particularities (Robertson, 1995; K. R. Cox, 1997). Likewise, large-scale globalization has not kept countless people from continuing to embrace national differences (Smith, 1990; Foster, 1991; Buell, 1994). Indeed, many groups have championed national, religious and other particularistic identities as a reaction to and defence against a universalizing 'McWorld' (Barber, 1996). For followers of Samuel Huntington, identity politics under contemporary globalization is marked by a clash of civilizations: Confucian, Eastern Orthodox, Hindu, Islamic, Judaeo-Christian, etc. (Huntington, 1993, 1996). Others argue that globalization has promoted fragmentation, with a flourishing of substate identities like ethno-nationalism and indigenous peoples' movements (Halperin and Scheffer, 1992; Wilmer, 1993; Connor, 1994; Brysk, 2000). In addition, some accounts suggest that global relations have increased opportunities for the development of nonterritorial identities and solidarities, for example, connected to class, gender, race, religion and sexual orientation.

A further tendency in debates about globalization and identity has highlighted the rise of more intercultural constructions of being and belonging. From this perspective, also developed in Chapter 7, globalization has encouraged countless new cultural combinations and blurred distinctions between nations and between civilizations. Various authors have in this respect associated globalization with 'creolization' and 'hybridization' (Hannerz, 1987;

Nederveen Pieterse, 1995; Hedetoft and Hjort, 2002). A number of commentators have moreover suggested that these tendencies have created a need for alternative forms and ethics of identity politics, away from the old communitarian habits of dualistic 'us–them' oppositions between neatly defined and separated groups (Blaney and Inayatullah, 1994; Shapiro, 1994; Scholte, 1996, 1999; Shapiro and Alker, 1996; Linklater, 1998).

Knowledge

Although most debates about globalization and social change have centred on questions of production, governance and identity, it is possible also to reflect on the implications of a more global world for structures of knowledge. Have dominant modes of understanding shifted as society has acquired more global qualities? Does globalization generate fundamentally different ontologies (notions of reality), epistemologies (conceptions of knowledge), and methodologies (ways of constructing knowledge)?

Most accounts of globalization have been silent on its consequences for knowledge frameworks. Indeed, many researchers on globalization have apparently not regarded structures of knowledge as an important part of their study. Implicitly these analyses have thereby suggested that no significant changes have unfolded in this area.

However, some commentators have explored questions of knowledge and suggest that globalization has promoted shifts in the ways that people comprehend their situation. In terms of ontology, for example, certain authors have associated globalization with basic changes in understandings of space and time (Robertson, 1992). In terms of epistemology, various arguments have linked globalization with contemporary trends of religious revivalism (Robertson and Chirico, 1985). In terms of methodology, some scholars have regarded globalization as an occasion to depart from disciplinary divisions and other established academic conventions (Breton and Lambert, 2003; Scholte, 2004c).

The present book raises these issues in Chapter 8 and concludes that contemporary globalization has in certain respects encouraged challenges to the prevailing rationalist framework of knowledge. As a result, even staunch defenders of rationalism have tended to become more reflexive about their mode of understanding. However, this more self-critical awareness has by no means displaced rationalism as the predominant knowledge structure in today's world.

Systemic transformation?

The preceding survey makes it plain that no easy answers are available to questions of globalization and social change. Do global economics reproduce capitalism or introduce postcapitalist modes of production? Do global politics perpetuate statism or create poststatist modes of governance? Does global culture reinforce nationalism or advance alternative frameworks of identity? In terms of knowledge, does globalization sustain rationalism or promote new frameworks of understanding?

Putting together various observations concerning globalization and social change, can one conclude that the process carries epochal significance? Does a more global world entail a fundamentally different kind of society? Is contemporary globalization propelling a systemic transition of the sort that in earlier history bridged feudalism and capitalism, or the medieval and the modern? Again, opinions are divided.

For some analysts, contemporary globalization entails the dawn of a postmodern era. For example, the geographer David Harvey has applied the label 'postmodernity' to global capitalism and associated cultural changes (Harvey, 1989). For his part, the sociologist Martin Albrow has declared that 'the Global Age' lies beyond modernity, because globality allegedly supplants rationality and the nation-state as the primary bases of social organization (Albrow, 1996). Meanwhile other theorists have identified postmodernity as a global world of 'informationalized', 'mediatized', 'hyperreal', 'virtual', 'simulated' social experiences in which people lose a stable sense of identity and knowledge (Axford, 1995; Luke, 1995; Ó Tuathail, 1996: ch 7; Peterson, 2003).

In contrast to such transformation theses, other accounts have seen only continuities of modernity in contemporary globalization. From such perspectives, a more global world exhibits the same basic modern attributes as preceding social relations. Globality is just as capitalist, just as industrialist, just as bureaucratist, just as militarist, just as nationalist, just as individualist, just as rationalist as earlier forms of modernity. Indeed, some analysts have regarded globalization as an extension of modernization. Such authors claim that, by spreading and deepening the hold of modern social structures across the world, globalization is generating 'high', 'advanced', 'radical' or 'super' modernity (Giddens, 1990, 1991; Augé, 1992; Spybey, 1996). In a variation on this theme, Ulrich Beck has associated globalization with a 'new' and 'reflexive' modernity, a 'modernization of modernization' that replaces industrial society with a risk society wrought by insecurities (Beck, 1986, 1997).

The present book's account of globalization and social change falls somewhere between a high-modernity argument and a postmodernity thesis. From the perspective adopted in Part II, there is an intimate but not necessary connection between globality and modernity. The main structural impetuses to contemporary intense globalization have indeed come from modern social patterns like capitalist production, bureaucratic governance, communitarian identity, and rationalist knowledge. Likewise, for the moment most historical shifts associated with globalization can be understood as changes within continuities of modernity: hypercapitalism is still capitalist; polycentric governance is still bureaucratic; heterogeneous identities still tend to be formed through communitarian 'us–them' dynamics; reflexive rationalism is still rationalist. That said, however, transplanetary and supraterritorial connectivity could conceivably also be generated by and sustained with non-modern social forces. Thus, even if Giddens is right that 'modernity is inherently globalizing' (1990: 63, 177), it does not follow that only modernity can evoke globalization or that globalization is inherently modernizing. Other globalizations (including postmodern globalizations) are possible, as various alternative social practices within current globalization already intimate.

Liberation or shackles?

Next to disputes over starting premises and arguments about social change, a third cluster of globalization debates highlight normative issues. In a word, is globalization a good or a bad thing? Does the process enhance or degrade the human condition? Does the trend produce a utopia or a hell? Does globalization take history to a peak of progress or a trough of decay?

On these matters, too, opinions have been highly divided. On the one hand, many people have welcomed globalization as an emancipatory force. For these enthusiasts, global relations increase efficiency, sustainability, welfare, democracy, community, justice and peace. Globalization is a 'win–win' scenario where everyone in world society benefits. Against this rosy picture, many other people have rejected what they have variously described as 'global pillage', 'global *apartheid*' and 'the global trap' (Brecher and Costello, 1994; Alexander, 1996; Martin and Schumann, 1996). For critics, global relations undermine security, equality and democracy. The rest of this section considers normative debates about globalization in more detail under these three general headings.

Security

The first of these themes, security, encompasses various issues connected with human experiences of safety and confidence. Does globalization encourage protection or vulnerability, stability or uncertainty, well-being or misery, social integration or alienation, calm or stress, hope or fear? Is a more global world a more endangered world, objectively and/or perceptually?

Security has various dimensions: bodily safety, ecological integrity, material welfare, cultural protection, rule of law, and more. Indeed, one effect of contemporary globalization debates has been to broaden the security agenda in world politics beyond the military affairs of states (Booth, 1991; Krause and Williams, 1997; Thomas and Wilkin, 1999). Yet major disagreements have reigned regarding the effects of globalization on the different dimensions and issues of security.

The traditional focus of security has concerned peace and violence. Analysts who link globalization with a spread of free trade and democracy have often connected these developments to a decline in warfare. Observe, they emphasize, that armed conflict has disappeared between states in the more globalized parts of the world. By this account, globalization involves the growth of international cooperation and a one-world community. On broadly such lines, Hans-Henrik Holm and Georg Sørensen have in their assessment of globalization described an emergence of 'postmodern states' for which warfare is unthinkable (1995: 204; also Shaw, 2000).

From a contrary angle, prophets of doom have forecast 'the coming anarchy' of 'global disorder' (Harvey, 1995; Kaplan, 2000). From this pessimistic perspective, globalization has bred intolerance and violence, as manifested in ultra-nationalism, racism, religious fundamentalism, warlordism and terrorism. Civil wars have proliferated as globalization has weakened the state, especially in the East and the South. The technologies of globalization (computers, missiles, satellites) have produced a barbarism of techno-war and a voyeurism of media war. Global resource wars allegedly loom over oil, diamonds, fresh water and more. The pains of global economic restructuring, often pursued through policies sponsored by global institutions like the IMF, have sparked urban riots (Walton and Seddon, 1994). At the same time global sex tourism, global trade in prostitutes, and the mail-order marriage business have increased violence towards women (Pettman, 1996; Skrobanek *et al.*, 1997; Kempadoo and Doezema, 1998). Globalization has also generated new types of illegality such as computer crime and money laundering, as well as transworld criminal networks such as the Sicily-based Cosa Nostra and the Colombia-based Cali cartel (Williams, 1994; Shelley, 1995; Mittelman and Johnston, 1999; Berdal and Serrano, 2002).

A second major security concern in globalization debates is ecological integrity. On this subject the optimists have stressed how global conferences, global research programmes and global environmental movements have raised ecological awareness throughout the contemporary world (McCormick, 1989). The technologies of globalization can – in the case of digital computers, for example – vastly enhance environmental management. Global laws and institutions can provide indispensable frameworks of ecological protection and regeneration (Haas *et al.*, 1993; Young *et al.*, 1996). To take one outstanding example, global conventions and monitoring bodies have been successfully 'healing the sky' from ozone depletion (Tanner, 1997).

For other observers, however, globalization has entailed environmental catastrophe. Since the 1960s a spate of Cassandras have warned of 'the chasm ahead', 'the closing circle', and 'global collapse' (Peccei, 1969; Commoner, 1971; Meadows *et al.*, 1992). A number of global ecological problems allegedly threaten human survival. Consider exhaustion of natural resources, excessive world population growth, nuclear holocaust, acid rain, climate change, species extinction, HIV/AIDS, BSE ('mad cow disease'), SARS, and GM (genetically modified) food crops. Meanwhile global trade has taken pollution to new heights, and global institutions like the World Bank have engineered ecologically unsustainable 'development' (Rich, 1994; Reed, 1996). Worries about global ecological despoliation have lain at the heart of Beck's previously mentioned 'risk society' (Beck, 1988).

Next to bodily security and ecological security, globalization is generally held also to have far-reaching implications for economic security. The enthusiasts have emphasized the gains in economic efficiency and growth that allegedly result when the world becomes a single open marketplace (Bergsten, 1996; Bryan and Farrell, 1996; Burtless *et al.*, 1998: ch 2). Moreover, global trade is said to enhance consumer satisfaction, distributing more products to more people at lower prices. With regard to employment, global investment creates jobs at host sites, and technological advances connected with globalization reduce the burdens of human labour in many industries. Globalization has also served as a primary engine of economic development, particularly in the so-called 'newly industrializing countries' (NICs) like Malaysia and South Korea and the so-called 'emerging markets' like Brazil, Russia, India, China and South Africa (BRICS). Meanwhile, when disasters strike, global communications and global organizations make possible humanitarian relief operations with a speed and on a scale never before available. In short, for its champions, globalization is a formula for unprecedented material prosperity across the planet.

For the critics, however, globalization has had calamitous consequences for economic security (Mander and Goldsmith, 1996). Global capitalism, warns William Greider, 'appears to be running out of control toward some sort of abyss' (1997: 12). The 'mad money' of 'casino capitalism' in global financial markets threatens even the largest of fortunes (Strange, 1986, 1998). Wild fluctuations in foreign exchange rates, stock prices and other financial values can destroy livelihoods in an instant. Global capital outflows have brought even major national economies like Mexico, Korea, Russia, Argentina, Brazil and Turkey to their knees in a matter of days. In the South and the East, global finance has saddled countries large and small with crippling debts. Concurrently, the pressures of global competition have reduced aid flows to poor countries. 'Globalization' and 'development' are antithetical, say the critics (Raghavan *et al.*, 1996; McMichael, 1996a; Thomas and Wilkin, 1997; Hoogvelt, 2001). 'Structural adjustment' in the face of globalization has unravelled welfare provisions for vulnerable sectors of society (Cornia *et al.*, 1987–8; Ghai, 1991; Chossudovsky, 1997). Unemployment has burgeoned as countless companies relocate and 'downsize' in response to global competition. Full employment has become unrealizable. Some analysts have even foreseen a 'jobless future' and 'the end of work' (Aronowitz and DiFazio, 1994; Rifkin, 1995). As for people who remain in waged employment, they have allegedly been caught in a 'race to the bottom' of working conditions between 'lean and mean' global firms (Brecher and Costello, 1994; Tilly, 1995; Kapstein, 1996). In this 'world war' of 'savage capitalism' (Robinson, 1996a: 13, 27), governments and workforces do anything to maintain the 'confidence' of global markets.

More ideational concerns in debates about globalization and security relate to culture. Do global circumstances make people secure in their ways of being, understanding and communicating? On this subject the optimists have celebrated the cultural pluralism and innovation that global relations purportedly promote. In line with previously described claims about heterogenization and hybridization, these commentators have argued that globalization creates space for thousands of flowers to bloom. Furthermore, the enthusiasts maintain, global communications through jet tourism, electronic mass media and the Internet promote greater intercultural understanding and are laying the foundations for a veritable world community.

In contrast, other commentators have suggested that globalization undermines security of identity and knowledge. From their perspective, global relations involve cultural imperialism (cf. Tomlinson, 1991; Petras, 1993; Golding and Harris, 1997). The new world order of globalization imposes 'western' and especially 'American' meanings that both obliterate older traditions and restrict the development of new alternatives. The resultant loss of cultural resources is not only tragic in its own right, but also limits the capacities of humankind to respond creatively and effectively to political, ecological and economic challenges.

From another angle, some analysts have affirmed that intense blending of cultures through globalization unsettles any and all truth claims. Even the Enlightenment vision of human progress becomes a casualty. Science is dead, relativism reigns, intellectual security dissolves.

In sum, globalization debates are littered with polarized claims and counterclaims about human security. At one extreme, enthusiasts have linked globalization to an 'end of history' where peace, sustainability, prosperity and truth are assured (Fukuyama, 1992). At another extreme, alarmists have warned of the 'global turmoil' of a 'new world disorder' (Brzezinski, 1993). These issues are treated at greater length in Chapter 9, where the evidence on these points is found on the whole to be rather negative. However, the fault for these unhappy outcomes lies with the policies adopted towards contemporary globalization rather than with the process as such.

Equality

Alongside security, social equality has been a second major focal point of normative debates about globalization. Do people have equal opportunities to participate in global relations; or does globalization arbitrarily bypass, marginalize and silence much of the world's population? Do people fairly share the costs and the benefits of globalization; or does the process increase maldistribution in the world? Is globalization a force for social justice or exploitation?

Many commentaries on globalization and equality have stressed the negative, with allegations that the process has sustained and indeed often deepened arbitrary social hierarchies. With respect to class, for example, many have claimed that globalization has increased the advantages of already privileged strata. Income gaps have grown in almost every country as wealthy circles have taken the lion's share of the material benefits from globalization. In the words of a peasant activist in Brazil, 'Globalization is a system where a few get a lot and a lot get too little' (Cervinski, 2004). At the same time, many argue, global markets have undermined the Keynesian welfare state as a mechanism for reducing social inequalities (Teeple, 1995; Gray, 1998; Mishra, 1999).

Critics have also frequently alleged that globalization has perpetuated if not heightened inequality in relations between countries (Hurrell and Woods, 1999). In these accounts, globalization is a postcolonial imperialism that has not only reinvigorated the exploitation of the South by the North, but also added former communist-ruled areas to the list of victims. For poor countries, globalization allegedly means perpetual financial and related economic crises, the immiserating effects of structural adjustment programmes imposed by the IMF and the World Bank, further subordination in world trade, ecological problems without economic benefits, and the cultural imperialism of global communications (Thomas and Wilkin, 1997). In the eyes of the pessimists, globalization has frustrated hopes and expectations that decolonization would give the South equal opportunity and self-determination in world affairs.

Meanwhile a number of feminist analyses have linked globalization with gender inequalities (Duggan and Dashner 1994; Eisenstein, 1998; Mies, 1998; Peterson and Runyan, 1999; Wichterich, 2000; Signs, 2001). For example, women are said to have had less access than men to global communications networks, global financial markets, global corporate management, and global governance institutions. The global trade regime has allegedly had gender-differentiated effects that can disadvantage women (Joekes and Weston, 1994; Moon, 1995; Fontana, 2003). Women have provided the bulk of low-paid and poorly protected labour in global service industries ('electronic sweatshops') and the 'global factories' of export processing zones

(Elson and Pearson, 1981; Fuentes and Ehrenreich, 1983; Runyan, 1996; Pearson, 1998). At the same time the pains of global economic restructuring (for example, reduced public services) are said to have fallen disproportionately on women (Vickers, 1991; Beneria and Feldman, 1992; Aslanbeigui *et al.*, 1994; Rajput and Swarup, 1994; Sparr, 1994; Marchand and Runyan, 2000).

Similarly, global relations have, by some claims, perpetuated and intensified racial inequalities. Like women, people of colour have, through what some have termed 'global apartheid', faced structural barriers to access global realms of travel, communications, organization, finance and markets (Falk, 1993; Mazrui, 1994; Richmond, 1994). Several critics have suggested – implicitly or explicitly – that global agencies like the IMF and the World Bank have harboured institutional racism (Budhoo, 1990: 7, 48–9; Rich, 1994: 246–9). Meanwhile declining economic security in the North as a result of globalization has purportedly encouraged a growth of racial intolerance in society at large. Racism has also been quite plain in immigration controls against people of colour in the so-called 'open' world economy (Alexander, 1996: 181–3, 253). More subtle subordination has occurred through the global mass media's usual portrayal of black people 'either as victims of disaster or as exotic extras' (Alexander, 1996: 252).

Other commentators have highlighted still further inequalities in globalization with respect to rural peoples (Flora, 1990; McMichael, 1996b). The countryside has allegedly benefited far less from global flows than towns, as globalization perpetuates an urban bias in development paradigms. Meanwhile the 'global agro-food system' is said to have promoted big industrial and finance capital in the countryside at the expense of smallholder livelihoods and food security (LeHeron, 1993; McMichael, 1993, 1994; Whatmore, 1994). In particular, the ongoing transformation of the world economy has purportedly accelerated a process of 'global depeasantization' whereby dispossessed rural populations have poured into sprawling urban slums (Araghi, 1995).

While many critics have regarded globalization as a catastrophe for social equality, others have made more positive diagnoses. For example, enthusiasts have argued that everyone is – or will be – better off in a global economy. These optimists often point to examples of Chile, China, Hungary, Kuwait and Uganda. Many people may struggle during the transition to a more globalized world, and some classes and countries may gain more, or sooner, than others. However, by following the right policies, in the long run substantial benefits will accrue to all. Already, the optimists affirm, global companies and industries have offered women more opportunities to enter paid employment, while global governance agencies and global social movements have helped to give gender equity issues a higher profile. Global regimes have also done much to advance principles of racial equality and human rights more generally, including for children and disabled persons. Global governance institutions like the World Bank and global nongovernmental organizations (NGOs) like Oxfam are, say some, addressing problems of rural development more effectively than state programmes have ever done.

So does globalization favour the privileged and exploit the vulnerable? Or does globalization open new avenues to greater equality? Chapter 10 assesses a range of available evidence and concludes that, while globalization offers important possibilities to create greater social equality, other significant impacts to date have been negative. Again, however, these downsides have flowed from policy choices rather than from globalization per se.

Democracy

A third area in the spotlight of contemporary normative debates about globalization is democracy (McGrew, 1997b; Holden, 2000). What does 'becoming global' imply for 'rule by the people'? Does globalization enhance or undermine the public's awareness of, involvement in, and control over the decisions that shape its destiny? Does globalization widen or restrict debate of public affairs? How does globalization affect participation, transparency and accountability in governance processes?

Many commentators have celebrated globalization as an occasion of unprecedented democratization. Following the end of the Cold War, liberal democracy has spread to more states than ever (Huntington, 1991; Shin, 1994; Diamond and Plattner, 1996). The military are out in Latin America and Asia. Apartheid is over in South Africa. The wall is down in Europe. Multiparty politics, 'free and fair' elections to representative institutions, and legal guarantees of civil rights have become the worldwide norm for national government. Global regulatory institutions and global civil society have greatly promoted human rights and norms of so-called 'good governance'. The global mass media have encouraged democracy activists from China to Nigeria, Georgia to Chile.

Many analysts have also championed purported democratizing impacts of the technologies of globalization (Abramson *et al.*, 1988; Rheingold, 1993; Budge, 1996; Hill and Hughes, 1998). With particular exuberance, Walter Wriston has enthused that 'the information age is rapidly giving power to the people in parts of the world and in a way that only a few years ago seemed impossible' (1992: 170–1). Electronic communications have given citizens access to unprecedented amounts of information at unprecedented speeds. Telephone, email, radio and television have allowed citizens to relay their views to governing authorities as never before. Electronic communications have also enabled civil society activists across the planet to exchange views and coordinate strategies in global democratic campaigns for progressive social change (Frederick, 1993; Lee, 1996; Harcourt, 1999).

However, against this applause, sceptics have painted globalization as antithetical to democracy (Gill, 1996; Robinson, 1996a: 20–1; Klein, 2000; Hertz, 2001). Various authors have associated this new world order with 'low-intensity democracy' and 'polyarchy' where a narrow élite holds control (Gills *et al.*, 1993; Robinson, 1996b). In apocalyptic terms, Claude Ake has described a 'deadly threat' of globalization that irreversibly shrinks democratic space and renders political participation irrelevant (1999: 179–80).

In particular, many critics have highlighted the alleged inadequacy in a globalizing world of democracy through the state. Of course, some objectors have rejected the principle that the state can ever be a suitable vehicle for democratic self-rule. For these dissenters, formal democracy of the ballot box is a cruel veneer for social injustice. What use, they ask, are referenda and multiparty elections organized by the state if these exercises do nothing to end class inequities, North–South gaps, gender hierarchies, and the subordination of minorities? For these critics, the modern state has never been democratic, and globalization has merely brought these intrinsic failings into sharper focus.

Other analysts have maintained that, while the state was an important agent of the popular will in an earlier era, forces of globalization have critically undermined the democratic capacities of country governments (Connolly, 1991; Held and McGrew, 1993; McGrew, 1997b). For example, say these commentators, states cannot tame the tyranny of global corporations (Korten, 1995). Global financial markets, too, have often constrained the possibilities for democratization through the state (Armijo, 1999). In addition, states – particularly small states – cannot ensure democracy for their citizens in respect of global governance bodies like the International Atomic Energy Agency (IAEA) and the WTO. On this line of argument, territorial mechanisms like the state cannot – certainly by themselves – secure democratic governance of supraterritorial phenomena such as global communications and global ecological problems. Ironically, then, unprecedented numbers of states have adopted liberal democracy at the very moment when statist democracy has passed its historical sell-by date.

On notions of electronic democracy, sceptics have emphasized a digital divide whereby only a minority of the world's population – and a highly privileged minority at that – has had access to the Internet (Loader, 1998). As for home voting via interactive television, this practice would 'privatize politics and replace deliberative debate in public with the unconsidered instant expressions of private prejudices' (Barber, 1996: 270). Meanwhile new information and communications technologies supply authorities with unprecedented capacities for intrusive surveillance and the manipulation of public opinion.

Yet the critics have not been only negative. Many of them have also regarded globalization optimistically as an opportunity to reconstruct democracy. The resultant new frameworks might well give voice and respond to public needs and wants better than state-centric mechanisms of old were ever able to do. For example, some commentators have welcomed globalization as a force that facilitates devolution and the principle of subsidiarity, whereby governing power is always located at the closest possible point to the citizen. Other reformers have stressed the need for a democratization of governance at the regional level, for instance, in relation to the European Union (EU). Meanwhile other analysts have advanced ideas of 'cosmopolitan democracy' through transworld institutions (Held, 1995a,b; Archibugi *et al.*, 1998). A number of specific proposals have suggested the creation in the United Nations of a People's Assembly of citizen representatives alongside the General Assembly of states. In other ways, too, promoters of innovation in democratic practice have endorsed the development of civil society as a 'multilateralism from below' that pursues the public good (Falk, 1992, 1995; Smith and Guarnizo, 1998; Smouts, 1999; Kaldor, 2003). Likewise, a number of political theorists have regarded globalization as a stimulus to develop new and more effective modes of citizenship (Steenbergen, 1994; Lacarrieu and Raggio, 1997; Castles and Davidson, 2000; Vandenberg, 2000). In short, for these authors democracy is historically contingent, and globalization by altering the contours of governance demands that democracy be refashioned anew.

As with issues of security and equality, then, considerable discord exists concerning the implications of globalization for democracy. For some a more global world is a blessing for collective self-determination, while for others it is a bane. The relative merits of the various arguments are evaluated in Chapter 11, where it is concluded that contemporary globalization has indeed generated very serious democratic deficits, but also significant opportunities to redress them.

What to do?

On top of disagreeing about starting premises, assessments of social change, and normative evaluations, people have also taken radically different positions concerning the policy courses that should be adopted towards globalization. Almost no one argues that all is well in the current globalizing world, but commentators have advanced widely varying prescriptions to improve the situation (Higgott, 2000).

Four broad lines of policy response to contemporary globalization can be distinguished. On the one hand, neoliberalists have championed globalization on a market-led path in which public authorities only facilitate and in no way interfere with the dynamics of demand and supply. In contrast, rejectionists have advocated 'de-globalization' and return to a pre-global status quo ante. A third approach, reformism, has argued that globalization should be deliberately steered with public policies, including substantially increased global governance. Finally, transformist strategies have variously drawn on anarchist, socialist, postmodernist and other radical visions to advocate a revolutionary globalization that transcends currently prevailing social structures like capitalism or rationalism.

Neoliberalism

As the name suggests, 'neo'-liberalism advances a new line on an old story. It draws on several centuries of modern thought dating back to treatises by the likes of John Locke and Adam Smith. Neoliberalism builds on the *laissez-faire* convictions of classical liberalism, which promise that unconstrained market forces will 'naturally' bring prosperity, liberty, democracy and peace to society. In particular, liberal trade theorists have argued since the seventeenth century that state borders should not form an artificial barrier (with tariffs and other officially imposed restrictions) to the efficient allocation of resources in the world economy.

Early intellectual exponents of neoliberalism between the 1930s and the 1960s included Friedrich von Hayek and Milton Friedman. Since the 1970s neoliberalists have revived classical liberal arguments for 'free markets' in relation to an economy that is becoming increasingly global (Gill, 1995a; Chomsky, 1998; Gore, 2000; Went, 2000; Gamble, 2001; Hovden and Keene, 2002; Scholte, 2003; Steger, 2004, 2005). According to neoliberalist tenets, globalization should be approached with large-scale removal of official interventions in the market, especially through measures of liberalization, deregulation, privatization and fiscal constraint. This policy package has often been termed 'the Washington Consensus', as the economist John Williamson dubbed the prevailing view of the US Government and the Washington-based global economic institutions in the 1980s (Williamson, 1990, 1997).

In a word, neoliberalists have reacted against the statist strategies of economic management that prevailed (whether in a socialist, a fascist or a welfarist form) across the world between the 1930s and the 1970s. With liberalization, neoliberalists have advocated the abolition of most state-imposed limitations on movements between countries of money, goods, services and capital. Logically, neoliberalism should also promote unrestricted cross-border movements of labour, but in practice its proponents have rarely pressed this point. With deregulation, neoliberalists have called for the removal of various state controls, for example, on prices, wages and foreign exchange rates. With privatization, neoliberalists have urged a major contraction of state ownership of productive assets and a transfer of many service provisions from government agencies to the private sector. And with fiscal constraint, neoliberalists have demanded tight controls on government spending in order to limit public-sector debt and reduce tax rates.

This is not to say, as some commentators have mistakenly assumed, that neoliberalist approaches to globalization accord no role to the state and other governance institutions. Deregulation does not mean no regulation. On the contrary, neoliberalism recognizes the need for laws and institutions that uphold markets and promote their efficient operation, for example, with guarantees of property rights and contracts. Moreover, when a population is reluctant, the implementation of a neoliberalist agenda can depend on strong pressure from the state and/or suprastate agencies like the IMF (A. Gamble, 1994). However, in neoliberalist eyes public-sector agencies should not attempt to direct the course of market forces in the global or any other realm. Hence neoliberalism prescribes a shift from state interventionism towards market-enabling governance.

Neoliberalism has generally prevailed as the reigning policy discourse for globalization since the early 1980s. Most governments – including in particular those of the major states – have adopted a neoliberalist orientation toward globalization over the past quarter-century. From the side of global institutions, agencies such as the IMF, the WTO and the Organization for Economic Cooperation and Development (OECD) have continually linked globalization with liberalization. Since the 1990s UN agencies have largely come to a neoliberalist orientation as well, albeit with greater hesitation and qualification. Meanwhile most schemes of regionalization in the contemporary globalizing economy have focused on the liberalization of cross-border traffic between the countries involved. Champions of neoliberalism have also abounded in commercial circles, particularly in the financial markets and among managers of global firms. Business associations like the International Organization of Employers (IOE) and the World Economic Forum (WEF) have likewise figured as bastions of neoliberalism. In the mass media, major business-oriented newspapers and magazines like the *Wall Street Journal* (*WSJ*) and *The Economist* have generally supported neoliberalist policies, as have business and economy programmes on mainstream radio and television. In academic quarters, conventional courses in Business Studies and Economics have extolled the virtues of global free markets from positions at renowned and obscure universities alike. Other researchers have promoted neoliberalist policies through influential think tanks such as the Institute for International Economics in Washington, DC (Bergsten, 1996).

Given this considerable hold on élite circles, neoliberalism has generally ranked as policy orthodoxy in respect of contemporary globalization. Indeed, neoliberalist ideas have held widespread unquestioned acceptance as 'commonsense'. Enjoying the strongest backing in official, business, media and academic circles, neoliberalist measures towards globalization have usually been the easiest to endorse. Moreover, as later chapters make clear, this approach has often generously served powerful interests, particularly those related to dominant classes and countries.

This is not to say that neoliberalist policies have been fully and consistently implemented. There have always been disconnects between ideology and practice. In particular, many powerful state and corporate actors have qualified or refused a 'free markets' approach when its adoption would disadvantage them. For instance, as already noted, few champions of global *laissez-faire* have taken the logical step of advocating unrestricted transworld movements of labour. In addition, the European Union and the US government have for many years obstructed efforts to liberalize trade in agriculture, a measure that would substantially benefit many poor countries. On these and other occasions, the practical application of neoliberalist principles has revealed glaring double standards. Yet in spite of these inconsistencies – or indeed perhaps because of them – neoliberalism has remained the dominant policy orientation towards globalization over the past quarter-century.

True, advocates of liberalization, deregulation, privatization and fiscal constraint have tended to become less dogmatic since the mid-1990s. While mainstream economists have vigorously rebutted 'anti-globalization' argments (Deardorff, 2003; Segerstrom, 2003; Bhagwati, 2004), many neoliberalists now concede that their policy instruments need to be formulated and executed with greater regard to particular contexts than was often done in the evangelical 1980s and early 1990s. Likewise, the 'Augmented Washington Consensus' of recent years has included more measures to address corruption, transparency, financial codes and standards, institution building, unsustainable debt burdens, better timing and sequencing of capital control removal, social safety nets, poverty reduction, corporate citizenship, civil society consultation, and so on (Burki and Perry, 1998; Stiglitz, 1998, 2002; Coyle, 2000; CFGS, 2001; Rodrik, 2001; World Bank, 2001, 2002). Yet at its core 'Washington Plus' has retained the neoliberalist commitment to globalization-by-marketization. Indeed, in this sense it is somewhat misleading to speak – as some have done – of a 'Post-Washington Consensus', given that the broad underlying strategy has remained the same (Martib, 2000).

As elaborated in Part III, this book aligns itself with critics of neoliberalism. It judges that, although some liberalizations, deregulations, privatizations and fiscal disciplines have enhanced efficiencies in the contemporary globalizing economy, the magnitude of these gains has fallen far short of what is needed to ensure prosperity for all. On the contrary, as at other times in history, 'free markets' have generally directed disproportionate benefits to the already privileged and increased the marginalization of the disadvantaged. Unconstrained global markets have also tended to encourage greater cultural destruction, ecological degradation and human rights abuses. 'Post-Washington' reforms have certainly been an improvement on the ultra-liberalism of the 1980–95 period, but they do not address the inherent shortcomings of a market-led strategy of globalization.

Rejectionism

The other three general policy approaches to globalization distinguished here have in different ways reacted against the harmful effects of neoliberalism. For their part, rejectionists have extrapolated from the failings of *laissez-faire* globalization to conclude that any and all forms of transworld connectedness have calamitous consequences. For these critics, globality is by its very nature deeply and unacceptably unsafe, unjust, undemocratic and unsustainable. Since these negative consequences are inherent in globalization, the rejectionists say, the process should be avoided in whatever guise. Only with a reversion to national and local spheres can people rebuild a good society. 'De-globalization' is needed to recover ecological integrity, economic welfare, cultural security, self-determination and peace (Mander and Goldsmith, 1996; Hewison, 1999; Hines, 2000; Bello, 2004).

Rejectionist calls for de-globalization have come in diverse forms, including economic nationalism as well as some streams of religious revivalism and radical environmentalism. Economic nationalists (a group that has included some old-style socialists like the Communist Party in post-Soviet Russia) have put the emphasis on reestablishing self-determination of countries by delinking them from global economic activities (Raghavan *et al.*, 1996). Religious revivalists among some Buddhists, Christians, Hindus, Jews and Muslims have prescribed 'going local' to retrieve the original beliefs and practices of their faith. (That said, not all religious responses to globalization have taken a rejectionist line. See, for example, Muzaffar, 1993 for a modernist Islamic approach to globalization and Sulak, 1999 for a modernist Buddhist view.) Meanwhile some 'deep green' ecologists have aimed to restore pre-modern respect of, and harmony with, nature through self-sufficient local communities (Norberg-Hodge, 1999a; Shuman, 2000).

Rejectionists are the veritable anti-globalizers in contemporary politics. Confusingly, many commentators have also applied the label of 'anti-globalization movement' to reformists and transformists who seek not to reverse globalization, but to redirect its course away from neoliberalism to alternative paths. Such critics would more accurately be called 're-globalizers' rather than 'de-globalizers'. Reformists and transformists are proponents of 'alter-globalization' (after the French *alter-mondialisation*) or 'counter-globalizations' rather than 'anti-globalization'. Only rejectionist circles are actually against globalization per se. Even that opposition is qualified to the extent that, paradoxically, rejectionist anti-globalizers have often relied on global telecommunications, the Internet, air travel and transworld civil society networks to pursue their causes.

The fact that even the greatest opponents of globalization are enveloped in it suggests the unviability of rejectionist strategies. Indeed, the present book takes the view that the forces behind globalization are currently far too strong to unravel the process. The (re)construction of nationalist or localist social orders, free of global links, is therefore not practicable. As indicated in Chapter 4, prevailing conditions with regard to capitalist development, governance arrangements, identity politics and knowledge structures all point decidedly towards sustained globalization for the foreseeable future. The idea of eliminating these powerful trends is unfeasible within current time horizons. The challenge is not to undo and abolish globalization, but to understand and shape the process in ways that avoid the pitfalls of neoliberalism.

Reformism

With the aim of building such alternative globalizations, a number of strategies have taken what can be termed a reformist approach. Like rejectionists, reformists oppose neoliberalist globalization for inflicting major cultural, ecological, economic, political and psychological harms. However, in contrast to rejectionists, reformists affirm that a more global world is here to stay, and they seek to redirect globalization more positively on non-marketist lines.

As the name suggests, reformists hold that capitalism can be a force for social good if it is 're-formed', that is, reorganized in non-liberalist ways that encourage economic efficiency and stability, promote equitable distribution, limit ecological damage, avoid cultural violence, and enhance democracy. In particular, reformists draw on social-democratic traditions such as Keynesian economics and the welfare state. In these visions, far-reaching proactive public policies backed by a strong and democratically controlled governance apparatus are required to achieve a socially progressive capitalist economy. For example, reformists have advocated controls on cross-border movements of resources when such constraints would reduce market volatilities, social inequities and environmental costs. Reformists have also often argued for anti-trust measures and other official controls to limit corporate power. In addition, reformists have prescribed various statutory guarantees of minimum standards (including basic incomes, labour protections and environmental controls) in order to protect vulnerable circles from the ravages of unfettered capitalism. Other reformist policies have sought actively to promote opportunities for structurally disadvantaged social groups like people of colour, the unemployed, small cultivators, and women.

Many reformist policies to tame global capitalism can be pursued through the state. A number of reformists have therefore argued for a reinvigoration of country-based social democracy to meet new global realities (Boyer and

Drache, 1996; Hutton, 1996; Martin and Schumann, 1996; Giddens, 1998; Hirst and Thompson, 1999; Held, 2004). These commentators have often expressed disappointment that purportedly social democratic governments have not done more to reign in global capital. Cardoso and Lula in Brazil, Blair in Britain, Schröder in Germany, and Mbeki in South Africa have, for these critics, conceded far too much to neoliberalism.

In part, as various social democrats have recognized, these failings of country governments arise because global capital cannot be effectively tamed through the state alone. To be effective, a reformist strategy of globalization also requires expanded global governance (Group of Lisbon, 1994; Carlsson *et al.*, 1995; Deacon, 1997; Reinicke, 1998; Cable, 1999; Falk, 1999; Kaul *et al.*, 1999, 2003; Brand, 2000; Nederveen Pieterse, 2000; Drache, 2001; Simmons and de Jonge Oudraat, 2001; Nayyar, 2002; Deacon *et al.*, 2003; Held and Koenig-Archibugi, 2003). For example, these reformists would argue, effective prevention of monopoly requires a global competition authority that works alongside state and regional anti-trust schemes. Likewise, labour standards and other social protections cannot be effectively secured in a context of global capitalism unless enforceable transworld conventions supplement and bolster relevant state statutes. Similarly, binding global ecological regimes administered through a World Environment Organization are needed as well as country and local laws. A fully-fledged global central bank is required to establish greater stability and justice in global financial markets. Redistributive global taxes (for example, on foreign-exchange transactions, air travel, carbon emissions, and the profits of transnational corporations) are needed to allocate the gains of global capitalism in more socially just ways.

Of course, global social democracy must be democratic. Reformists have therefore also urged that democracy be refashioned so that the prescribed enlargement of global governance involves appropriate forms and levels of public participation and public accountability. Reformist suggestions for such a democratization of globalization have included the creation of global parliamentary bodies, enhanced oversight of global governance by national legislatures, revised voting formulas for global institutions, and the promotion of an energetic global civil society.

Reformist strategies have on the whole held a weaker position in the politics of globalization than neoliberalism and rejectionism. Social-democratic proposals to *tame global capitalism* have gained much less support than 'post-Washington' measures to *improve global markets*. (Note the important difference of emphasis.) Nor have reformist visions of greater global governance mustered the mass appeal that some economic nationalists and religious revivalists have managed to attract for their de-globalization campaigns. Given this generally shallow support for reformist globalization, the strategy has to date yielded relatively few concrete results, except perhaps to push neoliberalists to greater moderation. Indeed, neoliberalist regimes have shown considerable adeptness in coopting reformist themes (like 'civil society' or 'sustainable development') and draining them of most social-democratic content.

Nevertheless, reformism has had important proponents. For example, several country governments have made pronouncements in favour of greater global governance. In this vein French President Jacques Chirac has, in rhetoric at least, supported the creation of an Economic and Social Security Council in the United Nations. Meanwhile several national parliaments (for example, in Belgium, Canada and Germany) have since 1999 passed resolutions in favour of a global tax on currency transactions. A vision of global social democracy has also underpinned notions of 'decent work' developed since 1999 at the International Labour Organization (ILO) and conceptions of a 'rights-based approach to development' pursued at the United Nations Development Programme (UNDP). In addition, UNDP has popularized many global reform proposals through the *Human Development Report*, issued annually since 1990. In civil society numerous activists, including some prominent participants in the World Social Forum (WSF) process, have promoted greater global governance on social-democratic lines. In a similar vein, the International Confederation of Free Trade Unions (ICFTU) has advocated 'international policies and institutions to manage the process of globalization in the service of the needs and aspirations of people' (ICFTU, 1998: 9).

As the tenor of the above remarks suggests, the present book is broadly sympathetic to reformist visions of global social democracy, albeit with several qualifications. For one thing, reformism tends to take an overly materialist approach, offering many proposals to reshape capitalism and governance while giving minimal attention to matters of identity and knowledge. Indeed, reformist ideas have been mostly drawn from Western Europe, and their proponents have generally given little thought to the intercultural negotiations that are necessary to make the strategy democratically viable in global spheres. More broadly, too, reformists have tended not adequately to think through the technicalities and the politics of implementing their programmes. Finally, reformist ideas concerning global democracy have often merely transposed models of national democracy to the global sphere, when globalization arguably calls for more far-reaching innovations in democratic practices.

Transformism

A fourth category of strategies towards globalization covers policies that go beyond reformism to advocate more fundamental social change. These approaches treat the emergence of a more global world as an occasion to create a thoroughly different society. Transformists do not seek, like reformists, only to produce new laws and institutions that make the existing social order work better. Rather, these advocates aim to transcend prevailing social structures with radically new arrangements. Whereas reformists accept primary ordering principles of contemporary life like capitalism and rationalism, transformists regard these frameworks as incorrigible and look to use globalization to build a fundamentally different society.

Like neoliberalism, rejectionism and reformism, transformist strategies have come in various guises. For example, many in a new generation of anarchists and socialists have seen contemporary globalization as a moment to resist and transcend capitalism and associated violences (Gills, 1997; Rupert, 2000; Bircham and Charlton, 2001; Epstein, 2001; Broad, 2002; Graeber, 2002; Danaher and Marks, 2003; Kingsnorth, 2003; Notes from Nowhere, 2003; Sandbrook, 2003; Mertes, 2004; Eschle and Maiguashca, 2005; Starr, 2005). Often these radicals have dismissed as outdated the traditional socialist strategy of overturning capitalism through a proletarian capture of the state. Instead they have championed new global social movements of the oppressed that include indigenous peoples, peasants, sexual minorities and women as well as working classes. For their part, a number of postmodernists have argued for radically different kinds of global identity politics and radically new forms of global knowledge (Ó Tuathail, 1996; Shapiro and Alker, 1996). With a religious emphasis, certain theologians have regarded expanded globality as a context for a post-rationalist spiritual revolution (Küng, 1990; Rifkin, 2003).

Transformist visions of globalization have mainly been pursued outside conventional politics: away from governments and political parties; away from mainstream media and large publishers; away from leading universities and academic conferences; indeed, often away from formal organizations of any kind. Instead, transformists have often worked outside the spotlight through loose and decentralized networks. The casual observer can therefore readily overlook these activities.

Examples of transformist initiatives in contemporary politics of globalization include the grassroots peasant activists of the worldwide Vía Campesina coalition, including the media-savvy Zapatistas of Chiapas State in southern Mexico (Bové and Dufour, 2001; Olesen, 2002). In addition, globally oriented socialism has inspired the efforts of some alternative labour movements that work outside traditional trade union arrangements (Waterman, 1998). Students and other youth have figured prominently in transformist groups such as Reclaim the Streets in Britain, Montreal Anti-Capitalist Convergence in Canada, Ya Basta in Italy, and Direct Action Network in the USA. Postmodernist politics have marked various dissident academic and artistic circles, mainly in the OECD countries. Liberation theology has assembled followings among radical priests in the global Catholic Church, while Hindu revivalists and Islamists have also formed transplanetary networks.

On the whole, however, transformist policies toward globalization have attracted even weaker support than reformist strategies. These visions have taken no noteworthy hold in official governance of globalization. The numbers of transformist activists and academics have remained small, and the relevant grassroots movements in particular have generally suffered from very limited resources. For the moment it seems highly unlikely that transformist campaigns can gain the upper hand in globalization politics. Even in their present weak position, these radicals have experienced some pretty violent suppression by official authorities.

Transformist initiatives have also had their own limitations. For example, these visions have tended to be incompletely articulated, saying much more about what is opposed than what is proposed. Moreover, it is not always clear that the new worlds on offer through transformation would indeed improve upon the limitations and failings of currently prevailing social structures. For example, transformist movements have often struggled with their own internal age, class, country, culture, gender and race hierarchies. White middle-class Anglo-Saxon Protestant males (WMCASPMs) have readily dominated movements to overcome domination, too!

In its final chapter this book adopts some caution towards transformist strategies and draws more from reformist programmes of global social democracy (with the qualifications noted earlier). Transformist critiques of other approaches to globalization have the vitally important effect of stimulating searching debates of what is and creative explorations of what could be. However, transformist strategies of globalization are not sufficiently developed either intellectually or politically to be practicable in the short or medium term. Indeed, the achievement of global social democracy within the next generation might provide riper ground for deeper progressive transformations in the longer run.

Conclusion

As this opening chapter has indicated – and as the summary in the box below recapitulates – the only consensus about globalization is that it is contested. People have held widely differing views regarding definition, scale, chronology, explanation, impact and policy. Everyone – including each reader of this book – has to see their way through the debates to their own understanding and practice of globalization.

The remaining chapters return to the different contentious points surveyed in successive sections of this opening chapter. Chapters 2 to 4 elaborate starting premises. Chapters 5 to 8 examine implications for social structures. Chapters 9 to 11 explore impacts on the human condition. Chapter 12 considers policy options.

Globalization debates in summary

Starting premises

- competing definitions: internationalization or something different?
- varying measurements of scale: globalism or scepticism?
- contrasting chronologies: old or new?
- diverse explanations: materialist or idealist, individualist or structuralist?

Implications for social change

- old capitalism, new capitalism or postcapitalism?
- persistent statism or poststatist governance?
- homogenization or heterogenization of identities?
- old lines or new turns in knowledge?
- extension of modernity or dawn of postmodernity?

Impacts on the human condition

- increased or decreased security?
- more or less social equality?
- greater or reduced democracy?

Policy responses

- neoliberalist reliance on market forces?
- rejectionist reliance on localism?
- reformist reliance on public policies?
- transformist reliance on social revolution?

However, before entering into that more detailed discussion, what does the preceding review of research and policy reveal concerning the present state of knowledge about globalization? Clearly a great deal has been pronounced on the subject. Indeed, thanks to burgeoning studies we are today much better placed than we were only a decade ago to make sense of globalization. Nevertheless, our understanding of the process remains quite limited in important respects. Although some of the literature has become conceptually more sophisticated and empirically more rigorous, the overall level of globalization debates is still disappointing. Too much discussion continues to be couched in soundbite, overgeneralization and blatant prejudice. Too little research breaks out of disciplinary corners to draw together the various dimensions of globalization: cultural, ecological, economic, geographical, historical, legal, political and psychological.

It may be hoped that this book makes some inroads on these limitations; however, it can do little to counter another key shortcoming. As noted earlier, the protagonists in globalization debates have been disproportionately urban, white, middle-class, Judaeo-Christian, older English-speaking men resident in the North (especially the USA and the UK). Notable books on globalization have appeared in Argentina (Ferrer, 1997; Seoane and Taddei, 2001), Brazil (Ianni, 1992, 1996; Gómez, 2000), China (Wang Ning, 2002), Japan (Kaneko, 1999; Inoguchi, 2001), Malaysia (Khor, 2001; Mittelman and Othman, 2001), Poland (Aniol, 2002), Russia (Gorbachev Foundation, 2003), South Africa (Mhone and Edigheji, 2003), Thailand (Sulak, 1999) and elsewhere. However, these works are few in number and tend to have small circulation. As a result, many views on globalization are marginalized or silenced altogether. Much of the debate is never heard. The present book can alert the reader to these sidelined voices, but it cannot speak for them.

Chapter 2

Defining Globalization

Main points of this chapter
Rise of the g-word
Starting premises for definition
Redundant concepts of globalization
A way forward
Qualifications
Conclusion

Main points of this chapter

- general notions of global-ness have a long history, but talk of 'globality' (the condition) and 'globalization' (the trend) has mainly arisen since 1980
- a clear and precise definition of the global is crucial to advance both knowledge and policy in contemporary society
- when taken to mean internationalization, liberalization, universalization or westernization, ideas of globalization reveal little new and can have objectionable political implications
- important new insight is provided when globalization is understood in spatial terms as the spread of transplanetary – and in recent times more particularly supraterritorial – connections between people
- globality in the sense of transworld connectivity is manifested across multiple areas of social life, including communication, travel, production, markets, money, finance, organizations, military, ecology, health, law and consciousness
- notions of globalization as the rise of transplanetary and supraterritorial links between people need to be carefully qualified in order to avoid globalist excesses

Definition is not everything, but everything involves definition. Knowledge of globalization is substantially a function of how the word is defined. Thus every study of globalization should include a careful and critical examination of the term itself. A muddled or misguided core concept compromises our overall comprehension of the phenomenon. In contrast, a sharp and revealing definition promotes insightful, interesting and empowering knowledge, an understanding that helps people to shape their destiny in directions of their choosing.

Notions of globalization have grabbed many an intellectual imagination over the past two decades. In academic and lay circles alike, many have pursued an intuition that this concept could provide an analytical lynchpin for understanding contemporary society. 'Globalization' is not the only (or necessarily the best) entry point for such an enquiry, of course, but it has generated a lot of provocative and sometimes highly insightful commentary on present times.

Yet what lies in this word? What, precisely, is 'global' about globalization (Maclean, 1999)? The present chapter develops a definition in five main steps. The first section traces the rise of the vocabulary of globalization in academic and lay thinking. The second section elaborates some general principles about the nature and role of definition. The third section identifies several analytical cul-de-sacs with respect to globalization: that is, definitions that generate redundant and in some respects also unhelpful knowledge. The fourth section sets out a conceptualization of globalization as the spread of transplanetary and, in present times more specifically, supraterritorial social relations.

To stress that this analysis does not succumb to globalist exaggerations, the fifth section adds half a dozen key qualifications to this definition. First, territorial geography continues to be important alongside increased supraterritoriality. Second, globality is interrelated with, rather than separate from, other social spaces. Third, the global is not inherently contradictory to the local. Fourth, globalization is not intrinsically a culturally homogenizing process. Fifth, global relations have spread unevenly across regions and social sectors, so that people experience globality to different extents. Sixth, globalization is a thoroughly political matter, empowering some people and disempowering others.

Rise of the g-word

Although the term 'globalization' was not coined until the second half of the twentieth century, it has a longer pedigree. In the English language, the noun 'globe' dates from the fifteenth century (derived from the Latin *globus*) and began to denote a spherical representation of the earth several hundred years ago (Robertson, 2001: 6,254; *MWD*, 2003). The adjective 'global' entered circulation in the late seventeenth century and began to designate 'planetary scale' in the late nineteenth century, in addition to its earlier meaning of 'spherical' (*OED*, 1989: VI, 582). The verb 'globalize' appeared in the 1940s, together with the term 'globalism' (Reiser and Davies, 1944: 212, 219). The word 'globalization', as a process, first surfaced in the English language in

1959 and entered a dictionary two years later (Webster, 1961: 965; Schreiter, 1997). Notions of 'globality', as a condition, began to circulate in the 1980s (Robertson, 1983).

The vocabulary of globalization has also spread in other languages over the past several decades. The many examples include the terms *lil 'alam* in Arabic, *quanqiuhua* in Chinese, *mondialisation* in French, *gorobaruka* in Japanese, *globalizatsia* in Russian, *globalización* in Spanish, and *küreselleşme* in Turkish. Among the major world languages, only Swahili has not (yet) acquired a globalization concept, and that exception is perhaps largely explained by the widespread use of English in élite circles of the African countries concerned. Yet less widely used languages, too, now incorporate words such as *globalisaatio* (Finnish), *bishwavyapikaran* (Nepalese), *luan bo'ot* (Timorese), and so on.

Talk of 'globalization' has become rife among academics, journalists, politicians, business people, advertisers and entertainers. Everyday conversation now includes regular reference to global markets, global communications, global conferences, global threats, the global environment, and so on. A recent children's T-shirt was inscribed with the words 'Global Generation' – and well they might be.

When new vocabulary gains such wide currency across continents, languages and walks of life, can it just be explained away as fad? Or does the novel word highlight a significant change in the world, where new terminology is needed to discuss new conditions? For example, when Jeremy Bentham coined the word 'international' in the 1780s the concept caught hold because it resonated of a growing trend of his day, namely, the rise of nation-states and cross-border transactions between them (Bentham, 1789: 326; Suganami, 1978). The current proliferation of global talk also seems unlikely to be accidental. The popularity of the terminology arguably reflects a widespread intuition that contemporary social relations are undergoing an important shift in character. The challenge – indeed, the urgent need – is to move beyond the buzzword to a tight concept.

As a deliberately fashioned analytical tool, notions of the global appeared roughly simultaneously and independently in several academic fields around the early 1980s. In Sociology, for example, Roland Robertson began to 'interpret globality' in 1983 (Robertson, 1983). Concurrently, in Business Studies, Theodore Levitt wrote of 'the globalization of markets' (Levitt, 1983). These years also saw some researchers in International Relations shift their focus to 'global interdependence' (Rosenau, 1980; Maghroori and Ramberg, 1982). Economists, geographers and others picked up the concept later in the 1980s.

Since the 1990s globalization has become a major academic growth industry. The problem is now explored across disciplines, across continents, across theoretical approaches, and across the political spectrum. Countless academics have rushed to claim the cliché of the day. The number of references to 'globali[s/z]ation' in titles held by the United States Library of Congress multiplied from 34 in 1994 to 693 in 1999 and 5,245 in early 2005 (Waters, 1995; LoC, 1999, 2005). Google hits for 'globali[s/z]ation' on the World Wide Web have risen to 23.3 million as this book goes to press. A host of research institutes, degree programmes, course modules, textbooks and websites now focus on the problem. The recent appearance of several globalization anthologies, the preparation of the first *Encyclopedia of Globalization*, and the development of an online 'Globalization Compendium' further attest to the consolidation of a new field of enquiry (Beynon and Dunkerley, 2000; Higgott and Payne, 2000; Lechner and Boli, 2000; Robertson and White, 2002; Held and McGrew, 2003; Michie, 2003; Global Compendium, 2005; Robertson and Scholte, 2006). Since 2000 several new professional groups have also emerged: Global Studies Associations in Britain and the USA; and a Globalization Studies Network with worldwide membership. Some theorists have even presented globalization as the focal point for an alternative paradigm of social enquiry (cf. Shaw, 1994, 1999; Cerny, 1996; Mittelman, 2002).

Yet ideas of globalization tend to remain as elusive as they are pervasive. We sense that the vocabulary means something – and something significant – but we are far from sure what that something is. Anthony Giddens has observed that 'there are few terms that we use so frequently but which are in fact as poorly conceptualized as globalization' (Giddens, 1996).

Persistent ambiguity and confusion over the term has fed considerable scepticism about 'globaloney', 'global babble', 'glob-blah-blah', 'glob-yak-yak'. One critic has pointedly dismissed the idea of lending analytical weight to the notion of globalization as 'folly' (Rosenberg, 2001, 2005). True, some of these objectors have had dubious motives, such as vested interests in orthodox theory, or an intellectual laziness that resists rethinking conceptual starting points. However, other doubters have quite rightly demanded a full conceptualization before they will treat globalization as a serious scholarly category.

Starting premises for definition

Before addressing the challenge of tightly conceptualizing the global, it is well to reflect on the nature and purpose of definition. The exercise of naming and identifying things is much more than a lexicographical curiosity. Five points deserve particular emphasis.

First, definition serves – or should serve – to advance knowledge. A definition should pave the way to greater insight. Thus, to be maximally helpful, a new notion like globality/globalization should be defined in a way that opens new understanding. The word should not merely restate what can already be known with other terminology.

Second, no conceptualization is normatively and politically neutral. It is therefore necessary carefully to reflect on the priorities and power relations that any definition reflects – and also helps to (re)produce. Different definitions of globalization may promote different values and interests. Indeed, certain critics find that the word 'globalization' itself is so loaded with an imposed alien ideological agenda that they prefer to avoid the term in scholarly analysis (Grzybowski, 2004). Farsi speakers make a political statement in their choice between the terms *jahanisasi* and *jahanishodan*. The first word, 'making global', carries connotations of a US-led imperialist project, while the second, 'becoming global', carries connotations of an open process that can be shaped in various future directions.

Third, every definition is relative to a context. Each understanding of a key concept reflects a historical moment, a cultural setting, a geographical location, a social status, an individual personality and – as already noted – a normative and political commitment. Indeed, in the details if not in the general framework, every account of an idea is unique. Each person develops a conception that corresponds to their particular experiences and aspirations. No universally endorsable definition is available. To ask everyone to conform to a single view would be to ask many people to abandon themselves. The object of definition is not to discover one sole understanding that secures universal acceptance, but to generate insight that can be effectively communicated to, and debated with, others.

Fourth, no definition is definitive. Definitions of core concepts are necessary to lend clarity, focus and internal consistency to arguments. However, knowledge is a constant process of invention and reinvention. Hence every definition is tentative and subject to reappraisal. Definition is in motion rather than fixed. The point of the exercise is not to end in a full stop, but to stimulate discussion that prompts further redefinition as situations change and (one hopes) wisdom deepens.

Fifth, the variability of definition means that each formulation should be as clear, precise, concise, explicit, consistent and cogent as possible. With clarity, a good definition readily captures and communicates insight. With precision, it brings the issue at hand into sharp focus. With conciseness, it encompasses the greatest understanding in the fewest words. With explicitness, it leaves a minimum unspoken and to the reader's inference. With consistency, it lends internal coherence from start to finish of an argument. With cogency, it relates convincingly to empirical evidence and policy needs. To be sure, no definition ever fully meets these criteria, but the better conceptions come closer to the ideal.

Not everyone agrees with these starting premises, of course. For example, some commentators accept that globalization is a vague concept and see little point in trying to define it in a clear, specific, succinct, distinctive way. On this relaxed approach, globalization is a malleable catchall term that can be invoked in whatever way the user finds convenient. Thus many a politician has blamed an undefined 'globalization' for a variety of policy difficulties, sometimes to divert attention from their own failures. Many a social activist has rallied under an unspecified 'anti-globalization' banner, so that this movement has encompassed enormously diverse (and sometimes strikingly contradictory) elements. Many an author and publisher have put 'globalization' into the titles of writings that actually say very little on the subject.

While such loose approaches may be politically and commercially useful, they are deeply unsatisfactory for serious social analysis and the policy implications that flow from it. Definitions fundamentally shape descriptions, explanations, evaluations, prescriptions and actions. If a definition of a core concept is slippery, then the knowledge built upon it is likely to be similarly shaky and, in turn, the actions pursued on the basis of that knowledge can very well be misguided.

Unfortunately, as the next section indicates, a great deal of thinking about globalization has not followed one or several of the above principles of definition. However, the fact that many conceptions have gone astray does not mean that there is no way forward with the term. On the contrary, too much is at stake in globalization debates – both theoretically and practically – to abandon the journey.

Redundant concepts of globalization

Much if not most existing analysis of globalization is flawed because it is redundant. Such research does not meet the first criterion above, namely, to generate new understanding that is not attainable with other concepts. Four main definitions have led into this cul-de-sac: globalization as internationalization; globalization as liberalization; globalization as universalization; and globalization as westernization. Arguments that only build on these conceptions fail to open insights that are not available through preexistent vocabulary. Deployed on any of these four lines, 'globalization' provides no distinct analytical value-added. Commentators who reject the novelty and transformative potential of globalization in contemporary history have almost invariably defined the term in one or several of these four redundant ways. Moreover, these conceptions can also raise political objections.

Internationalization

When globalization is interpreted as internationalization, the term refers to a growth of transactions and interdependence between countries. From this perspective, a more global world is one where more messages, ideas, merchandise, money, investments, pollutants and people cross borders between national-state-territorial units. For certain authors, like Hirst and Thompson, globalization is an especially intense form of internationalization, so that the global is a particular subset of the international (1999: 7–13). Many other analysts are less discriminating and simply regard the words 'global' and 'international' as synonyms to be used interchangeably.

Most attempts to quantify globalization have conceived of the process as internationalization. Thus, for example, Dani Rodrik has measured globalization in terms of current account transactions as a proportion of GDP (Rodrik, 2001). Similarly, globalization indexes issued by A. T. Kearney consultants and *Foreign Policy* (*FP*) magazine since 2001 and by the Centre for the Study of Globalization and Regionalization (CSGR) since 2005 have been largely calculated with reference to amounts of cross-border activities between countries. That is, the scores mainly relate to FDI, international travel, membership in international organizations, international telephone traffic, etc. Moreover, the calculations measure and compare the indicators on a territorial basis, so that one country is said to be more, or less, globalized than another (Kearney/*FP*, 2001, 2002, 2003, 2004; CSGR, 2005).

Ideas of globalization-as-internationalization are attractive insofar as they entail a minimum of intellectual and political adjustments. Global relations of this kind can be examined on the same ontological and methodological grounds as international relations. Global economics can be the same sort of enquiry as international economics. The study of global politics need not differ substantially from traditional international politics. Global culture would be considered equivalent to international culture. Globalization-as-internationalization gives the comforting message that the new can be wholly understood in terms of the familiar.

Indeed, most accounts of globalization-as-internationalization stress that contemporary trends are replaying earlier historical scenarios. In particular, these analyses frequently note that, in proportional terms, levels of cross-border trade, direct investment, and permanent migration were as great or greater in the late nineteenth century as they were a hundred years later. The suggestion is that globalization (read greater international interdependence) is a feature of the modern states-system and world economy that ebbs and flows over time. So today's social researchers can relax and carry on their enquiries more or less as previous generations have done.

Yet these very claims of familiarity and historical repetition constitute strong grounds for rejecting the definition of globalization-as-internationalization. If globality is nothing other than internationality – except perhaps larger amounts of it – then why bother with new vocabulary? No one needed a concept of globalization to make sense of earlier experiences of greater international interaction and interdependence, and this notion is similarly redundant today.

Ideas of globalization-as-internationalization can also be politically objectionable. They readily imply that world social relations are – and can only be – organized in terms of country units, state governments, and national communities. As such, the vocabulary of internationality tends to ignore, marginalize and silence other modes of organization, governance and identity that exist and are highly valued by, for example, indigenous peoples, regionalists, and various kinds of cosmopolitans.

Liberalization

A second common analytical dead-end in discussions of globalization has equated the notion with liberalization. In this case, globalization denotes a process of removing officially imposed constraints on movements of resources between countries in order to form an 'open' and 'borderless' world economy. On this understanding, globalization occurs as authorities reduce or abolish regulatory measures like trade barriers, foreign-exchange restrictions, capital controls, and visa requirements.

Using this definition, the study of globalization is a debate about contemporary neoliberalist macroeconomic policies. On one side of this argument, many academics, business executives and policymakers have supported neoliberalist prescriptions, with the promise that worldwide liberalization, privatization, deregulation and fiscal restraint would in time bring prosperity, freedom, peace and democracy for all. On the other side, critics in what is often called the 'anti-globalization' movement have opposed neoliberalist policies, contending that a *laissez-faire* world economy produces greater poverty, inequality, conflict, cultural destruction, ecological damage and democratic deficits.

To be sure, large-scale globalization and widespread economic liberalization have frequently transpired concurrently in the past quarter-century. For example, average tariff rates for non-agricultural products have fallen to record low levels. Moreover, this wave of neoliberalism has often played a significant (albeit not necessary) facilitating role in respect of contemporary globalization. However, it is quite something else to conflate the two concepts, so that globalization and liberalization become the same thing. Furthermore, such an equation can carry the dubious – and potentially harmful – political implication that neoliberalism is the only available policy framework for a more global world.

Indeed, on cross-examination most 'anti-globalization' protesters are seen to reject *neoliberalist* globalization rather than globalization per se. True, some of these critics have adopted a rejectionist, mercantilist position that advocates 'de-globalization' to a world of autarkic regional, national or local economies. However, most opponents of neoliberalism have sought different approaches to globalization – 'alter-globalizations' or 'counter-globalizations' – that might better advance human security, social justice and democracy. Many in mainstream circles, too, have recently suggested that globalization can be rescued with social, environmental and human rights safeguards. They have thereby also acknowledged that neoliberalist policies are not intrinsic to globalization.

In any case, the language of globalization is unnecessary to rehearse arguments for and against *laissez-faire* economics. People have debated theories and practices of 'free' markets for several centuries without invoking talk of globalization. For example, no one needed the concept of globalization when the international economy experienced substantial liberalization in the third quarter of the nineteenth century (Marrison, 1998). Likewise, globalization-as-liberalization opens no new insight today.

Universalization

A third cul-de-sac appears in analyses of globalization when the notion is conceived as universalization. In this case, globalization is taken to describe a process of dispersing various objects and experiences to people at all inhabited parts of the earth. On these lines, 'global' means 'worldwide' and 'everywhere'. Hence there is a 'globalization' of the Gregorian calendar, tobacco, business suits, the state, curry dinners, bungalows, school curricula, Barbie dolls, shotguns, and so on. Frequently, globalization-as-universalization is assumed to entail standardization and homogenization with worldwide cultural, economic, legal and political convergence. For example, some economists have assessed globalization in terms of the degree to which prices for particular goods and services become the same across countries (Bradford and Lawrence, 2004).

Yet this third type of conception, too, opens no new and distinctive insight. To be sure, some striking worldwide diffusion has transpired in contemporary history. Moreover, substantial cultural destruction in recent times has appeared to lend credence to the homogenization thesis (although, as is elaborated later in this chapter, the cultural dynamics of globalization are actually more complex). However, universalization is an age-old feature of world history. Indeed, Clive Gamble has written of 'our global prehistory', arguing that the transcontinental spread of the human species – begun a million years ago – constitutes the initial instance of globalization (1994: ix, 8–9). Various aptly named 'world religions' have extended across large expanses of the earth for centuries, and several of these faiths have held explicit universalistic pretensions. Transoceanic trade has distributed various goods over long distances on multiple prior occasions during the past millennium. No concept of globalization was devised to describe universalization in earlier times, and there is no need to create new vocabulary to analyse this old phenomenon now either.

Moreover, inasmuch as notions of globalization-as-universalization carry misguided assumptions of globalization-as-homogenization, this definition can have unhappy political consequences. Cultural protectionists can be led to oppose globalization per se, when they are in fact only against one of its possible results. Indeed, as later chapters show, globalization can when handled in certain ways promote cultural diversity, revival and innovation.

Westernization

A fourth common conception of globalization has defined it as westernization. As such, globalization is regarded as a particular type of universalization, one in which social structures of modernity (capitalism, industrialism, rationalism, urbanism, individualism, etc.) are spread across all of humanity, in the process destroying pre-existent cultures and local autonomy. Globalization understood in this way is often interpreted as colonization, Americanization and (in the vocabulary of the Iranian intellectual, Ale Ahmad) 'westoxification'. For these critics, talk of globalization is a hegemonic discourse, an ideology of supposed progress that masks far-reaching subordination by the West of the rest (Petras and Veltmeyer, 2001).

To be sure, a cogent case can be made that current large-scale globalization has resulted mainly from forces of modernity like rationalist knowledge, capitalist production, and bureaucratic governance (cf. Giddens, 1990). At the same time, early global consciousness arguably facilitated the onset of modernity, too (Robertson, 1992: 170). In turn, contemporary globalization has often inserted patterns of modern, western social relations more widely and deeply across the planet. Sometimes this westernization has involved violent impositions that could indeed warrant descriptions as imperialism. Moreover, it is true that governance institutions, firms, mass media, academics and civil society associations in Western Europe and North America have ranked among the most enthusiastic promoters of contemporary globalization.

Yet it is one thing to assert that globalization and westernization have had interconnections and quite another to equate the two developments. After all, modernity and western civilization have appeared in many other guises besides contemporary globality. Moreover – and it is politically important to acknowledge this – globalization could in principle be taken in non-western directions: for example, Buddhist globalizations, Confucian globalizations, Islamic globalizations, or possible future postmodern globalizations (cf. Pettman, 2005). Also, it is by no means clear that globalization is intrinsically imperialist, given that there are emancipatory global social movements as well as exploitative global processes.

In any case, westernization, modernization and colonization have a much longer history than contemporary intense globalization. Perhaps currently prevailing forms of globality could be analysed as a particular aspect, phase and type of modernity. On this reading, a definition of globalization would need to specify what makes *global* modernity distinctive. Yet in this approach, too, westernization and globalization are not coterminous.

In sum, then, much talk of globalization has been analytically redundant. The four types of definition outlined above between them cover much current academic, corporate, journalistic, official and popular discussions of things global. Critics of 'globaloney' are right to assail the historical illiteracy that marks most claims of novelty associated with these conceptions of globalization.

Of course, this is not to suggest that debates about international interdependence, neoliberalism, universalism-versus-cultural diversity, modernity, and imperialism are unimportant. Indeed, a well-fashioned concept of globalization could shed significant light on these issues. However, it is not helpful to define globalization as – to treat it as equivalent to – internationalization, liberalization, universalization or westernization. Not only do we thereby merely rehash old knowledge, but we also lose a major opportunity to grasp – and act upon – certain key circumstances of our times.

A way forward

Fortunately, the four definitions critiqued above do not exhaust the possible conceptions of globalization. Important new insight into historically relatively new conditions is available from a fifth notion. This approach identifies globalization as the spread of transplanetary – and in recent times also more particularly supraterritorial – connections between people.

A global (in the sense of transplanetary) social relation is one that (like an Internet chat room and certain communicable diseases) can link persons situated at any inhabitable points on the earth. Globalization involves reductions of barriers to such transworld social contacts. With globalization people become more able – physically, legally, linguistically, culturally and psychologically – to engage with each other wherever on planet Earth they might be.

In this fifth usage, globalization refers to a shift in the nature of social space. This conception contrasts with the other four notions of globalization discussed above, all of which presume (usually implicitly rather than explicitly) a continuity in the underlying character of social geography. To clarify this crucial point, the following pages first note the general importance of space in social relations and then elaborate on the features of transplanetary and, more specifically, supraterritorial links between persons. The far-reaching methodological implications of this understanding of globalization are also noted, although the final section of the chapter highlights several major qualifications to the definition of globalization as growing transplanetary connectivity.

To clarify the vocabulary, in the approach adopted here, the words 'global', 'transplanetary' and 'transworld' are treated as synonyms. They are therefore used interchangeably in the rest of this book. References to 'supraterritoriality' are made whenever that more particular quality of globality comes into play.

Space

The term globality resonates of spatiality. It says something about the *arena* and the *place* of human action and experience: the *where* of social life. In particular, globality identifies the planet – the earth as a whole – as a field of social relations in its own right. Talk of the global indicates that people may interact not only in built, local, provincial, country and macro-regional realms, but also in transplanetary spaces where the earth is a single place.

Why highlight issues of space? Most social analysis takes the spatial aspect as an unexplored given. Yet geography is a defining feature of social life (cf. Lefebvre, 1974; Gregory and Urry, 1985; Massey, 1994; Thrift, 1996; Brenner *et al.*, 2003). Relations between people always occur somewhere: in a place, a location, a domain, a site. No description of a social circumstance is complete without a spatial component.

Moreover, no social explanation is complete without a geographical dimension either. Space matters. To take one ready example, geographical differences mean that desert nomads and urban dwellers lead very diverse lives. Space is a core feature – as both cause and effect – of social life. On the one hand, the geographical context shapes the ways that people formulate knowledge, relate to nature, undertake production, experience time, organize governance, construct identities, and form collectivities. Concurrently, culture, ecology, economics, history, politics and psychology also shape the spatial contours of social relations.

Given these dense interconnections, a major change of spatial structure affects society as a whole. A reconfiguration of social geography is intimately interlinked with shifts in patterns of knowledge, production, governance, identity, and social ecology. So a transformation of social space – like large-scale globalization – is enveloped in larger dynamics of social change.

Globality: transplanetary relations and supraterritoriality

Globality in the conception adopted here has two qualities. The more general feature, transplanetary connectivity, has figured in human history for many centuries. The more specific characteristic, supraterritoriality, is relatively new to contemporary history. Inasmuch as the recent rise of globality marks a striking break from the territorialist geography that came before, this trend potentially has major implications for wider social transformation.

Globality in the broader sense of transplanetary ('across the planet') relations refers to social links between people located at points anywhere on earth. The global field is in these cases a social space in its own right. The globe, planet Earth, is not simply a collection of smaller geographical units like regions, countries and localities; it is also itself a specific arena of social life. A fundamental distinction can therefore be drawn between 'international relations' (as exchanges between countries) and 'global relations' (as exchanges within a planetary realm).

Of course, this more general kind of globality – transplanetary connections between people – is by no means new to the past few decades. As the next chapter stresses, long-distance and intercontinental domains have had age-old importance in human history. On the other hand, as Chapter 3 also shows, contemporary transplanetary links are denser than those of any previous epoch. More people, more often, more extensively and more intensely engage with the planetary arena as a single social place. Volumes of transworld associations, communications, diseases, finance, investment, travel and trade have never been as great.

However, the distinctiveness of recent globalization involves more than the quantity, frequency, scope and depth of transplanetary social links. Qualitatively, too, much of today's global connectivity is different. Unlike earlier times, contemporary globalization has been marked by a large-scale spread of supraterritoriality.

As the word suggests, 'supraterritorial' relations are social connections that substantially transcend territorial geography. They are relatively delinked from territory, that is, spatial domains that are mapped on the land surface of the earth, plus any adjoining waters and air spheres. Territorial space is plotted on the three axes of longitude, latitude and altitude. In territorial geography, place refers to locations situated on this three-dimensional grid; distance refers to the extent of territory separating territorial places; and border refers to a territorial delimitation of sections of the earth's surface. (For more on territorial geography, see Gottman, 1973; Sack, 1986; Storey, 2001; Paasi, 2003; Elden, 2005.)

Yet territorial locations, territorial distances and territorial borders do not define the whole geography of today's transplanetary flows. These global connections often also have qualities of *transworld simultaneity* (that is, they extend anywhere across the planet at the same time) and *transworld instantaneity* (that is, they move anywhere on the planet in no time). Thus, for example, on average 3,000 cups of Nescafé are reputedly drunk around the planet every second (Nescafé, 2003), and telephone links permit immediate communication across the ocean as readily as across the street. Global relations with supraterritorial features are not adequately mapped on a territorial grid.

Supraterritorial forms of globality are evident in countless facets of contemporary life. For instance, jet aeroplanes transport passengers and cargo across any distance on the planet within twenty-four hours. Telecommunications networks effect instantaneous links between points all over the earth, so that a call centre or data processing bureau for customers in North America may be located twelve time zones away in India. The global mass media spread messages simultaneously to transworld audiences. The US dollar and the euro are examples of money that has instantaneous transplanetary circulation. In global finance, various types of savings and investment instruments (for example, offshore bank deposits and eurobonds) flow instantaneously in transworld domains. Ecologically, developments such as climate change, stratospheric ozone depletion, and losses of biological diversity unfold simultaneously on a global scale. Ideationally, many people have a supraterritorial experience of place, for instance, when watching televised moon landings and global sports events simultaneously with hundreds of millions of other people scattered across the planet. Global human rights campaigns do not measure their support for a cause as a function of the territorial distance and territorial borders that lie between advocates and victims.

With these and many more instances of supraterritoriality, current globalization has constituted more than an extension of the compression of time relative to territorial space that has unfolded over a number of past centuries. In this long-term trend, developments in transportation technology like motor ships, railways and early aircraft progressively reduced the time needed to cover a given distance over the earth's surface. Thus, while Marco Polo took years to complete his journey across Eurasia in the thirteenth century, by 1850 a sea voyage from South East Asia to North West Europe could be completed in 59 days (PTT, 1951: 11). In the twentieth century, motorized ships and land vehicles took progressively less time again to link territorial locations. Nevertheless, such transport still required substantial time spans to cross long distances and moreover still faced substantial controls at territorial frontiers.

Whereas this older trend towards a shrinking world occurred *within* territorial geography, the newer spread of transplanetary simultaneity and instantaneity takes social relations substantially *beyond* territorial space. In cases of supraterritoriality, place is not territorially fixed, territorial distance is covered in no time, and territorial boundaries present no particular impediment. The difference between territorial time–space compression and the rise of supraterritoriality is qualitative and entails a deeper structural change of geography.

A number of social researchers across a range of academic disciplines have discerned this reconfiguration of space, albeit without invoking the term 'supraterritoriality' to describe the shift. Half a century ago, for example, the philosopher Martin Heidegger proclaimed the advent of 'distancelessness' and an 'abolition of every possibility of remoteness' (1950: 165–6). Forty years later the geographer David Harvey discussed 'processes that so revolutionize the objective qualities of space and time that we are forced to alter, sometimes in quite radical ways, how we represent the world to ourselves' (1989: 240). The sociologist Manuel Castells has distinguished a 'network society', in which a new 'space of flows' exists alongside the old 'space of places' (1989: 348; also Castells, 1996–7; 2001). The anthropologist Marc Augé has described an instantaneity that puts 'any person into relation with the entire world' (1994: 95). In the field of International Relations, John Ruggie has written of a 'nonterritorial region' in the contemporary world (1993: 172).

Might such a geographical transformation in the longer term prove to be as epochal as the shift to territorialism was at an earlier historical juncture? After all, social relations have not always and everywhere operated with a macro spatial framework that is overridingly territorial. For instance, cultures with a metaphysical cosmology have assigned only secondary if any importance to territorial referents. In fact, a territorial grid to locate points on a map was not introduced anywhere until the second century AD, by Zhang Heng in China (Douglas, 1996: 22). Medieval people in Europe did not have a notion of territory defined by three-dimensional geometry applied to the earth's surface (Zumthor, 1993; Hanawat and Kobialka, 2000). Images of the world showing the continents in anything like the territorial shapes that are commonly recognized today were not drawn before the late fifteenth century. It took a further two hundred years before the first maps depicting country units appeared (Campbell, 1987; Whitfield, 1994). Not until the high tide of colonialism at the end of the nineteenth century did a territorial logic dominate the construction of macro social spaces across the earth.

From then until the third quarter of the twentieth century, social spaces of a macro kind (that is, as opposed to directly perceived micro social spaces like built environments) nearly always took a territorial form. Indeed, one could say that a structure of territorial*ism* governed social geography. In a territorialist situation, people identify their location in the world primarily in relation to territorial position. (In most cases the territorial reference points are fixed, though for nomadic groups the spots may shift.) Moreover, in territorialist social relations the length of territorial distances between places and the presence or absence of territorial (especially state) borders between places heavily influences the frequency and significance of contacts that people at different territorial sites have with each other.

However, like any social structure, territorialism as the prevailing mode of geography was specific to a particular historical and cultural context. True, many people today still use the terms 'geography' and 'territory' interchangeably, as if to exclude the possibility that social space could have other than territorial forms. Yet world geography today is in an important respect not like that of the period to the mid-twentieth century. Following several decades of proliferating and expanding supraterritorial connections, territoriality has lost its monopoly hold. Territorial domains remain very important, but they no longer define the entire macro spatial framework.

As Chapter 3 indicates in detail, most of the rise of supraterritoriality is recent. As with any development, longer-term antecedents can of course be found. However, supraterritorial connectivity has reached by far its greatest extents during the past half-century. Earlier periods did not know jet travel, intercontinental missiles, transworld migrants with transborder remittances, satellite communications, facsimiles, the Internet, instant transplanetary television broadcasts, intercontinental production chains, transworld retailers, global credit cards, a continuous diet of global sports tournaments, or large-scale transplanetary anthropogenic ecological changes. Contemporary history is supraterritorial to degrees well beyond anything previously known.

True, enthusiasm at discovering something new – a significant reconfiguration of social geography – must not prompt overstatements of its extent. Globalization in the more specific sense of the spread of supraterritoriality has been less extensive than globalization in the more general sense of the growth of transplanetary connections. The supraterritorial aspects of contemporary globalization have far-reaching transformative potentials, but they constitute only part of the larger trend, and assessments of currently unfolding social change need to be correspondingly tempered.

Global, world, international and transnational

Further clarification of the idea of globality that is suggested here may be obtained by comparing the term with cognate concepts such as 'world', 'international' and 'transnational' links. All of these words put the spotlight on social relations beyond society conceived on nation/state/country lines. However, the four notions imply different emphases and should not be conflated.

At first glance, 'world' might seem synonymous with 'global', since in contemporary modern society 'the world' is generally conceived as planet earth. Indeed, this book invokes 'transworld' as a synonym for 'transplanetary'. The so-called Stanford School of sociologists in the USA has explored themes of globalization under the label of 'world society theory' (Meyer *et al.*, 1997; Boli and Thomas, 1999). In Germany Niklas Luhmann and his followers have developed arguments about *Weltgesellschaft* (Luhmann, 1982; Albert and Hilkermeier, 2004). In the field of International Relations a number of scholars have also invoked notions of 'world society' to designate a transplanetary cobweb of human interaction (Burton, 1972; Bull, 1977).

However, 'world' can denote the totality of social relations in other than planetary contexts. People in other eras and cultures have identified their 'world' in non-global ways. For example, the ancient Chinese mapped their 'world' in terms of a Middle Kingdom surrounded by peripheries of barbarians. Other ancient civilizations unfolded in a Mediterranean 'world'. Medieval Europeans conceived of the 'world' in terms of relations between humanity, nature and God, without resort to an atlas. Hence 'world' is a more generic notion. Globality (in the sense of connectivity across the earthly planetary realm) has featured in some social 'worlds' throughout history, but far from all.

Moreover, the contemporary world has multiple spatial dimensions in addition to the global. World social relations today have regional, country, local, household and other geographical aspects alongside the transplanetary facets. Thus 'world' is the social-geographical whole, while 'global' is only one of its spatial qualities.

The distinction between 'global' and 'international' has been stressed already, but it bears reiteration. 'International' exhanges occur between country units, while 'global' transactions occur within a planetary unit. Whereas international relations are *inter*-territorial relations, global relations are *trans*- and sometimes *supra*-territorial relations. Thus global economics is different from international economics, global politics is different from international politics, and so on.

Finally, a number of researchers have since the 1970s adopted a discourse of 'transnational' relations to analyse social interchange beyond the state and national society (Merle 1974; Keohane and Nye, 1977). This conception has the merit of highlighting non-governmental relations between countries and non-national forms of social bonds (e.g., transnational religious and class solidarities). However, ideas of transnationalism offer less when it comes to elaborating a more specific conception of the character of these non-statist and non-nationalist circumstances. In contrast, notions of global relations positively identify the transplanetary and supraterritorial qualities of various social relations.

Another objection to the vocabulary of trans*nationality* is that it still takes the nation-state-country as its reference point and to that extent retains traces of methodological nationalism and statism. Indeed, transnational relations are usually conceived as transactions across state borders. On the other hand, ideas of globality avoid domestic/foreign, internal/external dichotomies and thereby foster a clear and important methodological reorientation.

Methodological implications

If contemporary social geography is no longer territorialist in character, then traditional habits of social research need to be adjusted. Methodological territorialism has exercised a pervasive and deep hold on the conventions of social enquiry. The spread of transplanetary and supraterritorial links requires an important shift of approach.

Methodological territorialism refers to the practice of understanding and investigating social relations through the lens of territorial geography. Territorialist method means formulating concepts, asking questions, constructing hypotheses, gathering and interpreting evidence, and drawing conclusions in a spatial framework that is wholly territorial. These intellectual habits are so engrained that most social researchers reproduce them more or less unconsciously.

Methodological territorialism lies at the heart of currently prevailing commonsense notions of geography, economy, governance, history, literature, culture and society. Thus the vast majority of social and political geographers have conceived of the world in terms of bordered territorial (especially country) units. Likewise, macroeconomists have normally studied production, exchange and consumption in relation to national (read territorial) and international (read inter-territorial) realms. Students of politics have conventionally regarded governance as a territorial question, that is, as a matter of local and country governments, with the latter sometimes meeting in 'international' (again, code for inter-territorial) organizations. Similarly, mainstream historians have examined continuity and change over time in respect of territorial contexts such as localities and countries (cf. Mazlish and Buultjens, 1993; Geyer and Bright, 1995; Schäfer, 2003). Literature has generally been classed in terms of national-territorial genres: English literature, Indonesian literature, etc. For their part, anthropologists have almost invariably conceived of culture and community with reference to territorial units, in the sense of local and national peoples (Ekholm and Friedman, 1985). Meanwhile territorialist premises have led sociologists usually to assume that society by definition takes a territorial (usually national) form: hence Albanian society, Bolivian society, Chinese society, etc. (Mann, 1986: 13–17; Wallerstein, 1986).

Like any analytical device, methodological territorialism involves simplification. Actual social practice has always been more complicated. Nevertheless, this assumption offered a broadly viable intellectual shortcut for earlier generations of scholars. Methodological territorialism reflected the social conditions of a particular epoch when territorial places situated within bordered territorial units and separated by territorial distances formed far and away the overriding framework for macro social geography.

However, territorialist analysis is not a timeless or universally applicable method. The emergence of the states-system, the growth of mercantile and industrial capitalism, and the rise of national identities all understandably encouraged researchers of earlier times to adopt methodologically territorialist perspectives. Yet today large-scale globalization – including the substantial spread of supraterritoriality – should stimulate a reconstruction of methodology on alternative, nonterritorialist premises.

This call for different intellectual foundations no doubt provokes resistance in some quarters. It is difficult and even painful to change taken-for-granted knowledge, to reassess a cornerstone of understanding of social relations, to endure the disruption and confusion that comes in the transition between abandoning one set of first principles and consolidating another. Moreover, a postterritorialist methodology has political implications that vested interests could oppose. For example, postterritorialist social knowledge would logically undercut the primacy of both state-centric research and state-centric governance.

Yet it can arguably be quite dangerous to give methodological territorialism further lease on life in the contemporary more global world. For example, territorialist assumptions are obviously unsuitable to understand – and address – transplanetary ecological issues. Likewise, if significant parts of capitalism now operate with relative autonomy from territorial space, then old intellectual frameworks cannot adequately address the issues of distributive justice that invariably accompany processes of surplus accumulation. Similarly, a political theory that offers today's world only territorial constructions of community, citizenship and democracy is obsolete. Hence the stakes in the call for postterritorialist enquiry are much more than academic alone.

Manifestations of globality

The character and scale of globalization as the spread of transplanetary connections – including many (mainly recent) links that have a supraterritorial quality – may be further clarified with a survey of transworld activities. Such a review indicates that globality can touch pretty well all aspects of social life. That said, as the final section of this chapter emphasizes, it does not follow that global relations have become anything close to the only feature of social geography, either today or in the foreseeable future.

A great deal of globality is manifested through communications, that is, exchanges of ideas, information, images, signals, sounds and text. Transworld communication can be effected by means of the book trade, postal services, telegraph, telephone, facsimile, telex, text messaging, videoconference, computer networks, newspaper, magazine, radio, television, video and film. Supraterritoriality comes into global communications when, for example, certain publications (like Harry Potter books) and recordings (like Eminem CDs) are released simultaneously across the planet. In addition, satellite broadcasts and transoceanic cables enable communication to be effected instantaneously between any points on earth, irrespective of the territorial distances and territorial borders that lie between them. Thus toll-free numbers can link up to a call centre on any continent.

The Internet is supraterritorial communication par excellence, instantly relaying a full range of visual and auditory signals anywhere on the planet that terminals exist to send and receive them. Much of today's globality is an 'e-world' of e-commerce, e-friendship, e-government, and e-mail. Indeed, in September 2001 the Internet allowed doctors in New York, USA to perform transoceanic robot-assisted telesurgery on a patient in Strasbourg, France (Pogue, 2001). The notion that the Internet involves new kinds of social geography is well conveyed by the term 'cyberspace' (Kitchin, 1998; Kitchin and Dodge, 2002).

Other globality occurs in the transplanetary movement of people. Global travel is undertaken by many migrant labourers, professionals, pilgrims, refugees, tourists, adventurers, adopted children and more. Relevant modes of transworld transport include caravans, ships, trains, motor vehicles and aeroplanes. Jet aircraft in particular have introduced something approaching a supraterritorial quality into contemporary global travel, as passengers can be flown between any two locations on the earth within a day. Transworld travel enables the occurrence of large global convocations like the *haj*, professional congresses, tourist resorts, trade fairs, and United Nations summits. Transplanetary movements of domestics and sex workers have brought globalization into many a household and brothel (Ehrenreich and Hochschild, 2002). Some business travellers have the globe as their office, working from hotels and airport lounges as much as a fixed home base. Increasing numbers of pensioners have undertaken 'retirement migration' for their sunset years (King *et al.*, 2000). Conflicts in Afghanistan, Bosnia, Somalia and elsewhere have generated global waves of refugees and asylum seekers. Although state border controls restrict global travel in many cases, millions upon millions of people each year move about the planet as a single place.

Further globality is manifested in certain production processes. In so-called 'global factories' (Fuentes and Ehrenreich, 1983) or 'global commodity chains' (Gereffi and Korzeniewicz, 1994), different stages of the production of a commodity are sited at several (perhaps very widely scattered) locations on the planet. Thus, in principle, the research centre, design unit, procurement office, fabrication plant, finishing point, assembly line, quality control operation, data processing office, advertising bureau and after-sales service could each be situated in different provinces, countries and continents across the planet. Global production involves intra-firm trade within a transworld company as well as, if not more than, inter-national trade between countries. Through so-called 'global sourcing', a producer draws the required inputs from a transplanetary field, rather than being restricted to a particular country or region. Differences in local costs of labour, raw materials, regulation and taxation often figure more importantly in these business calculations than the costs of transport across territorial distance and borders between the various sites in the global production chain. This type of manufacture has developed especially in respect of textiles, clothing, motor vehicles, leather goods, sports articles, toys, optical products, consumer electronics, semiconductors, aircraft and construction equipment. A global production process has supraterritorial qualities inasmuch as it occurs simultaneously and with tight coordination across a transworld space.

Globality can be manifested in consumption as well as production. Many commodities are distributed and sold through global markets, sometimes in the context of a tightly coordinated supraterritorial business strategy. In this way consumers dispersed across the planet purchase the same good or service, often under a single brand name like Nike, Pepsi-Cola or Toyota. Already in the 1980s, Howard Perlmutter of the Wharton Business School identified 136 industries where a global marketing strategy had supposedly become vital to commercial success (Main, 1989: 55). The vast range of global products has come to include many raw materials, GM plants, packaged foods, bottled beverages, cigarettes, designer clothes, household articles and appliances, pharmaceuticals, music recordings, audio-visual productions, printed publications, online information services, financial instruments, office equipment, armaments, transport vehicles, travel services and much more. Citicorp has proclaimed itself to be 'your global bank', and Peter Stuyvesant has marketed itself as 'the global cigarette'. Transworld products have come to figure in the everyday lives of much of humanity, whether through actual purchases or through unfulfilled desires evoked by global advertising.

Global communications, global travel, global production and global markets have all promoted, and been facilitated by, global money. That is, some units of account, means of payment, stores of value and mediums of exchange have transplanetary circulation. For example, the 'US' dollar, the 'Japanese' yen, the 'British' pound and other major denominations are much more than national currencies. As supraterritorial monies, they are used anywhere on earth at the same time and move (electronically and via air transport) anywhere on earth in effectively no time. In addition, the Special Drawing Right (SDR) and the euro have emerged through the IMF and the EU, respectively, as suprastate monies with transworld circulation. Many bankcards can extract cash in local currency from automated teller machines (ATMs) connected to supraterritorial networks like Maestro and Cirrus. Several credit cards like Visa, MasterCard and American Express can be used for payments at countless establishments in almost every country across the planet (Mandell, 1990; Ritzer, 1995). An exception like Iran stands out by outlawing global credit cards. Although not yet in wide usage, digital money can be stored on certain smart cards (so-called electronic purses) in multiple currencies at once, creating something of a global wallet.

Globality also appears in many areas of finance. For instance, most foreign exchange transactions today take place through a round-the-globe, round-the-clock market that connects the dealing rooms of New York, Sydney, Tokyo, Singapore, Hong Kong, Zürich, Frankfurt and London. In global banking, depositors place their savings in a global currency and/or at a global bank and/or at a global branch location such as a so-called 'offshore' financial centre. These practices contrast with territorial banking, in which clients deposit their savings in their national currency at a local or national bank within their country of residence. With transworld payments, migrant workers use global banking networks to remit some of their earnings to relations at another corner of the planet. Meanwhile global bank loans occur when a lender (or syndicate of lenders, perhaps spread across several countries) provides credit in a global currency. Thus, for example, a group of banks based in Austria, the Netherlands and the UK might issue a loan in US dollars to a borrower in the Dominican Republic. The level of interest on such a credit is generally not the prevailing national percentage, but a function of a supraterritorial benchmark like the London Inter-Bank Offered Rate (LIBOR). At the same time, micro-credit schemes in local communities can be linked to global institutions like the World Bank. Similarly, global bonds (often called 'eurobonds') involve a transworld currency as well as borrowers, investors, a syndicate of managers, and securities exchanges that are spread across multiple countries. Global financial transactions also occur on similar lines in respect of medium-term notes and short-term credit instruments like treasury bills and commercial paper. In equity markets, meanwhile, global shares are company stocks that are: (a) listed on several securities exchanges across the earth; and/or (b) held by investors spread across the planet. For their part derivatives have a global character when, for example, the same futures contract is traded simultaneously on the Chicago, Singapore and London markets, as well as through electronic links between them. Insurance policies, too, can have global coverage in a global currency and/or are handled by global companies in global financial centres. In addition, many private and institutional investors maintain global portfolios. That is, they spread their funds across banks, stocks, bonds, money-market tools, derivatives contracts and insurance policies from around the globe. Indeed, with supraterritorial dealing, a broker can buy and sell financial instruments anywhere on the planet instantaneously with a telephone call or the click of a mouse. Several major financial markets like the National Association of Securities Dealers Automated Quotation system (Nasdaq), set up in 1971, and its European counterpart (Easdaq), launched in 1996, have no fixed territorial meeting place at all. In sum, then, much of today's foreign exchange, banking, securities, derivatives and insurance business occurs globally and with considerable delinkage from territorial space.

Through all of the activities already mentioned, people may be globally connected through organizations, that is, associations that coordinate the activities of individuals spread across the planet. Many of these organizations pursue mainly commercial purposes as global companies (often imprecisely named 'multinational corporations'). The thousands of examples include

Inter Press Service, Mitsubishi, Nokia, Novartis, Standard Chartered, and Royal Dutch/Shell. In addition, many businesses have developed various types of transworld coalitions, often termed 'strategic alliances' (for instance, joint ventures, subcontracting arrangements, franchises, and so on). Highly visible examples include the One World and Sky Team airline groups. Other transplanetary organizations have mainly regulatory functions and can suitably be called global governance institutions. For instance, activities of the IMF, the WTO and the United Nations Educational, Scientific and Cultural Organization (UNESCO) extend across the planet. Some regionally, country-, and locally-based governance bodies like the EU, the United States government and the London municipal authorities also have significant global reach. Along with commercial and governance agencies, many civil society associations also have a global organization. They include faith-based groups like the World Fellowship of Buddhists, labour movements like the ICFTU, NGOs like Amnesty International, peasant coalitions like Vía Campesina, and philanthropic bodies like the Ford Foundation. In addition, many localized civil society associations organize globally through coalitions and other networks. For example, the global Oxfam network encompassed nearly 3,000 local associations in some 80 countries in the year 2000 (Hajnal, 2002: 57, 60). Still other global organizations involve clandestine operations like transworld criminal networks (Berdal and Serrano, 2002).

Globality is further manifested in some military activities. Contemporary arsenals include a number of global weapons that can range across pretty well any distance over the earth. Examples include spy satellites, long-range bomber and surveillance aircraft, and unpiloted intercontinental missiles. Global warfare occurs when a campaign of armed combat is pursued from widely spread points across the planet. For instance, although the battlefields lay in Iraq, the 2003 war against Saddam Hussein's Ba'ath regime involved command headquarters in the USA and Qatar, air bases in Europe and Kuwait, troops and arms from several continents, and satellites in outer space. Likewise, the British military has maintained a global presence with contingents in over 80 countries as of 2002, whereas 250,000 US troops were stationed in 120 countries as of 2005 (*FT*, 12 July 2002). So-called 'rapid reaction forces' can be deployed anywhere on the planet within hours. UN peacekeeping operations involve multinational armies deployed anywhere on earth. Certain paramilitary groups like Al-Qaida and the Irish Republican Army (IRA) have also operated as transworld networks. The attacks of 11 September 2001 brought home as never before the potential impact of informal global militias using global communications and global finance.

Ecologically, a planetary life-support system has of course operated from the moment that the first organisms appeared on earth. However, some matters of *social* ecology can also have global qualities. Several major anthropogenic (i.e., human-induced) environmental changes have had a pronounced transworld dimension. For example, the anthropogenic greenhouse effect is allegedly producing planetary climate change, popularly known as 'global warming'. Neither the causes nor the effects of this trend can be territorially specified and restricted. Similarly, stratospheric ozone depletion (and its reversal) is largely a distanceless and borderless process. With respect to the biosphere, the contemporary more global world is experiencing major reductions in the diversity of ecosystems, in the number of species of life, and in the variety of genes that circulate within individual species. In contemporary genetic engineering, recombinant DNA techniques allow a gene to be taken from one organism anywhere on earth and put into a second organism at any other location. Another headline global ecological issue asks how many people the planet can support at one time. Further environmental conditions with global aspects include radioactive fallout, atmospheric flows of sulphur dioxide and nitrogen oxide (so-called 'acid rain'), the depletion of tropical moist forests, desertification, changes in sea level, marine pollution, management of ocean fish stocks, big dams, possible future shortages of fresh water and arable soil, and waste disposal in outer space. Although the severity of these various ecological problems can be debated, it is clear that none of them is confined to a particular country or region.

Sometimes closely related with ecological concerns, a number of health matters, too, have global dimensions (WHO, 2001; Lee, 2002, 2003; Pirages, 2006). Since prehistory natural forces of waters and winds have transported micro-organisms across the planet. In addition, people have for many centuries carried a number of communicable diseases across and between continents, including plague, small pox, anthrax, cholera, syphilis, measles, tuberculosis and influenza. Yet contemporary times have raised the speed and magnitude of global spreads of various human, animal and plant diseases. Examples include HIV/AIDS, SARS, BSE, foot and mouth disease, and gemini viruses. For bacteria and viruses, the planet is one microbial pool in which pathogens don't carry passports. Other questions of human health with transplanetary aspects include bodily harms related to tobacco consumption, illicit drug use, and occupational conditions. In 2002 the World Health Organization (WHO) warned of a 'globesity' pandemic of overweight middle classes across the planet. Needless to say, successful strategies to address these health issues also require a partly global approach.

Much globality is also found in the area of law. Countless formal rules and regulations have acquired a transworld character. The widely diverse examples include various arms control schemes, criminal laws, environmental agreements, human rights conventions, technical standards, and trade rules. In addition, some law firms have developed transworld networks of offices, while police forces have pursued transplanetary cooperation through the

International Criminal Police Organization (Interpol). Global suprastate courts include the International Court of Justice (ICJ), ad hoc war crimes tribunals, and the recently established International Criminal Court (ICC). In addition, some national courts hear cases that relate to transworld issues, such as various global intellectual property claims that are brought before US tribunals.

Finally, globality is evident in social relations through global consciousness. In other words, people often think globally. In addition to holding microcosmic conceptions of the social realm as a district or a country, people can also hold macrocosmic notions, where the planet is regarded as a 'global village'. Globally minded people regard the planet as a principal source of their food supplies, their entertainments, their threats and their friends. Some workers like Ghanaian traders and Filipina domestics see the whole earth (as opposed to a particular locality or country) as their potential workplace. Transworld consciousness also takes form in certain languages (e.g., English, Esperanto and Spanish), certain icons (e.g., Coca-Cola labels), certain narratives (e.g., soap operas), certain fashions (e.g., blue jeans), certain rituals (e.g., sending postcards), and other symbols. Awareness of the planet as a single social place is furthermore evident in events like global sports competitions (including global supporters clubs for some teams), global exhibitions, global film festivals, global tours by music superstars, global conferences, and global panics (Taylor, 1997; Giulianotti, 1999). Since 1982 Disney World has taken thousands of visitors through its 'Spaceship Earth' attraction, a ride through world history (Schäfer, 2005). Over 750 properties have been placed on UNESCO's World Heritage List of sites holding 'outstanding value to humanity' since the launch of that programme in 1972 (WHC, 2004). The UN has nurtured global culture through the dedication since 1949 of over 125 decades, years, weeks and days, including a succession of Development Decades, the International Year of Indigenous Peoples, and World AIDS Day (Drori, forthcoming). In addition, global consciousness has arisen when people conceive of their social affiliations in transplanetary and supraterritorial terms, for instance, with transworld solidarities based on class, gender, generation, profession, race, religion, sexual orientation and indeed humanity as such. Stories of aliens from outer space seem telling in this regard: the foreign other is conceived not as another nationality from another territory, but as another life form from another planet, thereby defining humanity and the earth as one.

All of the many instances of globality just described (and summarized in the following box) are discussed in greater detail later in this book, where these activities are also related to questions of deeper social structure. The present concise survey merely serves to demonstrate the widespread incidence of transplanetary – including more particularly supraterritorial – circumstances across contemporary social life. Cumulatively, all of this global communication, global travel, global production, global consumption, global money, global finance, global organization, global military, global ecology, global health, global law and global consciousness indicates that contemporary social relations cannot be described without extensive reference to transworld spaces.

Manifestations of globality in summary

Communications
- post
- telecommunications
- mass media

Travel
- migrant labour
- pilgrims
- refugees
- tourists
- business travellers

Production
- transworld production chains
- global sourcing of inputs

Markets
- global products
- global marketing and sales strategies

Money
- global currencies
- bank cards with access to global ATM networks
- global credit cards
- digital cash in electronic purses

Finance
- foreign exchange markets
- banking (deposits, payments and loans)
- securities markets
- derivatives trading
- insurance business

Organizations
- global commercial enterprises
- global governance agencies
- global civil society associations

→

Military
- global weapons
- global campaigns

Ecology
- global atmosphere (climate change, ozone depletion, radioactive fall-out, acid rain)
- global biosphere (loss of biological diversity, deforestation)
- global hydrosphere (rising sea level, marine pollution, reduced fresh water)
- global geosphere (desertification, loss of arable soil)

Health
- global communicable diseases
- global aspects of diet, drug use and occupational conditions
- global campaigns of health improvement

Law
- global rules and regulations
- transworld networks of lawyers and police
- global courts

Consciousness
- conceptions of the planet as a single place
- global symbols
- global events
- transworld solidarities

Qualifications

The preceding discussion has made a strong case for what globalization *is*, in terms of a change in social space that is both quantitatively and qualitatively significant. However, it is equally important to emphasize what the growth in transplanetary connections and the spread of supraterritoriality do *not* entail. In particular it is crucial to reject the following six non sequiturs: globalism, reification, global/local binaries, cultural homogenization, universality, and political neutrality.

Globalism

First, then, the rise of transplanetary and supraterritorial connectivity in no way means that territorial space has ceased to matter. We should not replace methodological territorialism with a globalism that looks *only* at transplanetary relations and ignores the importance of territorial spaces. We do not live in a 'borderless world' where territory is 'obsolescent' (Ohmae, 1990, 1995; O'Brien, 1992; Rosecrance, 1995; also Badie, 1995). Although contemporary history has witnessed the end of territorial*ism* (where social space is effectively reducible to territorial grids), we have certainly not seen the end of territorial*ity*. To say that social geography can no longer be understood in terms of territorial spaces alone is of course not to say that territoriality has become irrelevant.

On the contrary, territorial production arrangements, territorial governance mechanisms, territorial ecology and territorial identities remain highly significant at the start of the twenty-first century, even if territoriality does not monopolize the situation as before. For example, many communications links like airports, roads, railways and shipping lanes remain territorially fixed. Several recent economic studies have suggested that territorial distance remains a strong influence on trade in manufactures as well as – perhaps more surprisingly – financial assets (Portes and Rey, 1999; Aviat and Coeurdacier, 2004). In other words, people are still more likely to do foreign business with countries that are territorially closer. In addition, territorial borders continue to exert strong influences on movements of material goods and people (Helliwell, 1998). It can take months to complete the dozens of official documents required to export legally from India. Meanwhile countless localized products remain bound to particular territorial markets. Largely territorially bound commodities derived from agriculture and mining have persisted at the same time that largely supraterritorial commodities like information and communications have risen to prominence. While US dollars and Visa card payments cross the planet instantly, many other forms of money continue to have restricted circulation within a given territorial domain, and national currencies show no sign of disappearing altogether (Gilbert and Helleiner, 1999). Most people today still hold their bank accounts at a local branch or do no banking at all. Much ecological degradation is linked to specific territorial locations, for instance, of overgrazing, salination, or dumping of toxic wastes. In terms of social affiliations, some observers have suggested that territorially bound identities could even have become more rather than less significant in a world of diminishing territorial barriers (Mlinar, 1992; Harvey, 1993). Certainly territorial politics surrounding Palestine and Taiwan remain as heated as ever.

So the end of territorialism has not marked the start of globalism. The addition of supraterritorial qualities of geography has not eliminated the territorial aspects (Brenner, 1998, 1999). Indeed, as later chapters in this book indicate, contemporary globalization has been closely connected with certain forms of *re*territorialization like the rise of micro-nationalist politics, urbanization and the growth of globally connected cities, and the proliferation of offshore arrangements.

Perhaps the most striking reterritorialization to accompany recent globalization has been regionalization (Gamble and Payne, 1996; Frankel, 1998). Some of this regionalization has occurred within states, in cases like Flanders in Belgium or Siberia in Russia. Other regionalization has had a trans-state character, such as the Basque area across France and Spain or the Kurdish movement across Iran, Iraq, Syria and Turkey. Still other regionalization has happened intergovernmentally, in projects like the East African Community (EAC) and Asia-Pacific Economic Cooperation (APEC). And considerable regionalization has had an unofficial character, as in citizen action initiatives like the European Social Forum (ESF) or academic networks such as the Organization for Social Science Research in Eastern and Southern Africa (OSSREA).

Clearly, social space in today's world is *both* territorial *and* supraterritorial. Indeed, in social practice the two qualities always intersect. Supraterritoriality is only relatively deterritorialized, and contemporary territoriality is only partly supraterritorialized. Territorial relations are no longer purely territorial, and supraterritorial relations are not wholly non-territorial.

Thus, for example, every Internet user accesses cyberspace from a territorial location. Global products, global finance and global communications always 'touch down' in territorial localities. Supraterritorial military technologies like spy satellites are generally directed at territorial targets. So-called 'global cities' such as London and Tokyo still have a longitude, latitude and altitude. Global ecological changes have territorially specific impacts: for example, rising sea level has different consequences for coastal zones as against uplands.

In short, contemporary society knows no 'pure' globality that exists independently of territorial spaces. The recent accelerated growth of supraterritoriality has brought a relative retreat from territoriality rather than its complete removal from social life. In this sense the term 'deterritorialization' can have misleading connotations and is therefore avoided in this book (Ó Tuathail, 1998, 2000). Global relations today substantially rather than wholly transcend territorial space. Although territoriality does not place insurmountable constraints on supraterritoriality, global flows still have to engage with territorial locations. The present world is globalizing, not totally globalized.

By the same token, however, little if any territoriality today exists independently of supraterritoriality. Most contemporary regional, country, provincial and local conditions coexist with – and are influenced by – global circumstances. Indeed, territoriality is changed by its encounters with supraterritoriality. For example, as indicated in Chapter 6, territorial states act differently in a globalizing world than in a territorialist one. Similarly, territorial identities obtain different dynamics when they are associated with global diasporas (e.g., of Armenians and Sikhs). Territorial environmental issues like local water shortages acquire different significance when they form part of a transworld problem.

In sum, current globalization is not replacing one compact formula of spatiality (territorialism) with another (globalism). Rather, the rise of supraterritoriality is bringing greater complexity to geography – and by extension to culture, ecology, economics, history, politics and social psychology as well. The relative simplicity of a territorialist-statist-nationalist world is fading.

Reification

The preceding point regarding the interrelation of supraterritorial and territorial spaces points to a second caution, namely, regarding reification. While globality is a discrete concept, it is not a discrete concrete condition. It is helpful, analytically, to distinguish different spheres of social space; however, concretely, the global is not a domain unto itself, separate from the regional, the national, the provincial, the local, and the built environment. There is no purely global circumstance, divorced from other spaces, just as no building, locality, province, country or region is sealed off from other geographical arenas.

So social space should not be understood as an assemblage of discrete realms, but as an interrelation of spheres within a whole. Events and developments are not global *or* national *or* local *or* some other scale, but an intersection of global *and* other spatial qualities. The global is a dimension of social geography rather than a space in its own right. It is heuristically helpful to distinguish a global quality of contemporary social space, but we must not turn the global into a 'thing' that is separate from regional, national, local and household 'things'.

For example, a government may be sited at a country 'level', but it is a place where supranational, national and subnational spaces converge. Thus states are involved in transworld law and regional arrangements as well as national regulation and relations with provincial and local authorities. Likewise, firms and other actors in today's globalizing circumstances are meeting points for co-constituting transworld, regional, national and local aspects of geography. Hence the vocabulary of interconnected 'scales' is preferable to that of separated 'levels'.

Avoidance of reification is especially important in these early days of global studies. Several centuries of international studies have suffered dearly from a reified distinction between the national and the international, where the 'internal' and 'domestic' was ontologically separated from the 'external' and 'foreign'. In practice, of course, the 'inside' and the 'outside' of countries are deeply intertwined. These old errors of reifying the international must not be carried over into new research of the global.

Global/local binaries

The interrelatedness of dimensions of social space (as opposed to the existence of separate domains) suggests that it is mistaken – as many have done – to set up oppositions between the global and the local. Such a binary resurrects in new form the misguided domestic/international dichotomy of old. Typically, local/global polarizations have depicted the local as 'here', immediate and intimate, as against the global being 'there', distant and isolating. The local is concrete, grounded, authentic, and meaningful, whereas the global is abstract, unconnected, artificial and meaningless. The local purportedly provides security and community, while the global houses danger and violence. The local is innocent, the global manipulative. The local is the arena for autonomy and empowerment, the global the realm of dependence and domination. On such assumptions, some critics have rejected globalization with calls for localization (Hewison, 1999; Hines, 2000).

Yet these global/local binaries do not bear up to closer scrutiny. After all, people can have very immediate and intimate transworld relationships with each other via jet travel, telephone and Internet. In contrast, many next-door neighbours in contemporary cities do not even know each other's names. Supraterritorial communities of people (for example, sharing the same class position, disability, religious faith or sexual orientation) can have far-reaching solidarity, whereas localities can experience deep fear, hatred and intolerance. Global flows frequently involve ordinary people leading everyday lives (listening to radio and munching brand-name fast food), while various exhibits of local culture are contrived. Indigenous peoples have used transworld networks and laws to promote their self-determination, while many a local élite has exercised repression over a district. Local officials can be as inaccessible, unsympathetic, secretive, arbitrary and unaccountable as authorities in global spheres. Devolution has brought greater popular control through the regions in Spain, but it has also brought oppression through many provinces in the Russian Federation. In short, there is nothing inherently alienating about the global and nothing intrinsically liberating about the local.

Instead, both the local and the global have enabling and disabling potentials. Indeed, as already stressed, the two qualities are inseparable in social practice; so terming one circumstance 'local' and another 'global' is actually arbitrary and confusing. For example, globally mobile companies may follow locally tailored marketing strategies, while locally grounded peasants may be globalized through their televisions and religions. A social condition is not positive or negative according to whether it is local as against global, since the situation is generally both local and global at the same time. It is the particular blend of local and global (and other spatial spheres) that matters, not locality versus globality.

Cultural homogenization

The complexity of multidimensional social space likewise suggests that it is mistaken – as many observers have done – to associate globalization with homogenization. The growth of transplanetary and supraterritorial connectivity does not ipso facto reduce cultural diversity. After all, the global, the regional, the national, the provincial, and the local aspects of social space can intertwine in innumerable different combinations. Indeed, by injecting a further dimension into the geographical spectrum – thereby adding to its complexity – globalization could just as well increase cultural pluralism.

True, the contemporary world has experienced considerable cultural destruction. For example, languages have been disappearing at rates as worrying as those for species extinction (Wurm, 1996). Indigenous peoples' heritages have been undercut or erased across the planet. 'Science' has triumphed worldwide as the most authoritative form of knowledge, often running roughshod over religious and other thought (Drori *et al.*, 2003). A high tide of consumerism has seemingly imposed cultural levelling across the world, including via a multitude of global agents such as Carrefour, Michael Jackson, Microsoft, and Madison Avenue advertisers.

On the other hand, perceptions of cultural homogenization in the context of globalization can be exaggerated. For example, what appears on the surface to be the same transplanetary language can in fact harbour widely varying vocabularies and understandings across different social contexts. So the English of Nairobi markets is not the English of the Scottish Highlands, and the Spanish of East Los Angeles barrios is not the Spanish of Santiago office blocs (Rhedding-Jones, 2002). Likewise, as reception research has shown, different parts of a transworld audience can read hugely different meanings into a Hollywood blockbuster. In this regard it can be questioned how far the diverse viewers actually 'see' the same global film (Tomlinson, 1991). Similarly, global marketers often have to adjust the design and advertisement of transworld products in ways that appeal to diverse cultural contexts. Even an icon of global Americanization like McDonald's varies its menu considerably across the planet in relation to local sensibilities, with kosher Big Macs in Jerusalem, vegetable McNuggets in New Delhi, and McHuevo in Montevideo (Watson, 2000: 122). Even global laws like labour standards could be applied variably in accordance with local contexts. Thus globalization is also glocalization (Robertson, 1992: 173–4; Kraidy, 1999; Salcedo, 2003).

In any case, losses of cultural diversity are not intrinsic to globalization as such. On the contrary, transplanetary and supraterritorial relations can host great cultural heterogeneity (cf. Breidenbach and Zukrigl, 1998). For instance, female genital cutting remains a matter of heated global cultural contention (Boyle, 2002). Multiple world religions occupy sites on the

Internet, and all manner of peoples from racial diasporas to sexual minorities have formed transworld associations.

Indeed, globalization has offered opportunities to reassert cultural distinctiveness. For example, indigenous peoples have used UN mechanisms and electronic mass media to promote their particularity (Dowmunt, 1993; Wilmer, 1993). Various movements of religious revivalism have used global communications like Internet and satellite television to considerable effect in advancing their causes. As elaborated in Chapter 7, globalization has also promoted the growth of a host of other supraterritorial identities.

By breaking down territorial distances that previously effected considerable segregation of cultures, globality can also foster innovative blends of traditions. For example, ethnic minority youth in Frankfurt-am-Main have combined aspects of African-American rap music and hip-hop culture with elements of their North African and Turkish heritages to create novel modes of expression for their hybrid identities in contemporary Germany (Bennett, 1999). So-called 'world music' has mixed different strains to the point that the original elements are no longer distinguishable. Similarly, fusion cooking combines elements of traditional cuisines from widely scattered parts of the planet to create new menus. Some observers take such developments as evidence that contemporary globality is increasingly less west-centric (Appiah and Gates, 1997: ix; Leclerc, 2000).

In any case, it is clear that globalization can have heterogenizing as well as homogenizing effects. There can be, and are, many globalizations (Berger and Huntington, 2002). Globalization can – and many argue should – be pursued under a rainbow motif of diversity. The overall balance between cultural divergence and convergence lies not in globality as such, but in the way that transworld relations are handled. The social power relations that shape transplanetary connections are particularly important in this regard. Thus, to the extent that cultural imperialism afflicts contemporary history, it is largely a problem of the voracity of western modernity rather than an outcome of globalization per se.

Universality

A further qualification to notions of globalization as increased transworld and supraterritorial connectivity must note that the trend has not touched all of humanity to the same extent. Globality links people *anywhere* on the planet, but it does not follow that it connects people *everywhere*, or everywhere to the same degree. To repeat the earlier disclaimer, under the definition suggested here globalization is not universalization. On the contrary, the incidence of contemporary transplanetary connectivity has varied considerably in relation to territorial location and social status. Indeed, some people continue to live lives that are relatively untouched by globality.

In terms of territorial position, global networks have generally involved populations of North America, Western Europe and East Asia more than people in other world regions. For example, although McDonald's had over 25,000 outlets in 119 countries as of June 1999, four-fifths of them were found in just 10 countries (Watson, 2000: 122–3). Variations in the intensity of globality have also occurred among regions within countries. For example, coastal provinces of China have undergone greater globalization than the interior of the country. In the USA, residents of Silicon Valley have been more enveloped in global communications than inhabitants of the Dakotas. Across the earth, patterns of contemporary globalization have broadly followed urban–rural lines, with cities and towns generally experiencing more transplanetary connectivity than countrysides.

With regard to social position, wealthy people have on the whole accessed transworld relations more than the poor. While those with the means rush from their global bank to the airport lounge, hundreds of millions of low-income people alive today have never made a telephone call. With respect to gender, men have generally linked up to the Internet much more than women (HDR, 1999: 62). Other patterns of uneven entry to, and benefit from, global flows can be discerned in respect of civilization and race.

Contemporary globality has not been an exclusively Northern, urban, élite, male, western, white preserve. At the territorial margins, for example, transworld links have extended to remote villages in Africa (Piot, 1999; Mendonsa, 2001). At the social margins, the homeless of Rio de Janeiro often request a television even before they demand running water (Mariana, 2002). Yet, although globality may have become pervasive, prevailing cultural frameworks, resource distributions and power relationships have produced a highly uneven spread of transplanetary and supraterritorial relations in today's world.

Political neutrality

The foregoing remarks concerning unequal opportunities to use and shape transworld connections highlight the thoroughly political character of globalization. Human geography is no more politically neutral than any other aspect of social relations like culture or economics. Space always involves politics: processes of acquiring, distributing and exercising social power. A social field is never a level field. Thus transplanetary and supraterritorial connections invariably house power relations and associated power struggles, whether latent or overt. Global links are venues of conflict and cooperation, hierarchy and equality, opportunity and its denial.

Indeed, nothing in globalization is apolitical. Even seemingly tame questions of transplanetary technical harmonization have provoked power struggles. For example, in the nineteenth century the British and French governments competed to have the prime meridian (for the measure of longitudes and universal standard time) pass through their respective capitals, with Greenwich eventually winning out. More recently, different computer operating systems have offered users different degrees of initiative and control (Raymond, 1999). It is illusory to think that anything in globality can be divorced from issues of power – and thus also justice.

Any analysis of globalization must therefore examine the political aspects involved. On the one hand, these politics involve actors: that is, power relations among individuals, households, associations, firms and governance organizations. In addition, the politics of globalization involve social structures: that is, power relations between age groups, between civilizations, between classes, between genders, between races, between people holding different sexual orientations, and so on. Like any significant historical trend, the growth of transplanetary and supraterritorial connections empowers some people and disempowers others.

So, as a political process, globalization is about contests between different interests and competing values. The spread of globality is – and cannot but be – normatively laden and politically charged. It is important to determine whose power rises and whose suffers under currently prevailing practices of globalization and to consider whether alternative policies could have better political implications.

Indeed, much of the politics of globalization is about choices. True, powerful forces connected with dominant actors, deep social structures and long-term historical processes have promoted the recent large-scale expansion of transplanetary and supraterritorial connectivity. However, all social actors – including the writer and readers of this book – have opportunities (admittedly unequal) to respond to and mould this trend.

Multiple globalizations are possible. There is nothing inevitable about the scope, speed, direction and consequences of the trend. In particular, as stressed earlier, globalization as a geographical process and neoliberalism as a political project are not the same thing. Alternative paths of globalization might be more desirable than the directions that have prevailed over the past quarter-century. Personal and collective decisions (both active and passive) can make a substantial difference.

These ethical choices and political moves include the way that one defines globalization. As ever, theory and practice are inseparable. Who gets to define globalization, and who benefits (and loses) from the resultant definition? In particular, does a given conception of globalization help or hurt the subordinated and the oppressed? Each definition and associated understanding of globality reflects certain interests and political positions and feeds into struggles to sustain or alter prevailing power relations.

Hence part of the justification for the definition of globalization adopted here must be political. To address the challenges of contemporary society people need a conception of globalization that not only provides intellectual clarification, but also helps to make relevant, wise, responsible and empowering decisions. As the third part of this book suggests, notions of globality as transplanetary and supraterritorial connectivity can well serve the promotion of human security, social equality, and democracy in contemporary history.

Conclusion

This book argues that, when defined in a particular geographical fashion, notions of 'globality' and 'globalization' can be valuable additions to the conceptual toolkit for understanding social relations. Yes, much globe-talk of recent years has revealed nothing new. And yes, loose thinking and careless politics have devalued many ideas of 'globalization'. However, these shortcomings do not discredit the concept in every form. After all, widespread sloppy usage of other key ideas – 'class', 'democracy', 'rationality' and 'soul', to name but a few – has not been reason to discard these notions altogether.

On the contrary, a definition of globalization as a respatialization of social life opens up new knowledge and engages key policy challenges of current history in a constructively critical manner. Notions of 'globality' and 'globalization' can capture, as no other vocabulary, the present ongoing large-scale growth of transplanetary – and often also supraterritorial – connectivity. Such an insight offers a highly promising entry point for research and action on contemporary history.

To reiterate, this conception of globalization has a distinctive focus. It is different from ideas of internationalization, liberalization, universalization and westernization. The transterritorial connections of globality are different from the inter-territorial connections of internationality. The transborder transactions of globality are different from the open-border transactions of liberality. The transplanetary simultaneity and instantaneity of supraterritoriality is different from the worldwideness of universality. The geographical focus of globality is different from the cultural focus of western modernity. Although globalization as defined in this book has some overlap with, and connections to, internationalization, liberalization, universalization and westernization, it is not equivalent to any of these older concepts and trends.

Of course, the conception of globalization elaborated in this chapter is in no way intended to be the last word about what the term might mean. As stressed earlier, no definition is definitive. The aim of this book is not to issue a final pronouncement, but to offer ever-provisional ideas that provoke further reflection, debate and, in time no doubt, another rewrite of this text.

Chapter 3

Globalization in History

Main points of this chapter
Intimations of globality: to the nineteenth century
Incipient globalization: to the mid-twentieth century
Contemporary accelerated globalization
Conclusion

Main points of this chapter

- when understood as transworld connectivity, globality has figured (at least marginally and in prototypical forms) in human history for centuries
- transplanetary relations, including some with supraterritorial qualities, experienced growth to unprecedented levels from around the middle of the nineteenth century
- the main, greatly accelerated rise of globality, including pronounced supraterritorial aspects, has occurred since the middle of the twentieth century

Where is globalization located historically? When did globality first become part of social relations? How has globalization spread over time? How does the extent of contemporary globality compare with the scale of earlier periods? How far will globalization figure in future society?

Next to arguments over definition, some of the most frequent and deepest debates about globalization concern its history. The two issues are inextricably linked, of course. Different definitions generate different chronologies and periodizations.

The principal debate regarding the history of globalization is whether this development is new or old. On the one hand, proponents of a novelty thesis assert that globalization is entirely recent. Globalists tend to adopt this position that contemporary society is experiencing something that no previous time has known. In contrast, proponents of an 'old-hat' argument affirm that today's globalization repeats earlier scenarios and/or is part of far longer historical processes. Conceptions of globalization as internationalization, liberalization, universalization and westernization tend to hold a longer chronology.

If, as in this book, globalization is conceived as the spread of transplanetary and more specifically supraterritorial relations between people, then the trend has both long-term and distinctive contemporary aspects. Some presence of globality can be traced back centuries, while greater growth of transplanetary links occurred from the middle of the nineteenth century onwards, and large-scale supraterritoriality has appeared for the first time in recent decades. Thus today's globalization is both old and new.

Before this three-part periodization of globalization is elaborated, several points warrant emphasis. First, to stress once more, the historical survey presented in this chapter reflects a particular definition of globalization. Notions of globalization as internationalization, liberalization, universalization or westernization would generate different accounts of history.

Second, even definitions of globalization as the growth of transplanetary connectivity can have different chronologies and periodizations, particularly if those accounts do not highlight the issue of supraterritoriality to the degree done in this book. Thus, for example, Roland Robertson has distinguished five phases of globalization between the early fifteenth and late twentieth centuries (1992: 58–9). For their part, David Held and Anthony McGrew have discerned four epochs of globalization: premodern, early modern, modern industrial, and contemporary (1999: 26).

Third, any periodization is artificially neat. In practice sociohistorical developments cannot be divided into wholly discrete phases. Hence transitions between the three phases of globalization distinguished here have not occurred clearly and completely at precise dates. Nevertheless, the historical shorthand of periods provides helpful general bearings.

Fourth, although recent decades of globalization have shown progressive acceleration, the trend is not inherently linear. In principle the growth of transplanetary and supraterritorial relations between people could in future slow, stall, or even reverse. However, owing to the strong forces that currently propel globalization (as discussed in Chapter 4), most current signs point to considerable additional increases of globality in the years to come.

Finally, a caution must be added concerning the data that are presented in this and other chapters as evidence of the scale of globality and the pace of globalization at various points in time. As matters currently stand, it is often necessary to infer *global* connectivity from *international* data, with corresponding dangers of slipping into a (redundant) conception of globalization-as-internationalization. Some of the statistics refer, for example, to inter-national telephone calls, inter-national civil society associations, and inter-national bank loans. Yet such figures underestimate the extent of global connections, inasmuch as intra-national telecommunications, intra-national civil society activities that address global issues, and intra-national electronic finance also manifest supraterritorial qualities. Unfortunately, many established indicators continue to be rooted in a methodological territorialism that at best only partially recognizes transplanetary flows and indeed can readily distract attention from the distinctiveness of globality in relation to internationality.

Indeed, the development of specifically *global* measures is a priority for contemporary social statistics (cf. EU, 1998). Historically, the term 'statistics' shares a common root with 'state' and has been a largely state-driven activity (Poovey, 1998: 308). Yet today transworld as well as country-based data are often required. For instance, global demographic mapping is needed for effective global ecological planning. Trends of inequality in the world population as a whole are different from trends of inequality within countries (Bhalla, 2002). However, thus far many distinctively *global* statistics are unavailable.

What about having a single aggregate measure of globalization? Several researchers (like the Kearney and CSGR teams mentioned in Chapter 2) have in recent years sought to construct a 'globalization index' that would permit comparisons of levels of globalization both between countries and across time. Yet such statistical exercises are enormously problematic, to the point that one team of scholars has described 'globalization as an inherently unquantifiable metric' (Riezman *et al.*, 2004: 25; also Lockwood, 2004). Therefore, rather than rely on one measure of the trend, the following account traces the historical growth of globality with reference to a wide range of indicators, almost all of which have shown marked upward trajectories.

Intimations of globality: to the nineteenth century

Globalization has no historical origin, in the sense of an exact starting point. Any attempt to identify 'the first global act' would be arbitrary. Rather than parachuting onto the historical stage fully matured overnight, globality gradually appeared as many intermittent and diffuse whispers.

Going back several millennia, various ancient civilizations had conceptions of the world – as they knew it – as a single place. For example, the ancient Chinese had a concept of *tian xia* that referred to everyone living below heaven. Similarly, ancient Greek notions of *oikoumenê* in the sixth and fifth centuries BC conceived of the total habitable world as a single realm (Heidel, 1937; Kroebner, 1945; Hannerz, 1996). Somewhere between 425 and 375 BC, Socrates and Plato affirmed that the earth was spherical rather than flat, a principle further developed by Aristotle (Heidel, 1937: ch 7). By the third century BC cartographers at the Alexandria Library had mapped a world that extended from India to the Atlantic shore of Europe (Jacob, 1999).

The first (tellingly characterized) *world* religions emerged during the fifth and sixth centuries BC with Zoroastrianism and Buddhism. Christians had an incipient transplanetary notion of their prospective communion long before

Isaac Watt published his hymn 'Jesus Shall Reign Where'er the Sun' in 1719. Similarly, Muslim faithful of the eighth and subsequent centuries were inspired by a vision of a transworld Islamic community, the *umma*.

Early intercivilizational contacts also gave a prototypical global quality to various premodern contexts. For example, ancient Greek society developed from a blend of Indo-European, Egyptian, Phoenician and local Aegean influences (Bernal, 1987). More or less continuous contacts between people across Eurasia, from China to Spain, existed from the second century AD onwards, including along the renowned Silk Road of transcontinental commerce from Ch'ang-an to Constantinople (McNeill, 1963: ch 7). Janet Abu-Lughod has described a 'world system' of the thirteenth century that extended from Flanders to China (J. Abu-Lughod, 1989).

Premodern intimations of globality surfaced in a number of other activities as well. For example, a succession of 'dollars of the Middle Ages' served as monies across the Mediterranean world: namely, the Byzantine *solidus* from the fifth to seventh centuries; the Muslim *dinar* in combination with the *solidus* from the eighth to the middle of the thirteenth century; and the *fiorino* of Florence during the next 150 years (Cipolla, 1956: ch 2). Precursors of 'transnational corporations' can be seen in the banks and merchant houses of twelfth-century Italian city-states, who maintained branches across Europe (Braudel, 1979a: 390–5). Between the thirteenth and fifteenth centuries, these bankers also made long-distance loans to England, Flanders and the Balkans. Prototypical global traders sold coffee between and across continents as early as the thirteenth century. Fourteenth-century Mongol expansions from Central Asia brought bubonic plague to China, India, the Middle East and Europe (McNeill, 1976: ch 4). At the same time several writers including Dubois, Dante and Marsilius of Padua made proposals for suprastate governance that would encompass at least all of Christendom (Hinsley, 1963: ch 1). Early long-distance movements of books gave hints of future transworld communication (Febvre and Martin, 1958).

The preceding evidence suggests that globality has not, as some have implied, been solely a feature and product of western modernity. As is argued in Chapter 4, modern capitalism and rationalism do seem to have spurred the greatest expansions and accelerations of globalization in contemporary history. However, it would be wrong to say that transworld connectivity is uniquely western and modern.

On the other hand, veritable transplanetary relations that encompass all continents did not figure anywhere in significant measure until the middle of the second millennium AD. A global imagination inspired voyagers in the fifteenth and sixteenth centuries to attempt a circumnavigation of the earth, a feat first accomplished in 1522. The first known globe, as a depiction of the world, was constructed by Martin Behaim in Nuremberg in 1492 (Brotton, 1999: 75). Cartographers in Europe sketched maps of the entire planet's surface starting in the sixteenth century, including the production in Venice in 1688 of a printed globe that measured more than a metre in diameter and included considerable detail on most of the world's coasts (Agnew, 1998: ch 1; Wills, 2001: 9–10).

In the commercial arena, early modern times saw the slave trade ply between Africa, the Americas and Asia, forcibly taking some 8–10.5 million involuntary migrants across the Atlantic (Curtin, 1969: 87). The so-called 'Columbian Exchange' after 1492 brought a transworld diffusion of American foodstuffs such as cassava, chocolate, potatoes and tomatoes, while the transatlantic transfer of major diseases like smallpox, syphilis, typhus and measles wrought devastating consequences on the Aztec, Inca and other indigenous peoples of the Western Hemisphere (Crosby, 1972; McNeill, 1976; Watts, 1997). Other transoceanic commerce took tea, cane sugar, spices, tobacco, furs and precious metals across the world. To conduct this trade the English, Dutch, French and Danish East India Companies as well as other prototypical 'global corporations' maintained networks of head offices and overseas posts.

In terms of money and finance, early modern times saw gold and silver circulate across the globe. In the eighteenth century two merchant banks, Hope & Co and Barings, operated on stock exchanges in several countries (Born, 1977). Meanwhile commercial houses in Amsterdam and Geneva lent money to governments across Europe as well as to the newly founded American federation (Cameron and Bovykin, 1991).

With such developments in trade and finance, Immanuel Wallerstein, Fernand Braudel and others have emphasized that capitalism has from its earliest days had transworld components (Wallerstein, 1974; Braudel, 1979b). Indeed, during the eighteenth century a number of London-based transatlantic traders considered themselves to be 'citizens of the world' (Hancock, 1995). David Hume wrote, with reference to the rentier class of his day, 'These are men who have no connections with state, who enjoy their revenue in any part of the globe in which they choose to reside' (1741–2: 363). On similar lines that could have been written 200 years later, Adam Smith declared in the concluding paragraphs of *The Wealth of Nations* that:

> A merchant . . . is in great measure indifferent . . . from what place he carries on his trade; and a very trifling disgust will make him remove his capital, and together with it all the industry which it supports, from one country to another (1776: 519).

Global consciousness also figured in other Enlightenment thought of the eighteenth century. Philosophers such as A. R. J. Turgot, Johann Gottfried Herder, and the Marquis de Condorcet were concerned with the history of humanity as a whole, and moreover discerned a trend towards a social unification of the world (Kilminster, 1997: 262–4). Turgot, for example, forecast that, 'finally, commercial and political ties unite all parts of the globe' (1750: 41). Indeed, the Enlightenment itself was an intercontinental movement, linking thinkers 'from Edinburgh to Naples, Paris to Berlin, Boston to Philadelphia' (Gay, 1966: 3).

In respect of governance, notions of international law consolidated from the sixteenth century onwards and advanced the premise that a single set of secular rules should apply across the whole 'civilized' world. Among social movements, anti-slavery campaigns of the eighteenth century included transatlantic collaboration among Quakers. Meanwhile the Seven Years' War of 1756–63 might be regarded as the first 'world war', with its simultaneous battlefields in Europe, North America and South Asia.

However, the scale of all this proto-global activity remained very limited. Early transplanetary commerce involved only a few articles, traded in relatively small quantities, by a handful of companies, for a tiny minority of the world's population. The Hudson Bay Company sent one transoceanic message per year, while today's large global corporations despatch thousands of emails each day. Similarly, long-distance financial dealings of early modern times were quite rare and invariably had a bilateral character, linking financiers in one country with a client in a second country. Global consciousness touched relatively few minds of these earlier times, and even for that small minority globality was usually a passing intuition rather than a central well-developed conception.

Moreover, other forms of global connectivity did not figure in human history at all before the nineteenth century. There were no anthropogenic transworld ecological changes like global warming or ozone depletion. No global institutions were available for an effective transplanetary implementation of global regulations. No global postal services or telecommunications operated. True, a few creative minds of the sixteenth century were already beginning to imagine the possibility of supraterritorial communication. Shakespeare's Puck in *A Midsummer Night's Dream* thought to 'put a girdle round the earth in forty minutes' (1595–6: 38), while Mother Shipton of Yorkshire prophesied that 'around the world thought will fly, in the twinkling of an eye' (Young, 1991: 1). However, actual global communication as it is experienced today was not in the picture.

Indeed, supraterritoriality was absent from the incipient globality described above. Money and finance of early capitalist development did not have qualities of simultaneous and instantaneous exchanges involving any place on earth. For example, although the speed was remarkable for its time, it still took a number of days for financial panic to travel several hundred kilometres between London and Amsterdam in 1745 and between London and Paris in 1825 (Neal, 1985). Nor were the early global products distributed, priced and sold in the context of a tightly coordinated transworld marketing strategy. Hence, to the extent that transplanetary connections existed before the nineteenth century, they unfolded entirely in territorial space.

Incipient globalization: to the mid-twentieth century

Substantially increased transplanetary links – including some with a distinctively supraterritorial quality – developed during the late nineteenth and early twentieth centuries. The hundred years after 1850 saw the advent of major new global communications technologies, a multiplication and consolidation of global markets, increased elements of global finance, two 'world wars', and a degree of supraterritorial connectivity in certain organizations. Indeed, the global swine flu epidemic of 1918–19 afflicted numbers of people (50 million deaths) comparable to the global scourge of AIDS today (20 million dead to date).

However, the two periods of globalization are different. In scale, quality and impact, globalization of the nineteenth century cannot be likened to the hugely accelerated rise of intense transplanetary connectivity that has unfolded since the middle of the twentieth century. Most of the relevant statistics for the nineteenth century show far smaller numbers. Indeed, transworld production chains and significant anthropogenic global ecological problems were altogether absent from the earlier time. Nor did nineteenth-century globality have anything like the degree of supraterritoriality that marks the present day.

Communications

Global communications grew in the nineteenth century as never before. Transworld postal services consolidated. Distance-conquering transoceanic telegraph lines spread from the 1850s. Cross-border telephone connections and radio communications developed from the 1890s.

The telegraph, invented in 1837, provided the first means of substantially supraterritorial communication. Submarine telegraph cables became available in the early 1850s across several seas within Europe. A transatlantic telegraph link came permanently into use from 1866. Five years later telegraph lines stretched continuously between Australia, China, Europe and Japan, although the first transpacific cable did not become operational until 1903 (Ahvenainen, 1981). With these connections, information could circle the planet in a few days rather than a month. Several press agencies like Reuters were formed to take advantage of these opportunities. The telegraph's significance for the rise of supraterritoriality was presciently articulated at mid-century by the novelist Nathaniel Hawthorne, who exclaimed through one of his characters that 'by means of electricity, the world of matter has become a great nerve, vibrating thousands of miles in a breathless point of time' (1851: 273).

The late nineteenth century also introduced distanceless voice communication via the telephone, invented in 1876. The first telephone calls between countries became possible with a line connecting London and Paris in 1891. Two-way telephone messages across the Atlantic Ocean were first achieved via radio waves in 1926. During the next five years radio telephony also came to link Buenos Aires with Madrid, Batavia (now Jakarta) with Amsterdam, and London with Cape Town, Sydney and Auckland. By 1933 an advertisement of the American Telephone and Telegraph Company (AT&T) could justifiably claim that 'the world is bound together by telephone' (Young, 1991).

As for radio, the first wireless transmission between countries occurred in 1899, across the English Channel. A transatlantic radio signal was successfully received for the first time in 1901. World services on the wireless developed from 1924. The first veritably transplanetary radio event occurred in January 1930, when the speech of King George V to open the London Naval Conference was relayed simultaneously to 242 radio stations spread across six continents. By the mid-1930s the world counted 57 million radio receivers, more than 1,100 radio stations, and 1,354 international radio programmes (Huth, 1937).

That said, until the mid-twentieth century global communications were quite limited on the whole. Early transworld telegraphy and telephony had relatively slow speeds, very low capacities, notoriously poor reliability, and extremely high costs. For example, in the late nineteenth century telegraphic messages between Australia and Europe took several days to be relayed; and a message of 20 words cost £10, five times the average weekly wage of that time. The price of a telephone call from London to New York in 1927 was almost a thousand times higher in real terms than the rate prevailing in 1996 (*FT*, 23 December 1996: 17). Matters improved with the introduction of coaxial cables in the 1930s, but the fax machine exhibited at the World's Fair of 1939 required eighteen minutes to transmit a single sheet of paper (Gelernter, 1995). Although television was invented in 1926, the broadcasts remained localized until the 1960s. The digital computer first appeared in 1946, but computer networks were unknown before 1969.

Travel

The nineteenth century also brought global movements of people on an unprecedented scale. The 50 years after 1850 saw the creation of major new diasporas, as about 50 million people migrated from India and China to various destinations in the tropics, while around the same number made permanent moves from Europe to the Americas, Australasia and South Africa

(Lewis, 1978: 14). Indeed, passports and tight surveillance of cross-border movements of people were in their infancy at this time (Torpey, 2000).

Temporary transworld travel also increased in this period. For example, black vocal choirs from the USA toured Europe, and the pioneering travel agent Thomas Cook led his first round-the-globe excursion in 1872. The first world fair, drawing exhibits from across the planet, was staged in London in 1851. The modern Olympic Games were launched in Athens in 1896. The *haj* drew tens of thousands of pilgrims to Mecca annually in the 1920s.

Several key developments in global infrastructure abetted this greater transworld mobility. The Suez and Panama Canals, completed in 1867 and 1903 respectively, greatly reduced the length of many transoceanic voyages, as did the introduction of steamships in place of sail. Concurrently, large-scale railway construction greatly facilitated transcontinental travel. The early twentieth century saw the advent of mechanized air transport. Airmail services began in 1918, and the first nonstop transatlantic flight was achieved in 1919. By 1957 more passengers crossed the Atlantic by aeroplane than by ship. A team of pilots crossed the Eurasian landmass from Amsterdam to Batavia in just over four days in 1933. In 1942 a recently defeated candidate for the US presidency could experience what he called 'one world' by flying around the planet in 160 hours (Willkie, 1943).

However, Wendell Willkie had very small company with his jet lag in the 1940s. The 1896 Athens Olympiad involved only several dozen athletes from a few countries and attracted minimal press coverage (MacAloon, 1981: ch 7). Early global tourism was undertaken by only handfuls of people. Package holidays – which spurred the idea that anyone could take vacations anywhere in the world – were not introduced until 1949. Although the liquid-fuelled rocket was invented in 1927, intercontinental missiles did not arrive on the scene until 30 years later.

Markets

Next to transworld communications and transworld travel, the period of incipient globalization also saw unprecedented growth of transplanetary commodity markets and global brand names. In terms of primary commodities, for example, a prototypical global market in copper consolidated from the 1850s onwards, interlinking shipments from Australia, Chile, Cuba, England and the USA. The London Metal Exchange (LME), established in 1876, handled any deal in copper, tin, lead and zinc, wherever on earth the supplies originated and regardless of whether the cargoes ever landed on British soil (EIU, 1957). Global pricing dynamics also developed at this time in respect of grains and cotton, especially between the commodities exchanges at Buenos Aires, Cairo, Calcutta, Chicago, Liverpool, New York, Rio de Janeiro and Winnipeg (Baer and Saxon, 1949).

Global markets in brandname packaged goods also started to emerge in the late nineteenth century, aided by the creation of automated bottling, canning and refrigeration processes. For example, products such as Campbell Soup and Heinz foods became household articles across several countries from the mid-1880s. Coca-Cola was marketed in Britain, Canada, Cuba, Mexico and the USA within 20 years of the drink's introduction in 1886. Office equipment from Remington Typewriter, agricultural machinery from International Harvester, and appliances from Western Electric also began to be marketed between and across continents from the late nineteenth century. By the 1880s Singer covered three-quarters of the world market in sewing machines (Chandler, 1986: 415–16). With the expansion of colonial settlement and other transoceanic migration during this period, expatriates from Europe, Asia and North America took their demand for 'home' products with them to all corners of the earth. In 1899 J. Walter Thompson was the first advertising agency to open an office outside its country of origin, presaging the development of global commercial promotion campaigns (Mattelart, 1989: 3).

The range of global products continued to grow in the early twentieth century. Transworld marketing was started for Bayer aspirin, Gillette razors, National Cash Register and Otis Elevator. From the outset in 1908, Henry Ford regarded his best-selling automobile, the Model T, as a 'world car' (Spybey, 1996: 41). By 1929 Coca-Cola was bottled in 27 countries and sold in 78 lands. The supraterritorial character of the beverage was explicitly recognized during World War II, when it was promoted as 'the global high-sign' (Pendergrast, 1993). The basis for other well-known global products was laid with the arrival of Nescafé in 1938, the long-play phonograph in 1948, the Marlboro cowboy in 1954, and the first McDonald's restaurant in 1955.

Global markets in primary products also developed further in the first half of the twentieth century. While the LME and other commodities exchanges continued their operations, governments took the first initiatives (via multilateral commodity agreements) to establish transworld price controls on certain products, including sugar, coffee, rubber and tin. During World War II, the Allies created a number of so-called Combined Boards for the global coordination of production and distribution of several dozen strategic raw materials and manufactures. After the war an International Emergency Food Council briefly operated a global programme to combat world hunger in 1946–7.

However, the globalization of markets prior to the mid-twentieth century must not be overestimated. Products with transplanetary distribution and sale were few in number at this time. Moreover, even in these limited cases, marketing strategies lacked the tight transworld coordination that became possible in the past half-century with digital computers, advanced telecommunications, and electronic mass media.

Money and finance

An incipient globalization of money and finance also occurred in the nineteenth and early twentieth centuries. The sterling-based gold standard that prevailed from around 1870 to 1914 gave certain national currencies transworld circulation (De Cecco, 1974). The British pound was the prime global money of this day, but the Dutch guilder, the Japanese yen, the Mexican silver dollar and other denominations also figured in some trade and finance that were not directly connected to their 'home' jurisdictions. An employee of the American Express Company invented the traveller's cheque in 1890 (Mandell, 1990: 28). After the disruptions of World War I, a gold exchange standard was incompletely and temporarily restored in the 1920s. That said, foreign exchange trading during this phase of globalization was minute compared to the levels of recent decades, and governments held small foreign exchange reserves. By the end of 1913, official foreign exchange holdings across the globe had a total value of only around $1 billion (Cohen, 1977: 284), as compared with $1,600 billion in 1997 (BIS, 1998: 105).

Money became almost completely territorialized between the 1930s and the 1950s. True, a number of countries were at this time associated with the so-called sterling bloc or the dollar bloc. In addition, as colonies many other lands had their money closely linked to the currency of a distant metropole. However, these arrangements applied to rigidly bordered regional and imperial territories, not to the planet as a whole.

Indeed, even under the two gold standards most money was shipped in paper and metal form over territorial distances and across territorial borders. Apart from limited sums of money wired by telegraph, currencies at this earlier time lacked the supraterritorial mobility made possible on a large scale later in the twentieth century by airborne shipments and transworld electronic fund transfers. Nor did incipient globalization involve distinct suprastate monies (like the SDR), global bank passes or global credit cards.

In finance, the gold standard and colonialism encouraged a number of commercial banks to develop overseas branch networks. On the eve of World War I, British-based institutions held between a quarter and a third of all bank deposits in countries including Argentina, Australia, Brazil and New Zealand (Jones, 1993: 40). The major banks of the day lent large sums across borders and suffered an international debt crisis in the 1870s when a world economic downturn stopped many repayments. Indeed, the first Latin American debt crisis for European banks occurred in the 1820s.

However, global banking of the nineteenth and early twentieth centuries was heavily constrained by territorial distance and borders. Apart from expatriate colonials, very few people maintained bank accounts outside their country of residence. Offshore banking facilities did not appear (and then only on a small scale) until Luxembourg passed relevant legislation in 1929, followed by Guernsey in 1936, and Jersey and the Netherlands Antilles in 1940. In the 1930s wealthy Canadian and US citizens also started to use the Bahamas to locate offshore trusts and holding companies (Hampton, 1996).

A more pronounced *global* debt dynamic (that is, one that potentially encompasses places anywhere on earth and has transworld effects) emerged after World War I. The German state owed huge reparations to the Allies, who among themselves owed some $26.5 billion in war debt, much of it to the USA, which in turn made substantial loans to Germany in order to facilitate reparations payments. A string of multilateral conferences grappled with this complex web of transworld financial obligations from 1920 until all war debts and reparations were cancelled in 1932. However, globally syndicated commercial bank loans were not known at this time.

In securities markets, meanwhile, the gold standard facilitated a proliferation of foreign bond issues in the late nineteenth century. For example, bonds issued in Europe funded much of the California Gold Rush as well as railway construction in the Americas, China and Russia. In total, the tsarist regime in Russia borrowed some $1.5 trillion in present-day US dollar values on the Paris bond market between 1880 and 1913.

In regard to stocks, listings of nonresident companies figured (as a proportion of total quotations) as significantly on the Amsterdam and London stock exchanges in the 1870s as they did in the 1980s (Neal, 1985: 226). On the other hand, no amount of discounting for inflation could take the £5 billion worth of externally listed shares in world finance of the late nineteenth century anywhere close to the figure of several trillion pounds today.

In any case, such securities transactions of the nineteenth century had a distinctly bilateral, international character. That is, savers in one country invested in a second country using the currency of either the originating or the receiving country. The transactions involved no global syndicates of fund managers, no global pool of investors, and no global portfolios. Moreover, brokers lacked the technology for instantaneous transworld trading. Nor were electronic global clearing and settlement systems available.

In short, some money and finance obtained certain global features in the period 1870–1914. These characteristics resurfaced to a limited extent and temporarily during the 1920s. However, these monetary and financial transactions retained a heavily territorial character. They occurred for the most part between country units and under major constraints of distance and borders.

Organizations

Incipient global communications, travel, markets, money and finance encouraged – and were at the same time encouraged by – the formation of prototypical global organizations in the nineteenth and early twentieth centuries. These institutions included a number of market actors, regulatory agencies (covered below under the heading of law), and civil society bodies.

In terms of firms, the cross-border activities of certain banks, mining companies, agricultural businesses and manufacturers have already been mentioned. A few industrial concerns began not only to sell their goods across several countries in the nineteenth century, but also to establish subsidiaries to pursue production outside the base country. In the first such instance, the US-based gun maker Colt opened a factory in Britain in 1852 (Stopford and Strange, 1991: 13). Similarly, Siemens of Germany built a facility in Russia in 1855, and Kikkoman of Japan set up soy sauce manufacture in the USA in 1892 (Jones, 1996). By the early twentieth century several hundred firms operated across colonial empires or in several state jurisdictions at once. On the other hand, these companies did not pursue global production chains, in the sense that different stages of a process were sited at widely dispersed locations.

More civil society associations, too, began to acquire incipient global features between the nineteenth and mid-twentieth century. For example, a number of Christian missionary societies and several Islamic revival movements coordinated their respective proselytization efforts across several continents at this time. The World Zionist Congress was formed in 1897. Transatlantic peace movements held a sequence of meetings in the 1840s and again around the turn of the century (Beales, 1931; Calvocoressi, 1987). Frequent cross-border consultations also transpired towards in the later nineteenth century among campaigners for women's suffrage (Berkovitch, 1999). Marcus Garvey's Universal Negro Improvement Association encompassed over 900 chapters across five continents in the mid-1920s (Leanne, 1994: 86–9). The labour movement maintained its First International in 1864–72, a Second International in 1889–1914, and a Third International (the Comintern) in 1919–43. By 1914 unions had set up more than two dozen International Trade Secretariats to support workers in particular industries (Lorwin, 1953; Holthoon and Linden, 1988; Silver, 2003). Meanwhile business circles founded the International Chamber of Commerce in 1920. In the area of humanitarian relief the International Red Cross and Red Crescent Movement dates back to 1863, while the Save the Children Fund was started in 1919. In respect of environmentalism, the first cross-border initiatives at wildlife conservation were taken around the turn of the century (McCormick, 1989). Also early in the twentieth century, Mahatma Gandhi took his campaigns for social transformation to South Africa, India and Britain.

However, like the regulatory bodies discussed below, all of these prototypical global firms and civil society associations lacked much supraterritorial character. In general, they operated between countries rather than across the globe as a single place. The territorially based members of the organization (that is, company affiliates or branch associations) maintained a high degree of autonomy from any global head office. Indeed, the global communications infrastructure of the time was not adequate to conduct tightly coordinated transworld campaigns and policies. Moreover, these prototypical global organizations had heavily restricted mobility, with limited possibilities to relocate offices and facilities to other places in the world.

Military

Globalization of military activity was increasingly evident after the middle of the nineteenth century in, for example, the so-called 'new imperialism' of greatly enlarged overseas colonial empires. Half a dozen West European states were joined in the 1890s by the USA in maintaining large military garrisons thousands of kilometres from their respective capitals. American and Spanish armies fought in the Philippines, Belgian soldiers in the Congo, British troops in Afghanistan, Dutch military in what would become Indonesia, French forces in West Africa, German units in East Africa.

Military campaigns of unprecedented transworld scope came in the first half of the twentieth century with the aptly named 'world wars'. The major combatant states coordinated operations across theatres in Africa, Asia, Europe and the Pacific. In terms of global weaponry, World War II saw the arrival of radar and long-distance bomber aircraft. In 1945 V1 and V2 rockets fired by German forces on London introduced long-range missiles into battle (Neufeld, 1995).

Law

The nineteenth century brought expanded globality in the legal field, too. Inter-state treaties increased to unprecedented numbers at this time, and more of them took a multilateral rather than bilateral form. Over 20 times as many multilateral accords were concluded in the period 1851–1950 as in the period 1751–1850 (Ku, 2001: 4). Multilateral conference diplomacy also intensified after 1815, with some congresses like those of Berlin in 1884–5 and Paris in 1919 addressing far-flung parts of the planet.

The second half of the nineteenth century witnessed the creation of the first permanent regulatory agencies with a transplanetary remit (Murphy, 1994). These bodies included the International Telegraph (now Telecommunication) Union (ITU), founded in 1865, and the General (now Universal) Postal Union, founded in 1874. Systematic transworld monitoring of disease began following major cholera outbreaks in the 1840s, with the first multilateral scientific conference on transboundary disease in 1851. Institutions for transworld tracking of weather also emerged before the turn of the century.

Important global standards were set during this period as well. Arrangements for universal time coordination (UTC) in relation to a prime meridian at Greenwich were concluded in 1884. Institutionalized transworld technical standardization began with the establishment of the International Electrotechnical Commission (IEC) in 1906. The International Organization for Standardization, source of the now pervasive ISO numbers, started operations in 1947.

In the 1920s and 1930s the League of Nations developed an unprecedented breadth – if perhaps still relatively shallow depth – of transworld governance. Interpol launched its transborder pursuit of lawbreakers in 1923. The formation of the Bank for International Settlements (BIS) in 1930 introduced the first multilateral institution devoted specifically to monitoring transborder financial flows. The basis for still larger expansion of global governance was laid in the 1940s with the creation of the UN system, the Bretton Woods institutions (the IMF and the World Bank), and the General Agreement on Tariffs and Trade (GATT).

Consciousness

All of the above incipient material globalization helped to spread global thinking to more contexts and to wider circles of people from the nineteenth century onwards. Newly created mass-circulation newspapers also began to bring information from around the planet within easy reach of literate people everywhere.

Meanwhile prototypical global organizations gave expression to, and in turn deepened, a sense of transplanetary community in various circles. Supraterritorial religious and labour solidarities have already been mentioned. In addition, the late nineteenth century witnessed several projects to foster transworld racial solidarity. For instance, white Anglo-Saxon imperial federalism gathered adherents across the British Empire in the 1870s and 1880s, and the first intercontinental Pan-African Congress was held in 1893. Meanwhile first-generation feminists of the late nineteenth and early twentieth centuries developed some transworld solidarity based on gender. In this vein the writer Virginia Woolf made her renowned declaration that: 'As a woman I want no country. As a woman my country is the whole world' (1938: 197).

Global thinking continued to surface during this period in other literary and academic circles as well. In the early nineteenth century the social theorist Claude-Henri de Saint-Simon proclaimed a 'religion of humanity' that was promoted *inter alia* through a Parisian newspaper by the name of *Le Globe* (Taylor, 1975: 51). Karl Marx and Friedrich Engels recognized a global dimension in capitalism, writing in *The Communist Manifesto* of a 'universal inter-dependence of nations' (1848: 64). Pioneer sociologists like

Summary chronology of incipient globalization, 1850s–1950s

1851	first world's fair
1852	establishment of the first foreign manufacturing subsidiary
1863	start of the first transworld relief organization
1864	creation of the first transworld labour organization
1865	formation of the first global governance agency
1866	first permanent transoceanic telegraph cable
1870	emergence of the first transworld monetary regime
1872	first round-the-world tourist excursion
1890	invention of the traveller's cheque
1891	first cross-border telephone connection
1896	first global sports event, the Athens Olympiad
1899	first cross-border radio transmission
1918	inauguration of airmail
1919	first nonstop transatlantic flight
1920	inauguration of the League of Nations
1926	first transatlantic telephone call
1929	first offshore banking arrangements
1930	formation of the Bank for International Settlements
1944	creation of the International Monetary Fund and the World Bank
1945	V1 and V2 ballistic missiles fired from Germany on London
1945	formation of the United Nations system
1947	signing of the General Agreement on Tariffs and Trade
1949	first package holiday
1951	first international credit card
1952	first scheduled jet airline service
1954	advent of the Marlboro cowboy
1956	first transoceanic telephone cable

Emile Durkheim and Leonard Hobhouse also made perceptive observations of emergent globality (Scholte, 1993: 21). One or two researchers of the late nineteenth century had premonitions of transborder ecological problems like acid rain and global warming (McCormick, 1989: 182; Myers, 1996: 1). Over 50,000 precious stones were assembled to form a Globe of Jewels (using emeralds for sea and rubies for land) in Iran in 1869. Efforts to chart a global star map began in 1890, involving twelve observatories across the earth (although the complete catalogue of the heavens was not published until 1964) (Daston, 1999). Esperanto was introduced in 1887 to answer a newly perceived need for a distinctly global language that transcended territorial locations. In 1926 the Fabian Society in London saw fit to convene a series of lectures on 'The Shrinking World' (Toynbee, 1948: 97). A few years later José Ortega y Gasset declared that 'the content of existence for the average man of to-day includes the whole planet' (1930: 29).

That said, global consciousness was at this time not central to everyday life. Few people attended the Fabian lectures, and almost no one spoke Esperanto. Indeed, a UNESCO survey conducted in 1962 estimated that 70 per cent of the world's population was unaware of happenings beyond the village (Connor, 1994: 27). Relatively few people acted out a strong sense of global class, gender, racial or religious solidarity. Territorial identities, especially those linked to state and nation, tended to sweep aside all other constructions of community.

The evidence reviewed in the summary box on the preceding page clearly indicates that globality – as transplanetary connectivity – took many forms and reached substantially greater extents in the late nineteenth and early twentieth centuries than ever before. Moreover, this period also saw certain global relations – like radio, a handful of brandname goods, and a few regulatory arrangements – acquire something of a supraterritorial quality. However, as the next section shows, it is quite something else to suggest – as some observers have asserted – that contemporary globalization repeats the scale and significance of trends a hundred years earlier.

Contemporary accelerated globalization

So, if conceived as the growth of transplanetary – and more specifically supraterritorial – spaces, then globalization has unfolded mainly since the mid-twentieth century. Although transworld relations are not completely novel, the pace and scale of their expansion has become qualitatively greater over the past five decades. These years have seen far and away the greatest increases in the number, variety, intensity and influence of global social phenomena. To take one general indicator, the rigorously calculated CSGR Globalization Index for the world as a whole shows an impressive rise from 0.18 in 1982 to 0.40 in 2001 (CSGR, 2005).

Communications

Some of the most striking contemporary accelerations of globalization have occurred in respect of communications, especially those of an electronic supraterritorial kind (Cairncross, 1997; Mowlana, 1997). The relevant infrastructure has vastly grown since the mid-twentieth century. Transoceanic cables became available for telephone as well as telegraph messages from 1956, when the first such link connected Scotland and Newfoundland. Direct dialling between countries was introduced between London and Paris in 1963, the same year that a 'hot line' was installed in the spirit of détente between the Kremlin and the White House. By 1990 transworld direct-dial telephony was available in over 200 countries.

Over the same period the introduction of satellites has hugely increased the carrying capacities of the global communications infrastructure. Orbital satellites became available in 1958, followed by geostationary satellites (which hold a fixed position above the earth) in 1963. AT&T launched the first telecommunications satellite in 1962. The International Telecommunications Satellite Organization (INTELSAT), founded in 1964, today links more than 20 orbitals with thousands of earth stations in over 200 countries (INTELSAT, 2005). In addition, other operators between them maintain some 150 further communications satellites (Demac, 1986).

Meanwhile optical fibres have offered ever-rising capacities for global communications since their invention in the late 1960s. The maximum load of a single strand of fibre-optic cable increased to 6,000 simultaneous voice conversations by the early 1980s and 600,000 concurrent telephone calls by the mid-1990s. The introduction since the 1980s of broadband technologies such as Integrated Services Digital Network (ISDN) and very high-speed Asynchronous Transfer Mode (ATM) has allowed fibre-optic cables to carry not only voice, but also large concentrations of digitized data, text, sound recordings, graphic material, and motion pictures. Several transoceanic and transcontinental fibre-optic cables have been laid since 1988. Whereas the submarine telephone cable laid in 1956 could carry a maximum of 60 calls simultaneously, the Fibreoptic Link Around the Globe (FLAG) constructed in 1996–2002 can transmit up to 600,000 conversations concurrently. Another major project, the Global Crossing fibre-optic network, has connected more than 200 cities across the planet with over 100,000 miles of cable. Given the enormous capacities offered by satellites and fibre optics, cross-border telephone traffic burgeoned from 33 billion minutes in 1990 to 70 billion minutes in 1998 (HDR, 1999: 25).

Telephone connection points have likewise proliferated in the past half-century. The 1965 world total of 150 million fixed lines rose to 851 million by 1998. Moderately priced fax machines came on the market in the mid-1980s and numbered nearly 30 million worldwide by the mid-1990s. More recent developments in telephony include videophones and videoconferencing technology.

In addition, reduced costs and improved performance have turned mobile telephones into a mass consumer good. The world count of these devices increased from less than a million in 1985 to 700 million at the end of 2000 and over a billion in 2004 (*FT*, 8 October 1998: VIII; *FT*, 8 October 1999: VIII; *FT*, 20 June 2001: 13). The late 1990s saw the introduction of satellite-based mobile telephone systems in which a handset can be reached instantly with a single telephone number at any location on earth. New generations of mobiles have acquired a wider menu of capacities, for example, to convey text, fax, email and image as well as voice messages.

Recent developments in the global telecommunications infrastructure have also created large supraterritorial spaces for computer networks. The first transoceanic computer link, using a telex connection, was achieved in 1963. Communication between dispersed computer networks occurred for the first time in 1969, in the so-called ARPANET between researchers at four universities in the western USA. Email was introduced through ARPANET three years later. Company-wide so-called 'intranets' have grown since the late 1980s to coordinate production and sales operations, wherever on the planet the various bureaux and employees might be situated. Other key events in the development of global computer networks have included the introduction of commercial silicon microchips in 1971, personal computers (PCs) in 1981, and portable laptops shortly thereafter.

The publicly accessible Internet, a transworld 'meganetwork' linking millions of individual computers, emerged in the 1980s and quickly underwent enormous expansion. The number of computer systems connected to the Internet (or 'hosts') burgeoned from 213 in 1981 to 313,000 in 1990 and 318,000,000 in 2005 (ISC, 2005). Estimates of current and projected Internet use vary widely; however, a fair guess calculates that 934 million people across the world were online by 2004 (CIA, 2004). Internet take-up has been faster than that of any previous communications technology.

The Internet has also developed a graphical dimension, the so-called World Wide Web, which became available for general public use in 1991. The millions of supraterritorial 'sites' on the Web provide near-instantaneous access to all manner of information for readers anywhere on earth. The search engine Google covered more than 8 billion web pages as of 2005 (Google, 2005).

Like computer networks, supraterritorial communications via television are new to contemporary accelerated globalization. Transoceanic television transmissions via satellite were first achieved in 1962. The first live satellite television broadcast occurred in respect of a concert by the Beatles in 1967. Since then, hundreds of millions of people have simultaneously watched other global events such as championship sports, moon landings, and war reports. The number of television receivers across the planet rose from 75 million in 1956 (the first year of mass production of affordable sets) to 1,400 million in 1997 (Brown, 1990: 115; UNESCO, 1999: IV.S.3). Television density nearly doubled from 121 per 1,000 people worldwide in 1980 to 235 per 1,000 in 1995 (HDR, 1999: 4). Only one state, Bhutan, has attempted to exclude television from its jurisdiction, and even this government relented and legalized the medium in 1999. Television transmissions via direct broadcast satellite (DBS), first achieved in 1976, have taken the additional step of bypassing earth stations and beaming signals straight to individual dwellings via parabolic rooftop dishes. Global television stations such as Cable News Network (CNN), BBC World, and Al-Jazeera have multiplied since the 1980s. CNN now transmits to over 200 countries and other territories.

With respect to an older global mass medium, the world count of radio sets increased dramatically to over 2.4 billion in 1997, more than 40 times the level of the 1930s (UNESCO, 1999: IV.S.3). The transistor radio, introduced in 1955, has offered greater portability and much improved reception. More recently, digital radios that receive satellite transmissions are opening new opportunities for low-cost, high-capacity global broadcasting. The amount of world service programmes by major government-sponsored radio stations doubled between 1960 and 1988, to a total of some 16,000 hours per week (UNESCO, 1989: 154). Incalculable additional amounts of globally relayed information have been broadcast through local and national radio stations.

Travel

Transplanetary movements of people have likewise grown to unprecedented levels since the middle of the twentieth century. Much-enlarged infrastructures of paved roads and air corridors have coupled with pre-existent transcontinental railways and transworld shipping lanes to make global travel more available than ever. The average number of people crossing state frontiers across the world per day rose from 69,000 in 1950 to over two million in 2000 (French, 2000: 6).

The decades since 1960 have brought massive increases in the numbers of aeroplanes, airports, routes and flights. The speed, range and carrying capacities of the craft have improved with the advent of commercial jets in the late 1950s, wide-body aircraft in 1969, and supersonic carriers in the early 1970s. Jet engines have given something of a supraterritorial quality to air travel, connecting almost any points on earth to one another within 24 hours. The world total of air traffic between countries grew from 25 million passengers per annum in 1950 to over 400 million in 1996. The number of air travellers flying within as well as between countries on scheduled commercial flights reached nearly 1.5 billion per annum in 1997 (ICAO, 1998). Passenger kilometers flown on scheduled airlines rose from 1.8 trillion in 1991 to 2.9 trillion in 2001 (ICAO, 2003).

With aircraft and other means of cross-border transport, people took 425 million holidays abroad in 1990, a figure that rose to 693 million in 2001 and is expected to reach 937 million by 2010 (*FT*, 7 January 1997: VII; WTO-1, 2002). Total receipts from travel between countries rose twenty-fold from $19 billion in 1970 to $389 billion in 1996, thus at rates far ahead of world GDP growth (WTO-1, 1991: 11; UN, 1997: 184).

Meanwhile large numbers of people have made longer-term transworld movements. Between voluntary migrants and involuntary refugees, around 100–120 million people resided outside their country of citizenship as of the early 1990s (Sutcliffe, 1998: 325; Stalker, 2000: 7). Nearly four million Filipina domestic workers are currently employed in 130 countries across the planet (Hawkesworth, 2003: 51; also Parreñas, 2001). Remittances from migrant labourers (totalling $88 billion from North to South in 2002) constitute a significant proportion of GDP in several countries (UN, 2002). Moreover, transworld movements of professionals from South to North have created a 'brain drain' of tens of thousands per year (Stalker, 2000: 107). Study abroad has become fairly commonplace in higher education, involving an estimated 1.5 million people in 1993 (Stalker, 2000: 108). A new phenomenon of transworld (often airborne) asylum seekers emerged in the 1980s and reached a peak flow of 700,000 to the European OECD countries in 1992, before declining to 300,000 three years later (Castles and Miller, 1998: 88–9).

That said, heavy state-imposed restrictions have severely limited many global movements of people, particularly those involving low-skilled labour. In this vein, a Ugandan recently despaired that 'obtaining a visa from the British High Commission [in Kampala] is harder than getting into heaven' (UMU, 2003).

Organizations

Not surprisingly, growth in global communications and travel has gone hand in hand with growth in global organizations since the 1960s. This rise of globality has occurred not only in terms of the numbers of institutions that have a transplanetary field of activities, but also in terms of the degree of supraterritorial mobility and coordination that marks their operations.

In the business sector, the count of firms that work simultaneously in several countries multiplied more than ninefold from 7,000 in the late 1960s to 61,000 (with over 900,000 foreign affiliates between them) in 2003. Total world stock of FDI went from $68 billion in 1960 to $1,700 billion in 1990 and $7,100 billion in 2002 (UNCTAD, 1994: 131; UNCTAD, 2003: 1; UNCTAD, 2004: 8). Along with global organization through direct investment, companies have also formed thousands of transworld strategic alliances, particularly since the 1980s (Gilroy, 1993; Dunning, 1997). Organized crime syndicates like the Columbia-based Medellín cartel and the China-based Triads have added further to the volume of transworld 'business'. The current collective annual income of these globally operating mafias may be as high as $1.5 trillion (HDR, 1999: 42; Mittelman and Johnston, 1999).

At the same time as proliferating in quantity, contemporary corporate connections have also become more deeply global in quality. For one thing, transplanetary communications have permitted much more intensive supraterritorial coordination of contemporary business operations. In addition, FDI today has much greater transworld mobility, with companies more ready and able to relocate facilities within a global space. In one striking example, athletic suppliers Nike during a five-year period closed 20 factories and opened 35 others at new sites often thousands of miles away (Abegglen, 1994: 26).

Like the expansion of cross-border firms, the greatest historical proliferation and growth of cross-border civil society organizations (CSOs) has also transpired since 1960. Of the more than 20,000 active bodies of this kind counted by the Union of International Associations in 2000, less than 10 per cent were over 40 years old (UIA, 1998: 1764; UIA, 2001: 33, 35). In this light Lester Salamon (1994: 109) has spoken of: 'a global "associational revolution" that may prove to be as significant to the latter twentieth century as the rise of the nation-state was to the latter nineteenth'.

Countless further transworld associations (like many newsgroups on the Internet) have had a less formal and more transient character. For example, Peoples' Global Action against 'Free' Trade and the World Trade Organization (PGA) promoted public demonstrations against the WTO in the late 1990s as a loose transplanetary network without offices or officers.

Law

Global governance agencies have likewise grown at unprecedented rates in recent decades. The increase in the number of these organizations has been relatively modest, since many transworld regulatory bodies were created in the period of incipient globalization. That said, the UN system has acquired various additional agencies and programmes since the 1960s, and the OECD was established in 1962. Moreover, most transworld governance institutions have in recent decades experienced unprecedented expansion in their competences, memberships, staffs and budgets.

Transplanetary legal instruments have proliferated at the same time. The half-century after 1950 saw the conclusion of 70 per cent more multilateral treaties than in the preceding full century (Ku, 2001: 4). A number of these laws have related to so-called 'global commons' (a concept popularized in the 1970s) like Antarctica, the deep seabed, and outer space.

As is elaborated in Chapter 6, these various transworld frameworks have added wide-ranging and influential supraterritorial qualities to contemporary regulation. It is in this regard not surprising that the phrase 'global governance' was coined in the late 1980s and rapidly acquired common currency in the 1990s. Talk of the need for global public policy has not been far behind.

Production

As previously noted, transworld production processes and associated intra-firm trade did not exist in earlier phases of globalization. These activities first gained substantial proportions in the 1960s, when supraterritorial coordination developed especially in the production of semiconductors and consumer electronics. Subsequently the trend spread to the assembly phase in the manufacture of clothing, motor vehicles and appliances. More recently, many service industries have turned to global production, for example, by siting data processing operations in the Caribbean, India and Ireland.

As the preceding points indicate, global production has developed mainly, though not exclusively, through the location of the labour-intensive phases of a process at low-wage sites, particularly in the South. Indeed, many states with large and on the whole relatively poorly skilled labour forces have sought to lure global corporations to their jurisdictions with special tax and regulatory measures. These advantages have generally applied to designated areas known by names such as special economic zones (SEZs), export processing zones (EPZs), and free production zones (FPZs). Within these enclaves of so-called 'offshore' manufacture, global companies may enjoy subsidies, tax exemptions, advantageous investment codes, the suspension of restrictive social and environmental regulations, and other privileges (World Bank, 1992; ILO, 1998).

Like the global production processes that flow through them, offshore zones are new to contemporary history. Although the first of these arrangements appeared in the late 1950s (in Columbia and Ireland), host states have created most of these special areas since the mid-1970s. By the late 1980s there were around 260 EPZs in 67 countries, most prominently in Asia and the Caribbean (Lang and Hines, 1993: 82). The number multiplied further in the 1990s with, for example, several former communist-ruled countries joining the trend. Some 3,000 EPZs were in place in 116 countries across the globe by 2002 (ILO, 2003: 2).

Markets

Contemporary globalization has also seen far more transplanetary distribution of finished products through global trade. The value of world cross-border trade rose from \$629 billion in 1960 to \$7,430 billion in 2001 (Balaam and Veseth, 2001: 111; WTO-2, 2002: 13).

A number of new transport technologies have facilitated this growth. Many vehicles have become larger and faster. Standard twenty- and forty-foot container units, introduced in the late 1960s, are easily transferred between trucks, trains, boats and aeroplanes, thereby permitting ready intermodal movements of goods across the planet. In addition, air express services have given a supraterritorial quality to some deliveries. Companies such as DHL, UPS and TNT have offered 24-hour transworld shipments since the late 1960s.

Aided by these and other technological developments, the principal spread of global products has occurred since the second half of the twentieth century. Today many supermarkets and department stores are mainly stocked with transworld articles. To mention just a few of the thousands of global brand names, Twinings teas are now sold in 120 blends across over 100 countries. Kiwi shoe polishes are marketed in 130 countries. The global Interflora network of 58,000 florists allows intimates to exchange bouquets in and between 140 countries. Each month *Reader's Digest* reaches nearly 100 million people across more than 60 countries through 48 editions and 19 languages. Promoting its religious product, the Church of Jesus Christ of Latter Day Saints has provided the *Book of Mormon* with translations into 86 languages for its ten million members across 159 countries. Global trade has also taken malevolent forms with transworld trafficking in body parts, illicit drugs, and women and children.

Not only countless goods, but also some of their retail distributors have gone global since the 1970s (Treadgold, 1993). Well-known examples of such chains include Italy-based Benetton clothing shops, Japan-based 7-Eleven convenience stores, and Sweden-based IKEA furniture warehouses. Alternatively, today's global consumer can – equipped with a sales catalogue, credit card, and telephone, television or Internet links – shop the earth without leaving the house. Mail-order outlets and telesales units have undergone exponential growth, while e-commerce on the World Wide Web has expanded several thousand times from less than $3 billion in 1996 to nearly $6.8 trillion in 2004 (Bacchetta *et al.*, 1998: 23; HDR, 1999: 60; Global Reach, 2004b). A few commodity exchanges (for example, the New York Mercantile Exchange and the Sydney Futures Exchange) have established electronic links that enable instantaneous transworld trading between them.

Yet the contemporary accelerated globalization of markets has involved more than exponential growth in the numbers of affected products and outlets. Equally important has been the greater intensity of supraterritoriality in today's markets. Advances in transplanetary telephony, computer networks and air transport have allowed managers considerably to increase their supraterritorial coordination of distribution, promotion and sales activities. Local circumstances have often continued strongly to influence marketing decisions at the level of individual sales outlets, but in many companies the primary strategic framework has become global.

Money

As noted earlier, money was thoroughly territorialized in the mid-twentieth century. The Bretton Woods Agreements of 1944 provided for the creation of a dollar-centred gold standard, and this regime of fixed exchange rates became fully operational in 1959. Under the Bretton Woods arrangements the US dollar became a global currency, so much so that, by the early 1970s, the value of dollars circulating outside the USA exceeded the value of gold stocks held by the Federal Reserve Bank. In these circumstances the Nixon Administration halted dollar–gold convertibility in 1971.

However, in contrast to the return to monetary territorialism that followed earlier collapses of a gold standard in 1914 and the early 1930s, the demise of the Bretton Woods regime did nothing to halt the globalization of money. On the contrary, in the new situation of floating exchange rates the German mark, the Japanese yen, the Swiss franc and a dozen other national currencies joined the US dollar as global stores of value, units of account and means of exchange. Today trillions of dollars' worth of national denominations are used in innumerable transactions that never touch the 'home' soil. Meanwhile the aggregate value of official foreign exchange reserves in the world rose from $100 billion in 1970 to $1,579 billion in 1997 (Spero, 1990: 41; BIS, 1998: 105).

At the same time other global monies have appeared in the shape of suprastate currencies. The previously mentioned SDR was created in 1969 as a reserve denomination under the supervision of the IMF. Two releases of SDRs, one in 1970–2 and the other in 1979–81, added around $30 billion of this currency to the world money supply. In 1997 the Board of Governors of the IMF approved an as-yet still unratified doubling of SDR allocations. The most important regional suprastate money, the euro, entered into electronic circulation in 1999 and took tangible form in 2002. The euro had its forerunners in the European Unit of Account, devised in 1961 as a denomination for certain bonds, and the European Currency Unit (ECU), created in 1978 with wider uses. Both the ECU and the SDR have resided only in computer memories for accounting purposes, whereas the euro has slipped into purses for the transactions of everyday life.

Several other forms of supraterritorial money have also been new to the period of accelerated globalization: international credit cards from 1951, chip or 'smart' cards from 1981, and debit cards in the 1990s. In 2002 over one billion Visa credit cards were accepted in over 150 countries for transactions amounting to $2.4 trillion. Visa, a name adopted by BankAmericard in 1976, expounds a vision of universal or u-commerce done 'anywhere, anytime, any way' (Visa, 2003). Meanwhile, rival MasterCard had come to be recognized at more than 32 million establishments in 210 countries and other territories (MasterCard, 2003). These and other bank passes allow the holder to extract cash from ATMs, first introduced in 1969 and numbering 900,000 in over 120 countries by 2003 (MasterCard, 2003).

Through the developments just described, territorial currencies have lost the near-monopoly position that they held in respect of money in the middle of the twentieth century. Moreover, monetary globalization since the 1970s has far exceeded anything witnessed under the gold standards or before. For one thing, the amounts of money involved are far greater. In addition, the supraterritorial quality of this money has much increased, particularly with the advent of electronic finance.

Finance

Unprecedented financial globalization has transpired in contemporary history with respect to foreign exchange dealings, banking, securities markets, derivatives business and the insurance industry. The average volume of daily transactions on the world's wholesale foreign exchange markets rose a hundredfold in a quarter of a century between 1973 and 1998, from $15 billion to $1,500 billion. The introduction of the euro and other developments prompted turnover to drop to the still massive figure of $1,210 billion per day in 2001, which rose once more to an average daily figure of over $1,900 billion at the end of 2004 (BIS 2001a, 2001c: 98–100; CLS, 2004; Gilpin, 2001: 261). Now more is traded in six hours on the forex markets than the World Bank has lent in its entire history (Clark, 2001: 17). The Continuous Linked Settlement (CLS) process introduced in 2003 ensures same-day final settlement of transactions across currencies between the leading global commercial banks. Meanwhile the retail sector has seen a worldwide proliferation of 'bureaux de change' where customers can walk off the street to buy and sell a score of currencies on demand.

In banking, the second half of the twentieth century introduced the phenomenon of global deposits. In these accounts, savers use transworld bank networks to place their funds anywhere on the planet. The world total of bank deposits owned by nonresidents rose from $20 billion in 1964 to $7.9 trillion in 1995 (IMF, 1993: 60–70; BIS, 1996: 7). Commercial banks in the world's main financial centres saw the share of their assets attributable to nonresident depositors rise from around 5 per cent in 1960 to around 40 per cent by 1990 (Porter, 1993: 54). In addition, several trillion US dollars' worth of bank deposits now lie in offshore finance centres, which have proliferated from the handful created before 1950 to 60 jurisdictions at the turn of the century (Doggart, 1993; Roberts, 1994; Palan, 1998, 2003; Hampton and Abbott, 1999; TCO, 2001). Among the larger centres, the Cayman Islands today host more than 500 offshore banks (alongside only six branches for local business), while over 200 are registered in Luxembourg and over 70 in Guernsey (Roberts, 1995).

With electronic transfers, the globalization of finance also allows monies to be moved instantaneously between bank offices over whatever distance. Key conduits for these transactions are the computerized systems of CHIPS (the Clearing House Interbank Payment System) and SWIFT (the Society for

Worldwide Interbank Financial Telecommunications). Begun in 1970, CHIPS typically processed $148 billion per day of US dollar payments across the globe in 1980, rising steeply to $1.37 trillion through 270,000 transactions per day in 2005 (CHIPS, 2005). Started in 1977, SWIFT operations in 2004 carried an average of 9.1 million messages per day (with an average transit time of less than 20 seconds) between over 7,500 financial institutions in 202 countries (SWIFT, 2005).

Contemporary globalization has also affected the lending side of banking as never before. Credit was first created from global accounts in 1957, when Moscow Narodny Bank issued a loan of $800,000 in London. In other words, a bank based in one country made a loan in a second country using a globally circulating currency that originated in a third country. Supraterritorial lending by transplanetary syndicates of commercial banks began on a significant scale in the early 1970s and has expanded massively since. The value of new transworld syndicated bank credits totalled around a trillion dollars per annum in the late 1990s (BIS, 2000b: 120, 122). Aggregate outstanding balances on these loans rose from less than $200 billion in the early 1970s to well over $8,000 billion in 2001 (BIS, 1998: 144; BIS, 2001b: 10). Other global lending has taken place on a large scale since the 1960s through official multilateral financial agencies like the IMF, the World Bank Group, and regional development banks for Africa, the Americas, Asia, the Caribbean and Europe. The capital base of the IMF has risen tenfold since the 1960s, to reach almost $300 billion in 1999.

Veritably supraterritorial securities markets started in the 1960s with the advent of the eurobond market. The first eurobond issue came in July 1963, when the state highways authority in Italy issued debt in London denominated in US dollars through financial managers in Belgium, Britain, Germany and the Netherlands. The annual volume of new eurobonds grew to $5 billion in 1972, $43 billion in 1982, and $371 billion in 1995 (Kerr, 1984: 30–1, 51; OECD, 1996b). By the end of the 1980s only the secondary market for US domestic bonds remained larger than that for global bonds (Honeygold, 1989: 19). Net issuance of all cross-border bonds and notes rose from $247 billion in 1994 to $1,157 billion in 1999 (BIS, 2000b: 112).

In the equity markets, the quotations of US-based corporations Gillette and ITT on the London Stock Exchange were rare instances of extraterritorial share listings in 1950. Forty years later externally based companies accounted for nearly half of the quotations on the Amsterdam and Frankfurt bourses, a third of those on the Zürich and Paris markets, and over a fifth of those on the London Stock Exchange (O'Brien, 1992: 45). A few global companies like Nestlé and Alcatel Alsthom have issued equities on as many as a dozen bourses across the world. The 1990s also saw the appearance of American Depository Receipts (ADRs) and Global Depository Receipts (GDRs). In these instruments, shares of companies based in Asia, Eastern

Europe and Latin America are bundled into packages and traded at global financial centres.

Globality has arisen not only in relation to individual security instruments, but also in the ways that they are assembled in investment portfolios. Numerous investors (especially institutions such as pension funds, insurance companies, unit trusts and hedge funds) today operate transplanetary portfolios. Many of these investment companies have further deepened their supraterritorial character by registering offshore, particularly in Luxembourg, the Bahamas, Dublin and the Channel Islands.

Meanwhile electronic communications have enabled investors and dealers instantly to transmit and execute orders to buy and sell securities – in principle anywhere across the planet. Moreover, since 1985 a number of stock exchanges have established transworld electronic links between themselves. Before 1980 transactions in bonds and equities between resident and non-resident investors were negligible. The value of cross-border dealings in shares increased (in constant 1994 dollars) from $1.4 billion in 1987 to $2.6 billion in 1994 (Scott and Wellons, 2000: 17). By 1997 the value of cross-border securities transactions was equivalent to 672 per cent of GDP in Italy, 253 per cent of GDP in Germany, and 213 per cent of GDP in the USA (BIS, 1998: 100). In 1980 the figure for the USA had been only 9 per cent of GDP (*Economist*, 18 October 1997).

Most payments connected with global securities trading are effected through one of two computerized transplanetary clearinghouses. Euroclear was established in Brussels in 1968, while Cedel has operated since 1971 from Luxembourg. These giant electronic bookkeeping operations fulfil a role in global securities trading akin to that of CLS in foreign exchange dealing and CHIPS and SWIFT in supraterritorial banking. Euroclear alone processed 118 trillion euros' worth of bonds, stocks and investment funds in 2003 (Euroclear, 2005).

Globalization has also burgeoned since the 1970s in regard to financial derivatives. This market started on the Chicago Mercantile Exchange in 1972 and has subsequently spread to several score of trading sites around the world. Global markets in futures, options and other types of derivatives contracts have developed in respect of foreign exchange rates, interest levels, bond and share prices, stock market indices and more. The total world annual turnover on organized derivatives exchanges alone (thus not counting the larger number of over-the-counter deals) stood at more than $350 trillion in 1997 (BIS, 1998: 155–6). The notional amount of outstanding over-the-counter financial derivatives contracts reached $88 trillion at the end of 1999 and $197 trillion at the close of 2003 (BIS, 2000a: 26; BIS, 2004: 1). Like most major contemporary securities markets, the financial derivatives business is mainly electronic, using telephone lines and information display terminals that connect traders anywhere in the world. Moreover, several derivatives exchanges in different time zones (for example, London and Singapore, Chicago and Sydney) have established direct links to enable round-the-world, round-the-clock dealing in certain futures and options.

Still further transplanetary connectivity has spread in the insurance sector. All of the major insurance companies now operate across the major global financial centres. Meanwhile the six largest insurance brokers have developed a World Insurance Network (WIN) that allows them to transact business across the earth from their office computers.

In sum, then, finance has shifted very substantially out of the territorialist framework that defined most banking, securities, derivatives and insurance business before the middle of the twentieth century. The amounts transacted are staggering: multiple trillions of US dollars' worth per day. Such figures dwarf the numbers associated with sales turnover in other global markets and investment in transworld production processes. It is understandable that many worries concerning 'globalization out of control' have centred on the financial sector.

Social ecology

Many other worries about the course of contemporary globalization have focused on its environmental aspects. Anthropogenic global ecological changes did not occur on any notable scale before the middle of the twentieth century. Prior to the early 1970s, no question of transplanetary environmental degradation held any sustained prominence on the political agenda. Since then, however, governments have signed over a hundred multilateral treaties on environmental issues. Scientists have undertaken several dozen major initiatives to study transworld ecological developments. Millions of citizens across the globe have joined environmental NGOs like the World Wide Fund for Nature (WWF) and Greenpeace.

Three global ecological problems have gained greatest attention. One, the depletion of stratospheric ozone, accelerated from the 1960s and began to raise alarms in the 1980s. As of the mid-1990s, this shield to protect the earth's surface from biologically active ultraviolet radiation from outer space was thinning at a rate of 3 per cent per decade (GACGC, 1995: 1). The main assault on stratospheric ozone has come from chlorofluorocarbons (CFCs), invented in 1931 and widely used in industrial and consumer products from the 1950s.

A second widely discussed supraterritorial environmental issue – popularly known as 'global warming' – involves anthropogenic increases in greenhouse gases and their consequences for the planetary climate. This human interference with the chemical composition of the atmosphere has come through the industrial production of carbon, methane, halocarbons and nitrous oxide. This activity dates back to the beginnings of industrialization in the middle of the eighteenth century, but the main, accelerated rises in levels of greenhouse gases have occurred since the second half of the twentieth century. For example, carbon emissions from fossil fuel combustion grew from about 1.5 billion tons per annum in 1950 to an average of around 5.5 billion tons per annum in the 1980s (GACGC, 1995: 12; Porter and Brown, 1996: 6). Carbon dioxide levels have increased from 200–275 parts per million by volume (ppmv) in the preindustrial era to 370 ppmv at the start of twenty-first century (*Guardian*, 24 July 2001: 5). The Intergovernmental Panel on Climate Change, formed in 1988, has concluded that the anthropogenic greenhouse effect has brought a rise in the mean surface temperature of the earth of between about 0.3°C and 0.6°C since the late nineteenth century (IPCC, 1995: 22). This global warming may have any number of consequences, including a rise in the average sea level, intensified soil erosion, altered patterns of disease, and increased species extinction.

Loss of biological diversity is already large enough to constitute a third main instance of contemporary global ecological change. For example, it is estimated that three-quarters of crop varieties were lost in the course of the twentieth century (Porter and Brown, 1996: 12). Meanwhile whole packages of genes disappear when a species becomes extinct. Owing mainly to the exponential growth of human consumption of environmental assets over the past 150 years, the pace of species extinction has increased between 1,000 and 10,000 times (Wilson, 1988: 13). Different authorities have calculated that an average of anywhere between 20 and 200 species died out each day in the late twentieth century (Myers, 1993: 179; GACGC, 1995: 32). A middle-range estimate suggests that the rate of loss rose from around one species per annum at the turn of the century to six species per year in 1950, before skyrocketing to some 10,000 species annually in 1990 (Myers, 1985: 155). In spite of this exponential increase in extinctions, biodiversity is arguably still underappreciated as a global resource.

Other global ecological problems mentioned briefly in Chapter 2 have also mainly emerged since the middle of the twentieth century. In respect of acid rain, for instance, annual world emissions of sulphur dioxide rose from some 70 million metric tonnes in 1950 to around 180 million metric tonnes in 1990 (Porter and Brown, 1996: 8). Transplanetary fallout from nuclear devices dates from the first detonations of atomic weapons in 1945 and spread to civilian facilities in 1986 with the explosion of the Chernobyl nuclear reactor. The depletion of tropical moist forests (or 'rainforests') has also mainly transpired since the second half of the twentieth century, thereby reducing one of the Earth's principal sites of photosynthesis and major concentrations of biomass (crucial for the creation of new species). The worldwide construction of large dams in recent history has shifted ten trillion metric tonnes of water from the oceans to the continents and moved the earth's axis of rotation sixty centimetres from the North Pole towards western Canada (Myers, 1996: 1).

Annual world consumption of fresh water quadrupled between the 1950s and the 1990s, while world per capita availability of fresh water declined by more than a third, raising fears of a developing global water shortage (Porter and Brown, 1996: 11). At the same time between a quarter and a third of the earth's land surface, home to 600–900 million people, is threatened to some degree with desertification (McCormick, 1989: 117; GACGC, 1995: 33).

The jury is still out on many questions concerning the precise character, causes, magnitude, rate and locational distribution of anthropogenic global environmental transformations, as well as the severity of their consequences for human and other life on earth. However, the substantial supraterritorial quality of these phenomena and their generally increased scale since the mid-twentieth century is indisputable.

Military

Also eminently apparent is the major expansion of military globalization since the 1950s. Although no 'Third World War' has as yet been waged, the so-called Cold War between the USA and the USSR extended to all corners of the planet. In the name of saving humanity from communism, American armed forces intervened everywhere from Turkey to Korea to Vietnam to Grenada, not to mention a host of clandestine operations and proxy wars. For their part Soviet troops and military advisers surfaced in Cuba, Afghanistan, Ethiopia and Angola as well as in major concentrations across Eastern Europe and along the USSR's border with China.

Other global military campaigns have continued after the end of the Cold War. For example, state armies from far-flung parts of the planet have converged on Somalia, Bosnia, Kosovo and Iraq. In addition, UN peacekeeping operations, first started in 1956, have multiplied to unprecedented numbers since the 1990s. As discussed further in Chapter 9, global paramilitary and terrorist violence has grown to become a major source of human insecurity in contemporary history.

The decades since the 1950s have also seen the main development of global weapons. Intercontinental ballistic missiles (ICBMs) with nuclear warheads were introduced by the USA in 1957 and the USSR three years later. Originally launched from land, ballistic and cruise missiles can now also be fired from submarines, trucks and aircraft. Originally carrying conventional bombs and nuclear devices, the missiles can now also transport chemical weapons and biological agents. Meanwhile advances in guidance systems have greatly enhanced the precision with which the long-range missiles can hit targets (Mackenzie, 1990). The US military has proposed satellite-based defences against missiles since the 1980s, but so far has refrained from full-scale development of what has popularly been termed a 'star wars' system (Fitzgerald, 2000; Wirtz and Larsen, 2001).

Consciousness

No numerical measures of global consciousness are available; however, it seems safe to venture that people today are generally more aware than ever before of the planet as a single place and are more inclined to conceive of the earth as a whole as humanity's home. 'World records' were not registered until the twentieth century, with the first edition of the best-selling Guinness Book appearing in 1955. The popular 'global village' metaphor was coined in the 1960s (McLuhan and Fiore, 1968), while the Gaia hypothesis that the planet exists as a single living being was formulated in the 1970s (Lovelock, 1972, 1979). Earth Day was first marked in 1970. A hundred years ago global consciousness was generally limited to fleeting perceptions in limited élite circles. Today, with globes in the classroom, world weather reports in the news, and global products in the cupboard, transworld dimensions of social life are part of everyday awareness for hundreds of millions of persons across the planet. Global consciousness perhaps gained its single greatest boost by the transworld diffusion in 1966 of pictures taken from outer space showing the earth as one location. Now the symbol of the globe surfaces in every corner of daily life.

At the start of the twenty-first century globality is widely and deeply embedded in academic, commercial, official and popular thinking. Seasoned travellers boast a global collection of souvenirs. Meanwhile television daily takes even the most sedentary viewer across the planet in an instant. Every week brings a global news sensation, a global sports competition, and a global conference of some prominence. Recent decades have brought a growth of so-called 'world music' and 'world literature' that blend and transcend territorial cultures. In recognition of the growing importance of transplanetary spaces, some (albeit far from enough) statistics are now calculated on a global basis. For example, providers of financial data have devised several transplanetary share price indices, including the FT/S&P Actuaries World Index, started in 1987, and the International Herald Tribune World Stock Index, started in 1992.

Accelerated globalization since the mid-twentieth century has also brought some growth in transworld solidarities. On the one hand, human disasters connected with disease, hunger, natural catastrophes and war have elicited global sympathies and assistance with a frequency and a scale not known in earlier times. Newer transworld social movements concerned with consumer protection, environmental concerns and human rights have joined older global labour and peace movements. In addition, as is discussed further in Chapter 7, a host of transplanetary bonds have deepened in contemporary history with respect to class, disability, gender, generation (especially youth culture), profession, religion, race and sexual orientation. People living under conditions of globalization have increasingly constructed significant aspects of their identity in supraterritorial terms.

Summary indicators of accelerated globalization in contemporary history

telephone lines (fixed and mobile)	from 150 million in 1965 to over 1,500 million in 2000
mobile telephones	from 0 in 1978 to over 1 billion in 2004
Internet users	from 0 in 1985 to 934 million in 2004
radio sets	from 57 million in the mid-1930s to 2,400 million in 1997
television receivers	from 75 million in 1956 to 1,400 million in 1997
international air travellers	from 25 million in 1950 to 400 million in 1996
receipts from international travel	from $19 billion in 1970 to $389 billion in 1996
export processing zones	from 0 in 1957 to 3,000 in 2002
foreign exchange reserves	from $100 billion in 1970 to $1,579 billion in 1997
daily foreign exchange turnover	from $15 billion in 1973 to $1,900 billion in 2004
bank deposits by nonresidents	from $20 billion in 1964 to $7,900 billion in 1995
international bank loans	from $9 billion in 1972 to $1,465 billion in 2000
balances on international bank loans	from $200 billion early 1970s to $10,383 billion in 1997
issuance of global bonds	from 0 in 1962 to $371 billion in 1995
over-the-counter financial derivatives contracts	from 0 in 1971 to $197 trillion in 2003
world stock of FDI	from $66 billion in 1960 to $7,100 billion in 2002
international trade	from $629 billion in 1960 to $7,430 billion in 2001
international companies	from 7,000 in late 1960s to 65,000 in 2001
international CSOs	from 1,117 in 1956 to over 20,000 in 2000
annual species extinction	from 6 in 1950 to 10,000 in 1990

Conclusion

Hence, when conceived as the rise of transplanetary and supraterritorial social connections, globalization is mainly new to contemporary history.

Only since the middle of the twentieth century has globality figured continually, comprehensively and centrally in the lives of a large proportion of humanity. Hundreds of millions of people now experience direct and often instantaneous written, auditory and/or visual contact with previously distant others several times per day.

Again, contemporary globalization is not a rerun of earlier times, including in particular the late nineteenth century. Arguments of repetition between the two periods have mainly rested on comparisons of just three indicators: namely, levels of cross-border merchandise trade, foreign direct investment, and permanent migration. A number of economists have noted that, on certain proportionate calculations, international trade and investment reached similar extents in the 1890–1913 period as in the 1990s (Baker *et al.*, 1998: 5, 9, 339; Balaam and Veseth, 2001: 168). Moreover, numbers of permanent migrants were similar in the two periods in absolute terms.

Yet to conclude a broader rerun of history on the basis of this evidence alone is unsustainable (cf. Baldwin and Martin, 1999; Sutcliffe and Glyn, 2003). For one thing, these accounts overlook many other instances of globality whose current levels are incomparably higher than anything experienced in the nineteenth century. Take for instance the scale of contemporary telecommunications, air travel, transworld goods, transplanetary financial transactions, transworld civil society associations, global regulations, global festivals, and global awareness among general publics the world over. In addition, the repetition thesis ignores various key aspects of contemporary globalization that were wholly absent in the late nineteenth century, such as digital computers, advanced telecommunications, television, electronic money and finance, transworld production chains, and measurable anthropogenic global ecological changes.

Even the three key indicators that underpin the repetition thesis are problematic. The trade and investment statistics refer to *proportionate* amounts, whereas *absolute* numbers are far higher for the present day than in the nineteenth century. The trade figures only cover merchandise exports, while the scope of contemporary global commerce involves many more goods and services. The similarity in absolute numbers of migrants becomes less striking when one considers short-term transworld travel and tourism as well as permanent relocations. In other words, total global movements of people (temporary as well as permanent) are far greater today than a hundred years ago. Finally, nineteenth-century trade and investment lacked the far greater supraterritorial characteristics that are manifested today; thus even if quantities might on certain calculations be similar, the spatial qualities of many contemporary global transactions are significantly different. For instance, intra-firm trade barely existed a century ago, but accounts for up to a quarter of cross-border commerce today.

In sum, then, although globalization has a longer history, the antecedents to recent trends must not be exaggerated. A sense of range, scale and impact is lost when people argue that there is nothing new in contemporary global connectivity. It makes ample sense that the vocabulary of 'globality' and 'globalization' was absent in the nineteenth century and has only surfaced in recent times.

To be sure, as emphasized before, it is important not to exaggerate the extent of globalization even today. After all, world telephone density in 1995 was still limited to 12 sets per 100 head of population. At present only about 15 per cent of humanity accesses the Internet. Transborder corporations directly employ only a small proportion of the world workforce, namely, 73 million persons as of 1992 (ILO, 1995: 45). A large majority of people alive today have never joined – let alone been actively involved in – a transworld civil society association.

Nor, to repeat a qualification from Chapter 2, has globalization involved all people on earth to the same extent. For one thing, the large majority of global transactions has occurred between people in the North. In addition, the rise of supraterritoriality has touched urban centres (especially so-called 'global cities') more than rural areas. The trend has involved propertied and professional classes more than poorer and less literate circles. Women and people of colour have generally had less access to global spaces than men and white people. On various counts, then, contemporary globalization has often gone hand in hand with marginalization. This unevenness between countries and social groupings is elaborated in Chapter 10 with reference to the inequalities of contemporary globalization.

That said, accelerated globalization of recent decades has left almost no one and no locale on earth completely untouched, and the pace has on the whole progressively quickened with time. This does not mean that the process is linear and irreversible. For example, as noted earlier, money has over the past two centuries had alternating phases of territorialization and globalization. Perhaps ecological constraints like exhaustion of natural resources and climate change could put a brake on globalization in the long or maybe even medium term.

However, at present the forces behind globalization (identified in the next chapter) would seem to rule out any major reversal in the short or medium run. Several authors (cited in the preface to this second edition) who have recently suggested that globalization is finished can marshal little convincing evidence to support such a claim. Current trends in technological innovation and regulation heavily favour a further expansion of transplanetary connectivity. For example, prospective advances in fibre-optic cables will yield capacities running into the millions of telephone calls per hair-thin strand. Likewise, both capitalism as a mode of production that promotes globalization and rationalism as a mode of knowledge that stimulates globalization are today deeply entrenched. For the moment, to take a phrase from the *Wall Street Journal*, globalization 'is one buzzword that's here to stay' (26 September 1996: R2).

Maybe the expansion of transplanetary and supraterritorial links will not continue across the twenty-first century at the often breakneck speeds that have been witnessed during the past 50 years, but most current signs point to further rather than less globalization in future. The coming years could bring the end of certain policies towards globalization (like neoliberalism); hence when Elmar Rieger and Stephan Leibfried have written of the 'limits to globalization' they have meant the limits to *neoliberalist* globalization (Rieger and Leibfried, 2003). However, the growth of transworld spaces as such seems set to continue. The key question for the future is therefore less 'whether' and more 'whither' globalization. The trend is in this sense very much 'an unfinished revolution' (Shaw, 2000).

Chapter 4

Explaining Globalization

Main points of this chapter
Contending theories
An eclectic synthesis
Conclusion

Main points of this chapter

- explanations of globalization can be approached through a number of theoretical frameworks, including liberalism, political realism, Marxism, constructivism, postmodernism, and feminism
- each of these perspectives offers insights into the dynamics that have propelled globalization, but each is also overly narrow, missing important aspects of the process
- an eclectic approach that interlinks developments in geography (like globalization) with trends in production, governance, identity and knowledge offers a more encompassing explanation

Having developed a definition of globalization and tracked a history of the trend, this book's analysis can proceed to the no less thorny issue of explanation. Why and by what dynamics has the spread of transplanetary (including supraterritorial) connectivity occurred? What has made globalization happen? This question is crucial not only to satisfy intellectual curiosity, but also to inform policy action. In order to anticipate possible future courses of globalization and to shape those processes in desired directions, it is necessary to understand the forces that have generated the development and brought it to its present position. Viable explanation provides grounds for sound prediction, prescription and action.

Given this crucial importance of explanation, it is surprising – and disappointing – to find that existing research on globalization has given this matter comparatively little attention. In fact, the present book is one of relatively few in the burgeoning literature on globalization that devotes a chapter specifically to explaining the trend. Most other works have tended to make only passing and fairly unspecific reference to conditions such as capitalism, modernity, technological change, or US hegemony as forces behind globalization. Many accounts have not explicitly addressed issues of causation at all. Of course no explanation of globalization can be completely adequate, but that unavoidable shortfall does not justify skirting the question.

Much as there are multiple possible definitions and periodizations of globalization, so too there are multiple explanations on offer. Some accounts have, methodologically, a more materialist character, locating the forces that produce globalization in economics and ecology. Other explanations take a methodologically more idealist approach, putting the emphasis on cultural and psychological causes. In addition, the various theoretical frameworks advance different accounts of the key actors, structures and historical dynamics that have generated globalization. The diverse perspectives also highlight different core issues and (implicitly if not explicitly) promote different interests. Accordingly, each type of explanatory framework tends to point towards different sorts of policy prescriptions.

The first part of this chapter reviews a broad menu of available theories for explaining globalization. In turn a succession of subsections examine liberalism, political realism, Marxism, constructivism, postmodernism, and feminism. Each of these six perspectives is found to provide distinctive insights towards an explanation of globalization, but all are also limited by excessive parsimony. That is, in each case the analytical need to simplify is taken to the point of oversimplification, where the explanation offered is unsustainably narrow. Too much is left out.

The second part of the chapter synthesizes key insights from the various theoretical frameworks in a multifaceted social explanation of globalization. This eclectic approach attributes the growth of transplanetary connectivity to interrelated impulses from the realms of production (namely, certain turns in capitalist development), governance (namely, various enabling regulatory conditions), identity (namely, particular ways of asserting being and belonging), and knowledge (namely, certain logics of rationalist consciousness). By this argument it is not one variable that has generated globalization, but a complex interplay of several forces (cf. Held *et al.*, 1999; Waters, 2001; Urry, 2003).

Nor is causation held to flow in one direction with respect to globalization. The trend is treated here as both explanandum (something to be explained) and explanans (something that explains – or at least contributes to an explanation of other trends). The present chapter considers the 'explanandum' side: namely, how circumstances in the areas of production, governance, identity and knowledge have combined to produce globalization. Conversely, subsequent chapters in Part II of the book examine the 'explanans' side: namely, how the geographical shift to greater globality has influenced developments in the four other spheres.

Contending theories

In principle globalization can be explained in a host of different ways. Any of the main schools of social and political theory can offer a story of why transplanetary connections have developed, and why global relations have proliferated with particular speed and intensity in recent history. The various approaches are surveyed below to give a sense of the possible range of explanations, before the second half of the chapter elaborates a more specific account that is adopted for this book's analysis.

The review that follows distinguishes six main types of social explanation for globalization: liberalism, political realism, Marxism, constructivism, postmodernism, and feminism. Each of these approaches is seen to take a different perspective on:

- the central issue for investigation in respect of globalization;
- the material and/or ideational generators of global social relations;
- the key actor(s) that have propelled globalization;
- the principal structure(s) that have produced globalization; and
- the core dynamic(s) of history that have driven globalization.

What follows is a very general survey. The accounts of the various schools of thought are highly compressed and simplified. Only the basic premises of each approach are identified and assessed. Other writings have elaborated much more sophisticated versions of the various positions. The more limited purpose in the present context is to offer a summary overview of the range of possible explanations of globalization, as a prelude to setting out the explanatory framework that informs this volume. More detailed treatments of contending perspectives can be found in theory textbooks (e.g., Baylis and Smith, 2005: pt 2; Burchill *et al.*, 2005).

Nor is the sixfold typology of theories laid out below complete. This review covers the main *social* explanations of globalization. A more comprehensive survey could in addition consider environmentalist theories that focus on the ecological dynamics of globalization (Lovelock, 1979) and spiritual approaches that explore globalization in relation to the metaphysical (Rifkin, 2003). More restrictedly, this chapter limits its range to accounts that explain globalization in terms of social action and social structure.

The sixfold categorization of explanations presented here is also overly neat. Many scholars and writings do not fit precisely and consistently into one or the other school of thought. Instead, lots of researchers take inspiration from more than one approach and/or shift their positions over time. Moreover, many thinkers adopt less explicit and/or more nuanced stances on core premises than the stark positions that are presented here. The tenets of contending perspectives are expressed below as blunt ideal-types in order to emphasize contrasts between different possible points of view. In practice accounts of globalization often do not fall obviously and wholly under one of the six headings.

Likewise, there is plurality within each type of explanation distinguished in the following paragraphs. For example, while all political realists focus on the struggle for power among states, some examine this contention in terms of hegemony, while others frame interstate competition in terms of the balance of power. Similarly, there are numerous variations on the Marxist theme of class relations within the capitalist mode of production. In recognition of this diversity, headings below describe each approach in the plural (i.e., liberalisms, postmodernisms, feminisms, etc.).

Liberalisms

Liberalist explanations of globalization tend to see the process as a market-led extension of modernization. This type of approach is generally taken by people who are interested in maximizing human progress through the pursuit of currently dominant models of 'development', with an emphasis on economic growth and liberal democracy. Most mainstream accounts of globalization – including those that promote neoliberalist policies of the kind described in Chapter 1 – adopt some variant of liberalist explanation. Most other perspectives on globalization develop their alternative explanations largely out of critiques of liberalism.

From a liberalist position globalization is, at the most elementary level, a result of 'natural' human desires for economic welfare and political liberty. As such, increased transplanetary connectivity is ultimately derived from human drives to maximize material well-being (through markets) and to exercise basic freedoms (as guaranteed by publicly accountable government). For liberalists globalization is an outcome of people's strivings to escape poverty as well as to achieve civil and political rights. On a liberalist account it is inherent in market dynamics and modern democratization that these forces should eventually interlink humanity across the planet.

On top of these assumed primordial human motivations for wealth and freedom, liberalist explanations generally highlight two sorts of conditions as being necessary for the realization of globalization. First, technological advances – particularly in the areas of transport, communications and information processing – are required to effect transplanetary connections physically. Second, suitable legal and institutional arrangements must be in place to enable markets and liberal democracy to spread on a transworld scale.

As technological innovation is mainly the work of engineers, liberalist social researchers generally focus their studies on institutional circumstances that further or hinder globalization (cf. Keohane and Martin, 1995; Keohane, 1998; Ruggie, 1998). Hence liberalists investigate issues such as: the effects of different state policies in promoting or hampering globalization; whether regional institutions act as stepping stones or stumbling blocks to globalization; the construction of global governance arrangements to support global markets and global human rights; the role of market self-regulation in advancing globalization; and the organization of firms and civil society associations for effective global action.

Given these emphases, most liberalist explanations of globalization have emanated from the fields of Business Studies, Economics, International Political Economy, Law, and Politics. Indeed, most work on globalization in these disciplines has taken a broadly liberalist approach. In addition, some economic geographers and economic sociologists have developed market and institutionalist analyses of the development of global production and global governance (e.g., Dicken, 2003). Work of the so-called Stanford School of world society theory on global modernity has also fallen in a broadly liberalist frame (Boli, 2006).

Liberalist accounts of globalization have not generally been advertised with this label. Whereas many political realists, Marxists, constructivists, postmodernists and feminists have declared their affiliation with those respective theories, most adherents of liberalism have taken this approach without calling it such. In most cases readers have to infer this perspective from the types of arguments that the author in question advances.

Liberalism has ranked as the principal orthodox account of globalization, with particular support from circles of power. Liberalist explanations have underpinned the neoliberalist prescriptions that are favoured in mainstream policy circles. To the extent that liberalist attributions of globalization to market forces, technology and institutions have had widespread acceptance as 'commonsense', scholars taking this line of argument have faced less pressure to specify, verify and justify their approach compared to researchers who adopt more critical perspectives.

To their credit, liberalist explanations have helpfully highlighted the importance of technological change and institutional arrangements in promoting globalization. Transplanetary connectivity could not have accelerated and intensified as it has over the past half-century in the absence of air travel, advanced telecommunications, digitization, and so on. Liberalists have also astutely stressed the necessity of constructing institutional infrastructure to support globalization. Transworld relations have not appeared spontaneously, but have required conducive regulatory circumstances of *inter alia* technical standardization, administrative harmonization, translation arrangements between languages, laws of contract, and guarantees of property rights.

That said, liberalist explanations also have several major limitations. For one thing, these accounts do not probe further to ask what social forces lie behind the creation of technological and institutional underpinnings for globalization. It is not satisfactory to attribute these developments to 'natural' human drives for economic growth and political liberty. After all, such strivings have been manifestly absent from many sociohistorical contexts. If, as seems empirically to be the case, these impulses in their current pronounced form are peculiarly modern, then researchers need to delve more deeply into the structures of contemporary society for the conditions that have prompted the technological and institutional bases of globalization. Other theories considered below seek in different ways to do this.

A second significant shortcoming in liberalist explanations is their culture-blindness. These accounts locate the causes of globalization in material conditions of technology and institutions, without exploring the socially and historically situated life-worlds and knowledge structures that have promoted these technological and institutional developments. Instead, liberalist accounts tend to suppose that culture (and cultural diversity) do not matter in determining when, where and how globalization occurs. People everywhere are assumed to be equally amenable to and desirous of increased globality in their lives, when this is plainly not the case.

A third critical failing in liberalist explanations of globalization is their inadequate attention to power. These arguments do stress that firms compete for markets and that interest groups compete for benefits. However, liberalists ignore the importance of structural power inequalities in prompting globalization and shaping its course. Liberalist explanations therefore have little or no regard for entrenched power hierarchies between states, classes, cultures, sexes, races, etc. Yet even the most cursory glance indicates that globalization has been steeped in such structural inequalities and associated political struggles.

Political realisms

Where liberalist accounts underplay questions of power, political realists put struggles for power at the heart of their explanations of globalization (e.g., Gilpin, 2001). Political realism is the traditional power politics understanding of international relations. This approach is generally adopted by researchers who are interested in questions of state power, the pursuit of national interests, and conflict (including warfare) between states.

Political realists assume that territorial sovereign states are the principal actors in world politics. Proponents of this approach further presume that states are inherently acquisitive and self-serving, making for inevitable competition as their insatiable appetites for power clash. To manage this unavoidable interstate conflict, some political realists have advocated the use of a balance of power, where any attempt by one state to achieve world dominance is countered by collective resistance from other states. Other political realists have suggested that a dominant state can bring stability to world order if this so-called 'hegemon' maintains international rules and institutions that both advance its own interests and at the same time contain conflicts between other states.

In the vein of hegemonic stability theory, globalization can be explained as a way that the dominant state of the day – in the case of recent history the USA – has asserted its primacy and concurrently created an environment of controlled competition among states. On this account large-scale contemporary growth of transplanetary connectivity has allowed the US state to promote its national interests and further its power. By implication, globalization would recede if and when it was no longer in the interest of the US state to sponsor the process, or if and when the US state lost the resource dominance that underwrites its hegemonic status. No published account has systematically explained globalization on quite these lines, but the general logic of hegemonic stability theory has featured in some analyses of post-1945 US foreign policy (Kennedy, 1987; Nye, 1990).

In another variant of political realism, globalization could be explained as a strategy in the contest for power between several major states in contemporary world politics. On this line of argument, transplanetary connectivity has advanced as the governments of Britain, China, France, Japan, the USA and other large states have exploited the potentials of global relations to bolster their respective power positions. Such states have aimed to attract global firms into their jurisdiction to strengthen the domestic economy and have supported global expansion by firms based in their jurisdiction to gain influence over other states. Likewise, political realists would say, strong states have in the pursuit of power developed global military capabilities, promoted their currencies as global monies, and drawn in global migrants to raise their country's human capital.

Political-realist explanations of globalization have the merit of highlighting issues of power and power struggles, something that liberalist accounts tend to ignore. Power politics perspectives also helpfully draw particular attention to the role of states in generating global relations. As such, political realism usefully counters unsustainable suppositions in some quarters that globalization is antithetical to and undermines territorial states. Political realism also rightly stresses that states have not been equal in globalization, with some being dominant and others subordinate in the process.

On the other hand, political realism arguably takes the emphasis on power too far. The theory's politics-centrism suggests that everything in globalization comes down to the acquisition, distribution and exercise of power. Not surprisingly, proponents of this approach are found almost exclusively in the fields of International Relations and Politics. Yet globalization also has cultural, ecological, economic and psychological logics that are not reducible to politics. Globalization is also about the production and consumption of resources, about the discovery and affirmation of identity, about the construction and communication of meaning, and about humanity shaping and being shaped by nature. To be sure, culture, ecology, economics and psychology are bound up with power relations: these other aspects of social relations are anything but apolitical. However, they are also more than political and require consideration in their own right, too.

The state-centrism of political realism is also a weakness, inasmuch as this approach tends to neglect the importance of other actors in generating globalization. Within governance circles, for example, it is not only national governments that have provided the regulatory frameworks for transplanetary connections, but also substate authorities, macro-regional institutions, global agencies, and private-sector bodies. Nor is it viable to explain the globalizing activities of nongovernmental actors like firms, civil society associations, and households wholly in terms of the pursuit of national interest and the assertion of state power. When going global these other types of actors have followed motivations and exerted influences that are partly – and sometimes quite substantially – autonomous from the policies of country governments.

Similarly, political realism oversimplistically reduces power relations in the creation of transplanetary spaces to a question of state hierarchies. The primacy of the USA and other major governments has certainly helped to stimulate contemporary globalization, to orient the process in particular directions, and to skew the benefits of increased transworld connectivity in favour of dominant states. However, additional types of power relations – for example, on lines of class, culture and gender – have also affected the course of globalization. These other structural inequalities cannot be adequately explained as an outcome of interstate competition. Power politics among states has no doubt had implications for hierarchies in globalization between managers and workers, between various world religions, and between men and women. Yet there is more to these other social dynamics than conflict between major states. After all, class inequality, cultural hierarchy, and patriarchy predate the modern states system.

Marxisms

Marxist theories offer explanations of globalization that bring one of these other power structures to the fore, namely, class relations. Marxism is the principal political economy critique of liberalist orthodoxy. This approach is adopted by researchers who are principally concerned with modes of production, social exploitation through unjust distribution, and social emancipation through the transcendence of capitalism. Marxist arguments about globalization have emanated from all fields of social enquiry, albeit most especially from Geography, Politics and Sociology (Bromley, 1999; Rupert and Smith, 2002; Rosenberg, 2005).

Marxists explain the expansion of transplanetary relations as an outcome of the capitalist mode of production. Karl Marx himself presciently anticipated the growth of globality when he wrote in *Grundrisse* that 'capital by its nature drives beyond every spatial barrier' to 'conquer the whole earth for its market' (1857–8: 524, 539). Thus on Marxist accounts globalization happens because transworld connectivity enhances opportunities of profit making and surplus accumulation. In particular, say Marxists, globalization is a strategy that enables the capitalist, bourgeois, accumulating class to increase its resources and power over the labouring, proletarian, exploited class.

Marxists reject both liberalist and political realist explanations of globalization. On Marxist accounts, the technological advances that enable globalization have not been propelled, as liberalists argue, by 'natural' human drives for economic growth, but by historically specific impulses of capitalist development. Likewise, say Marxists, the legal and institutional infrastructures that facilitate globalization have emerged not so much to spread market efficiency across the planet, but to serve the logic of surplus accumulation on a global scale. Meanwhile Marxists dismiss liberalist talk of 'freedom' and 'democracy' as being not real impulses behind increased transplanetary connectivity, but a legitimating ideology for exploitative global capitalist class relations. Similarly, for Marxists, state policies and inter-state struggles for power are not, as political realists claim, the actual drivers of globalization, but rather expressions of deeper forces of capitalism and class struggle. Dominant states may be exercising power when they promote globalization, but they do so in the service of capital rather than in some notional 'national interest'.

Like liberalism and political realism, Marxist explanations of globalization have appeared in a variety of guises. More traditional Marxist arguments have focused on the growth of transplanetary circuits of capital through global companies and global commodity flows, accompanied by the consolidation of transworld networks among the capitalist class and transworld fragmentation among the working class (cf. Burnham, 1997; Harris, 1998–9; Pijl, 1998; Tabb, 2001). Meanwhile so-called neo-Marxists in dependency and world-system theories have examined capital accumulation on a global scale more on lines of core and peripheral countries than in terms of bourgeois and proletarian classes (cf. Wallerstein, 1979; Chase-Dunn, 1989; S. Amin, 1997). What some have dubbed 'neo-Gramscian' accounts have highlighted the significance of underclass struggles to resist globalizing capitalism: not only by traditional labour unions, but also by new social movements of consumer advocates, environmentalists, peace activists, peasants, and women (cf. Cox, 1987; Gill, 1993; Gills, 1997; Mittelman, 2000).

Marxist approaches offer important contributions to understanding globalization. Attention to capitalism and class relations takes explanations of growing transplanetary connectivity beyond liberalism and political realism to some of the deeper social forces that have generated relevant technological advances, institutional developments, and state strategies. Marxist accounts of capital and class also reveal a great deal about social power relations and the generation of inequality in a globalizing economy.

Yet, much as political realism focuses too narrowly on state hierarchy, the Marxist focus on class stratification likewise presents an overly restricted account of power. Other relations of dominance and subordination have also operated in globalization on lines of state, culture, gender, race, sexual orientation, (dis)ability and more. These additional structural inequalities and violences certainly intersect with and are affected by class relations. However, the workings of US hegemony, west-centric cultural domination, masculinism, racism, heterosexism and ablism are not reducible to class dynamics within capitalism. Thus weak states, aboriginals, women, people of colour, sexual minorities and disabled persons have found good reason to form cross-class solidarities in their respective struggles for emancipation and social justice. Class is a key axis of power in globalization, but it is not the only or always the most important one.

Likewise, it is too simplistic to explain globalization solely as a result of drives for surplus accumulation. Capitalism accounts for a lot in globalization, but far from all. For example, people have not undertaken global communications and global travel only to feed surplus accumulation, but also to explore identities and investigate meanings. People have not acquired global consciousness solely to supply capitalism with a mindset conducive to transplanetary accumulation, but also owing to various other secular and religious promptings. People have not developed global weapons and pursued global military campaigns only for capitalist ends, but also due to inter-state competition, masculinist behaviour, and militarist cultures that predate capitalism.

In particular, Marxism is limited by its methodological materialism. The approach is often characterized as one of 'historical materialism' and 'political economy', where ideational aspects of social relations are treated as outcomes of, with no autonomy from, the mode of production. Yet it oversimplifies matters to suggest that culture and psychology are reducible to political economy, that structures of identity and knowledge are wholly results of, and entirely subordinate to, those of production and governance. To take one example, nationalism as an identity structure has shaped capitalism as well as vice versa. Likewise, aesthetics and language are more than by-products of accumulation. In short, while capitalism has played a key part in generating globalization, social forces are more multidimensional, complex and interesting than a narrow historical materialism posits.

Constructivisms

In contrast to the methodological materialism of liberalist, political realist and Marxist explanations of globalization, a range of other accounts have taken methodologically idealist approaches. In these cases, transplanetary connectivity is said to have arisen because of the way that people have mentally constructed the social world with symbols, language, interpretation, and so on. From ideational perspectives, globalization has resulted from particular forms and dynamics of consciousness. For methodological idealists, patterns of production and governance are second-order structures that derive from deeper cultural and socio-psychological forces. Such accounts of globalization have come especially from the fields of Anthropology, Humanities, Media Studies, and Sociology, although idealist arguments have also influenced some researchers in Geography, Politics and even Business Studies.

One type of ideational explanation is constructivism, an approach that has been popular particularly since the 1990s among International Studies scholars in North America and Western Europe who wish to develop an alternative perspective to liberalism and political realism (Adler, 2003; Barnett, 2005). As the theory's name suggests, constructivism concentrates on the ways that social actors 'construct' their world: both within their own minds and through inter-subjective communication with others. In particular, constructivists examine how inter-subjective communication generates common understandings of reality, shared norms for social behaviour, and notions of group identity and solidarity. Conversation and symbolic exchanges lead people to construct ideas of the world, rules for social interaction, and ways of being and belonging in that world.

Constructivist research to date has not focused on explaining globalization; however, such an account can be extrapolated from existing works and the general premises of the theory. These would suggest that transplanetary connectivity has increased as people have reimagined society on transworld rather than, or in addition to, country-national-state lines. By following inter-subjective dialogue down new avenues, people would develop global-scale understandings of social units, social rules and social identities. These mental reorientations would in turn underpin a larger process of economic and political globalization.

Constructivist theory offers a helpful corrective to materialist explanations of globalization by affirming that social geography is a mental experience as well as a physical fact. The growth of transplanetary connections is indeed facilitated to the extent that people conceive of themselves as inhabiting a global world and as sharing values and interests with others spread across the continents. Moreover, this mental reorientation to global identities and solidarities would seem to result at least in part from inter-subjective social-psychological dynamics of forming 'in' and 'out' groups of 'us' and 'them'. National, class, religious and other identities respond in part to material conditions like state power and capital accumulation, but group affiliations also depend on inter-subjective construction and communication of shared self-understandings.

Yet constructivist explanations can also go too far down the road of methodological idealism. In this case a social-psychological reductionism unacceptably ignores the significance of economic and ecological forces in shaping mental experience. What is needed is an explanation of globalization that recognizes the significance of knowledge and identity but at the same time interlinks ideational influences with material social forces.

Moreover, like liberalism, constructivist explanations are limited by their neglect of issues of structural inequalities and power hierarchies in social relations. With this apolitical tendency, constructivism fails to appreciate that individuals who engage in inter-subjective communications invariably do so under conditions of structural domination and subordination. As often as not, the construction of social reality occurs in a context of political struggle and as an expression of resistance. To take one obvious example, national identities in the South developed largely through opposition to colonial rule.

Postmodernisms

In contrast to constructivism, other ideational explanations of globalization do highlight the significance of structural power in the construction of identities, norms and knowledge. For shorthand convenience these approaches are here grouped under a single label of 'postmodernism'. However, others have pursued this broad genre of argument under the names of 'poststructuralism' and 'postcolonialism'.

Whatever the precise appellation, these perspectives understand society first of all in terms of knowledge power: that is, how power structures shape knowledge; and how certain knowledge structures support certain power hierarchies. For example, one leading exponent of postmodernism, Michel Foucault, has posited that each epoch is marked by a prevailing *episteme*, or mode of knowledge (1966). This reigning structure of understanding (or 'discourse') determines what can and cannot be known in a given socio-historical context: i.e., what passes as 'truth' and 'real'; and what dissolves as 'mythical' and 'imagined'.

For postmodernists the dominant framework of knowledge in 'modern' society is rationalism. This mode of understanding emphasizes the earthly world, the subordination of nature to human control, objectivist science, and instrumentalist efficiency. Modern rationalism breeds a society obsessed with economic growth, technological control, bureaucratic surveillance, and discipline over desire. Moreover, say postmodernists, the rationalist mode of knowledge has an inherent expansionary logic that leads it through processes of cultural imperialism to subordinate if not destroy other epistemologies.

Only a few postmodernist writings have focused on the problem of globalization per se (e.g. Luke, 1995; Ó Tuathail, 1996; Dirlif, 1997; Ling, 2000; Cameron and Palan, 2004). Extrapolating from the general premises of the theory, however, globalization could be understood as a process whereby western rationalism imposes itself across the planet on indigenous cultures and other non-modern life-worlds. Different authors in this genre have linked knowledge power in the modern (globalizing) world with racism, sexism and US hegemony (Said, 1978; Campbell, 1998; Chowdhry and Nair, 2002).

With their emphasis on modes of knowledge as power, postmodernist and postcolonialist arguments succeed in incorporating ideational elements into explanations of globalization while also keeping questions of politics to the fore. Postmodernist theories highlight the significance of modern rationalist epistemology as a mindset that has been vital to the techno-scientific advances and bureaucratic institutions that have made globalization possible. Like Marxism, then, postmodernism helps to go beyond the relatively superficial accounts of liberalism and political realism to the deeper social conditions that have prompted globalization.

That said, postmodernist explanations also have their limitations. Where Marxist accounts of globalization are restricted by their methodological materialism, postmodernist arguments are constrained by their methodological idealism. Predominant discourses have most certainly had far-reaching impacts on economy and ecology, but the notion that these material forces can be reduced to modes of consciousness seems unsustainable. Again, what is wanted is an explanation that interconnects ideational and material forces rather than looking to one or the other.

Feminisms

For their part, feminist accounts of globalization have brought gender relations to the fore. Whereas other theories have identified the principal dynamics behind the rise of transplanetary and supraterritorial connectivity in terms of technology, state, capital, identity or discourse, feminists have put the spotlight on the social construction of masculinity and femininity. That is, the roles and behaviours assigned to biological sex are held to mould the overall social order and significantly to shape the course of history, including the spread of globality.

Feminist perspectives on globalization are adopted by researchers whose main concerns lie with the status of women, particularly the structural subordination of women to men. These arguments stress that women have tended to be marginalized, silenced and violated in global communications (e.g., lower Internet access), global migration (e.g., abused domestics and sex workers), global finance (e.g., limited availability of credit), global organizations (e.g., few leadership positions), and global wars (e.g., rape on the battlefield). Feminist approaches to globalization have appeared across all fields of social studies and humanities, albeit perhaps most frequently in Politics and Sociology (Duggan and Dashner, 1994; Wichterich, 1998; Peterson and Runyan, 1999; Signs, 2001; Peterson, 2003; Rai, 2004).

Many feminist arguments have come as corrective supplements to other theories rather than as fully fledged explanations of globalization in their own right. Thus, for example, feminist liberals have urged that more attention be given to the inputs of and consequences for women in respect of the laws and institutions that govern globalization. Feminist takes on political realism have highlighted male dominance of state power and the masculinist character of inter-state competition and war. Feminist contributions to Marxist research have emphasized the pervasive gendered character of surplus accumulation, for example, with low-paid female sweatshop work and unpaid female domestic work. Feminist postmodernism has identified a close relationship between masculinism and rationalist knowledge, while feminist postcolonialism has highlighted the subordination of women in imperialist contexts. In these different ways, much feminism has advocated an 'add-gender-and-stir' approach to other theories.

Certain other feminist arguments have made gender relations themselves the principal causal force in social relations. On these more radical accounts, patriarchal subordination of women and masculinist behaviour patterns are *the* primary forces that have generated other social structures such as capitalism, the state, nationalism and rationalism. By a radical feminist logic, the growth of transplanetary connections would also be driven in the first instance by masculinist strivings and patriarchal oppressions.

Feminist accounts of globalization have provided welcome antidotes to the gender-blindness that has generally afflicted other perspectives. Everyday experience makes plain that people in global as in all other spaces act partly in accordance with socially constructed sex roles. The 'private' sphere of the household and intimate relations is obviously as integral and influential in most people's lives as the 'public' sphere of the workplace and citizenship. The reproductive economy is clearly as central to the sustenance of social relations as the productive economy. Yet 'malestream' research on globalization (and social life generally) has tended to render these crucial matters invisible.

That said, feminist explanations can overplay the significance of gender relations, much as political realism can overemphasize inter-state competition and postmodernism can overstress knowledge power. Arguments concerning masculinism and patriarchy can clarify a great deal about the causes, courses and consequences of globalization. However, the gender reductionism of a radical feminism that roots everything surrounding transplanetary connectivity in social constructions of sex roles seems overly simplistic. Hence, much as Marxist preoccupations with class inequality can breed neglect of other types of social subordination, so feminist focus on gender hierarchies can distract attention from other important oppressions, for example, on lines of culture and race.

Contending social explanations of globalization

Liberalisms

- main focus on markets
- globalization explained as a result of technological advances and the construction of facilitating institutional infrastructures

Political realisms

- main focus on inter-state relations
- globalization explained in terms of competition among major states and/or US hegemony

Marxisms

- main focus on the mode of production and class relations
- globalization explained as an outgrowth of capitalism

Constructivisms

- main focus on social construction of reality
- globalization explained in terms of mental (re)constructions of the social world

Postmodernisms

- main focus on knowledge power
- globalization explained as a result of the imperialism of rationalism

Feminisms

- main focus on gender relations
- globalization explained as a product of masculinist behaviours and patriarchal subordinations

An eclectic synthesis

The preceding assessment of six ideal-type social theories has identified a number of possible explanations of globalization. Each approach highlights certain forces that could contribute significantly to the large-scale growth of transplanetary connectivity in contemporary history: technology and institution building in the case of liberalism; national interest and inter-state competition in the case of political realism; capital accumulation and class struggle in the case of Marxism; identity and knowledge construction in the case of constructivism; rationalism and cultural imperialism in the case of postmodernism; and masculinism and the subordination of women in the case of feminism. On the other hand, each perspective is also limited by reducing the dynamics of globalization to just one or two principal causes.

The approach in the present book is to synthesize insights from several theoretical frameworks in a multifaceted explanation of globalization. In a word, the perspective adopted here understands globalization as part of a socio-historical dynamic involving five interrelated shifts in macro social structures. One trend – the growth of transplanetary and supraterritorial connectivity – is interlinked with four other developments: a shift from capitalism towards hypercapitalism in respect of production; a shift from statism towards polycentrism in respect of governance; a shift from nationalism towards pluralism and hybridity in respect of identity; and a shift from rationalism towards reflexive rationality in respect of knowledge.

The resultant account of globalization is not amenable to conventional theory labels. The argument draws substantially from liberalism and political realism regarding the significance of states and other governance arrangements, from Marxism regarding the importance of capitalism, from constructivism regarding the relevance of identity patterns, from postmodernism regarding the role of knowledge power, and from feminism regarding the pervasive significance of gender relations. The approach developed here, therefore, does not fit a textbook category. Rather, the explanation weaves together insights from these perspectives to form a distinctive (and in some eyes no doubt peculiar) outlook.

The notion of 'weaving together' is key here. In other words, none of the five highlighted trends (with respect to geography, production, governance, identity and knowledge) is regarded as the original source of the other four. Each is taken to be simultaneously cause and effect of the others. Globalization is argued to be concurrently both an outcome of and an input to other core aspects of contemporary social change. The rest of this chapter indicates how developments around production, governance, identity and knowledge have combined to generate large-scale globality. Then Chapters 5 to 8 consider how, conversely, intense globalization has contributed to changes (as well as continuities) in the four other areas.

Forces of production in globalization

The contemporary rapid growth of transplanetary and supraterritorial social connections has resulted partly from economic conditions. More specifically, globalization has unfolded in the context of certain turns in capitalist development. Although this book does not advance a Marxist argument that globalization can be understood entirely in terms of capitalism, no explanation of this shift in geography would be complete without significant attention to the capitalist mode of production.

Capitalism characterizes a social order where economic activity is oriented first and foremost to the accumulation of surplus. In other words, capitalists (who might be individuals, private firms, publicly owned enterprises, or other collective actors) attempt to amass ever-greater resources in excess of their survival needs. Capitalist production contrasts on the one hand with a subsistence economy (where no surpluses arise) and on the other hand with profligacy (where any surplus is immediately depleted through luxury consumption). Under capitalism surpluses are invested in further production, with the aim of acquiring additional surplus, which is then reinvested in still more production, in the hope of obtaining still more surplus, and so on.

A capitalist economy is thoroughly monetized. Marx in this light characterized money as 'the universal commodity' of capitalist social relations (1867: 89). Money greatly facilitates accumulation, particularly since surpluses are easily stored and shifted in this fungible form. In addition, the manipulation of value by means of monetary calculations (including prices, wages, interest charges, dividends, taxes, currency revaluations, accounting formulas, etc.) offers abundant opportunities to transfer surplus, especially from the weak to the powerful.

Since most parties in a capitalist order are seeking to accumulate to one degree or another, this mode of production involves perpetual and pervasive contests over the distribution of surplus. Such competition occurs both between actors (individuals, firms, etc.) and along structural lines (of class, gender, race and more). Some of the struggles are overt, for example, in wage disputes. Other conflicts remain latent, for instance, when many poor people in the South are unaware that much of their country's limited surplus value is being transferred to wealthy people in the North through the repayment of global debts. These and countless other experiences have shown historically that capitalism tends to breed exploitation and other inequities unless deliberate countervailing measures are implemented.

Surplus accumulation has transpired in one way or another for many centuries, but capital*ism* is a comparatively recent phenomenon. When accumulation occurred in earlier times, it was temporary, limited, and involved only small circles of people. Not until the past several hundred years has capital become an 'ism', reigning as a foremost and ubiquitous framework of production over large populations for sustained periods of time. From beginnings in Western Europe around the fifteenth century, capitalism spread to all continents over the next half-millennium (albeit to different degrees). Today the structural power of capitalism is such that most people across the planet regard surplus accumulation as a 'natural' circumstance and can scarcely imagine, let alone enact, an alternative mode of production.

Capitalism has spurred globalization in four principal ways: related to market expansion, accounting practices, asset mobility, and enlarged arenas of commodification. Regarding the first point, Marx and Engels wrote over 150 years ago that 'the need of a constantly expanding market for its products chases the bourgeoisie over the whole surface of the globe' (1848: 39). Many firms have indeed pursued global markets as a means to increase their sales volume. Greater turnover at a given rate of profit obviously yields larger aggregate profits. Moreover, higher production runs to supply global markets can bring significant economies of scale and thereby raise profit margins. Capitalist enterprises have thus had major incentives to develop transworld distribution and sales networks for global products. To make transplanetary markets possible, capitalism has spurred much technological innovation in communications, transport and data processing as well as developments in global organization and management.

Second, capitalism has encouraged globalization inasmuch as global accounting practices offer major opportunities to enhance accumulation. For example, managers can vary and alter prices in a coordinated fashion across transplanetary domains so that overall company profits are maximized. Indeed, higher profit margins at mature market locations can allow a firm to cover the temporary losses that might be involved in establishing new sites at whatever other points on earth. A transworld pricing strategy can thereby yield greater overall profits in the medium and long term.

In addition, manipulations of global accounting have given capitalists the possibility to concentrate profits at points of low taxation within transplanetary spaces. In territorialist circumstances, surplus was generally confined to a particular state jurisdiction, and the capitalist was compelled to work within its tax regime. However, by moving into the cyberspace of electronic finance, capital can readily escape such territorial bounds. Profits that have in practice been achieved, say, in Italy can through the ruses of so-called 'transfer pricing' be made to appear on the balance sheet of a Luxembourg subsidiary with offshore taxation status. Likewise, 'hinwis' ('high net worth individuals') may significantly reduce their tax charges by registering their assets at offshore financial centres rather than in their country of residence.

Third, capitalism has promoted globalization owing to the opportunities for enhanced accumulation offered by global sourcing. Capitalist interests are well served when firms can place their production facilities wherever on Earth the needed resources are most easily accessed and the costs are lowest. Indeed, the fear of seeing globally mobile corporate assets go to more attractive sites can induce territorially bound workers and governments to temper demands regarding their share of surplus value *vis-à-vis* business.

In particular, global mobility has provided capitalists with an escape from the reduced rates of profit that accompanied corporatist arrangements in the OECD countries by the late 1960s (cf. Marglin, 1988). True, in the mid-twentieth century corporatist compromises between big business, organized labour and country government – epitomized in the Keynesian welfare state – secured capitalism in the North by reducing overt class conflict at a time when socialism was gaining unprecedented strength across much of the planet. However, this stability was bought at a price of progressive taxation, considerable social insurance charges, and fairly tight guarantees of wide-ranging workers' rights. In these ways corporatism reduced the scope for accumulation by companies and investors. In contrast, contemporary globalization has allowed big business to retrieve an advantaged position over government and labour, inasmuch as capital thereby gained far greater transplanetary mobility than the other two parties (Kurzer, 1993). Transworld relocations – or merely the threat of such departures – have rebalanced the trilateral bargain heavily in favour of large capital. Many workers and governments have felt constrained to lower wages, corporate taxation, business regulation, and various public expenditures on social security.

In broadly similar ways, globalization has offered capitalists a way to counter the strategies of socialism and economic statism that rose in much of the South during the mid-twentieth century. In the wake of large-scale decolonization, many states in Africa, Asia, the Caribbean and Latin America took initiatives to control capitalist development within their jurisdictions. These governments expropriated many assets and often introduced centralized state planning of the country's economy. Some voices in the South even called for reparations from the North as compensation for past capitalist-imperialist exploitation. However, increased transplanetary mobility has given big (mainly North-based) capital a means to counter these efforts at a major redistribution of world wealth. Indeed, apart from the major exception of China, little remains of state socialism today in either the South or the East.

Fourth and finally, capitalism has spurred globalization insofar as the commodities that circulate in transplanetary spaces have offered major additional opportunities for surplus accumulation. In other words, global communications, global travel, global monies, global financial instruments and global consumer goods have done more than enhance the possibilities for accumulation through primary production and traditional manufacturing. In addition, the information, communications, finance and consumer sectors have offered vast potentials for further accumulation in their own right. Indeed, telephone systems, Internet operations, foreign exchange dealing, global retail chains and the like have often generated high profits. Thus, as is further elaborated in Chapter 5, the very process of expanding global spaces has been a boon to capitalism, so that globalization has been integral to the emergence of what can be termed 'hypercapitalism'.

The preceding points should not be read to imply that every global capitalist venture has yielded the expected windfalls. On the contrary, 'going global' has hurt many corporations and investors who believed that this strategy offered a short, one-way street to superprofits. Global financial and information industries in particular have experienced enormous volatility over the past quarter-century, including major losses for some players. Nevertheless, hopes of enhanced accumulation have continued to stimulate accelerated globalization, and (as is detailed in Chapter 5) many of those capitalist dreams have been substantially realized.

So capitalism clarifies a lot about why and how respatialization through globalization has occurred. As David Harvey has said, 'Capitalism cannot do without its spatial fixes' (2000: 54). A former social order marked by territorialist geography, statist governance and nationalist identity well served an earlier day of commercial and industrial capitalism. However, a different spatial framework with considerable global aspects better serves the current phase of capitalist development.

That said, capitalism has not generated contemporary globalization by itself. For one thing, global capitalism has depended on regulatory arrangements and identity frameworks that have enabled surplus accumulation though transplanetary spaces. In addition, the capitalist mode of production has depended on the concurrent existence of a rationalist mode of knowledge that creates the secular, anthropocentric, instrumentalist mindset through which capitalism thrives. In short, as stressed earlier, the various principal forces behind globalization have been co-dependent.

Forces of governance in globalization

As just noted, a mode of production cannot operate in the absence of an enabling regulatory apparatus. Social relations are always marked by governance mechanisms of some kind, even if the rules are sometimes loose, variable or implicit. There is no such thing as an unregulated social context, and no social change takes place in the absence of rules that stimulate, facilitate and confirm the transformations. Hence globalization could not unfold without governance arrangements that promote the process, and an explanation of the trend must be sought partly in the regulatory realm.

The term 'governance' is subject to many different understandings (Rhodes, 1997; Pierre, 2000; Hermet *et al.*, 2005). In the present context the word is taken to mean regulation in a generic sense; thus governance refers to processes whereby people formulate, implement, enforce and review rules to guide their common affairs. Much governance happens through government, in the sense of regulatory activities through local and national public authorities. However, governance can entail more than government. Governance can extend beyond state and substate institutions to include suprastate (macro-regional and global) regimes as well. Moreover, governance can span private regulatory mechanisms along with public sector arrangements. Hence governance goes beyond government to cover the full scope of societal regulation.

Society might be considered to have a 'mode' of governance (a general way of making, implementing, enforcing and reviewing rules), much as it has a mode of production (a general way of extracting, processing, distributing and consuming resources). Moreover, just as a mode of production may change over time (say, from feudalism to capitalism, or from early to advanced capitalism), so the prevailing structure of governance can also alter through history. Indeed, as is discussed at length in Chapter 6, globalization has transpired in conjunction with a shift from a statist towards a polycentric mode of regulation. Whereas statism concentrates the construction and application of social rules in centralized national territorial governments, polycentrism disperses regulation across multiple substate, state, suprastate and private sites, as well as dense networks that interlink these many points of governance.

Hence it is perhaps not accidental that the words 'globalization' and 'governance' have entered common usage roughly simultaneously over the past two decades. Inasmuch as 'government' tends to be associated with the state, this notion does not apply comfortably as an umbrella term for the polycentric condition of multi-scalar and diffuse regulation. The vocabulary of 'governance' works better as a generic concept that covers statism, polycentrism, and other modes of regulation.

To be sure, the end of stat*ism* in recent decades has by no means entailed the end of the state. On the contrary, much of the regulation that has advanced contemporary globalization has emanated from states. Confounding the assumptions of many commentators, including those cited in Chapter 1, globalization and the state have been anything but mutually contradictory. On the contrary, most transplanetary relations would not have developed – or would have grown far more slowly and ponderously – if state policies had not encouraged globalization (Panitch, 1996; Weiss, 1998). Even many neoliberalists like staff of the IMF and the World Bank have in the past decade come to acknowledge the importance of the state for an effectively functioning global economy (Dhonte and Kapur, 1997; World Bank, 1997).

Globalization and the state have thus been quite compatible and indeed co-dependent in contemporary society. (That said, the growth of global relations has in several important respects tended to alter the character of the state, as is elaborated in Chapter 6.) State regulation has furthered globalization in four principal ways: provision of infrastructure; liberalization of international transactions; guarantees of property rights for global capital; and sponsorship of global governance arrangements. At the same time, in keeping with emergent polycentrism, states have not provided the entire regulatory infrastructure for accelerated globalization; hence the following discussion also notes contributions from macro-regional, transworld, and private regimes.

Regarding infrastructure, state programmes have supplied much of the initial transport, communications and organizational bases for transplanetary links. In the nineteenth century states (including colonial administrations) supported or themselves undertook the construction of most key canals and harbour facilities for expanded global shipping. In the twentieth century states built most airports and sponsored most early airlines. States provided many of the initial telecommunications networks, while the US military laid the foundations for the Internet in the third quarter of the twentieth century. States have furthermore advanced the organizational infrastructure of globalization by legalizing and often also actively promoting the operations of thousands of global companies, global civil society associations, and (as elaborated below) global governance institutions.

Regarding the liberalization of cross-border money and financial flows, most states have in recent decades relaxed or abandoned foreign exchange controls, thereby greatly facilitating global movements of currency. As of 2004 a total of 158 states had accepted Article VIII of the IMF, under which they undertake not to impose any restrictions on payments related to cross-border trade in goods and services (IMF, 2004). Dozens of states (starting with the USA in 1974 and the UK in 1979) have also removed restrictions on capital movements in and out of their jurisdictions (Helleiner, 1994; Kapstein, 1994).

On the other hand, states have thus far baulked at proposals to amend the IMF Articles of Agreement to require all members of the organization to remove statutory controls on cross-border capital flows. Likewise, although the OECD has promoted liberalization of capital movements since its inception in the early 1960s, intergovernmental negotiations through that body in 1995–8 towards a Multilateral Agreement on Investment (MAI) failed to establish a general 'free flow' principle under which states would not discriminate between capital of foreign and domestic origin. Instead, national governments have concluded thousands of bilateral investment treaties (BITs) that collectively have had broadly the same effect as an MAI (UNCTAD, 2004: 6).

A host of other state measures have also encouraged the growth of global finance. For example, numerous national governments have amended legislation to allow nonresident ownership of bonds and equities on securities markets within their jurisdiction. In addition, scores of states have since the 1980s established rules to permit entry into their country of global banks and global securities firms. The proliferation of offshore finance facilities has likewise required states to construct enabling statutory frameworks. As previously indicated in Chapter 3, states and/or substate governments have also created hundreds of offshore manufacturing sites; thus many companies have opted for global production partly because of the regulatory bait laid by country and provincial authorities in EPZs.

States' liberalization of cross-border trade has also encouraged the growth of global production and global markets. It is clearly harder to pursue global commerce when government-imposed tariffs, quotas, licensing procedures, technical standards, subsidies and other regulatory measures favour intra-state over cross-border transactions. Already some trade liberalization in the second half of the nineteenth century aided the early development of global products. Then high protectionism in the second quarter of the twentieth century discouraged further growth of transplanetary markets (outside inter-continental colonial empires, that is). Thereafter eight rounds of multilateral negotiations between 1948 and 1994 under the GATT reduced average import duties on manufactures from over 40 per cent to only 3 per cent. More recently, the WTO regime has encouraged states also to liberalize cross-border trade in agriculture and various service sectors.

Other state-led trade liberalization conducive to global production, exchange and consumption has occurred through regional agreements. The past half-century has witnessed the creation of multiple regional free trade areas (FTAs), customs unions, and (in the case of the EU) a common market. FTAs are regional associations of states with zero-tariffs between the member countries. These schemes have appeared in – or are currently projected for – most of Europe, the Americas, South Asia, South East Asia, Southern Africa, and elsewhere. Particularly in Europe, FTAs and customs unions (the latter involve the introduction of a common external tariff as well as the abolition of internal tariffs) have greatly encouraged global investment.

Along with infrastructure projects and liberalization measures, a third general way that states have advanced globalization has been through guarantees of property rights for global capital. Legally enforced support of ownership claims has of course been integral to capitalist development for several centuries, and the globalization of accumulation processes has constituted no exception. Firms would be far less inclined to invest in multiple jurisdictions across the planet if host states did not erect and uphold property laws that protected business and investor interests. Whereas many governments undertook nationalizations and expropriations of corporate assets in the third quarter of the twentieth century, the tendency since the 1980s has been to shower companies with legal protections and to privatize the greater part of state enterprises, often transferring the ownership to global capital.

States have also encouraged the globalization of capital by constructing multilateral regimes that guarantee intellectual property rights (IPRs) such as patents, trademarks, copyrights, and designs. In the late nineteenth century, governments erected global agreements like the Paris Convention for the Protection of Industrial Property (1883), the Berne Convention for the Protection of Literary and Artistic Works (1886), and the Madrid Agreement for the International Registration of Marks (1891). In more recent times, the World Intellectual Property Organization (WIPO) has seen the annual number of applications for global patents rise from under 3,000 in 1979 to over 54,000 in 1997 (HDR, 1999: 67). The 1994 Agreement on Trade-Related Aspects of Intellectual Property Rights (TRIPS) strengthened guarantees of IPRs in global markets through the WTO. Meanwhile two intergovernmental treaties concluded at the end of 1996 have extended copyright law to cyberspace.

Developments around IPRs illustrate a fourth manner that states have sponsored a regulatory environment that is conducive to globalization, namely, through the creation of transworld governance mechanisms. For reasons elaborated in Chapter 6, transplanetary and supraterritorial links cannot be administered through territorially based arrangements alone. Globalization also requires significant elements of global governance: that is, rules and permanent regulatory bodies with a transworld scope. Most of these global regimes (covering *inter alia* communications, conflict management, ecology, finance, health, human rights and trade) have been established through intergovernmental agreements. With time, bodies like the Bretton Woods institutions and the United Nations agencies have acquired some autonomy from their member states. Nevertheless, most global governance has emerged and grown through states and inter-state relations, and it is hard to see how it could have done otherwise. True, as elaborated in Chapter 6, some important contemporary global governance has developed not through the public sector, but through private institutions like the International Securities Market Association (ISMA) and the Internet Corporation for Assigned Names and Numbers (ICANN). However, this market-based governance has required at least the acquiescence of states, and often it has had their active encouragement, too.

Once in place, transworld governance institutions have greatly furthered globalization through standardization. Needless to say, transplanetary connectivity has been facilitated to the degree that people across the earth have come to operate with similar bureaucratic, legal and technical arrangements. For example, the ITU has issued hundreds of recommendations governing technical standards in electronic mass media and telecommunications, running to more than 10,000 pages in all. Meanwhile the International Organization for Standardization has published over 10,000 measures covering pretty well all areas of technology (UIA, 1998: 1093). The Warsaw Convention of 1929 (amended in 1955) has prescribed a transworld format for airline operations, while the International Civil Aviation Organization (ICAO) has overseen global rules for air navigation, *inter alia* to prevent in-flight collisions. The OECD has promulgated a Model Tax Convention to further the standardization of bilateral tax treaties that have proliferated with the globalization of capital. Several private-sector associations like the

International Accounting Standards Board (IASB) and the International Federation of Accountants (IFAC) have since the 1970s developed global guidelines for corporate accounting and auditing. The International Organization of Securities Commissions (IOSCO), created in 1983, has promoted transplanetary standards for stock and bond markets, while the International Association of Insurance Supervisors (IAIS), formed in 1994, has done the same for the insurance business. Starting in 1996, the IMF has coordinated major initiatives to set global frameworks for the calculation and presentation of macroeconomic statistics. The WHO has promoted regulatory harmonization in the area of disease control, while other parts of the UN system have overseen the codification of universal standards of human rights.

In sum, then, a host of measures especially from states – but also from regional, transworld, and private regulatory institutions – have together provided a major governance input to globalization. The construction of a supportive legal infrastructure has not been the sole cause of globalization, but the trend could not have developed without this administrative grounding. This is not to say that every regulation in contemporary history has favoured the growth of transplanetary connectivity. Certain state actions have inhibited globalization, for example, with bans on Internet software, harassment of transworld civil society activities, and discouragement of global capital flows. Moreover, state restrictions on immigration have rarely been as tight as at the start of the twenty-first century. However, the balance of relevant regulation has greatly favoured globalization.

Indeed, states and other governance bodies have been heavily constrained to establish regulatory arrangements that facilitate the expansion of global social spaces. Conditions in respect of capitalism (discussed above), together with circumstances related to identity and knowledge (discussed below), as well as the sheer momentum of global respatialization itself, have put policymakers under considerable pressure to provide supportive frameworks of rules. Given the strength of these other forces, it seems highly unlikely that regulators could have blocked most or all globalization had they wished to do so. Even governments with strong reservations about globalization have succumbed to at least a partial accommodation of the trend. Thus, for example, the King of Bhutan no longer outlaws television (as he once tried to do), and Fidel Castro's Soviet-style regime has actively promoted global tourism for Cuba. To this extent the question has been less *whether* regulators would enable globalization and more *what kind* of regulatory frameworks they would erect to govern the process. Contemporary policymakers cannot deny the growth of transworld relations, but they do have a variety of options for shaping the trend in certain directions rather than others.

What of the particular role of the US state in generating contemporary globalization, given the significance that some political realist theories attach to the role of a hegemon in world politics? US governments have often played a pivotal role in the regulatory developments described above. For example, US administrations were key proponents of the establishment of the UN, the Bretton Woods institutions, the OECD, and the GATT/WTO. The US state has also actively supported the creation of macro-regional regimes that have facilitated globalization, especially in Europe and the Americas. In addition, the very name 'Washington Consensus' identifies where pressure for liberalization of global trade and finance has been strongest. The political culture of US foreign policy has also had several historically entrenched traits that especially encourage the development of global connectivity (Thorne, 1992). For instance, the metaphor of the melting pot suggests that all of humanity has crossed the planet to realize the American dream. Looking outward, prevailing US myths have affirmed that America is an exceptional society with a mission to bring liberty and prosperity to every corner of the earth. Where ideological persuasion has failed, the US state has had unequalled military resources to further its favoured path of globalization by force of arms (Mosler and Catley, 2000).

However, recognizing the far-reaching influence of the US state in shaping contemporary globalization is not the same as arguing that US hegemony has been a necessary condition for, and primary cause of, intense growth of transplanetary connectivity since the middle of the twentieth century. US preeminence among states has deeply affected the *type* of accelerated globalization that has occurred over the past 50 years, but US primacy has not generated globalization itself. Other pervasive and deeply embedded forces in respect of regulation, capitalist production, identity dynamics and rationalist knowledge would in any case have generated the past half-century of large-scale globalization. However, globalization would have proceeded in different directions in the absence of a dominant US state. Likewise, as is stressed in Chapter 12, US policies will greatly condition the possibilities for more progressive future courses of globalization.

Forces of identity in globalization

Thus far this explanation of contemporary globalization has concentrated on political-economic forces; however, in keeping with the premise that a fuller explanation needs to synthesize material and ideational elements, the rest of this account highlights psychological and cultural dynamics at the core of globalization. The next paragraphs examine impulses to the growth of transplanetary connectivity coming from the area of identity construction, while the last section considers the significance of forces related to knowledge.

As seen earlier in this chapter, many theories underplay (and in some cases utterly neglect) the role of identity in social life. However, people engage with one another in society not only to obtain resources and to exercise power, but also to discover who they are, where they belong, and what they might become. Understanding and affirming the self – both as an individual and as a group member – is a prime motivation for, and major preoccupation of, social interaction. People seek in social relations to explore their class, their gender, their nationality, their race, their religious faith, their sexuality, and other aspects of their being. Constructions of identity moreover provide much of the basis for social bonds, including collective solidarity against oppression. Notions of identity underpin frameworks for community, democracy, citizenship and resistance. In short, identity matters (a great deal).

Society may be said to have a 'mode of identity' (a general way of defining and expressing who people are) alongside its mode of production and its mode of governance. Prior to the onset of intense globalization half a century ago, the prevailing structure of identity was nationalism. (In this context 'nationalism' is not taken to mean unbridled patriotism, but a circumstance where people construct their being, belonging and becoming first and foremost in terms of national affiliation. The concept of nationhood is further elaborated in Chapter 7.) Like structures of production and governance, modes of identity change over time. As indicated in Chapter 7, globalization has unfolded in tandem with – both reflecting and reinforcing – a broad shift in the reigning framework of identity from nationalism towards greater pluralism and hybridity.

Forces of identity have causal significance in social relations. Identity is not reducible to, and wholly an outcome of, forces of geography, production and governance. Certainly the rise of nationalism as the previously prevailing mode of identity was greatly encouraged by concurrently predominant patterns of social space (territorialism), economy (industrial capitalism), and regulation (statism). These four structures had strongly parallel logics in an earlier time. Similarly, the recent emergences of supraterritorial space, hypercapitalist production, and polycentric governance have spurred the contemporary turn towards more plural and hybrid identities. These four developments, too, have been largely complementary. However, identity cannot be wholly understood as an outcome of economics, geography and politics. Social-psychological processes also have dynamics of their own, and causality has simultaneously operated in converse directions, with identity having impacts on space, production and governance. Thus nationalism helped to promote territorialism, capitalism and statism in an earlier day, and more plural and hybrid identities have tended to feed more globality, hypercapitalism and polycentrism in recent times.

Circumstances surrounding the construction of identities have promoted globalization in three main ways. First, national 'selves' have been substantially formed and sustained in relation to foreign 'others' within a transworld realm. Second, a number of nations have developed in part as transplanetary diasporas. Third, increased attention to various nonterritorial identities (like those based in faith, gender and race) has promoted the growth of supraterritorial social connections more generally.

Regarding the first of these three influences, it is often mistakenly assumed that national identities have developed endogenously out of some primordial essence of a self-contained territorial home environment. Certainly the particular characteristics of each nation – its language, its customs, its art forms, its sensibilities, etc. – arise largely from local circumstances. However, the consolidation of such distinctive features into a large collective national identity has invariably occurred in the context of wider world contacts. In other words, *inter-national* relations have provided a core dynamic for the construction of nations themselves. The process of nation building has thereby drawn social relations into global realms.

National identities have several striking inter-national qualities (Scholte, 1995: 191–4; Scholte, 1996: 567–71). For example, definitions of nationhood have always rested on claims to difference and uniqueness of one group *vis-à-vis* the rest of the humanity. National 'selves' have been constructed in terms of contrasts with external 'others'; the content of the national 'us' has invariably been defined in relation to the foreign 'them'. Thus nineteenth-century imperialism did much to consolidate nationalism in Western Europe. Indeed, national identities have characteristically been established through the exclusion of 'outsiders' in the rest of the world. Nationality has intrinsically been a question of privilege within an inter-national sphere. In addition, nations have generally emerged and/or been sustained in the context of self-protective reactions against interventions from afar. Thus inter-national warfare, commercial rivalries and cultural intrusions have spurred many a nationalist reaction. At the same time, many national campaigns have depended on support from inter-national sponsors in the broader world. For example, the USA with its Monroe Doctrine supported national assertions in Latin America during the nineteenth century. Similarly, Bolshevik Russia promoted national projects in Central Asia in the early twentieth century. Japanese occupiers advanced national programmes in the colonies of South East Asia during World War II. The UN has championed Timorese and other national self-determination struggles in recent decades.

Contrary to many intuitions, then, the affirmation of national identities has on the whole actually spurred rather than slowed globalization. Nations have only looked inward within the purported homeland to the extent that they have simultaneously looked outward to the wider (and eventually global) world. Nationality and globality have been largely co-dependent in the area of identity, much as the state and globality have been substantially mutually reinforcing in the area of governance.

Indeed, many nations have spread across the planet in global diasporas (Cohen, 1997). Prominent examples include the Chinese and Palestinian nations. Although these diasporas have constructed their identities with reference to a particular territorial homeland, in fact they have existed as transworld networks. Diasporas have given impetus to globalization through their efforts to maintain connections with the country of origin as well as among various outposts across the planet. Thus, for example, the diaspora of Filipina care workers has played its part in deepening global finance with large-scale remittances to the home islands. Meanwhile associations like the World Union of Free Romanians have contributed to the globalization of civil society.

Other impulses to the growth of transplanetary connectivity have come from the affirmation of supraterritorial identities. Constructions of the self and group affiliations in terms of age, class, gender, race, religious faith, and sexual orientation intrinsically transcend territorial place, distance and borders to encompass people dispersed across the earth. For example, the spread of world religions provided significant stimulus for prototypical globalization in previous epochs. Incipient globalization of the nineteenth and early twentieth century gained boosts from transworld working class solidarities of the socialist and communist internationals, transworld racial solidarities of Pan-Africanism and the White Commonwealth, and transworld women's solidarities in the first wave of feminism. In addition to these supraterritorial identities, recent accelerated globalization has had encouragements from global youth culture and transworld expressions of lesbian, gay, bisexual and transgender identities, as described further in Chapter 7.

In several ways, then, forces of identity have operated alongside those connected with production and governance to promote a significant expansion of global relations in contemporary social life. In turn, the rise of diasporas and supraterritorial solidarities through globalization, together with the continuing importance of various forms of nationality, have contributed to a shift in the prevailing structure of identity from nationalism towards greater pluralism and hybridity. This aspect of globalization and social change is explored more fully in Chapter 7.

Forces of knowledge in globalization

Next to identity, other significant ideational spurs to globalization have come in the area of knowledge. The theoretical perspective adopted here agrees with those schools of social and political thought which maintain that the way that people know their world has significant implications for the concrete circumstances of that world. Hence globalization has occurred in part because of certain powerful patterns of social consciousness. Knowledge frameworks have a significance that is not reducible to forces of production, governance and identity. In short, the rise of globality could not transpire in the absence of mindsets that encourage such a development.

Modern rationalism is a general configuration of knowledge that has greatly promoted the spread of global thinking and, through it, the broader trend of globalization (Boli and Thomas, 1999; Drori *et al.*, 2003). This framework of knowledge has four main distinguishing features. First, rationalism is secularist: it defines reality in terms of the tangible earthly world, without reference to transcendent and divine forces. Second, rationalism is anthropocentric: it understands reality primarily in terms of human interests, activities and conditions (rather than, for example, in terms of ecological systems). Third, rationalist knowledge has a 'scientist' character: it holds that phenomena can be understood in terms of single incontrovertible truths that are discoverable by rigorous application of objective research methods. Fourth, rationalism is instrumentalist: it assigns greatest value to insights that enable people efficiently to solve immediate problems.

When secular, anthropocentric, scientific, instrumental rationality reigns as the predominant knowledge structure, it tends to subordinate other ways of understanding and acting upon the world. Rationalism elevates one kind of 'making sense' over all others. Rationalists readily dismiss aesthetics, spirituality, emotion, and fantasy – or rather accept these and other 'irrationalities' only inasmuch as they complement, advance, or at least do not interfere with rational knowledge. 'Irrationality' is not seen to contain any important truth in its own right.

Indeed, rationalism is something of a (secular) faith. Rationalists maintain that science enables humanity to discover a single, definitive, objective truth about each phenomenon. This knowledge could then be applied to harness natural and social forces for human purposes. Techno-scientific rationality would thereby allow people to conquer disease, hunger, poverty, war, etc., and as a result to maximize the potentials of human life.

The effects of rationalist knowledge are manifested in all that is regarded as 'reasonable' in modern society. For example, rationalism has prompted modern people to separate 'society' from 'nature' and to seek through scientific and technical means to subordinate natural forces for instrumental human ends. Secular, anthropocentric, instrumental calculations have also provided a knowledge framework for capitalist production and a cult of economic efficiency. A rationalist mindset has likewise underlain the power of 'objective' secular law in modern social relations and the pervasiveness of bureaucracy in modern organizations (governments, firms, civil society associations, schools, hospitals and so on). Rationalism has furthermore propelled the production of scientific knowledge through universities and think tanks.

Like any social structure, rationalism is a product of history. It has arisen at particular times and places under particular conditions. True, instances of secular, anthropocentric, scientific, instrumental thinking can be found in various pre-modern contexts. However, a rationalist social structure – one that systematically marginalizes other forms of knowing – is distinctive of modern society. Rationalism first consolidated in the so-called 'Enlightenment' that took hold in the North Atlantic area during the eighteenth century. Enlightenment thought removed the label of 'knowledge' from myth, faith and other 'traditional' ways of understanding. Subsequently rationalism has been carried, particularly through colonialism and informal imperialism, to all corners of the earth.

Rationalist thought has encouraged the rise of globality in several general ways. For one thing, this structure of knowledge has laid an ideational basis for the principal material causes of globalization. The reliance of capitalist production on rationalist knowledge has already been noted. In addition, rationalist frameworks of law and institutional organization have formed a backdrop for the regulatory frameworks that have encouraged globalization.

Other impulses to create global social spaces have come from the logic of rationalism itself. For example, the secularism of rationalism has encouraged people to construct 'the whole' of their existence in terms of planet earth rather than, say, in terms of the divine. Indeed, before the sixteenth century 'maps' of 'the world' often depicted relations between people and their god(s) as well as, or instead of, some terrestrial realm. For a secularist mindset, truth comes in the form of earthly – indeed, global – principles that transcend the particularities of locality and prevail for humankind across whatever territorial distances and borders. A number of significant impulses to globalization have therefore come from efforts to discover transplanetary realities. This quest has motivated both so-called 'explorers' of earlier times and global travellers of recent generations. Rationalism encourages a belief that people can maximize knowledge when they access and understand the earthly world as a whole. Globalization can be seen, in part, as the pursuit of this secularist holy grail.

Meanwhile the anthropocentrism of rationalism has directed social consciousness to the space occupied by humanity, namely, planet Earth. In an anthropocentric conception, the cosmos is seen not as a metaphysical realm of the gods, nor as a biosphere of interdependent life forms, nor as the localized domain of a particular tribe. Rather, the rationalist lens focuses on the space of *homo sapiens*, that is, on the planet as a single place. This conception of the Earth as the human home within the universe, too, has provided a crucial mental orientation for globalization.

The scientism and instrumentalism of rationalism have also been conducive to globalization. Scientific knowledge is nonterritorial: the truths revealed by 'objective' method are purportedly valid for anyone, anywhere, anytime on earth. This objectivist orientation can feed expectations that certain products, regulations, technologies, art forms and the like can apply across the planet. Meanwhile territorialism (especially the hindrances of state borders) has frequently contradicted utilitarian notions of efficiency. For example, the instrumentalist logic of mainstream economic analysis has held that territorial distance should be overcome and territorial borders should fall in order to achieve the most productive world division of labour.

In a variety of ways, then, rationalist thinking has encouraged the growth of a global imagination and the various material transworld activities (communications, markets, travel, etc.) that global thinking promotes. For two hundred years, the Enlightenment mindset has in important respects opposed the principle of a territorial division of society. As Martin Albrow has succinctly put it, 'Reason knows no territorial limits' (1996: 32).

Conclusion

In sum, then, the perspective adopted in this book explains globalization as an outcome of multifaceted dynamics of social relations. Not every impulse of production, governance, identity and knowledge has advanced globalization. Moreover, conditions in some social settings have been more conducive to an expansion of transplanetary connectivity than others: e.g., the New York Stock Exchange as against subsistence farms in Uzbekistan. However, the balance of forces in contemporary society has heavily favoured the emergence of a more global world.

Indeed, the explanation of globalization outlined above suggests that the growth of transplanetary connections between people is unlikely to reverse in the foreseeable future. The various dynamics of capitalism, state and other regulation, national and other identity construction, and rationalism are deeply embedded in large parts of contemporary society, including its most powerful quarters. In combination, these forces have generated enormous momentum for globalization. To be sure, as is particularly stressed in Part III of this book, policymakers as well as citizens at large have ample opportunities to affect the speeds, directions and consequences of growing globality. However, it is hard to see how political action could stop, let alone reverse, the powerful combination of forces that are currently assembled behind this reconfiguration of social space. Only a possible systemic ecological calamity would appear to stand in the way of continuing large-scale globality and considerable further globalization in the period ahead.

The account of globalization presented here is admittedly complex. It explains contemporary globalization in terms of interrelations between four aspects of capitalism, five features of state and other governance, three qualities of national and other identity construction, and four implications of rationalist knowledge. Such an approach violates the demands of conventional social science for parsimony. Why not, some critics might object, explain globalization more simply as the result of one main cause such as technology, or US power, or capitalism, or cultural imperialism?

Principal dynamics of globalization

Capitalist production
- global markets to increase sales volumes and enhance economies of scale
- global accounting of prices and tax liabilities to raise profits
- global sourcing to reduce costs of production
- supraterritorial commodities to increase the channels of accumulation

Regulation
- governance agencies' provision of the infrastructure to effect global connections
- states' liberalization of cross-border transactions
- legal guarantees of property rights for global capital
- establishment and growth of transworld governance mechanisms
- transplanetary standardization of technical specifications, legal principles and administrative procedures

Identity construction
- national 'selves' constituted in relation to foreign 'others' within a global realm
- assertions of various national identities through transplanetary diasporas
- affirmations of various nonterritorial identities through transworld networks

Rationalist knowledge
- secularist constructions of the social world in terms of planet earth
- anthropocentric orientation to the planetary home of the human species
- scientific notions of objective truths with transplanetary validity
- instrumentalist efficiency arguments against 'irrational' territorial divisions

The view adopted here is that more compact formulas of the kind covered in the first half of this chapter are oversimplified and omit more than is acceptable. Shorthand equations tend to offer highly partial explanations and illusory degrees of predictive powers. Moreover, in terms of theory–practice relations, policies and actions based on excessively narrow understandings of globalization can produce substantial harm through omission. Thus, for example, political engagement of globalization from perspectives like liberalism and Marxism has often wrought considerable cultural violence, however unintended, because these theories brush over issues of identity and knowledge. Meanwhile constructivist theories have generally been insufficiently sensitive to the power relations of social hierarchies, while the relative economic illiteracy of postmodernist approaches can have unhappy consequences for material welfare.

In contrast, a more complex explanation that is alert to an intricate combination of multiple forces could encourage the development of more viable positive policies towards globalization. Indeed, this book's 'critical introduction' is meant to promote more secure, equitable and democratic courses of globalization. The approach developed above constantly turns the spotlight on insecurity, inequality and marginalization within globalization to date, in the hopes of fostering future globalizations that limit – or better yet overcome – these violences.

Of course, some readers will find this critical theory to be insufficiently radical, or to be radical in the wrong ways. For example, eco-centric thinkers and activists may object that the approach taken here gives insufficient attention to globalization as a process of environmental degradation. Feminists may argue that gender relations should figure more centrally than they do in this account. Indigenous peoples may regard the theory of globalization developed here as yet another manifestation of the imperialism of westernist-modernist-rationalist knowledge. Theists may reject the secularist character of the theory and its failure to grasp the possibilities that globalization offers for spiritual revival. Anarchists may say that the argument does not sufficiently challenge what they take to be the inherently oppressive nature of states and other bureaucratic governance frameworks.

Admittedly, like any theory, this account embodies and furthers certain interests and values. The approach here tries to be ecologically aware while keeping the principal focus on social problems. It seeks to promote gender sensitivity while also keeping attention on other social hierarchies such as inequalities related to class, culture and race. The argument attempts to be reflexively rationalist: that is, to maximize the emancipatory potentials of modern knowledge while recognizing that modernity has tendencies towards ecological destruction, bureaucratic oppression, spiritual vacuum, and suppression of other life-worlds. To theists and anarchists one can only answer that, for better or for worse, the author has a secularist outlook and a faith in the potentials of formal public regulation to improve the human condition. Theory cannot but rest, in part, on the theorist's politics.

Part II

Change and Continuity

Has globalization changed the social order? If so, in what ways and to what extent have such changes taken place? Chapters 2 and 3 have shown that the large-scale rise of transplanetary and more specifically supraterritorial connections between people has significantly shifted the geography of contemporary society. But has this respatialization also reverberated more widely to alter other primary social structures?

Chapter 4 examined forces in contemporary history that have generated – and seem likely to continue generating – a major expansion of global social spaces. These causes of globalization were seen to emanate from interrelated spheres of production, governance, identity and knowledge. The next chapters investigate reverse causalities, whereby developments in geography are not only an outcome of, but simultaneously also an influence on, circumstances in the other four aspects of social relations.

Hence the central question for the second part of the book is whether globalization, an important respatialization of social relations, has encouraged broader changes of social structure. Chapter 5 considers the consequences of contemporary globalization for the mode of production. Chapter 6 assesses the implications of widespread transplanetary connectivity for the apparatus of governance. Chapter 7 explores the repercussions of greater transworld relations for patterns of identity. Chapter 8 examines the effects of globalization on social structures of knowledge.

Taken together, the overall conclusion of these chapters is that unprecedented growth of transplanetary links during the past half-century has involved an intricate interplay of changes and continuities. Not utter transformation or full constancy, but blended shifts and perpetuations. In Chapter 2 it was established that contemporary globalization has brought an end to territorialist geography, but together with a persistence of socially significant territorial spaces. Following a similar theme of mixed change and continuity, Chapter 5 indicates that globalization has encouraged the development of various different forms of accumulation, while also reinforcing older forms and furthering the maintenance of the overall capitalist mode of production. Chapter 6 shows that large-scale transplanetary relations have helped to make statist regulation non-viable, but also that the state retains a major role in the emergent polycentric structure of governance. Chapter 7 notes likewise that intense transworld connectivity has contributed to undermine the previous effective monopoly of the nationality principle on constructions of social identity, although nationhood remains an important element in current more plural and hybrid identities. Finally, Chapter 8 argues that recent large-scale globalization has tended to qualify the hold of rationalism as the prevailing knowledge structure, although modern rationality continues to have a central place in contemporary, more global society.

As is ever the case in history, nothing involves total change or total continuity. Globalization has promoted important shifts in social structures, but not a complete social transformation. The trend has accommodated important continuities, but not a complete historical standstill. Contemporary intense globalization has been a notable force of social change, but the shifts to date have not been so great as to constitute an epochal transition from one historical age to another.

In any case, as will already be apparent from Chapter 4, this book does not maintain that globalization is the only or primary cause of the changes and continuities that are described in the next chapters. The discussion is therefore couched in a language whereby globalization has 'encouraged', 'promoted', 'helped', and 'furthered' various trends, rather than 'producing', 'generating', 'determining' or 'necessitating' them. According to the perspective adopted here, the full causal force behind developments in geography, production, governance, identity and knowledge lies in their interrelations and mutual determination. Hence globalization is only one of several key forces in the dynamics of current history, and thus only part of a multifaceted explanation of social change.

On a methodological note, readers may ask how it can be established that globalization has the causal significance claimed for it in the following chapters. How can we know that globalization has been causally important? This question raises deep problems in the philosophy of explanation that cannot be fully addressed here. However, in brief, the arguments presented here about the significance of globalization for social change can be defended on a combination of four broad grounds. First, theory (on the lines laid out in the second half of Chapter 4) generates a logically coherent supposition that globalization as a reconfiguration of spatial structure should manifest interconnections with concurrent developments in production, governance, identity and knowledge structures. Second, extensive empirical evidence (as elaborated in Chapters 5 to 8) confirms multiple correlations in times and places between globalization and these other social trends. Third, countless actors who have lived through the experiences described in these chapters have given testimony (in interviews and writings documented here) that globalization has had the sorts of effects indicated. Fourth, counterfactual thinking (i.e., imagining that globalization had not unfolded, on the lines covered in Chapter 3) suggests that the social changes examined in Chapters 5 to 8 would not have happened – or would not have happened in the same ways or to nearly the same extent – in the absence of growing transplanetary connectivity. Thus a combination of theory, data, perceptions, and counterfactual thinking provides ample grounds for affirming that globalization has mattered as a force of social change.

The chapters in Part II focus on structural developments and structural forces, with the result that agency may seem to play less of a role in shaping the contemporary globalizing world. However, in accordance with the structuration approach described in Chapter 1, the analysis in this book assumes that all of the structural trends covered in the following chapters have occurred through actor decisions. After the more structural orientation of Part II, the importance of policy choice for the course of globalization is reemphasized in Part III.

Chapter 5

Globalization and Production: From Capitalism to Hypercapitalism

Main points of this chapter
Expanded commodification
Altered organization
Conclusion

Main points of this chapter

- intense globalization of the past half-century has substantially strengthened the position of capitalism as the prevailing world structure of production
- the growth of transplanetary social spaces has helped to increase surplus accumulation in areas such as primary production and heavy industry, while in addition facilitating the extension of commodification to consumer, finance, information, communications, genetic, atomic and care sectors
- the expansion of transworld links has encouraged significant shifts in the organization of capitalism, including the rise of offshore centres, global companies, corporate mergers and acquisitions, and oligopoly

The preceding chapter indicated that the capitalist mode of production has figured centrally in the generation of globality in modern history. The present chapter now considers the reverse direction of influence: namely, what the rapid growth of transworld spaces in recent decades has meant for the way that production is ordered. Has globalization entailed any changes to the prevailing economic framework? How, if at all, has increased transplanetary connectivity altered the forms that capitalism takes and the ways that surplus accumulation happens? Has globalization, as a major respatialization of social life, on the whole bolstered or undermined capitalism? Does the more global world of the early twenty-first century show harbingers of a postcapitalist order?

As mentioned in Chapter 1, a few authors have associated contemporary globalization with a retreat of capitalism. Yet if capitalism is conceived as a structure of production dominated by processes of surplus accumulation, then it seems difficult to confirm such propositions. After all, as earlier chapters have noted, globalization has involved the creation of thousands of transworld companies and strategic alliances, as well as the appearance of innumerable global products, as well as huge expansions of transplanetary money and financial flows, as well as the development of major additional sectors of accumulation in the information, communications and biotechnology industries. None of these developments points to a decline of capitalism, let alone its end. On the contrary, the trends sooner indicate that contemporary globalization has helped capitalism to become more widespread and more entrenched than ever. If anything, globalization has contributed to the advent of 'hypercapitalism'.

This is by no means to affirm that the rise of transplanetary and supraterritorial social relations has left capitalism unaffected. Although the overall structure of capitalism would seem as robust as ever, globalization has helped to alter the manner in which accumulation occurs. These shifts relate, on the one hand, to the scope of commodification and, on the other hand, to the organizational circumstances of accumulation.

In respect of commodification, globalization has not only reinforced older arenas of accumulation such as primary production and heavy industry, but also promoted the growth of other sectors such as consumer capital, finance capital, information capital, communications capital, and most recently also genetic capital (through biotechnology), atomic capital (through nanotechnology), and care capital (through the 'maid trade' and the like). Aided by globalization, then, more production than ever has acquired a capitalist logic. These points are elaborated in the first part of this chapter.

With regard to the organization of capitalism, globalization has furthered much-enhanced accumulation through offshore centres and transworld companies. In addition, the growth of transplanetary spaces has encouraged an unprecedented wave of corporate mergers and acquisitions, which in turn has contributed substantially to an increased concentration of capital in current history. These organizational aspects are covered in the second part of the chapter.

In short, although globalization has not transformed the primary structure of production – that is, taking society from capitalism to some postcapitalist circumstance – this respatialization has stimulated important developments within capitalism. Together, the expansion of commodification and the greater organizational efficiency of accumulation have created a situation that can suitably be termed 'hypercapitalist'. This larger and faster accumulation has, as ever with capitalism, raised normatively and politically charged questions of inequality and fair distribution, points that are examined at length in Chapter 10.

Expanded commodification

Following a Marxian conceptualization, 'commodities' are the objects through whose production and exchange surplus is created, extracted and amassed. Hence a resource becomes 'commodified' when it is incorporated into capitalist accumulation processes. For example, timber becomes commodified when foresters move from subsistence use to market sale of wood products for profit. A song becomes commodified when it is no longer just sung among friends, but recorded and sold through the music industry. Biological material like a plant variety becomes commodified when it is patented for commercial exploitation. One of the key features of capitalism therefore relates to the kinds of objects that function as commodities. Likewise, the range of resources that become commodified provides a broad indicator of the scope and intensity of capitalism in a given social context.

The character of commodities (in the specific Marxian sense just described) has shifted throughout the history of capitalism. The following sentences perhaps present an overly neat periodization, but the general point holds that, over the past centuries, a continually widening spectrum of economic activity has turned capitalist. Early surplus accumulation chiefly involved commercial capital: that is, profit was acquired mainly through trade in agricultural and mining output as well as in certain luxury goods like furs and spices. From the late eighteenth century onwards, commercial capital was joined by industrial capital: that is, the range of commodified articles expanded to include manufactures from large-scale factory production. Subsequently, mainly from the late nineteenth century onwards, commercial and industrial capital were joined by finance capital: that is, financial instruments like stocks and bonds were also increasingly commodified. Trade in these 'articles' became a means of accumulation in its own right, and the financial assets became to some degree divorced from 'real' assets.

Accelerated globalization since the middle of the twentieth century has helped further to expand commodification through a combination of six developments. First, global markets have increased the scale of older forms of commodification in primary and industrial goods. Second, consumerism – much of it related to global products – has considerably extended the range of industrial capital. Whereas manufacturing previously concentrated on bulk textiles, steel, chemicals, armaments and so on, it has over the past century increasingly also encompassed a plethora of branded articles that are destined for immediate personal consumption. Third, the growth of supraterritorial connectivity has greatly expanded finance capital beyond its far more modest scope of a hundred years ago. Global banking, securities, derivatives and insurance markets have hugely increased both the volume and the variety of financial instruments that serve not only to facilitate other kinds of production, but also as channels of accumulation in themselves. Fourth, globalization has encouraged a spread of commodification into new areas involving information and communications. As a result, items such as computer software and telephone calls have also become means to achieve surplus accumulation. Fifth, global companies and global markets have promoted the emergence of biotechnology and nanotechnology industries. Sixth, global migration has contributed to increased commodification of care work.

Primary and industrial capital

Emphasis on the rise of new forms of commodification in recent history can easily distract attention from the persistence and indeed growth, on a planetary scale, of older arenas of capitalist production. As noted in Chapter 1, some contemporary social commentators have spoken of de-industrialization and the dawn of 'postindustrial' society. By these arguments, efforts at surplus accumulation are being redirected away from agriculture, mining and heavy industry to the 'information economy' of a 'network society'.

It may be true that primary and industrial production have declined as a proportion of capitalist activity. The share of agriculture and manufacturing in measured world output dropped from 38.8 per cent in 1960 to 25.8 per cent in 1990 (ILO, 1995: 27). However, a relative reduction is of course not the same as an absolute decrease. On the contrary, the period of intensified globalization has seen continued large-scale world growth of capitalist farming, forestry, fisheries and mining, as well as the manufacture of steel, chemicals, armaments, and so on. Agricultural products have figured prominently in the globalization of markets, especially in the hands of transworld agribusiness enterprises. Mining output remains the key export to global markets for countries like Russia (oil and gas) and Zambia (copper). Construction companies, in some cases like ABB and Bechtel Group operating as transworld organizations, have undertaken countless infrastructure projects to build the roads, ports, electricity grids, and power plants that underpin today's more global economy. Some localized de-industrialization has occurred as certain older factory centres have become rust belts; however, new manufacturing sites, including across parts of the South, have more than compensated for these declines to yield an overall rise in world industrial production.

Hence the new economy of global capitalism retains much of the old. It has not been a case of abandoning earlier arenas of commodification in favour of fresh fields of accumulation. Rather, older sectors have survived and grown at the same time that new sectors have burgeoned.

Consumer capital

One of the principal greatly expanded newer areas of commodification has been consumer capital. 'Consumerism' describes behaviour where people frenetically acquire (and usually fairly quickly discard) a variety of goods that provide the user with some kind of instant but ephemeral gratification (cf. Featherstone, 1991; Sklair, 1995). This consumption centres on the satisfaction of transient desires, especially cravings for novelty, entertainment, fantasy, fashion and pleasure. Consumerism rejoices in excess – or indeed denies any such thing. 'Consumer capital' refers here to surplus accumulation that is realized in the context of this hedonistic consumption.

Although consumerism has antecedents prior to the mid-twentieth century, its main expansion has occurred since then. Today consumer capitalism involves an enormous range of articles, including brand-name foods and beverages, designer clothing, (purported) health aids, motorcars, licit and illicit recreational drugs, tourism, dates arranged through commercial agencies, photographs, audio-visual productions, and mass spectacles like lotteries and sporting fixtures. In all of these cases, the consumer purchases an instant (and usually temporary) pleasurable experience. Indeed, many people have also taken consumerist expectations to settings such as education and health care where immediate gratification is often not available. Nevertheless, many contemporary universities and hospitals, too, have been reoriented towards achieving 'customer satisfaction'.

Consumerism involves the generation as much as the satisfaction of desire. People must be induced to purchase articles and experiences that they would otherwise consider unnecessary. Hence design and presentation have become major preoccupations in contemporary markets. As of 2000, the world packaging industry produced 1.4 billion tonnes of materials (70 per cent of them used for consumer goods) at a value of 443 billion euros through around 100,000 companies (*FT*, 18 May 2000: V). Likewise, a clever branding strategy can turn the mundane into the exceptional. To this end advertising has, especially during recent decades, become a crucial adjunct to much capitalist enterprise. Expanding at rates well ahead of GDP growth, world expenditure on product promotion burgeoned from $39 billion in 1950 to $299 billion in 1997 (Paehlke, 2003: 83).

A core ritual of consumerism is 'shopping'. Over the past half-century this performance has become routine activity for hundreds of millions of people. With seeming inexorability, shop-opening hours have increased in most corners of the world, sometimes against objections from traditional religious quarters. Indeed, for many residents of the contemporary world, Descartes could with only minimal exaggeration be repackaged to read: '*Je shoppe donc je suis.*' Department stores and glittering arcades appear as temples, demanding at least a weekly visit, or more by the especially devout.

Another quintessentially consumerist activity is tourism (Urry, 2002). Desires to experience 'unique' and 'exotic' places have burgeoned since the 1960s. In contrast to self-organizing *travellers* of earlier generations, *tourists* of the present day purchase a packaged and branded product with largely prearranged and staged presentations of the would-be extraordinary. In 2004 travel and tourism generated $5.5 trillion in annual expenditure (10.4 per cent of world GDP) and involved some 214 million jobs, or 8.1 per cent of the world's waged workforce (WTTC, 2005).

Consumerism has pervaded all corners of the contemporary world, although it has tended to affect city dwellers, middle classes and youth relatively more than other social circles. Moreover, this sphere of capitalism has on the whole been more concentrated in the North than the South and the East. However, by the 1990s consumerism had also become prominent in urban centres of East and South East Asia, Eastern Europe and Latin America. Even a postage stamp issued in 1992 by purportedly 'communist' Vietnam unabashedly depicted a clearly marked Suzuki motorcycle draped in the insignia of Pepsi-Cola. After 1991 the government of India's New Economic Policy opened the country to consumerist icons like Pizza Hut and Kellogg's. Meanwhile Coca-Cola, expelled from India in 1977, has returned to the country since the 1990s on a larger scale than ever.

The significance of consumerism in contemporary capitalism is evident in the strength (both demonstrated and potential) of the consumer movement, a form of citizen activism that was scarcely known 50 years ago. Founded in 1960, Consumers International, the self-proclaimed 'global voice for consumers', now has over 250 member organizations in 115 countries (CI, 2005). Whereas capitalists of an earlier era worried about workers withdrawing their labour, today many business executives sooner worry about consumers withholding their purchases, as witnessed for example in boycotts of Nestlé and Nike. Over the past decade companies have turned increasingly to so-called 'corporate social responsibility' (CSR) schemes in good part to head off such consumer campaigns.

Consumerism has been intimately interconnected with globalization in three general ways. First, most of the principal consumerist articles have been transworld products. For example, British American Tobacco sold 900 billion cigarettes per year in 180 countries as of 2000 (Maguire, 2000). Over a billion Barbie dolls were sold in 150 countries in the 40 years after this toy first came to market in 1959 (*Volkskrant*, 29 April 2002: 6). Goods like Sony, Lego, Armani and Microsoft have thrived as global brand icons (Klein, 2000). Shopping malls – and airport duty-free zones foremost among them – are in large part celebrations of supraterritorial offerings. Transworld production chains have also furthered consumerism insofar as much of the output of these global processes has consisted of packaged brand-name articles.

Second, many objects of consumerist desire have lain in the technologies that lie at the heart of contemporary intensified globalization. Needless to say, mass tourism could not have developed on so large a scale without air travel. Meanwhile global communications technologies like electronic mass media have ranked among the chief suppliers of consumerist fad and fantasy, for example, with television programmes and countdowns of pop music hits.

Third, global contexts have often played an important role in generating the hedonistic desires on which consumerism thrives. Advertising has largely operated through supraterritorial mass media like radio, television, and transworld magazines. More recently cable television, call centres and online e-commerce have opened new and distanceless ways of shopping. A global event such as the Olympic Games has become as much a 'Gathering of the Brands' as a 'Gathering of the Nations' (*FT*, 22 July 1996: 21). On other occasions, globality has itself served as a marketing ploy, for example, when an advertisement for Coca-Cola stresses how people all over the planet crave the drink.

The preceding remarks are not meant to imply that globalization has been a prerequisite for, let alone the sole cause of, the spread of consumer capitalism. However, global products, transplanetary markets, and transworld communications have greatly facilitated this expansion and intensification of commodification. In these ways globalization has made consumerism a far stronger force in the twenty-first century than it would otherwise have been.

Moreover, consumerism has provided a boon for surplus accumulation. On the one hand, branding and packaging have allowed suppliers heavily to mark up prices, thereby generating higher rates of profit. In addition, the ephemeral character of consumerist fashions and pleasures has ensured that most of the products in question have a relatively short use life. Thus, when their incomes allow it, consumers quickly return to market for a new video, pack of cigarettes, automobile, paperback novel, holiday, music recording, or other pleasure article.

Thanks both to marked-up prices (yielding higher returns) and to relatively short product lives (generating higher frequencies of purchase), consumerism has figured centrally in the survival and growth of contemporary industrial capitalism. Indeed, leading lights of consumerism have ranked prominently among the world's largest companies. A 1996 list of the top 100 corporations by market capitalization (that is, total share value) contained over 20 suppliers of consumerist items. Their number included Coca-Cola, Philip Morris, Nestlé, Walt Disney, McDonald's, Gillette, 7-Eleven, Sony, and five automobile manufacturers (*WSJ*, 26 September 1996: R27).

Finance capital

Finance is 'commodified' when dealings in foreign exchange, securities, derivatives and the like are employed not only to assist capitalist production in other sectors like agriculture and manufacture, but also as a means of accumulation in their own right. For instance, currencies might be bought and resold in the hope of realizing profit (through commissions and exchange rate fluctuations) as well as – or indeed instead of – to enable cross-border commerce. Likewise, investors may trade securities to gain profit from shifts in the prices of stocks and bonds rather than from payments of dividends and coupons. Financial derivatives, too, have since the 1980s often become only loosely connected to tangible resources. The derivatives then turn into objects of investment in themselves as much as (if not more than) tools of risk management. Insurance policies are bulk traded as objects of accumulation in their own right through a secondary reinsurance market. In all of the cases just mentioned, financial instruments come to have only partial – and perhaps only negligible – relation to other objects of value. The trade in financial instruments becomes a fairly self-contained circuit of accumulation.

The large-scale globalization of finance in current history has greatly stimulated the commodification of financial instruments. As recognized in pioneering analyses of the phenomenon by Rudolf Hilferding (1910), Vladimir Ilich Lenin (1917) and Karl Polanyi (1944), early instances of finance capital appeared in the late nineteenth century. However, the commodification of finance has become hugely more significant within contemporary capitalism. In the past 50 years the variety of financial instruments, the number of financial markets in the world, the magnitude of investments in financial instruments, and the volumes of financial trading have all skyrocketed well beyond any previous level. Much of this enormous expansion of financial activity has come through electronic, supraterritorial transactions that move instantly across the planet.

Many indicators point towards an increased commodification of financial instruments. For example, the proportion of foreign exchange dealings that relate to transactions in 'real' goods fell from 90 per cent in the early 1970s to around 2 per cent in the late 1990s. In the 1970s the value of transworld movements of portfolio capital was roughly equal to that of global flows of foreign direct investment, but by the 1990s these financial transfers had become three times as large as FDI (*FT*, 30 September 1994: XII). Although the following two figures are not directly comparable, it remains striking that the annual turnover on world financial markets in the mid-1990s topped $1,000 trillion, while world GDP was less than $30 trillion. In other words, the value of around *ten days* of transactions on world financial markets had come to approximate the value of *annual* world production of goods and services. Such figures imply that financial dealings have developed a capitalist logic that goes well beyond the so-called 'real' economy.

The contemporary proliferation of types of financial instruments also suggests a deeper commodification of finance. In the bond and money markets, for example, the traditional straight bond has been joined by floating-rate bonds, bonds with equity warrants, zero-coupon bonds, commercial paper, repurchase agreements, asset-backed securities and so on. Similarly, new forms of financial derivatives have appeared constantly in recent years.

By the mid-1990s Euroclear handled about 90,000 different kinds of securities, with projected further increases to over half a million (*FT*, 19 June 1997: 20). Many of today's retail banks have become financial supermarkets, offering a dizzying array of saving and borrowing instruments as well as various brokerage services.

Contemporary finance capitalism has also involved new kinds of institutional investors, including unit trusts, mutual funds, pension funds, and insurance companies. For example, the number of US-based mutual funds grew from 100 in 1951 to over 8,000 in 2003 (ICI, 2004: ii, 13). The total invested in these funds topped $1 trillion in 1990 and $3 trillion in 1996, before reaching $8.1 trillion at the end of 2004 (*FT*, 27 March 1996: 29; ICI, 2005). Meanwhile the value of world pension fund assets amounted to $13 trillion in 2000 (*The Economist*, 20 May 2000: 127).

Concurrently, financial trading centres have multiplied throughout the world. In the 1990s new stock exchanges opened in 70 countries across Africa, Asia, Eastern Europe and the former Soviet Union (Harris, 1998–9: 23). Securities exchanges have appeared in places such as Malawi and Burma where such an institution would have seemed very unlikely only a decade before. Most derivatives exchanges have been created since the early 1980s, in cities such as Kuala Lumpur and São Paulo as well as major financial centres in the OECD countries.

Meanwhile turnover in the financial sector has burgeoned at market sites old and new. As mentioned in Chapter 3, foreign exchange dealing reached well over a trillion dollars per day by the mid-1990s and nearly two trillion per day in 2004. The level of secondary trading in bonds likewise has risen to many trillions of dollars' worth per annum. The average value of dealing on the world's five most active stock exchanges (Hong Kong, London, New York, Singapore and Tokyo) totalled more than $1 trillion daily in 1995 (*FT*, 28 March 1996: II). Average turnover on the New York Stock Exchange (NYSE) grew more than tenfold in the last quarter of the twentieth century. Whereas 30 million shares traded was a record day for the NYSE in the mid-1970s, in the mid-1990s this figure regularly topped 450 million shares. Derivatives dealings have skyrocketed as the value of outstanding exchange-traded contracts rose from $0.7 trillion in 1987 to $14.3 trillion in 2000 (IMF, 2001: 22–3). Outstanding over-the-counter derivative contracts added a further $197 trillion to this global market as of 2003 (BIS, 2004: 1).

Increased turnover in financial markets has on the whole brought increased accumulation. For instance, foreign exchange business has since the 1970s provided banks with a major source of revenue. In one especially large 'killing', forex traders made £3 billion from the Bank of England's attempts in 1992 to stabilize sterling within the EU exchange rate mechanism of that day. George Soros alone acquired $1 billion betting against the pound on this occasion. Large swings in the Argentine peso, the Brazilian real, the

Indonesian rupiah, the Korean won, the Russian rouble, the Thai baht and the Turkish lira have also given currency speculators field days in the past decade.

More generally, too, bank dealings – and those of transworld banking corporations prominently among them – have been a principal conduit of surplus accumulation during the period of accelerated globalization. True, banks have faced a number of crises. For example, looming defaults on massive commercial loans to the South suppressed profits across much of global banking in the mid-1980s. Likewise, property bubbles have burst in several countries at considerable cost to the banking sector. Nevertheless, on the whole profits for global banks have remained high and secure. Banks constituted the single largest group (18 in number) among the 100 largest world companies by market capitalization in the mid-1990s (FT500, 1997: 6–7). Banking was also the biggest sector among the largest 500 corporations in 2004, with 66 companies holding a collective stock market value of $2.6 trillion (Pretzlik, 2004).

Steep rises in stock market indexes through the 1980s and 1990s likewise indicated a large growth in stores of surplus as a result of the heightened commodification of financial instruments. In London, for instance, the FTSE-100 Index rose from a level of 1,000 at its launch in 1984 to more than 7,000 in 2000. In New York the venerable Dow Jones Industrial Index not only finally broke the 1,000 level in early 1980s, but proceeded to exceed the 10,000 mark in 1999. In all, world stock market capitalization more than tripled in a decade: from $6.5 trillion in 1986 to $20.2 trillion in 1997 (IFC, 1996: 17; UGI, 1999: 3). Investments on equity markets in the USA alone totalled $17 trillion in early 2001, before the subsequent slump.

Figures for profits from trade in financial derivatives are not generally publicized. However, the eagerness with which traders and institutions have developed this business implies that it has provided handsome returns. In any case large sums must have flowed into the coffers in order that the firms involved could pay dealers and managers salaries of often astronomical proportions. Meanwhile insurance (including reinsurance) ranked as the sixth largest sector in terms of world stock market capitalization in 2004 (Bolger, 2004).

In sum, then, finance capital has generated many windfall profits in the present time of transworld trading. A large proportion of contemporary market transactions have been undertaken in a spirit of short-term speculation rather than for long-term investment. In consequence, as detailed in Chapter 9, global finance capital has often been hugely volatile, placing participants on permanent alert and subjecting them to recurrent panics.

Like any casino, global finance has yielded major losses as well as big wins. For example, next to his massive gains Soros also lost $800 million on one day in 1987 and $600 million on another in 1994. World bond markets crashed in February 1994. A lone dealer in government bonds, Toshihide Iguchi of Daiwa Bank, accumulated losses of $1.1 billion until he was exposed in 1995. In equity markets, meanwhile, the Dow Jones Index has on several occasions since 1987 plummeted over 300 points in a single trading day. The 2001–2 slump in US stock markets at one point wiped $8 trillion off of capitalization (Miller *et al.*, 2004). The FTSE-100 Index only slowly recovered to 5,000 points after its parallel plunge. Long after the bubble burst on the Tokyo Stock Exchange, the Nikkei 225 Index has yet to come anywhere close to the level of 37,000 that it reached in 1989.

Securities exchanges in the so-called 'emerging markets' have tended to be even more volatile. For example, the devaluation crisis of the Mexican peso in December 1994 triggered massive sell-offs throughout Latin American stock markets in the first half of 1995. Likewise, a large-scale withdrawal of global capital from the Bangkok market in mid-1997 provoked similar investor stampedes across much of East and South East Asia. Further such crises have subsequently afflicted Russia, Brazil, Argentina and Turkey.

Global derivatives markets, too, have produced a succession of spectacular losses. In 1994 a trading subsidiary of MetallGesellschaft lost an estimated $1 billion on oil derivatives. At the end of the same year Orange County, California, went bankrupt after losing almost $1.7 billion in the derivatives market. The rogue trader Nick Leeson brought down the venerable house of Barings with losses of $1.3 billion in February 1995. In another spectacular case, a copper futures dealer at Sumitomo Corporation, Yasuo Hamanaka, built up losses of $2.6 billion in the decade to June 1996. A hedge fund specializing in equity derivatives, Long Term Capital Management (LTCM), was saved from collapse in September 1998 with a $3.6 billion rescue package. True, these figures become less astounding when they are considered as a proportion of overall amounts of contract trading, and so far no other major hedge fund crisis has occurred since LTCM. Nevertheless, such scenarios have reinforced fears that the speed and volume of transactions through transworld electronic channels could produce a domino effect in the derivatives market, whereby the bankruptcy of one participant could generate a systemic collapse.

Thus far, however, the global financial casino has found stability in its instability. Even taking major slumps and crises into account, on the whole finance capital has yielded investors many more gains than losses, and the structure of capitalism has emerged as the clear overall winner. With little exaggeration it can be concluded that the contemporary growth of global finance has given surplus accumulation one of its greatest boosts in history.

The justice or otherwise of the ways that these gains have been distributed is a different question, of course. As elaborated in Part III, only a minority of the world's population has held bank accounts and securities, and many poor people and poor countries have suffered from limited access to credit and/or crippling financial debts. Understandably, then, anti-poverty groups and development NGOs have reserved some of their sharpest critiques for global finance.

Information and communications capital

In addition to primary, industrial, consumer and finance capital, globalization has also created conditions for major growth in information and communication capital. Like financial instruments, data, messages, ideas and images circulate with particular ease in transplanetary, supraterritorial spaces by means of electronic networks. Information technology (IT), telecommunications, and mass media have thereby become primary sites of surplus accumulation in recent decades.

As noted earlier, other commentators have discussed the growth of these new industries with concepts like 'postindustrial society', 'the information society', 'the information age', 'the services economy', 'the network economy', 'the knowledge revolution', and so on. Yet these accounts have tended to downplay or ignore the capitalist character of the contemporary production of information and communications. So-called 'postindustrial society' (if one can speak of such a thing) has been even more steeped in capitalism than was its 'industrial' predecessor. In this light references to 'reflexive accumulation' and 'cybernetic', 'digital', 'electronic', 'high technology' and 'virtual' capitalism better capture the nature of these developments (Robins and Webster, 1988; Dyer-Witheford, 1999; Schiller, 1999; Paehlke, 2003; Peterson, 2003).

Contemporary production of information and communications has extended the reach of commodification in four major respects: hardware, software, servicing and content. Hardware refers to the operating equipment through which information and communications are processed. The production of telephones, computers, satellites, television sets and the like has entailed a major expansion of factory-centred industrial capital since the middle of the twentieth century. Companies, governments, educational establishments, and households have spent huge sums to enhance their data processing capacities. World sales of PCs topped 80 million units in 1996, while receipts from the provision of semiconductors reached $50 billion in 1989 and $155 billion in 1995 (*FT*, 9 January 1996: 21; 26 September 1996: 5). Annual world revenues from telecommunications equipment have also far exceeded $100 billion. In many countries, investment in information and communications infrastructure has come to exceed investment in agriculture and 'smokestack industries' (Sweezy and Magdoff, 1985). One oft-quoted business analyst has estimated that a third of investment in the North since the 1960s has gone into equipment to handle data and information (Drucker, 1993: 75). Reflecting this shift, the share of office and telecommunications equipment in cross-border trade grew from 5 per cent in the early 1980s to 12 per cent in 1995, when it surpassed the value of agricultural exports (*FT*, 28 March 1996: 3).

Much surplus accumulation in contemporary history has also been pursued through the production of software, that is, the thousands of digital programmes that process information and communications through the hardware. Interestingly, the inventor of the World Wide Web, Tim Berners-Lee, forwent patent rights in 1991, so making this major software innovation freely available for public use. However, this exception shows the rule that computer programmes have been significant money spinners. Already in the mid-1990s, programmes to effect Internet communications alone generated sales of $2 billion per annum (*FT*, 9 April 1996: 15). Commercial software producers have included corporate giants such as Microsoft and Cisco Systems as well as hundreds of smaller suppliers.

Servicing of the hardware and software just described has also grown to become a large and profitable industry. Computer technology in particular has required major support. In this field specialized IT consultancy companies like Electronic Data Services (EDS) and Integris have deployed tens of thousands of employees across the world and generated multiple billions of dollars in annual revenue.

Finally, information and communications industries have widened the scope of capitalism with large-scale commodification of the content that passes through electronic processing systems. In other words, the conveyance of data, ideas, messages and images through supraterritorial spaces has become a highly profitable business. Telephone calls, databases, mailing lists, Internet connections, television broadcasts, DVD releases, news services, market surveys, and the like have presented enormous new opportunities for accumulation. Telephone companies, online service providers, cable and satellite television suppliers, polling agencies and so on all levy subscriptions and/or other user charges in the pursuit of profit. In this way information and communications have become important to capitalism not only as infrastructure to facilitate other processes of accumulation, but also as major objects of accumulation themselves (cf. Mosco, 1988). Indeed, some critics fear that information which is not amenable to commercial exploitation through digitization is becoming increasingly scarce. In the words of Spike Peterson, 'what does not conform to the informational codes and economy does not count' (2003: 137).

Globalization has lain at the heart of this commodification of information and communications. For one thing, the technologies in question are largely those of supraterritorial communications. In addition, transworld organizations have generated much of the increased demand for commodified information and communications. The operations of global companies, global civil society associations and global governance bodies have been thoroughly dependent on telecommunications networks and computerized data transfers. Meanwhile publishers, broadcasters, filmmakers and Internet service providers have flourished with transworld customer bases.

Initially the contemporary increased commodification of information was an unqualified boon for accumulation. A study by the American Federation of Information Processing Societies estimated that revenues of the computer sector in the USA quadrupled in real terms during the 1980s (Schiller and Schiller, 1988: 149). Hardware providers like Intel, IBM and Hewlett Packard shot up the ranks to join the world's largest corporations. Shares in IT firms rose in the 1980s and 1990s to rank among the high earners on equity markets. IT stock launches and mergers and acquisitions between IT companies provided investment banks with some of their most lucrative business.

Yet, much as other new technologies in the past, information industries have subsequently had a bumpy ride in capitalist markets. Like the railways sector in the nineteenth century, the initial IT boom was followed by large-scale bust. The PC gold rush likewise receded in the mid-1990s, as even former market leaders Apple Macintosh and Olivetti struggled. The Internet bubble burst with many investor casualties in 2000–1, particularly on the Nasdaq market. Nevertheless, overall the IT sector has blessed capitalism, and high profits on software have placed industry leaders like Marc Andreessen, Michael Dell and Bill Gates among the world's wealthiest individuals.

Telecommunications, too, have generated great accumulation in contemporary history. In terms of market capitalization the value of this sector across the planet quadrupled between 1986 and 1995, to over $600 billion (*FT*, 12 February 1996: 24). Annual turnover on telecoms equipment and services exceeded $600 billion in 1996 (*WSJ-E*, 17 February 1997: 2). Both fixed-line and mobile telephone providers enjoyed large profits in the 1990s, although a slump in the market capitalization of several leading mobile telecoms companies in 2001 temporarily dampened some of the capitalist exuberance in that industry. Lucrative capitalist potential helps to explain the flood of – and urgency behind – privatizations of telephone services around the world since the mid-1980s. Sixty-one telecoms privatizations occurred between 1990 and 1996, and several dozen more sell-offs followed in the late 1990s (EST, 1997: 5). In only one country anywhere in the world, Uruguay, has the privatization of the service been explicitly rejected. Concurrently, the WTO has given considerable priority to liberalizing the telecoms sector in cross-border commerce. As one commentator has summarized, 'deregulation and technological change are transforming the phone industry from a sleepy utility business into a high-growth competitive free-for-all' (Kuhn, 1995: 48). For example, over 80 new telecommunications companies were established in the Asia-Pacific region between 1990 and 1997 (EST, 1997: 6).

Other large-scale accumulation has occurred in the context of globalization through mass media corporations. Sales of the world's 50 largest multimedia businesses reached $110 billion in 1993, while the value of cross-border trade in printed materials, music, visual arts, cinema and associated equipment nearly tripled from $67 billion in 1980 to $200 billion in 1991 (HDR, 1999: 33). Global media empires such as Time Warner Inc., Walt Disney Company, Bertelsmann AG, Viacom, and News Corporation have loomed large on the contemporary capitalist landscape (Herman and McChesney, 1997; McChesney, 1997; Williams, 2001). The largest player in the sector, Time Warner Inc., generated revenues of $40 billion in 2003 (Time Warner, 2004: 12). Media tycoons like Rupert Murdoch and Silvio Berlusconi have ranked among the most colourful entrepreneurs in contemporary capitalism. True, flamboyance has not always enhanced the bottom line. Nevertheless, capitalist ambitions have continued to fuel the growth of the media sector, whose value in Europe more than doubled during the first half of the 1990s (*FT*, 17 June 1996: 26). Indeed, in the mid-1990s broadcast media and publishing were the two most profitable industries in Europe (FT500, 1997: 17). In the USA, almost a fifth of the 400 richest persons as of 1989 obtained their wealth from the mass media (Petras, 1993: 141).

Spurred largely by globalization, then, information and communications industries have moved to the core of capitalism for the twenty-first century. Expecting that this trend will proceed further, global investment bankers like Merrill Lynch and Salomon Brothers have maintained large telecommunications, media and IT divisions. In the light of such developments, Peter Drucker has conceded that his purported 'postcapitalist society' may in fact be an economy dominated by information capitalism (1993: 166–7).

Genetic and atomic capital

The seemingly ever-widening range of commodification under globalizing capitalism can be further seen in emergent sectors of biotechnology and nanotechnology. At the moment these new arenas of accumulation remain relatively small next to well-established primary, industrial, consumer, finance, information and communications capital. However, genetic and atomic capital have the potential to figure large in future global accumulation.

Biotechnology – an integration of biochemistry, microbiology and engineering – involves the mapping and manipulation of the elementary building blocks of life. Originating in the discovery of DNA in 1953, and mainly developed since the 1970s, advanced genetic engineering has applications in a host of sectors, including agriculture (e.g., GM crops), chemicals (e.g., plastics), energy (e.g., biofuels), forestry (e.g., pulp and paper), medicine (e.g., cell and tissue culture), military (e.g., biological weapons), and pharmaceuticals (e.g., hormones and insulin). Champions expect that biotechnology can greatly advance struggles against disease, poverty and ecological degradation, while critics warn that the emergent field opens the way to clones, designer babies, and new diseases with unpredictable consequences for human and other life (Rifkin, 1998; Ruse and Castle, 2002).

One undoubted consequence of biotechnology is its extension of capitalist activity. Although much of this work remains experimental at the present time, the research has often been undertaken through life science companies backed by venture capital. Some of the resultant new products have already gone to market, for example, GM crops in the USA since 1996. As of 2001 over 3,000 biotech companies in the USA and Europe between them generated over $32 billion in revenue (McKelvey *et al.*, 2004). This figure seems likely to rise many times over in the years to come.

Nanotechnology is even earlier in development than biotechnology. Nano production covers processes whereby materials are constructed at the level of atoms and molecules. Whereas traditional manufacturing technologies have involved the assembly of large visible parts, and biotechnology has involved constructing items on a microscopic level, nanotechnology operates at an even smaller scale. One nanometre (nm) is one-billionth of a metre, or approximately ten atoms of hydrogen in width. Nanotechnology permits the manufacture of metals, tissues, etc. on an atom-by-atom or molecule-by-molecule basis (Wood *et al.*, 2003; Mehta, 2006).

At the moment nanotechnology remains even more experimental than biotechnology. Total world revenue for all nano-scale products was only $7.6 billion in 2003 (ETC, 2004: 4). Wider economic applications – with larger and as-yet little studied social impacts – will probably not appear for several decades. However, if the science is successfully developed, it holds enormous potentials for additional accumulation. Like mechanization and digitization before it, the 'atomically modified' outputs of nanotechnology could revolutionize the production of foods, medicines, metals, textiles, weaponry, and more. Patents on these innovations could generate huge profits and reinforce capitalism still further in the middle of the twenty-first century and beyond.

Globalization has fostered the emergence of both biotechnology and nanotechnology in a number of ways. For one thing, transplanetary networks have enabled a critical mass of widely dispersed specialist scientists to undertake accelerated research and development of these two areas. In addition, each of these new spheres of accumulation has looked to a global pool of finance to acquire the large amounts of requisite venture capital and to a transworld scale of market to recoup investments and maximize earnings. Several global companies like Du Pont, Eli Lilly, Monsanto and Syngenta have been leaders in the commercial exploitation of biotechnology. These and other transworld corporate players have begun to take on the market application of nanotechnology as well. Global governance has figured importantly in both new sectors, *inter alia* by enshrining the intellectual property rights that provide much of the legal framework for profit making from these technologies.

Care capital

Finally, globalization has contributed to an expansion of commodification through the growth of what might be termed 'care capital'. The care sector encompasses services to promote the well-being of persons who cannot perform such activities themselves, such as disabled, elderly, ill and young people (Yeates, 2004: 371). It also includes the provision of emotional and material supports to intimates.

Traditionally care work has not been commodified. Childrearing, homemaking, healing, listening, and sexual relations have generally not been objects of commercial transactions. True, small circles of wealthier households have long included waged domestic servants. In addition, many modern medical professionals have received pay for their therapies, and prostitutes have for centuries supplied remunerated sexual labour. However, most day-to-day care work (predominantly supplied by women) has not been monetized.

Of course care labour has been indispensable to the workings of capitalism as a whole (Mies, 1998; Peterson, 2003: ch 4). For example, the nurturing and socialization of children has been vital to the provision of the next generation of capitalist investors and workers. Likewise, unpaid material, affective and sensual sustenance in the 'private' sphere of the household has underpinned other commodified labour in the 'public' arena of the waged workplace. Moreover, unremunerated homemakers (again, overwhelmingly women) have provided a major client base for much consumer capitalism. However, in the past care has generally buttressed accumulation in other sectors rather than itself being a site of direct and deliberate accumulation. Indeed, to this day household work is invisible production in an informal economy that does not figure in conventional macroeconomic statistics.

Yet under emergent hypercapitalism the provision of care too has become increasingly commodified. This trend is evident, particularly in the North, with the growth of commercial health services, childcare provision, nursing homes for the elderly, housecleaning agencies, professional counselling and other psychological therapies, marriage and adoption bureaux, surrogate mothering, and an expanded (and often legalized) sex industry with erotic dance clubs and the like as well as prostitution. In many cases hired care labour within the household has also promoted increased female wage labour in the 'public' sphere, whether in lowly paid clerical and retail jobs or in high-earning professional careers.

Although globalization has not been essential to the commodification of care, transplanetary connections have facilitated this trend in important respects. A few medical services (particularly for expatriate professionals working in major cities in the South) have operated as global companies. Some marriage and adoption services have drawn brides and children from all corners of the earth. The expanded sex industry has often been linked to global tourism when the client travels to the provider and global (usually illicit) migration when the sex worker is brought to the client. Transworld migration from the South to the North has also supplied a substantial proportion of the lowly paid and poorly protected (usually female) domestics that underpin highly lucrative care capital (Heyzer *et al.*, 1994; Anderson, 2000; Wichterich, 2000; Parreñas, 2001; Ehrenreich and Hochschild, 2002). Several authors have discerned 'global care chains' in which migrant domestics both service care needs in the North and, through remittances, sustain family in the South (Hochschild, 2000; Yeates, 2004).

Summary

Taking the above remarks concerning commodification in sum, globalization has played an important role in widening the range of capitalism and reorienting the relative weights of accumulation away from 'merchandise' (commercial and industrial capital) toward 'intangibles' (finance, information, communications, genetic and nano capital). To this extent the 'real' economy has acquired a different 'reality'.

As emphasized earlier, this is not to claim that primary and older industrial commodities have become insignificant in contemporary capitalism. However, they do not dominate accumulation in a more global economy as they once did in territorialist capitalism. Among the world's largest 100 firms by market capitalization in 1995, a full three-fifths concentrated on consumer, finance and/or information industries. Chemicals and oil companies still carry weight, but other sectors that were prominent in the territorialist world of the late nineteenth century (e.g., mining, iron and steel, and railways) barely figure in the top corporate ranks today (FT500, 1996: 2). Only one of the top ten sectors in Europe in terms of shareholder returns over the period 1996–2001 came from older heavy industries (namely, oil and gas). All nine others involved consumer, finance, information and communications sectors (*FT*, 29 June 2001: II).

It would seem telling in this light that, in general, countries where production has continued to focus predominantly on extractive activities and old industrial plant have become relatively poorer in the contemporary globalizing world. This is arguably one reason for the widened North–South gap since 1960, especially with respect to the poorest countries. Likewise, the collapse of state socialism in Eastern Europe and the former USSR might be attributed in part to the failure of central planning in those countries adequately to generate consumer, finance, information, and communications sectors. The Soviet bloc could make a running in the mid-twentieth century, when primary and industrial capital were dominant, but the regimes failed to meet the challenges of emergent hypercapitalism in the globalizing economy of the late twentieth century.

Altered organization

Apart from shifts in respect of commodification, another general area where globalization has promoted changes in the operations of capitalism is the organizational conditions of accumulation. Two developments in this regard – the growth of offshore centres and the proliferation of transworld companies – have been mentioned earlier while discussing the definition, history and explanation of globalization. At the present juncture, however, the concern is to assess the consequences of these developments in global organization for surplus accumulation. In addition, two further trends in respect of capitalist organization are newly introduced below, namely, increased merger and acquisition (M&A) activity and a greater concentration of capital in many sectors. Like the expansion of commodification, these organizational shifts have on the whole enhanced the possibilities of surplus accumulation. In these respects, too, globalization has thus far been a bonanza for (hyper)capitalism.

Offshore centres

As intimated in Chapters 3 and 4, the offshore phenomenon has provided a major fillip to surplus accumulation. Offshore centres generally offer nil or minimal rates of corporate, sales, and personal taxes. These sites also entice capital with low input costs, limited regulation, subsidies, and statutory guarantees of confidentiality. Euphemisms affirm that offshore arrangements provide 'tax efficiency' and 'discretion'. To put the matter more explicitly, offshore arrangements have created much enhanced opportunities for accumulation.

As indicated earlier, states have created offshore zones mainly for global production processes and for global financial activities. In addition, offshore registration has offered so-called 'flags of convenience' for shipping vessels and leased aircraft. The Internet has opened further possibilities of offshore dealings in respect of gambling, telecommunications and e-commerce (Palan, 1998: 625). Inasmuch as duty-free shopping occurs in special areas that escape normal taxation arrangements, it could also be considered an offshore activity.

Many of these sites of special taxation and regulation are islands like the

Bahamas or Bahrain that literally lie 'offshore'. Yet in countries like Bangladesh and Romania, EPZs are located 'onshore' in or near coastal areas. Meanwhile certain so-called 'offshore' centres such as Liechtenstein and Luxembourg are in fact landlocked. In this respect the term 'offshore' is somewhat of a misnomer.

It should be noted as well that offshore arrangements have not been a preserve of small states alone. Several major states have also passed the relevant legislation. For example, in the 1980s both Britain and China launched special economic zones for manufacturing. Offshore financial facilities were introduced in New York in 1981, in Tokyo in 1986, and in Bangkok in 1993.

Since so much of the relevant data (particularly in relation to offshore finance) is not publicly available, it is difficult to calculate with any precision the repercussions of these arrangements for contemporary capitalism. However, it would not seem far-fetched to suggest that offshore legislation has in recent decades channelled more than a trillion extra dollars' worth of accumulation to corporations and private individuals.

The offshore phenomenon has arguably also benefited accumulation for companies and wealthy persons in indirect ways. For example, many governments have arguably lowered upper tax bands and loosened restrictive regulations on economic activity partly in order to discourage capital flight to offshore zones. In addition, many trade unions have probably moderated their demands in respect of wages and other working conditions for fear of otherwise encouraging enterprises to relocate plants in EPZs (and other low-wage areas).

Global companies

As noted in earlier chapters, thousands of firms have in the context of globalization given their organization a substantial transworld dimension, either by establishing affiliates in multiple countries across the planet or by forging strategic alliances with enterprises based in several regions. Some of these global corporate organizations are huge. For example, as of 2004 the Unilever company encompassed more than 500 subsidiaries in around 100 countries, and the mass media conglomerate Bertelsmann AG covered more than 600 affiliates in 50 countries. In the realm of strategic alliances, the WorldPartners Association, formed in 1993, has linked 19 telecommunications carriers in operations across over 35 countries. The advertising firms FCB and Publicis have since 1988 developed collaboration between their several hundred offices in over 70 countries.

Global companies have acquired a very prominent place in contemporary capitalism. For example, the collective annual sales of the 50 largest unitary global enterprises rose from $540 billion in 1975 to $2,100 billion in 1990, equivalent to around 10 per cent of recorded world product (Carnoy *et al.*,

1993: 49). Yearly sales by all foreign affiliates of transborder firms increased from $2.7 trillion in 1982 to $17.6 trillion in 2003, equivalent to almost half the value of world GDP (UNCTAD, 2004: 9). By 1990 the largest 350 global companies between them conducted almost 40 per cent of the world's cross-border trade, and the largest 500 companies collectively accounted for over half (Rugman and Verbeke, 1990: 1; Lang and Hines, 1993: 34).

Although 'going global' has not opened a capitalist paradise to all firms, on the whole the fruits of transplanetary mobility and coordination have figured very positively in company profit margins. Global corporations have often sited their production and markets at the commercially most advantageous locations, wherever on earth those places might be. Moreover, even when plant and equipment remain fixed at certain locations, transworld companies have (as mentioned in Chapter 4) also increased their earnings through global accounting formulas. With transfer pricing, for instance, a firm can set prices on its intra-firm cross-border trade at such levels that profits flow to the balance sheets of those subsidiaries that are sited in countries with the most advantageous tax, auditing or other regulatory conditions. Sometimes, then, the tricks of global accounting have been as important to corporate accumulation as transplanetary production and marketing.

A number of rough indicators suggest that global organization has served the purpose of surplus accumulation very well. For instance, the annual profits of the largest transplanetary enterprises have exceeded the GDPs of many smaller countries. Other studies have shown that, among US-based firms at least, the bigger transworld corporations have tended to generate higher returns than intra-country firms, particularly since 1980. Some analysts have in this regard discerned a two-tiered stock market, with a clear contrast between global and national companies (Kuhn, 1995: 46, 48). By no means is it clear that, as some Marxists have suggested, the contemporary proliferation and growth of global corporations has been *necessary* to the survival of capitalism. Nevertheless, globalization of the firm has certainly – for the time being at least – yielded plentiful capitalist returns.

'Alliance capitalism', too, has generally had positive implications for accumulation (Dunning, 1997). True, some of these initiatives have yielded disappointing results. Indeed, certain studies have suggested that over 40 per cent of parties to strategic alliances have not regarded their partnerships as successful (Gilroy, 1993: 137). Yet even on this pessimistic assessment more than half of early strategic alliances bore fruit. Moreover, the proportion of profitable strategic alliances would seem likely to grow as firms acquire more experience with this mode of organization. Already many strategic alliances have allowed companies to pool resources, achieve economies of scale, share risk, and shape markets to their joint advantage. For example, cross-licensing agreements between global pharmaceutical companies have generated very high profits in that sector (Gilroy, 1993: 152). Indeed, in some cases 'strategic alliance' appears to be a euphemism for 'cartel'.

Mergers and acquisitions

In a third general organizational trend of contemporary capitalism that is substantially connected with globalization, many companies have gone beyond strategic alliances to full-scale fusions through mergers and acquisitions. In the words of one investment banker, 'As companies go global, more acquisitions result' (*Fortune*, 1995: 40). Indeed, with 'conquests' by 'corporate raiders' and many 'hostile takeovers', M&A activity among firms has acquired a vocabulary of (supraterritorial) warfare once reserved for (territorial) states.

Since the 1980s capitalism has seen successive flurries of M&A (Kang and Sakai, 2000). The annual world total of these transactions more than doubled from 11,300 in 1990 to 24,600 in 1997 (HDR, 1999: 32). The aggregate value of M&A deals rose to unprecedented levels of $1.1 trillion in 1996, $1.5 trillion in 1997 and nearly $2.1 trillion in 1998 (*WSJ-E*, 2 January 1998: R9; *FT*, 29 January 1999: I). Fusions across state borders numbered 2,141 with a total value of $67.3 billion in 1993, then skyrocketed to a peak of $1.1 trillion in 2000, and subsequently declined year on year to 4,500 deals with a total value of $297 billion in 2003 (Went, 1996: 13; UNCTAD, 2001: 52; UNCTAD, 2004: 6).

The rise of transplanetary relations has not constituted the sole force behind 'merger mania' and 'takeover fever'; however, the growth of global economic activity has spurred the trend in several respects. For example, cross-border M&A has given many companies a means of quick entry into a target country. Rather than needing to build up an affiliate from scratch, the global company can purchase a going concern and in the process also dispense with a competitor. Governments have generally been loath to hinder such acquisitions, partly for fear of alienating globally mobile capital that might otherwise locate in another jurisdiction.

Globalization has also encouraged much M&A activity within countries. Many 'domestic' fusions have had the specific aim to create a larger national firm that can hold its own in globalizing capitalism. In short, corporate combination has been a strategy for company survival in the face of global competition. On these occasions, too, governments have been reluctant to hamper M&A, for fear of prompting relocation and/or of undermining the position of 'their' firms in global markets.

Increased transplanetary connectivity has also stimulated burgeoning M&A activity insofar as the deals have been especially prevalent in areas of production that lie at the heart of globalization. For example, a number of aircraft manufacturers have merged with an eye to global positioning. In this spirit Lockheed acquired Martin Marietta in 1994, while Boeing merged with McDonnell Douglas in 1997. In consumer industries, corporate acquisitions have made major global players still larger in cases like Nestlé, Philip Morris, RJR Nabisco and Unilever. The pharmaceuticals sector witnessed some $80 billion of M&A business in the mid-1990s, including 16 deals of $1 billion or more (*FT*, 7 March 1996: 21). Several principal transworld hotel chains (Hilton, Sheraton, etc.) have also expanded by the M&A route.

In finance, various mergers between commercial banks have created veritable global giants like Tokyo-Mitsubishi Bank, Chase Manhattan (incorporating Chemical Bank) and HSBC (incorporating Midland Bank). Multiple other bank mergers and takeovers occurred within and between EU countries in anticipation of their economic and monetary union. Most Canada-based banks have been involved in mergers, largely so that these institutions might survive in global financial markets.

A number of global banks have since the 1980s also taken over global securities houses, thereby ending the traditional separation of commercial and investment banks. Prime examples of these combinations include Credit Suisse First Boston, Deutsche Morgan Grenfell and ING Barings. In addition, numerous banks have acquired insurance companies (or vice versa) to become so-called 'bancassurance' combinations. In the largest such transaction to date, Travelers Group took over Citicorp in 1998 in a deal worth $73 billion. Among themselves, too, insurance firms have undergone dozens of fusions largely in order to enhance their global market position.

As for the information and communications sectors, IT enterprises experienced 2,913 mergers and acquisitions in 1995 alone (*FT*, 29 January 1996: 22). Dozens of major telecommunications companies have likewise undertaken M&A to create veritable transworld carriers. For instance, Telefónica de España, newly privatized and the largest global company based in Spain, has bought into businesses in 18 countries. Various global media firms have also fused since the late 1980s, including Sony with CBS and Time Life with Warner Brothers (with further expansions in 1996 to acquire Turner Broadcasting and in 2000 to merge with America Online).

True, the 1990s also witnessed some important demergers, especially in respect of multi-business conglomerates. For example, IBM disaggregated into 14 smaller and potentially mutually competitive companies in 1991. Sandoz hived off its industrial chemicals division as a new company in 1995, before fusing with Ciba-Geigy in 1996 to form the pharmaceuticals giant Novartis. AT&T, Hanson, ICI, and ITT have also embarked on demerger initiatives.

However, the list of breakups is relatively short next to the concurrent plethora of mergers and acquisitions. Moreover, 'spinning off' appears to have been a temporary fashion, mainly circulating in the boardrooms of UK- and US-based companies, along with a few other firms headquartered in

France and Germany. No headline demergers have occurred since 2000. The overall trend in present times of accelerated globalization has pointed decidedly towards increased combinations.

Mergers and acquisitions are not by themselves guarantees of profitability in globalizing markets, of course. Indeed, many fusions have failed in terms of subsequent share price performance, earnings growth, turnover of top executives, new product development, etc. Time Warner failed to report a profit for many years after the 1989 merger and struggled again after acquiring other businesses a decade later. The costs of major takeovers are also astronomical (although they bring high earnings to the investment banks that coordinate them). Nevertheless, even if the returns have sometimes fallen below expectations, global market opportunities and competition have propelled a major trend to fuse companies.

Concentration

Due largely to expanded M&A activity, globalizing capitalism has brought substantially increased concentration to many areas of production. Often the fusions have involved not a bolt-on acquisition of a small firm by a sector leader, but a 'mega-merger' of giants that radically transforms the competitive balance in a market. The peak year of 2000 saw 175 cross-border mergers involving assets of over $1 billion each (UNCTAD, 2004: 6). As a result, globalizing capital has, thus far, on the whole meant bigger and more centralized capital.

A handful of big firms now dominate many sectors. For example, in the mid-1990s the largest five companies in the respective areas of production accounted for 70 per cent of world markets in consumer durables, 60 per cent of air travel, over half of aircraft manufacture, over half of electronics and electrical equipment, over 40 per cent of global media, a third of chemicals, and some 30 per cent of world insurance sales (Harvey, 1995: 194). In 1998 the ten biggest firms in the respective world markets controlled almost 70 per cent of computer sales, 85 per cent of pesticides, and 86 per cent of telecommunications (HDR, 1999: 67). Likewise, ten companies have come to control two-thirds of the world semiconductor industry (Lang and Hines, 1993: 35–6). Meanwhile business in the issuance and secondary trading of debt instruments has become more and more concentrated in a small group of investment houses (ISMA, 1995: 10). By 1998, just three firms between them handled over 75 per cent of the value of worldwide M&A deals (*FT*, 29 January 1999: 1). In cross-border trade, as of the early 1990s, five companies accounted for 77 per cent of cereal shipments, and four companies covered 87 per cent of tobacco shipments. Meanwhile the top three companies in their respective sectors effected 80 per cent of the banana trade, 83 per cent of the cocoa trade, and 85 per cent of the tea trade (Madden, 1992: 46). Global chains owned almost a third of the world's hotel rooms in 1993, up from a quarter in 1989 (*FT*, 31 January 1997: 15). A few companies such as Associated Press, Reuters and Agence France Presse have dominated global news provision. Visa, MasterCard and American Express between them process 95 per cent of the world's credit card business (*FT*, 12 June 1996: 1). As of 1995, the five giants of the music industry controlled more than two-thirds of the $40 billion world market in recordings (*FT*, 2 September 1996: 21; 27 September 1996: X). Following several major mergers and acquisitions, the big four of accountancy firms (Deloitte Touche Tohmatsu, Ernst & Young, KPMG, PricewaterhouseCoopers) dominate across six continents.

In these circumstances, the largest 100 global companies (0.2 per cent of the total number) have controlled 12 per cent of total world FDI and 14 per cent of world sales by foreign affiliates (UNCTAD, 2004: xvii). The top 300 global firms have held anywhere between a quarter and a third of all corporate assets (Dunning, 1993: 15; Harvey, 1995: 189). The 15 largest global companies have each reached annual sales turnovers whose value exceeds the GDP of over 120 countries (Went, 1996: 18).

To be sure, some developments have gone against the prevailing trend towards concentration. Indeed, new technologies and new methods of management have encouraged a growth of small firms in some sectors, including computer software, Internet service providers and biotechnology. That said, these small companies have often conducted most of their transactions with large global concerns. To that extent their autonomy has been severely restricted.

Overall, the past half-century of intense globalization has yielded conditions of considerable oligopoly in the world economy. Indeed, many corporate leaders have assumed that only the largest companies in a sector can profit in a global market. The much-discussed 'pressures of global competition' have made governments and citizens more ready to allow 'their' corporate flag carriers to acquire an oligopolistic position. Meanwhile no global anti-trust or competition authorities have emerged to monitor and if necessary check this concentration, a point for future policy that is discussed in Chapter 12.

Conclusion

The analysis in this chapter (see the summary box) suggests that significant trends in capitalism have been not only a major cause, but also a chief consequence of globalization. Taking these developments in sum, it is clear that the growth of transplanetary and supraterritorial spaces has to date helped to widen the range of surplus accumulation and deepen the hold of capitalism in contemporary society. Alternative modes of production have arguably never been as weak in the world economy. In this light theses concerning 'late capitalism' and 'postcapitalism' seem decidedly misplaced.

Implications of globalization for production in summary

Expanded capitalist commodification

- continued growth of primary and industrial capital
- rise of consumer capital
- exponential expansion of finance capital
- development of information and communications capital
- emergence of genetic and atomic capital
- growth of care capital

Reorganization of surplus accumulation

- creation of profit-enhancing offshore arrangements
- proliferation of transworld corporate networks
- large waves of company mergers and acquisitions
- rise of global oligopolies

As elaborated in Chapter 9, the reinvigoration of capitalism through the growth of globality has been accompanied by considerable volatility and periodic crises. In addition, as specified in Chapter 10, the move from capitalism to hypercapitalism has exacerbated a number of inequalities between classes, countries, genders and races, as well as between urban and rural areas. Moreover, as seen in Chapter 11, so far the contemporary growth of transworld capitalism has tended to reduce democratic controls on economic policy. Yet these negative developments do little to suggest a decline of capitalism as a structure of production. Surplus accumulation has continued robustly, however unstable and unjust the circumstances may have been for many individuals, firms and governments. Hence for the time being analysis should concentrate not on risks that globalization might pose to the survival of capitalism, but on harms that globalizing processes of surplus accumulation can do, particularly to vulnerable social circles.

Chapter 6

Globalization and Governance: From Statism to Polycentrism

Main points of this chapter
The obsolescence of statism
The reconstructed state
Multi-scalar public governance
Privatized governance
(Global) civil society
Conclusion

Main points of this chapter

- contemporary large-scale and accelerated globalization has rendered the statist mode of governance non-viable and encouraged the emergence of polycentric (multi-sited and networked) regulation
- states remain crucial nodes in this polycentric governance, although globalization has spurred several important shifts in their attributes
- globalization has opened considerable possibilities for substate (municipal and provincial) authorities to engage directly with realms beyond their state
- inadequacies of the state as a sole site for governance of global relations have promoted a growth of suprastate (macro-regional and transworld) sites of regulation
- dominant neoliberalist policy frameworks in contemporary globalization have encouraged a major expansion of private sites of governance
- civil society activity has followed the trend from statism to polycentrism by shifting its focus from the state alone to a multi-scalar diffuse governance apparatus

Alongside, and often in close relation with, shifts in the social structure of production, contemporary globalization – and the rise of supraterritoriality more particularly – has also encouraged a number of changes in the organization of governance in the contemporary world. Territorialism as the previously prevailing framework of social space was closely interlinked with statism as the previously prevailing mode of regulation. Hence a move away from territorialism in geography has, not surprisingly, unfolded together with a move away from statism in governance. As a result, society in today's more global world is regulated in what can be termed a polycentric manner.

'Statism' refers here to a condition where societal governance is more or less equivalent to the regulatory operations of territorial bureaucratic national governments. In statist circumstances, all formulation, implementation, monitoring and enforcement of societal rules occurs more or less directly through the state and inter-state relations. Under statist governance, macro-regional and global regulatory mechanisms are small in scale, if present at all, and fall more or less completely under the thumb of country governments. Likewise, in a statist mode of governance local governments have no significant autonomy from central governments regarding national policy questions. Moreover, local authorities in a statist situation lack substantial possibilities to engage directly with the wider world outside their state. In short, as the term suggests, statism entails governance that is for all intents and purposes reducible to the state.

Following – and spurred on by – half a century of accelerated globalization and growing supraterritorial connections, statist conditions no longer mark governance today. To be sure, country governments remain major and indispensable sites of regulation in the contemporary more global world. The end of stat*ism* in no way entails the end of the state itself. However, governance now also involves suprastate (regional and transworld) regimes that operate with some autonomy from the state. In addition, many substate (municipal and provincial) governments today engage directly with spheres beyond their country.

In other words, governance in the more global world of the twenty-first century has become distinctly multi-layered and trans-scalar. Regulation occurs at – and through interconnections among – municipal, provincial, national, macro-regional and global sites. No single 'level' reigns over the others, as occurred with the primacy of the state over suprastate and substate institutions in territorialist circumstances. Instead, governance tends to be diffuse, emanating from multiple locales at once, with points and lines of authority that are not always clear.

The dispersal of governance in contemporary history has occurred not only across different layers and scales of social relations from the local to the global, but also with the emergence of various regulatory mechanisms in private quarters alongside those in the public sector. Many rules for global companies, global finance, global communications, global ecology and other global matters have been devised and administered through nongovernmental arrangements. Although this private governance has generally depended on support, or at least tolerance, from government agencies, it too has maintained substantial autonomy from the state.

This situation of multi-scalar and diffuse governance might be called 'polycentrism', to denote its distinctive feature of emanating from multiple interconnected sites. Polycentrism is not the only possible name for this situation, of course. For example, Michael Hardt and Antonio Negri have invoked the term 'empire' to describe 'a decentered and deterritorializing apparatus of rule that progressively incorporates the entire global realm' (Hardt and Negri, 2000: xii). John Keane has introduced the concept of 'cosmocracy' to denote a 'much messier' and 'far more complex type of polity' with 'multiplying, highly mobile and intersecting lines of governmental powers' (Keane, 2003: 98). Other analysts have for their part referred to a 'new medievalism' to designate conditions where, as in the European Middle Ages, multiple authorities operating on different scales exercise overlapping and sometimes conflicting competences over the same realms (Bull, 1977: 254–5, 264–76; Anderson, 1996; Kobrin, 1998a; Friedrichs, 2001). Or one can describe a 'new multilateralism' or a 'plurilateralism' involving both states and non-state actors (Cerny, 1993; R.W. Cox, 1997; Schechter, 1999a, b). Another alternative is to speak of 'networked governance' or 'netocracy', where regulation occurs through webs of interconnected agencies (cf. Rhodes, 1997; Reinicke, 1999–2000; Stone, 2004). James Rosenau has talked of 'mobius-web governance' with intricate and overlapping dynamics among multiple levels of regulatory authority (2003: 396–7).

Polycentrism seems the least problematic of these labels. 'Empire' has existed in such diverse forms in so many historical contexts that the word does not easily evoke something distinctive about governance in the present-day more global world. The term 'cosmocracy' and the related 'cosmopolitics' (Archibugi, 2003) could be read to imply: (a) that the larger, global scale has primacy over other spheres, possibly with a tendency towards world government; and (b) that the inhabitants of this polity have overriding cosmopolitan impulses towards universal human solidarity and global citizenship. Yet neither of these conditions holds today. The notion of 'new medievalism' is objectionable since, apart from superficial similarity in the broadest outlines of the governance structure, there is very little of the medieval in the twenty-first century. The phrase 'networked governance' captures important qualities of the contemporary poststatist mode of regulation, but this name perhaps tends to overplay the significance of the links relative to the nodes, overemphasizing the connections between agencies relative to the agencies themselves. In contrast, 'polycentrism' both captures the multi-sited character of current governance and invites an exploration of the interplay between sites.

The rest of this chapter further elaborates the shift from statism of an earlier era to polycentrism as the prevailing mode of governance in the twenty-first century. The first section below indicates how contemporary large-scale globalization – and the rise of supraterritoriality more particularly – have rendered statist regulation non-viable. The second section shows how globalization has not undermined the state, but rather repositioned it in certain important respects. The third section explains the recent growth of multi-scalar public governance (with transborder relations between substate authorities and a proliferation of macro-regional and global institutions) as largely a response to inadequacies of the state as the sole site for governance of global relations. The fourth section reviews the expansion of private regulatory arrangements as a consequence of rapid contemporary globalization and its prevailing neoliberalist policy orientation. The fifth and final section notes that the shift from statism to polycentrism has prompted changes in the object of civil society activity away from the state alone to a multi-scalar and diffuse governance apparatus.

The obsolescence of statism

The statist mode of governance peaked between the mid-nineteenth to the mid-twentieth century. At this point territorial bureaucratic centralized states reigned supreme over the vast majority of humanity, including through state-based colonial empires. Governance through local councils, religious orders and market actors was everywhere superseded by or subordinated to regulation through the state. States supplied rules to govern pretty well every aspect of social relations: money, language, armed violence, sexual behaviour, employment, formal education, health standards, heritage, nature conservancy, etc.

World politics in this statist era was very much an international (or, to be more precise, inter-state) system. Provincial and municipal authorities had no significant transstate relations. Suprastate regionalism did not exist apart from a few international river commissions. A few small and minimally resourced international organizations showed but the faintest trappings of global governance. The situation fell very much into what international relations theorists have typically called a 'Westphalian' mould, after the 1648 Peace of Westphalia that formalized the modern concept of a system of sovereign states.

Westphalian sovereignty held that each state would exercise supreme, comprehensive, unqualified and exclusive rule over its territorial jurisdiction. With supreme rule, the Westphalian sovereign state would answer to no other authority; it always had the final say in respect of its territorial realm and its cross-border relations with other countries. With comprehensive rule, the Westphalian sovereign state governed all areas of social life. With unqualified and absolute rule, Westphalian sovereign states respected a norm of non-intervention in one another's territorial jurisdictions. With exclusive and unilateral rule, the Westphalian sovereign state did not share governance over its realm with any other party.

Since the mid-twentieth century, accelerated globalization and the rise of supraterritorial connectivity have made Westphalian constructions of state sovereignty obsolete. Westphalian practices of sovereignty depended on a territorialist geography where all social transactions occur at fixed locations: either within territorial jurisdictions, or at designated points across tightly patrolled territorial borders. However, supraterritorial circumstances cannot be fixed in a territorial space over which a state might aim to exercise absolute control. An era of large-scale globality does not allow a state – even the most highly endowed state – to exercise supreme, comprehensive, unqualified and exclusive rule over its territorial domain. Indeed, on many occasions transplanetary relations influence circumstances in a country without ever directly touching its soil.

Many material conditions in the current globalizing world have made statist governance unviable. Computerized data transmissions, radio broadcasts, satellite remote sensing and telephone calls do not halt at customs posts. Moreover, such communications occur: (a) at speeds that make it difficult for state surveillance to detect them in advance; and (b) in quantities that a state, even with greatly enhanced capacities, cannot comprehensively track. Even a long-time arch-sceptic of globalization theses has conceded that Internet use by transborder criminal networks presents states with major challenges (Krasner, 2001). Electronic mass media have also detracted from a state's dominion over language construction and education. Nor can a state exercise complete authority over transplanetary associations or global companies. In addition, as detailed below, many regulations now come to the state from suprastate bodies and global law rather than from that state itself. Likewise, governments intervene in, rather than control, global trade. How can the Maritime and Port Authority of Singapore possibly inspect the 18.5 million containers that crossed its wharves in 2003 (MPA, 2004)? With the development of global currencies, credit cards and the like, even the most powerful state has lost unqualified authority over money supplies and exchange rates. Nor can a state successfully assert supreme and exclusive rule over the global financial flows that pass through its jurisdiction (or do they?). Electronic commerce, intra-firm trade, offshore financial centres, derivatives, and hedge funds have all substantially compromised state abilities to raise tax revenues (Tanzi, 2000). Transworld ecological developments such as ozone depletion and biodiversity loss have similarly contradicted the material territorialist preconditions of statist governance.

Contemporary globalization and the rise of supraterritoriality have also loosened crucial affective underpinnings of statism (in ways that are detailed in Chapter 7). On the one hand, the new geography has advanced various nonterritorial identities and solidarities. Transworld bonds on lines such as class, disability, gender, profession, race, religion and sexual orientation have diluted, rivalled and sometimes also overridden feelings of national community that have in the past so buttressed statist governance. At the same time, contemporary globalization has also often reinvigorated more localized solidarities. When faced with a seemingly vast, intangible and uncontrollable globality, many people have turned away from the state to their local 'home' in hopes of enhancing their possibilities of community and self-determination (Strassoldo, 1992). In addition, citizens and governors alike have in general become increasingly ready to give values such as economic growth, human rights and ecological integrity – none of which is strictly bound to territory – a higher priority than loyalty to the state.

On both material and ideational counts, then, contemporary large-scale globalization – and its supraterritorial aspects in particular – have contradicted and subverted the statist mode of governance. In this light various authors have observed that the world has moved into 'the twilight of sovereignty' or 'beyond sovereignty' (Soroos, 1986; Wriston, 1992). These commentators have noted that 'sovereignty is no longer sacrosanct' or 'has lost much of its relevance' (Chopra and Weiss, 1992; Lapidoth, 1992: 345). The Westphalian notion of sovereignty has indeed become obsolescent (Czempiel and Rosenau, 1989; Rosenau and Czempiel, 1992).

Other analysts have argued that sovereignty has not ended but rather taken new form to fit poststatist conditions (cf. Williams, 1996; Clark, 1999: ch 4; Cohen, 2001; Osiander, 2001; Krasner, 2003). These theorists rightly emphasize that key ideas and practices like sovereignty are social constructs that evolve as historical contexts change (Onuf, 1991; Biersteker and Weber, 1996; Sørensen, 1999). In this regard some commentators have spoken of emergent 'partial' or 'shrunken' sovereignty, as states surrender their prerogatives in certain areas. Other observers have introduced notions of 'limited', 'qualified' and 'semi' sovereignty, as states acquire numerous legal commitments to regional and global regimes. Or analysts have coined phrases concerning 'pooled' and 'shared' sovereignty, in respect of various instances like the EU where regulation is undertaken jointly among states. The head of the WHO has promoted the idea of 'enlightened sovereignty', where states cede control in areas subject to universally agreed norms and values (Brundtland, 2000). Global environmental problems might elicit a 'greening of sovereignty' (Litfin, 1998; also Schrijver, 1997). Still other scholars have reconceptualized sovereignty to mean a state's 'capacity to manage', thereby removing inferences of unilateral, supreme and unconditional rule (cf. Gelber, 1997: xi). Yet whether one abandons or refashions the concept of sovereignty, it is clear that the statist conditions to which sovereignty referred in the past are gone.

True, even in statist times practice sometimes fell short of the Westphalian principle of sovereignty (Krasner, 1999; Teschke, 2003). For example, many states at one time or another undertook military invasions and covert interventions into foreign jurisdictions. Westphalian states also never enjoyed full control of cross-border movements of money (Helleiner, 1999). In addition, colonial administrations sometimes exercised only limited control over peripheral districts of their claimed territory. Meanwhile weaker states often lacked the resources to make good their legal pretensions to absolute control over their territorial jurisdiction. And a scattering of religious universalists, liberal cosmopolitans and Marxist internationalists rejected the Westphalian principle of sovereign statehood on moral grounds long before the onset of contemporary intense globalization.

In spite of these earlier challenges, however, Westphalian sovereign statehood remained hypothetically realizable in the territorialist world of old. A state could, by strengthening its means, graduate from mere legal sovereignty to approximate full substantive sovereignty. Major states could generally make good their claims to supreme, comprehensive, unqualified and exclusive governance over a designated territorial space. Moreover, the principle of sovereign statehood enjoyed largely unquestioned acceptance in Westphalian times. The few cosmopolitans around were normally dismissed as misguided utopians.

Yet today, amidst large-scale globality (and widespread supraterritoriality more particularly), statist constructions of sovereignty cannot be made operative, whatever the resources that a country government has at its disposal. Although a number of technological developments have greatly enhanced capacities for state surveillance and intervention, these innovations have not kept pace with rises in global mobility. For example, determined Internet users can find ways to circumvent state-controlled firewalls and service providers (as in China). No amount of unilateral state mobilization can halt climate change at the border, or monitor all electronic financial transfers, or locate every undocumented worker.

That said, states are anything but impotent in the face of contemporary globalization. The end of Westphalian state sovereignty has not marked the end of state power. On the contrary, as noted in Chapter 4, states have ranked among the prime forces that have generated the major acceleration of globalization in recent decades. Moreover, governments can shape the effects of globalization on their territories and populations: with fiscal policies, monetary policies, consumer policies, labour policies, environmental policies, data protection policies, and so on. Arguably many governments have not used their full room for manoeuvre in respect of globalization (McQuaig, 1999). Indeed, many politicians have sought to escape responsibility for their own policy failures by blaming a purported juggernaut of globalization.

Stronger states in particular can substantially influence transplanetary and supraterritorial activities and indeed exploit the new geography to considerable advantage. For example, the US government has become a sole 'superpower' in good part thanks to its use of global rules and institutions, global money, global finance and global military operations. Arguably major states – such as those of the OECD and the Group of Seven (G7) – have in fact gained new power as they have lost traditional sovereignty.

In contrast, weaker states have tended to lose relative power in the face of expanded globality. Clearly, for example, the Japanese state has generally been able to exert far more influence in global spaces than the Bolivian state. The authorities in Burkina Faso or El Salvador have had very limited capacities to manage global flows in regard to their respective countries, with but a handful of relevant experts and hardly any of the necessary equipment and data. Indeed, with cruel irony most new, postcolonial states (established in the time of accelerated globalization and the major rise of supraterritoriality) obtained Westphalian sovereignty in name at the very moment that the principle ceased to be realizable in practice.

But none of this has meant the end of the state. Although, as noted in Chapter 1, a number of commentators have linked contemporary globalization to a retreat or even demise of the state, these death notices have been recklessly premature. Yes, recent decades have witnessed several striking implosions of government, for example, in Lebanon and Somalia. In addition, several states like ex-Czechoslovakia, Eritrea/Ethiopia, the former Soviet Union, and Yugoslavia have fragmented. Yet states threatened with collapse have almost invariably survived, and recompositions of states have been the stuff of world politics for centuries. None of these developments point to the death of the state as such.

Thus, just as territoriality has remained important with the passing of territorialism, so states have remained important with the passing of statism. Whatever new world order might be emerging in the course of contemporary globalization, the state remains a significant part of it (Weiss, 1998; Sørensen, 2004). There is no basis to assumptions that globality and the state are inherently contradictory. States remain prominent players in contemporary governance and show no sign of disappearing in the foreseeable future.

The reconstructed state

Yet to conclude that the state persists – and persists prominently – in contemporary times of large-scale accelerated globalization is not to conclude that the state remains the same. As many a political theorist has stressed, the state has never in its history been fixed. It is perpetually 'in motion, evolving, adapting, incorporating . . . always in some condition of transition' (Jarvis and Paolini, 1995: 5–6).

The accelerated growth of transplanetary connectivity over the past half-century has promoted several significant shifts in the character of the state. One change, the end of sovereignty in its Westphalian incarnation, has already been elaborated above. In addition, states have had to develop new capacities to address global matters such as ecological change, electronic finance, human rights, and transworld production. Other features of post-Westphalian statehood, discussed in further detail below, include: (a) reorientations of states to serve global as well as national constituencies; (b) adjustments to state provisions of social welfare; (c) altered features of warfare; and (d) increased transstate connections in regulatory processes.

Turns towards global constituencies

Contemporary globalization has encouraged increased complexity in respect of the constituencies that states serve. The territorialist state of old generally represented so-called 'domestic' or 'national' interests. It sought to advance the pursuits of its citizens in the wider world and to defend them against harmful so-called 'external' or 'foreign' intrusions. To be sure, Westphalian states often favoured the interests of certain sectors of their resident population more than others, for example, particular classes, religious denominations or ethnic groups. However, such privileged constituencies almost always lay within the given state's territory and among its citizens.

Under the influence of contemporary globalization, states have become less consistent in holding a territorial line of defence of their 'inside' against their 'outside'. States no longer always clearly promote 'domestic' interests against those of 'foreigners'. Instead, states in a more global world have tended to become arenas of collaboration and competition between a complex array of national and transnational players.

To take one prominent example, contemporary states have often served the interests of global capital in addition to (and sometimes ahead of) national capital. (Needless to say, global capital here includes not only 'foreign'-based enterprises, but also 'home'-based concerns with transworld operations.) Much contemporary state policy has thereby addressed the needs of global production chains, transplanetary financial markets, supraterritorial mass media operations, transworld telecommunications companies, and so on. Many governments have feared that, if they do not provide sufficiently appealing and predictable taxation and regulation environments, footloose global capital will desert them. For instance, in 1995 alone 65 states liberalized their rules governing foreign direct investment (HDR, 1999: 29; see also UNCTAD, 2004). Likewise, many governments have offered subsidies and reduced corporate tax rates in scarcely disguised interstate tax competition for mobile global business (Tanzi, 1996). Offshore privileges of the kind described in Chapter 5 are another symptom of the tendency for contemporary states to serve global capital. In addition, some states (or parts of states) have collaborated in the illicit business of global criminal networks.

On the judicial side of government, various global actors have increasingly used national courts, sometimes also in regard to situations outside the territorial jurisdiction of the state in question. For example, many transworld companies have gone to US-based courts regarding alleged violations of patent rights outside the USA. In another case, human rights groups sought to indict former President Augusto Pinochet for abuses in Chile through the Spanish courts. (For more on extraterritorial jurisdiction of state courts, see Akehurst, 1972–3; Born, 1996; Lowenfeld, 2002.)

The above remarks are not meant to suggest that states have prostrated themselves before transworld companies, with no attention for 'internal' business interests. On the contrary, many states have responded to contemporary globalization with intensified commercial protectionism in respect of certain 'domestic' sectors (agriculture, steel and textiles are prominent examples). Indeed, the contemporary state has often been a site of struggle between territorial and supraterritorial capital. For example, even the radically neoliberalist Thatcher Government prevaricated in the face of Nestlé's 1988 takeover of a 'British' institution, Rowntree Mackintosh. Likewise, Vodafone's proposed purchase of Mannesmann in 2000 initially sparked nationalistic opposition in Germany, although the agitation quickly dissipated when it was realized that Mannesmann shares already lay largely in non-German hands.

Post-Westphalian states have sometimes also sided with other types of global constituents besides firms. For example, many governments in the South have taken heed of the priorities of global economic institutions, foundations and NGOs when designing and executing development policies. In terms of social movements, the Iranian state after 1979 gave extensive support to Islamicists across the planet. Other states have from time to time carried the banner for global environmentalism or for a global human rights campaign. For instance, in 1995 the Danish, German and Swedish governments joined transworld protests by environmentalists against Royal Dutch/Shell's plan to sink the Brent Spar oil platform in the North Atlantic. Likewise, many states backed global civil society campaigns against apartheid rule in South Africa.

In short, with increased globalization the clientele of governments has become increasingly global as well. National-territorial constituencies remain very important, but *raison d'état* has become more than *raison de la nation*. A state's attempts to serve both country-based and global interests can breed ambiguous policy, particularly when the two constituencies conflict.

Pressures on state welfarism

Greater state orientation towards global constituencies is a fairly indisputable consequence of greater transplanetary connections in contemporary society. However, a second issue, the implications of greater globality for state provision and regulation of social welfare, is far more debateable (cf. Esping-Andersen, 1994; M. Rhodes, 1996; Bowles and Wagman, 1997; Baker *et al.*, 1998; Yeates, 1999, 2001; Alber and Standing, 2000; Swank, 2002; Södersten, 2004). On the one hand, many analysts have argued that the growth of transworld relations has put (or could be expected to put) considerable downward pressures on state guarantees of social protection (Teeple, 1995; Gray, 1998; Stryker, 1998; Mishra, 1999). On this line of argument, the welfare state and progressive social reform would be the casualty of a 'race to the bottom' of government interventions in the market economy. In contrast, other researchers have argued that states (especially stronger states in the North) have far more discretion in their choices regarding social policy in a globalizing world. Such governments can, if they so decide, sustain considerable programmes of social welfare (Garrett, 1998; Rodrik, 1998; Hirst and Thompson, 1999; Yeates, 2001; Clift, 2003).

The history of states during the half-century prior to the onset of accelerated globalization was in good part a case of growing public-sector guarantees of nutrition, health care, housing, education, minimum income and other human welfare needs. At the same time, many states introduced regimes of progressive taxation to effect a substantial redistribution of wealth among their resident populations. Such programmes of state-centred social reform unfolded (in different ways and to different extents) across the planet: North and South, East and West. A number of circumstances encouraged this trend, including the spread of universal suffrage in national politics, pressures from organized labour, the global communist movement, and promises made by governing élites to suffering masses during the world wars and decolonization struggles.

In contrast, the last decades of the twentieth century saw considerable attenuation of state-supplied welfare guarantees and other measures for progressive redistribution. 'Transition economies' in Eastern Europe and the former Soviet Union experienced major declines in state provision of social services and large increases of social inequalities. 'Opening up' the economy to private market activity under surviving communist regimes in China and Vietnam also went hand in hand with growing welfare gaps. Across the South, postcolonial socialist projects gave way to 'structural adjustment' in the direction of liberalized markets and less direct state provision and regulation of welfare programmes (Rudra, 2002). Would-be social reformers like Museveni in Uganda or Lula in Brazil have, once in state office, tempered or abandoned programmes to increase state-supplied welfare and state-led redistribution. In the North, Britain under Thatcher, the USA under Reagan, and New Zealand under Lange pursued especially severe reversals of state guarantees of welfare needs in the 1980s. In addition, François Mitterand, failed as President of France in the early 1980s to resurrect policies of nationalization and

Keynesian demand stimulation. Even governments in Scandinavia, after largely resisting pressures to retrench during the 1980s, scaled back their public welfare measures in the 1990s (Geyer *et al.*, 2000). Almost no government anywhere in the world of the early twenty-first century dares openly to pursue a major programme of progressive redistribution of wealth to finance expanded state guarantees of social welfare.

Instead, responsibilities for the provision of education, health care, housing, pensions, and the like have tended to shift from the state to non-state actors. There are exceptions, for instance, where statutory health insurance has been substantially extended in Costa Rica, South Korea and Tunisia. However, in many more countries citizens have been encouraged to supplement or supplant public health and pension programmes with private commercial schemes. At the same time many states have contracted out much delivery of social services to NGOs. In addition, families (and particularly women) have often been expected to fill in welfare gaps left by the failures and omissions of states (Dalla Costa and Dalla Costa, 1993).

This general retreat from state-led progressive social reform has unfolded concurrently with major growth in transplanetary and supraterritorial relations. Does this correlation imply that the two trends are causally connected? Certainly some links can be discerned. As noted in earlier chapters, opportunities to escape the profit-constraining corporatist welfare state have provided considerable impetus to the globalization of capital. In response, many governments have told their citizens that cuts in higher rates of tax and reductions of costly social protections are necessary steps to face 'global competition'.

Has globalization limited the state's ability to raise tax revenues needed to pay for more generous social guarantees? Opinion on this point is divided. Some analysts have suggested that globalization has undermined the fiscal capacities of states (McKenzie and Lee, 1991; Steinmo, 1994). Other studies have argued that so-called 'big government' can be quite compatible with globalization (Rodrik, 1998; Garrett, 2001) and that taxation of business remains as viable as ever (Swank, 1998). Both sides in this debate have tended to define globalization as liberalization, so that the argument concerns the consequences of certain policies towards globalization rather than globality (as transplanetary connectivity) per se. In this sense the implications of greater transworld relations for state guarantees of welfare are perhaps more a question of policy choice than the new geography as such. Needless to say, stronger and wealthier states have far more scope to make such choices than weaker and poorer states, so that globalization would sooner constrain government fiscal positions in the South than in the North.

In any case it would be overly simplistic to attribute developments in Northern welfare states entirely to globalization. Quite apart from increased transplanetary relations, other demographic, economic and political conditions were already putting substantial strains on social programmes in most OECD countries by the last quarter of the twentieth century. Circumstances like ageing populations, altered family patterns, transformations in labour markets, government budget deficits, increased costs of health care, and the rise of neoliberalist ideology all presented challenges to social welfare policies built up through Northern states during the so-called 'golden age' of 1945–75. Hence, although pressures from globally mobile capital for lower taxation and reduced regulatory constraints created additional problems for Northern welfare states in the late twentieth century, substantial difficulties existed anyhow.

Moreover, governments of the North have responded to pressures on the welfare state in diverse ways and to varying extents. For example, strongly neoliberalist regimes in Australia and the USA have retrenched more severely, while more social democratic governments in Denmark and the Netherlands have maintained comparatively high state-supplied social protections. In other words, to understand the impact of globalization on a given welfare state it is necessary to examine national particularities like electoral politics, cultural traditions, and the relations between state, labour and business in a given country (Esping-Anderson, 1996; M. Rhodes, 1996; Garrett, 1998; Geyer, 1998; Yeates, 1999; Weiss, 2003).

In any case, cuts in state guarantees of social protections should not be exaggerated, particularly in respect of the North. In fact, in EU countries social expenditure as a percentage of GDP remained broadly steady during the 1980s and 1990s, and at considerably higher levels than in the 1960s. In some respects people in the North have sometimes perceived a decline of the welfare state, when it may actually be their expectations of still greater public provision of pensions, health care, education, housing and other social services that have been disappointed.

Outside the North, too, there could be greater room for manoeuvre on state welfare policies than is often imagined. It may transpire that, with time, governments in 'transition countries' can improve their provisions of social protection in a more global world. In the South, economic restructuring programmes have increasingly incorporated so-called 'social safety nets' since the 1990s, with the aim of reducing the worst pains for poor and disadvantaged people. Indeed, in 1999 the IMF and the World Bank changed the label of what had until then been called 'structural adjustment programmes' to 'poverty reduction strategies'. It is a matter of dispute how far the new name has brought different substance with it, but the shift has at least given explicit acknowledgement of a need for social policy delivered through states.

Finally, there are cases where globalization appears actually to have promoted growth of state welfare programmes. For example, many governments have expanded education and training budgets on the argument that such spending will enhance their country's competitive position in global markets. In a more specific case, the Republic of Korea responded to pressures of globalization, including in particular the Asia financial crisis of the late 1990s, with increases in state-supplied social protection (Lee, 1999: 34–7; Kwon, 2000).

In sum, then, globalization has had complex implications for state guarantees of social welfare. Depending on the specific circumstances, growing global relations can have the effect of contracting, reorienting, or expanding state delivery of social protections. In any of these scenarios, however, globalization is but one of several relevant factors. Wider macroeconomic conditions, national institutions, and political choices also figure importantly in determining the fate of state welfare programmes in a more global world.

Altered patterns of warfare

Next to welfare, contemporary globalization has also had implications for warfare. Preparation for and engagement in organized armed violence was a major spur to the early formation of Westphalian states and subsequently also remained one of their chief preoccupations (Shaw, 1984; Mann, 1988; Tilly, 1990). That said, the means and purposes of state war-making have shifted over time. The large spread of global relations in recent decades has encouraged several further such changes in relation to the post-Westphalian state (Sørensen, 2004: ch 7).

For one thing, unprecedented levels of globality in contemporary history have reduced some incentives for interstate warfare. With its focus on territorial conquest, war has limited utility for the capture of supraterritorial resources. Armed operations by land, sea and air are not terribly effective ways to gain control of the Internet, electronic finance, transworld production chains, global consumer markets, transplanetary ecological trends, or global governance regimes. Of course, states may continue to pursue warfare for territorially based objectives like securing access to natural resources or overthrowing country governments, but conventional armies are poor tools in relation to supraterritorial phenomena.

Indeed, interstate warfare arguably serves little purpose for governments and social circles that have become deeply intertwined with one another through global relations. States have little reason to embark on war against each other – and on the contrary have every reason to avoid armed conflict – when they host the same global companies, promote the same global currencies, support the same global élites, enjoy the same global entertainments, collaborate in the same global governance regimes, and so on. In this light Martin Shaw has suggested that the end of warfare between advanced industrial states reflects their transformation into a relatively coherent single Western state conglomerate (Shaw, 2000). Thus perhaps it is no accident that states with McDonald's outlets in their jurisdictions have only once gone to war against each other. Even in the single exception to this rule, the Kosovo War of 1999, the six McDonald's restaurants in Belgrade only closed during the hostilities between Serbian and NATO forces and quickly reopened after the ceasefire (*New York Times*, 2 July 1999).

While the rise of global connectivity may in certain respects have discouraged *inter*-state warfare, it has in other ways encouraged states to pursue greater *inward* application of armed violence (Kaldor, 1999; Shaw, 2000; Hironaka, 2004). All but three of the 61 major armed conflicts recorded between 1989 and 1998 were civil wars (HDR, 1999: 5; Wallensteen and Sollenberg, 2000). Many of these cases have involved the suppression of micro-nationalist strivings or religious resurgence movements, both of which have, for reasons elaborated in Chapters 7 and 8, often been fed by globalization (Gurr, 1994, 2000). On various other occasions states have unleashed armed force to secure the position of global companies, the implementation of structural adjustment programmes, or the privileges of an exploitative local élite that puts greater stakes in global economics and politics than in its purported 'homeland'.

In addition, as already noted in Chapter 2, recent globalization has brought changes to the conduct of war, including new kinds of weapons (like long-range fighter aircraft) and new kinds of operations (like rapid reaction forces). With chief reliance on precision bombing, NATO forces suffered not a single troop casualty in the Kosovo War. Meanwhile the recent 'war on terrorism' has involved satellite remote sensing, monitoring of bank accounts, and hacking into computers as much as armed combat.

So large-scale globalization has by no means heralded the end of militarization. The state in a more global world is anything but a postmilitary state. On the contrary, globalization has given states military equipment of unprecedented sophistication and destructive potential. Although world military expenditures declined for several years after the dissolution of the Soviet Union, by 2000 they had risen once again to $800 billion (FPIF, 2002). The events of 11 September 2001 have stimulated still further remilitarization. Hence the post-Westphalian state has not abjured warfare so much as pursued it differently.

Increased transstate relations

So far this discussion of states in an increasingly global world has mainly considered the state acting individually: how it deals with constituents; how it does or does not provide social protections; how it engages in warfare. But contemporary globalization has also affected the ways that states act collectively. As noted earlier, large-scale transplanetary connections and the pronounced growth of supraterritorial relations have made *unilateral* state control of territorial jurisdictions impossible in many important fields of policy, yet *joint* efforts by states can often have considerable effects in regulating globality and its consequences. As discussed in the next section, much of this multilateralism has developed through macro-regional and global regimes with permanent suprastate agencies. In addition, however, considerable multilateral governance has grown in recent decades more informally (and often outside the public eye) through transstate regulatory processes.

Others have termed these transstate connections 'transgovernmental relations' or 'government networks' (Keohane and Nye, 1977; Slaughter, 2000, 2004). In these instances, officials holding similar functions in different states interact with each other on matters of common concern. Such transstate information sharing and policy coordination generally occurs without formal treaties or permanent suprastate secretariats.

Interstate exchanges between heads of government, diplomatic services and armed forces go back to the earliest days of modern national governments, of course. However, in contemporary history transstate networks have also developed across a much wider span of the government apparatus. For example, justice ministries and police from different states now often collaborate to combat transborder criminal activities. Judges and human rights commissioners from different country jurisdictions meet to exchange experiences. Securities and insurance supervisors from multiple states consult in their oversight of (increasingly globalized) financial markets. Environmental regulators from various governments cooperate in respect of ecological problems that transcend state boundaries. Defence, trade and foreign ministry officials from different states collaborate in non-proliferation export control regimes like the Nuclear Suppliers Group and the Missile Technology Control Regime in respect of materials that could be used to produce weapons of mass destruction (Joyner, 2004). Health officials from numerous states work together on transplanetary disease control, while immigration services from different states collaborate on asylum and refugee issues. Other transstate networks respectively link central bankers, intellectual property regulators, labour officials, and parliamentarians.

The scale of this transgovernmental activity should not be underestimated. Innumerable state bureaucrats maintain daily telephone and email contact with their counterparts in other states. To take a more particular illustration, around 40,000 country officials convene each year around issue-based committees and working groups of the OECD in Paris.

Probably the most pronounced manifestation of transstate governance to date has been the G7/8 process (Hajnal, 1999; Hodges *et al.*, 1999; Bayne, 2000; Kirton *et al.*, 2001; G8, 2004). This transgovernmental collaboration on global economic, financial and later also wider questions started as a Group of Five in 1975, soon expanded to the G7, and became the Group of Eight (G8) with the addition of Russia in 1998. Begun as a summit for heads of government, the G7 established a separate finance ministers group in 1986 that normally meets 3–4 times per year. Between summits and ministerial meetings, considerable G7/8 activity takes place outside public view between senior officials of the respective governments.

Other 'Gs' in transstate relations include the Group of Twenty (G20), created in 1999 as an expansion of the G7 finance ministers to include representatives from so-called 'emerging markets' like Brazil, South Korea and South Africa. The Group of Ten (G10) central bank governors from advanced industrial countries have met regularly at Basel since 1962 to discuss monetary and financial matters of common concern. An Intergovernmental Group of Twenty-Four on International Monetary Affairs (G24) was established in the early 1970s as a South-based counterpart to the G10, although it has had far less policy impact (Mayobre, 1999). Meanwhile the Group of Seventy-Seven (G77), started in 1964 and now in fact numbering 133 states, has linked governments of the South on questions of the global economy more generally.

Whereas inter-state cooperation of the past normally took formal shape in treaties, much of contemporary transstate governance has no basis in conventional international law. At most, the collaboration is set down in a memorandum of understanding (MOU) among the officials concerned. In contrast to treaties, these MOUs do not require ratification by legislative bodies, so that transstate relations can easily become technocratic networks that operate outside democratic oversight.

Indeed, transgovernmental networks can tend to disaggregate and fragment the state. A Westphalian state conducted its foreign policy in a relatively coordinated manner through a single department of external affairs. In contrast, the state in a more global world engages with other states through multiple ministries, regulatory agencies, legislatures and courts, all of which can come to operate with considerable autonomy from each other. In some cases transministerial cooperation among states can be greater than interministerial collaboration within the same state. Transgovernmental activities may also increase divisions within states. For instance, in the United Nations Environment Programme (UNEP) environment ministers from around the world have regularly complained about their difficulties with economics ministers. Likewise, officials from finance ministries and central banks have often found more commonality of views among themselves in G7/G10/G20 circles than with other departments of their respective states. In such cases global concerns and connections have loosened the cohesiveness of the state.

In sum, as the preceding pages have indicated, accelerated globalization of the past half-century has promoted some significant shifts in the character of the state: different kinds of constituencies; different kinds of welfare and warfare; and different kinds of interstate relations. Intense globalization has not meant the end of the state, which is as entrenched in social life as ever; however, it has meant a transition from Westphalian to post-Westphalian statehood.

Multi-scalar public governance

As previously emphasized, the story of governance in the contemporary globalizing world does not end with the state. The move from Westphalian to post-Westphalian states is only one aspect of the larger structural shift from statism to polycentrism. Not only have states themselves become more decentred and fragmented in current governance, as seen with the rise of transstate relations. In addition, regulation under conditions of intense globalization has been increasingly diffused from states to other sites 'above' and 'below' the country government. This has created a multi-scalar and (inasmuch as the layers are densely interconnected) trans-scalar situation.

Globalization has furthered this dispersion of public-sector governance in three principal ways. First, as already discussed, the rapid contemporary growth of global (and especially supraterritorial) relations has made country-based statist regulation impracticable. Other institutions at municipal, provincial, macro-regional and transworld levels have moved in to fill the many resultant gaps in effective governance. Second, globalization has involved a number of problems (global health issues, global environmental changes, etc.) in which substate and suprastate agencies may hold a comparative advantage over states, or at least an important complementary role. Third, the growth of global communications, global travel, global organization, global finance, global law and global consciousness has provided substate and suprastate authorities with infrastructures and mindsets to sustain their operations, including many activities that bypass states.

Indeed, many substate and suprastate governance arrangements have acquired relative autonomy from states. In other words, these bodies now often take their own initiatives in regulating a more global world and are not wholly subordinated to states. Weaker states in particular have become liable to influence and sometimes even outright domination by public governance agencies at other levels. The power of regional and global financial institutions in much of the South is a well-known example. On the other hand, the autonomy of substate and suprastate regulatory agencies from states is limited insofar as these bodies continue to interact with and be shaped (often heavily) by country governments, especially those of more powerful states.

Thus in polycentric circumstances no site or level of governance has one-way sway over the others. Regulation occurs through interconnections among multiple locations with different but overlapping spheres of jurisdiction. The following pages consider in more detail the expansion of transborder substate governance, the development of suprastate regional regimes, and the growth of global governance arrangements.

Transborder substate governance

Even in statist times, before contemporary large-scale globalization, government was never completely centralized in national bureaucracies. Smaller territorial sections of state jurisdiction – variously called provinces, federal states, counties, districts, cantons or departments – had their own governance institutions. In addition, most villages, towns and cities had their own governments. Apart from in micro-territories like Andorra or San Marino where country and local government were the same thing, Westphalian states delegated a number of regulatory tasks from central bodies to provincial and municipal agencies.

However, under statist conditions of the territorialist past, non-central authorities worked entirely within the state context. Only very rarely would local governments reach out beyond their country to the wider world. Moreover, if municipal and provincial bodies had contacts with governance institutions abroad, it would be with the intermediation of their state authorities. Aside from rare exceptions like the first Basque government of 1936–9 (Zubiri, 1999), substate agencies had no 'foreign policy' of their own.

These circumstances have altered in the present-day more global world. For one thing, most states have in recent years undertaken significant additional devolution from national to subnational spheres. The many examples include decentralization by the 74th amendment to the Indian Constitution in 1996, the construction of Flemish and Walloon governments in Belgium by the constitutional revision of 1980, power transfers from the centre to the provinces in Argentina, increased autonomy for the Government of Quebec within Canada, and greater competences for the districts in Uganda.

These devolutions have transpired largely owing to cultural, economic, historical and political circumstances connected to the particular state in question; however, globalization has also often encouraged the trend. As previously emphasized, the growth of transplanetary and supraterritorial relations has loosened the supreme and absolute rule that states could aim to exercise in the preceding territorialist context, thereby increasing possibilities for substate sites of governance to take greater initiative. Indeed, provincial and municipal authorities can be better suited to handle matters like the organization of global spectacles, the provision of infrastructure for global companies, and some aspects of the control of transworld infectious diseases and transworld crime. Moreover, devolution from states to substate institutions has often come with the explicit urgings and financial sponsorship of suprastate agencies like the EU or the multilateral development banks.

In a further departure from statist practices, many substate authorities have in recent decades developed direct transborder contacts with parties abroad (Duchacek *et al.*, 1988; Michelmann and Soldatos, 1990; Brown and Fry, 1993; Hocking, 1993; Aldecoa and Keating, 1999; Breslin and Hook,

2002; Dai, 2003). These 'supralocal' connections have often unfolded without intermediation by central state governments. Indeed, the 'paradiplomacy' pursued in these transborder substate relations has sometimes run counter to policies prevailing at the state level.

Considerable transborder substate governance has developed between municipalities. This trend is hardly surprising insofar as transplanetary telecommunication webs, air corridors, capital flows, diasporas and ecological problems have connected so-called 'global cities' like Hong Kong, London, Los Angeles, Moscow, Paris and Singapore as much to one another as to their respective hinterlands (Eade, 1997; King, 2000; Sassen, 2001, 2002; Cross and Moore, 2002; Erie, 2004). Yet in small and medium-sized towns, too, local governments have taken global policy initiatives on matters such as development cooperation, crime control, environmental degradation and human rights promotion.

Formal regular transworld contacts between town councils began on a small scale in the early twentieth century through the International Union of Local Authorities (IULA), founded in 1913. The practice of twinning towns began in the 1950s (Handley, 2001). However, global links between municipal governments have mainly intensified since the late twentieth century. The various networks include the World Association of Major Metropolises, launched in 1985, and regional organizations of urban authorities set up for Arab countries (1967), Africa (1975), Asia (1989), Europe (1990) and Latin America (1995). In 2004 the IULA, the World Federation of United Towns (UTO), and the World Associations of Cities and Local Authorities Coordination (WACLAC) came together to form the World Organization of United Cities and Local Governments, with several thousand members in over a hundred countries.

In regard to global ecological issues more specifically, the International Council for Local Environmental Initiatives, established in 1990, connected 455 municipal authorities across the world as of 2003, in order 'to achieve and monitor tangible improvements in global environmental conditions' (ICLEI, 2003; also UIA, 1998: 951). In addition, the CityNet group has shared information on sustainable development among dozens of cities in the Asia-Pacific region. In a more ad hoc fashion, virtual policy forums have involved city managers from across the planet in electronic consultations on a variety of issues.

At the level of provinces and federal states, a number of substate governments have developed their own departments of foreign affairs. This trend has gone furthest in Quebec, where the provincial ministry of external affairs has maintained a staff of 360 people and 24 offices in 17 countries. The ministry has moreover conducted over 120 missions abroad per year and concluded more than 400 agreements with foreign governments (Teitelbaum, 2001; Fry, 2006). Other Canadian provincial governments in Alberta, British

Columbia and Ontario have pursued transborder relations on a smaller scale. Nearly 40 of the 50 states of the USA had permanent representations abroad in 2002, up from just 4 states in 1980; the number of these offices rose from 151 in 1992 to 240 in 2000 (Fry, 1995, 2006). For their part the *Länder* in Germany between them have opened some 130 offices around the globe since the 1970s, mainly as foreign trade and investment bureaux in major export markets of Asia, Eastern Europe and North America (Kaiser, 2005). In China the various provincial governments have their own foreign affairs departments that operate with considerable autonomy from the central authorities in Beijing (Goodman and Segal, 1994; Segal, 1994; Breslin, 2000). Australian states, French regions, Japanese prefectures and Swiss cantons have also joined the trend of setting up overseas offices.

Some provincial governments have also bypassed the central state to develop direct links with suprastate agencies. For example, federal states in both Brazil and India have had direct dealings with the World Bank. Several provincial regulatory bodies have their own affiliation to the International Organization of Securities Commissions (IOSCO), separately from the country authorities. In Europe, a Committee of the Regions established under the 1992 Maastricht Treaty has formalized direct consultations between suprastate institutions of the EU and substate tiers of government in the member-states. By 1996 there were 115 representative offices of substate regions in Brussels (Keating, 1999: 6). Launched in 1989, the INTERREG programme of the EU has provided several billion euros to fund transborder cooperation between substate governments on issues such as energy, environmental protection, tourism, and transportation. In 1999 the UN Human Settlements Programme (UN-HABITAT) launched a Global Campaign on Urban Governance that gave the transplanetary organization direct connections with municipal governments.

In some other cases substate regional governments have pursued their own multilateral collaboration with one another, separately from both state and suprastate authorities. For example, in Western Europe the so-called 'Four Motors' network, in operation since 1988, has linked Baden-Württemberg, Catalonia, Lombardy and Rhône-Alpes in collaboration on commercial, cultural, educational, environmental and technological matters. Meanwhile substate authorities in Bavaria, Quebec, Shandong, Upper Austria and the Western Cape have formed a multilateral partnership in respect of hi-tech industries. In northern Scandinavia the Saami Council has linked the local parliaments of indigenous peoples in Finland, Norway and Sweden.

Other ventures by substate authorities into transborder relations have been more ad hoc. For example, local authorities in Tatarstan have asserted their independence from the Kremlin in dealing with global capital. Likewise, many provincial governments in China have bypassed Beijing to pursue direct relations with global companies. Governors from three southern states of the

USA travelled to Germany to present competing incentive packages for a global firm to invest in their jurisdictions. State, county and city governments took the lead in imposing sanctions by the USA against the apartheid regime in South Africa when the country government under Ronald Reagan was slow to adopt restrictive measures (Fry, 1998: 5). Similarly, the State of Massachusetts put its own sanctions on Burma in 1997, although on this occasion a federal court overruled the policy.

As this last example well illustrates, none of the growth of transborder substate relations has signalled the end of states as significant sites of regulation. The European Commission's Director of Science and Technology almost certainly exaggerated when declaring in 1994 that: 'in just a few decades, nation-states . . . will no longer be so relevant. Instead, rich regions built around cities such as Osaka, San Francisco and the four motors of Europe will acquire effective power' (quoted in Runyan, 1996: 242).

Moreover, although substate authorities have often gained greater autonomy from the state in the context of accelerated globalization, they have not necessarily gained greater policy initiative overall. After all, like states, municipal and provincial governments have faced pressures to accommodate global companies, global financial markets and global civil society associations as well as (or more than) their local constituents. In addition, substate agencies have in contemporary history had to contend not only with the state, but also with growing sites of suprastate governance that hold macro-regional and transworld remits.

Macro-regional governance

In addition to the micro-regionalization within states just described, globalization has also unfolded together with – and in several ways encouraged – a trend of macro-regionalization among states (Fawcett and Hurrell, 1995; Gamble and Payne, 1996; Mansfield and Milner, 1997; Coleman and Underhill, 1998; Hettne *et al.*, 1999, 2000, 2001; Hook and Kearns, 1999; Hout and Grugel, 1999; Schulz *et al.*, 2001; Breslin *et al.*, 2002). No fewer than 109 regional trade agreements were reported to the GATT between 1948 and 1994 (*The Economist*, 1995: 27–8). The decade of the 1990s alone saw 93 such accords reported to the GATT/WTO. Other macro-regional schemes like the League of Arab States and the Organization of American States (OAS) have focused more on diplomatic and military concerns. To be sure, some of these regional governance initiatives have not developed beyond paper agreements. However, others have involved a substantial growth of suprastate laws and institutions.

Macro-regionalization of governance has transpired across the world. The most far-reaching instances have occurred in Europe, where 50 years of progressive widening and deepening of macro-regional regulation has culminated in today's European Union, encompassing 25 countries after a fifth enlargement in 2004, and Council of Europe, with 45 member states. Outside Europe, other significant macro-regional governance projects have developed in Central America (1960), East Africa (1967–77, relaunched in 1991), South East Asia (1968), the Caribbean (1973), West Africa (1975 and 1994), Southern Africa (1980 and 1993), the Persian Gulf (1981), Central Asia (1984), South Asia (1985), Central Europe (1989), the Black Sea area (1993), North America (1994) and the cone of South America (1995). Negotiations to form a Free Trade Area of the Americas (FTAA) across the Western Hemisphere have stalled since 2003, but the vision has not been abandoned.

In addition, the decades of accelerated globalization have witnessed the development of several intercontinental transregional initiatives. For instance, as its name suggests, the North Atlantic Treaty Organization (NATO) has spanned North America and Europe since its creation in 1949. Meanwhile the Organization for Security and Cooperation in Europe (OSCE) has come to link 55 participating states from Central Asia, Europe and North America. In the Southern Hemisphere 23 states of Africa and South America have since 1986 formed a Zone of Peace and Cooperation of the South Atlantic with periodic ministerial meetings. Asia-Pacific Economic Cooperation, an intergovernmental forum with 21 member economies from along the Pacific Rim, has pursued economic and security questions through multiple gatherings since 1989 (Ravenhill, 2001; Rüland *et al.*, 2002).

Certain macro-regional entities have embarked on their own relations with each other, introducing a new multilateralism of regions alongside the old multilateralism of states. For example, the EU has maintained formal connections with the Association of South East Asian Nations (ASEAN) since 1980, the Andean Pact since 1983, and the Gulf Cooperation Council (GCC) since 1989. The EU and the Southern Common Market (MERCOSUR) launched an Inter-Regional Framework Cooperation Scheme in 1995. Since 1996 regular Asia-Europe Meetings (ASEM) have linked the EU and so-called 'ASEAN+3' (China, Japan and South Korea) (Stokhof and Van der Velde, 1999; Gilson, 2002). On the whole, however, this trend toward inter-regionalism has so far remained modest (Rüland *et al.*, forthcoming).

Like substate agencies with transborder relations, some macro-regional governance frameworks have acquired a notable degree of autonomy from states. True, states have instigated regional projects and remain prominent participants in regionalization. However, in some ways states have also been constrained to 'go regional', for example, in order adequately to respond to global capital and transplanetary ecological problems. Moreover, macro-regional governance has in a number of cases developed to a point that the regimes have acquired authority over member states as well as vice versa.

The EU in particular has gone beyond an interstate arrangement to a suprastate regime (Marks *et al.*, 1996; Richardson, 1996; Cram *et al.*, 1999; Hix, 1999; Rosamond, 2000; Wallace and Wallace, 2000). It has its own Commission, Parliament, Court of Justice, and Central Bank, together with a distinct European currency launched in 2002 and some 80,000 regulatory measures generated by 2000. By the early 1990s some 40 per cent of all civil servants (local and national) within the member countries regularly were in contact with EU matters (Risse, 2000). The EU has also emerged as a distinct actor in global politics, with its own Common Foreign and Security Policy (CFSP), its own overseas development regime (the Yaoundé, Lomé and Cotonou agreements), its own delegations in over 120 countries, its own participation in G7/8 and WTO meetings, and observer status in most UN bodies (C. Rhodes, 1996; Piening, 1997; Bretherton and Vogler, 1999; Jørgensen and Rosamond, 2002). On the other hand, the scale of the EU apparatus should not be overstated, as its budget in 2000 amounted to only 1.2 per cent of the collective GDP of its member countries (Jørgensen and Rosamond, 2002: 194). Indeed, some of the major EU member governments have proposed to reduce even this low figure to 1.0 per cent.

How is macro-regionalization related to globalization: as stepping-stone or stumbling block (Hettne *et al.*, 1999: xix)? In some respects, the two trends have been complementary. For one thing, technologies of supraterritorial communication and travel have made possible tight coordination of activities on both macro-regional and global scales. In addition, macro-regional common markets have provided efficiency and economies of scale for the production, distribution and sale of global products (Chesnais *et al.*, 2000). In this vein one critical research and advocacy group has talked of globalization being 'corporate led and EU fed' (Balanyá *et al.*, 2000). Furthermore, macro-regional governance arrangements have often proved to be an effective mechanism for the administration of global norms, for instance, in areas such as human rights and technical standardization. Moreover, the growth of global consciousness has prepared people intellectually for the construction of suprastate regional frameworks. Indeed, various observers have suggested that macro-regional integration serves as an intermediate stage towards full-scale globality (Tober, 1993: 101; Hettne, 1994).

On the other hand, in some respects regionalization can also unfold in opposition to globalization. After all, regionality carves up the planet, whereas globality spans the planet. Regionality follows territorial logic, whereas globality often transcends territoriality. Regionalism can be a reaction against globalism, serving as a macronationalist, neoprotectionist defence against the turbulence of globalizing capitalism, the imposition of global cultures, and so on. Some EU controls on external trade and ever-tightening restrictions on immigration into the region well illustrate this reactive dynamic. Thus Helen Wallace (1996: 17) has suggested that 'European integration can also be seen as [an] effort to contain the consequences of globalization . . . and to harden the boundary between [West Europeans] and the rest of the world.'

Yet others have looked to macro-regionalization as a positive strategy towards globalization, as a way to enhance self-determination in the governance of a more global world. Many Japanese policymakers have promoted regionalization in East Asia in this vein after the crisis of 1997–8, for example, with proposals for an Asian Monetary Fund (AMF) and the New Miyazawa Initiative to strengthen financial systems in the region. Meanwhile many Japan-based firms have pursued a regionalization of production in East Asia to sustain their global competitiveness (Hughes, 2005).

To be sure, globalization has not been the only force propelling the proliferation and growth of suprastate regional projects in contemporary history. Local, country and region-specific circumstances have also determined where and when regionalization has taken place, how far, in what forms, at what speeds, and so on. However, macro-regional schemes would not have appeared in such numbers – and developed as far as they have – in the absence of a concurrent large-scale growth of global relations.

Transworld governance

Of course suprastate governance involves more than regional arrangements. As noted in Chapter 2, globality has legal aspects in terms of formal rules and regulatory agencies that have a transplanetary scope. As indicated in Chapter 3, the greatest growth of global governance institutions and associated legal instruments has occurred in recent decades. Indeed, as described in Chapter 4, these regulatory organizations have established many norms and rules that have facilitated accelerated globalization over the past half-century.

Large-scale contemporary globalization has created needs for significant elements of transworld governance. HIV/AIDS, the Internet, air travel, refugee movements, transplanetary money flows, climate change, and much more cannot be effectively regulated without a substantial global dimension to the regime. Unprecedented amounts of global governance are therefore unavoidable and indispensable in the twenty-first century (although *how* one pursues global governance is substantially a matter of political choice).

Today several thousand multilateral agreements on culture, ecology, finance, health, human rights, military affairs and trade apply to global spheres. Organs of the United Nations, the Bretton Woods institutions, the WTO, the BIS, the OECD, and the Commonwealth are prominent examples of governance bodies with a global remit. Several transworld institutions have a direct presence globally. For example, UNDP has some 150 Country Offices, while the IMF and the World Bank each maintain resident missions in over 70 countries. Moreover, these global governance organizations execute their mandates using transworld communications networks and transplanetary bureaucracies with staff and funds drawn from all corners of the world.

One outstanding example of expanded global governance is the World Trade Organization (Hoekman and Kostecki, 1995; Jackson, 1998; Krueger, 1998; Sampson, 2001; Cohn, 2002). Established in 1995, the Geneva-based WTO has obtained a larger membership, a far wider agenda, and substantially greater enforcement capacities than any previous transplanetary trade regime. Over 140 states have joined the WTO, and a queue of others waits to enter. The organization has addressed not only traditional concerns with cross-border exchange of merchandise, but also matters such as trade in services, intellectual property issues, electronic commerce, trade-related investment, competition policy and environmental questions.

The contemporary global trade regime has powers that extend beyond those of its state members. Under the 1994 Marrakech Agreement that created the WTO, member-states commit themselves (with no reservations allowed) to alter their national statutes and procedures to comply with suprastate trade law. Even the US Supreme Court has recognized, in a 1999 judgment, the higher authority of WTO rules. The Trade Policy Review Body of the WTO conducts periodic surveillance of member governments' commercial measures. Alleged violations of WTO rules are submitted to a Dispute Settlement Body (DSB), where panels of experts reach decisions that are binding unless every state party to the global trade regime (including the initial complainant) votes to overturn the advice. In the first nine years of the WTO's existence over 300 trade disputes were tabled for DSB consideration. Many more WTO-related cases have been settled through informal negotiation and pressure. Formally, of course, states have had the 'sovereign prerogative' whether or not to join and comply with the WTO. However, the forces of a globalizing economy, coupled with the prevailing neoliberalist discourse that extols trade liberalization, have heavily constrained this supposed 'free will'. Indeed, to date no state has rejected the Marrakech Agreement outright.

Other considerable growth in public global economic governance has occurred through the International Monetary Fund (Denters, 1996; James, 1996; Blustein, 2001; Boughton, 2001). During the first 30 years after it started work in 1946, the Washington-based IMF held a modest brief to establish and then manage the Bretton Woods regime of fixed exchange rates. However, since the 1970s the Fund has intervened more intensely with its client governments. For one thing, the 'second-generation' IMF has undertaken comprehensive and detailed surveillance of economic performance: of its 184 member-states (annually); of the world economy as a whole (biannually); and since 1998 of certain macro-regions as well. In addition, the IMF has supplied major training and technical assistance services, largely in order to provide poorly equipped states with staff and tools that can better handle the policy challenges of globalization. The IMF Institute has taken over

21,000 officials from around the globe through its programmes since it opened in 1964 (IMF, 2003c). Furthermore, the Fund has gone beyond its traditional stabilization measures (which correct short-term problems with the balance of payments) to sponsor wide-ranging economic restructuring programmes in over 80 countries. Finally, the IMF has since the 1980s played a pivotal role in responding to crises in global finance, including emergencies of recent years in Asia, Russia, Latin America and Turkey. To the extent that the Fund has acted as a lender of last resort in such situations and has addressed questions concerning the supervision of global capital markets, it has acted as something of a suprastate central bank. Meanwhile the Bank for International Settlements has since 1974 developed some general principles for the oversight of global commercial banking, for example, on matters including capital adequacy ratios as well as payment and settlement systems.

The much-expanded activities of the Organization for Economic Cooperation and Development further illustrate the contemporary growth of global economic governance (Sullivan, 1997; Ougaard, 2004: ch 5). With a Paris-based secretariat expanded to 2,300 people, the OECD today convenes some 200 committees, working parties, and expert groups. In the 30 years after 1970, the number of OECD instruments (that is, decisions, recommendations, agreements, etc.) multiplied more than tenfold. These measures have especially addressed the environment, taxation, and transworld investment, although they have also extended across every major policy area except military affairs. Like the WTO and the IMF, the OECD has acquired a significant role in policy surveillance. At regular intervals (usually every 18 months) the organization releases an authoritative assessment of the macroeconomic conditions of each of its 30 member-states, including suggestions for policy adjustments. Increasingly, officials from certain non-member governments have observed OECD proceedings on issues of concern to them, so that, for example, states with offshore finance centres have closely followed OECD deliberations on taxation questions and money laundering.

The acceleration of global ecological degradation has also prompted a significant expansion of transworld governance in recent history (Porter *et al.*, 2000; Miles *et al.*, 2002). Some 900 multilateral environmental agreements have come into force to date, including conventions signed in respect of supraterritorial problems such as depletion of stratospheric ozone (1985), climate change (1992), and loss of biological diversity (1992). Other treaties have addressed so-called 'global commons' such as Antarctica and the deep seas. Since the 1970s most of the principal transworld regulatory agencies have created special organs and programmes to address ecological issues. The many initiatives of this kind include the OECD Environment Committee (1970), the World Bank Environment Department (1987), the UN Commission on Sustainable Development (1993), and the WTO Committee on Trade and Environment (1995). That said, other major initiatives in transplanetary ecological governance like the Kyoto Protocol on global warming have struggled to gain acceptance (Victor, 2004).

Elsewhere, global governance has grown as an instrument of conflict management. In this vein the United Nations has undertaken over 30 peacekeeping operations since 1956 and several humanitarian interventions in the 1990s (Mayall, 1996). Even the usually sovereignty-obsessed government of China has endorsed the concept of UN peacekeeping and has since 1989 moreover participated in some of these activities (Kim, 1994: 49–53). A global Nuclear Nonproliferation Treaty (NPT) has been administered through the International Atomic Energy Agency since 1970. Other global arms control regimes have addressed biological and chemical weapons.

The period of accelerated globalization has also witnessed unprecedented growth of suprastate governance in respect of human rights. In the area of workers' rights, for example, the ILO has come to monitor a transplanetary code encompassing (as of 2003) 185 Conventions and 194 Recommendations. Several other global legal instruments on human rights (for example, concerning torture, racial discrimination and the protection of children) have acquired supervisory committees under the UN Secretariat. Interestingly, from the perspective of global governance, these UN committees consist of experts who act in their personal capacity rather than as representatives of states. Meanwhile the UN Commission on Human Rights, which is composed of government delegates, has since 1970 undertaken over 60 official examinations of country situations. Hardly any state now invokes (as Burma did in 1996) the 'domestic jurisdiction' clause of the United Nations Charter to deny entry to a UN human rights mission.

On occasion global human rights governance has even brought individuals (rather than states) to justice, intimating the introduction of something like cosmopolitan law. Ad hoc global tribunals to investigate crimes against humanity were created after World War II and again in the 1990s to address genocide in Rwanda and war in former Yugoslavia. The extradition of Slobodan Milosovic to the Hague Tribunal in 2001 marked the first time in history that a person was charged under international law for offences performed as a head of state. A permanent International Criminal Court was established in Rome in 2002, although its statute has not been ratified by several major states including China, Russia and the USA. In addition, the UN and other suprastate agencies have promoted the creation of national human rights commissions and ombudspersons, helping to raise their number during the 1990s from around a dozen to around a hundred (Cardenas, 2003).

Global regulatory agencies have also engaged in other aspects of state building. For example, in postconflict situations the UN has undertaken direct administration of Bosnia, Cambodia, East Timor, Haiti, Kosovo and

South West Africa (now Namibia) (Wilde, 2001). The UN has also provided assistance and supervision for scores of national elections after 1990 (Findlay, 1995: 49). The World Bank has since the mid-1990s given considerable attention to reforming state and substate governance in areas such as the civil service, the judiciary and labour legislation. Technical assistance from the IMF has developed central bank and finance ministry capacities in many weak states. Thus the construction of governance institutions has not been a one-way affair: not only have states built up macro-regional and transworld institutions, but suprastate bodies have on numerous occasions also built up states.

Of course, it is important not to overestimate the growth of global governance just described. Transplanetary regulatory frameworks have been riddled with neglected issues, double standards, limited enforcement, poor coordination between institutions, understaffing, underfunding and low legitimacy. To note but one neglected issue, global governance has accomplished little in the area of public schemes for binding regulation of transworld companies. In terms of resource limitations, the UN has a smaller budget than the New York Fire Department and a smaller staff than the City of Stockholm. Global economic institutions, too, have had restricted operating budgets (in 1996) of only $1,375 million for the World Bank, $471 million for the IMF, and just $93 million for the WTO (World Bank, 1996: 155; IMF, 1996: 217; WTO-2, 1996a: 153). The BIS is unique in being able to fund its work from the income of its own activities, without needing to solicit contributions from member states.

Thus, contrary to some expectations, global governance is not – and currently shows no sign of becoming – global government (Zolo, 1997; Heinrichsohn, 2000). Globalization is not leading to the creation of a centralized world state, where Westphalian-style sovereignty is transferred 'upwards' from the country to the global level. As this chapter has made plain, regulation in today's globalizing world occurs in a polycentric manner through macro-regional, state and substate authorities as well as global arrangements. Moreover, the principle of subsidiarity has generally weighed strongly in contemporary governance, so that global regulation has tended to devolve for implementation to macro-regional, state and local institutions. Indeed, on the whole global governance frameworks currently have very limited and fragile legitimacy in the public eye. Most citizens are barely aware that transworld regulatory arrangements exist.

Yet these substantial shortcomings do not negate the crucial point that post-Westphalian governance involves notable global laws and institutions. The rapid growth of transplanetary regulation has not heralded a demise of the state, but it has confirmed the end of statist governance. Although it is states that have created transplanetary governance institutions, they have done so under substantial constraints of globalization. Nor have states fully controlled the actions and further development of transworld authorities once the latter are established.

Privatized governance

Governance has become polycentric under the influence of globalization not only with the diffusion of regulation across multiple layers of the public sector, but also by the spread of private, non-statutory frameworks of rules (cf. Cutler *et al.*, 1999; Ronit and Schneider, 2000; Brühl, 2001; Haufler, 2001; Knill and Lehmkuhl, 2002; Hall and Biersteker, 2003). Given statist conditions of the past, one might easily assume that governance is by definition a public operation through governmental and intergovernmental agencies. However, the formulation, implementation, monitoring and enforcement of societal rules could in principle also occur through nonofficial channels like market-based agencies and civil society organizations.

Contemporary globalization has encouraged a substantial privatization of governance in two main ways. First, a number of private regulatory arrangements have arisen to fill regulatory gaps in suprastate governance. Although transworld and macro-regional regimes have undergone unprecedented degrees and rates of expansion in recent history, this growth has often still lagged well behind the regulatory needs of expanded global relations. Various areas – including global markets and global finance – have suffered major governance deficits as a result. In a number of cases non-governmental actors have stepped in where public regulatory frameworks have been deficient or absent. The private agencies have then constructed the necessary standards and norms that enable increased global relations to develop.

Second, the prevailing neoliberalist approach to contemporary globalization has also promoted the rise of private regulation. The logic of neoliberalism can easily move from prescribing the privatization of production to advocating the privatization of governance. At an extreme, neoliberalists might affirm that the global private sector can – together with consumer and other stakeholder pressure in the marketplace – adequately regulate itself.

Like most phenomena connected with contemporary globalization, private global governance is not completely new to recent history. For example, in the second half of the nineteenth century a number of business associations created standard forms of contract to govern cross-border trade in commodities such as corn and cotton (Wiener, 1999: 165). However, the scale of current private regulation far outstrips anything seen in the past.

Moreover, private global governance of earlier times tended to be sanctioned by intergovernmental treaty, so that states retained considerable initiative and control of the overall process. To be sure, approval or at least tolerance of states (especially big states) remains necessary for the operation of today's private regulatory arrangements. Yet much recent private governance has arisen with little direct involvement of governments.

One major contemporary growth area of private governance of globalization are schemes of so-called 'corporate social responsibility', sometimes also termed 'corporate citizenship' (Zadek *et al.*, 1997; Zadek 2001; Andriof and McIntosh, 2001). Official suprastate measures to regulate transborder companies have remained either moribund (like the UN Centre for Transnational Corporations code of 1979), or weak (like the UN Global Compact launched in 2000), or unratified (like the draft UN Norms on the Responsibilities of Transnational Corporations of 2003), or highly general in terms (like the OECD Guidelines for Multinational Enterprises, first issued in 1976 and subsequently revised), or very narrow in focus (like the 2003 WHO Framework Convention on Tobacco Control). However, non-statutory rules for transborder enterprises have proliferated since the 1990s, especially regarding labour, environmental and human rights practices (cf. Hopkins, 1999; Richter, 2001; Jenkins *et al.*, 2002; Abrahams, 2004; Bendell, 2004). By 2002 around 4,000 of the 65,000 transnational corporations were promising social and environmental reports (Utting, 2006).

Private CSR frameworks have taken several forms. Some of these voluntary codes for transborder firms are self-regulatory arrangements. That is, the schemes are operated either by a single company over its own activities or by a group of companies over their own sector. For example, Nike and Unilever have developed company-based codes (which notionally also cover their subcontractors and suppliers), while the International Council of Toy Industries has overseen an umbrella code for the sector. Outside consultants have devised other CSR arrangements like the Global Reporting Initiative (GRI), started in 1997, and the Social Accountability Standard SA8000, operational since 1998. Some civil society groups have also promulgated CSR standards. For example, Amnesty International issued its Human Rights Principles for Companies in 1998, while scores of Christian associations have used the Interfaith Center on Global Corporate Responsibility to screen firms for investment. Recent years have also seen the emergence of so-called 'multi-stakeholder initiatives' involving firms, labour unions and NGOs in jointly pursued nonofficial regulatory arrangements for global business. Like the consultancy schemes, multi-stakeholder initiatives involve standard setting, independent monitoring, certification and reporting. Examples include the Forest Stewardship Council (FSC), which has since 1993 linked timber companies, workers, environmentalists and indigenous peoples in efforts to promote sustainable logging (Humphreys, 1996, 2003).

Other significant private global governance has expanded since the 1970s in respect of commercial adjudication. Whereas states have submitted their trade conflicts to a public body, the GATT/WTO, global companies have tended to handle their disputes through private arbitration, thus avoiding litigation in state or suprastate courts (Dezalay and Garth, 1996; Mattli, 2001; Lehmkuhl, 2003). The available mechanisms include the International Court of Arbitration of the International Chamber of Commerce, the London Court of Arbitration (LCA), and the China International Economic Trade Arbitration Commission (CIETAC). The New York Convention on the Recognition and Enforcement of Foreign Arbitral Awards (1958) stipulates that national courts cannot review the judgements of arbitrators on core issues. To give one indication of the scale of this private governance practice, the Secretariat of the ICC had received 10,000 requests for arbitration by 1998, more than two-thirds of them since 1976 (Craig *et al.*, 1998: 2).

In addition to global production and trade, much private governance has also applied to transplanetary finance (Porter and Coleman, 2002). The many relevant sites include the International Chamber of Commerce Commission on Banking Technique and Practice, the World Federation of Exchanges (for securities markets), and the Derivatives Policy Group (with members drawn from academics and investment bankers). Bodies like the International Accounting Standards Board and the International Federation of Accountants have respectively developed the main global accountancy and auditing norms currently in use. Rating agencies like Moody's and Standard & Poors have also played something of an unofficial policing role in the contemporary global economy, rewarding governments and companies that score well and punishing those that rate poorly (Levich, 2002; Sinclair, 2005).

Considerable additional privatized governance has emerged in relation to global information and communications. For example, the International Telecommunication Union has moved from being an intergovernmental organization to a hybrid construction with 600 affiliated companies as well as 189 member states (Salter, 1999). Titles and addresses in cyberspace are regulated through the Internet Corporation for Assigned Names and Numbers, created in 1998 with operations that involve business, technical, academic and user inputs (Franda, 2001: ch 2).

Multiple further instances of private governance of globalization can be found across other sectors. The International Organization for Standardization, formally a nongovernmental body, has often agreed its measures together with the major companies involved (Clapp, 1998). The ICC's Uniform Customs and Practice for Documentary Credits have been accepted by banking associations in 175 countries (Wiener, 1999: 183). The International Air Transport Association (IATA) has standardized airline documentation. The Rome-based Codex Alimentarius Commission has set global food standards with considerable inputs from industry. The World Tourism Organization ('the other WTO') has a Business Council that includes representatives of different facets of the industry in 70 countries. The Bill and Melinda Gates Foundation has donated more for health care programmes in Africa than WHO has had available from governmental contributions. Between 1974 and 2004 some 90 so-called 'public–private partnerships' were established to combat global diseases. The vast majority of these 'PPPs' have emerged since the mid-1990s (IPPPH, 2004; also Reich, 2002).

Finally, substantial privatization of governance has occurred in the course of contemporary globalization in the form of 'contracting out' the delivery of public services to private providers. For instance, non-profit organizations have come to figure prominently in the supply of humanitarian relief. The mid-1990s annual budgets of the giants in this field included $586 million for CARE International, $419 million for World Vision International, and $350 million each for Oxfam and Save the Children (Smillie, 1999: 17–18). By comparison, the operating budget for the UN High Commissioner for Refugees (UNHCR) has run at about $1,000 million per annum. Not surprisingly, in view of these resource constraints, UNHCR in 1998 maintained connections with more than 500 non-profit organizations as 'Partners in Action' (UNHCR, 1999). Likewise, bilateral and multilateral donor organizations have since the 1970s made far more use of non-profit bodies (rather than official agencies) to execute development assistance projects.

Outsourcing has even extended to military operations. Mercenaries more or less vacated the world scene by the late eighteenth century, but these soldiers-for-hire have reappeared (usually on a small scale) in recent decades in various armed conflicts, for example, in Angola, Chechnya, former Yugoslavia, and elsewhere. Moreover, the 1990s saw the rise for the first time of private military companies. Examples include South Africa-based Executive Outcomes and US-based Military Professional Resources, Inc. These firms have mainly provided logistical support for state armies or protection for business premises, but they can also offer direct combat capacities. For example, Executive Outcomes was contracted to undertake humanitarian operations in Sierra Leone in the mid-1990s (Shearer, 1998; Zarate, 1998; Brayton, 2002; Mandel, 2002; Singer, 2003).

The merits or otherwise of private governance – in regard to social justice and democracy, for example – are considered in Part III of this book. The point at the present juncture is to note that contemporary globalization has brought with it a considerable privatization of regulation. Polycentric governance involves not only multiple scales of regulatory activity, but also the spread of private alongside public mechanisms of governance. Inasmuch as this privatization has responded to the slow development of official regulatory arrangements in various areas of globalization, together with prevailing neoliberalist doctrine, the trend could be reversed as and when neoliberalism recedes and more public-sector frameworks are constructed.

(Global) civil society

Given all of the developments reviewed above, globalization has fostered a considerable dispersal of regulatory competences across substate, state, suprastate and private sites of governance. This shift from statism to polycentrism has in turn had important implications for civil society activity.

The concept 'civil society' has meant many things since it appeared in sixteenth-century English political thought (Chambers and Kymlicka, 2002; Cohen and Arato, 1992). In today's context we might conceive of civil society as a political space, or arena, where self-generated associations of citizens seek, from outside political parties, to shape the rules that govern social life. Civil society groups bring citizens together non-coercively in deliberate attempts to mould the formal laws and informal norms that regulate social relations.

Civil society associations assemble people who share concerns about a particular policy issue. The many examples of civil society activity include anti-poverty campaigns, business forums, consumer advocates, criminal syndicates, pro-democracy groups, development cooperation initiatives, environmental movements, ethnic lobbies, faith-based associations, human rights promoters, labour unions, local community groups, peace advocates, peasant movements, philanthropic foundations, professional bodies, relief organizations, think tanks, women's networks, youth associations, and more. Civil society therefore includes – but also ranges far wider than – NGOs. The huge diversity of civil society groups is evident not only in their broad range of focal issues, but also in their multifarious organizational forms, constituencies, capacity levels, geographical scopes, ideological persuasions, strategic visions, and campaign tactics.

With its concern to shape the rules of social life, civil society activity unfolds in relation to a governance apparatus. In former circumstances of statism, when governance came down to government, civil society functioned in relation to the state. However, when the framework of governance changes – as it has done with contemporary globalization – the character of civil society may be expected to alter in tandem (Scholte, 2002a). In today's more polycentric condition, civil society associations have redirected some of their attention from states to other sites and networks of governance, including global regulatory arrangements. An unofficial 'new multilateralism' of civil society associations has arisen alongside the official multilateralism of global governance agencies (Schechter, 1999b; O'Brien *et al.*, 2000).

Recent history has therefore witnessed a major rise of what analysts have variously called transnational/global social movements (Smith *et al.*, 1997; Porta *et al.*, 1999; Cohen and Rai, 2000; Guidry *et al.*, 2000; Khagram *et al.*, 2002; Smith and Johnston, 2002), transnational advocacy networks (Keck and Sikkink, 1998), global citizen action (Edwards and Gaventa, 2001), and transnational/global civil society (Lipschutz, 1992; Drainville, 1998; Florini,

2000; Scholte, 2000; Anheier *et al.*, 2001; Glasius *et al.*, 2002; Clark, 2003; Kaldor, 2003; Taylor, 2004; Germain and Kenny, 2005). Like most features of contemporary globalization, civil society mobilization beyond the nation-state-country is not completely new. As noted in Chapter 3, labour, peace, racial, religious and women's movements had already developed a transworld dimension in the nineteenth century. However, the scale of this earlier global civil society activity was much smaller than that of today.

Contemporary civil society has 'gone global' in at least seven important ways. First, many civil society associations have begun to address the governance of transplanetary problems. The multiple examples include arms control, asylum seekers, climate change, cultural protection, debt relief, digital inclusion, gender equity, HIV/AIDS, human rights, labour standards, religious revivalism, and trade agreements. Indeed, recent years have seen considerable civil society activism around the general theme of globalization itself, in what have been variously termed 'anti-globalization', 'alter-globalization', 'counter-globalization' and 'global justice' movements (Bourdieu, 1998; Klein, 2000, 2002; Rupert, 2000; Starr, 2000; Broad, 2002). Prominent initiatives in this vein have included Peoples' Global Action (PGA), started in 1998, and the World Social Forum process, launched in 2001 (Houtart and Polet, 2001; Sen *et al.*, 2004).

Second, civil society activities have obtained global qualities by engaging with transplanetary governance institutions. Countless civil society associations have addressed themselves to UN agencies, the World Bank, the IMF and the WTO, often 'leapfrogging' over states to contact the global bodies directly (Weiss and Gordenker, 1996; Willetts, 1996; Fox and Brown, 1998; Foster with Anand, 1999; Scholte, 2002b; Scholte, 2004d). Indeed, a number of civil society associations have opened bureaux near the headquarters of suprastate governance organizations. For instance, the ICFTU, the Institute of International Finance (IIF), and Oxfam all maintain offices in walking distance from the headquarters of the IMF and the World Bank. In response, as is considered further in Chapter 11, many governance agencies dealing with global issues have devised mechanisms of one kind or another to engage (at least to some extent) with civil society associations.

A third global aspect of much contemporary civil society activity is its use of transplanetary and supraterritorial travel and communications. Air transport has enabled civil society actors from across the planet to convene in frequent global meetings, including parallel forums alongside many official global governance conferences (Pianta, 2001). Between such face-to-face encounters, telecommunications, computer networks and electronic mass media have allowed today's civil society groups to maintain more or less instantaneous connections with one another across the world. The Internet has proved to be a particular boon to global citizen activism (Lee, 1996; Harcourt, 1999; Naughton, 2001; Warkentin, 2001).

Civil society has also become global in the fourth sense of adopting global organizational forms. Some of these transplanetary associations are unitary and centralized, like the Geneva-based World Economic Forum, which has since the early 1970s assembled transworld companies (now numbering some 900) under the motto of 'entrepreneurship in the global public interest'. Alternatively, the transplanetary association may take a federal form, as in the case of the Brussels-based ICFTU, with several hundred affiliated national labour organizations. Initiatives like Shack/Slum Dwellers International and the StreetNet alliance of street vendors have developed transworld networks among local initiatives. Meanwhile other global civil society associations have operated without a coordinating secretariat. An illustrative example is the aforementioned PGA, which has mainly operated through a website.

Fifth, parts of contemporary civil society development have been helped by global finance. Several foundations with global operations have been particularly important in this regard. For example, the Friedrich Ebert Stiftung has funded many labour movement initiatives across the world. The Ford Foundation has supported NGOs in dozens of countries. George Soros has ploughed some of his billions gained from foreign exchange speculation and hedge funds into civil society development through his Open Society Institutes in former communist-ruled countries and Turkey.

Sixth, considerable elements of contemporary civil society have become global inasmuch as they are motivated by sentiments of transplanetary solidarity (Johnson and Laxer, 2003). For example, as is elaborated further in Chapter 7, many civil society groups have built on a sense of collective identity that transcends territory – for example, on lines of age, class, disability, gender, profession, race, religious faith or sexual orientation. In addition, significant amounts of civil society activity are today driven by cosmopolitan inspirations to provide security, justice and democracy for humanity across the planet.

Finally, some civil society associations have turned global by themselves undertaking transworld regulatory activities. That is, these organizations have become directly involved in mechanisms to formulate, implement, monitor and enforce global governance measures. For example, in the late 1990s hundreds of civil society associations joined with the World Bank in a Structural Adjustment Policy Review Initiative to assess the effects of macroeconomic reforms in eight countries (SAPRI, 2004; SAPRIN, 2004). The Ethical Trading Initiative, established in 1998 with sponsorship from the British government, has involved 18 NGOs and 4 trade union federations. NGO forums have often influenced the declarations and programmes of action that emanate from UN-sponsored global issue conferences. Such impact was especially apparent during the population meeting at Cairo in 1994, when interventions from the NGO forum were instrumental in preserving commitments to family planning.

Environmental NGOs have taken a particularly prominent part in global governance of their issue-area (Princen and Finger, 1994; Lipschutz with Mayer, 1996; Wapner, 1996; Newell, 2000). In 1980 the World Conservation Union (IUCN) and the World Wide Fund for Nature collaborated with UNEP to launch a World Conservation Strategy that developed guidelines for states. On a similar pattern the World Resources Institute (WRI) formulated the Tropical Forestry Action Plan in 1985 jointly with the UN Food and Agriculture Organization (FAO) and UNDP. Since 1997 Global Forest Watch has tracked illegal logging and its impacts on local populations in ten countries across the world. The International Council of Scientific Unions played an important advisory role to the World Meteorological Organization and UNEP in setting up the Intergovernmental Panel on Climate Change in 1988. The Secretariat for the Convention on International Trade in Endangered Species of Wild Fauna and Flora (CITES) has worked in close cooperation with the IUCN and the WWF. The IUCN, WRI and UNEP have jointly organized the Biodiversity Conservation Strategy Programme.

Of course civil society interventions have also sometimes blocked global governance initiatives, prompting some observers to speak of an '*anti*-globalization movement'. For example, NGOs played an important role in thwarting negotiations in the OECD toward a Multilateral Agreement on Investment in 1998 (Kobrin, 1998b; Henderson, 1999; Goodman, 2000; Smythe, 2000). Civil society opposition to neoliberalist globalization has also played a part in frustrating WTO Ministerial Conferences at Seattle in 1999 and Cancún in 2003 as well as cancelling a World Bank meeting in Barcelona in 2001 (Cockburn and St Clair, 2000; Kaldor *et al.*, 2000; Yuen *et al.*, 2001). Coalitions of NGOs and grassroots groups have halted several World Bank-funded dam constructions or obtained better compensation arrangements for people adversely affected by these projects (Udall, 1998; Khagram, 2000).

Civil society engagement with global governance has sometimes also reverberated back on state regulation. Employing a so-called 'boomerang effect', civil society groups have worked through global arenas in pursuit of changes to state policy (Keck and Sikkink, 1998). For example, civil society associations in Kuwait have utilized global events and measures to press their government to change budget allocations, economic planning, and environmental laws. Some women's associations in Eastern Europe and Central Asia did not meet their country authorities until both sides attended UN meetings on gender issues.

Conclusion

From the above (and as summarized in the box below) it is plain that globalization has significantly affected the mode of governance. In tandem with this reconfiguration of social space, the statist mould of old has given way to a polycentric framework of regulation. States continue to figure very significantly in this poststatist condition, but they are embedded in multi-scalar and diffuse networks of regulation. Polycentric governance occurs through diverse and often interconnected public and private arrangements on varying scales from local to global. The situation has lacked a clear centre of command and control of the sort that the Westphalian sovereign state once provided.

Implications of globalization for governance in summary

Refashioning of states

- removal of the material and ideational conditions for statism and Westphalian constructions of sovereignty
- reorientation of states to serve global as well as national constituencies
- complex and differential effects on state delivery of social protections
- shifts in the incidence of warfare and the tools with which it is waged
- major growth in transstate networks

Diffusion of regulation

- widespread devolution and increased cross-border relations of substate authorities
- proliferation and growth of macro-regional governance agencies
- expansion of public global regulation
- development of private, non-statutory frameworks to govern various aspects of global affairs

Growth of global civil society

- rise of organized citizen activism on global issues
- increased engagement by civil society groups of suprastate and private governance agencies as well as the state

With such a dispersion of regulatory activities, polycentric governance involves major challenges of producing coherent and effective policy. No single actor or committee of actors plays an overall coordinating role in, say, the regulation of climate change, epidemics, intellectual property, the Internet, or refugee flows. The possibilities of gaps, overlaps, confusions and contradictions between agencies are considerable. Moreover, with no final site of adjudication, people in a situation of polycentrism can always appeal their case to another authority.

To take one prominent example, regulation of a global financial crisis involves governments of the countries directly affected, as well as transstate networks like the G7, G20 and G24, as well as global agencies such as the BIS and the IMF, as well as macro-regional institutions like the European Central Bank, as well as private bodies with regulatory functions such as the IASB and the International Securities Market Association, as well as civil society associations like the IIF and Friends of the Earth (Scholte, 2002c). Nothing like a World Financial Authority exists to provide general oversight and coordination. In this situation, responses to global financial crises – like in Asia in 1997–8 – have tended to be rather ad hoc and muddled. Similar comment could be made about the governance of many other global problems.

Of course a dispersion of regulatory activities does not necessarily entail a diffusion of power. On the contrary, as already stressed in Chapter 2, and as further elaborated in Part III, contemporary globalization has very much been a question of hierarchy and dominance. Decentralization in respect of the institutions of governance has also been a context for considerable concentration of power in certain states and social circles. As a result, today's globalizing world confronts critical democratic deficits, as considered at length in Chapter 11.

Chapter 7

Globalization and Identity: From Nationalism to Hybridization

Main points of this chapter
Globalization and the nationality principle
Plural national identities
Nonterritorial identities
Hybridization
Conclusion

Main points of this chapter

- contemporary globalization has helped to undermine the previous near-monopolistic position of state-nations in the construction of collective identities
- globalization has encouraged the growth of national identities on scales other than the state, in respect of substate, macro-regional and transworld spheres
- the spread of transplanetary relations has encouraged some rise in universal-cosmopolitan attachments to humanity as a whole
- the growth of transworld spaces has facilitated the development of various nonterritorial identities **inter alia** on lines of faith, class, gender and race
- pluralization of identities in the context of globalization has increased tendencies of hybridization

So far this discussion of globalization and social change has interlinked structures of space, production and governance. Socio-psychological aspects of the dynamics are now added in the current chapter with a focus on frameworks of identity. Identities – that is, constructions of being, belonging and becoming – hold key significance in terms of both defining the self and forging collective bonds with others. Moreover, structures of identity have far-reaching implications for resource distributions, regulatory apparatuses and citizenship. Not surprisingly, then, identities often lie at the heart of, and give shape to, political struggles.

Territorialism as the previously prevailing structure of social space was closely interlinked with nationalism as the previously prevailing structure of collective identity. Given this relationship, the currently ongoing shift away from territorialism in social geography has, not surprisingly, unfolded together with an attenuation of nationalism as the overriding basis of macro social identification. Instead of the monochrome fixation on nationality (especially state-centred nationhood) that reigned in the mid-twentieth century, identities in today's more global world have tended to adopt a more plural and hybrid character. Today faith, class, gender, race, age, sexual orientation and other aspects of self and solidarity have acquired increased prominence alongside – and in complex mixes with – nationality. The general situation with respect to identity has moved from one of nationalism to one of considerable pluralism and hybridity.

'Nationalism' is taken here to be a circumstance where people construct their being, belonging and becoming first and foremost in terms of national affiliation. Ideological nationalism – the zealous promotion of one's nation – is one reflection of the deeper social structure of nationalism. Other manifestations of this structure include the construction of states, firms and civil society associations as primarily if not exclusively national organizations, often adorned with national symbols. In addition, under nationalist conditions literature, music and other art forms are principally described on national lines: 'the American novel', 'Dutch painting', etc. Although other touchstones for identity such as class and religion exist under conditions of nationalism, they are invariably subordinated to the overriding nationality principle, for example, in national business confederations and national churches.

In the middle of the twentieth century, prior to accelerated and large-scale globalization, nationalism ranked as the predominant world structure of collective identity. Across the planet national sensibilities were either well entrenched or, in the case of decolonizing areas, on a sharp ascent. Reflecting these times, the theologian Reinhold Niebuhr declared that the nation was 'the most absolute of all human associations' (1932: 83). On similar lines the political scientist Rupert Emerson in 1960 dubbed the nation 'the terminal community' that invariably prevailed 'when the chips are down' (1960: 95–6).

Several decades of intensified globalization and spreading supraterritoriality have helped to loosen the hold of nationality as the overriding basis of group identity. National solidarity has rested in good part on a population's shared devotion to and struggle for a specific territorial homeland. A relative deterritorialization of social space could therefore be expected to transpire hand in hand with a relative denationalization of social identity. At the same time, the general rise of supraterritorial connections might logically be reflected in, and encouraged by, a growth of nonterritorial identities and solidarities, for example, on lines of bodily condition (e.g., AIDS sufferers), generation (e.g., teenage culture), or religion (e.g., Baha'ism).

This is by no means to suggest that contemporary globalization has brought an 'end of the national project' in regard to identity (Smith, 1990a; Brown, 1995; Guéhenno, 1995), any more than the trend has yielded the fall of capital in respect of production or the demise of the state in respect of governance. Many nations survive and indeed thrive in today's more global world. Just as the passing of territorial*ism* has not meant the passing of territorial*ity* in the sphere of geography, so the end of national*ism* has not entailed the end of national*ity* in the sphere of identity. Notions of a 'postnational' era would seem at best premature (Habermas, 1998; Hedetoft and Hjort, 2002; see also Kennedy and Danks, 2001).

Rather, much as the expansion of transplanetary and supraterritorial links between people has helped to alter various attributes of capitalist production and state governance, so globalization has also encouraged changes in the manifestations of national identity. For example, next to state-nations (that is, national identities connected with a state jurisdiction), the contemporary globalizing world has experienced a proliferation of micro-nations that reside within and sometimes also across state jurisdictions. In addition, regionalization against the backdrop of globalization has promoted some development of macro region-nations, especially in the case of European identity. And globalization has furthered a growth of transworld national identities in peoples like Armenians and Chinese that are dispersed in diasporas across the planet.

At the same time as shifting the forms of nationhood, accelerated globalization and the rise of supraterritorial connectivity have also encouraged some notable growth of non-national, non-territorial collective identities during the past half-century. For one thing, recent decades have seen modest increases in universalistic cosmopolitanism, where people identify themselves with a single community of all humankind that extends everywhere on earth. In addition, other nonterritorial identities and accompanying transworld solidarities and struggles have been based on a particular attribute that is shared by certain persons scattered across the planet. Thus what might be termed 'partial cosmopolitanisms' have developed in relation to shared faith, class, gender, race, age, sexual orientation and disability.

These various trends in the social construction of identities in a globalizing world have often converged on the individual. That is, the same person might experience several identities at once, with a mix of state-nationalities, micro-nationalities, region-nationalities, global diasporas, and nonterritorial identities. Indeed, few people living more globalized lives have a one-dimensional identity of the old nationalist sort. Globalization has tended to generate hybridity, where persons have complex multifaceted identities and face challenges of negotiating a blend of sometimes conflicting modes of being and belonging within the same self.

The rest of this chapter elaborates these implications of contemporary globalization for identity in turn. The first section considers the general relationship between globalization and the nationality principle. The second section examines the proliferation of different kinds of national projects under contemporary intensified globalization, including micro-nations, region-nations and transworld nations in addition to traditional state-nations. The third section explores connections between globalization and the growth of nonterritorial identities. The fourth section analyses the dynamics of hybridization within globalization.

Globalization and the nationality principle

Before further elaborating how accelerated globalization of recent history has affected national identities it is advisable to consider what constitutes a nation. This is not to attempt (fruitlessly) a resolution of long-running, complicated and often heated debates about defining nationality. However, for the purpose of the present discussion nationhood may be said to exhibit four general distinguishing features.

First, a nation encompasses a large population. Its size is substantial enough that each member has face-to-face contacts with only a minor proportion of the total national group. Nations are thereby distinguished from smaller-scale affiliations like neighbourhoods and traditional kinship circles whose members have regular direct interactions with one another.

Second, a nation is distinguished as a form of collective identity by attachment to a specific territorial homeland, which usually has larger proportions than a district or province. Each nation roots itself in a particular country, even if (as in the case of certain diasporas) a majority of the group resides outside that domain. In some instances, two or more national projects have laid claim to the same tract of land. As a result, long and bitter nationalist conflicts have developed over, for example, Kashmir and Northern Ireland.

Third, a nation defines itself through an emphasis of attributes that set it apart from other national groups. Each nation declares itself to be unique on the basis of difference. These distinguishing features may relate to language, customs, sensibilities, art forms, religion, race or more. Nationalists generally connect these marks of distinction to a shared heritage in the past, a joint struggle in the present, and/or a common destiny in the future.

Fourth, as previously noted in Chapter 4, nations are mutually constitutive. They do not arise autonomously, but through *inter-national* relations. Thus a nation identifies its purportedly unique characteristics largely by drawing contrasts with 'foreigners'. In addition, nations have usually forged and sustained themselves in good part through acts of collective defence against 'external' intrusions such as military attacks or colonial domination. At the same time, nations have tended to consolidate in part by asserting privileges (like citizenship and welfare entitlements) for 'insiders' that are denied to 'outsiders'. On each of these counts, nationality and inter-nationality have been two sides of the same coin.

Some might add statehood (including the aspiration to statehood) as a fifth distinguishing feature of nationhood; however, states and nations are far from the same. A nation is a type of group identity, while a state is a type of governance apparatus. A nation-state is a territorial government that means to rule over a corresponding national homeland. A state-nation is a territorial community that means to be ruled by a corresponding state apparatus. However, many states are not nation-states (e.g., city-states and multinational states like the Austro-Hungarian Empire). Likewise, many nations are not state-nations (e.g., the micro-nations and region-nations discussed later in this chapter).

True, historically the governance structure of statism and the identity structure of nationalism have often had close interconnections. The main form of national identity between the mid-nineteenth and mid-twentieth centuries was the state-nation. Thus the Brazilian nation was linked with the Brazilian state, the German nation with the German state, the emergent Indonesian nation with the emergent Indonesian state, and so on. Notions of 'nation' and 'state' were so tightly interwoven in this earlier day that many people treated the two notions as synonymous (for example, saying 'international' relations when they meant 'inter-state' relations). Indeed, to this day many people conflate the terms 'citizenship' and 'nationality', even though the words refer to different issues of governance and identity, respectively.

Yet nations can also take non-state forms. Many large groupings of people that claim distinctive collective attributes and attachment to a territorial homeland lack a corresponding state. Examples include substate nations like Luo and Québecois, transstate nations like Basques and Kurds, and globally dispersed nations like Africans and Palestinians. Indeed, as later parts of this chapter elaborate, one of the significant consequences of contemporary heightened globalization has been to loosen the connections between states and nations, including to the point that many national projects today no longer involve an aspiration to acquire their own sovereign state.

Although nationalists usually affirm that their identities are primordial and natural, national projects on the lines just described were not consolidated anywhere on earth until well into the nineteenth century. Only then did a fully fledged national sensibility emerge: deeply rooted in consciousness; spread across all provinces in a country; enveloping all classes and religions in a population; and central to political organization and aspirations. Even in France, often depicted as the birthplace of the national idea, social consciousness was not comprehensively 'nationalized' until the late nineteenth century (Weber, 1977). Indeed, viewed in the long term of history, national unity has been an aberration rather than the norm (McNeill, 1986).

If nationalism is a historically bound social structure, might contemporary globalization – with its expansion of supraterritorial spaces and growth of planetary connections – herald the end of the national identities? In certain ways, globalization has unsettled and indeed challenged the position of the nation as the predominant touchstone of collective identity in society. As is elaborated later in this chapter, the spread of transworld relations has promoted a rise of nonterritorial identities and cosmopolitan solidarities. Given this increased plurality of group affiliations, appeals to an overriding state-bound 'national interest' today generally fall on less steady ground than they did in the first half of the twentieth century.

In addition, globalization has disrupted several aspects of social structure that have in the past encouraged the development of nations. For example, nationalism has historically thrived in the context of territorially based commercial and industrial capitalism. However, as indicated in Chapter 5, globalization has shifted the scope of accumulation to include commodities that are much less tied to territorial geography. Moreover, most major national projects have historically developed in the context of territorial states. States sponsored the language, symbols, education systems, infrastructure and wars that were crucial to the creation of nations. Yet trends in governance described in Chapter 6 (with the move from statism to polycentrism) have attenuated the dynamics that previously bolstered state-nations. Indeed, European governance institutions have promoted a suprastate European identity, while global governance agencies have often advanced notions of a cosmopolitan 'international community'.

In experiences of daily life, too, globalization has made the question of national distinctiveness still more problematic than it has always to some extent been. The growth of transworld relations has greatly intensified the interpenetration of languages, customs, artefacts, races and other purported hallmarks of 'unique' national character. As a result, it has often become more difficult clearly and precisely to distinguish nations from one another.

But do such tensions between globalization and nationalism mean that national identities have no future? Little evidence points to so radical a conclusion. After all, many of the circumstances that have historically encouraged the growth of national affiliations have persisted in the midst of contemporary intense globalization. As stressed before, older territorially bound commerce and industry have not disappeared with the rise of global capitalism. Similarly, states have shown no sign of becoming irrelevant, even if they have lost their earlier monopoly on governance. Meanwhile entrenched national languages, national festivals, national transportation infrastructures, national historiographies, national legal systems, national statistics, national medical styles, national academic traditions, and so forth hardly seem likely to disappear in the short or even medium term. The discourse of nationality has remained prominent in global governance agencies such as the United *Nations* and the

Inter-national Monetary Fund. Many a transworld women's organizer, global company manager, and supraterritorial religious revivalist has retained at least a secondary national self-definition along with their nonterritorial identity.

Moreover, current accelerated globalization has in some ways positively reinforced national sensibilities. For instance, price structures of telecommunications have generally been set so that 'domestic' calls within the nation cost much less than 'foreign' calls over a similar distance (albeit that such cost differentials have substantially declined of late in many countries). In addition, electronic mass media can be harnessed in the service of a national project, as wartime propaganda has illustrated for decades. Newspaper websites mainly attract readers (including expatriates) from the nation where the respective journals are based. Global broadcasters like CNN International draw tiny audiences relative to national channels in most parts of the world most of the time. Nationalist pride has put much impetus behind the entry of flag-carrying companies into global capitalism. Korean corporate conglomerates, the *chaebols*, present a clear example in this regard. Global tournaments like the Olympic Games and various World Cups have also thrived on nationalist sentiment.

Indeed, increased contact with the 'foreigner' through global connectivity has in many cases heightened rather than reduced awareness of, dedication to, and determination to preserve national distinctiveness. Although the growth of transworld spaces can in some ways blur national differences, closer inter-national encounters in global markets, global media and the like can also sharpen self-awareness of national identity. Many a global tourist is only too glad to get back to their national home!

Moreover, by removing the protection previously afforded by territorial distance and borders, the rise of supraterritoriality has sometimes prompted nationalist reactions. Adopting a rejectionist position of the sort described in Chapter 1, many people have feared that global capital destroys national jobs, that global communications threaten national cultures, that global governance undermines national self-determination, that global ecology endangers national health. These fears have provoked many a defensive move to preserve national identities. For example, contemporary times of accelerated globalization have seen widespread calls for trade protectionism and tighter immigration controls. Many parts of Europe have experienced revivals of xenophobic nationalism, witnessed *inter alia* in the electoral advances of the Freedom Party in Austria, the Flemish Bloc in Belgium, the National Front in France, the Progress Party in Norway, and the Greater Romania Party. In Australia the One Nation party briefly flourished in the late 1990s. Meanwhile one White House aspirant of the 1990s, Patrick Buchanan, urged 'cultural war' and the construction of an impenetrable 2,000-mile steel fence along the US border with Mexico, allegedly to protect the American worker from the ills of globalization (Buchanan, 1998). Thus deepening transworld connectivity has in some quarters provoked greater determination to retain national identities. In these circles, the more that territorial distances and borders have disintegrated, the more national differences have seemed precious.

Plural national identities

Although, owing to the logics just described, contemporary intensified globalization has not heralded the end of national identities, the reconfiguration of geography has affected the forms that nationhood takes. On a broad pattern seen previously with respect to capital and the state, the growth of transplanetary connections has wrought change-within-continuity as regards the nation. That is, the general feature of nationhood has remained, but its specific manifestations have altered in important ways. In particular, the globalizing world has witnessed a pluralization of national identities. Instead of the previous effective monopoly of state-nations, national identities have come increasingly to take substate, transstate and suprastate forms as well. Indeed, many individuals have acquired a plurinational sense of self.

The persistence of state-nations

As already implied in earlier paragraphs, many state-nations have proved to be quite resilient under contemporary conditions of accelerated globalization. For instance, the spread of transworld relations apparently did nothing to reduce the urgency with which the Bonn/Berlin government sponsored German national reunification under an enlarged German state after 1989. Likewise, most of the new post-communist states in Central Asia and Eastern Europe (Kazakstan, Slovenia, etc.) have enthusiastically sought to forge a national community that matches their territorial jurisdiction. Elsewhere in the South, large-scale globalization has not deterred most newly decolonized states from pursuing strategies of nation-building in respect of their populations (albeit with mixed records of success).

Moreover, state-nations old and new have often actively reaffirmed their cultural distinctiveness in the face of intensified globalization. For example, governments in France, Iceland, the Philippines and Russia have taken measures to counter the encroachments of global English on their respective national languages. Meanwhile in the 1980s the Thatcher government in the UK reformed the school curriculum with a specific goal of giving greater emphasis to British history. Steps in recent decades to deepen the European Union have also often reinvigorated state-nationalist sentiments, with electorates in several member countries using popular referenda to block advances in that regionalist project. In this vein Danes at first rejected the Maastricht Treaty in 1993, and Swedes refused the euro ten years later. Several national electorates may well soon turn down the proposed EU constitution.

Some governments have taken steps to reduce global flows in an effort to preserve state-national identities. For example, authorities in China, Malaysia, Saudi Arabia and elsewhere have at one time or another outlawed 'foreign' satellite broadcasts into their respective countries. Other regimes have adopted different technical standards for satellite television in the hope of repelling this 'invasion' (Webster, 1984: 1172). In the 1970s and 1980s, states of the South led an (unsuccessful) drive for a New World Information and Communications Order (NWICO) that aimed among other things to enhance national control over mass communications and to give greater national character to the communicated material. In Hanoi the government passed rules in 1995 to enhance the 'Vietnamese' nature of advertising. The next year police dismantled various billboards promoting 'foreign' goods in a campaign of 'protection against poisonous cultural items' (*FT*, 2 February 1996: 14).

In other cases governments have sought to harness forces of globalization in the service of a state-nation project. For example, state-sponsored airlines (now largely privatized) have in the past stimulated considerable national pride in many countries. Meanwhile state-owned and state-regulated electronic mass media have often promoted national consciousness through their news and entertainment programmes. The Globo network in Brazil and the Televisa group in Mexico have helped to advance state-national identity via television in those two countries. The governments of India and Indonesia have used satellite broadcasting to the same end (Ploman, 1984: 102–3, 121). States have furthermore often sponsored national pavilions at World Fairs and national teams in global sports competitions. The African National Congress (ANC) and the Revolutionary Front of an Independent East Timor (Fretilin) have used global governance agencies to considerable effect in their struggles to gain a state for their respective national projects.

All of this said, however, globalization has in other important respects tended to weaken state-nations. For one thing, as elaborated below, the trend has promoted the growth of alternative frameworks of collective identity, both national and nonterritorial. In addition, the rise of transplanetary connections has compromised the state's previous capacity to dominate the construction of nations. For example, under prevailing neoliberalist policies, the globalization of capital has made it next to impossible for states to expropriate enterprises in the purported 'national interest'. Through privatization under neoliberalist globalization, a much smaller proportion of communications networks (crucial to the formation of cultural bonds) are today owned and operated by the state. With the growth of transworld relations, money has come to involve much more than state-sponsored national currency. In short, the state in a more globalized world is unable to control many of the circumstances that spawn and sustain group solidarities.

Some of the alternative collective identities that have developed in this situation are also nations, but national associations that do not correspond to an existing state. These groupings have all of the distinguishing features of a nation, namely, large population, attachment to a territorial homeland, emphasis of cultural distinctiveness, and international reciprocal identification. However, these nations are not connected to a sponsoring state – and in many cases do not aspire to old-style sovereign statehood either.

The rise of micro-nations

Hundreds of national identities in the contemporary globalizing world have operated on a smaller scale than traditional state-nations. Many of these micro-nations like the Flemish in Belgium and the Kikuyu in Kenya have lain within a single state jurisdiction. However, others like the Baluchis in West Asia, the Tutsis in Central Africa, and the Roma in Central Europe have resided across several states. Some micro-national movements have sought secession from an existing state in order to create their own nation-state. Yet other campaigns have parted from traditional nationalist strategies and have instead aimed for greater national autonomy within and across established states (Keating, 2001).

Contemporary micro-nations take several forms. So-called 'indigenous peoples' or 'aborigines' group the descendants of the original human inhabitants of subsequently conquered territories. Examples include Amerindians in Amazonia, Aboriginals in Australasia, Tribals in the Indian Subcontinent, Bushpeople in the Kalahari, First Nations in North America, and Saami in Scandinavia. Micro-nations also include other sub- and transstate peoples who have felt alienated from and/or marginalized by established states. Examples include Corsicans in France, Ibo in Nigeria, Québecois in Canada, Tamils in Sri Lanka, and Tibetans in China.

Certain micro-nationalist strivings for recognition and autonomy appeared as early as the end of the nineteenth century. Examples include the Acehnese, the Basques, the Catalans, and the Scots (Smith, 1995: 52). However, most micro-national movements have grown more recently. True, like state-nationalists, micro-nationalists have usually affirmed that their identity derives from some age-old primordial essence. However, in most cases full-scale efforts to forge a micro-national identity have been new to the past half-century. One source has counted, as of 1990, over 800 micro-nationalist movements in a world of fewer than 200 states (Falk, 1992: 202; see also Halperin and Scheffer, 1992).

Micro-nationalist campaigns have booked a number of advances in recent decades, including the segmentation of several states. In some instances (such as the former Czechoslovakia, Soviet Union and Yugoslavia) the division has gained recognition in international law. In other cases (such as Cyprus and Sudan) *de facto* splits have developed. Micro-nationalist resistances have also stimulated major constitutional reforms without state fragmentation in Spain (1978), Lebanon (1990), and Belgium (1993). Aboriginal peoples have gained greater statutory protection of their identities within existing states in Australia, Brazil, Canada, New Zealand and Scandinavia. The post-apartheid government of South Africa has declared eleven languages to be official.

Yet, striking though recent advances of micro-nations may be, the trend has in important respects not marked a transformation of underlying structures of identity. 'Tribes', 'ethnic groups', 'indigenous peoples' and 'national minorities' have only redrawn the map of nations. These collective identities have not contradicted the nationality principle as such. Like state-nations, micro-nations involve sizeable populations. With the exception of nomadic peoples, micro-nations are devoted to a fixed territorial place. Like state-nations, micro-nations identify themselves by highlighting their purportedly unique attributes. Following another well-known pattern, micro-nations establish their identity and solidarity largely through processes of international 'othering': some of it defensive and some of it aggressively exclusionary. In short, micro-national movements have not challenged the principle of nationhood, but rather have reproduced it in new forms. Most significantly, the spread of micro-nations in today's world has often loosened the connection between nation and state, a development that in turn has promoted greater pluralism in identities.

Globalization has encouraged the growth of micro-nations in three general ways. First, to draw again on a major previous point, globalization has reduced the relative power of the state, decreasing its capacity to forge a single united nation to the exclusion of other identities. The retreat of statism has opened new regulatory venues including devolved government and suprastate institutions through which micro-nations can advance their autonomy. Moreover, in some countries micro-nationalism has partly entailed a reaction against the state's service of supraterritorial constituents. For example, protests at collaborative interventions between the Nigerian state and Royal Dutch/Shell have spurred the Ogoni movement in the Niger Delta. In such cases micro-nationality has emerged as a form of identity that promises to fulfil collective needs in a more global world better than the state-nation. Such a dynamic has also unfolded among, for example, the Moros, the Québecois and the Scots in their struggles with the Philippine, Canadian and British states, respectively.

Second, micro-national movements (especially indigenous peoples' campaigns) have on various occasions exploited transworld relations to advance their causes (Wilmer, 1993; Brysk, 2000). Representatives of different aboriginal groups have met together in global gatherings since the mid-1970s. On a more regular basis, too, air, telephone and Internet have allowed, for example, the Navajo in the USA to aid the Saami in Scandinavia and the Cree in Canada to assist the Miskito in Central America. Indigenous peoples have also created their own 'multilateral institutions'. On a regional scale the Inuit Circumpolar Conference (ICC), formed in 1977, has linked this aboriginal group across Alaska, Canada, Chukotka (Russia), and Greenland. On a transworld scale the Unrepresented Nations and Peoples Organization (UNPO) has since its creation in 1991 furthered the causes of more than 50 member communities (UNPO, 1995). In official circles, meanwhile, United Nations bodies have promoted the recent codification of indigenous peoples' rights in suprastate law (Anaya, 1996). The UN also declared 1993 to be the International Year of the World's Indigenous People. Concurrently, publicity via the global mass media has helped to generate transworld support for aboriginal movements like the Zapatistas of Chiapas State in Mexico and the Free Papua Organization (*Organisasi Papua Merdeka*, OPM) in Indonesia (Olesen, 2002).

Third, globalization has encouraged the growth of micro-national movements in a reactive sense. Thus, much as the rise of globality has reinvigorated the defensive dynamic of some state-nations, so it has also sometimes fuelled self-protective resistance in micro-nations. In this vein a Québecois trade unionist has affirmed that 'our values and distinctiveness are very important to us. We don't want globalization in the sense of a culture-grinder of uniformization' (St-Denis, 2002). Global tourism has intensified aboriginal Hawaiian sensibilities. Global deforestation has spurred indigenous activism in Amazonia. More generally, too, global ecological degradation has given indigenous peoples occasion to assert the worth of their alternative ways of engaging with nature. The activation of the North American Free Trade Agreement (NAFTA) at the beginning of 1994 provided the immediate trigger for the Zapatista rebellion. In these and other cases, micro-nationalism has held out a promise of cultural integrity and political autonomy through smaller communities, against fears of homogenizing tendencies and externally imposed rule in globalization.

To be sure, globalization has not been the only force behind the contemporary upsurge in micro-national movements. Circumstances connected with particular countries and localities have also determined whether, when, and in what form micro-nationalist strivings have emerged. Indeed, globalization seems to have played a lesser role in some of these campaigns, such as the long-running struggles of various hill peoples in South Asia. On the whole, however, the rise of transworld connectivity has figured significantly in making micro-nationalism a major force of contemporary politics.

The emergence of region-nations

Whereas the micro-nationalist campaigns just described have sought to build national identities and communities on a scale smaller than the state, regionalist projects have developed ideas of nationhood 'above' the state. These macro-nationalisms have included Pan-African, Pan-Arab, Pan-Asian, Pan-European, and Pan-Turkish movements. Often such strivings have enjoyed collective state sponsorship through, for example, the African Union, the League of Arab States, the Council of Europe, and the European Union.

Proponents of region-nations have usually linked these putative collective identities to a common heritage that stretches far into the past. Shared experiences like the slave trade, Islam, Christendom or the Ottoman Empire are said to provide deep historical roots for present-day solidarity. The categories 'African', 'Arab', 'Asian' and 'European' became deeply institutionalized under colonialism of the late nineteenth and early twentieth centuries. Yet strivings to foster collective identities linked to a suprastate region are mainly a recent phenomenon. Some modest manifestations of Pan-Africanism appeared as early as the 1890s, albeit more on racial than regional grounds. Various associations to promote European unity emerged between the two world wars. However, the principal rise of macro-nations on a regional scale has occurred since the second half of the twentieth century, concurrently with and often aided by accelerated globalization.

On the whole, region-nations have so far made more limited advances than micro-national identities. For example, the Pan-Asian movement stalled after several conferences in the 1940s. (However, the last years of the twentieth century saw some determined assertions of 'Asian values' in economic development, especially with respect to human rights.) Perpetual quarrels among Arab governments have severely hampered the development of that region-nation. Notions of an African identity have enjoyed widespread popular currency across that continent. Since 1983 a Pan African News Agency (PANA) has attempted to assert an autonomous regional voice in global journalism. However, on the whole Africanist sentiments have to date produced little in the way of sustained and focused campaigns for a deeper and more institutionalized transcontinental identity. Pan-Turkism grew following the disintegration of the Soviet Union, but has thus far not developed beyond a vague aspiration. Meanwhile most other regionalist schemes (for example, in Central America, South Asia and elsewhere) have been primarily commercial projects with little if any accompanying drive to deepen identity bonds across the populations of the participating countries.

By comparison, European regional organizations (especially the Council of Europe and the EU) have done most to promote a common identity alongside a common market. European symbols and experiences now abound in daily life around this macro-region. Article 8 of the 1992 Maastricht Treaty even formalized an institution of EU citizenship. The idea of a European collective solidarity has gained considerable hold among some élites and younger generations in the EU. However, commitment to a region-nation remains pretty shallow in the hearts and minds of many residents of Europe today.

These limitations noted, region-nations have nevertheless figured more prominently in contemporary world culture than in earlier times and could well show further growth in years to come. Globalization has not been the sole impulse for this rise, but it has encouraged the trend. The connections between the two developments have followed broadly the same lines that were previously mentioned in regard to micro-nations. Namely, globalization has: (a) ended statism and thereby enhanced opportunities for the growth of suprastate identities like region-nations; (b) supplied important means of communication and organization for building macro-regional identities; and (c) provoked nationalist reactions, in this case on a macro-regional rather than a country or more local scale. The spurs that globalization has given to regional governance institutions (discussed in Chapter 6) have also furthered the growth of corresponding regional identities.

Like micro-nations, region-nations have proved to be nations in an alternative guise rather than a qualitatively different form of identity. The various 'Pan' movements have all shown the four broad distinguishing features of nationhood: that is, large population; attachment to a specific territory; stress on cultural uniqueness; and inside–outside differentiation. Hence in respect of region-nations, too, globalization has brought changes *in* rather than changes *of* the national framework of identity in contemporary society.

The growth of transworld nations

In addition to state-nations, micro-nations and region-nations, the nationality principle has persisted in contemporary society in the form of nations that have dispersed across the planet. Joel Kotkin has called these diasporas 'global tribes' (Kotkin, 1992). Others have spoken of 'deterritorialized nations' and 'long-distance nationalism' (Anderson, 1992; Basch *et al.*, 1994). In this vein, for example, Jean-Bertrand Aristide as President of Haiti declared that his country existed wherever on earth there were Haitians (Glick Schiller and Fouron, 1999: 354; 2001). Other prominent examples of transworld nations include Africans, Armenians, Chinese, Indians, Jews, Lebanese, Palestinians and Sikhs (Cohen, 1997). On a smaller scale, shared national identities have also bonded transworld networks of Ghanaian traders, Filipina domestics, Chilean exiles, and other migrants (Rex, 1998).

In the nineteenth century, many immigrants continued for several generations after arrival in the new country to embrace the national identity associated with their previous homeland. Often these groups lived in distinct neighbourhoods, segregated from (and often subordinated by) the population at large in a 'Chinatown' or 'Little Italy'. Yet territorial distance and borders also separated these immigrant communities from their national roots. Hence their bonds with the homeland often lay mainly in the imagination rather than in regular concrete interactions. In these circumstances the experiences of, for example, Africans, African-Americans and Afro-Caribbeans substantially diverged. Likewise, the Ashkenazy (European), Falasha (Ethiopian), and Sephardic (Middle Eastern) Jews developed significantly different cultures during their centuries of isolation from one another. Today's descendants of nineteenth-century immigrants to the Americas have little specific shared experience with their supposed co-nationals in the old country.

In contrast, large-scale globalization of recent times has greatly enhanced the capacities of transworld nations to sustain substantial contacts. Mass air travel has enabled many members of a diaspora to make regular transworld visits to one another. Supraterritorial communications such as direct-dial telephony and satellite television have permitted close day-to-day interchanges within a global nation. For instance, television reports in the early 1990s reconnected the 250,000 ethnic Koreans living in Uzbekistan with 'compatriots' in East Asia who had all but forgotten them.

Meanwhile Internet connections can help to sustain collective identities among immigrants with a common national origin. Examples include the Vietnet listserv (linking the transplanetary Vietnamese diaspora) and the Nikkei Nexus website (linking associations of persons of Japanese ancestry across the world) (My Vuong, 1999). As another website has put the more general point, 'people speaking the same language form their own online community no matter what country they happen to live in' (Global Reach, 2004a).

Transplanetary finance has made it easier for families and other circles within a global nation to give each other pecuniary support. For example, funding from expatriates in Britain, Canada and the USA has supported Sikh activism in the Punjab. Meanwhile global markets have brought 'home' goods within easy reach of expatriates worldwide, enabling them more easily to sustain their national cuisine, national dress and national festivals.

Global organizations have given some transworld nations an institutional basis. For instance, the World Union of Free Romanians, active in the period 1984–96, and the World Romanian Council, founded in 2000, have linked the global Romanian diaspora. The California-based International Basque Organization for Human Rights, founded in 2003, has served to bring together that global nation. A number of governments – including those of Brazil, China, Mexico and Portugal – have promoted the development of community abroad associations. Since 1995 an *Agence de la Francophonie* has linked 50 states in the transworld promotion of French language and culture. For its part the Commonwealth with 53 state members has advanced a transworld Anglophone identity through professional associations, cultural festivals, and sports like cricket and rugby (Shaw, 2004).

In recognition of the global mobility of significant sectors of their subjects, some states have recently increased the scope for dual citizenship. In cases like Turkey and the USA the change has been enacted with legal directives. In many other instances officials have turned a blind eye to statutory offences of holding more than one passport. True, as part of its general turn from the Commonwealth towards the European Union, the British state has during the period of accelerated globalization narrowed the possibilities of dual citizenship *vis-à-vis* former colonial populations. However, on the whole governments have (at least implicitly) acknowledged that they can no longer demand that all their subjects hold only one exclusive national affiliation and loyalty.

In sum, then, the relationship between globalization and national identities has shown several contrary tendencies. In some ways transworld relations have contradicted the nationality principle, but in other ways they have reinforced it. On no account has the rise of transplanetary and supraterritorial relations spelled the end of national identities; however, nations in contemporary globalizing times have been different from those of earlier generations. In particular, the state-nation framework has become less dominant as a specific kind of nation, and globalization has encouraged a diversification of types of nations to include also micro-nations, region-nations and transworld nations.

Nonterritorial identities

The pluralization of identities under contemporary globalization becomes still greater when the growth of various nonterritorial affiliations is added to the diversification of national bonds discussed above. Whereas national identities involve attachment to a particular homeland, other aspects of being such as age, bodily condition, class, faith, gender, profession, race, sexual orientation, and belonging to the human species itself are not bound to territorial location. A blind person's visual impairment is not place-specific and is a struggle shared with similarly disabled people the world over. A religious person's faith applies wherever they might be and provides a basis for transplanetary solidarity with co-believers. Likewise, women, peasants, people of colour, teenagers, engineers and sexual minorities have core aspects of identity that lack a territorial referent and link them with others anywhere on the globe. Humanity, too, is a supraterritorial, transworld category of identity.

As might be expected, accelerated growth of global relations during the past half-century has gone hand in hand with a growth in transplanetary identities. In the words of Zdravko Mlinar, globalization has radically altered experiences of proximity and social connectedness, shaking 'traditional territorial identities based on *contiguity*, *homogeneity*, and clearly (physically and socially) identifiable *borders*' (1992: 1, his emphases; also Shapiro and Alker, 1996). For Nicholas Negroponte, the currently emergent more global generation of children is 'released from the limitation of geographic proximity as the sole basis of friendship, collaboration, play, and neighborhood' (1995: 230).

To be sure, nonterritorial affiliations existed prior to contemporary large-scale globalization. For example, as noted in Chapter 3, adherents of the world religions have for centuries affirmed a notional unity with their co-believers everywhere, even though these long-distance communities usually in practice never had regular direct contacts with one another. For centuries a number of political theorists have advanced notions of a cosmopolitan unity of humankind (Carter, 2001: pt 1). Transworld solidarities among workers, women, and people of colour gained some following in the late nineteenth and early twentieth centuries. In addition, several global associations of students and other young people were active in the first half of the twentieth century.

However, large-scale globalization since the middle of the twentieth century has spurred unprecedented growth in nonterritorial identities and associated networks of solidarity and struggle. Supraterritorial affiliations now touch more people more regularly and more intensely than ever. As transworld spaces have spread, more persons have placed important aspects of their social bonds in nonterritorial as well as (and to some extent instead of) territorial groupings.

This is not to suggest that people holding a nonterritorial identity are all the same, any more than to presume that people sharing a national identity are uniform. On the contrary, nonterritorial groupings have, like nations, in practice housed considerable diversity and tension. Thus, for example, claims of cultural specificity have often complicated the discourse of human rights. Local and national loyalties have frequently frustrated the development of transworld class solidarity. Global gender politics have spawned multiple feminisms, including liberal, socialist, black, pacifist, radical and ecological strands. Indeed, some parts of transworld women's movements have rejected the 'feminist' label altogether. Considerable diversity and various internecine disputes have also marked transworld networks among sexual minorities. That said, identity can house diversity, and differences can coexist with solidarity.

Keeping in mind these qualifications concerning history and diversity, the following paragraphs trace the rise of various nonterritorial identities in the context of – and partly as a result of – accelerated globalization of the past half-century. The growth of universalistic self-identifications with humanity as a whole is examined first. Thereafter the growth of a number of 'partial cosmopolitanisms' linked with nonterritorial social positions like faith and gender is considered.

Humanity

The most encompassing nonterritorial identity for people relates to their species, to their human-ness. Contemporary globalization does seem to have increased conceptions of 'our own kind' in terms of humanity as a whole. Growing transplanetary connections have given people unprecedented degrees of intimacy with one another as human beings, wherever on earth they might be. Global products, global organizations, global broadcasts, global monies and global symbols (like photographs of Earth from outer space) have given people across the planet common reference points as never before. As Anthony Giddens has observed, with heightened globalization 'humankind in some respects becomes a "we", facing problems and opportunities where there are no "others" ' (1991: 27).

Increased self-identification as 'human' – with bonds and responsibilities to other humans anywhere on the planet – is evident in widespread references to a 'global village' and the 'world community', phrases that were rarely if ever heard 50 years ago. As a priest in the Russian Orthodox Church has put it, 'Our world today is like a communal flat in Soviet times. We must live together, be tolerant, do something together' (Tchistiakov, 2002). Similar perceptions have spurred a burgeoning academic literature on cosmopolitanism over the past decade (Held, 1995a; Nussbaum *et al.*, 1996; Archibugi, 1998; Cheah and Robbins, 1998; Linklater, 1998; Jones, 1999; Robbins, 1999; C. Brown, 2001; Featherstone *et al.*, 2002; Singer, 2002; Vertovec and Cohen, 2002). Increasingly, there is a sense that, in important respects, the situation of human beings anywhere in the world concerns human beings everywhere in the world and that some global challenges are common human struggles. To be sure, the extent of self-identification with a global humanity must not be exaggerated, but these sentiments have certainly grown relative to previous generations.

One prominent area where globalization has increased awareness of bonds with humanity as a whole is the environment. Climate change, stratospheric ozone depletion, biodiversity loss, planet Earth's possible collisions with comets, and the like affect humanity as such. No nation, class, gender, race or other social category is exempted. Global ecological degradation has prompted the creation of a number of transworld associations and campaigns (Greenpeace, WWF, etc.) whose members work together for the (supposed) good of humankind as a whole. Likewise, many have accepted the principle that a 'human interest' above and beyond national and sectoral interests requires increased global governance of transworld ecological problems. To be sure, the distribution of the costs of environmental repair remains a matter of considerable political contention, but the fact of humanity's shared ecological fate is broadly accepted.

The growth of global relief campaigns provides further evidence of increased nonterritorial self-identification with the transplanetary human species. Wars, famines, epidemics and natural disasters have since the mid-twentieth century elicited transworld assistance with much greater frequency and on a much larger scale than in earlier times. The aid is tellingly characterized as 'humanitarian', i.e., it is extended on the basis of shared identity as human beings. Global mass media in particular have often played a key role in mobilizing the so-called 'world community' to provide emergency relief. In July 1985, for example, satellite transmissions brought the Live Aid pop concerts simultaneously to half the countries of the world and yielded almost $4 billion in donations for 20 drought-stricken countries of Africa. Likewise eliminating distance between the self and the suffering other, television pictures of the Indian Ocean tsunami of 26 December 2004 provoked a transplanetary response that was absent following the devastating Krakatoa eruption in the same region 120 years earlier. In the contemporary more global world, as the philosopher Peter Singer has declared, 'it makes no moral difference whether the person I help is a neighbor's child ten yards from me or a Bengali whose name I shall never know, ten thousand miles away' (1972: 231–2).

In some cases self-identification with humanity has legitimated military engagements. Several so-called 'humanitarian interventions' took place in the context of the nineteenth-century Concert of Europe, but the practice is mainly recent (Wheeler, 2000; Coker, 2001). However tardy and inadequate in many cases, the frequency and scale of contemporary humanitarian interventions is unprecedented: in Cambodia, Haiti, East Timor, 'safe havens' for Kurds in Iraq, Somalia, Bosnia, Rwanda, Kosovo, Sierra Leone, and so on. Against this backdrop one might speak of a new genre of 'cosmopolitan militaries' (Elliott and Cheeseman, 2004).

Collective solidarity with fellow human beings anywhere on earth has also motivated substantial peace movements since the middle of the twentieth century. As noted in Chapter 3, protests against war and militarization united people from multiple countries on several occasions in the nineteenth and early twentieth centuries. However, the size and global spread of these previous initiatives did not match the scope of contemporary mobilizations for peace. Examples of these struggles include transworld campaigns against nuclear weapons since the 1950s (with a peak in the early 1980s) and against US military intervention in Indochina in the 1960s. Most recently, large-scale opposition to the harm inflicted on human beings through warfare was evident on 15 February 2003 with demonstrations by anywhere from 5 to 30 million people in 600 cities in 60 countries against an impending US-led military invasion of Iraq (Koch, 2003).

Other solidarity with transworld humanity has grown since the 1950s around the theme of 'development'. The specific content of this term has remained ambiguous and contested, but a broad transplanetary consensus has emerged that all of humanity should benefit from certain economic, political, cultural and ecological standards of living. Moreover, millions of individuals have undertaken acts of solidarity (in terms of financial donations, voluntary labour, etc.) with the aim of assisting 'development' to a 'humane' condition anywhere and everywhere on Earth. A smaller circle of people has been ready furthermore to contemplate a fundamental reallocation of world resources in the name of distributive justice for global humankind.

In addition, some policy thinkers have recently begun to promote a notion of 'global public goods', where the 'public' that needs to be served by collectively enjoyed materials and services is a transworld humanity. In economics theory, public goods are things that everyone needs and which should be denied to no one. Examples include disease control and transport infrastructure. Traditionally, in territorialist times, public goods have been conceived in relation to a national economy. Of late, however, some policy discourse has reformulated the concept in global terms (Kaul, 1999, 2003).

Further increased social identification with the global species is evidenced through the growth since the 1940s of a substantial transworld human rights regime (Dunne and Wheeler, 1999). The Universal Declaration of Human Rights, issued in 1948, has gained the adherence of all but a handful of the world's states. Governments have also since the 1950s acceded in large numbers to UN-sponsored human rights treaties. There are now 189 state parties to the 1949 Geneva Convention, 148 state parties to the 1966 International Covenant on Civil and Political Rights, and 132 state parties to the 1948 Genocide Convention. The installation of a permanent International Criminal Court in 2002 had seemed a utopian fantasy ten years earlier. Outside official circles, millions of citizens have supported transworld human rights organizations like the Anti-Apartheid Movement, launched in 1959, and Amnesty International, formed in 1961.

The global human rights regime arguably contains within it an incipient notion of global citizenship, that is, the principle that individuals hold certain entitlements and obligations as members of a transplanetary polity (Hutchings and Dannreuther, 1999; Castles and Davidson, 2000; Delanty, 2000; Carter, 2001; Münch, 2001; Dower and Williams, 2002; Heater, 2002; Linklater, 2002; Pogge, 2002; Dower, 2003; O'Byrne, 2003). In spite of increased discussion of the subject, however, it remains far from clear what global citizenship would precisely entail. Moreover, to date formal citizenship has only existed in relation to states and, in the exceptional case of the European Union, to a regional governance framework. Nevertheless, growing talk of global citizenship reflects greater self-identification with a transplanetary human community. The principle may well obtain more formalized expression in years to come.

In sum, global environmental concerns, transworld humanitarian relief operations, the transplanetary human rights movement, and emergent discourses of global public goods and global citizenship all show increasing self-identification with humanity as a whole in the contemporary globalizing world. This is not necessarily to endorse the trend. After all, cosmopolitan universalism can have objectionable aspects, for example, if it dogmatically imposes a particular religious vision or western liberal modernism across the planet and denies any validity to other life-worlds, including national self-understandings (Kessler, 2000; Fine, 2003). In any case, there is little sign that increased attachments to global humanity are displacing national and other communitarian identities. Other sections of this chapter amply indicate that globalization has not negated these other identities and on the contrary often bolsters them. Humanity is one of multiple – and sometimes competing – touchstones of identity in the contemporary globalizing world.

Religion

One of the other types of transworld identity that has markedly grown with contemporary globalization relates to religious faith. True, key events in a religion's history and its main shrines are usually associated with particular territorial places. Thus, for example, Bethlehem has been a key site in Christian belief, and the temple at Ayodhya has had core importance for Hindu revivalists. In addition, some nationalist campaigns have focused on religious differences as a primary basis for drawing boundaries between territorial communities, say, in Ireland and former Yugoslavia.

However, the core tenets of a world religion are in principle nonterritorial: they can be embraced and practised anywhere on earth. The key identity distinction for a person of faith is not between a proximate 'native' and a distant 'foreigner', but between believers and non-believers. Thus Ayatollah Ruhollah Musavi Khomeini declared that his return to Tehran in 1979 after prolonged exile evoked no special emotion, for his 'homeland' was Islam (Simpson, 1988: 29–30).

Contemporary globalization has provided a context for considerable religious resurgence across multiple confessions: Baha'i, Buddhist, Christian, Hindu, Islam, Judaic, Sikh, and various so-called New Age faiths (Robertson and Garrett, 1991). As discussed in Chapter 8, some of this resurgence has challenged the prevailing rationalist structure of knowledge. In other cases people have attempted to synthesize religious belief with modern science (Golshani, 2004). However, the key concern in the present chapter is with identity frameworks rather than knowledge structures. The important point at this juncture is that faith has obtained greater significance as a nonterritorial touchstone of identity in today's more global world.

Accelerated globalization of recent times has enabled co-religionists across the planet to have greater direct contact with one another. Global communications, global organizations, global finance and the like have allowed ideas of the transworld *umma* of Muslims and the universal Christian church to be given concrete shape as never before (Mandaville, 2001). Aeroplanes have taken Popes anywhere and drawn *haji* from everywhere. The scale of the yearly pilgrimage to Mecca has grown from around a hundred thousand in the 1920s to well over two million today. Satellite broadcasts have enabled televangelists to preach global sermons. Thousands of Mormons and pentecostalists have undertaken global missions. Promoters of every major faith have maintained websites: Hindu Matrimonial International, Islam Online, Totally Jewish, etc. In 1995, the Vatican website attracted over 300,000 hits from 70 countries at Christmas (*FT*, 19 February 1996: 13). The Organization of the Islamic Conference (OIC), founded in 1971 with headquarters in Jeddah, has occupied a spot in global governance. Its International Islamic News Agency has aimed to spread awareness of Muslim causes and views. A Universal Islamic Declaration on Human Rights was promulgated in 1981 as a Muslim alternative to the purportedly west-centric human rights regimes emanating from the United Nations.

At the same time as being pursued through global channels, assertions of religious identity have, like nationalist strivings, often also been partly a defensive reaction to globalization. In these cases religious revitalization has waxed into a kind of nonterritorial cultural protectionism, particularly for those who have associated globalization with oppressions of westernization and Americanization. On the other hand, these faith-based resistances have also used transworld connections to promote their own cultural visions. Thus with global communications the Islamic Revolution in Iran found echoes across the planet at greater speeds and (non)distances than any previous Muslim revivalist initiative (Esposito, 1990).

Certain former proponents of containment in the Cold War have highlighted religious revivalism in contemporary globalization to claim that a 'clash of civilizations' has replaced the planetary rift between Soviet-led and US-led blocs of states (Huntington, 1993, 1996). On this account, faith-based identities have become the principal fault line in global politics. Such a view is overly simplistic, however. It overlooks diversities within and commonalities across religions, so that faith-based groups do not form monolithic, neatly separable, and diametrically opposed blocs. In addition, the thesis neglects the significance of other frameworks of identity, like nationality and class, which often shape social life in ways that work contrary to religious affiliations. Yet it is not necessary to adopt a 'clash of civilizations' perspective to acknowledge the significance of religious faith as a basis of identity in – and promoted by – contemporary globalization.

Class

Whereas the category of 'humanity' covers all people on earth, and several messianic religions would like to encompass the entire population of the planet, other nonterritorial identities have a sectoral character that inherently limits them to only part of humankind. One such affiliation is class: that is, identity based on socio-economic role and corresponding privileges and/or disadvantages. Class can be conceived in broad binary categories of bourgeoisie/proletariat, capital/labour, or managers/workers. In addition, more specific class groupings can be identified in terms of domestics, factory workers, investors, peasants, professionals and the unemployed.

Like most things in globalization, transworld class identities have a long history. For example, the European aristocracy has for centuries constituted itself as a class network on a macro-regional scale. During colonial times this circle was extended, to a limited degree, to include traditional hereditary rulers from other parts of the globe. Likewise, as mentioned in Chapter 3, a number of early capitalists in Europe regarded themselves as a supranational social group, and labour internationals have existed since the 1860s. However, as also with most things in globalization, the main concrete manifestations of transplanetary class identities have come in recent times.

Much of the most striking evidence of growing supraterritorial class bonds in contemporary history has related to élite circles. Globally mobile business, civil society, governance and media figures have increasingly identified with each other in what Susan Strange has termed 'a transnational managerial class' (1994: 138; see also Fennema, 1982; Cox, 1987; Pijl, 1989; Embong, 2000; Robinson and Harris, 2000; Sklair, 2001). Commonalities that bond this transworld group include global English, degrees from leading Northern universities, global professional attire, frequent flyer programmes, global job mobility, investments in global financial instruments, multiple citizenships, and children educated in international schools. Indeed, shared experiences of these kinds permit many in this class to move with ease between jobs in the corporate, civil society, regulatory and journalistic sectors.

Global élite circles tend to congregate around a number of global associations and conferences. Prominent venues of this kind include the Paris-based International Chamber of Commerce, annual and spring meetings of the IMF and World Bank, UN summits and, perhaps best known, the World Economic Forum. Since its inauguration in 1971, the WEF has organized hundreds of country, regional and global meetings of business executives, senior governance officials, politicians, and civil society leaders, including its widely publicized annual jamborees in Davos, Switzerland. The three-day

Davos meetings attract some 3,000 participants at a cost of some $10,000 per head. Membership of the WEF, with annual subscriptions starting at $12,000, requires that a firm have a capital base or a yearly turnover of at least $1 billion. The WEF has been instrumental in launching the Uruguay Round of trade negotiations that produced the WTO and in forging links between local and global capital in China, India, Latin America, Russia and post-apartheid South Africa (Pigman, 2002; Graz, 2003; Simonson, 2006). Given this profile and power, the Davos meetings have since 2000 been a major target of so-called 'anti-globalization' protests.

To be sure, the influence of global élite associations like the WEF can be overplayed. Global managers do not have a single and tightly coordinated strategy of planetary rule. Nevertheless, with contemporary globalization something like the supraterritorial union of capitalists described (prematurely) on the eve of World War I in Karl Kautsky's speculations on 'ultra-imperialism' has arguably taken shape (Kautsky, 1914).

Certainly transplanetary élite links have developed further than nonterritorial working class identities. Although globalization has proceeded much further in the present day than in the early twentieth century, transworld organizations of labour have strengthened relatively little in the interim. True, the ICFTU as of 2005 grouped 234 national trade union centres from 152 territories, while membership of the World Confederation of Labour (WCL) as of 2001 spanned 144 unions from 116 countries. (The two global organizations are likely to agree a merger in 2005.) Sectoral global trade secretariats like the International Metalworkers Federation (another IMF!) and Public Services International (PSI) have also remained active. Other global working-class identity has found expression outside traditional labour hierarchies in initiatives like the Union Network International (UNI), an online 'cybertariat' founded in 2000. In addition, certain new social movements (for example, concerning human rights) have embraced nonterritorial working-class interests.

Global workers' solidarity has found expression in a number of labour disputes (Kamel, 1990: ch 5). For example, the miners' strike of 1984–5 in Britain attracted transworld backing (Saunders, 1989). Sacked dockers from Liverpool in England toured 15 countries in 1995–6 to garner support for their cause (Waterman, 1998: 258). Workers across North America campaigned against the NAFTA accord in 1993 (Kidder and McGinn, 1995). Various labour activists have used the Internet to build a 'new internationalism' of resistance to global capital (Lee, 1997b).

Underclasses have also constructed some transworld solidarities outside the labour movement. For example, since 1993 the *Vía Campesina* has given global form to peasant struggles, now with members in 60 countries (Desmarais, 2002). Representatives of the urban poor in Asia and Southern Africa have maintained community exchange programmes since the late

1980s and organized themselves formally as Shack/Slum Dwellers International in 1996 (Patel *et al.*, 2001). Another small-scale initiative, the Participation Resource Action Network, has linked poor people across four continents (Gaventa, 1999). Thousands of transworld partnerships between North-based and South-based development NGOs have likewise championed the interests of the poor, although the NGO activists themselves have often come from more privileged circles.

Yet the illustrations just given have marked the exception rather than the rule. On the whole transplanetary solidarities based on underclass identities have figured fairly marginally in contemporary global politics. Most shop floors have known no transworld organizations or Internet links. Indeed, in the contemporary situation of mobile global capital and considerable structural unemployment, wage earners at different corners of the planet have sooner been set in competition against each another.

Gender

Other pronounced deterritorialization of collective identities has occurred in the context of contemporary globalization in respect of gender. These transplanetary solidarities have built on differences between femininity and masculinity, including various gender inequalities that are explored in Chapter 10. Formal organizations with an explicit focus on gender have developed mainly among women, although recent history has also seen the emergence – halting, mainly reactive, and on a much smaller scale – of men's movements (Pease and Pringle, 2001).

An unprecedented proliferation and growth of transworld networks that are devoted specifically to the advancement of women's interests has occurred since the 1970s (Rowbotham and Linkogle, 2001; Naples and Desai, 2002; Mohanty, 2003; Antrobus, 2004). Gender politics have turned matters such as physical abuses of women, reproduction strategies, equal opportunities between the sexes, and women's labour into 'global gender issues' (Peterson and Runyan, 1999). Six UN-sponsored global women's conferences with attendance running into many thousands have taken place at five-yearly intervals between 1975 and 2005. Women's associations have also figured prominently in the NGO Forums that have been held almost annually since the 1990s alongside special UN meetings (Pietilä and Vickers, 1996). Like indigenous peoples, women's struggles have on various occasions found support from global governance agencies and global conventions that was lacking from a patriarchal state and its territorial law (Stienstra, 1994). More informally, women activists have developed much solidarity through the Internet as 'a global room of our own' (Harcourt, 1999: xiv).

Race

Along with faith, class and gender, race has provided another important nonterritorial framework of identity in the contemporary globalizing world. On these occasions collective solidarity has developed in relation to shared bodily features, especially skin pigmentation, and shared social experiences (often oppressive) associated with those phenotypical characteristics. In the words of one black activist based in São Paulo (Carneiro, 2002),

> Globalization provides us with an opportunity to recognize that people of African descent throughout the world form a community of destiny and face similar problems. My identity as a person of African descent can be greater than my national identity.

Racial consciousness – in particular 'black'/'white' and 'yellow'/'white' dualisms – emerged as a significant social circumstance several hundred years ago and became pervasive throughout the world in the second half of the nineteenth century. As noted in Chapter 3, some racially based transworld solidarity developed in the 1880s and 1890s among Anglo-Saxons and Pan-Africanists. In contemporary times, global associations that put an explicit emphasis on race have mainly linked people of colour. However, some transworld coalitions of white supremacists have also developed, including through the Internet.

Shared experiences of racial discrimination were one important stimulus to the development of transplanetary Third World solidarity in the 1960s and 1970s. Global governance agencies and global communications have greatly facilitated the activities of *inter alia* the Non-Aligned Movement and the Group of 77, both formed in the early 1960s. Global connections likewise lent much strength to the Anti-Apartheid Movement during its 35-year campaign against legalized racism in South Africa.

In addition, consultations between leading Africans and prominent African-Americans gained some prominence in the 1990s. For instance, a Policy Summit joining these circles at Abidjan in 1991 drew 1,500 participants. In another initiative, the first black governor of a US state hosted 25 African heads of government in the capital of Virginia in 1993 (Leanne, 1994: 2). Among other things, such conferences have generated substantial contributions from black Americans to education efforts in Africa. The Congressional Black Caucus and its foreign policy lobby TransAfrica, both formed in the 1970s, were influential in prompting the introduction of wide-ranging official US economic sanctions against apartheid in 1986 as well as US military intervention in Somalia and Haiti during the early 1990s (Johnson, 1998). A Strategic Alliance of Afro-Descendents of Latin America and the Caribbean has linked groups in 14 countries of that region since 1994.

Alongside this overtly political activity, electronic mass media have played an important role in forging notions of nonterritorial black identity and solidarity. On the Internet, for example, African-Americans have carved distinctive racial spaces like NetNoir and The Black World Today, in some cases including links to the broader African diaspora (Lekhi, 2000). In the context of global consumerism, many marketers have deliberately promoted the 'blackness' of certain music, literature, sitcoms and celebrities. At a grassroots level, many members of the African diaspora have taken to donning 'native' dress as an identity statement. More negatively, globalization can advance nonterritorial black solidarities insofar as the pains of the accompanying economic restructuring have been perceived – often correctly – to fall disproportionately on people of colour.

Youth

Other nonterritorial identity has developed in the course of globalization with respect to youth. Nominally this category relates to a particular age group, though more generally it encompasses lifestyles and phases of psychological development that are identified as 'young'.

Much contemporary global culture has been youth culture. Global consumerism has linked young people across the planet through shared cult films, music hits, slang, and fashion trends. Satellite music television stations have since the 1980s come to reach several hundred million households on all inhabited continents. Global audio-visual media have arguably made many of today's youth more familiar with Hollywood's constructions of America than with many parts of their 'home' countries. Global backpacking has brought young people (mainly from wealthier circles in the North) into contact with their generational peers at all corners of the earth.

That said, it is not clear that these increased transworld contacts have created deep and lasting bonds of global youth solidarity. True, student activism of the late 1960s took encouragement from intercontinental support between Berlin, Chicago, London, Paris and Prague. Many so-called 'anti-globalization' protests of recent years have likewise created global networks of young people that converge in periodic public meetings and maintain other links virtually through the Internet. On the whole, however, youthfulness has been a touchstone for transworld identity without corresponding politics of transplanetary solidarity and struggle.

Sexual orientation

Another touchstone of growing nonterritorial identity has related to sexual preference, in particular lesbian, gay, bisexual and transgender (lgbt) orientations. True, sexual minorities are age-old. Indeed, some evidence suggests that these proclivities have genetic as well as social bases. However, apart from some shortlived gay activism in the early twentieth century, it is only in the time of accelerated globalization that sexual minorities have identified themselves as 'peoples'. In other words, sexual disposition has become a touchstone of collective identity, solidarity and strivings for self-determination (Adam, 1987; Cruickshank, 1992; Adam *et al.*, 1999).

The historical concurrence of the lgbt revolution with the growth of supraterritorial spaces is significant. As with the other cases already discussed, globalization has made room for affiliations based on sexuality by loosening the hold of territorial identities. It bears remembering in this regard that, historically, the modern state criminalized homosexuality and drove it underground (Mosse, 1985). In addition, much 'coming out' has occurred at supraterritorial locations: on television and in film; through telephone switchboards; in global music and sport (including the first World Outgames scheduled for 2006); with gay tourism and migration; by lobbying of supra-state institutions; via the 'queerplanet' and other computer conferences; and, unhappily, in response to the global AIDS epidemic and its attendant homophobic backlash. In territorial spaces sexual minorities have tended to be isolated and hidden from one another; yet in global arenas lgbts can veritably claim, 'we are everywhere' (cf. Manalansan, 1997; Altman, 2001: ch 6).

Various transworld and regional organizations to support sexual minorities have appeared since the formation in 1978 of the International Lesbian and Gay Association (ILGA). Today the Brussels-based ILGA includes over 400 member groups in around 90 countries (ILGA, 2005). In addition, Amnesty International has since the 1990s actively campaigned against persecution of lgbt people the world over (AI-LGBT, 2005).

In sum, the disruption, through globalization, of the equation of 'space' and 'territory' has encouraged the growth of social mobilization around various nonterritorial identities in contemporary history. In addition to the seven types of affiliation discussed in more detail above, other global solidarities have focused on a particular disability, profession, or recreational activity. In this way computer bulletin boards, telephone help lines and the like have encouraged the development of 'electronic tribes' of cancer patients, lawyers, football fanatics, etc. (S. Jones, 1994). Likewise, email, global journals, multilateral research teams, and transworld conference circuits have forged nonterritorial 'epistemic communities' that have come to figure centrally in many academic professions (Haas, 1992).

True, the extent and depth of nonterritorial affiliations must not be exaggerated. Globalist enthusiasts often celebrate the potentials of transplanetary human solidarities more than their actual impacts. Nevertheless, it would be equally mistaken to reiterate today Heidegger's conclusion, spoken on the eve of contemporary intense globalization, that 'the frantic abolition of all distances brings no nearness' (1950: 165). On the contrary, transworld identities related to humanity, faith, class, gender, race, age, sexual orientation and disability have come to figure significantly in the social networks and political struggles of hundreds of millions of people.

Hybridization

Taken together, the different trends described so far suggest a general structural shift in the construction of identity under contemporary conditions of intense globalization, namely, towards increased hybridization (Nederveen Pieterse, 1995, 2004). A hybrid identity draws from and blends several different strands in substantial measure, so that no single marker holds clear and consistent primacy over others. For example, a hybrid self might encompass several nationalities, or might be of mixed race, or might have a multifaceted sexuality, or might combine different class contexts. Likewise, a hybrid identity can give strong emphasis to several types of being and belonging, with the result that, for instance, national loyalties, religious bonds, and gender solidarities could compete and conflict.

Hybridization has not been new to the present period of accelerated globalization, of course. In earlier times, too, identities were in practice often not centred on a single state-nation as completely and unreservedly as the previously cited quotations from Niebuhr and Emerson affirmed. For example, a century ago intimate contacts between colonizers and colonized induced many experiences of plural and in some ways contradictory identities on both sides of those encounters. Immigrants, too, were frequently torn between their original and adopted territorial homelands well before air travel and telephone calls allowed migrants to 'stay' in their place of birth from a distance.

However, the immediacy of the whole planet in contemporary globality has greatly multiplied and intensified experiences of being several selves at once. In the author's current place of residence, for example, the evening television news can, in a matter of minutes, emphasize notions of 'us' in relation to the Midlands, England, Britain, Europe and humanity. A Chinese family living in Mexico deposits its wealth in euros at a Saudi-owned bank located in Switzerland: where are their attachments? A Fijian citizen of Indian descent works in Paris for a US-based accountancy firm: who is she? What collective identity do we ascribe to the computer programmer (sitting beside me on a flight from Chicago to London) who moves between South Africa, Western Europe and North America, having no fixed address and never staying in any country for more than a fortnight? What does one make, in identity terms, of sex workers from Africa lining Tverskaya Street in Moscow, dressed in traditional Russian costume that hardly any local would today wear? In countless such situations, globalization has produced striking cultural mixes.

Global relations can in this way decentre the self. Fredric Jameson has spoken along these lines of a 'postmodern' condition where 'everyone "represents" several groups all at once' (1991: 322). Anthony Smith has depicted a global culture that is 'tied to no place or period . . . a true melange of disparate components drawn from everywhere and nowhere' (1990b: 177). In like vein Octávio Ianni has characterized globalization as 'a vast and intricate process of transculturation' (Ianni, 1992). James Rosenau has similarly described a 'turbulence' of multidirectional shifts in identity and legitimacy sentiments in the context of globalization (Rosenau, 1990). According to Lothar Brock, globalization has encouraged 'identity surfing', where people slide from identity to identity in borderless realms of unconnectedness (1993: 170).

These quotations depict more intense instances of hybridity than most people experience in their day-to-day lives at the start of the twenty-first century. Nevertheless, globalization has tended to increase the sense of a fluid and fragmented self, particularly for persons who spend large proportions of their time in supraterritorial spaces, where multiple identities readily converge and create 'lost souls' (Iyer, 2000). In more globalized lives, identity is less easily taken for granted; self-definitions and associated group loyalties are much more up for grabs.

Hybrid identities present significant challenges for the construction of community. How can deep and reliable social bonds be forged when individuals have multiple and perhaps competing senses of self – and indeed often feel pretty unsettled in all of them? How can populations – including those united in disadvantage – fix a 'we' when so many people are polycultural?

Hybridity can hardly be reconciled with a communitarian approach to forging social cohesion and advancing political struggle. In this tradition, solidarity in large-scale communities is established primarily through 'othering': that is, drawing neat distinctions and oppositions between 'in' and 'out' groups. However, identities in a more global world are too multiple and overlapping to make sustainable 'us'/'them' divisions into discrete communities. Under conditions of hybridity, persons who belong with 'them' in one respect belong with 'us' in another. Thus, for example, individuals who are bonded together when they emphasize a national aspect of their identity readily find themselves affiliated with other circles when they emphasize class, gender, race or other dimensions. In a world of widespread hybridity it is impossible to follow the communitarian formula with clarity and consistency, as done in territorialist–nationalist times of old.

If globalization, through associated pluralization and hybridization, contradicts communitarianism, what are the implications for citizenship? Can citizenship be based on state-national identity alone, as previously, when so many other aspects of identity are foregrounded in the contemporary more global world? If being, belonging and becoming are experienced in more diverse and more blended ways, do institutions of citizenship require a fundamental reconstruction to accommodate this multidimensionality? References earlier in this chapter to dual-national citizenship, regional citizenship and global citizenship suggest that older assumptions that citizenship is singular, national and fixed are already not viable in a globalizing world of hybridization. Whether wanted or not, circumstances are in a transition, as Andrew Linklater puts it, 'to a condition in which sovereignty, territoriality, nationality, and citizenship are no longer welded together to define the nature and purpose of political association' (1998: 44). Constructing democratic community for this kind of world is a major challenge for the future.

Conclusion

As with production and governance, then, globalization has had important cause-and-effect relations with structures of identity. On the one hand, as

Implications of globalization for identity in summary

Proliferation of national identities

- persistent and in many cases reinvigorated state-nations
- growth of micro-nations, including indigenous peoples' movements
- modest emergence of region-nations
- deepening ties within transworld national diasporas

Encouragement of nonterritorial identities

- growth of self-identifications with a globally spread human species
- resurgence of faith-based identities, especially in religious revivalist movements
- rise of a number of global class identities
- rise of gender identities, particularly through global women's movements
- rise of racial identities, especially among people of colour
- spread of global youth culture
- growth of sexual orientation as a basis of social identity and group affiliation

Greater hybridization

- more plural and mixed identities
- resultant non-viability of communitarian approaches to building collective solidarity

seen in Chapter 4, the growth of transplanetary spaces has flowed in part from certain dynamics of identity construction. At the same time, as seen in the present chapter, the spread of global connectivity has had significant implications for identity frameworks. These consequences are recapitulated in the summary box.

In short, then, the significance of globalization has lain not in eliminating nationhood, but in substantially complicating the construction of identity. Globalization has facilitated an upsurge of multiple identities that has in past decades eroded the position of the state-nation as the preeminent structure of self-definition and collective solidarity. In the resultant process of hybridization, constructions of collective identities have tended to become more multidimensional, fluid and uncertain. Although globalization has not dissolved the nationality principle, this transformation of geography has ended the near-monopoly that this notion held on structures of identity in the first half of the twentieth century and thereby raised fundamental questions about the nature of citizenship and the shape of political struggle.

Chapter 8

Globalization and Knowledge: From Rationalism to Reflexivity

Main points of this chapter
Epistemology
Ontology
Methodology
Aesthetics
Conclusion

Main points of this chapter

- contemporary globalization has not substantially weakened the hold of rationalism on the social construction of knowledge, although some rationality has become more reflexive
- the rise of transplanetary connectivity has encouraged some growth in anti-rationalist knowledges like religious revivalism, ecocentrism and postmodernism
- the growth of transworld relations has promoted some shifts in ontology, methodology and aesthetics

Together with frameworks of space, production, governance and identity, the structure of knowledge is, in the perspective adopted in this book, a fifth primary facet of a social order. How people understand is a key social question alongside (and interrelated with) issues of how people bond, regulate, produce, and construct space. Moreover, just as prevailing structures in regard to identity, governance, production and geography vary by setting, so too underlying frameworks of knowledge shift with socio-historical context. It is therefore important to consider whether and how globalization has affected knowledge patterns.

Questions of knowledge have already surfaced at a number of earlier junctures in this book. For example, it was indicated in Chapter 2 that global consciousness (that is, awareness of the planet as a single place) is one of the main manifestations of transplanetary connectivity. It was noted in Chapter 3 that a global imagination has figured in the history of transworld relations for at least half a millennium. And it was seen in Chapter 4 that the predominant modern structure of knowledge, rationalism, has been vital to the creation of global social spaces. Now the present chapter assesses the consequences of contemporary globalization for rationalism and knowledge patterns more generally.

As mentioned in Chapter 1, several authors have linked globality with a purported decline or even demise of modern rationality. Martin Albrow has presented a particularly explicit and articulate statement of this thesis (Albrow, 1996). Certain other sociologists have linked globalization with the challenge to rationalism posed by contemporary religious resurgence movements, including what has popularly often been called 'fundamentalism' (Robertson and Chirico, 1985; Robertson and Garrett, 1991; Beyer, 1994; Bastian *et al.*, 2001; Hopkins, 2001).

Yet announcements of the death of modern rationality in the face of globalization are no less premature than proclamations of the end of territoriality, capital, state and nation. True, as is elaborated in the first section below, global flows have in some ways made room for non-rationalist knowledges such as religious revivalism, ecocentrism and postmodernist thought. However, most knowledge that has circulated in contemporary expanded global spaces has continued to exhibit the core rationalist attributes of secularism, anthropocentrism, scientism and instrumentalism. To this extent, globalization to date has tended to spread and strengthen the position of modern rationality.

This is not to say, though, that the rise of transplanetary connectivity has left rationalist knowledge untouched. On the contrary, as later parts of this chapter indicate, this respatialization of social relations has contributed to several broad shifts in the attributes of modern rationality. In respect of epistemology, for example, global problems such as ecological degradation and financial crises have encouraged a greater appreciation of the limitations and potential dangers of rationalism. In terms of ontology, contemporary globalization has fostered a different conception of 'the world' (now more global) to which reason is applied, as well as different appreciations of time. With regard to methodology, the spread of globality has helped to promote new fields of study, new approaches to education, new literacies, and new kinds of scientific evidence. In the area of aesthetics, globalization has facilitated the emergence of new forms and appreciations of beauty.

To be sure, the growth of transworld spaces has not been the only cause of these contemporary developments in the social construction of knowledge. For one thing, localized circumstances have strongly influenced whether or not reactions against rationalism occur and, if so, how intensely and in what guises. In addition, contemporary shifts in knowledge have emerged partly out of developments within science, philosophy and religion themselves. However, in combination with other impulses, globalization has exerted some important influences on knowledge structures in contemporary history.

Epistemology

One key aspect of a knowledge system is the underlying notion of knowledge, or what philosophers formally call epistemology. Epistemology (of which people are often only minimally conscious) prescribes what counts as 'fact', 'explanation' and 'understanding'. In what ways, if any, has contemporary globalization altered conceptions of the character of knowledge?

Once again the answer is one of change and continuity. The growth of global relations in recent history has in some respects promoted a rise of antirationalist epistemologies, in forms including religious revivalism, ecocentrism and postmodernism. However, in the main globalization has thus far reinforced and extended the hold of modern notions of reason. At the same time, contemporary globalization has also encouraged turns toward greater reflexivity in some rationalist thinking. In reflexive rationality the main precepts of rationalism continue to reign, but people subject this epistemology and the knowledge that results from it to more critical examination.

Persistent rationalism

Rationalism has ranked as the most powerful epistemology in modern social relations. Yet, like any other construction of knowledge, the rationalist perspective is socially and historically bound. It ascended in particular places (starting with the North Atlantic area), in particular social circles (starting with middle-class intellectuals), and in particular times (especially from the eighteenth century onwards). In turn, rationalism may be expected to give way to other epistemologies when socio-historical conditions become ripe for such a transformation.

Has the contemporary rise of transplanetary connectivity constituted an occasion for a transition to a postrationalist epistemology? Have this reconfiguration of geography and accompanying shifts in production, governance and identity made modern rationality unsustainable? Although rationalism has figured as a major cause of globalization, has the contemporary reorganization of social space reverberated to undermine that knowledge structure?

Such a proposition is difficult to sustain, particularly since rationalism has remained integral to most transworld relations. For one thing, global communications technologies have well served modern science and its chief production sites, like universities and research institutes. Global markets, global production, global finance and global organizations have likewise mainly reproduced secular and instrumental thinking. Global ecological problems and prevailing policy responses to them have reflected a persistence of anthropocentric attempts to subordinate nature to human purposes with science and technology. Similarly, most global consciousness has had a decidedly secular character.

Moreover, the currently most influential policy approaches to globalization, summarily described in Chapter 1, have rested firmly on rationalist premises. Neoliberalism, reformism and economic nationalism have exhibited a thoroughly secular, anthropocentric, techno-scientific and instrumentalist orientation to knowledge. Among transformist perspectives, anarchist and socialist views on globalization, too, have involved a rationalist epistemology. By comparison, non-rationalist approaches to knowledge like revivalist religion and postmodernism have generally had far less influence in the politics of globalization.

In these ways contemporary globalization can be associated with a further ascendance of rationalism to unprecedented strength. Indeed, religious practices have declined in many circles across the planet during the period of accelerated globalization, particularly in the OECD countries where transplanetary connections have become most widespread. (Continuing high levels of church attendance in the USA have formed an exception in this regard.) The thought patterns of global managers have in most cases been as anthropocentric as knowledge comes. Capitalist production and bureaucratic governance – both of them substantially advanced through contemporary globalization – each involve intensely instrumentalist orientations. In short, the growth of global relations has in various ways extended rationalist knowledge to more parts of the planet and to more parts of human lives.

Indeed, people who construct knowledge in secular, anthropocentric, techno-scientific, instrumental terms have generally exercised the greatest power in global spaces. Rationalist epistemology has reigned supreme in global enterprises, global governance agencies and the more influential parts of global civil society like think tanks and professional NGOs. People who espouse Hindu revivalism, deep ecology or an ultra-relativist postmodernism have not tended to work for British Petroleum (BP), the Bank for International Settlements, or Amnesty International.

Religious revivalism

On the other hand, global spaces have in some respects also accommodated nonrationalist epistemologies and have in some cases even facilitated antirationalist movements. For instance, the decades of accelerated globalization have witnessed numerous instances of religious revivalism, where believers have sought to regain their faith's original, premodern, essential truth. This 'fundamentalism' has appeared across all of the major world religions (Kepel, 1991; Marty and Appleby, 1991). For one thing, charismatic and evangelical movements have proliferated in Protestant circles across the continents in contemporary times (Poewe, 1994). Meanwhile many quarters of Eastern Orthodoxy and Roman Catholicism have experienced heightened conservatism, the latter especially since 1978 under the pontificates of John Paul II and Benedict XVI. Concurrently, Islamic revivalism has attained considerable strength in many parts of Central, South West, South and South East Asia as well as North Africa. Judaic revivalism of groups like *Gush Emunim* ('Bloc of the Faithful'), founded in 1974, has motivated many Jewish settlers in territories occupied by Israel in the Six-Day War of 1967. In India the *Rashtriya Swayamsevak Sangh* (RSS), the *Vishwa Hindu Parishad* (VHP), and the *Bharatiya Janata Party* (BJP) have sought to Hinduize politics and radicalize Hinduism. Meanwhile various forms of Buddhist revival have unfolded in Mongolia, Sri Lanka and Thailand.

Contemporary globalization has encouraged religious revivalism in several ways. On the one hand, many of these anti-rationalist strivings can be understood in part as defensive reactions against encroachments by global forces on established cultures and livelihoods. This point has been previously elaborated in discussions of rejectionist discourses and transworld religious identities. Yet at the same time, as also noted in Chapter 7, a number of revivalist movements have exploited global relations to advance their causes. To give further examples in this regard, the leading mullah in Tajikistan has maintained many of his communications by fax and mobile telephone (Juergensmeyer, 1993: 5). Meanwhile Ayatollah Khomeini used world service broadcasts to pronounce his *fatwa* against the author Salman Rushdie in 1989.

However, we should not overestimate the scale of religiously based anti-rationalism under contemporary globalization. George Weigel surely exaggerated in asserting that 'the unsecularization of the world is one of the dominant social facts of life in the late twentieth century' (cited in Huntington, 1993: 26; also Berger, 1999). True, several religious revivalist movements have attracted large followings and exerted notable political influence. However, on the whole religious resurgence has enlisted only a limited proportion of humanity and stimulated relatively few major alterations of public policy, although changes such as increased restrictions on abortion can have severe consequences for those directly affected.

Moreover, these religious upsurges have not been completely new to contemporary times of intense globalization. Revivalist reactions against the secularist character of modern rationality have emerged from time to time ever since the Enlightenment. For example, the 1920s saw the creation of the Hinduist RSS and the rise of Islamic revivalism in a number of anti-colonial struggles (Peters, 1979). An earlier phase of Protestant 'fundamentalism' in the USA culminated in the mid-1920s with a court challenge (in the Scopes trial) against teaching Darwinian ideas of biological evolution.

Indeed, just as previous rises of religious revivalism have proved temporary, little evidence suggests that recent instances are on course to displace rationalism as the dominant epistemology in today's globalizing world. Transplanetary relations have helped to stimulate and sustain some renewals of anti-rationalist faith, but global networks have more usually promoted activities involving rationalist knowledge. Contemporary revivalist movements have largely replayed a long-term tendency – one that well predates contemporary accelerated globalization – whereby certain religious circles have from time to time revolted against modern secularism and scientism.

Meanwhile today, as during much of the past two centuries, many if not most influential religious thinkers have sought to marry faith and reason, that is, to combine and reconcile experience of the transcendent with scientific and instrumental knowledge. Thus, for example, the director of a global bank might be a techno-scientific economist by day and a practising Buddhist after hours. Modernizing tendencies in Islam have rivalled revivalist movements. Likewise, reform Judaism has on balance exerted as much influence as revivalist Judaism. Many if not most Christians, Confucians and Hindus, too, have sought to adjust their religious understanding to accommodate modern rationality. In short, revivalist anti-rationalism has been a minority tendency even in many faith circles.

Ecocentrism

Next to religious revivalism, ecocentrism has formed a second noteworthy reaction in contemporary history against prevailing rationalist epistemology. The term 'ecocentrism' is borrowed from Robyn Eckersley (1992), although it is here applied to a wider range of authors and arguments. Whereas religious revivalisms have taken principal aim against the secularist character of modern rationality, ecocentrisms have in the first place opposed anthropocentrism and the attendant drive to control nature for human ends. In ecocentrist knowledge, humanity exists within – and as but one part of – a larger life system. For ecocentrists, *homo sapiens* is subordinate to nature rather than vice versa, and human desires need to be renounced in favour of ecological integrity when the two conflict.

Ecocentrism has taken a number of guises in contemporary history. For example, many indigenous peoples have as part of the assertion of their collective identity promoted notions of aboriginal knowledge where human beings are integrated within and subservient to a natural order. Ecocentrist premises have also underlain notions of 'deep ecology', which reject the 'shallow' environmentalism of those who advocate so-called 'sustainable development' using rationalist knowledge frameworks (Naess, 1976; Devall and Sessions, 1985). From another angle, ecofeminists have identified rationalism with masculinism and have opposed both forces in terms of their purported violence against nature and women (Warren, 1996). For his part, the inventor James Lovelock has popularized the so-called 'Gaia' notion that regards planet Earth as a living creature to which people owe their greatest responsibility, ahead of country, state and nation (Lovelock, 1979). Various grassroots environmentalists like anti-road campaigners and animal liberation groups have likewise tended to understand society in ecocentrist terms.

Globalization has not been the only circumstance to promote the rise of ecocentrist knowledge, but the growth of transplanetary relations has played an important part in the trend. In particular, global ecological changes have raised awareness of the damages that anthropocentric rationalism can inflict. An appreciation of humanity's dependence on ecological conditions is heightened in the light of supraterritorial developments (like climate change and biodiversity loss) from which there is no escape, short of leaving the planet. In addition, some people have been drawn to ecocentrist thought by the ecological irrationality of much global economic activity. In this vein it might be asked why foods are shipped between continents, at a cost of considerable air and sea pollution, when adequate (and often more nutritious) supplies are usually available from local cultivation. Finally, much as some religious revivalists have exploited global communications and transworld associations to further their causes, so some ecocentrists have benefited from the transplanetary social movement activities that globalization has made possible.

Yet the scale of current ecocentrist challenges to rationalism must not be exaggerated. Aboriginal knowledge, deep ecology, ecofeminism and the Gaia hypothesis have, even collectively, attracted relatively small followings. Nor do present trends suggest that ecocentrism is on the way to becoming more than a marginal epistemology. Insofar as ecological sensitivities have gained ground in the context of contemporary globalization, policymakers have mainly opted for rationalist responses in the vein of so-called 'sustainable development'. Such a strategy seeks to perpetuate humanity's subordination of nature and to find techno-scientific fixes for environmental problems.

Postmodernism

In addition to religious revivalism and ecocentrism, the time of accelerated globalization has also witnessed a rise of so-called 'postmodernist' epistemologies. These perspectives on knowledge, briefly introduced in Chapters 1 and 4, have generally retained the secular and anthropocentric orientations of rationalism. However, postmodernists have rejected scientific claims concerning objective facts as well as instrumentalist notions that the primary purpose of knowledge is technical problem-solving.

Against rationalism, postmodernism adopts an anti-universalist and antiessentialist view of knowledge. Instead, this alternative epistemology regards all knowledge as bound to its time and place, as well as the particular person who constructs it. Every truth is therefore contingent upon its context. No understanding transcends its specific personal, cultural and historical setting. For postmodernists, rationalist notions of scientific objectivity are – like any other knowledge claim – a myth with no absolute truth about them (Anderson, 1990). It is social power relations – rather than any fundamental truth – that have elevated rationalism over other modes of knowledge in modern times.

Logically, it would be possible to conclude from the relativism of postmodernism that all knowledges are equally valid. Some postmodernists have indeed adopted an ultra-sceptical position toward knowledge, where no grounds other than personal whim are available for ranking certain values and beliefs over others. At this extreme, fascism could not be condemned relative to liberalism, and no basis would exist to distinguish good art from bad. In such a situation postmodernism would replace the objectivism of rationalism with an 'anything-goes' subjectivism.

However, postmodernists do not – as some of their critics charge – have to take the rejection of objectivism to a nihilistic conclusion. On the contrary, many proponents of this alternative epistemology have advanced strongly held value claims about culture and politics. Postmodernist philosophers like Michel Foucault and Julia Kristeva have taken very overt and public moral stands. Some feminists have integrated postmodernist knowledge into struggles against gender hierarchies (Peterson, 1992). Postmodernist security studies have employed the epistemology in value-inspired critiques of military violence (Campbell and Dillon, 1993). In contrast to religious revivalists, however, postmodernists regard their truth claims to be contingent and contestable.

As mentioned in Chapter 1, postmodernism has attracted most of its explicit adherents in academic circles and the arts. Among academics the exponents have concentrated mainly in the humanities (especially Literary Criticism and Philosophy) and on the fringes of social research (including Anthropology, Geography, Linguistics, Politics and Sociology). In the arts postmodernist thought has reshaped significant parts of architecture, cinema, literature, music, painting, sculpture and theatre.

The contemporary growth of postmodernist epistemologies can be connected to globalization in several ways. For one thing, global relations have, by eliminating territorial buffers, intensified intercultural contacts and heightened general awareness of cultural diversity and contingency. Many people have thereby come – in line with postmodernist precepts – to regard their knowledge as socially and historically relative. Persons who have experienced intense hybridization of the kind described in Chapter 7 are perhaps most especially susceptible to postmodernist relativism. Indeed, exponents of postmodernism have included disproportionate numbers of migrants and exiles.

Globalization has also promoted postmodernist thought through the technologies of supraterritorial communications. For example, mass media news reports have often involved obvious manipulations of 'facts'. After all, the story depends largely on where the camera is pointed. Computer-generated 'virtual realities' have likewise blurred lines between fact and fiction. Indeed, by increasing communication through images as opposed to verbal exchanges, global relations have perhaps given more reign to 'irrational' unconscious associations in human thought (Lash, 1990: ch 7).

In addition, globalization has encouraged the rise of postmodernist epistemology through consumer capitalism. The consumerist mindset is oriented more to ephemeral experiences than to fixed facts. As a way of knowing the world, consumerism (through shopping, tourism, etc.) gives greater weight to sensation than to science. Also, against instrumentalist logic, consumerism accords higher priority to gratifying desires than to solving problems.

All of this said, the novelty and power of postmodernist epistemologies in contemporary society should not be overestimated. Like religious revivalist movements, relativist philosophies date back well before the onset of accelerated globalization. The nineteenth-century nihilism of Friedrich Nietzsche gives but one prominent example. Moreover, to this day fully fledged postmodernist thought has figured mainly on the margins of social life. The overwhelming majority of academics, entrepreneurs, officials and civil society organizers have so far stuck with a predominantly rationalist orientation.

Reflexive rationalism

Thus, in spite of various important challenges, rationalist knowledge has retained primacy in contemporary times of growing global relations, yet this prevailing epistemology has not come through the twentieth century unchanged. In particular, modern rationality has in recent history often become more reflexive.

A number of sociologists have invoked the term reflexivity to describe rationalist thought that is acutely self-conscious, self-searching and self-critical (Beck, 1994; Giddens, 1994). Reflexive rationalists 'think about what before they did unthinkingly' (Smart, 1999: 33). Reflexivity brings less confidence in rationalist knowledge claims and reduced faith in the modern project of perpetual progress through the application of human reason.

Reflexive rationalism is still rationalist. It rests on long-standing core tenets of secularism, anthropocentrism, scientism and instrumentalism. However, reflexivity takes away the conviction element: modern knowledge is no longer taken for granted. Thus many modernist thinkers today, while still regarding rationalism as the most promising epistemology currently available, have also recognized its limitations and flaws. With this attitude, reflexive rationalists have tended to be less dismissive of alternative knowledges and more ready to experiment with different epistemologies (for example, in unconventional approaches to health care).

Indeed, reflexive rationalism and postmodernism overlap at points. Like postmodernists, reflexive rationalists view knowledge as uncertain and contingent. Also like postmodernists, reflexive rationalists see that modern reason can have harmful outcomes, for instance, in the form of military–industrial complexes and ecological degradation.

However, the two epistemologies also part ways. In particular, postmodernists regard rationalism as irredeemable and actively pursue alternative epistemologies, whereas reflexive modernists conclude that, for all its limitations, rationalism is still the best game in town and indeed can be reformed. In the latter vein André Gorz has called for a 'rationalization of rationality', and Ulrich Beck has prescribed a 'new modernity' of more self-critical and self-limiting science (Gorz, 1988: 1; Beck, 1986). Thus reflexive modernists seek a regeneration of rationalism in forms where it does not promote ills such as centralized power and the suppression of cultural diversity. In contrast, postmodernists doubt that rationalism is susceptible to such corrections.

Reflexive rationalism is not completely new to recent history, of course. A sceptical bent has been intrinsic to modern rationality from the outset. Science has constantly questioned and perpetually revised knowledge in the light of new information and analysis. To be modern is in part to 'stand outside' of and critically reflect upon one's being.

Yet the self-monitoring aspects of rationalism have gained unprecedented intensities in contemporary history. Anthony Giddens has in this light characterized the current situation as one of 'high modernity' marked by extreme reflexivity (1991: 28–9). In these circumstances people have become less trusting of science and technology. Thus, for example, current times are replete with food scares and calls for greater spirituality in modern life. Even many professional scientists have retreated from claims to hold objective facts and full truths: the scepticism of science has turned upon science itself (Beck, 1986: 155). In an 'age of relativization' (Sakamoto, 1997), the enlightened are questioning their Enlightenment. Modernists are questioning modernity.

Globalization has not been the only force behind the growth of reflexive rationalism, but this rearrangement of social space has encouraged this turn in knowledge in several ways. For one thing, much as with the spread of postmodernism, the rise of globality has promoted heightened reflexivity by intensifying intercultural encounters. Transplanetary travel, supraterritorial communications, and transworld marketing of artefacts such as Rastafarian music and certain alternative therapies have made rationalists more aware that the world contains a plurality of knowledge systems, each with its own internal coherence. For many people the posited hierarchy of 'reason' over 'folk wisdom' has become more qualified in consequence. Also querying ahistorical objectivism, the philosopher Sandra Harding has asked, 'Is science multicultural?', a question that few if any people would have thought to pose 50 years ago (Harding, 1998).

Computer technologies at the heart of globalization have also injected uncertainties into the rationalist project. On the one hand, digital computers have enabled people to access much more information and to manipulate it faster and in more complex ways. These capacities have often advanced the rationalist cause of subordinating natural and social forces to human interventions. On the other hand, computers have also generated far more data than human minds can effectively monitor and control. Furthermore, continually advancing digitization brings the prospect of increasingly sophisticated artificial intelligence that operates with relative autonomy from human decision. Already, for instance, self-monitoring computer programmes have contributed to 'irrational' runs on currencies and stock markets.

As these undesirable outcomes of electronic finance illustrate, globalization can encourage greater reflexivity insofar as transplanetary relations have produced harms that call into question the rationality of rationality. Other examples include the destructive potential of global weapons, the damage of anthropogenic global ecological changes, and the cruelty of liberalized global markets for vulnerable social circles. Such threats (which are elaborated in Part III) have prompted many rationalists to reflect that modern rationality can sometimes be the problem rather than the solution.

To repeat, however, reflexivity marks a shift within rather than a change of knowledge structure. In reflexive rationality, 'reflexive' is the adjective and 'rationality' is the noun. Although reflexive rationalists may show greater openness to alternative knowledges than traditional 'conviction rationalists', they remain rationalists. 'High modernity', if one accepts that label for present-day society, is still modernity.

Giddens and others have sometimes spoken of 'high modernity' as being also 'late modernity'. This characterization intimates that reflexive rationalism could mark the start of a transition to some kind of postmodern knowledge. Indeed, as noted above, reflexive and postmodernist epistemologies do have some notable overlap. Yet it seems too early to draw the further implication that increased reflexivity is taking rationalism toward the historical exit door.

On the contrary, it is well to remember that much rationalism in the early twenty-first century has not acquired a heightened reflexive character. There is still plenty of evangelical scientism about. Many a manager bows before the shrine of productivity, and many an economist kneels at the temple of efficiency. Many people – in particular the majority of those in positions of power – still regard science and technology as the salvation of our earthly lives. Globalization has (so far) not on the whole displaced that faith.

Ontology

Next to its effects on epistemology, globalization has also contributed to some important turns in other aspects of knowledge. Several of these developments relate to ontology, that is, the broad way that people define 'reality'.

All groups and individuals hold particular conceptions of the entities and relationships that constitute their world. Key ontological concerns include the character of God (if any), life, self, society, time and space. Notions of such conditions form a backdrop to, and shape, every thought and purposeful action, even if people may only rarely express these ideas explicitly. Shifts in mental constructions of elementary realities may also occur so subtly as to be little noticed.

Ontologies vary by sociohistorical context; so the question arises whether contemporary globalization has promoted any changes in this respect. To some extent, all of the developments described in earlier chapters involve adjustments of assumptions about reality as well as shifts in concrete circumstances. However, the key ontological changes at the heart of globalization relate to understandings of space and time.

Space

As noted in Chapter 2, a number of social thinkers from different disciplines have in the context of globalization redefined geography in postterritorialist terms. The present book adds to that trend. To the extent that these academic articulations of revised notions of space strike a chord in lay circles, the accounts are expressing a broader ontological shift in ideas of place.

Different conceptions of space have indeed emerged in wider circles than a cluster of social theorists. As noted in Chapter 3, an awareness of globality has in recent history become commonsense for a notable proportion of humanity. The sociologist Roland Robertson has in fact defined globalization as a growth in 'the scope and depth of consciousness of the world as a single place' (1992: 183). The different conception of space elaborated in this book will resonate with far more readers today than it would have done 50 years ago.

Current widespread talk of 'virtual reality' seems a revealing illustration of an adjusted ontology. People recognize that globally conveyed images on computer and television screens are 'real'; yet these electronic depictions do not fit conventional understandings of geographical 'reality'. People are therefore prompted to construct alternative, postterritorialist definitions of space, in order to restore a fit between their understandings and their experiences. The mediated picture becomes as 'real' as the directly observed scene. With such an ontological shift people move cyberspace and other global realms from fantasy to actually lived reality.

However, this shift to a postterritorialist understanding of space is far from complete. Many people at the start of the twenty-first century still equate 'space' and 'geography' with 'territory'. Perhaps global maps conveying supraterritorial realities will one day be as commonsense to people as territorial maps have been in modern history. Then it would no longer be necessary, as in this book, to express postterritorialist ontology with constant references back to old terminology, that is, invoking notions of supra*territoriality* and de*territorialization*. The vocabulary of globality would at this point be able to stand on its own.

Time

Contemporary globalization has gone to the heart of conceptions of time as well as space. As noted in Chapter 2, supraterritoriality involves a qualitative change in space–time relations insofar as it dissolves the connection (within the confines of planet Earth, at least) between time and distance. Transplanetary instantaneity has brought the advent of globally unifying 'real time'.

In this situation, people living more globalized lives are less inclined to think of time with reference to distance. For example, inhabitants of a more global world do not, as in many earlier contexts, understand a day in terms of the time it takes to travel to the next village or some other destination. In addition, the hour has today lost its once close connection (in many countries) with the railway timetable.

Globalization has tended to shift the ontology of time from a link with distance to a connection with speed. For example, air passengers are usually more conscious of how fast they are travelling than how far they are going. In respect of fax and email, people are more concerned with the speed than with the distance of communications: it is not how far correspondents have to respond, but how quickly they answer. In global production the issue of how swiftly suppliers can deliver ('just in time') often has little to do with how far they have to deliver. By putting greater stress on speed in these and other ways, globalization has contributed to a general acceleration of the experience of life.

In addition, globalization has tended to heighten people's sense of overcrowded time. By removing the buffers previously afforded by distance, supraterritorial connections have allowed ever more activity to descend on a person's time. For those who lead intensely globalized lives, a day becomes a deluge of telephone calls, emails, channel hopping between radio and television transmissions, electronic money transactions, and charges down airport concourses. In a word, life becomes more hectic.

Excessive global time arguably carries significant costs for the quality of life. In this vein Sohail Inayatullah and Ivana Milojevic have worried about 'temporal impoverishment' in 'a world of quick inattentive time . . . where data and information are far more important than knowledge and wisdom' (1999: 77). Indeed, the combination of faster and busier time in highly globalized lives can present substantial coping challenges. In this regard it is probably little accident that stress and supraterritoriality have grown concurrently in contemporary history. Indeed, like notions of 'globalization', the concept of 'stress' has in recent decades spread to countless languages across the planet.

Methodology

Along with epistemology and ontology, methodology is a third area of knowledge where globalization might have effects. Methodology refers to the manners in which knowledge is built: that is, the ways that questions are asked; and the principles and procedures of inquiry that are used to answer the questions posed. Methodology involves issues both of general approach to knowledge construction and of specific research tools.

Globalization has *not* had significant impacts on several core methodological issues in social inquiry. For example, concerning the agent–structure question (discussed in Chapter 1), globalization has not prompted a mass conversion of voluntarists into structuralists, or vice versa. Likewise, the spread of transplanetary relations has not turned materialists (those who root social causation in economic and/or ecological processes) into idealists (those who explain social relations in terms of cultural and/or psychological forces), or vice versa. Increased globality has not induced general changes of perspective on the relationship between facts and values; neither has the rise of transworld connectivity altered views on the links between theory and practice. These methodological issues (explored at greater length in Scholte, 1993) are not directly affected by the shape of social space. Thus globalization is a new subject of study around which long-running debates about methodology can be replayed (Taylor *et al.*, 1996; Germain, 1999; Shaw, 1999). However, the expansion of global spaces has not changed the balance in these arguments, let alone resolved them.

That said, contemporary intense globalization has arguably had some consequence for several other methodological issues. As elaborated below, these impacts have related to the role of academic disciplines, to processes of teaching and learning, and to the nature of empirical evidence.

Disciplinarity

The growth of global problems has accentuated the need to transcend conventional academic divides when undertaking social inquiry. Some theorists have called for *multi*disciplinarity in studies of globalization, where researchers from several fields each contribute their respective approaches to a joint investigation. Others have appealed for greater *inter*disciplinarity, where researchers take the additional step of integrating principles and tools from different fields of study. Some academics have gone still further and argued for *post*-disciplinarity, namely, the creation of substantively new methodologies that do not rely on separated fields of study. The so-called 'world-system approach', associated especially with the work of Immanuel Wallerstein, provides one example of post-disciplinarity (Wallerstein, 1991).

The rise of transplanetary relations has contributed to some retreats from discipline-bound research inasmuch as academic divides have often hampered rather than advanced knowledge of transworld relations. Global communications, global economic restructuring and global ecological degradation are among various contemporary issues that can be only partially – and often but poorly – understood through single disciplines. Little wonder, then, that recent history has seen the emergence of interdisciplinary enterprises such as Business Studies, Media Studies, International Political Economy, and Environmental Sciences. The US Committee on the Human Dimensions of Global Change has concluded that 'the need to understand global change may well become a powerful force for change in the existing structure of scientific disciplines' (Stern, 1992: 33). Likewise, several world-system theorists have cited globalization as a justification for their post-disciplinary approach to social enquiry (Taylor *et al.*, 1996).

However, recent moves away from disciplinarity must not be overplayed. So far, exhortations to transcend the old academic divides have well exceeded actual multidisciplinary, interdisciplinary and post-disciplinary research practices. Like contemporary social inquiry in general, most studies of global issues have drawn from a single field. Several transdisciplinary academic journals for the study of global problems have appeared, such as *Global Networks*, *Global Social Policy*, and *Globalizations*; yet most professional research continues to be published through discipline-related organs. Similarly, most academic conferences have remained tribal conclaves on disciplinary lines. Most research funding has continued to flow through disciplinary channels, and adherence to disciplinarity normally still provides professional academics with a faster track to promotion than alternative approaches. In short, some minor inroads aside, disciplinary methodology remains quite firmly entrenched in the contemporary globalizing world.

Teaching and learning

Other methodological shifts promoted in part through globalization have related to education processes (Breton and Lambert, 2003). For example, the growth of global publishing has meant that millions of schoolchildren and older students now acquire part of their learning from transworld textbooks. A number of (mainly US- and UK-based) academics, including Paul Samuelson in Economics, Kenneth Waltz in International Relations, and Anthony Giddens in Sociology, have in this way become global teachers.

Several colleges and universities have embarked on transworld franchising of entire courses. For instance, Monash University in Melbourne has marketed its programmes in standardized packages throughout Asia (Waters, 1995: 172). Several UK-based institutions have embarked on similar enterprises. In addition, universities can – thanks to air transport, faxes and the Internet – use academics in different countries or continents as external examiners for their programmes. At secondary-school level the International Baccalaureate (IB) has emerged as a global diploma: it draws from no country and is recognized across continents.

Meanwhile mass air travel has in recent history facilitated large increases in study abroad activities. Children from wealthier circles in the North can today expect at least one school trip overseas as part of their secondary education. Hundreds of thousands of university students in the North have completed a period of study abroad, albeit that complications of credit transfer and grade conversion often still arise. At postgraduate level a few institutions have begun to experiment with transworld programmes, where students spend different parts of their course in different countries or continents. The Universitas 21 initiative has linked institutes of higher education in several countries to offer global degrees.

Other 'distance learning' has developed on 'virtual campuses' via television and computer networks. For instance, the Open University in Britain, the Télé-Université in Québec, and Item/Seis in Mexico have delivered prerecorded lectures and demonstrations to their students via television. Countless other teachers have used the Internet as a classroom tool, with websites at least partially displacing books and journals as source material.

Indeed, technologies at the heart of contemporary accelerated globalization have substantially broadened the character of literacy. In many lines of work the ability to use computer applications has become as important as the ability to read and write with paper and pen. In addition, television, film and computer graphics have greatly enlarged the visual dimensions of communication. Many people today 'read' the globalizing world without a book. Sociologists Scott Lash and John Urry have in this regard contrasted a 'literary paradigm' of modernism with a 'video paradigm' of postmodernism (1994: 16). In a world suffused with electronic mass media, journalists, advertisers and disk jockeys have come to rank among the principal teachers.

Finally, the growth of transplanetary spaces has spurred the development of English as a global lingua franca (Pennycook, 1994). Esperanto, the deliberately designed transplanetary language, has only attracted a few million speakers worldwide. In contrast, English is now spoken by 1.7 billion people across the earth (BT, 2000: 10), including many who have never set foot in a country to which English is native. One might even distinguish a 'global dialect' of English, namely, the version that is spoken in tourist resorts and professional conferences. This 'global English' uses vocabulary and turns of phrase that have little currency on the streets of Glasgow, Brisbane and Omaha. More critically, Mary Snell-Hornby suggests that this 'free-floating lingua franca . . . has largely lost its original cultural context, its idioms, its hidden connotations, its grammatical subtleties, and has become a reduced standardised form of language for supra-cultural communication' (2000: 17). The globality of English has spawned several diplomas such as TOEFL (Teaching of English as a Foreign Language) and has raised the Cambridge Proficiency Examination to a transworld standard. At the same time, native speakers of English have found it increasingly easy to get by in the world without learning other languages.

Evidence

While widening the scope of literacy, globalization-promoting technologies have also enlarged the amounts and types of empirical evidence that are available to researchers. Air travel, telecommunications and computer networks have enabled investigators to gather data in no time from any and all corners of the planet. An era of global research has dawned (at least for those who can obtain the required funding).

The Internet in particular has changed the character of research. Increasingly, academic writings (like the present book) include references to online sources. No longer is a 'document' limited to hard-copy sheets with static, monochrome text. In some ways the Internet approximates the 'world brain' that H. G. Wells anticipated many years ago as 'an efficient index to *all* human knowledge, ideas and achievements . . . a complete planetary memory' (1938: 60, his emphasis).

Digital information processing has also enabled researchers in the contemporary globalizing world to handle much greater quantities of data. Large-scale number crunching and bulging bibliographies have become the order of the day. Whether greater wisdom has resulted is another matter, of course. In the so-called 'information age' it is arguably often harder to see the wood for the trees.

In sum, then, when it comes to methodology globalization has: (a) created greater urgency to abandon narrow disciplinary studies; (b) altered some aspects of education processes; and (c) increased amounts of empirical material and broadened the ways that researchers handle evidence. Yet these developments have not, in a deeper structural sense, substantially altered the kinds of knowledge that result from academic endeavours or from learning generally. As noted earlier, rationalism has remained the prime order of the day in global knowledge, if perhaps tinged with greater reflexivity.

Aesthetics

What, finally, of aesthetics? Has globalization affected prevailing appreciations of beauty or, to put it another way, the ways that people know art? As the next paragraphs indicate, beauty has exhibited some different facets in transplanetary spaces. However, older ideas of what constitutes art have not disappeared in the process.

To begin with, globalization has helped certain art forms to obtain transworld currency. Electronic mass media and global markets in particular have promoted some kinds of music, dance, film, dress and cuisine to the top of fashion across all continents. Ronaldo's turns on the football pitch, Andy Warhol's images, and tinted-glass office blocks have become transplanetary marks of beauty, unconnected to any specific country and appreciated (in some circles, at least) the world over. That said, increased globality has, in the vein of greater reflexivity, given many contemporary artists more awareness of the diversity of viewpoints from which art is received (Poissant, 2004).

Much as globalization has encouraged greater hybridization in collective identities, as discussed in Chapter 7, so transplanetary spaces have also provided increased possibilities for intercultural combinations in the arts. For example, an Indian sitarist has linked up with an American guitarist to produce a new variant of jazz (if it can still be called that). An evening's entertainment in a global city can readily encompass an Ethiopian meal, a Russian play, and transport by Korean car with Canadian pop music on the stereo. In Berlin, home to people from 181 countries, *Multikulti* radio has issued broadcasts in 19 languages (Velea, 1996). Beauty has thereby increasingly lain in melanges as well as in the 'purity' of traditions.

Moreover, the growth of transplanetary connections has contributed to the creation and spread of certain new forms of beauty. For instance, computer-generated images and global brand symbols have often fallen outside pre-existent categories of art. Global relations have also tended to endow speed with beauty, *inter alia* in the sensation of jet travel, the pulse of electronic music and the flurry of still motion on television and cinema screens.

Together, these three trends in art – of importations, combinations and new creations – have arguably brought greater diversity and flexibility to appreciations of beauty. David Harvey has on these lines described 'the ferment, instability and fleeting qualities of a postmodernist aesthetic that celebrates difference, ephemerality, spectacle, fashion, and the commodification of cultural forms' (1989: 156). On the other hand, contemporary times of globalization have also witnessed many a traditionalist reaction against new turns in the arts.

Conclusion

So, as with production, governance and identity, globalization has had a number of repercussions for knowledge (summarized in the box). In regard to epistemology, increased globality has encouraged several anti-rationalist reactions as well as promoted greater reflexivity within rationalism. With respect to ontology, spreading globality has involved some shifts in conceptions of space and time. In terms of methodology, the growth of transworld networks has furthered some altered approaches to research, teaching and learning. As for aesthetics, globalization has advanced some different experiences of beauty. From all of these angles the reconfigured geography has encouraged greater pluralism and contestation in the construction of knowledge.

Implications of globalization for knowledge in summary

Epistemology

- global relations have largely reproduced rationalist knowledge
- increased transplanetary connectivity has in some ways also encouraged anti-rationalist reactions such as religious revivalism, ecocentrism and postmodernism
- globalization has promoted a growth of reflexive rationalism

Ontology

- growing globality has entailed altered conceptions of space
- supraterritorial relations have shifted experiences of time

Methodology

- global issues have intensified the need for multi-, inter- and post-disciplinary modes of inquiry
- many educational tools and programmes have gained transplanetary circulation
- supraterritorial spaces have raised the importance of visual literacies
- English has increasingly become a transplanetary medium of communication
- technologies of globalization have generated greater quantities and different qualities of empirical evidence

Aesthetics

- transplanetary relations have facilitated the worldwide spread of certain forms of art
- globalization has encouraged increased hybridization in art
- transworld spaces have helped to produce new types of art

However, thus far, respatialization through globalization has on the whole affected the margins more than the core of knowledge power structures. Rationalist epistemologies have retained primacy in global flows and contemporary social relations generally. Discipline-based methodologies have continued to thrive under accelerated globalization, and most shifts in education practices have affected form more than content. New types of art have in general supplemented rather than displaced the old. Knowledge has witnessed considerable creative ferment in the current globalizing world, but on the whole the reigning primary principles of understanding have not radically altered.

This general conclusion of mixed change and continuity has applied throughout Part II of this book. The preceding four chapters have successively identified important shifts in production, governance, identity and knowledge that have accompanied the respatialization of social life through globalization. To this extent contemporary globalization has certainly not marked 'the end of history'. On the other hand, contemporary globalizing circumstances have also been marked by underlying continuities: of capitalism, of bureaucratism, of communitarianism, and of rationalism. To this extent proclamations that globalization involves epochal transformation to a wholly new era seem misplaced, or at least premature.

Part III

Normative and Policy Issues

Having elaborated a concept of globalization, having traced the historical course of the trend, having examined its causes, and having traced the consequences of this respatialization for parallel and interrelated social structures, this book now has a substantial base from which to assess the costs and benefits of the new geography. What has been going right and what has been going wrong in the past decades of intense globalization? Who has been winning and who has been losing from the trend, and in what ways? In the light of such a balance sheet, has the rise of transplanetary connectivity to date been a good and/or a bad thing? Inasmuch as globalization has caused harms, what corrective measures might be taken?

This book examines these normative and policy questions around three main themes: human security, social equality, and democracy. The next chapters examine these three broad questions in turn. Chapter 9 considers the implications of expanding globality for human security: that is, the types and levels of safety and confidence that people do and do not experience in society. Chapter 10 assesses the repercussions of recent decades of intense globalization for social equality: that is, the forms and intensities of arbitrary hierarchies between people (in terms of class, country, gender, race, urban/rural divides, and age). Chapter 11 explores the consequences of spreading transplanetary relations for democracy: that is, the ways and degrees that people are able to take policy decisions regarding the globalizing circumstances that affect their destinies.

In respect of each of these headline themes contemporary globalization is found to have yielded both positive and negative outcomes. As a critical introduction, this book places greater emphasis on the downsides, particularly as they are largely avoidable. In other words, the harms have resulted not from increased globality as such, but from the policies that have been adopted towards it.

Chapter 12, on future globalizations, then considers what alternative policies might be available to counter the insecurities, inequalities and democratic deficits that have flowed from currently prevailing (that is, mainly neoliberalist) approaches to globalization. It is argued that contemporary social forces and political constellations present severely limited prospects for rejectionist and full-scale transformist strategies in the short and medium term. However, a host of practicable ambitious reforms could make the globalizing world a more humane place within the next few decades.

Chapter 9

Globalization and (In)Security

Main points of this chapter
Peace
Crime
Ecological integrity
Health
Poverty
Financial stability
Employment
Working conditions
Identity
Knowledge
Social cohesion
Conclusion

Main points of this chapter

- globalization has had important repercussions for various facets of human security: military, ecological, physiological, economic, psychological and cultural
- on all of these dimensions contemporary globalization has had both positive and negative consequences
- in each case globalization has not been the sole source of human (in)security, but one of multiple interrelated factors
- negative impacts of contemporary globalization on human security have generally resulted not from the growth of transplanetary connectivity as such, but from the policies (often along neoliberalist lines) that have been adopted toward the trend

AIDS, GM, CFCs, LTCM, ICBMs, SARS, 9/11, Y2K. Much of the shorthand of today's more global world resonates of insecurity. Contemporary public discourse, particularly through the mass media, is replete with threats, scares, crises and emergencies. Some sociologists have in this light described the present circumstance as a 'risk society' (Beck, 1986, 1999), and 'human security' has become a popular policy buzzword (CHS, 2003).

Often people have drawn associations between this heightened vulnerability and increased globality. Many have endorsed the sentiments of Suwan Mingkwan and Tern Tarat, fisherfolk near the Thai–Lao border, when they proclaim that 'globalization is a chaos and creates a disaster' (Mingkwan and Tarat, 2002). Problems of human security have thereby fuelled much unease about, and protest against, current globalization.

However, does the historical coincidence between globalization and greater experiences of danger and risk also entail a causal relationship? In what ways and to what extents has recent full-scale globalization undermined – or on the contrary perhaps enhanced – people's safety and confidence? Absolute security is of course not available, as every human situation carries uncertainties and exposures. The challenge is to maximize the potential benefits and minimize the possible problems of globalization for human security. What does the record to date suggest?

Many of today's headline insecurities have readily evident connections with globality. Some of these misfortunes strike suddenly, like aeroplane crashes, nuclear accidents, financial crises, terrorist assaults, computer viruses, and globally spread physiological diseases. Other insecurities with links to globalization carry on from day to day, such as transworld crime, global warfare, purported 'floods' of immigrants, job insecurity in a global economy, and worries about a so-called 'race to the bottom' of social and environmental protections. Then there are longer-term global risks of harm like those associated with the tobacco trade, HIV/AIDS, mobile telephones, biotechnology, nanotechnology, climate change, natural resource depletion, and cultural destruction.

In addition to these substantive problems, globalization also has links to human insecurity at a deeper structural level. As an ongoing major reconfiguration of social geography, the rise of transplanetary relations has undermined many of the former securities connected with the certainty and predictability of one's place in the world. As seen in Part II, contemporary globalization and the growth of supraterritoriality have unsettled previously familiar terrains of production, governance, identity and knowledge. The new geography has in many ways disturbed previous, relatively clear, and largely unquestioned social bearings in terms of territorialist economy, statist governance, nationalist identity, and rationalist knowledge. The resultant intensified sense of a loss of ties and groundedness has arguably contributed to a general environment of increased human insecurity.

On the other hand, contemporary globalization has in various respects also enhanced human security. For example, transplanetary connections have facilitated emergency relief activities and peacekeeping missions. Globalization has also encouraged heightened ecological sensitivity and (in some cases) greater economic efficiency. As suggested in Chapter 7, a number of groups such as indigenous peoples and sexual minorities have arguably gained greater security of identity in a postnationalist era. Hence, as ever with globalization, there are multiple sides to the story.

Moreover, it should be remembered that human security is not an objective fact, but rather an interrelation of the material (i.e., concrete conditions) and the ideal (i.e., perceptions and understandings of those situations). Hence, for example, a constant barrage of press reports of threats arguably heightens the sense of vulnerability even if the actual incidence of harmful events remains unchanged. Paradoxically, many people today have felt increased risk at a historical moment when technological developments have provided unprecedented means to control danger.

(In)security is also experienced differently – and with regard to different priority issues – depending on the social context involved. As repeatedly stressed in this book, globalization does not entail simple universalization and homogenization; thus people in the contemporary globalizing world have experienced different vulnerabilities to different extents in different contexts. For example, the destitute of Sri Lanka have not focused on dangers of climate change, while IT millionaires have rarely if ever worried about threats of malaria. Similarly, Rwandans and US-Americans have been relatively unaffected by each other's respective experiences of genocide and 9/11. Politics generally decides which insecurities obtain greatest attention and response, who is secured, and who does the securing.

The rest of this chapter assesses connections between contemporary globalization and multiple issues of human security. In turn the sections below consider questions of peace, crime, ecological integrity, health, poverty, financial stability, employment, working conditions, identity, knowledge, and social cohesion. Given its character as 'a critical introduction', the present account often puts particular emphasis on the downsides of globalization for security to date. The vulnerabilities associated with the contemporary growth of transplanetary and supraterritorial links have indeed been great. These ills are the more regrettable insofar as many of them could be substantially reduced. In other words, the problems for human security have generally resulted not from globalization as such, but from the particular policies (often in a neoliberalist vein) that have so far been adopted towards the trend. As Chapter 12 elaborates, different strategies of globalization could yield greater security.

Peace

As noted in Chapter 6, contemporary globalization would seem to discourage warfare insofar as armed conflict between states for control of territory serves little purpose in respect of most supraterritorial concerns and interests. In those parts of the world where globalization has gone furthest, governments face – and are to a considerable degree dependent on – powerful transplanetary markets and communications networks whose operations would be greatly disrupted by military adventures. In addition, as seen in Chapter 7, many citizens – including significant elements of élite circles – have developed commitments to global issues and attachments to global communities, ties that make them less disposed to support old-style armed campaigns to conquer territory.

Thus it is arguably in part (albeit not only) owing to large-scale globalization that the OECD states have not gone to war against each other since 1945. Military conflict between states of East Asia, Europe and North America also seems unlikely in the foreseeable future. To this extent there is some cause to applaud a correlation between globalization and greater peace.

In addition, the growth of suprastate governance in the context of globalization has brought some greater possibilities of arms control and disarmament. For example, a number of multilateral treaties (some with regional scope and others with transworld coverage) have restricted the testing and deployment of nuclear warheads. The nuclear non-proliferation treaty regime, established in 1968 through the IAEA, has discouraged (albeit not with total success) the spread of nuclear weapons to more state arsenals. At the end of 2003 a total of 158 states had ratified the Chemical Weapons Convention of 1993, administered since 1997 through a permanent Organization for the Prohibition of Chemical Weapons (OPCW, 2004). Global controls have also advanced for biological weapons and landmines. The transworld campaign against landmines in particular has demonstrated that substantial popular support can be mobilized for tighter control of global production and trade of arms (Price, 1998; Mekata, 2000).

Suprastate governance has also opened up new means of conflict management. Since the 1950s the UN has developed so-called peacekeeping operations in inter-state conflicts, and in the 1990s the organization substantially expanded humanitarian assistance in civil wars as well (Weiss *et al.*, 1994; Minear and Weiss, 1995). True, some of these efforts have had limited success, and proposals to create UN peace *enforcement* units have thus far not borne fruit. However, important positive UN contributions to conflict limitation have been made, for example, in Cambodia, Cyprus and Namibia. Meanwhile regional governance bodies like the Organization of African Unity (OAU – now African Union) and the Organization for Security and Cooperation in Europe have undertaken conflict management initiatives in their respective areas. Global humanitarian NGOs have often assisted both transworld and regional official agencies in alleviating the harms of war.

Yet contemporary globalization has not in every respect reduced the dangers of armed violence. For one thing, inter-state warfare has persisted in the contemporary more global world outside the North. Recent decades have witnessed several military conflagrations between states, including Vietnam and Cambodia, Iran and Iraq, Ecuador and Peru, Eritrea and Ethiopia. Indeed, global reach with 'rapid reaction forces' and the like has facilitated military interventions by states of the North into conflicts in the South and the East. The US government in particular has despatched armed forces to Afghanistan, the Balkans, the Caribbean, Central America, West Africa, the Horn of Africa, and the Persian Gulf. Territorial interests still drove the Argentine and British governments to war over the Falklands/Malvinas in 1982. Nor has half a century of large-scale globalization ended the state of war on the Korean peninsula, where the will for territorial reunification under a single nation-state has persisted, irrespective of South Korea's deep involvement in transworld relations.

Meanwhile, as mentioned earlier, widespread micro-nationalist and religious revivals encouraged in part by globalization have promoted a substantial rise in intrastate warfare outside the North. The many instances have included Afghanistan, Angola, Congo/Zaire, Georgia, Indonesia, Russia, Sri Lanka, Sudan, and former Yugoslavia. In total, recent wars in the South (mostly intrastate) have cost some five million civilian lives. Many of the weapons that wrought these casualties have emanated from the global arms trade. Efforts to halt illicit shipments of small arms and light weapons have had limited success. In addition, global diasporas have on a number of occasions injected considerable financial backing for civil wars in their countries of origin.

Even 'peace' between major states since the mid-twentieth century has prevailed under a spectre of destruction such as people have never before experienced. In spite of the end of the Cold War, and even after implementation of existing disarmament agreements, a handful of states still possess enough nuclear warheads to eliminate the entire human race. A Comprehensive Test Ban Treaty in respect of nuclear weapons was signed in 1996; however, the US Senate's subsequent refusal to ratify prevented implementation of the agreement. Global weapons such as fighter jets, ballistic and cruise missiles, and spy satellites have sown insecurity in the target populations, whether or not those tools have been used in actual raids. In addition, the holders of such weapons have lived with a constant anxiety that prospective enemies could acquire similar capabilities – or worse, develop still more sophisticated technologies for global attacks.

The technologies of globalization have also been closely interlinked with militarization in other ways. For example, the telephone was used on the battlefield within two years of its invention (Young, 1991: 49). Likewise, supraterritorial connections by radio and laser have acquired important military purposes. Computer networks were first developed in the US armed forces in 1969 and have become a key tool of contemporary warfare for major states. Future military operations involving powerful states could well focus on invading computer systems as much as on occupying territorial domains.

Globalization has furthered warfare in non-technological ways, too. Global finance largely paid for the Gulf War of 1990–1, whose oil fires also provoked a major global ecological scare at the time. Global companies have figured prominently in the production of military equipment. Global organization has featured in military alliance structures such as NATO, in armed violence pursued by global criminal networks, and in the transworld activities of various terrorist bodies.

Indeed, global terrorism has figured as a prominent source of insecurity since the 1970s. Terror politics are not new, insofar as various state and non-state actors have long used campaigns of fear, death, disruption and destruction to promote their causes; however, intensified globalization has given terrorists new tools and higher profile (Booth and Dunne, 2002; Gunaratna, 2002; Mackinlay, 2002). Global news media coverage of a bombing or a hostage seizure has allowed both large military divisions and small guerrilla cells to obtain immediate worldwide publicity. Attacks on aeroplanes, airports, cruise ships, embassies, corporate offices, Olympic Games and other venues of globality have made particularly spectacular impacts. Global trade in weapons has supplied many of the means for terrorist acts, while global finance has often channelled the necessary funds. Certain individual terrorists have lived as global itinerants, while global communications have enabled terror units across the planet to exchange information and coordinate operations.

In short, globalization and the rise of supraterritoriality in no way inherently reduce military and paramilitary threats to human security. Indeed, it is conceivable that general warfare between major states could recur in spite – or even because – of globalization. As is elaborated in further sections below, adjustment to global relations can produce many harms in terms of ecological damage, increased poverty, job losses, deterioration of working conditions, cultural destruction and social fragmentation. In certain circumstances such heightened insecurities could encourage a return of large-scale interstate warfare. On this count, too, equations of globalization and peace could prove to be dangerously complacent.

Crime

Next to war, multiple further worries of violence in contemporary society have related to crime. Indeed, many if not most people in today's world experience crime as a more immediate and intense threat than warfare. Criminal violence in fact currently kills three-quarters of a million people across the world per year, so broadly equivalent to numbers of military casualties. However, in what ways and to what extent is insecurity from crime related to globalization?

Certainly global relations have often provided contexts for criminal activity.

Thus, for example, the Internet has proved a boon for many fraudsters and paedophiles. Global finance has greatly enhanced opportunities for money laundering, which now stands at levels equivalent to 2–5 per cent of world GDP per annum (FATF, 2004). Criminal elements have also often exploited transplanetary trade at a time when only 4 per cent of shipping containers are inspected. Many gangs have dealt globally in restricted goods (like culturally protected art), prohibited goods (like illicit drugs), taxed goods (like cigarettes), stolen goods, and undocumented migrants.

Indeed, transworld criminal networks have figured as a powerful form of global organization in contemporary history. Prominent examples include the triads of China, drug barons of Latin America, and some oligarchs of Russia. Several of these criminal circles have moreover been embedded in global diasporas. One leading authority on the subject has gone as far as declaring that organized crime could be the largest beneficiary of globalization. For example, the Colombia-based Cali cartel ranks as the most successful 'global corporation' in the South, generating $6 billion per annum in revenue and $3 billion in profit (Williams, 2000).

To be sure, expanded global spaces have also created new opportunities to combat crime. The significance of transstate judicial cooperation was mentioned in Chapter 6. In addition, Interpol has operated as a global governance agency to pursue lawbreakers across the planet since 1923 (Anderson, 1989). New information technologies have increased possibilities for transworld tracking of criminals. A Financial Action Task Force (FATF) based at the OECD has worked since 1989 to counter money laundering with strengthened state regulation and closer multilateral cooperation (Reinicke, 1998: 156–72; Wiener, 1999: ch 3). In general, however, people today sooner associate globality with more crime rather than less.

Ecological integrity

Along with avoidance of war and crime, security in a more global world also depends crucially on maintaining a viable relationship between people and their natural surroundings. It goes without saying that human life requires certain atmospheric, hydrospheric, geospheric and biospheric conditions. Humanity needs breathable air, potable water, arable soil, and sustainable coexistence with other life forms.

Thanks in good part to global ecological challenges and global initiatives to meet them, environmental issues have risen to considerable prominence on the contemporary security agenda. Countless civil society groups, companies, media organs, official agencies and research institutes have since the 1960s put the spotlight on environmental questions as never before. On the whole, this greater sensitivity has tended to heighten awareness of ecological risks and to foster a general atmosphere of insecurity.

True, some technologies associated with globalization – like telecommunications, digital data processing, and satellite surveillance – have provided highly sophisticated tools for anticipating natural disasters and monitoring ecological trends. On the other hand, many technologies of globalization have also been highly polluting. Aeroplanes have dirtied the skies, and the motor ships that support global trade have dirtied the seas. Much of the electricity to run global communications has been generated with nuclear and fossil fuels whose by-products contaminate air, land and sea. Contrary to some expectations, computers have tended in practice to increase rather than decrease paper use, thereby adding pressure on forests. Rapid turnover in global consumer goods has added massively to non-degradable solid waste, however well intentioned recycling activities might be. Meanwhile spent rockets and satellites have started a further junkyard in outer space.

Global capitalism has often undermined ecological security in other ways, too. For instance, some companies (especially producers of toxic substances like pesticides and heavy metals like zinc) have 'gone global' in part to relocate at sites where environmental regulations are less stringent (Heerings and Zeldenrust, 1995: ch 4). Some have exaggerated the extent of 'pollution havens' and a 'race to the bottom' of environmental standards in poorer countries, but these problems have figured significantly in some situations (Mani and Wheeler, 1998; Neumayer, 2001; Clapp, 2002). Global trade in toxic wastes (so-called 'pollution flight') has also posed dangers for populations in the South. One source on 'garbage imperialism' has calculated that firms made over 500 attempts between 1989 and 1994 to export a total of more than 200 million tons of waste from the OECD countries to the South (Bellamy Foster, 1994). Likewise, as governments in the North have restricted or banned a number of tobacco products, pharmaceuticals and pesticides, global marketing has enlarged outlets for many of these goods in the South and the East. Global lending, too, has sometimes promoted environmental degradation as, for example, governments have intensified exports beyond sustainable levels in order to obtain foreign exchange earnings for debt repayment (Miller, 1991). Likewise, certain ministries in the South have abandoned environmental projects and policies in an effort to achieve fiscal targets connected with globally sponsored structural adjustment programmes (Reed, 1996). In spite of a proliferation of 'socially responsible investment' schemes, few bankers and brokers have adjusted their global financial activities to promote greater ecological integrity (Bouma *et al.*, 2001; Durbin and Welch, 2002).

Meanwhile each of the major anthropogenic global environmental changes of contemporary history has presented threats (imminent and/or long term) to ecological integrity. Transboundary air pollution could, it is feared, destroy forests and lakes. Nuclear accidents and thinned ozone yield the spectre of increased cancer rates. Declining biological diversity might take the earth to a species depletion threshold beyond which the entire biosphere would collapse; recent losses have already cost some 10–15 per cent of species on earth (Speth, 2001). Rising sea level associated with climate change could submerge highly populated coastal areas and small island countries. Large-scale contamination of soil and freshwater could threaten human subsistence.

Given such prospects, the emergence of global social ecology has, not surprisingly, produced a succession of popular scares. For example, rapid growth in world population led in the late 1960s to widespread fears of a 'time bomb'. The global oil crisis of the 1970s fed worries of an impending exhaustion of many vital natural resources. Further anxiety has accompanied the spread of genetically modified foodstuffs through the transworld markets of agribusiness and biotechnology firms. In a word, then, global environmental issues have become a prime source of insecurity, particularly among people who face few direct economic and military threats.

To be sure, as mentioned in Chapter 6, global governance of ecological matters has made some notable advances. Whereas the UN Charter made no mention of the environment in 1945, UN-sponsored global summits on the environment at Stockholm (1972), Rio de Janeiro (1992) and Johannesburg (2002) have raised awareness of the problems among official circles and the general public. In terms of concrete progress, the ozone regime established through the 1985 Vienna Convention and the 1987 Montreal Protocol has proved particularly successful. By 1997 world production of the main ozone-depleting substances had fallen to 76 per cent of the 1988 level (Edwards, 2004: 22). Meanwhile the Global Environment Facility (GEF) – operative since 1994 and administered between UNDP, UNEP and the World Bank – has pledged some $2 billion to help poor countries make investments that benefit ecological integrity. That said, when spread across a decade and across the entire planet, the GEF sum is pretty modest in relation to the challenges at hand.

More generally, too, the advances of global environmental care must not be exaggerated. Efforts to address global warming have proved especially frustrating, as implementation of the 1992 Framework Convention on Climate Change has proceeded with painful slowness. Various proposals have circulated for carbon taxes and other 'clean development mechanisms', but half a dozen UN conferences since 1992 on climate change have yielded limited concrete results. Indeed, refusals by the Chinese and US governments to ratify the 1997 Kyoto Protocol have severely undercut this key attempt to set legally binding limits on emissions of greenhouse gases.

As for connections between global commerce and environmental degradation, the Doha Declaration of 2001 for the first time promised that a future cycle of trade liberalization talks would deal specifically with environmental issues. However, it is not yet clear when such a 'green round' of WTO negotiations might take place. Nor has general backing yet developed for a World Environment Organization that would work on a par with the WTO and other global governance agencies (Newell and Whalley, 1999; Biermann, 2000).

Hence at least some of the ecological insecurities associated with contemporary globalization can be attributed to *laissez-faire* policies rather than to the fact of transplanetary connectivity itself. Many global relations are polluting, but others do not have to be, and suitable global regulations can promote ecological integrity, not lower it. The primary indictment for environmental degradation should therefore be addressed to neoliberalism as a particular kind of globalization and not to globality as such.

Health

Like global ecological issues, global health problems have generated considerable insecurity in recent decades (Garret, 1994; NIC, 2001; Lee *et al.*, 2002; Lee, 2003; Pirages, 2006). Global transmission of diseases via people and produce has triggered a succession of popular panics since the 1980s. Transplanetary travel has greatly accelerated the spread of HIV/AIDS and, more briefly, SARS. AIDS induced 20 million deaths worldwide by 2001 (leaving over 10 million orphans), while more than 40 million other people are currently living with the disease (Barnett and Whiteside, 2002; Poku and Whiteside, 2002). Mainly as a consequence of AIDS, average life spans are declining by 20–40 years in a number of countries of Sub-Saharan Africa. Owing to global trade rules, most AIDS sufferers have lacked access to the more effective drug treatments. Meanwhile, the global food trade has diffused BSE across the planet, with the associated human risk of variant Creutzfeldt-Jakob disease (CJD).

Globalization has also complicated health problems that do not attract the media spotlight. For example, greater global mobility has increased the spread of older illnesses like cholera, malaria and tuberculosis. Global markets in alcohol, asbestos, junk food, tobacco, and various other licit and illicit drugs have raised numerous health risks across the planet. 'Race to the bottom' arguments have suggested that global commercial competition can undermine health and safety standards for workers (Fustukian *et al.*, 2002). Onerous global debts have undercut public spending on primary health care in dozens of poor countries since the 1980s. Global migration has facilitated the movement of thousands of health professionals, often away from places of the greatest need to the more lucrative working conditions of medically privileged areas.

To be sure, some of the problems just mentioned have developed due to the policies adopted towards globalization rather than as a consequence of greater transplanetary connectivity per se. Thus, for instance, debt and structural adjustment in poor countries can be handled in ways that do not so greatly compromise public health expenditures. In addition, more proactive global regulation could reduce or halt trade in products detrimental to health. For example, agreement was reached in 2003 through the WTO to improve poor countries' access to essential medicines, though it is as yet unclear how far the rather complicated provisions can be effectively implemented.

Indeed, when taken in certain directions globalization can also enhance human health. For instance, global communications media have upgraded the knowledge and practice of health care for professionals and laypersons alike. Telemedicine (the provision of health advice through telecommunications) has improved health services and reduced the need for referrals. Although their power can be abused and their profits can be excessive, global pharmaceutical companies have provided many positive health treatments. From the side of charity, global philanthropists like the Gates and Rockefeller Foundations have sponsored major programmes to better health, for example, through the large-scale provision of children's vaccines. Global civil society has contributed to health improvement with relief agencies like *Médecins sans frontières* (MSF), consumer groups like Health Action International (HAI), and other advocacy bodies like the International Women's Health Coalition. The promotion of 'health for all' has also been a primary aim of several (unfortunately poorly financed) global governance agencies, including the United Nations Children's Fund (UNICEF), the United Nations Fund for Population Activities (UNFPA), and the WHO. In 2001 the G8 set up a Global Fund to Fight AIDS, TB and Malaria, although this initiative has to date fallen far short of its target budget of $10 billion per year. Transstate collaboration among national health authorities has also helped to share knowledge and coordinate policy responses.

In sum, it is not possible to make a blanket denunciation or endorsement of the health effects of globalization. As with peace, crime and ecology, the balance sheet on globalization and health is mixed. Certainly major harms can arise in the absence of carefully crafted public policies. To this extent the problems have lain in the *laissez-faire* attitudes of neoliberalist globalization rather than globalization as such.

Poverty

Along with debates over peace, crime, ecology and health, some of the most intense arguments about globalization and human security have concerned poverty. On the one hand, neoliberalists have promised that *laissez-faire* globalization will yield material prosperity for all humanity (Dollar and

Kraay, 2000). Reformists and transformists have countered that globalization conducted on neoliberalist lines sustains or worsens poverty, whereas alternative approaches to transplanetary connectivity could improve matters. In contrast, rejectionists have dismissed any form of globalization as detrimental for the poor. What does the evidence of past decades suggest?

To begin with, assessments of the poverty effects of globalization confront huge problems of definition and indicators. After all, subsistence requirements are not transculturally and transhistorically fixed. Determinations of the nature and amounts of basic needs vary considerably by context. Minimum living standards are different in Siberia as against Sumatra, or in 1840s Ireland as against the present day. Moreover, poverty is a subjective as well as an objective condition. For example, many people whose material survival is assured may nevertheless feel poor because they perceive themselves as having far fewer resources than the average person in their society. Given these complexities of definition, it is difficult to compile statistics of any reliable precision for global poverty. Per capita GDP and daily income are generally recognized to be inadequate indicators, but these crude measures are often used nevertheless in the absence of straightforward alternatives.

Indeed, much of the debate about rising or falling poverty in the contemporary globalizing world has revolved around this kind of unsatisfactory data. For example, a lot of attention has gone to World Bank figures regarding the number of people across the planet who live on less than the equivalent of $1 per day. Neoliberalists have seized upon the suggestion that, even with major world population growth, this total dropped from 1.4 billion persons in 1980 to 1.2 billion in 2001. However, critics have argued that the methodologies used in these calculations changed over this period, so that the figures cannot be safely compared (Wade, 2002).

Yet a number of other measures have also suggested declines in world poverty during the contemporary period of accelerated globalization. For example, in terms of UNDP's Human Development Index (HDI), the proportion of the world's population living in destitution more than halved between 1960 and 1992 (HDR, 1994: 1–2). In absolute numbers, more people escaped from poverty in the second half of the twentieth century than in the preceding 500 years (HDR, 1997: 2). The ranks of the indigent in China declined by more than half between 1978 and 1985, and from 280 million in 1990 to 125 million in 1997 (Rohwer, 1992: 4; AP, 1999b). In the South, home to most of the world's poor, average life expectancy lengthened by 17 years between 1960 and the mid-1990s (*FT*, 2 February 1996: 1). Child mortality for under-5s fell from 196 per 1000 live births in 1960 to 82 in 2002 (UNICEF, 2003b: 105). The proportion of one year-olds immunized rose from 70 per cent in 1990 to 89 per cent in 1997, while malnutrition decreased from 177 million children in 1990 to 150 million in 2000 (*Globe and Mail*, 6 May 2002: A8). Adult illiteracy in the South declined from nearly 60 per cent in 1970 to 35 per cent in 1994. The share of the world's population with access to safe water rose from 40 per cent in 1990 to 72 per cent in 1997 (DFID, 1997: 13; HDR, 1999: 22). Advances of these kinds have been especially pronounced in so-called 'newly industrializing countries' in parts of East and South East Asia and Latin America.

Nevertheless, poverty remains a major problem in the twenty-first century world. It is safe to say that several billion people today subsist on the most marginal of earnings. As of the mid-1990s around a seventh of humanity (828 million people) was chronically malnourished (FAO, 1998). There were 880 million illiterate adults across the world in 1998 and 113 million children out of school in 2000 (UNESCO, 2000: 8, 11). Most countries of the South have not become NICs. In fact 70 lands experienced no increase in per capita income between 1980 and the mid-1990s, and 43 countries had a lower per capita income in the mid-1990s than in 1970 (HDR, 1996: 1). The scale of poverty in Sub-Saharan Africa was as great in the mid-1990s as in the mid-1960s (UNCTAD, 1995: 11). In addition, certain so-called 'transition countries' of Eastern Europe and the former Soviet Union experienced striking increases of poverty in the 1990s. Life expectancy actually declined in seven of these countries after 1989 (HDR, 1999: 79). Meanwhile slum residents in Chicago's South Side have endured deprivations alongside the shack dwellers of Lima's favelas. Between the early 1980s and the mid-1990s, child poverty rose by a third in the USA and by half in Britain (Jolly, 1995). It increased in Canada from one in seven children in 1989 to nearly one in five in 1999 (*Globe and Mail*, 7 May 2002: A8).

If poverty has in some ways decreased, in other ways increased, and in any case remained a significant problem during recent times of large-scale globalization, to what extent have these trends resulted from globalization? How far can the improvements and/or continuing difficulties be attributed to the growth of transplanetary and supraterritorial connectivity? Statistics are inconclusive, although some general connections can be discerned.

In terms of global trade, most of the NICs have prospered in a context of significantly increased exports of global goods and services. To take the most outstanding case, the gross national product (GNP) of China tripled between 1978 (the year of 'opening up' to global commerce) and 1993. On the other hand, global markets in primary commodities have on the whole given the poor countries that most rely on these exports steadily declining terms of trade since the 1970s (Coote, 1996). Indeed, world prices of primary commodities in the mid-1990s stood at their lowest level since the 1930s (ul Haq *et al.*, 1995: 29). Moreover, a study by the United Nations Conference on Trade and Development (UNCTAD) has concluded that the world's 48 poorest countries would collectively lose \$300–600 million per annum as a result of reduced exports and increased food imports under the Uruguay Round agreements (Went, 1996: 126). In addition, trade liberalization has deprived many poor states of one of their chief sources of tax revenue (namely, customs duties), thereby increasing the squeeze on public-sector programmes for poverty reduction. Given this mixed evidence, even mainstream economists are now divided about the welfare consequences of trade liberalization (McCulloch *et al.*, 2001).

Global finance has also had some unhappy impacts on poverty. In principle one might hope that a global pool of savings could provide unprecedented levels of poverty-reducing investments. However, all too often 'development' has worked for global finance rather than, as one would hope, the other way around. Nowhere has this maldistribution of resources occurred more blatantly than in global loans to poor countries. The transworld debts of the South grew sixteen-fold between 1970 and 1997, to nearly $2.2 trillion, and little of this sum appears to have helped poor people. Most of the $1.3 trillion in increased debt between 1980 and 1994 involved an accumulation of unpaid interest rather than fresh credits (Childers, 1994: 10; World Bank, 1994: 192). By 1996, 41 of the world's poorest countries between them had accumulated some $250 billion in global debts, a burden that severely limited their governments' capacities to attack poverty. In Latin America during the debt crisis of the 1980s, the ranks of indigent people expanded from 130 to 180 million (Bello *et al.*, 1994: 52). By now even the most hard-nosed bankers concede that the debt burdens of many poor countries are unsustainable and have damaging impacts on vulnerable sectors of their populations. However, in spite of multiple debt relief programmes since the late 1980s – with partial debt cancellation, long-term rescheduling, and interest rate reductions – most of the countries concerned remain saddled with crippling debts. Much was expected from the Highly Indebted Poor Countries Initiative (HIPC) introduced by the IMF and the World Bank in 1996 and enhanced in 1999. However, this relief too has proved small, slow and grudging. Long and dogged efforts by global development campaigners to address the debt burdens of the South have borne much less fruit than hoped. Indeed, far more money was mobilized far more quickly to rescue the Long Term Capital Management (LTCM) hedge fund in 1998 than has been garnered to support the HIPC initiative.

The general volatility of global financial markets has also adversely affected the poor. In Indonesia, for example, concerted efforts reduced the number of destitute people from 70 million (60 per cent of the populace) in 1970 to 25.9 million (13.7 per cent of the populace) in 1993. However, the Asia crisis of 1997–9, induced largely by developments in global capital and currency markets, may have put up to 130 million people in Indonesia in poverty by early 1999 (AP, 1999a). Similarly, vulnerable social circles in Thailand and Argentina suffered from collapses of the baht and the peso in global currency markets in 1997 and 2001, respectively.

More generally, too, macroeconomic adjustments to a more global economy have, when followed on neoliberalist lines, often brought cuts in public services to poor people. For example, although average incomes have risen substantially in China since 1978, access to social protections has not. Likewise, a number of governments in the North (especially those in the 'Anglo' countries) have reduced certain welfare provisions at least partly in the name of enhancing global competitiveness. Particularly during the 1980s and early 1990s, structural adjustment policies sponsored in the South and the East by the IMF and the World Bank often cut substantially into social security programmes. A study by the ILO has suggested that if governments would return to earlier social policies, world poverty in terms of people living under $1 per day would decline by a third from 1.2 billion to 0.8 billion (Hoeven, 2002). In fact the Bretton Woods institutions have since the mid-1990s increasingly incorporated social safety nets into their recommended macroeconomic packages. In the Asia crisis of 1997–9 the two bodies moreover departed from their traditional fiscal conservatism to condone substantial public-sector deficits, with a view to protecting food security, primary health care, basic education and employment.

Indeed, poverty eradication has over the past decade become a headline theme of global policy. In 1999 the Bretton Woods agencies made 'poverty reduction' their explicit foremost priority in regard to countries of the South. Following this line, the World Bank's subsequent *World Development Reports* have regularly highlighted problems of the poor (World Bank, 2001, 2004). At the United Nations Millennium Summit in 2000, some 150 governments committed themselves to reach eight Millennium Development Goals (MDGs) of significant poverty reduction by 2015 (UN, 2000; HDR, 2003). Likewise, the Commission on Human Security and the World Commission on the Social Dimension of Globalization have put the spotlight on poverty concerns (CHS, 2003; WCSDG, 2004). The ILO has launched a Global Campaign on Social Security and Coverage for All, against the current situation where less the 10 per cent of people in poor countries have access to statutory social insurance and social assistance.

However, for the most part it remains to walk the talk. The United Nations declared a succession of 'development decades' starting in the 1960s to little avail. In practice most OECD states have diminished their levels of overseas development assistance (ODA) to poor countries. Per capita aid to the 'least developed countries' declined by nearly a third in the second half of the 1990s. Since 2002 African governments have attempted to revive ODA with the so-called New Partnership for Africa's Development (NEPAD), but it remains to be seen whether this scheme will attract significant donor support.

Although global trade, finance and governance agencies have in the above-mentioned ways worked to perpetuate and sometimes deepen poverty, it would of course be mistaken to attribute these difficulties entirely to globalization. After all, local social structures, country policies, natural calamities and other forces have also had their negative impacts. Moreover, it might not necessarily be globalization per se so much as the approaches adopted towards globalization that generate the problems. The adverse effects noted above are a matter of policy, not geography. Neoliberalist globalization may have worsened the lot of many poor people, but (as explored further in Chapter 12) alternative policies could build up the poverty-alleviating potentials of global relations.

Financial stability

If the connections between contemporary globalization and poverty are hotly debated, few dispute that the considerable volatility of global financial markets has had some damaging consequences for human security. As seen in Chapters 3 and 5, expanded globality has made far more finance capital available far faster for investment across the planet. However, the sums and speeds of transactions have also – particularly in a context of liberalization and deregulation – carried greater risks of large and rapid movements in the values of currencies, securities and derivatives.

Some degree of instability is inherent in capitalist financial markets. Indeed, fluctuations can sometimes encourage greater economic efficiency, as investors perpetually look out for higher returns. However, problems arise when rumour, herd behaviour, computer-automated trading and the like generate inordinate short-term movements in the prices of financial instruments. Moreover, full-scale crises in currency, stock, bond and derivative markets can spill over to harm the wider economy with disruptions to banking, trade, fiscal balances, consumer spending, and employment.

Global finance of the past three decades has involved considerable instability. The debt crisis of the South mentioned above called the solvency of a number of major commercial banks into question in the 1980s and has saddled dozens of low- and medium-income countries with damaging fiscal and wider economic burdens ever since. Major stock and bond market collapses in the chief global financial centres in 1987, 1994 and 2001 substantially undermined general economic confidence. Wild swings in global foreign exchange markets and short-term capital flows have helped to trigger financial crises in Britain, Italy and Sweden in the early 1990s, Latin America in 1994–5, Asia in 1997–8, Russia in 1998, Brazil in 1999, and Argentina and Turkey in 2001. The string of debacles in derivatives markets include the Metall Gesellschaft and Orange County affairs in 1994, Barings in 1995, Sumitomo in 1996, and Long Term Capital Management in 1998. More recently, accounting scandals in major global corporations such as Enron, WorldCom, Ahold and Parmalat not only put their own shares in freefall, but also undermined confidence in the integrity of stock markets more generally.

These volatilities in global financial markets have heightened insecurity among the world's wealthy and poor alike. Many savers have anxiously watched their investments from hour to hour on televised tickertape. This environment of pervasive unease has generated a new 'science' of financial risk management, with some practitioners grouped in a Global Association of Risk Professionals. Meanwhile, as already stressed, the reverberations of global financial crises have often afflicted poor people in resultant general economic downturns and structural adjustment programmes.

Insecurities born of global finance have prompted some regulatory responses. Regarding transworld banking, for example, the Basle Committee on Banking Supervision at the Bank for International Settlements has issued multiple recommendations, guidelines and standards since its establishment in 1974. Prominent among these measures is the Basle Capital Accord – first adopted in 1988 and subsequently modified several times – which has provided a framework for assessing the capital position of banks as they engage in large-scale global lending (Wood, 2005). In 1997 the Basle Committee moreover published a set of *Core Principles for Effective Banking Supervision* with global applicability (BIS, 1997). Meanwhile the BIS Committee on Payment and Settlement Systems, established in 1990, has monitored the integrity of computer technologies used in global banking. Since 2000 an International Association of Deposit Insurers has sought to promote best practice in the protection of account holders.

Mainly since the 1990s, a number of other suprastate and private governance initiatives have aimed to increase stability in global finance beyond banking. The International Organization of Securities Commissions, the International Association of Insurance Supervisors, the OECD Committee on Financial Markets, the WTO Committee on Financial Services, the BIS Committee on the Global Financial System, the International Securities Market Association and the Group of 30 have between them developed a host of principles and standards for transworld foreign-exchange, securities, derivatives and insurance markets. Since 1996 the Basle Committee, the IAIS and IOSCO have coordinated a Joint Forum on Financial Conglomerates that enhances cooperation among banking, insurance and securities supervisors (given that global financial companies have increasingly operated across the three sectors). On the initiative of the G7, a Financial Stability Forum was established among major state and multilateral authorities in 1999 'to promote international financial stability, improve the functioning of markets, and reduce systemic risk' (FSF, 1999).

Other measures have sought to increase disclosure and transparency of relevant statistics, on the premise that global financial markets will be less prone to panics if investors have access to more (and more reliable) information. To this end the IMF established a Special Data Dissemination Standard in 1996 and a General Data Dissemination System in 1997. In 1999 the

International Federation of Accountants, the IMF and the World Bank launched an International Forum on Accountancy Development that aims to build accounting and auditing capacity in countries of the East and the South. Meanwhile the International Accounting Standards Board has formulated transworld standards on accounting specifically for financial instruments (Bryant, 1999: 22).

Yet such modest initiatives have to date not brought adequate levels of stability to global finance. High market volatility has continued to generate intense insecurity. The rapid succession of debt, currency, securities and derivative crises through the 1980s and 1990s finally provoked greater discussion towards the end of the century about major reforms of the so-called 'global financial architecture' (Blinder, 1999; Bond and Bullard, 1999; Eichengreen, 1999; Bryant 2000; Eatwell and Taylor, 2000). There was even, briefly, some high-level talk of convening a new Bretton Woods-like conference in order to overhaul global financial governance institutions. However, as the crisis of the late 1990s receded, the prevailing approach quickly shifted back to one of incremental adjustments to liberalized markets. Even the United Nations initiative on Financing for Development (FfD), launched in 1997, has largely sidestepped questions of proactive public regulation to attain greater financial stability (Herman, 2002; Langmore *et al.*, 2002).

Indeed, with finance as with ecology and poverty, the problems of insecurity relate largely to the policies followed (often of a neoliberalist kind) rather than to globality per se. Alternative regulatory strategies could bring more acceptable levels of stability to global finance. These possibilities are explored in Chapter 12.

Employment

On top of poverty and finance, much discussion of connections between globalization and economic security has focused on questions of employment. This is hardly surprising, given that work is central to the human condition, with major implications for health, material welfare, personal identity and social cohesion. The following paragraphs assess the consequences of globalization for the availability of jobs, while the next section examines the repercussions of globalization for working conditions.

Champions and critics of globalization alike agree that unemployment constitutes a major challenge for the twenty-first century. According to UN estimates, the world labour pool of 2.8 billion people in the early 1990s included about 800 million unemployed (120 million of them officially registered as such) and over 700 million underemployed (Simai, 1995: 4). Apart from the NICs, most countries in the South have suffered dire shortages of opportunities for waged labour. The end of central planning has also brought large-scale unemployment to the so-called 'transition countries'. Meanwhile countries in the North have moved from effective full employment in the 1960s to persistent unemployment (often in double-figure percentages) since the 1980s. Many more wage earners (estimated at 15 million across the OECD countries in 1994) have endured involuntary part-time employment (ILO, 1995). Concurrently, a large proportion of workers in the North have experienced continual worries about their job security in the short or medium term. Even corporations in Japan have since the early 1990s abandoned their traditional commitment to lifelong employment for their staff. Across the North the goal of full employment has largely disappeared from macroeconomic policy.

However, are these unhappy trends of the past 30 years a result of the globalization that has transpired at the same time? As noted in Chapter 1, the impact of globalization on employment opportunities has attracted many claims and counterclaims. Proponents suggest that the contemporary globalizing economy has created new jobs and could in the longer term provide waged work for all. In contrast, critics argue that globalization has generated huge job losses and eliminated the possibility of full employment.

As ever with globalization, the situation is more complicated than soundbites would have it. Certainly it is overly simplistic to attribute all unemployment problems to increases in transplanetary connectivity. For example, a host of new labour-saving technologies like digital computers and robotics have produced large staff cuts since the 1970s irrespective of globalization. 'Jobless growth' in many manufacturing and service industries has seen production rise while employment levels fall. Other unemployment has occurred when prospective workers have lacked the required education and training. This question of skills, too, is largely independent of changes in social geography. In short, any rejectionist proposition that de-globalization would in and of itself yield jobs for all should be treated with scepticism.

Indeed, the balance sheet on globalization and employment opportunities has shown some positive entries. For example, service industries such as retail trade, finance, communications, and information technology have significantly expanded their payrolls in recent decades. As seen in Chapter 5, these sectors have lain at the heart of global capitalism. Meanwhile global enterprises in these and other sectors have often created new jobs at their host sites. By 1992 transworld corporations directly employed some 29 million people outside their country of origin (ILO, 1995). Countless other workers have indirectly gained a livelihood from FDI, that is, through subcontracting and other services to global firms.

However, the job-creating effects of contemporary globalization have remained modest on the whole. As of the late 1990s, over 800 EPZs across the world had between them generated only 27 million jobs (HDR, 1999: 86).

Total increased employment in the South from exports to global markets averaged less than 700,000 new jobs per annum over the 30-year period from 1960 to 1990, thus only a fraction of concurrent population increases (Wood, 1994: 13). As of 1992, global companies collectively employed only 73 million people, amounting to less than 6 per cent of the overall world payroll (ILO, 1995: 45). Meanwhile, the expanding financial, information and communications sectors of global capitalism have generally required smaller labour:capital ratios than older extractive and manufacturing industries. For example, with its payroll of 15,000 the global IT giant Microsoft has employed far fewer people than the largest manufacturers of earlier generations.

In certain other ways contemporary globalization has had positively detrimental effects on employment security. In particular, some job losses have occurred in the North when firms have exploited the possibilities of globality to move their production facilities to low-wage sites in the South and the East, particularly in the NICs and in EPZs. Such relocations are estimated to have reduced demand for unskilled labour in the North by some 6–12 million person-years between 1960 and 1990 (Wood, 1994: 11). The trend has continued since 1990 as, for example, commercial liberalization through the WTO and regional trade agreements has further encouraged transfers from the North of various manufacturing operations, as well as some service industries like call centres. In a survey of 10,000 firms in Germany in 1993, one in three respondents said that they planned to transfer production to Eastern Europe or Asia in order to take advantage of lower labour costs and environmental standards (Axford, 1995: 118).

That said, it would be mistaken – as some commentators have done – to exaggerate the connections between job losses in the North and job gains elsewhere in a global economy. As noted earlier, 'lost jobs' in the OECD countries have often gone not to the South and the East, but to machines. Moreover, many global enterprises have established facilities in the South and the East not as a relocation strategy from the North, but as an expansion strategy in order to produce locally for new markets. Also, many of the 29 million jobs directly attributable to inward FDI have appeared in the North rather than the South or the East (when, for example, a Japan-based company has invested in the European Union).

In any case, in other respects global mobility has cost the South and the East dearly on the labour front, especially through the so-called 'brain drain'. For example, Africa alone has been exporting 60–70,000 professionals per year. To the extent that the resultant capacity gaps in the South are filled, it has mainly come through the import of expensive consultants from the North.

On another front, globalization has contributed to substantial job losses in the context of corporate mergers and acquisitions. In the global pharmaceuticals sector, for instance, the fusion of Glaxo and Wellcome saw the payroll shrink by 11 per cent, while Pharmacia and Upjohn closed 40 per cent of plants in the course of their merger (*FT*, 5 March 1996: 23; 7 March 1996: 1). When Chase and Chemical Banks merged, 12,000 people became redundant (*FT*, 1 April 1996: 23). As seen in Chapter 5, M&A activities have proliferated in good part as a response to global market competition and consolidation.

Contemporary globalization has further encouraged greater unemployment insofar as the massive growth of finance capital has shifted much investor interest from job-creating projects in the 'real' economy to financial instruments as objects of investment in their own right. Debt instruments, equities and currency speculation have enticed investors with promises of high and fast returns. By comparison, investment in more labour-intensive 'real' production has in contemporary capitalism tended to yield lower profits over a longer term. True, casino capitalism has generated some expansion of payrolls in the financial sector. However, today's banking, securities and derivatives businesses are largely automated, and mergers in the sector have brought substantial job losses in a number of firms. In any case, the extra employment created through the expansion of finance capital has probably been considerably smaller than the job growth that could be had were investments to be placed in 'real' production.

Finally, globalization has often undermined job security in the context of structural adjustment programmes. Most of these policy packages agreed by governments with multilateral financial institutions have prescribed a significant contraction of the civil service. In most cases no accompanying measures have redeployed the redundant officials in new jobs. Likewise, privatization and liberalization policies at the heart of neoliberalist structural adjustment have often brought job losses when local trade and industry are exposed to global competition. Proponents of conventional structural adjustment programmes have argued that rejuvenated market forces will correct these problems with expanded employment opportunities in the medium and long term. However, little evidence has as yet emerged in the South and the East to substantiate this claim.

Taking the various points above in sum, contemporary globalization has on balance had more negative than positive effects on employment opportunities. To be sure, the positive impacts should not be overlooked, and the unhappy consequences should not be exaggerated. Nor has globalization been the sole cause of growing un(der)employment in recent history. Nevertheless, globalizing capitalism has thus far reduced the certainty of job tenure for most people in work, and the new geography has to date come nowhere close to generating the positions needed to address structural deficits in world opportunities for waged employment.

However, as with other issues of human security, the problems with employment have lain less with the rise in transplanetary links per se and more with the ways that this trend has been (mis)managed. The prevailing neoliberalist spirit of the day has tended to treat job losses and high levels of unemployment as temporary pains that global free markets will in time redress. In this environment of *laissez-faire*, global employment policy has not developed much beyond platitudes emanating from occasional high-level meetings like the G7 Jobs Summits at Detroit in 1994 and Lille in 1996 or the UN World Summits for Social Development in 1995 and 2000.

Working conditions

Accelerated globalization in contemporary history has affected not only the opportunities for waged employment, but also the conditions of that work. As ever in globalization debates, analysts have disagreed on the nature of this impact, with some emphasizing the positive and others the negative. Indeed, the record has been mixed. On the plus side, for example, some global companies have offered workers in the South higher wages and larger benefits than local employers. However, other effects on labour conditions have been strikingly detrimental, and not enough has been done to mitigate and avoid these harms.

Prior to the present period of large-scale globalization, many waged workers in many parts of the world had obtained improved labour conditions through the state. In the East, workers made significant gains under state socialism. In the North, workers benefited from the welfare state. Trade unions held considerable power *vis-à-vis* the state in much of Latin America. Even some colonial administrations introduced greater labour protections in their later years.

Contemporary globalization has tipped the political balance substantially against workers. Global mobility of capital has not been matched with commensurate global mobility of labour, thereby considerably boosting the bargaining position of employers towards employees. Capital can move about the planet in search of profit-maximizing labour arrangements, while workers (especially less skilled workers) are far more bound to territorial place and much more constrained to accept the terms that this location offers. Moreover, global business lobbies have been much more strongly organized than global trade unions. Compare, for instance, the influence of corporate bodies and labour groups on WTO negotiations. Not surprisingly, therefore, the globalization of production has not been matched with an equivalent globalization of worker protections. The guarantees secured thus far for labour through contemporary polycentric governance have generally been weaker than the conditions obtained for workers in the later period of statist governance.

To put the point in Gramscian terms, neoliberalist globalization has been a key force in the decline of the so-called 'Fordist' social contract. Fordism developed, particularly in countries of the North, from the 1910s and peaked between the 1940s and the 1960s. It rested on an implicit trilateral pact between government, corporate business and organized labour. For their part, large trade unions delivered acquiescent and more productive workers to business. On its side, corporate business delivered higher wages, benefits and protections to workers. Completing the triad, the state delivered union protection and wide-ranging social welfare to workers as well as guarantees of property rights and various services to business. With these arrangements, Fordism produced 'the affluent worker' who had sufficient income and leisure time to consume mass-produced goods. To be sure, the fruits of Fordism were restricted to a minority of the world's workers: unionized white men in the North were the prime beneficiaries. Moreover, the labour in question often involved tedious assembly-line work. Nevertheless, Fordism marked a notable advance over earlier social contracts and held out the promise of more progressive capitalism.

In contrast, contemporary globalization has been associated with the displacement of Fordism by what neo-Gramscian theorists have called a 'post-Fordist' regime of accumulation. This new situation has been distinguished by 'flexibilization' (Standing, 1999). The 'flexible' worker lacks a job for life, but instead moves and retrains to meet altered market demands. To facilitate such mobility most OECD governments have loosened laws on hiring and firing. Post-Fordist workers are also expected to be 'flexible' in respect of hours, wages, benefits, health and safety standards, etc. 'Flexible' jobs are often casual, part-time and temporary, with few if any benefits beyond the (often low) wages offered. The workers involved frequently lack collective bargaining arrangements and other union protections. Under these conditions many households have needed more than one wage to make ends meet.

On these various counts the move from Fordism to post-Fordism has entailed significant deteriorations in working conditions, especially for less skilled labour. Many workers who have lost jobs on Fordist terms have returned to employment in 'flexible' positions. Most wage earners born after 1960 have never known Fordist securities during their working lives. Flexibilization has gone further in the UK and USA than in continental Europe and Japan, but the trend has not bypassed any OECD country. (For more on Fordism and post-Fordism, see Cox, 1987: ch 9; Amin, 1994.)

Increased insecurity in the workplace has readily spilled over to affect other aspects of life. The stresses induced by unceasing pressures for greater productivity and worries about pensions, health insurances, etc., can heighten tensions in the household and on the street. It would be difficult to demonstrate precisely that labour flexibilization has fuelled domestic strife, uncivil driving, hooliganism and other violence; and no doubt other factors have also played their part. However, it seems reasonable to posit that insecurity at work has fed insecurity elsewhere in everyday life.

In addition, the demands of flexibility in waged labour have tended to reduce the time and energy that people have available to execute unpaid caring duties. The consequences for children and the infirm can be particularly unhappy, as well as for women, who tend to bear the bulk of domestic caring tasks (a double burden of waged work plus housework). The repercussions of inadequate child rearing for the next generation may include asocial behaviour and unstable intimate relationships.

Apart from the change in power relations between capital and labour mentioned earlier, globalization has promoted the in many respects damaging shift to flexible labour in three other broad ways. First, some of the greatest flexibilization has occurred in the leading sectors of global capitalism. Major demands for 'flexibility' have fallen on support staff in the retail, financial, information and communications industries: that is, on shop assistants, bank clerks, data key punchers, telephone operators, and so on. Few of these workers have gained substantial wages and benefits, good promotion prospects, or long-term job security.

Second, flexibilization has generally accompanied the shift of jobs in the globalizing economy from older industrial centres in the North to new sites in the South and the East. As noted earlier, the scale of this transfer must not be overestimated. However, on those occasions when it has occurred, positions in the North with higher remuneration and greater worker protection have tended to give way to lower-paid jobs in the South with longer hours, less collective bargaining, and weaker health and safety standards. More generally, too, global companies have not provided their employees in the South and the East with the sorts of guarantees that workers in the North obtained under Fordist arrangements. For example, already since the middle of the twentieth century a number of shipping companies have used offshore 'flag of convenience' arrangements to compromise the working conditions of seafarers (ITWF, 2004). Employees in the subcontracted firms that serve global corporations have also often suffered poor work situations.

Third, much flexibilization has unfolded under the spectre of 'global competition'. Managers have pushed for 'flexible' labour in good part because they have believed, rightly or wrongly, that higher guarantees to employees would undermine a firm's position in global markets. For their part, workers have accepted 'flexible' contracts often because they have believed, rightly or wrongly, that demanding higher conditions of service would send jobs elsewhere in the world. Labour in the North has been constantly reminded that alternative and allegedly more pliant workforces are available in the East and the South.

The phrase 'rightly or wrongly' is added here since some would argue that the economic logic of flexibilization is flawed. Critics of these practices suggest that lower labour guarantees could yield less rather than greater competitiveness. Well-trained, well-remunerated, well-protected workers could provide a more motivated, reliable and productive labour force. To this extent reductions in wages and other working conditions could operate not only against human security, but against efficiency as well.

This is not to say that no efforts have been made to achieve better labour standards in a globalizing economy (Lee, 1997a; Standing, 1999; O'Brien, 2000; Rozendaal, 2002). The main site of global governance in respect of worker protection has been the International Labour Organization. Among other things the ILO created a Working Party on the Social Dimension of Trade Liberalization in 1994, launched an agenda of 'decent work' in 1999, and published a report on 'fair globalization' in 2004 (WCSDG, 2004). More concretely, since the late 1940s the ILO has promoted formalized core labour standards: for example, on freedom of association, the right of collective bargaining, the abolition of forced labour, the prevention of discrimination in employment, and a minimum wage. During the time of accelerated globalization the agency has also greatly increased the number of its other conventions and recommendations and has attracted many more signatories to those instruments. The ILO has in the past decade moreover broadened its conception of work beyond formal labour to cover also informal employment, household labour and the like. For example, the ILO Convention on Home Work (1996) has sought to protect homeworkers (a largely female sector) with minimum wages and conditions (HomeNet, 1999). An ILO Convention on Migrant Workers is under preparation. However, far from all states have ratified ILO measures, and relatively few states have endorsed recent conventions on subjects such as occupational safety, training, and health services. Moreover, the ILO has lacked means to enforce its codes, in the way that states can mobilize their courts or the WTO can invoke its Dispute Settlement Mechanism.

For their part, transworld trade rules have as yet included little in the way of labour standards. True, revisions to the Generalized System of Preferences effective from 1995 have involved some elements of a social clause (Jordan, 1995: 28). However, attempts in 1996 to incorporate a Working Party on Worker Rights into the WTO were rebuffed, with particularly strong resistance from governments of the NICs. Indeed, many in the South have worried that appeals to 'social protection' are a ruse to sustain Northern advantages in world trade (John and Chenoy, 1996). Much like the WTO, the proposed (and for now abandoned) MAI protected capital mobility and property rights, but neglected to safeguard labour rights. Nor have global financial institutions incorporated guarantees regarding working conditions into structural adjustment programmes.

On a macro-regional scale, the European Community adopted a Charter of the Fundamental Social Rights (otherwise known as the Social Charter) in

1989 and included a Social Chapter in the Maastricht Treaty two years later (Purdy, 1997). The Social Charter has enshrined principles such as equal treatment for women at work, works councils, and EU-wide collective bargaining with global companies. Elsewhere the NAFTA agreement of 1994 included a side accord regarding labour rights and standards, although these provisions have had even fewer teeth than the EU measures. In South America MERCOSUR has had a social committee that includes trade union representation, but this organ, too, has been quite marginal.

Elsewhere in suprastate governance the OECD in 2000 upgraded its Guidelines on Multinational Enterprises *inter alia* to cover core labour standards. In the same year the UN Global Compact for responsible business addressed three of its nine main provisions to labour issues. Again, however, the implementation mechanisms for such arrangements have remained weak. In a word, fully fledged official global labour legislation does not exist.

Private governance arrangements have taken some steps to fill the gaps, inasmuch as labour standards are enshrined in a number of corporate social responsibility schemes (previously discussed in Chapter 6). For example, various firms engaged in global production (especially in clothing, footwear and toy industries) have since the 1990s adopted voluntary codes of conduct on labour practices in their factories. However, CSR-related labour measures have often suffered from limited scope, unambitious targets, loose terms, mixed record of (voluntary) application, lack of independent monitoring and verification, and an absence of clear stakeholder participation and accountability mechanisms. Many CSR exercises have mostly focused on improving market image, particularly when the schemes have been introduced following adverse publicity from consumer campaigns.

In sum, despite some mild countervailing measures from official and private governance, on the whole flexibilization through globalization has had adverse repercussions for security in work. Once again, though, the problems have not lain with globalization as such, but with inclinations to take a *laissez-faire* approach to working conditions in global capitalism. More proactive policies towards labour standards could produce a more socially sensitive and sustainable globalization.

Identity

Human security not only has the military, environmental and economic aspects discussed so far, but psychological and cultural dimensions as well. A major issue in this respect is identity, given the importance for security of an assured sense of self. To be at ease in the world a person requires *inter alia* a comfortable concept of who one is, where one belongs, and what one wants to become, together with a confidence that the surrounding society will respect and preserve these ways of being, belonging and becoming.

What repercussions have the various developments regarding globalization and identity discussed in Chapter 7 had for human security? This question has attracted much less research and policy response than matters such as ecology, poverty and labour. Nevertheless, several general implications of globalization for the security of identity can be deduced.

On the positive side, contemporary globalization has in some ways provided wider scope for the exploration and expression of individual and collective identity. As noted in Chapter 7, territorialist geography tended to entail a restrictive bias toward state-centred national identities. Indeed, the world of nationalist identity coupled with statist governance often repressed indigenous cultures, racial and religious minorities, and homosexuality. In contrast, the growth of supraterritorial spaces has created more room for the expression of elements of identity besides state-nationhood, such as class, disability, gender, generation (especially youth), minority nationalities, profession, race, religion and sexual preference. Globalization has thereby encouraged a shift from the straitjacket of one-dimensional nationalism (as tended to prevail in the mid-twentieth century) to greater pluralism. Many people have gained the security of a more genuine sense of self as a result, for example, of religious discovery, women's activism, 'coming out' with minority sexualities, and celebrations of indigenous culture.

On the other hand, the turn toward plural, multidimensional and hybrid identities has removed the security of simplicity and predictability that marked a territorialist world where one's collective identity tended to be neatly defined by a single nationality connected to a corresponding state. The sense of self can become ambiguous and unsteady when a person holds several national identities at once: for example, the nationality of their country of residence; the nationality of their country of origin (in the case of migrants); the nationality of a substate or transstate territory; and so on. Further uncertainty can arise when the national self coexists in a person uneasily (and perhaps in contradiction and competition) with class, religious and other identities. In these ways a more global world can leave some individuals feeling torn and lost.

Contemporary globalization has also sometimes undermined the security of identity through cultural destruction. Various life-worlds have succumbed to an invasion of electronic mass media, transplanetary tourism, global English, global consumerism, and other supraterritorial interventions that have contradicted local traditions. For example, radio made little time for the 'long songs' of the Dayak people in Sarawak. As a result this age-old cultural form was obliterated less than 20 years after the introduction of the wireless (Rubenstein, 1991). The Internet, too, is not conducive to oral cultures. In addition, dams, roads and other major infrastructure projects financed by global institutions and/or built by global contractors have severely disrupted a number of indigenous ways of life. Indeed, to date the policies of transworld economic agencies like the BIS, IMF, IOSCO, OECD, WTO and World Bank have tended to be culturally blind, an approach that has arguably contributed to some wanton destruction of life-worlds. The Convention for the Protection of the World Cultural and Natural Heritage (1972), the World Commission on Culture and Development (1995), and the Universal Declaration on Cultural Diversity (2001) have offered rare and toothless antidotes. Likewise, the World's Bank Comprehensive Development Framework (CDF) announced in 1998 has advanced only modestly towards its objectives to integrate anthropological with economic concerns and to draw policy inputs from the grassroots as well as development professionals.

In these circumstances some observers have worried that globalization can crush cultural diversity along with biological diversity. For instance, up to half of the languages currently spoken by humanity are already threatened with extinction, and some linguists have forecast that over 90 per cent could die out during the twenty-first century (Wurm, 1996). Global media have encouraged this trend with their emphasis on a few major world languages. For example, as of 2004 nearly 90 per cent of Internet use occurred in just nine languages (Internet, 2004).

That said, cultural preservationists have discovered on various occasions that the technologies of globalization can be used to reinvigorate otherwise declining or dormant identities. For example, video productions have contributed to a revitalization of Bedouin culture in Egypt (L. Abu-Lughod, 1989). Television has fostered self-assertion among Aboriginals in Australia and among Catalans in Spain. Satellite broadcasts have furthered the survival of the Inuktituk language in the Canadian Arctic. Radio has fuelled Maori identity politics in Aotearoa (the indigenous name for New Zealand) (Dowmunt, 1993).

Thus, as with other aspects of human security, globalization has had mixed impacts on identity. Postterritorialist geography has carried constructive implications in some respects and destructive consequences in others. On the one hand, transworld relations have shown possibilities of cultural revival and innovation. On the other hand, contemporary globalization has shown potentials of violent cultural homogenization, particularly through westernization and Americanization. In respect of identity too, therefore, the problems of globalization and human security lie not so much in enlarged globality per se as in the way that this geographical trend is handled.

Knowledge

Next to identity, another cultural aspect of human security that needs to be evaluated in regard to globalization concerns the confidence that people feel in the knowledge that they hold. As indicated in Chapter 8, the rapid contemporary expansion of transworld relations has contributed to several shifts in prevailing structures of understanding. Have these developments promoted or undermined security?

In terms of security enhancement, the growth of religious revivalism associated with contemporary globalization has provided adherents with, for them, secure truths. Revivalists among Buddhists, Christians, Hindus, Jews and Muslims have all enjoyed the comfort of believing that they hold an indisputable knowledge. Likewise, secular fundamentalists who endorse an uncritical rationalism have felt sure in the gospel of science, the dogma of efficiency, and the cult of progress.

Yet each of these absolutisms has maintained its truth claims in part by denying a hearing to alternative beliefs. Fundamentalism has thereby tended to breed violence between contending dogmas. Thus, for example, many revivalist Sikhs have clashed, sometimes with force of arms, against Hindus. Many revivalist Hindus have sought to silence Muslims in India. Many revivalist Muslims have aimed to eliminate the state of Israel, while many revivalist Jews have tried to marginalize Christian and Muslim Arabs in Palestine. Many revivalist Christians have run roughshod over other faiths in their campaigns of proselytization. In these cases and more, the security of absolutist knowledge for some has come at a cost of insecurity for others, to the point of fatal consequences in some cases.

Like religious fundamentalists, devout rationalists have generally also had little ear for alternative forms of knowledge. The 'imperialism of science' has thereby constituted a threat to circles like indigenous peoples and religious traditionalists who have found their security of knowledge in nonrationalist thinking. True, globalization has, as seen in Chapter 8, created some additional room for different epistemologies to develop. However, transplanetary connectivity has at the same time given rationalists extra tools with which to marginalize and silence rival modes of understanding. For example, cyberspace, transworld publications and global conferences have served rationalist academics far more than holy persons and other nonrationalist teachers. Secularism has dominated in global foundations and think tanks. Technocracy has dominated in global governance. Instrumentalism has dominated in global business. These circumstances of the globalizing world have made it harder for nonrational knowledges to survive.

Meanwhile, insofar as it has encouraged the rise of reflexivity, globalization has also tended to undermine the security of knowledge among rationalists. Part of the secular intelligentsia has thereby lost objectivist certainties and Enlightenment confidence. Most rationalists are uncomfortable with the indeterminacy of truth in postpositivist epistemology. Even self-proclaimed relativists often carry too much residual rationalist baggage to feel genuinely at ease with knowledge that is held to have no validity beyond its particular personal, social and historical context. Meanwhile most rationalists have recoiled from what they regard as the 'meaninglessness' of postmodernist epistemology. Indeed, in academic circles scientists have often mobilized to suppress postmodernist challenges to rationalism with as much determination as they have opposed traditionalist myths.

Hence several turns in knowledge structures encouraged by globalization have tended to unsettle human security. Fundamentalism (both religious and secular) has provided confidence to some, but at a cost of violence to many. Meanwhile reflexive rationalism has tended to sow unsettling doubt, and postmodernism has tended to remove any trace of certainty.

Social cohesion

Many aspects of human security discussed above – including peace, crime, poverty, working conditions and identity – relate closely to a final issue, the security derived from social cohesion. A keystone of human safety and confidence is a firm sense of being integrated into and being supported by a larger collectivity. Recognizing the importance of this matter, the 1995 World Summit for Social Development promoted social integration as a leading theme next to poverty reduction and employment creation.

Certainly the logic of neoliberalist policies towards globalization has posed problems for social cohesion. Neoliberalism has approached social relations as a matter of competition in a global marketplace, a conception that makes little or no room for cooperation and collective interests. One arch-neoliberalist, Margaret Thatcher, has gone so far as to proclaim that 'there is no such thing as society'.

Most commentators now recognize that such extreme atomization is unsustainable in theory or practice. Social relations cannot be reduced to isolated individuals engaged in work and consumption. There is need for a social bond, but how is it to be forged in a globalizing world?

As intimated in Chapter 7, globalization has undermined the modern premise that social cohesion can and should be wholly guaranteed through the state-nation-country-society unit. On that principle previous generations have assumed that people would mainly secure social integration through a territorial homeland. True, already in earlier periods, lower levels of transplanetary relations made it impossible fully to parcel the world into discrete territorial blocs with neatly separated societies, each unified by a single nationality and ruled by a sovereign authority. However, strong forces of territorialist geography, statist governance and nationalist identity at this previous time combined to give the formula considerable viability and appeal. In contrast, contemporary large-scale growth of global spaces has made even an approximation of this model of social cohesion infeasible.

As noted in Chapter 1, some have looked to local communities to solve the problem of social integration in a more global world. This approach has much appeal at first blush, though it can easily romanticize the local. Moreover, intensified global relations have often weakened intimacy and mutual support within neighbourhoods as well as within countries. People who are glued to television and computer screens may have virtual bonds across the planet but little or no acquaintance with persons living next door. Similarly, globally mobile companies tend (exceptions duly noted) to hold limited long-term commitments to the localities where their facilities are situated at any particular time. Flexible workers, too, often have restricted opportunities to plant roots in a locality before the labour market calls them elsewhere.

Contemporary globalization has also undermined social cohesion by fuelling various divisive communitarian dynamics. Communitarianism is a mode of identity politics where the 'in-group' is constructed through an emphasis of difference from and polarized opposition to an 'out-group'. Communitarian 'us–them' logic is seen *inter alia* in binary divisions between compatriots and foreigners, between the West and the Rest, between whites and people of colour, between straights and gays, etc. In all of these cases, integration of part of a population is achieved by disintegration of the larger collectivity. Moreover, this negatively based cohesion – defining the purported community more for what it is not than for what it is – tends to yield only shallow solidarity.

Much communitarianism has been evident in the trends of identity politics described in Chapter 7. For example, the proliferation of nationalist movements has usually involved substantial degrees of aggressive othering. Nonterritorial solidarities, too, have often rested on the exclusion of a certain 'other': that is, a different class, a different race, and so on. Religious revivalists, radical feminists and others have usually created cohesion of their in-group largely by stressing separation from and conflict with 'outsiders'. In other words, these transplanetary communities have needed to fragment the world-societal whole in order to integrate their particular slice of humanity. Overall social cohesion – both within countries and on a world scale – has readily suffered as a result.

Given these limitations of nation-states, local communities, ethnic revivals, and transworld networks, there is pressing need to develop alternative models of social cohesion, together with associated new notions of citizenship and democracy. Unfortunately, little progress with such innovations has been booked to date. A few academics have contemplated reconstructions of citizenship for a more global world (Steenbergen, 1994; Lacarrieu and Raggio, 1997; Castles and Davidson, 2000; Vandenberg, 2000). However, these intellectual musings have filtered little into everyday practice.

Some firms have espoused notions of corporate citizenship as a way to contribute to a sustainable social fabric in a more global world. A number of business executives have recognized the limitations of neoliberalism with remarks like 'tomorrow's successful company cannot afford to be a faceless institution that does nothing more than sell the right product at the right price' (Thomas, 1999). The corporate social responsibility movement has stressed a 'triple bottom line' of social and environmental as well as financial balances. According to this vision, business should link 'three P's' of people, planet and profit. However, most companies have avoided CSR issues, and many CEOs have apparently signed up to the slogans mainly as a marketing ploy and/or to parry calls for greater official regulation of global capital. Yet even though fully developed and enthusiastically pursued CSR could promote greater social cohesion, it would not be sufficient. Society cannot be reduced to a market, however friendly that market might be.

To address this point, a number of reformists have advocated that the global public sector should join the global private sector to forge greater social cohesion amidst increased transworld relations. In this vision, global governance should do more than facilitate the growth of global markets, and also advance general social integration. Previously cited arguments for the development of global public goods have followed this reasoning that the provision of collective transplanetary benefits through global governance mechanisms can generate social bonds beyond the nation-state-country. However, global public goods initiatives have made little concrete progress to date.

Next to CSR and global public goods, a third possible source for greater social cohesion in a globalizing world is global civil society. Indeed, transplanetary associations have already built some significant transworld bonds between women, indigenous peoples and so on. The contemporary expansion of transworld humanitarian relief efforts has also promoted social cohesion beyond the nation-state-country. Global NGOs have also filled many gaps in social services in countries with weak states and markets, although the question remains whether NGOs have been providing foundations for socially sustainable globalization or only applying plaster to the crumbling walls of neoliberalist policies (Fowler, 1994; Devine, 1996). Moreover, global civil society has often operated with exclusions that undermine rather than forward social integration (Scholte, 2004b: ch 5).

In sum, globalization has made territorialist-statist-nationalist approaches to the construction of society non-viable, and no adequate alternative has yet been devised. This void has arguably encouraged a general decline in social responsibility, with particularly unhappy consequences for vulnerable circles. But all including the most privileged of élites suffer when a secure social bond is not in place.

Conclusion

The preceding discussion of globalization and human security has taken stock across a wide spectrum of issues. This review has indicated that contemporary social life is steeped in insecurities and that many of the problems have had significant connections with globalization. To be sure, people in different contexts across the globalizing world have faced different combinations of challenges to security, and some have confronted more imminent threats to survival than others. However, no one has been entirely safe – objectively and subjectively – and globalization has often received much blame for heightened insecurities.

As this chapter has shown, the relationship between increased globality and trends in human security is actually quite complex. For one thing, the implications of globalization have been positive as well as negative. As the boxed summary indicates, none of the eleven issue areas investigated in this chapter has had a completely one-sided balance sheet, where all is detrimental and nothing beneficial.

From this overview it is readily apparent that globalization has been associated with many harms to human security; however, this process of geographical transformation has never been the sole source of damage, and care should be taken not to overplay its significance. Each of the problems of human security discussed in this chapter has resulted from a confluence of multiple circumstances in which growing global connections is only part of the equation. Anti-globalization protesters are mistaken if they assume that the dissolution of transworld relations would by itself solve the problems of human security.

Moreover, some of the negative impacts of globalization on security have been overblown. For example, the Y2K millennium bug that was widely expected to paralyse global computer networks on 01/01/2000 did nothing of the sort. SARS was touted as the global plague of the twenty-first century, but in fact caused only 800 deaths. Likewise, aeroplane crashes and terrorist attacks have killed far fewer people than the barrage of often lurid media coverage would suggest. Some NGOs have played up global humanitarian emergencies and global ecological threats to attract publicity and raise revenue. 'Risk entrepreneurs' have induced people to buy more insurance than probabilities warrant. In these cases and more, people have experienced exaggerated degrees of distress in respect of globalization.

A number of other detrimental effects of globalization on human security have been largely unnecessary and avoidable. As indicated above, it has in no way been inevitable that increased transplanetary connectivity should perpetuate or worsen armed conflicts, crime, environmental degradation, financial instability, poverty, working conditions or cultural destruction. Where contemporary globalization has had negative implications in these

Globalization and (in)security in summary

Peace

- intense global connectivity has created significant disincentives to war among the OECD states
- the growth of global governance has brought increased possibilities of arms control and conflict management

but

- global reach has facilitated military interventions from the North into the South
- globalization has fuelled violence in the context of micro-nationalism and religious revivalism
- technologies of globalization have substantially raised the destructive capacities of war
- global arms markets have spread many destructive means of contemporary warfare
- globalization has greatly raised the profile of terrorist politics

Crime

- expanded global spaces have broadened opportunities to combat crime

but

- globality has provided criminals with important tools for their illicit activities
- transworld networks have given criminals a powerful form of organization

Ecological integrity

- global consciousness has promoted greater ecological awareness
- technologies of globalization have improved means to monitor environmental change
- a number of suprastate governance mechanisms have enhanced environmental care

but

- many global activities are heavily polluting
- global restructuring has often put downward pressures on environmental standards
- global ecological changes have generated much uncertainty and fear

Health

- global organizations have pursued multiple campaigns for health improvement
- global markets have made many more health treatments available to many more people

but

- global markets have also spread many goods that carry health risks

→

→

- global debts have undermined health expenditures in many poor countries
- global migration has encouraged many health professionals to leave countries with the greatest need of their services
- intense global movement of people and produce has accelerated the transmission of many diseases

Poverty

- global trade and investment have contributed to rapid welfare rises in the NICs

but

- comparatively few countries have achieved NIC status
- existing global trade rules have had some detrimental effects on poor countries
- global debt burdens in the South have severely compromised poverty reduction efforts
- several global financial crises have impacted negatively on poor people
- economic restructuring in the face of globalization has often increased poverty

Financial stability

- global finance has mobilized large sums of capital for investment
- moderate levels of financial market instability can enhance efficiency

but

- the high volatility of liberalized global financial markets has added considerably to feelings of economic insecurity
- crises in global finance have often harmed vulnerable circles as well as investors
- governance bodies have taken inadequate measures to curb wild fluctuations in global financial markets

Employment

- global companies and industries have generated millions of new jobs

but

- the supply of waged employment from global capitalism has lagged far behind the need
- global capitalism is generally less labour intensive than older sectors of production
- global finance capitalism has diverted substantial investment from the 'real' economy
- global corporate relocation has brought some job losses and many fears for job security
- economic restructuring in the face of globalization has brought job losses

→

→

Working conditions

- some global companies have improved terms of service for workers in the South

but

- globalization has undermined the Fordist social contract with flexibilization
- adequate guarantees of workers' rights have not developed under global capitalism
- poor labour conditions have often exacerbated insecurities of life outside the workplace

Identity

- global links have increased possibilities to develop multiple aspects of the self
- technologies of globalization have reinvigorated some declining cultures

but

- global relations have sometimes also contributed to cultural destruction
- the ambiguities and contradictions of a multidimensional self can be unsettling

Knowledge

- contemporary globalization has sometimes encouraged fundamentalisms that offer apparently secure truths

but

- fundamentalism has generally involved violence toward alternative beliefs
- global channels have often facilitated the imposition of rationalist dogmas
- reflexive rationalists have lost Enlightenment confidence
- few people feel secure with the postmodernist alternative of indeterminate knowledge

Social cohesion

- globalization has facilitated the growth of various transworld social bonds
- global NGOs have often supplied social services in countries where states and markets are deficient

but

- neoliberalist globalization has tended to neglect needs for social integration
- globalization has undermined possibilities of achieving adequate social cohesion through the nation-state-country alone
- alternative ways to achieve social cohesion have thus far remained underdeveloped

areas, the fault has lain with policy choices (often on neoliberalist lines) rather than with transworld relations as such. Alternative approaches towards globalization could alleviate or eliminate these harms – or indeed even generate positive outcomes.

However, after discounting for hyperbole and misguided policies, certain other contemporary troubles of human security have been to a significant degree intrinsic to the shift towards a more global social relations. For example, larger and faster transplanetary movements of people and produce have created greater problems of disease control; this problem is inherent to globalization, regardless of the policy framework adopted towards it. Likewise, labour-saving technologies in much of global capitalism have generated extra difficulties for provision of waged employment. Contemporary large-scale globalization has also imposed unavoidable challenges of building new strategies of cultural and psychological security that address a context of more plural and hybrid identities. Also, as a shift away from territorialist geography, globalization has brought inescapable problems of developing different bases of social cohesion to replace the nationalist-statist formula of old. More generally, globalization has invariably contributed to a backdrop of uncertainty that tends to accompany any significant social change.

Dealing with human insecurity is therefore a major political challenge in contemporary globalization. No social order can provide absolute security, of course, but the evidence assembled in this chapter gives good cause to ask whether globalization needs to produce as much insecurity as it has tended to do so far.

Chapter 10

Globalization and (In)Equality

Main points of this chapter
Class inequalities
Country inequalities
Gender inequalities
Other inequalities
Conclusion

Main points of this chapter

- globalization has had impacts on various types of social stratification, including with respect to class, country, gender, race, urban/rural divides, age and (dis)ability
- although contemporary globalization has helped to narrow social hierarchies in certain respects, in other ways the process has tended to widen structural gaps in life chances
- these inequalities are not inherent to globalization, but have mainly flowed from prevailing policy approaches to transplanetary connections

Social justice involves more than guarantees of certain minimum standards of human security for all. In addition, equity involves the promotion of equal life chances, so that people face a level playing field in society, free of arbitrary privileges and imposed exclusions. Equality in this sense means that social relations are not marked by structural stratifications of opportunity that accord some persons an inbuilt *a priori* advantage over others (for example, by accident of birth). From this perspective justice would entail moving society from a situation of hierarchical poles to one of inclusive circles.

Historically, various kinds of arbitrary privilege have arisen in social relations. Examples include dominance and subordination on the basis of class, caste, country, gender, race, urban/rural divides, sexual orientation, (dis)ability and age group. In relation to class, for instance, persons born into some socioeconomic circles have generally had fewer life chances than those born into others. Likewise, in terms of countries, individuals in the South or the East who have equivalent personal capacities and make similar efforts as individuals in the North have tended to harvest fewer fruits, simply by virtue of living in one geopolitical zone of the planet rather than another. In addition, hierarchical gender relations have generally given men built-in privileges in social life relative to women. Socially constructed racial inequalities have usually advantaged white people over people of colour. Meanwhile across the world urban-centred development strategies have tended to marginalize rural sectors. Lesbians, gays, bisexuals and transsexuals have often encountered discrimination on account of their sexual inclination. Similarly, mentally and physically handicapped people have frequently faced inordinate socially imposed obstacles to the realization of their potentials. In terms of age, more vulnerable groups such as children and the elderly have readily seen their interests systematically subordinated to those of people in mid-life who occupy most decision-taking positions.

The different lines of inequality intersect, of course. A person may be structurally subordinated in one sense (e.g., as a woman) but arbitrarily privileged in another (e.g., as an upper caste). Thus in assessing an individual's position in respect of social inequality the various hierarchies need to be considered in combination. A professional white urban middle-aged able-bodied heterosexual man in the North attracts the most structural advantages, whereas a low-trained rural elderly disabled homosexual woman of colour in the South has no social category in her favour. Not surprisingly, then, an Islamic black female mental health advocate in rural eastern Uganda has declared regarding globalization that (Wambedde, 2003): 'We are the grass that suffers when the elephants fight. No one comes to ask what our problems are and what alternatives we have. Things are imposed.'

This is not the place for an extended exploration of the intricate political-philosophical issues surrounding the principle of equality. These arguments are well summarized elsewhere (Clayton and Williams, 2000; Kymlicka, 2001). Suffice to say that, in the approach adopted here, equality does not require that social categories be eliminated and that all people become the same. Such uniformity is neither attainable nor desirable. However, it is manifestly inequitable when an embedded stratification of social positions largely determines whether or not people gain access to the resources they need to develop their capacities. Thus there is no justifiable reason why children from wealthier circles should have more life chances than children born into poorer circles, or why men should have greater opportunities than women on grounds of gender, or why rural inhabitants should be structurally disadvantaged relative to town dwellers. Greater rewards for greater accomplishments can be defended, but justice demands that all parties have equivalent possibilities to produce those greater accomplishments.

Social equality is not only right in principle, but it can also have positive repercussions for the issues of human security discussed in Chapter 9. To the extent that arbitrary social hierarchies prevail, there is less likely to be peace, sufficient care for the environment, good public health, poverty eradication, adequate labour protection, enhanced identity and knowledge, and social cohesion. Conversely, to the extent that people feel insecure, they are less likely to relinquish any unfair social advantages that they might have. In addition, as is elaborated in Chapter 11, greater social equality is deeply interconnected with greater democracy.

Needless to say, contemporary globalization does not constitute the original source of structural inequalities. Stratification by class, country, gender, race and other social categories long predates the current growth of transplanetary connections. Hence the question is how globalization has affected the forms and the intensity of social hierarchies in contemporary history. In what ways and to what extent has the accelerated spread of transworld relations since the mid-twentieth century either loosened or maintained – or perhaps even exacerbated – arbitrary subordinations in social life?

As noted in Chapter 1, claims and counterclaims about the effects of globalization on social inequality have filled academic journals and political speeches alike since the early 1990s. Even the World Bank has acknowledged the centrality of the issue by devoting its 2005 *World Development Report* to the theme of equity (World Bank, 2005). Proponents of globalization have promised enhanced opportunities for all, while critics have decried intensified subordinations. These arguments have key political importance. The expansion of global relations would be more sustainable to the extent that people perceive a fair distribution of chances to benefit from the process. In contrast, prevailing policies towards globalization – and maybe even transplanetary connectivity as such – would tend to fail to the extent that they are viewed as unjust.

No consensus is in prospect on the relationship between globalization and equality. The issues involved are enormously complex to analyse, both conceptually and empirically. Much research by economists in recent years has assessed the question in terms of trends in income distributions between and within countries (e.g., Aghion and Williamson, 1998; Stewart and Berry, 2000; Lindert and Williamson, 2001; O'Rourke, 2002; Sutcliffe, 2002; Wade, 2004). Unfortunately for the purposes of the present book, these economic investigations have generally defined globalization as marketization. That is, the studies have looked for correlations between the adoption of neoliberalist policies (especially trade liberalization) and trends in income disparities. However, as argued earlier, liberalization is only one aspect of contemporary globalization and is not intrinsic to the geographical change. In addition, social inequality involves much more than income differentials (e.g., other resource distributions, political hierarchies, cultural dominations and psychological oppressions). Besides, these studies employ such varying methodologies (in terms of different units of analysis, different indicators, different data sources, and different modes of calculation) that it is very hard to draw any firm conclusions even about income inequality. Moreover, on those occasions where statistical links can be drawn between globalization and trends in inequality (up or down), the correlations do not necessarily indicate causal significance. Indeed, by adopting different foci and formulas, different researches have yielded sometimes substantially contrasting results. The present chapter therefore does not aim to find precise and definitive quantitative evidence for causal links between globalization and inequality. The emphasis is put instead on identifying general connections that are described with illustrative examples.

Taking this approach, the record on globalization and inequality looks mixed. On the positive side, some developments in contemporary globalization have worked against structurally imposed hindrances on people. For example, as elaborated below, contemporary global capitalism has in some ways increased opportunities for women to engage in waged employment. However, the recent growth of global spaces has – under prevailing neoliberalist policies – often distributed costs and benefits in ways that further favour the already privileged and further marginalize the already disadvantaged.

As a result, global relations have, to date, in many instances widened resource gaps and reinforced social hierarchies, especially those related to class, country and urban/rural divides. Class stratification has meant that investors, managers, professionals and certain skilled workers have profited far more from globalization than less trained workers. In respect of countries, embedded hierarchies have thus far channelled the benefits of globalization disproportionately to lands of the North relative to those of the South and the East. With its generally urban-centric character, contemporary globalization has also tended to accentuate the marginalization of rural areas. Trends with regard to gender, race, (dis)ability and age stratifications have been more ambiguous or mixed, but neoliberalist policies towards globalization have in certain respects clearly operated against women, people of colour, the disabled and the elderly.

Given this record, the growth of global relations has not surprisingly unsettled many consciences and sparked resistance from a number of subordinated circles. As one trade union leader in France has noted, 'Globalization puts everyone on earth in the same boat, but some are in the hold while others travel first class' (Trogrlic, 2001). Whatever the precise impact, it is undeniable that several decades of accelerated globalization have not removed morally unacceptable gross inequalities from the world. Nor have prevailing policies towards globalization given priority to rectifying these problems. Authorities have not propounded targets for inequality reduction in the way that other targets have proliferated to raise efficiency, alleviate poverty, and enhance environmental protection.

To be sure, (neoliberalist) globalization has not been the sole cause of persistent and in some cases growing violences of inequality in today's world. However, the rise of transplanetary connectivity has contributed to these unhappy trends in at least four important general ways. First, people in different social categories have often had arbitrarily unequal opportunities to access purportedly 'free' and 'open' global spaces. Second, on its mainly neoliberalist course, contemporary global capitalism has often undermined the redistributive mechanisms that were built up through many states during the first three-quarters of the twentieth century. Third, global regimes (that is, the rules and institutions that govern transworld flows) have thus far tended to underwrite allocations of benefits and harms that favour the already advantaged. Fourth, contemporary globalization has substantially undermined the capacity of traditional, territorially based social movements like trade unionism and anti-colonialism to campaign for a fair distribution of life chances. More positively, though, globalization has often facilitated a growth of new, substantially supraterritorial social movements that have highlighted questions of gender justice, racial equity, children's rights, opportunities for disabled persons, and a so-called 'right to development' for all countries.

The rest of this chapter examines the dynamics of (mal)distribution under contemporary globalization in more detail. Most research on globality and social equality has addressed stratifications associated with class, North–South divisions, and gender; thus these three types of hierarchies are discussed at greater length below. Less evidence is currently available regarding the implications of globalization for racial stratifications, urban/rural divides, sexual minorities, (dis)abilities, and generational inequalities; hence remarks on these matters are more brief.

Throughout the discussion below it becomes apparent that social inequality is no more intrinsic to globality than to territorial geography. Yes, structural hierarchies between social groups have often persisted and grown in the context of contemporary globalization. However, these trends have mainly resulted from *laissez-faire* policies toward globalization and are not inherent in globalization itself. The adoption of different approaches to globalization could yield more just outcomes.

Class inequalities

As noted in Chapter 1, many critics have alleged that contemporary globalization has intensified class inequalities. 'Class' refers here to the division of a population in respect of different roles in the production process. In contemporary capitalism, for example, people generally contribute to production as investors, managers, professionals, skilled manual workers, or workers without formal qualifications (including homemakers). This division of labour is often further reflected in associated differences related to customs, dress, language, art forms, residential areas, etc.

Class diversity is to be accepted and in many cases welcomed; however, it is unjust when class categories generate unequal life chances. Certain forms of work may warrant higher rewards owing to the specialist competence and/or greater exertion demanded. However, the premiums can become excessive, and class distinctions have often restricted social mobility, educational opportunities, access to health care, and so on. In such situations class difference becomes class hierarchy.

Class inequalities existed long before the current period of accelerated globalization, of course; yet how has the growth of transplanetary and supraterritorial capitalism affected class gaps in more recent times? As noted above, statistical data on this question have focused on income differentials, with particular reference to a standard if somewhat crude measure known as the Gini coefficient. Historically this indicator has normally related to income inequality within a country's population; however, recently several researchers have calculated a Gini coefficient in respect of global humanity. These studies have suggested that world income inequality between households has seen little change during the period of accelerated globalization in the second half of the twentieth century (Berry, 2002). For example, a lead economist at the World Bank has calculated that the planetary Gini coefficient rose from 0.63 in 1988 to 0.67 in 1993 before dropping again to 0.63 in 1998 (Milanovic, 1999, 2005). Another thorough investigation by a respected economist has suggested a fall in the global Gini coefficient from 0.67 in 1980 to 0.63 in 2000 (Sutcliffe, 2002). Whatever the precise trend, it is noteworthy that all studies agree that the global Gini coefficient has remained greater than all but the very highest country Gini coefficients. In other words, income inequality between persons on a planetary scale has almost always been larger than such inequality within countries.

In national spheres, income inequality has over recent decades moved in different directions depending on the country in question and the statistical method used. However, one wide-ranging study has concluded that 48 out of 73 countries for which data of a sufficient standard are available experienced growth of income inequality during the 1980s and 1990s (Cornia, 2004). Thus, on this measure, two-thirds of countries would have seen widening class gaps during the heyday of neoliberalist globalization.

In the USA, for example, differences in household income between the top fifth and the bottom fifth of the populace narrowed between 1947 and 1973, but then increased by more than 50 per cent between 1973 and 1996 (Burtless *et al.*, 1998: 3). Wealth gaps of this kind have also grown in recent decades across almost all other OECD countries, albeit usually not as much as in the USA (Ghai, 1994: 30–2; HDR, 1999: 37). Wage differentials have tended to widen in the North between more trained labour (professionals, managers, technicians) and less trained labour (people with no more than general secondary education), after these gaps had decreased during the third quarter of the twentieth century (Wood, 1994).

In the East, meanwhile, most countries in the early transition from state socialism to market capitalism experienced a steep ascent to wealth for a few and a rapid descent to poverty for many. In Russia, for instance, the richest fifth of the population saw its proportion of national income rise from 32.7 per cent in 1990 to 46.7 per cent in 1997, while the poorest fifth had its share decline over the same period from 9.8 to 6.2 per cent (UNDP, 1998: 8). Across most of Central and Eastern Europe and the former Soviet Union in the 1990s, a limited circle reaped major material gains from the new connections to global capitalism, while the majority of people saw their standard of life worsen.

Huge class inequalities have marked much of the South in the contemporary globalizing world as well. To take the most extreme example, in the early 1990s the wealthiest fifth of the population in Brazil earned 26 times as much as the poorest fifth (HDR, 1991: 34). Major cities in Africa, Asia and Latin America today often house the ugliest shantytowns in the shadows of the shiniest skyscrapers. On the other hand, the Gini coefficient in Malaysia declined from 0.49 in 1980 to 0.45 in 1993 (HDR, 1999: 88). Given this variability it would seem important to look in greater detail at specific cases in order to determine how and why class gaps have enlarged or shrunk in one or the other country.

That said, a consistent trend has unfolded since the 1980s across countries of the North, the East and the South to concentrate greater wealth in the very rich. The most prosperous 5–10 per cent of country populations have increasingly separated themselves off from the rest. As of the mid-1990s, the value of the assets of 358 billionaires exceeded the combined annual incomes of countries with 2.3 billion inhabitants, or the poorest 45 per cent of the world's population (HDR, 1996: 2; Speth, 1996: 33). Hence, at the start of the twenty-first century some 7.7 million superrich each held more than $1 million in financial assets, while 2.8 billion others lived on less than $2 a day (World Bank, 2001: 3; CapGemini, 2004: 4). Even allowing for the objection that assets are not directly comparable to income, these numbers point to a deplorably uneven distribution of world resources that goes well beyond anything that can be justified on grounds of special skill and effort. Perhaps popular perceptions of growing general class inequality have tended to be greater than overall data indicate owing to this superaccumulation by the superrich. This explosion of wealth at the top end – and the general disinclination of governments to counteract it – has generated widespread unhappiness and cynicism.

Moreover, inequity on class lines has extended beyond matters of income and assets. For example, many countries across the world have in recent history witnessed a deterioration in publicly provided education. The alternative of private instruction or other supplements has generally only been available to wealthier households. As a result, class-based inequalities in educational opportunities have tended to increase. Widespread deterioration across the planet in public health, public housing and public transport has likewise tended to impact more heavily on disadvantaged classes, thereby deepening their subordination.

Yet how far, if at all, can greater class inequalities in contemporary history be attributed to globalization? The two developments have unfolded concurrently, but has the rise of transplanetary links *caused* the increases in class gaps? Some authors of a neoliberalist persuasion have explicitly rejected the proposition that globalization (understood as liberalization) could widen class stratification (cf. Burtless *et al.*, 1998: ch 4). At another extreme, many critics have regarded deepened class hierarchies as an inherent and incorrigible evil of global capitalism. Other studies have found no significant relationship between globalization (measured as increased cross-border trade and investment) and within-country income inequality (Vivarelli, 2004).

What conclusion can be drawn? In some ways globalization has indeed figured in the contemporary growth of class inequalities; however, this outcome is not inherent in transworld social relations. The problem has lain not in globality as such, but in the prevailing neoliberalist approach to managing transplanetary relations. Policymakers have generally pursued stabilization, liberalization, deregulation, privatization and fiscal constraint without specific attention to issues of class justice.

One major way that globalization has widened class gaps in contemporary history relates to access. 'Free' global markets have by no means been 'open' to all. As indicated in Chapter 5, expanded transworld spaces have generated considerable additional surpluses; however, different classes have had substantially different opportunities to tap that accumulation. Propertied circles, professionals and certain skilled workers have had far better chances to acquire the means (such as fax, air travel and financial advisers) to participate actively in global capitalism. Class divides have substantially skewed access to the Internet as well (Loader, 1998). Offshore banking and securities have mainly been reserved to the superrich, such as 78,000 citizens of Saudi Arabia who as of the mid-1990s had an average of $5.4 million each invested in global finance (FT500, 1997: 46). In contrast, salaried workers have tended to stay onshore, while most residents of today's world have lacked any bank account whatsoever. Several billion people have consumed global products, but only a small minority has owned the resultant profits.

A second way that globalization has generated greater class divisions follows from challenges to the redistributive state. Earlier in the twentieth century, many national governments developed a number of mechanisms to lessen class stratifications. Keynesianism in the North and various forms of socialism elsewhere in the world went some way to extract from richer circles that part of wealth accumulation which derived from class privilege. Governments used instruments such as progressive taxation, wage controls, price manipulations and improved public services to redirect much of that surplus to less advantaged socioeconomic circles. As a result, people from subordinated classes often gained increased opportunities to realize their potentials. To be sure, Keynesianism and socialism in practice frequently fell short of their promise to remove injustice based on class. At a minimum, however, the redistributive state that peaked in the third quarter of the twentieth century prevented class gaps from growing.

As indicated in Chapter 6, the expansion of globally mobile capital in contemporary history has constrained states to abandon a number of redistributive policies. Across the world, governments have retreated from progressive taxation (Tanzi, 1996). Top tax brackets fell in the OECD countries from an average of 52 per cent in 1985 to 42 per cent in 1990 (HDR, 1999: 93). In addition, widespread introductions and increases of value-added tax (VAT) have had a particularly regressive effect, especially when applied to essential goods like basic clothing and staple foods. Liberalization and deregulation have attenuated or terminated many redistributive wage and price policies. Fiscal austerity to improve 'global competitiveness' has often meant reductions in the amount and quality of state-provided education, housing, nutrition, health care, pensions and unemployment insurance. In sum, neoliberalist globalization has tended to erode the protective shield of the redistributive state. One aforementioned study has ascribed widespread growing income inequality largely to what they regard as excessively liberal economic policies and their rushed implementation (Cornia, 2004).

Emergent suprastate frameworks have not filled the regulatory gaps left by states in respect of countering arbitrary class hierarchies. On the contrary, global economic institutions such as the IMF, the OECD, the WTO and the multilateral development banks have figured as major promoters of neoliberalist policies since the 1980s. Indeed, many states have embarked on deregulation, liberalization, regressive tax reform and fiscal austerity in the context of structural adjustment programmes sponsored by suprastate agencies. Meanwhile these institutions have generally given short shrift to proposals for redistributive global taxes or to calls for a comprehensive clampdown on what in effect amounts to tax evasion by the wealthy through offshore finance facilities. Regional bodies, too, have mainly concentrated on market liberalization, with at best secondary attention to questions of class justice. Regional trade agreements like NAFTA and several thousand bilateral investment treaties have substantially strengthened the position of global capital relative to labour. For its part the ILO has focused on securing minimum workers' rights rather than pursuing a more ambitious agenda of class equity.

Nor have social movements succeeded in mounting effective opposition to growing class gaps in the context of neoliberalist globalization. The main traditional force for class equity, the trade union movement, has experienced substantial drops in membership across most of the world, particularly as old industries have declined and new 'flexible' labour practices have often excluded collective bargaining. Important trade union revivals such as the Central Workers' Union (CUT) in Brazil and the Confederation of South African Trade Unions (COSATU) have been rare. Moreover, contemporary trade unions have – notwithstanding some notable exceptions – tended to persist with nationally and territorially based campaigns (Munck and Waterman, 1999; Harrod and O'Brien, 2002; Munck, 2002). Such a strategy is decidedly inadequate when a large proportion of capital is globally mobile. In some countries where organized labour has retained significant strength, trade union credibility has suffered owing to bureaucratization, close ties with ruling circles, and self-aggrandizement of leaders. Meanwhile new global social movements (for example, of consumer advocates, environmentalists, human rights activists, and women) have tended to give only secondary if any attention to issues of class equity.

In sum, contemporary globalization has in various ways encouraged a greater entrenchment of class inequality. The *Human Development Report* has in this vein spoken of 'a breathtaking globalization of prosperity side by side with a depressing globalization of poverty' (HDR, 1994: 1). Even a bastion of neoliberalism such as the WEF has acknowledged a challenge of 'demonstrating how the new global capitalism can function to the benefit of the majority and not only for corporate managers and investors' (Schwab and Smadja, 1996). Access to global spaces has been highly uneven on class lines. Global capital has prompted states to undo many policies that previously reduced arbitrary class inequalities. Global regimes have not installed redistributive mechanisms to replace those lost in states. Global social movements have often underplayed questions of class stratification. None of these dynamics of social injustice is inherent in globalization. The problem of reinforced and enlarged class gaps, particularly in relation to the very wealthy, has mainly lain in prevailing neoliberalist policies toward expanding transworld relations.

Country inequalities

Arbitrary class hierarchies are of course not the only form of social inequality in the contemporary globalizing world. In addition, for example, theses concerning imperialism have since the nineteenth century highlighted a purported inequitable stratification of countries alongside that of classes. The modern world order, these accounts affirm, has unfairly discriminated against the 'South' (also termed the 'periphery', 'Third World', 'underdeveloped countries', etc.) and the 'East' (also called the 'semi-periphery', 'Second World', 'countries in transition', etc.) in favour of the 'North' (alternatively named the 'core', 'centre', 'First World' or 'developed countries').

To be sure, like any analytical categorization, the distinction of a North, a South and an East in world affairs involves substantial simplification. In practice the North, the South and the East have each contained considerable diversity. For example, the 'poor' South is normally taken to include the oil sheikhs of Kuwait and the financial traders of Singapore. Meanwhile the 'rich' North is normally taken to include the slums of Washington, DC and the marginalized farmers of Sicily. Indeed, poor people arguably form something of a 'South' within the North, and élites could be said to constitute a 'North' within the South and the East. It would clearly be perverse if global redistribution meant further enriching the wealthy of the South by further impoverishing the needy of the North.

Similarly, a country can contain large internal geographical welfare disparities. In Argentina, for instance, Chubut Province is much poorer than Buenos Aires Province. In India the state of Bihar has far greater poverty than Kerala. In England widespread wealth in the South East contrasts with pockets of need in the North East. China's economic boom of recent decades has concentrated on the coastal provinces, while many interior regions have remained stagnant. Owing to such differentials, too, analysis in terms of country units involves considerable simplification.

Yet social hierarchy within countries does not negate the fact of a concurrent hierarchy between countries. Although the notion of a North–South divide may be crude, it does capture an important configuration of world social relations. People living in lands whose governments are members of the G7, the OECD and NATO have generally held structural advantages over inhabitants of countries that have lain outside such clubs. Resource distribution, laws, institutions and inherited prejudices are such that the 'average' person born into a country of the South (where the 'South' has since 1989 arguably included much of the post-communist East) has had fewer life chances than the 'average' person born into a country of the North. Even when an individual from the South and an individual from the North have had equivalent personal means, the resident of the North has generally been able to obtain greater gains from the similar resource base. In these important senses a North–South divide has imposed a significant arbitrary hierarchy of opportunity in modern history.

A trend of increasing disparity between the world's richest and poorest countries can be tracked back to 1870, if not earlier (Pritchett, 1997); yet how has contemporary large-scale globalization affected inequality on North–South lines? Has the end of territorialism meant a reduction of stratification based on territorial units? Or have critics been right to attack globalization as a new imperialism of the North over the South? Evidence suggests that globalization to date has often reinforced arbitrary hierarchies between North and South. However, as with class inequalities, unjust outcomes in respect of North–South relations have often resulted from the (mainly neoliberalist) policies that have been adopted in respect of global spaces rather than from globality per se.

The general welfare gap between the South and the North has grown during the contemporary period of accelerated globalization. Inequality between countries has been calculated in at least seven different ways; yet all but one of the formulas has suggested that the gap grew between 1980 and 2000 (Wade, 2004). True, as seen in Chapter 9, many populations in both the North and the South have experienced various improvements in material conditions during these decades. Yet the advances have generally been greater in the already privileged North. As noted in the last chapter, a few previously 'less-developed' countries have during this period become NICs; however, other lands of the South have seen little improvement – and in some cases an actual decline – in the general welfare of their populations. These misfortunes can be partly attributed to local and national circumstances of the countries concerned, but globalization has also played a part in deepening North–South inequality.

One way that globalization has widened North–South differentials is through uneven access to global spaces. Pre-existent stratification has meant that, like subordinated classes, disadvantaged countries have been less able to share in the gains of global relations. For example, the great bulk of the infrastructure for global communications has been situated in the North. At the turn of the century countries with the richest fifth of the world's population had 74 per cent of all telephone lines, while the poorest fifth had a mere 1.5 per cent (HDR, 1999: 3). In 1996 there were more telephones in Tokyo than in the whole of Africa (*FT*, 7 June 1996: 3). The recent spread of mobile telephones in Africa has begun to improve matters, although as of 2003 still only 4 per cent of people in Africa had a mobile, as compared with 50 per cent in Europe (Poulin, 2004).

The so-called 'digital divide' between North and South in respect of information technology warrants particular mention (Everard, 1999; OECD, 2001; Warschauer, 2002). For example, a computer costs the average Bangladeshi eight years' wages, whereas the average American can purchase the equipment with one month's income (HDR, 1999: 6). As of 2000 Sub-Saharan Africa counted less than 3 million Internet users, while the USA with half the population of that region had 154 million users (Norris, 2001: 47). Users in the South have also generally had a lower quality of Internet connections in terms of smaller bandwidths and slower speeds. Southern contributions to Internet content have been even smaller, so that these parts of the world have normally been dependent data takers rather than proactive data makers. Although the dominance of English in cyberspace has subsided considerably since the late 1990s, some 90 per cent of both content and use of the Internet remains in European and East Asian languages as of 2004 (Global Reach, 2004a; Internet, 2004). All of the 13 main route servers of the

Internet are located in the North (one in Britain, one in Japan, and eleven in the USA). Moreover, the rules governing cyber-traffic have been such that the vast bulk of revenues from Internet use has flowed to the North, and the USA more particularly.

Similar concerns should be anticipated in regard to emergent biological and nano technologies. Already North-based biotechnology companies have established positions of dominance over South-based customers for genetically modified seeds. More generally, only a small percentage of medical research funding goes to illnesses (most prevalent in the South) that account for the lion's share of the world burden of disease. On a similar pattern, the next generation could bring far-reaching inequalities between countries that do and do not have control of nanotechnologies.

Other North–South inequalities have prevailed in the mass media. True, basic radio and television sets have spread to hundreds of millions of people across the planet, but hundreds of millions of others, mostly in the South, still lack access. Moreover, as with the Internet, Northern producers have supplied the vast majority of broadcast material. Bollywood is an exceptional Southern competitor for Hollywood and generally has only small audiences outside India.

Countries of the South have also tended to have secondary participation in global trade. Transworld products have circulated mostly in the North. For instance, consumers in 13 countries of the North have accounted for 80 per cent of the world market in music recordings (*FT*, 2 September 1996: 2). The 48 least developed countries, whose collective population accounted for about 13 per cent of the world total in 1997, had shares in world exports and imports that year of 0.4 and 0.6 per cent, respectively. Moreover, these meagre figures represented a decline of more than 40 per cent since 1980 (UNCTAD, 2000). Absolute volumes of merchandise exports from the South have grown substantially since 1980, but most of the countries remain focused on primary commodities whose prices have declined over this period (Morrissey and Filatotchev, 2000; UNCTAD, 2003).

With regard to global companies, the North as of 1995 held 75 per cent of the total accumulated stock of FDI and also attracted most of new FDI flows (Hirst and Thompson, 1999: 71). Moreover, when FDI went to the South in the 1990s, it concentrated in just ten countries, bypassing the vast majority. The least developed countries have attracted less than 1 per cent of recent world FDI flows (UNCTAD, 2000).

In respect of money US, European and Japanese currencies have dominated global transactions, not the Brazilian real, the Indian rupee and the South African Rand. The power of so-called 'hard' currencies is utterly arbitrary and has conferred enormous privileges on people in their countries of origin, especially the USA. While residents of the North have acquired several hundred million global credit cards, the 1.2 billion inhabitants of China between them held only 14 million of these plastic passes in the mid-1990s (*FT*, 19 September 1996: 37). Although many offshore finance centres have been 'located' (if sometimes only with brass plates) in the South, the tax advantages of these operations have accrued principally to wealthy 'hinwis' who mostly reside in the North.

In global financial markets, countries of the South long ago lost the substantial stream of transworld commercial bank loans that temporarily flowed their way during the 1970s. In the mid-1990s clients based in the North obtained nearly 90 per cent of new global borrowing (OECD, 1996a: 5). On a similar pattern, nearly three-quarters of both equity value and derivatives business were concentrated in the USA, Japan and Britain as of 1993 (Kidron and Segal, 1995: 70–1). True, global flows of securities to the South increased from only \$33 million in 1984 to \$89,000 million in 1993 (Haley, 1999: 75). On the other hand, at the end of the 1990s only 25 governments of the South had a credit rating that gave them access to global bond markets (HDR, 1999: 31). To the (limited) extent that financial trading sites have developed in so-called 'emerging markets' of the South, transworld electronic transfers have ensured that investors based in the North frequently own most of the assets and reap most of the profits. Moreover, when largely globally induced financial crisis has hit the South – for example, in Latin America 1994–5, Asia 1997–8, Russia 1998, Brazil 1999 and Argentina 2001–2 – investment houses based in the North have instantaneously withdrawn enormous funds.

Next to problems of uneven access, contemporary globalization has also furthered growing North–South gaps insofar as neoliberalist policies have discouraged public-sector interventions to counter this inequality of opportunity. During the third quarter of the twentieth century many states of the South attempted to promote 'development' with measures (like tariff protection for infant industries) that sheltered local producers from world market competition. At the same time most states of the North expanded programmes of official development assistance as a modest measure to redistribute wealth between countries.

Neoliberalist critics have rejected 'inward-looking' macroeconomic strategies and sometimes also 'foreign aid' as unhelpful disruptions to inherently progressive forces of the 'free market' (Bandow and Vásquez, 1994). On the neoliberalist wave since the 1980s, states across the South have (to varying degrees) reoriented their policies toward the world economy from protection to liberalization. Meanwhile, fiscal constraints and the rigours of global market competition have encouraged most governments in the North to reduce concessionary resource transfers to the South. By 1995 overseas development assistance (ODA) amounted to only 0.27 per cent of the GNP of the OECD countries, the lowest proportion since such statistics were first collected in 1950 and also a significant decline in real terms (*FT*, 6 February

1997: 5; UNCTAD, 2000). Although many OECD states have increased their ODA ahead of inflation rates since 1997, the proportion of GDP was down further to 0.25 per cent by 2003 (OECD, 2004: 64–5). Moreover, with the addition of clients in the post-communist East, these smaller sums of ODA have since the 1990s been spread across more potential recipients. The NEPAD initiative agreed between the G8 and African governments in 2001 is meant further to revive development support. Yet it will take far more to regain earlier levels of ODA, let alone to reach the long proclaimed and continually deferred UN target of 0.7 per cent of GDP.

Neoliberalists have rightly noted certain shortcomings in statist approaches to 'development' and the often less than optimal use of ODA. State ownership, government subsidies and statutory trade barriers have frequently encouraged inefficiencies and – through various forms of corruption – greater rather than less class inequality in the South. However, it is far from clear that the neoliberalist prescription simply to withdraw public-sector management of cross-border resource movements improves matters. After all, certain kinds of state steering have arguably allowed countries like the so-called 'Asian tigers' to narrow welfare gaps between themselves and the North. Moreover, while preaching liberalization to the South, OECD governments have retained many subsidies and other interventions in the market that have helped to preserve and enlarge their advantages over poor countries. As on earlier historical occasions, 'free trade' has often figured in contemporary neoliberalist globalization as an ideology of the strong whom it favours.

As for global regimes, these frameworks have on the whole promoted neoliberalist formulas with little regard to the detrimental effects that such policies might have on resource distribution between the North and the South. In the area of global communications, for example, institutions like the ITU and the WTO have concentrated on promoting 'free' flows of information. Global regulations have given principal priority to harmonizing technical standards and reducing statutory trade restrictions. Only secondary if any consideration has gone to public policies that would improve the South's access to telecommunications and electronic mass media. Inequities of the North–South digital divide have been recognized through the establishment of the G8 Digital Opportunity Task Force (DOT Force) in 1999 and the proceedings of the ITU World Summit on the Information Society (WSIS) in 2003–4. However, concrete countermeasures have remained modest to date. Indeed, when UNESCO in the late 1970s and early 1980s attacked arbitrary North–South hierarchies with its proposals for a New World Information and Communications Order, dominant states in the North suppressed the initiative. Neoliberalist governments in the UK and the USA went as far as to withdraw from the organization in 1984–5. The installation of a new leadership at UNESCO in 1987 brought a return to more orthodox policy directions, but even then Britain and the US did not rejoin the agency until 1997 and 2003, respectively (Wells, 1987; Imber, 1989).

Like global rules governing communications, the global trade regime centred on the GATT/WTO has focused primarily on liberalization, with limited regard to the possibility that 'free trade' might work against an equitable distribution of opportunities between countries. A so-called 'open' field favours the strong market players, who have been disproportionately situated in the North. Moreover, the GATT/WTO regime has over the half-century of its existence generally proved quickest to liberalize in areas like (most) manufactures and intellectual property where North-based interests hope to exploit opportunities in the South. Progress has tended to be slower in areas like agriculture and textiles where trade liberalization would give South-based interests greater market access to the North. Governance of global trade has therefore been riven with double standards that have usually fallen to the disadvantage of the South.

Economic studies have generally agreed that most of the income gains from the 1994 Uruguay Round agreements would accrue to the already advantaged North (Dubey, 1996: 14–16; Whalley, 1996: 428). For example, a study commissioned by the OECD and the World Bank calculated that the North would acquire 63.4 per cent of the income gains and that the new arrangements would also increase the income gap between Africa and all other regions (Goldin, 1993: 142, 205). The latest phase of multilateral trade negotiations, the Doha Round launched in 2001, is purportedly committed to a 'Development Agenda', but it is far from clear that the rhetoric will translate into meaningful pro-South outcomes.

The Trade-Related Aspects of Intellectual Property Agreement of the WTO is also widely regarded as increasing South–North gaps (UNCTAD, 1996; South Centre, 1997; Correa, 2000; Maskus, 2000; CIPR, 2002). Indeed, most governments of the South signed this accord before they adequately understood its terms and implications. Adopted largely under pressure from global pharmaceutical companies, TRIPS has put the cost of access to advanced technologies and medicines beyond the reach of many poor countries. At the same time, under TRIPS most income from patents, copyrights and trademarks flows to the North. Moreover, global patents on genetic material – henceforth to be guaranteed through the WTO – have given 'bio-prospectors' from the North control over, and income from, many varieties of plant life that originated in poor countries and with indigenous peoples (Shiva, 1997). The *Human Development Report* has spoken in this context of 'a silent theft of centuries of knowledge' (HDR, 1999: 68). Some improved access for poor countries to essential medicines, particularly to treat HIV/AIDS, was agreed on the eve of the 2003 WTO Ministerial Conference, but it has seen little implementation to date, and TRIPS' general bias in favour of the North remains.

True, several suprastate initiatives have stabilized prices and improved access for exports of the South to the North. In this vein, the Generalized System of Preferences (GSP) of the GATT has since the late 1960s offered some Southern producers better access to Northern markets in certain goods. Similarly, a succession of conventions between the EU and 71 African, Caribbean and Pacific (ACP) countries since 1975 has aimed *inter alia* to stabilize export earnings from the South to Europe. In addition, a Compensatory and Contingency Financing Facility was established through the IMF in 1988 for countries that experience temporary shortfalls in export earnings. However, the overall impact of these schemes has remained modest.

Outside official programmes, a number of alternative trading initiatives have linked producers in the South directly with nonprofit buyers in the North, thereby increasing the suppliers' earnings. Examples of such transworld NGO programmes include TWIN Trading and Traidcraft Exchange. Another alternative trade scheme, PEOPLink, has used the Internet to enable artisans from 42 countries of the South to sell their crafts directly to consumers worldwide (PEOPLink, 2004). An International Fair Trade Association was launched in 1989 and 15 years later grouped over 220 initiatives in 59 countries (IFAT, 2004). Nevertheless, these inspirational efforts have accounted for only a miniscule proportion of total world trade.

Meanwhile, proposals for a more comprehensive redistribution of the gains of global commerce have stalled. Reform of North–South trade lay at the heart of the unsuccessful campaign of the 1970s for a so-called New International Economic Order (NIEO) (Bhagwati, 1977; Sauvant and Hasenpflug, 1977). Even OPEC's quadrupling of oil prices in 1973 only reestablished the earlier level relative to manufactures, and the rate per barrel subsequently fell back to pre-1973 rates (Singer, 1995: 23). Many Northern agricultural subsidies remain in place, and steps to dismantle the protectionist Multi-Fibre Arrangement (MFA) dragged for years until its termination in 2005. In the 1990s barriers to trade in the North were estimated to cost the South twice the value of all development aid (Carlsson *et al.*, 1995: 166). Today countries of the North spend $311 billion per annum to subsidize their farmers while committing only $52 billion to ODA (Drache and Froese, 2003: 10). 'Generosity', indeed.

Further inequities in North–South relations have developed out of the regimes that govern global finance. In this issue-area, too, regulators have accorded priority to liberalization rather than equity (or they have assumed simplistically and uncritically that an 'open' economy automatically generates a just distribution). Neoliberalist policies have mainly removed statutory restrictions, for instance, on foreign exchange transactions, capital flows between countries, foreign ownership of financial assets, and so on. When the allocation of global loans and bonds is left to 'market forces', credit goes disproportionately to borrowers with the greatest means to repay. Moreover, in the market higher credit risks attract higher borrowing costs, so that the countries most in need of funds have tended to pay the highest charges. As seen in Chapter 9, some initiatives in global financial governance have sought to reduce the risks of systemic breakdown. However, the regulation of global finance has to date neglected questions of structurally unequal access between countries. The UN Financing for Development initiative has since 1997 sought to make global finance serve the South rather than the other way around, but as yet to little avail.

The North–South distribution of pains in global finance has likewise been unjust. Consider approaches adopted through the IMF and the London Club to 'resolve' the global commercial debt crisis of the 1980s. The losses fell far more heavily on borrowing governments in the South than on lending banks in the North. Indeed, in 1990 the interest on transworld debt due from the South to the North ($112 billion) amounted to nearly three times the flow of bilateral ODA from the North to the South ($41 billion) (Harrod, 1992: 106). Notwithstanding various initiatives since the late 1980s to reduce the burden of debt repayments, the scale of net South-to-North transfers in respect of official and commercial global loans has exceeded anything previously witnessed, including during colonial times.

Since the mid-1990s governments, firms and peoples of the South have also borne the brunt of the pain in financially driven economic crises in Asia, Latin America and Russia. Multilateral financial agencies have usually laid the blame for these misfortunes on flaws on the domestic laws and institutions of the affected countries. Accordingly the lion's share of recovery costs and corrective measures have applied to the South. In contrast, global regulators have generally underplayed the role in these crises of liberalized transplanetary capital flows. Hence global banks and investment companies (who hold mainly North-based funds) have avoided even the idea of contributing to the public costs of these downturns in 'emerging markets', for example, in terms of the alleviation of increased unemployment and destitution. Along similar lines, if a global bond-rating agency downgrades a poor country on the basis of faulty intelligence, the unfortunate victim has no way to recoup the damages that it suffers in terms of increased interest charges on its transworld debts.

The preceding remarks concerning global regimes are not meant to discount initiatives throughout much of the UN system since the 1960s to address issues of North–South inequity. Bodies like the United Nations Conference on Trade and Development (launched in 1964) and the United Nations Development Programme (created in 1965) have produced valuable research on North–South relations. These institutions have also helped more generally to keep questions of social justice on the global agenda. Yet since the 1980s UN agencies have generally taken a back seat in global economic governance. The initiative has lain far more with the Bretton Woods institutions and other organizations like the OECD and the WTO that have operated outside the UN purview.

Since official channels have largely failed to address – and indeed have often exacerbated – unjust distribution between the North and the South under contemporary globalization, one might expect social movements to have risen up in protest. After all, starting in the 1920s a global anticolonial coalition powerfully linked nationalists and socialists from across the South with various supporters in the North. Yet this progressive alliance largely dissipated after formal decolonization. To some extent certain faith-based associations, development NGOs and women's networks have taken the struggle against what was once popularly called imperialism forward into the twenty-first century. Owing in good part to these civil society efforts, many people would today broadly accept that countries have a 'right of development'. Yet active citizen participation in development promotion has on the whole remained limited. Meanwhile, other new social movements (for example, in respect of consumer protection, environmental conservation, and human rights) have usually not put questions of North–South equity high on their agenda.

On the whole, then, contemporary accelerated globalization has had unhappy consequences for the distribution of human life chances between countries. Inhabitants of the already privileged North have amassed disproportionate shares of the fruits of increased globality, largely on account of the accident of their country of birth. Currently prevailing state and suprastate policy frameworks have sooner reinforced than countered this structural inequality of opportunity, and to date social movement protests against growing North–South gaps have generally been weak and ineffectual. However, to repeat the key point, this dismal trend in injustice between countries has not been inherent in globalization. In particular, stronger social movements and alternative regulatory arrangements could yield more just outcomes.

Gender inequalities

In addition to highlighting problems of class and country hierarchies, a number of critics of contemporary globalization have (as noted in Chapter 1) alleged that the trend has perpetuated, if not exacerbated, the structural subordination of women to men. Feminist analyses in particular have highlighted the significance in globalization of gender inequity, that is, injustices that result from particular social constructions of femininity and masculinity. It is clearly arbitrary and unfair that biological and psychological differences between sexes become grounds for social inequalities.

Like class and North–South relations, gender refers to broad social patterns. Thus, just as certain individuals from underprivileged classes have beaten the odds to reach positions of influence, and just as certain countries of the South have attained accelerated 'development', so certain women have overcome gender obstacles to become leading managers, politicians and professionals. Yet exceptions at the level of individual women – as exceptions – sooner demonstrate than disprove the existence of social hierarchies on gender lines. Moreover, the 'successful' women have often achieved their accomplishments through the adoption of masculine behaviours.

The structural dominance of men over women is of course hardly new to the contemporary period of accelerated globalization. Patriarchy (as some analysts prefer to call this gender subordination) has a long history and had become embedded in most social contexts across the world before the proliferation of transplanetary connections in the past half-century. Globalization is no more the original source of gender injustice than it has been the wellspring of class or country stratifications. Yet has contemporary globalization intensified gender injustice, like it has often helped to widen class gaps and North–South hierarchies?

Trends in gender inequality are rather difficult to specify empirically. Even after several decades of social research on women and gender, most investigations (including most globalization studies) have continued to overlook these issues. Researchers have only recently begun systematically to assemble gender-based social data; hence few precise statistical indicators run historically from before, and then across, the period of accelerated globalization.

These limitations noted, it appears that, in a positive vein, some significant reductions have occurred since 1970 in gender gaps with respect to accessing health and education services (HDR, 1995: 3). For instance, the worldwide rate of girls' enrolment in secondary school rose from 36 per cent in 1990 to 61 per cent in 1997 (HDR, 1999: 22). By 2000 the world level of primary school enrolment for girls (79 per cent) was getting close to that for boys (85 per cent), though it remained highly uneven in some areas such as South Asia (UNICEF, 2003a: 39). In many parts of the world women have also gained greater access to paid employment. For example, participation in waged labour increased in the OECD countries from 48.3 per cent of women in 1973 to 60 per cent in 1990 (Simai, 1995: 12). In Western Europe between the 1970s and the 1990s, male jobs declined by one million while female employment grew by 13 million. Unskilled male workers have been particularly vulnerable to job insecurity in the contemporary globalizing economy (Wood, 1994). Moreover, between 1978 and 1988 the median wage of women workers in the North rose from 43 per cent to 54 per cent of the level for men (Lang and Hines, 1993: 74). In countries such as Germany, Sweden and the USA, women have since the 1960s obtained a larger proportion (albeit still a clear minority) of professional and managerial posts (Esping-Andersen, 1990: 212).

However, such improvements have remained far short of full equity. When researchers calculated a gender-related development index (GDI) for the 1995 *Human Development Report*, none of the 130 countries covered showed women to have equal opportunities with men (HDR, 1995: 2). Very often women still do not receive equal pay with men for the same work. In the former communist countries the position of women has generally deteriorated – both in absolute terms and relative to men – in respect of reproductive rights, employment opportunities, caring burdens, and participation in representative institutions (Einhorn, 1993; Funk and Mueller, 1993; Moghadam, 1993). In the 1990s almost 70 per cent of the world's poor people were female, and many girls in the South still lacked access to formal education (HDR, 1995: 36; Rivera *et al.*, 1995: 12).

Yet what specific role, if any, has globalization played in the continuities and changes of gender hierarchies in contemporary history? Available evidence suggests mixed consequences. In regard to employment, global capitalism has in several respects significantly boosted women's opportunities to undertake paid work. For one thing, female labour has figured prominently in the expanding service economy of global information, global communications, global retailing and global finance. Women have also occupied a large proportion of jobs in global manufacturing operations. For example, 4 million women held positions in 200 EPZs in the South alone as of 1994, up from 1.3 million in 1986 (Joekes and Weston, 1994: 37). Moreover, in the 1990s women in the *maquiladora* plants began to rise to some management positions (Suárez Aguilar, 1999). Increased trade, particularly within global production chains for clothing, has apparently narrowed wage inequalities between women and men in Bangladesh; however, increased trade in Zambia would seem to have widened this gender gap (Fontana, 2003).

That said, increased access for women to wage labour through global markets has also had downsides. After all, many of the new feminized workplaces in finance, information and communication sectors have had the quality of 'electronic sweatshops', with high stress and low remuneration. Largely owing to occupational sex-typing in global finance, men have taken most of the high salaries in management and on the trading floor, whereas women have provided most of the low-paid clerical support in the backroom (McDowell and Court, 1994). Any peek into an airport executive lounge reveals that women have gained relatively few places in global management circles.

True, jobs in global production through EPZs have often offered women better pay and benefits than other work (Lim, 1990), yet many of the positions have come with highly 'flexible' labour conditions. Moreover, the 1990s have witnessed some 'remasculinization' of the *maquiladora* workforces: partly due to a shortage of female labour; and partly owing to increased automation of the plants (with the stereotypical assumption that only men can handle heavy machinery) (Runyan, 1996: 240; Suárez Aguilar, 1999).

Still more dubious turns in gendered employment patterns have arisen in informal sectors of the global economy. Expanded transworld markets in domestics, mail-order brides, and sex workers have also enlarged job 'opportunities' for (mainly poor) women (Pettman, 1997; Skrobanek *et al.*, 1997; Kempadoo and Doezema, 1998; Anderson, 2000; Ehrenreich and Hochschild, 2002). For example, between 1988 and 1992 some 286,000 Filipinas and 50,000 Thai women arrived in Japan as 'entertainers' (Pettman, 1996: 197). Many migrant female domestic workers have suffered bodily violence as well as unacceptably arduous labour, although these problems have not as yet been systematically documented on a global scale.

Finally, women who have gained paid employment in the global economy have usually not lost other labour burdens in the process. Most have retained at least a second (unremunerated) job of family care. Some have furthermore kept a third job of household food cultivation. Such workloads have generally left the women concerned with little time or energy for a fourth job, namely, of political mobilization to improve their lot.

In sum, then, globalization to date has had mixed results for gender justice in respect of employment opportunities. On the one hand, global capitalism has substantially increased women's access to paid labour. On the other hand, particularly in the North, the terms attached to these jobs have generally been inferior to the conditions obtained by the preceding generation of (mainly male) workers. Meanwhile women across the world have tended to retain unpaid household chores as they have acquired greater waged work outside the home.

On issues other than employment, contemporary globalization has generally done little to reverse gender-based hierarchies of opportunity. For example, global finance has if anything exacerbated the exclusion of women from credit markets relative to men (Staveren, 2002; Porter, 2005: ch 10). True, several bilateral and multilateral agencies have, together with local advocacy groups, promoted innovative micro-credit schemes that have in particular offered poor women in the South increased borrowing facilities. However, the sums involved in these programmes have been tiny next to the huge flows of mainstream – 'malestream' – global finance capital.

Gender stratification has also persisted in regard to global communications. Various studies have shown that, in almost all countries (a few like France and Turkey being exceptions), men have formed a large majority of Internet users. As of the late 1990s, women made up 38 per cent of users in the USA, 25 per cent in Brazil, 16 per cent in Russia and 4 per cent in Arab countries (HDR, 1999: 62). On the other hand, some recent evidence suggests that gender gaps in Internet access are closing (Lekhi, 2000). Certainly multiple initiatives have called attention to the problem, including the Women's Networking Support Programme of the Association for Progressive Communications; the Working Group on Gender Issues of the

ITU; and the Gender Caucus and the NGO Gender Strategies Working Group at the WSIS.

However, access is only part of the problem of gender justice in global communications. The new technologies have often broadened the scope for sexist violence against women, for example, through web-based pornography, entrapment via email, and offensive text messaging. Sexist language and images have also pervaded much of the global mass media. Women have generally been absent from executive positions in ICT industries, and men have constituted the vast majority of directors and producers in the mass media (UNESCO, 1987). For example, only 7 per cent of Hollywood directors are female (*Financial Times*, 8 March 2005). These inequalities have limited women's influence on constructions of gender through global communications.

Along with unequal access to transworld spaces, contemporary globalization has also perpetuated and sometimes deepened gender hierarchies in the second general way named earlier, that is, through neoliberalist restructuring of the state. True, gender discrimination has recently become a more explicit concern in the economic and social development plans of many countries. Some states have moreover designated special ministers or even (in the case of Uganda, for example) created a distinct ministry specifically to address the status of women. However, the contraction of state services in line with neoliberalist prescriptions has tended to hurt women more than men. As the principal homemakers and carers, women have suffered disproportionately when the state has cut benefits for vulnerable citizens, reduced spending on health and education, decreased subsidies on food, lowered maternity and child care entitlements, and so forth. Likewise, the privatization of pension provisions has tended to disadvantage women, since they generally have lower incomes and shorter earning lives. In spite of substantial academic research on these negative gender impacts (as referenced in Chapter 1), to this day programmes of neoliberalist economic reform only rarely make even a passing mention of gender issues. Meanwhile, although relevant data are not available, the suspicion must be that gains in ownership and income from the privatization of industries have generally flowed disproportionately to men.

Trends in the treatment of gender stratification by global regimes have shown some positive signs, but the overall impact has again been mixed. In terms of progress, a number of suprastate legal instruments have put the spotlight on gender hierarchies. Examples include the 1979 Convention on the Elimination of All Forms of Discrimination Against Women (CEDAW) and several equal opportunity directives of the EU. The UN Convention for the Suppression of Traffic in Persons and the Exploitation of the Prostitution of Others, approved by the General Assembly in 1949, has over the years attracted 70 state ratifications (HDR, 1999: 103). The United Nations and its specialized agencies have also run a number of programmes to combat gender subordination, particularly through the UN Decade for Women in 1976–85 and six global conferences on women between 1975 and 2005 (Winslow, 1995; Pietilä and Vickers, 1996). Multilateral development programmes have also targeted certain projects specifically to advance the position of women. For example, the World Bank spent $1 billion on education and training of women in 1995, triple the amount expended annually under this heading in the 1980s (Balleroni, 1995).

However, women-centred initiatives have on the whole remained relatively marginal in global governance. Most suprastate agencies have at best relegated gender issues to a small and marginal office. For example, the United Nations created a fund for women in development at the launch of the Decade for Women, but thirty years later this programme, called UNIFEM, still had a modest annual budget of only $35 million (UNIFEM, 2004: 20). No World Gender Organization has emerged to complement the ILO on labour issues or UNCTAD on North–South questions. Meanwhile, global economic institutions like the World Bank have generally shown at best limited recognition of gender issues as they have promoted policies of neoliberalist restructuring (O'Brien *et al.*, 2000: ch 2).

Contemporary globalization has had some distinctly hopeful consequences for gender justice through the rise of transplanetary social movements. As noted in Chapter 3, civil society campaigns for women's rights have involved transworld networks since the late nineteenth century. However, global movements for gender justice have especially proliferated and grown in recent decades, as evidenced by the attendance of over 30,000 women at the Fourth United Nations Conference on Women, convened at Beijing in 1995 (Mawle, 1997: 155). A number of global mobilizations in respect of development cooperation, ecological sustainability and human rights have also emphasized concerns about gender hierarchies (Bunch and Reilly, 1994; Rowbotham and Linkogle, 2001). To date, however, most of these civil society initiatives have found it difficult to move people beyond a recognition of women's subordination to a commitment to implement concrete corrective steps.

In summary, contemporary globalization has had mixed impacts on gender inequality. In a positive direction, global capitalism has increased women's opportunities for paid employment; global governance has introduced a number of legal and institutional initiatives to promote the status of women; and global civil society has provided increased means to mobilize for gender equity. In a negative direction, gender stratification has limited women's access to many other global spaces; much female labour in the global economy has had poor conditions; and the costs of neoliberalist global economic restructuring have tended to fall disproportionately on women. Thus globalization has shown potentials to do both good and ill for gender justice. The challenge for future action is to devise policies that expand the gains and reduce the harms.

Other inequalities

Most research and argument about contemporary globalization and equality has addressed social hierarchies related to class, country and gender. However, stratification in global relations has extended to other social axes as well. Casual observation readily suggests that further arbitrary subordinations have existed in global spaces with respect to race, faith, urban/rural divides, age groups and disability. Regrettably, little specific data and analysis is currently available on the disproportionate effects of transplanetary flows along these lines. The relative brevity of the following remarks reflects this paucity of research and is not meant to suggest that discriminations related to race, religion, urban/rural gaps, age and disability are necessarily less severe or less important than those related to class, country and gender.

Indeed, the different categories have often overlapped and reinforced one another. For example, racial and religious hierarchies have frequently figured in North–South stratification. Likewise, class stratification has readily compounded the marginalization of rural cultivators. Gender and age hierarchies have combined to make the position of girls still more vulnerable than that of boys.

To be sure, categories of race, faith, urban/rural divides, age and disability are as ambiguous and contested as those of class, North–South divides, and gender. Nevertheless, it is apparent that, on the whole, people of colour have – both within and between countries – generally had smaller life chances than white people. Although globalization provides great opportunities for intercultural interchange, Judaeo-Christian traditions have tended to enjoy privileged positions on the main road, while other civilizations have occupied side streets and rarely visited cul-de-sacs (Nahavandian, 2004). The Christian calendar tends to define global time, for example. Likewise, exceptions duly noted, rural people have more usually suffered deprivation than city dwellers in the contemporary world. Across the continents, too, vulnerable age groups have often lacked adequate social protection, so that children and the elderly have experienced higher incidences of malnutrition, preventable illnesses and abuse than able-bodied adults.

Contemporary globalization has affected these hierarchies in the same broad ways that have been distinguished above with regard to class, country and gender. In terms of access to global spaces, for example, a number of critics have argued that contemporary society has been marked by 'global *apartheid*', where race forms a principal, arbitrary determinant of inclusion and marginalization (Falk, 1993; Mazrui, 1994; Richmond, 1994; Alexander, 1996; Castles, 2000). Unfortunately, research to date has produced little precise data to demonstrate racial hierarchies in access to global communications, global products, global finance and the like. Nor has a 'race and development indicator' appeared to complement similar statistics (problematic though they may be) for countries and sexes. Nevertheless, studies suggest that African Americans and Latinos have perceived greater threats from globalization to their wages and employment than other racial groups in the USA (Dawson, 1999). Racial stratification has arguably also been manifest when the mainstream mass media continually portrays Sub-Saharan Africa as only weak, poor and violent. Substantial anecdotal evidence suggests that people of colour have experienced institutional racism in the hiring and promotion practices of some global organizations. Racism in global travel is apparent to anyone queuing at a border checkpoint.

As for the dominance of town over countryside, rural settlements have tended to be marginalized in contemporary globalization relative to urban centres. This is not to suggest that global connectivity has benefited all city dwellers, at a time when rapid urbanization has left over 900 million people across the planet living in slums as of 2001 (HABITAT, 2003). Nevertheless, when the NICs have taken advantage of global production and markets to advance 'development', their cities have usually taken the lion's share of the benefits, while much rural poverty has remained relatively untouched. For example, in China metropolises such as Shanghai and Tianjin have seen marked rises in human development indicators, while the north-western areas of the country have had only a fifth the rate of economic growth (HDR, 2003: 62). Across the North, the South and the East, global communications, global markets, global finance and global organizations have used metropolitan centres as their primary nodes. For example, following deregulation of the telephone industry and the withdrawal of subsidies, telecommunications companies in the USA focused their services on urban concentrations (Lloyd, 1998). It may well be that, as the Unwiring the World Project at the Massachusetts Institute of Technology Media Lab has enthusiastically declared, 'it can now be cheaper to have first-class communications in the rural village than in Manhattan' (MIT, 2004). Some netizens do indeed exist among the rural poor, including the nearly 70,000 villagers in the Dhar district of the central Indian state of Madhya Pradesh who accessed a specially designed community intranet during the first 18 months of its operation in 2000–1 (Rajora, 2001). Yet such cases are exceptional. The cost of global communications remains well out of reach for most of the world's low-income rural people.

Meanwhile global agro-food industries have tended to weaken the often already precarious position of small-scale cultivators across the planet. The big corporate players have commanded high technologies, large credit facilities and advanced management techniques that traditional farmers have lacked. True, some smallholders have exploited the opportunities of globalization to their benefit. For example, peasants in the interior of South Sumatra have used radio reports on the BBC world service to determine the optimal moment, in terms of prices, to take their produce to market (Galizia,

1993). Yet such enterprising initiatives have been no match for the sophisticated market intelligence available to global companies. Meanwhile other farmers in the South have used the possibilities of global marketing to supply affluent consumers in the North with speciality crops and off-season fruits and vegetables (Llambi, 1994). However, this practice has dubious ecological rationality and can moreover reduce local food security when the cultivators in question neglect their staple crops and become dependent on (relatively expensive) imports.

In terms of age groups, contemporary globalization has in some ways tended to exclude older generations. For example, many workers over 40 have found it difficult to retool their skills in the face of global economic restructuring. As a result, permanent unemployment has loomed for substantial numbers of middle-aged people, especially in the rust belts of the North and the former centrally planned economies. In addition, many (though by no means all) older persons have found computer technologies daunting, thereby producing a considerable age bias in cyberspace. In contrast, certain technologies of globalization have in some ways offered children counterweights in their general subordination to adults. For instance, many young people have acquired more highly developed audiovisual literacy than older generations. Youth have likewise tended to access computers and advanced telecommunications with greater ease than their parents and teachers. For children, then, global communications can offer opportunities of empowerment. On the other hand, globally operating NGOs have often compromised the dignity of voiceless vulnerable children with degrading images in relief and development appeals through the mass media.

Contemporary globalization has similarly opened a number of opportunities to advance the lot of disabled persons. To be sure, 'ablism' has determined that most expansion of global spaces has occurred without regard to the needs of mentally and physically handicapped people. However, globalization has also involved human rights instruments, electronic communications, and transworld associations that have been used to advance the causes of disabled persons.

On the other hand, as already seen earlier with respect to class and gender, neoliberalist economic restructuring in the face of globalization has often hurt subordinated social circles. For example, people of colour have constituted a disproportionately high share of low-paid and unemployed workers; thus when 'global competition' has prompted reductions in state welfare entitlements, the pains have often been racially skewed. Moreover, popular fears of globalization's purported negative consequences for social welfare have often taken racist expressions, including objections to 'floods' of immigrants (Oloka-Onyango, 1999). On the age front, the young and the elderly have been particularly vulnerable during economic restructuring in the East and the South. Indeed, the harmful repercussions for children of the 1980s global debt crisis led UNICEF to spearhead calls for 'adjustment with a human face' (Cornia *et al.*, 1987–8). More recently, the Asia crisis of the late 1990s brought decreased school attendance and increased child malnutrition in some areas (Brown, 1999).

Meanwhile neoliberalist restructuring of agriculture – substantially sponsored by the Bretton Woods institutions and the WTO regime – has had mixed impacts on vulnerable smallholders. On the one hand, the liberalization of agricultural marketing has in some countries like Uganda freed cultivators from inefficient and oppressive state bureaux that previously denied farmers adequate earnings for their cash crops. On the other hand, structural reforms in Mexico have seen the government withdraw a number of crucial supports for poor farmers (Myhre, 1994). More generally, critics have worried that liberalization of agricultural trade is favouring strong corporate players and making little provision to help millions of 'inefficient' cultivators, especially in the South, to develop new livelihoods.

Fewer doubts exist regarding the benefits of the global human rights regime as an instrument against race and age discriminations. For example, concerted efforts through the United Nations against *apartheid* helped to bring down the racist order in South Africa. Meanwhile the International Convention on the Elimination of All Forms of Racial Discrimination, supported by a Committee on the Elimination of Racial Discrimination (CERD), has since 1969 promoted racial equity in the world generally. In 2001 the UN sponsored a World Conference Against Racism, held in Durban, South Africa, although only 14 heads of state and government attended.

Children's entitlements have been included in the global human rights regime through the Convention on the Rights of the Child, adopted by the UN General Assembly in 1989. This treaty, also overseen by a Geneva-based committee of experts, obtained ratifications in record time and is now, with over 190 state signatories, 'the most universally embraced human rights instrument in history' (UNICEF, 1998: 21). Only Somalia and the USA have not acceded to the convention. However, poor resourcing in terms of limited funds and personnel has so far restricted the enforceability of the treaty. For example, the Convention asserts a child's right to be registered immediately after birth, but UNICEF estimates that in 2000 around 41 per cent of births worldwide went unregistered (UNICEF, 2003a).

Global governance agencies have also promoted the position of children in other ways. For example, the UN-sponsored World Summit for Children in September 1990 attracted 71 heads of state and government and agreed several dozen specific targets for improving the lot of young people before the turn of the century (UNICEF, 1991: 72–4). Thanks largely to the efforts of UNICEF and the WHO, child immunization coverage in the South increased from 15 per cent in 1980 to 80 per cent in 1990, saving over 12 million lives (UNICEF, 1991: l, 3, 14). UNICEF has furthermore promoted breast-feeding, basic health and education for children, safe water and sanitation, care and support for mothers, high-quality family planning information and services, and the protection of children from abuse in households, workplaces, city slums, and war.

On the whole, however, global policymakers have not had children in their sights. Outside UNICEF, global governance agencies have rarely highlighted the specific needs of young people. It seems telling when a porter at the Marriott Hotel in Manhattan reports that he has never in his many years of employment seen a child lodging among the global managers (Escorcia, 1999). Meanwhile no quarter of transworld governance has attended at length to the distinctive problems of older age groups in globalization.

As with regard to poor countries, workers and women, a number of transborder social movements have sought to advance the causes of subordinated races, marginalized rural populations, and children (Starr, 2003). For example, the global Anti-Apartheid Movement was an influential civil society component of the struggle for racial justice in South Africa. Indigenous peoples have employed transworld coalitions to strengthen their political voice. *Vía Campesina* has promoted solidarity among peasants across all hemispheres (Desmarais, 2002). Global campaigns against child labour have also booked some successes. On the other hand, no global advocacy of note has promoted questions of social justice for the elderly, and transworld mobilizations for disabled people have generally attracted limited followings or media attention.

Conclusion

As shown in the summary box, the preceding examination of various forms of social stratification suggests that contemporary globalization has in various respects tended to perpetuate and sometimes also to accentuate the inequities that result from arbitrary hierarchies of life chances among people. The reduction of territorial barriers has not brought with it a reduction of social barriers. Classes, countries, sexes, races, urban/rural districts, generations and (dis)abled persons have had structurally unequal opportunities to shape the course of globalization, to share in its benefits, and to mitigate or avoid its pains.

Which of these structural subordinations is most important – and thus should be the primary focus of efforts to build a more equitable globalization? Different theories (reviewed in Chapter 4) and associated political strategies offer different answers to this key question. On the one hand, commentators who draw on Marxist frames of reference put the greatest

Globalization and (in)equality in summary

Stratified access to global spaces

- concentration of global communications on professional and propertied classes, countries of the North, men, urban dwellers and younger generations
- increased opportunities for women's employment, albeit often on lower terms and conditions than men
- global money and credit disproportionately available to already privileged circles
- offshore finance facilities effectively reserved to the wealthy
- concentration of global investments in the North and in cities
- predominance in the management of global organizations of middle-aged, white, urban men from the North and propertied classes

Decline of the redistributive state

- retreats from progressive taxation, with consequent widening of class gaps
- reduction in state-supplied social services, with disproportionately harmful effects on the disabled, children, the elderly, women, people of colour and less advantaged classes
- contraction of ODA under the pressures of 'global competition'

Social hierarchies in global regimes

- many global economic institutions have given at best passing attention to issues of social equality
- the 'free flow of information' principle in global communications has favoured dominant social circles
- the Uruguay Round and the WTO have disproportionately advantaged North-based interests
- the management of crises in global finance has generally favoured creditors (mostly in the North and usually wealthy) over debtors (mostly in the South and often poor)

Resistance to arbitrary hierarchies through global social movements

- persistent reliance on mainly territorial and national organization has weakened labour movements in the face of global capital
- many global NGOs and faith-based groups have highlighted inequities in North–South relations
- global women's networks have promoted awareness of gender justice issues
- global human rights movements have advanced causes of racial equity, child protection, and opportunities for the disabled

emphasis on class oppressions resultant from capitalism. In contrast, schools of thought such as political realism, dependency theory and world-system analysis give foremost attention to country and state hierarchies. Poststructuralists and religious revivalists look first of all to cultural stratifications imposed by modern rationalism. Feminists start with gender subordinations, while black liberation movements direct the spotlight to racial hierarchies. Social inequalities for young people, sexual minorities and disabled persons are generally most apparent to, and most sorely felt by, those groups themselves.

Hence there is no definitive rank order of inequalities in the contemporary globalizing world upon which everyone will agree. All of these arbitrary hierarchies produce significant injustice and suffering. Each demands corrective action. Moreover, none of the social hierarchies in global relations holds the key to completely resolving the others. After all, anticolonial struggles have not halted gender subordinations. Likewise, successful class resistance does not eliminate cultural and racial stratifications. The various structural inequalities in current globalization have significant overlap and mutual reinforcement, but they cannot be reduced to a single problem whose resolution would be a panacea for global social justice. Where one puts the emphasis – on class, country, culture, gender or some other social hierarchy – is a matter of personal judgement, as shaped by one's theoretical perspective and political commitments.

Whatever position each reader might choose to adopt, however, the general point to remember is that, as said at the outset of this chapter, globalization has not been the original cause of social inequalities. Nor has the rise of transplanetary connections been the only circumstance promoting social stratifications in contemporary history. Global relations – as a particular aspect of social geography – have not intrinsically discriminated between classes, countries, sexes, races, urban and rural areas, age groups, and the able-bodied and disabled. Yes, globalization can sustain and even increase social injustices, but such results only emerge when globalization is managed with policy frameworks that encourage unfair outcomes.

In short, it is not globalization per se that matters so much as the ways that the trend is handled. As seen in Part II of this book, the growth of transworld domains has involved new forms of capitalism and new forms of governance. Capitalism has always held potentials both for social progress and for social injustice. The mix of actual results has depended largely on the mode of regulation employed. Contemporary intense globalization has promoted greater unfairness not because of the changed geography itself, but mainly because of the accompanying broad policy shift since the 1970s from welfarism to neoliberalism. The implicit neoliberalist assumption that 'free' markets maximize equity as they maximize efficiency is fundamentally flawed. As shown above, most recent indicators suggest that neoliberalist preoccupations with competition, productivity and economic growth have exacerbated social inequalities.

To indict neoliberalism is not to advocate a return to old-style welfarism. The new contours of governance consequent upon globalization have rendered that statist approach unsustainable. However, neoliberalism is not the only policy approach available to the contemporary globalizing world. The challenge – as elaborated in Chapter 12 – is to formulate and implement workable alternatives, so that recent growth in gaps gives way to longer-term narrowing of inequalities.

Chapter 11

Globalization and (Un)Democracy

Main points of this chapter
The limits of statist liberal democracy
Citizen ignorance
Institutional process failures
Structural inequalities
Conclusion

Main points of this chapter

- the conventional framework of liberal democracy, with its focus on national self-determination through a territorial state, is not an adequate formula for 'rule by the people' in the polycentric governance of a more global world
- widespread ignorance among citizens about globalization and its governance has severely restricted the possibilities for democratic regulation of transplanetary relations
- across state, substate, suprastate and private regulatory institutions, the decision-taking processes that govern globalization have shown major shortfalls of public participation and accountability
- deeply entrenched structural inequalities (along the various lines discussed in Chapter 10) have highly skewed opportunities of citizen involvement in the governance of contemporary globalization

Next to – and deeply intertwined with – human security and social equality, democracy is a third core normative concern in respect of contemporary globalization. As noted in Chapter 1, widespread feelings that people lack choice and control with respect to globalization have aroused considerable disquiet about the process. Along with worries about insecurity and inequality, discontents about democratic deficits have fuelled much opposition to prevailing policies of globalization. In recent conversations with some 400 civil society actors across a wide spectrum of regional locations, social sectors, and political persuasions, almost all of them found democracy severely wanting in globalization today (Scholte, 2004b: ch 2).

Commentators have long drawn links between globalization and democracy. The term 'globalism' was in its first usage coupled with a purported process of worldwide democratization. Back in the 1940s Reiser and Davies anticipated stark alternative futures of 'global slavery or global freedom'. They urged coming generations 'to build a democratic world order on a planetary scale' (1944: xi, 57). How have actual developments in globalization unfolded over the 60 years since then?

To assess conditions of democracy under contemporary globalization it is first of all necessary to clarify terms. Democracy is no more susceptible to a single, universal, fixed, and final definition than any other key concept. On the contrary, notions of rule ('kratia') by the people ('demos') have varied enormously across different historical times, cultural settings and political commitments since the word was coined in ancient Greece. That said, the diverse notions all broadly concur that governance is democratic when decision-taking power lies with the people – a public, a 'community of fate' – whom the regulations in question affect.

More specifically, most approaches to 'rule by the people' build in one way or another on the following general principles. First, a public takes democratic decisions collectively, together, as a group. (To be sure, reaching collective positions often involves delicate negotiations between majority prerogatives, minority rights, and individual liberties.) Second, all persons qualified to participate in democratic governance do so on an equal footing, with equivalent opportunities of involvement. Third, people engage in democratic activities as autonomous agents: they are not coerced to participate or to take certain positions. Fourth, democracy is conducted in an open and transparent fashion, where everyone involved can see what decisions are taken and how. Fifth, democracy is a responsibility as well as a right: it combines opportunities and duties, liberties and accountabilities. In sum, then, democracy prevails when the members of a public determine – collectively, equally, freely, openly and responsibly – the policies that shape their joint destinies.

Needless to say, it is very difficult to realize democratic principles in practice. Full equality, full autonomy and full transparency rarely if ever prevail. In this sense it may well be that democracy is always pursued and never completely achieved; yet the quest remains worthwhile, indeed vital. Democracy is a cornerstone of human dignity and the good society. A public should shape its own destiny, even if some might doubt the wisdom of certain of the democratic decisions taken. A society that is not striving after democracy tends to be a less worthy and also more dangerous place.

Of course democracy is not the only core human and social value. Its promotion must be integrated with the pursuit of other primary concerns such as cultural promotion, ecological care, economic efficiency, and peace. Often democracy and these other pillars of a good society can be mutually reinforcing, so that more of one is also more of the other. In particular, it is not necessarily the case, as is sometimes assumed, that greater democracy comes at a cost of reduced efficiency. For example, workers in a democratic order could through the resultant greater legitimation of and commitment to their situation deliver higher productivity. However, where democracy clashes with other key objectives, then trade-offs must be faced.

The manner in which people conduct democratic governance depends on context. No single set of customs and institutions provides a formula for democracy that is relevant and workable in all times and at all places. The ways that principles of collective, equal, free, open, responsible decision-taking are enacted can vary enormously. Thus democracy as a general process needs to be distinguished from, for instance, liberal democracy as a particular approach to 'rule by the people'. The liberal formula of national self-determination through a state with periodic competitive elections to representative institutions offers but one model of democracy and might not be suitable or optimal in all contexts.

If practices of democracy are culturally and historically contingent, and if (as seen in Chapter 6) globalization has brought significant shifts in the mode of governance, then modern conceptions of democracy – centred as they have been on the territorial national state – might have become inadequate. Indeed, if pursued in inappropriate circumstances, conventional liberal-democratic practices could, paradoxically, promote authoritarian conditions. An altered mode of governance like polycentrism might call for altered practices of democracy.

Other political theorists have increasingly made similar suggestions. For example, R. B. J. Walker has urged that 'we may ask what democracy could be if not rooted in a territorial community' (1995: 323; also 1991). Anthony McGrew has affirmed that under globalization 'the core principles of liberal democracy . . . are made distinctly problematic' (1997a: 12; also 2006). Murray Low has noted that, if traditional democratic theory rested on a politics of bounded places, then globalization requires a new vision and mechanisms of democracy that are not organized around areal space (1997: 241–4). Responding to this need, a number of scholars have begun to explore a variety of postterritorialist, poststatist concepts of democracy (Connolly, 1991, 1995; Falk, 1995; Held, 1995a; Gill, 1997; Dryzek, 1999; Gilbert, 1999; Thompson, 1999; Holden, 2000; Picciotto, 2001; Morrison, 2003; Patomaki and Teivanen, 2004).

In principle the growth of multi-scalar diffuse governance and the accompanying demise of sovereign statehood could be a hopeful development for democracy. After all, sovereignty implies supreme, unqualified, comprehensive and exclusive power, whereas democracy generally emphasizes horizontality, checks on power, pluralism and participation. By this logic, the retreat of Westphalian sovereignty could encourage advances in democracy.

As noted in Chapter 1, enthusiasts have raised many hopes that globalization could reinvigorate democracy on new lines. By these accounts, global communications would open countless enhanced opportunities for civic education, public debate, and direct citizen involvement in official policy processes. Global civil society would create unprecedented possibilities for people to exercise voice and influence in politics. Global law would provide a framework for democratic deliberation in place of war in international relations.

In practice, however, experience to date has taught that increasingly polycentric governance under conditions of accelerated globalization is by no means inherently democratic. Although the contemporary growth of transplanetary connections has encouraged some innovations in democratic practices, on the whole regulatory processes in the altered political geography have suffered from severe democratic deficits. That said, as with the negative consequences for human security and social equality discussed in preceding chapters, the detrimental effects in regard to democracy have not been inherent to globality. Failures of democracy have resulted not from globalization itself, but from the prevailing ways that the trend has been handled to date. Different approaches could be more democratic.

To elaborate this general argument, the first section below indicates how contemporary globalization has generally weakened liberal democracy through the state. The second section considers democratic deficits that have resulted from widespread ignorance among citizens about globalization and its governance. The third section examines various shortfalls in democracy that have arisen owing to institutional failures (namely, in respect of elections, legislative processes, judiciary mechanisms, and civil society activities). The fourth section identifies frustrations of democratic globalization that have flowed from structural inequalities (namely, on lines of country, class, culture, gender, race, (dis)ability, urban/rural divisions, and age). Some thoughts on how to reduce democratic deficits in contemporary globalization are offered in Chapter 12.

The limits of statist liberal democracy

In the currently dominant liberal conception, democracy has existed when society is organized around self-determining nations that hold periodic 'free and fair' competitive elections of (most of) their supreme state authorities. Other qualities of liberal democracies include the rule of law, multiple political parties, nonpartisan civil and military services, a scrupulous judiciary, an independent mass media, a vibrant civil society, and civic education of all citizens. In the Westphalian international system, democracy was held to exist when people grouped themselves as distinct nations living in discrete territories ruled by sovereign states that are subject to popular control.

Accelerated globalization of recent decades has unfolded in tandem with a notable growth of liberal democracy in many states where it was previously absent. A so-called 'third wave' of democratization has – especially in the late 1980s and early 1990s – engulfed much of Africa, Asia, Latin America and the former Soviet bloc. In 1998 a Freedom House survey found that 117 of the world's 191 countries held regular competitive multiparty elections (Karatnycky, 1999: 114). Thus in many (especially neoliberalist) eyes, contemporary globalization has gone hand in hand with substantial democratization.

Several connections can indeed be drawn between global relations and the spread of liberal democracy to more states since the 1980s. For example, global human rights campaigns and other transworld civil society associations pressed (with some effect) for an end to many authoritarian governments, such as communist regimes in Central and Eastern Europe and military regimes in Latin America (Keck and Sikkink, 1998: ch 3). Global mass media gave sympathetic publicity to a host of national democracy movements in the late twentieth century. In the wired world of 1989, media images of Tienanmen Square, the triumph of Solidarity in Poland, and the breached Berlin Wall spread to spark mutually reinforcing popular uprisings throughout Central and Eastern Europe and beyond (Boden, 1990; A. Jones, 1994). In addition, suprastate agencies have supplied various forms of democracy support, including civil society development through EU programmes, election monitoring through the UN, and 'good governance' promotion through multilateral financial institutions. Indeed, a number of theorists and politicians have suggested that neoliberalist approaches to economic globalization encourage a democratization of the state (cf. Beetham, 1997).

However, these purported connections between globalization and democratization need to be qualified on at least six important counts. First, globalization has by no means constituted the sole force behind the contemporary wave of democratization. Each transition to multiparty regimes with 'free and fair' elections has drawn vital strength from locally based movements for change. Thus, for instance, local human rights campaigns played a key role in Argentina's transition to democracy. Likewise, student activists and local NGOs have made indispensable contributions to democratization in Indonesia and Thailand. In contrast, transborder democracy support has accomplished little in countries like a number of Central Asian republics where local mobilization for liberal democracy has been relatively weak. In short, global forces have normally only furthered a democratization of the state to the extent that these inputs have fallen on fertile ground in the country concerned.

A second criticism of the thesis that globalization has advanced democracy through the state is that many of the newly installed liberal mechanisms have run only skin-deep. In many cases multiparty elections have not led to broader democratic consolidation. Some new constitutions have remained paper instruments. Numerous 'independent' political parties and media outlets have become tools of narrow personal ambition and élite privilege. Pervasive graft has infested many court systems and government services. In a host of purported new democracies civic education has been limited and civil society frail. In these circumstances Fareed Zakaria has spoken of widespread 'illiberal democracy' in contemporary politics (Zakaria, 1997). Thomas Carothers has similarly distinguished a large category of 'semi-authoritarian' governments with shaky democratic credentials (Carothers, 2000). William Robinson has described new democracies in the South as 'polyarchies' where a small group dominates the state through tightly controlled electoral processes (Robinson, 1996b).

Indeed, to take up a third objection, it might be that liberal constructions of democracy are not culturally appropriate in all contexts across the world. As stressed on multiple occasions throughout this book, globalization need not – and arguably should not – entail universalization, where one set of meanings and ways of being is imposed across the planet, irrespective of whether locally prevailing circumstances are conducive to the import. Thus a western-style civil society of public-interest advocacy groups has taken limited root in most former Soviet republics, and multiparty legislative elections have made limited headway in most Arab states. This is not to argue for a return to communist rule or a perpetuation of absolute monarchy, but to consider that, in respect of democracy as well as so much else in social relations, one size does not fit all across the contemporary world.

Fourth, some critics have maintained that liberal constructions of democracy are inherently deficient, whatever the cultural context. From this perspective globalization would need to promote different kinds of public self-rule in order to be truly democratic. Democracy, according to this view, requires more than a multiplicity of political parties, periodic elections to representative state institutions, respect of civil rights, and nonpartisan bureaucracies. At best, these sceptics say, liberal arrangements can achieve a 'low-intensity democracy' that does little to mobilize the majority and to empower marginalized circles (Gills *et al.*, 1993). Chronic low voter turnouts in many countries and widespread cynicism about political parties and politicians would seem to reflect these limitations of liberal democracy (IDEA, 1997). For some social commentators, then, supplementary or alternative means are required to move from a democracy of form to a democracy of substance. On its own, liberal democracy cannot generate levels and types of public awareness, participation and accountability that would constitute a veritable democracy.

A fifth major qualification to claims that globalization has democratized the state notes that the state, being territorially grounded, is not sufficient by itself as an agent of democracy in a world where many social relations are substantially supraterritorial. A statist framework of democracy cannot adequately subject transworld flows to public direction. Global democracy needs more than a democratic state. For veritable democracy in a more global world, 'rule by the people' has to extend beyond the relationship between states and their respective national populations.

For one thing, as indicated in Chapter 6, no state can fully control its jurisdiction's involvement with global flows. Even the most powerful national governments cannot by themselves effectively regulate global health problems, global financial markets, global communications flows, global migratory movements, and global environmental changes. For example, the States-General in The Hague is unable to exercise full democratic governance over Netherlands-based global corporations like Philips and Royal Dutch/Shell. Likewise, the globally circulating Japanese yen is not subject to adequate democratic supervision through the Diet in Tokyo alone. Residents of Mexico cannot obtain much democratic regulation of the Internet by voting for members of their national congress. Each state rules over a limited territory, while global processes encompass the planet, often defying country borders. In this sense global flows can undermine even the best national democracy.

In addition, the inadequacies of statist democracy in contemporary globalization involve ideational conditions. The growth of substate, transstate and nonterritorial identities and solidarities of the kind described in Chapter 7 has reconfigured 'the public'. No longer can it be assumed that the 'demos' in democracy is always a state-nation. Indeed, insofar as democracy through the state is focused in the first place on education of, participation by, and accountability to the nation, other publics may be shortchanged. If states give precedence to a purported national interest, can they always – or even often – provide a sufficient framework of democratic involvement for transworld peoples like sexual minorities, communities of faith, women, and the disabled, let alone humanity at large? 'The people' has many sides in the contemporary globalizing world, and state-based democracy often proves to be an unsatisfactory framework for self-determination by collectivities other than state-nations.

Sixth and finally, globalization has undermined conventional frameworks of liberal democracy since, as indicated in Chapter 6, the mode of governance has moved from statism towards polycentrism. In the contemporary globalizing world, public awareness, participation and control need to be achieved not only in relation to the state, but also in respect of the various other parts of a multiscalar and diffuse regulatory apparatus. With polycentrism a host of substate, transstate, suprastate and private governance mechanisms have acquired a significant degree of autonomy from state-based democratic processes. The resultant democratic deficits cannot be corrected through the state alone. The rest of this chapter examines the democratic credentials of contemporary polycentric governance and generally finds the situation sorely wanting. The shortcomings fall under three broad headings – citizen ignorance, institutional process failures, and structural power inequalities – that are elaborated in turn below.

Citizen ignorance

A working democracy depends on knowledgeable citizens. A public that is unaware of its situation, and thus unmobilized, cannot pursue meaningful self-determination. To be democratically competent, people must have access to relevant information and an adequate understanding of the issues, concepts, principles, policies, procedures, and evidence at hand. Public participation in, and public control of, governance are ineffective if citizens are ignorant. When a director of the transworld association Doctors Without Borders (MSF) was recently asked what single development would most boost his organization's capacity to reform global governance of health, he replied, 'better public education about global affairs, so that people would understand what we are talking about and act' (Ooms, 2004).

Unfortunately, widespread public ignorance prevails today about globality and its governance. Most people recognize the term 'globalization', but few are clear about what, more precisely, the process entails and why it is significant. Public awareness of the nature, scope, scale, intensity, causes and impacts of globalization is deplorably low. Likewise, few citizens have well grasped the polycentric character of contemporary governance. Many individuals are ignorant of the involvement of their national and local governments in the governance of globalization. Most people have not even heard of many of the suprastate and private agencies that figure in the regulation of global flows. Even activists in the politics of globalization often confuse, say, the IMF with the World Bank. Few citizens have more than a loose intuitive sense of how arbitrary social hierarchies of country, class, gender, race and other structures are compromising democracy in polycentric governance of today's world.

This democratically unacceptable ignorance has by no means resulted from inherent stupidity on the part of citizens. Rather, the problem has been a general lack of sufficient opportunities to become cognizant of globalization and its governance. As the following paragraphs indicate, these failures of public education have been systemic across all the main sites of knowledge production: schools, universities, mass media, civil society, and governance agencies themselves.

Formal education

The perpetuation of general ignorance about the increasingly global character of contemporary society begins from an early age. School curricula have tended to include only passing and indirect coverage of global issues. True, children are often taught about other parts of the planet and may be introduced to cultural diversity among the world's peoples. However, schools have rarely focused on the global domain as a social field in its own right. In consequence, pupils normally do not consolidate notions of globality to the extent that they develop local, country and regional frames of reference.

Many primary and secondary school systems have lacked a significant civic education component of any kind, so that their graduates emerge with little understanding of governance whatsoever. Where the curriculum has included civics, the relevant courses have generally presented an obsolete statist picture of governance, neglecting features of polycentrism such as transgovernmental networks, suprastate agencies, and private regulatory mechanisms. At best, with regard to global governance, certain schools have staged a model United Nations; however, even that exercise has usually been framed in terms of state delegations rather than the wider UN apparatus. For the rest, attention to global governance matters vital to pupils' future destinies has been singularly lacking. School leavers thus assume the responsibilities of adult citizenship without basic understanding of, for instance, global environmental conventions that shape their health or global trade rules that govern supplies to local shops.

University curricula have also generally lagged well behind globalization and the shift toward polycentric governance. Although higher education courses on global aspects of society have proliferated in recent years, substantial coverage of globalization is still absent from most humanities and social science programmes. Moreover, all too often newfangled 'global studies' curricula have been scarcely distinguishable from the 'international studies' offerings that preceded them. Hence most of today's degree recipients – opinion leaders of the next generation – finish university with little more education on globality and its governance than when they started.

Mass media

Alongside formal programmes of learning at schools and universities, much informal public education occurs through the mass media. Most citizens obtain their day-to-day information and analysis regarding social life largely from newspapers, magazines, radio, television and websites. Thus the mass media significantly affect the amount and type of knowledge that people gain about global issues. Print, audio and visual journalism have certainly helped to raise citizen awareness of globalization and its governance; however, on the whole the mass media's potentials for citizen education on globalization have remained sorely underdeveloped.

Much of the problem has lain in low levels of media attention to globalization. On the whole, mainstream press and broadcasters have given scant coverage of the global dimensions of current affairs. The 'international' news often has a foreign rather than global character: that is, it addresses local and national events in other countries. Notable exceptions to this rule have existed, to be sure, including several business weeklies and certain satellite television news stations that regularly highlight issues that are distinctly global. Moreover, in certain countries like Canada and France, questions of governing globalization have regularly occupied the headlines and editorial pages of the principal media organs. However, on the whole news outlets with mass audiences have tended to leave global matters in the shadows relative to parochial stories. Large conferences on major global challenges (like the World Summit on the Information Society, the World Parliament of Religions, or the World Social Forum) can pass with barely a mention in most of the media. Likewise, problems such as crises in global finance, global epidemics of malaria and tuberculosis, and the political economy of global corporations can be lucky to get an occasional clip in the mainstream news. Given this dearth of reporting it is hardly surprising that most citizens remain substantially ignorant of globalization.

Not only the quantity, but also the quality of media coverage of global issues has often been wanting. To be sure, large press agencies and broadcasters have sometimes produced clear, detailed, probing and nuanced stories concerning global affairs. Such help from the mass media can promote sound public understanding of globalization and advance higher standards of citizen involvement in its governance. All too often, however, media treatments of globalization have been muddled and careless, with journalists themselves often poorly educated on global matters. Many media accounts have also been oversimplified and sensationalized, particularly in terms of exaggerated accounts of global threats to human security. It is sad comment on most of the mainstream media that celebrity interventions have often been required to boost coverage of global humanitarian issues. Regrettably, too, public demonstrations of citizen concern about currently dominant approaches to globalization did not gain notable column space and airtime until a minority of protesters resorted to violent tactics.

Moreover, mass media reporting about globalization has often lacked a sharp critical edge that would stimulate greater public debate on global politics. Many mainstream outlets have unquestioningly underwritten prevailing neoliberalist approaches to globalization. Indeed, much of the contemporary mass media are big businesses, many of them globally organized, which have profited from liberalization and privatization in the communications sector. Often the main media organs have also maintained close ties with governing circles, links that can further inhibit more probing investigative journalism on global political economy.

Sideline voices in the alternative media have countered some of these negative effects of much mainstream journalism. These outlets for different kinds of information and analysis about globalization include press agencies like Prachadharm News Net in Chiang Mai and ALAINET in Ecuador as well as radio stations like Açik Radyo in Istanbul, Mama FM in Kampala, and Making the Links in Saskatoon. In addition, the Internet has opened up substantial new spaces for citizen education about globalization and its governance, including through listservs and wikis. Social movements in particular have often used websites to obtain and spread information and analysis concerning global affairs that is not easily available from mainstream media.

On the other hand, alternative media have generally remained small operations that reach small and mostly self-selected audiences. These organs show little sign of leaving the margins of global politics to become major sites of mass education. Meanwhile the main press and broadcast outlets continue either to ignore questions of governing globalization or to cover these issues poorly, thereby sustaining general citizen ignorance on this subject. The vision of some digital utopians – where new information and communications technologies would generate informed and active 'netizens' in the electronic global democracy of a 'virtual polis' – is little in evidence today outside small quarters of civil society.

Civil society

Many political activists have placed considerable hope for more democratic globalization on the shoulders of civil society associations. This analysis expects that citizen groups like community organizations, NGOs, faith-based networks, and trade unions offer one of the most promising vehicles for increased public involvement in the governance of globalization. Civil society activities have certainly made important contributions in respect of public understanding of global problems and policies to address them. However, as with schools and the mass media, the civic education potential of civil society in regard to globalization has remained underdeveloped on the whole (Scholte, 2004b: ch 3).

Civil society groups have promoted citizen awareness about globalization and its governance in various ways. In terms of learning events, for example, civil society associations have sponsored countless teach-ins, lectures, symposia, colloquia, workshops, discussion groups, roundtables, artistic performances, and road shows. In addition, some civil society initiatives like the RITIMO network in France have built up publicly accessible libraries and documentation centres concerning global issues as well as many highly informative websites. With regard to learning materials, civil society groups like the Moscow-based Centre for the History of Globalization and worldwide Oxfam affiliates have collectively produced enormous amounts of leaflets, brochures, bulletins, newsletters, magazines, books, policy briefs, dossiers, training manuals, audio-visual productions, wall posters, comics, paintings, sculptures and more about the governance of globalization. As for mass media publicity, civil society groups like the Uganda Debt Network have often sought to raise public awareness of globalization matters through press releases, press conferences, articles in mass-circulation newspapers and magazines, television programmes and radio broadcasts (including audience phone-ins). In all of these ways, civil society activities of the past few decades have made many citizens more aware of – and more confident to speak out on – global concerns. Moreover, a number of civil society initiatives on citizen education about globalization have made particular efforts to reach underprivileged circles such as poor people, peripheral countries, and women.

All told, however, civil society contributions to greater public understanding of globalization have retained modest proportions. Many citizen groups have so concentrated their efforts on lobbying official and corporate circles that they have neglected public education. Those civil society associations that have given priority to this task have generally lacked the resources required to sustain long-term programmes of large-scale citizen education on global affairs.

Moreover, some civil society efforts have actually detracted from public learning about globalization, for instance, with inaccurate information and misrepresented views. Some well-intentioned activists have lacked sufficient competence on global issues, purporting to educate others about globalization when they have themselves also required considerable education on these matters. Thus, while civil society activities have made significant contributions to counter citizen ignorance on globalization, the magnitude of these benefits must not be exaggerated, and the effects on public understanding have not always been positive.

Governance agency transparency

Finally, the regulatory bodies themselves are another important source of public education regarding globalization and its governance. Here too, however, the potentials have generally been poorly realized. Although recent years have seen some notable improvements in the openness and transparency of many governance agencies that deal with global matters, much of these regulatory processes remain obscured from public view.

Governors have a democratic duty to inform the governed about their governance. Citizens should be able easily to discover what policy decisions are taken on global issues, at what time, where, by whom, from what options, on what grounds, with what expected results, and with what supporting resources. Similarly, in a democracy citizens should have ready access to official information concerning the implementation of policies and evaluations of their outcomes.

Elements of confidentiality in governance are of course justifiable in certain circumstances. For example, central banks and finance ministries arguably should not divulge policy decisions at moments when release of this information would cause major economic damage. Likewise, it is understandable that military and police units do not publish their operational plans for all to see. However, in a democracy secrecy about governance is the exception, and openness is the norm. A special case needs to be made for withholding information from citizens, and normally with an understanding that relevant documents will be released into the public domain once the period of sensitivity has passed.

To their credit, many agencies involved in the governance of globalization have raised their public transparency in recent years. The operations of various suprastate, state and substate institutions concerned with globalization are now considerably more visible to citizens than they were before the 1990s. Many governance organizations – including previously highly secretive bodies such as the IMF and the WTO – have constructed elaborate websites and have greatly expanded their output of press releases, newsletters, reports, pamphlets, audio-visual productions, in-person presentations, and public exhibitions. Far more official documents concerning the regulation of globalization have also become publicly available, both in hard copy and electronically through the Internet. Many more governance bodies now publish at least a partial staff list, often including contact details with which citizens can reach responsible officials. This greater visibility of governance activities better enables concerned citizens to make informed contributions to policy debates surrounding globalization.

However, the regulation of global spaces remains far from fully transparent. For example, as of the mid-1990s advance appointments were required before a visiting citizen could reach the 'public' information centre of the United Nations Office at Vienna. Only limited details have been publicly disclosed about the proceedings of the IMF and World Bank Boards, G8 gatherings, the BIS Board of Directors, and the OECD Council. Many state ministries remain tight-lipped about their dealings with global governance agencies and global corporations. Transgovernmental relations have generally operated outside the public eye, so that most citizens are not even aware that these policy networks exist. Likewise, the great majority of citizens are unaware that private regulatory schemes are important for various aspects of global communications, global finance, global investment and global trade. With minimal publicity, most people have never heard of bodies such as the IASB or ICANN.

Moreover, many governance agencies often fall short of *effective* transparency with respect to their dealings on globalization. It is one thing to disclose information; it is something else to make that information reach – and be comprehensible to – all people concerned. For example, many of the documents released by governance institutions are opaque for the uninitiated.

These papers and other public statements about policies are frequently laden with technical terms, obscure acronyms, professional jargon and other specialized vocabulary that can both confuse and alienate an audience of lay citizens. Often materials from suprastate bodies are not translated into all the relevant languages. Only 10 per cent of humanity today speaks English, after all. In many cases hard copies of documents are not readily available for people who lack Internet access. Moreover, governance institutions have often disclosed information to the public only *after* the decisions in question have been taken, thereby limiting opportunities for citizens to influence the policy process. In other words, 'transparency' has sometimes involved more lip service than veritable openness.

In sum, all the main sources of public education in society have failed adequately to counter citizen ignorance about globalization and its governance. Schools, universities, the mass media, civil society associations, and regulatory agencies themselves have neglected sufficiently to provide people with relevant information and analytical tools for effective political mobilization. To this extent, democratic engagement with one of the most important trends in contemporary history has been compromised.

Institutional process failures

Democracy rests not only on educated citizens, but also on participatory and accountable processes of public decision-taking. Members of a democratic polity must have adequate institutional mechanisms to make inputs into, and shape, policy formulation and implementation. Moreover, in a democracy the public must have ways to hold governors answerable for their actions (and sometimes inactions). Many democratic deficits have arisen in contemporary globalization because the institutional processes of governance have been wanting in terms of citizen involvement and control. As the following discussion elaborates, these deficiencies have reigned in respect of public referenda, legislative processes, judiciary operations, and civil society activities.

Public referenda

One way to obtain democratic input into policymaking processes is to conduct polls of the affected public. Such popular votes can take the form of official referenda on specific measures (e.g., whether or not to ratify a particular treaty). Alternatively, the poll can evaluate an overall policy package (e.g., with elections of representatives to governing councils). In addition, sample public opinion surveys by polling agencies constitute an informal and non-binding form of referendum. However, none of these channels has generated much democratic participation in global politics to date.

Official public referenda on specific policies have almost never figured in the governance of globalization. For example, Switzerland is the only state in the world that has put the question of joining global governance institutions to a binding popular vote. In 1992 the Swiss electorate approved their state's membership of the Bretton Woods institutions, but the voters rejected accession to the United Nations until 2002. The Uruguayan constitution allows for national plebiscites on particular policies, and under this provision a popular vote in 2004 rejected water privatization as widely promoted by multilateral financial institutions. In 1985 the government of Nigeria invited a public debate about a proposed structural adjustment programme, albeit without a formal referendum. President Babangida effectively ignored the resulting opposition by adopting the IMF/World Bank-sponsored package anyway (Herbst and Olukoshi, 1994: 472–7). Meanwhile macro-regional and global governance institutions have never formally polled their publics on any of their policy proposals. Likewise, private regulatory bodies that govern aspects of globalization have omitted this kind of public consultation.

Popular referenda can also figure in the politics of globalization more informally in the shape of public opinion surveys by professional pollsters. However, sampling exercises by the likes of Gallup and Latinobarómetro have rarely specifically addressed questions of globalization and its governance (Latinobarómetro, 2004). In the exceptional cases when commissioned polls have focused their attention on global affairs, the results have received little publicity, for example, through media reports.

In principle, citizens have significant other opportunities to raise questions about globalization and its governance in the context of elections of representatives to legislative assemblies and presidential offices. Indeed, proponents of indirect democracy would argue that public referenda on specific policies are not necessary so long as citizens have opportunities to vote in periodic competitive elections to representative governments. In between these plebiscites citizens are deemed to have delegated their day-to-day participation in and control over governance to designated officeholders.

Yet questions of globalization have figured so little in parliamentary and presidential elections that these exercises can hardly be deemed to constitute referenda on global policies. In local and national plebiscites, for example, the manifestos and platforms of contending political parties in most countries have barely addressed matters of global communications, global trade, global finance, global ecology, global health and so on. Likewise, debates and rallies in state-based electoral campaigns across the world have rarely highlighted the governance of globalization. Most voters cast their local and national ballots with only secondary if any attention to global regimes. And this is not to mention the hundreds of millions of people who live in countries without 'free and fair' legislative and/or presidential polls.

Meanwhile most suprastate institutions have operated without directly elected popular representatives. The chief exception is the European Union Parliament, which has obtained its deputies (numbering 626 as of 2004) through universal suffrage at five-yearly intervals since 1979. That said, voter turnouts in these elections have generally been low and have also declined over time in a number of EU member countries. Several distinctly European political parties have emerged in the European Parliament, including the European People's Party and the Party of European Socialists. However, these organizations have been run through centralized professional offices, with no direct input from, or accountability to, individual members and constituency branches, as would normally happen in country-based political parties.

Next to the EU's representative assembly, the only other directly elected regional body in the world is the Central American Parliament, which has operated since 1991 with meetings in Guatemala City. Every five years voters in the region select 22 representatives from each of six member countries. So far no distinctly regional political parties have emerged in this assembly, although the deputies have formed three main blocs (Parlamento Centroamericano, 2004).

Other macro-regional parliamentary organs have not been directly elected. Several of these bodies have drawn their members from sitting national legislators. Examples include the Parliamentary Assembly of the Council of Europe (operating since 1949), the NATO Parliamentary Assembly (since 1954), the Assembly of the Western European Union (since 1954), the OSCE Parliamentary Assembly (since 1992), and the Parliamentary Assembly of the Black Sea Economic Cooperation (since 1993). In 2001 the East African Community set up a small Legislative Assembly whose 27 members are selected by (albeit in this case not from within) the national congresses of the three member states. For the rest, dozens of other macro-regional frameworks such as ASEAN, the GCC, and the OAS have not had an elected permanent representative organ of any kind.

As for global governance institutions, none has direct election of its leadership. There is at present no prospect of UN People's Council or a WTO Parliament, although some reformers have urged the establishment of such organs. After 115 years of operations the Inter-Parliamentary Union (IPU) has failed to develop beyond a largely invisible and rather aimless talking shop toward something of an elected global congress. Nor is anyone seriously expecting popular selection of the IMF's Managing Director or WHO's Director-General.

Indeed, it is far from clear how plebiscites for global regulatory bodies could work in present circumstances. The technical means to conduct simultaneous transplanetary ballots are currently not available, and global political parties like the Liberal and Socialist Internationals are not equipped to pursue intercontinental electoral campaigns. Moreover, at a deeper philosophical level no consensus is in sight on a formula for representation in global parliaments. For example, would the constituencies in such bodies relate to countries, to regions or to nonterritorial configurations like functional groups, races or religions? Would global plebiscites operate on the principle of one person one vote, or would some weighted scheme be advisable that increases the relative voice of small country populations and/or minority peoples? Indeed, would an electoral model derived from modern western experience be appropriate for a global context that is marked by far-reaching cultural diversity?

Finally, it goes without saying that the various private regulatory mechanisms in contemporary governance of globalization have operated without public polls of any kind. Bodies like the Derivatives Policy Group and the Global Reporting Initiative (GRI) have no basis in popular referenda, formal or informal. Agencies such as the World Federation of Exchanges (for stock and bond markets) and the Business Council of the World Tourism Organization have lacked any systematic procedures of public consultation. Nor have private governance institutions, as private bodies, had publicly elected assemblies. The Forest Stewardship Council (FSC) is exceptional in having chambers to represent different stakeholders (business, environmentalists, indigenous peoples, labour), although the people involved have been largely self-appointed.

Legislation

It might be hoped that, once elected, representative legislative institutions would exercise democratic oversight of the governance of globalization. Unfortunately, however, the overall record in this regard has to date been very poor. Certain national parliaments and certain individual parliamentarians have monitored certain aspects of the regulation of global relations. Yet on the whole legislative assemblies have abdicated their duties of democratic oversight in this area.

To begin with the local sphere, few municipal or provincial councils have attended extensively to global affairs. To be sure, devolution of policy competences to substate authorities (as described in Chapter 6) could in principle substantially enhance democratic governance of globalization. After all, the growth of electronic communications notwithstanding, many citizens still find local government more immediate and accessible, given the smaller scale of the operations and the closer proximity of the offices for face-to-face contacts. Some elected substate authorities have indeed given substantial priority to global matters, for example, by implementing global environmental agreements in their localities or by assuring that global investments within their jurisdiction conform to democratically expressed local priorities. In addition, municipal governments in London, Paris and Porto Alegre have since 2001 given considerable support to the deliberative democracy of the

European and World Social Forums. However, on the whole the contemporary trend of devolution from country to provincial and district governments has not yielded greater democratic legislation with respect to globalization.

National parliaments have in general performed little better in providing legislative oversight of contemporary globalization. Most national representative assemblies have rarely debated global affairs (as distinct from foreign policies towards other states). For instance, hardly any state legislatures, anywhere in the world, carefully scrutinized the Uruguay Round agreements. Although a number of national constitutions require that the legislature ratifies treaties, much regulation of global domains today does not come in treaty form and thereby escapes the need for parliamentary approval. Governments, suprastate bodies and private regulatory bodies take countless important decisions on global questions without consulting the representative national assembly. Indeed, legislators are sometimes not even informed of their government's actions on global issues. In some cases parliamentarians have experienced just as much difficulty as ordinary citizens to obtain key official documents on global subjects. Few parliamentarians have brought personal expertise on global issues to their job. In most cases these politicians have also lacked adequate professional researchers and advisers to support them with global questions.

To be sure, some important instances of increased legislative activism concerning globalization have arisen in recent years. For example, Parliamentarians for Global Action, with over 1,300 members from 110 national parliaments as of 2004, has worked closely with a number of UN agencies since the late 1970s. The Global Legislators Organization for a Balanced Environment (GLOBE), founded in 1989, now brings together sitting representatives in more than a hundred national parliaments to enhance legislators' awareness of global ecological issues and policies. Most Northern parliaments now have one or more committees that monitor their government's participation in the Bretton Woods institutions, albeit that few of these legislatures have passed laws or motions on these agencies (Halifax Initiative, 2004: 43–6). A major exception on this point is the US Congress, which has since the early 1980s periodically held extensive debates about – and placed multiple conditions upon – increased funding for the IMF and the World Bank. In addition, since 2000 a Parliamentary Network on the World Bank has brought together national legislators from around 50 countries with the aim to promote greater transparency and accountability of that institution and global development assistance more generally. Efforts since 2003 to create a similar Parliamentary Conference on the WTO have thus far made less progress. Taken in sum, then, national assemblies have had a thin record of overseeing global governance agencies. Moreover, those legislatures that have occasionally debated global problems have not necessarily exercised much influence on what their government has gone on actually to do.

Potentials for macro-regional assemblies to exercise legislative oversight of the governance of globalization remain limited so long as such bodies are lacking in number and influence. Even the furthest developed regional representative body, the European Parliament, is to this day unable to initiate legislation or to block the rule-making directives of the (appointed) European Commission. That said, the European Parliament has had globalization prominently on its agenda, particularly through scrutiny of EU involvement in the WTO (Europarl, 2004).

Finally, as noted earlier, no global governance agency has a democratically representative and accountable legislative arm. In sum, then, nowhere in local, national, regional or global regulatory institutions has there been adequate legislative oversight of the governance of globalization. Rules to govern transplanetary connections have proliferated with little involvement from popularly elected assemblies. Indirect representative democracy is not working in contemporary global politics.

Judiciary processes

Democratic regulation of globalization has operated little better on the judiciary side of governance. In a working modern democracy, citizens are able to turn to non-partisan courts or other assessment mechanisms to adjudicate on claims that authorities have caused harm. However, such avenues are generally not (or only poorly) available in the governance of global issues.

In terms of courts, citizens normally cannot take grievances regarding global affairs to their national and local tribunals. True, state authorities can be brought before their own country's judiciary to answer for alleged wrongs committed on global policy matters within the territorial jurisdiction of that state. However, such cases are rarely pursued and would moreover be meaningless in the various countries that lack an effective non-partisan judiciary system in the first place. For the rest, national and local courts most of the time cannot pronounce on the activities of the state outside its territory or on the activities of suprastate authorities. Hence, for example, citizens of Nepal or Peru cannot call ICANN or the IMF to account in their respective national courts.

True, suprastate courts that cover larger jurisdictions exist for several macro-regional governance institutions. Examples include the European Court of Justice for the EU. Regional human rights regimes in Africa, the Americas, Asia and Europe also include a judiciary mechanism of some kind, whether a court or an investigative commission. However, these macro-regional judicial arrangements are in general not well developed and little known. Nor can regional mechanisms be used to try global actors for transworld actions any more than national judiciaries can.

Global courts are for the most part absent or unavailable for direct citizen petitions concerning the governance of globalization. Thus the International Court of Justice in The Hague only considers cases brought by states, not by individuals. The same holds true for the Dispute Settlement Mechanism at the WTO; citizens with a grievance about trade policy must find a state to sponsor their case. Advocates can alert the UN Commission on Human Rights to violations, but the findings of its committees have no binding effect.

True, where global courts are absent other possible official avenues for redress on global policy matters include public inspections, independent evaluations, and investigations by ombudspersons. In this vein the World Bank in the early 1990s acquired an Operations Evaluation Department and an Inspection Panel. Similarly, the IMF has since 1997 arranged several external reviews of certain of its policies. However, the scale of these accountability exercises has remained modest, and the resultant recommendations have generally been tame. Meanwhile, the BIS, the OECD, UN agencies, and the WTO lack even such limited policy review mechanisms. Likewise, private institutions in the governance of globalization such as the IASB and the GRI have no systems of public accountability that come into play if and when their regulatory activities cause harm. More is therefore needed in the way of open, outside, independent, published assessments of the performance of global governance bodies.

Civil society involvement

What, then, of civil society activity, through which citizens themselves can engage with policymaking processes rather than delegate their involvement to elected representatives and judicial bodies? As noted in Chapter 6, countless business forums, community organizations, faith-based groups, labour unions and NGOs have become increasingly involved in the politics of globalization. Many such associations have encouraged citizen participation in policymaking on global issues: both from the inside (through direct interactions with official circles); and from the outside (through public meetings, marches and the like). On the whole, however, the scale and impact of such activism has remained modest. Moreover, civil society groups have sometimes fallen short of democratic standards of participation and accountability in their own practices.

In terms of direct civil society engagement with official circles, many governance agencies concerned with the regulation of globalization have in recent decades created and expanded mechanisms for consultations with citizen groups. For instance, multiple suprastate institutions and state ministries dealing with global issues have established specific bureaux and appointed designated officials to handle relations with civil society groups. Thus most of the more than 70 World Bank missions across the planet now include a civil society liaison officer on their staff. In addition, a number of suprastate and state agencies have issued guidelines for staff interactions with civil society organizations (cf. ADB, 1999; World Bank, 2000; UNDP, 2002; IMF, 2003b). Civil society consultation has been formally built into a number of global policymaking processes. Prominent examples include the operations of the UN Commission for Sustainable Development and the preparation of Poverty Reduction Strategy Papers (PRSPs) for the Bretton Woods institutions. In addition, accredited civil society organizations have participated in many global governance convocations, including the annual meetings of multilateral financial institutions, WTO Ministerial Conferences, and a host of UN gatherings. Some civil society actors have even accepted invitations to join state delegations to such events, thereby gaining access to the more restricted zones of the meetings. Civil society associations have also injected citizen voices into policy processes on global issues by sitting on official committees, giving testimony at parliamentary hearings, submitting position papers, and lobbying authorities. Occasionally officials have also attended civil society events and engaged with citizen activists on the latter's own ground.

Yet the democratic consequence of civil society interactions with governance institutions must not be exaggerated. Only relatively small numbers of civil society organizations have acquired the competences and the connections to deal effectively with official agencies on transworld issues. Some global governance bodies (like the BIS and the OECD) have thus far done almost nothing to develop procedures of civil society consultation. Among macro-regional agencies, MERCOSUR is exceptional in having a formally institutionalized mechanism for civil society inputs, namely its Socioeconomic Advisory Forum. Civil society groups have also generally been locked out of G8 meetings and other transstate networks. ICANN is rare among private regulatory agencies in having arrangements for civil society engagement. Nor is the existence of formal consultative mechanisms enough, as many officials have treated civil society involvement with lip service or even undisguised hostility. All in all, then, civil society access to and engagement of official circles regarding global policymaking could be vastly improved.

Other civil society participation in global policy processes has occurred outside direct exchanges with official circles. After all, rulers often take account of activities where they are not present. For example, civil society associations have arranged countless public meetings where citizens can express concerns and make proposals regarding globalization. Many such gatherings have convened in the quiet of offices, conference halls, and exchanges over the Internet. Other meetings have taken the form of noisy rallies, marches and occupations. Civil society groups have also promoted public participation in the politics of globalization with petitions, letter campaigns, and boycotts on various issues. In addition, certain civil society associations have promoted more artistic means of public involvement in policy processes. This approach has opened opportunities for citizens who engage in politics more comfortably through dance, drawing, fashion, poetry, sculpture, song and theatre than through conversing and marching. All of these modes of participation have been actively nurtured in the World Social Forum process of globalization critiques since 2001 (Teivanen, 2002; Fisher and Ponniah, 2003; Sen *et al.*, 2004).

On other occasions civil society groups have worked to bring greater public accountability into global politics. Numerous civil society bodies have performed a watchdog role to check to see that authorities comply with their public declarations, national statutes, and international commitments in respect of global issues. In addition, countless studies undertaken by civil society organizations have documented the consequences of various policies regarding globalization. Some of these investigations have exposed error, incompetence, corruption and harm. Civil society associations have also provided channels through which citizens can seek correction of mistakes in the governance of globalization. In this regard civil society groups have pressed to have rules changed, officials replaced, institutions reconstructed, and reparations paid. To this end, civil society organizations have taken grievances about policies related to globalization to auditors, ombudspersons, parliaments, courts and the mass media. In addition, certain activists have staged symbolic 'trials' with informal 'tribunals' as a way to call authorities to task.

Again, however, the scale of these civil society initiatives on global matters must not be overplayed. Only a small proportion of the world's population has thus far participated in the sorts of citizen mobilizations just described. In most cases civil society organizations active on global issues have a small membership or (in the case of many NGOs) have no membership at all. Even when individuals have been members of a globally oriented civil society group, their involvement has often not extended beyond the payment of a subscription. Larger publics have tended to rally behind a civil society campaign only on a short-term and ad hoc basis, for example, in response to calls for humanitarian aid or debt relief. For the rest, global civil society has mostly been the preserve of relatively small numbers of full-time professional activists. Substantial parts of the world (like the Middle East and countries of the former Soviet Union) have had little inputs to policies on globalization from civil society associations. Hence much of the promise of civil society as an engine of transplanetary participatory politics is as yet unproven.

Moreover, civil society associations involved in global policy processes have often fallen short on democratic credentials in their own behaviour (Edwards, 2000; Scholte, 2004a; 2004b: ch 5). For example, although some civil society groups have provided inspirational examples of non-hierarchical, non-authoritarian, non-violent, highly participatory politics, others have been run with top-down managerial authoritarianism that stifles internal dissent. Many civil society bodies have failed to consult their constituents in a rigorous fashion. Some advocates who have claimed to speak for the grassroots have actually rarely ventured into the field. On the contrary, a number of the jet-setting staff have lost touch with their notional beneficiaries as they fly from one global conference to the next. Many civil society groups engaged in global politics have not held regular, independently monitored elections of their officers. Nor have these associations usually conducted and published independent external evaluations of their activities. Various civil society bodies concerned with globalization have not been public-interest organizations, but fronts (either openly or secretly) for governments, political parties, corporations, foundations, families or powerful individuals. Even civil society associations with considerable autonomy have sometimes lacked transparency about who they are, what objectives they pursue, where their funds originate, how they reach their policy positions, etc. Indeed, groups in 'uncivil society' such as neofascist and terrorist associations have deliberately subverted democratic practices.

As civil society organizations in global politics have matured, many of their leaders have become more alert to – and more determined to address – challenges regarding their own democratic practice (Brown *et al.*, 2001; Edwards, 2004). Critical voices in citizen movements have demanded more participation, transparency and accountability within their own ranks. As one democracy advocate in Uganda has put the matter, 'When you point a finger you need to do it with a clean hand' (Arituwa, 2003). However, far too many activists continue to hold the complacent view that civil society is inherently democratic.

Taking the above institutional questions in sum, shortfalls in effective referenda, legislative oversight, judiciary evaluation, and civil society activity have left policymaking processes for governing globalization with screaming democratic deficits. Local and national regulatory agencies have largely neglected global issues. Apart from the EU, few macro-regional governance arrangements have put self-democratization on their agenda. Transworld bodies like UN agencies and the Bretton Woods organizations have readily preached democracy to states, but have inadequately applied the strictures to their own workings. Indeed, to date global law has not articulated a principle of global democracy. Private mechanisms show some of the weakest democratic credentials of all, incorporating few if any mechanisms for public input and public control.

In a word, then, technocracy has won over democracy in the governance of globalization to date. Regulation of global affairs has mostly rested with bureaucracies that are largely insulated from public inputs and public controls. Some official circles have not regarded this 'depoliticization' of governance as a problem, presenting themselves as objective experts who operate most efficiently without ill-informed public interference. However, even the most dedicated technocrat ought to concede that purported trade-offs between efficiency and democracy in current governance of globalization have gone much too far one way.

Structural inequalities

As stressed at the start of this chapter, democracy is a three-faceted dynamic involving circumstances of education (citizen awareness and mobilization), institutional process (public participation and accountability), and social structure (equal opportunity of involvement for everyone concerned). All three aspects must be satisfied in order to realize veritable democracy. Thus it is not enough to overcome citizen ignorance and procedural shortcomings if governance is infused with structural hierarchies of the sort described in Chapter 10. To the extent that globalization systematically marginalizes certain groups, regulation tends to entail 'rule by *some* people' rather than by the public as a whole.

Indeed, given that individual, institutional and structural conditions are closely interconnected and mutually determining, the educational and procedural criteria of democracy cannot be fulfilled in the absence of social equality. That is, hierarchies on lines of country, class, gender, race and more are normally reflected in, and reinforced by, uneven access to education. Subordinated groups tend to suffer more from inadequate information about and limited analysis of globalization. Likewise, structural inequalities tend to be manifested in, and reproduced by, institutional mechanisms. Hence underprivileged circles usually have less access to plebiscites, legislators, judiciary agencies, and civil society activities.

Social inequalities present a major barrier to full democracy. As seen in the preceding chapter, globalization has far from eliminated arbitrary hierarchies of opportunity in the twenty-first century. On the contrary, under currently prevailing policy directions the growth of transplanetary connections has often sustained and even exacerbated structural inequalities. As the following paragraphs indicate, these stratifications of countries, classes, cultures and more have made contemporary global politics deeply undemocratic.

Country inequality

As noted in Chapter 10, hierarchies between countries constitute one of the principal axes of dominance and subordination in contemporary globalization. When it comes to governance, this inequality between countries has been reflected in an inequality between states (i.e., national governments). Democracy has therefore been structurally failing in respect of globalization partly because governments (and by extension their citizens) of subordinated countries have generally had far less opportunity for involvement and influence in regulatory processes than governments (and by extension their citizens) of dominant countries.

Owing to these inequalities, states in North America and Western Europe have had disproportionately greater say in the governance of global affairs than governments elsewhere. Regional, national and local authorities in the North have, structurally, had more resources and power in global regulation than their counterparts in the South. Also in conformity with the North–South hierarchy, most private mechanisms in the governance of globalization have operated from the dominant countries.

Among the major states, too, one government has been more equal than others in contemporary globalization. Indeed, some have characterized the dominance of the USA in global politics as 'unipolar' and 'hegemonic'. Washington has often used its advantages of resources and power heavily to shape the rules of global relations, sometimes blatantly ignoring what the majority of humanity might feel and want. Indeed, some have wondered why only 6 per cent of the world's population has the opportunity to elect the President of the United States, when many White House decisions (e.g., on climate change and nuclear proliferation) have profound transplanetary effects. Even if the US government had impeccable democratic credentials towards its own citizens – and it is far from clear that it does – this one state has no democratic grounds to speak for billions of people across the rest of the globe.

Glaring undemocracy of state inequality has also arisen when Northern governments have grouped together in the governance of global affairs. As discussed in Chapter 6, the G8 is a major force of global regulation, but it has offered seats to only a handful of powerful states, whose collective population amounts to a small minority of humanity. Likewise, the G10 in global financial governance has excluded most of the world's states from membership. Governments in the South have formed several coalitions of their own, including the G77 and the G24; however, these Southern bodies have exercised no notable influence next to the G8. The creation of the G20 in 1999 was meant to incorporate some governments of so-called 'emerging markets' in the highest councils of global governance, but this initiative has still excluded most states of the world, including the poorest, and has so far remained a sideshow next to the G8.

Inequality of countries has also marked formal multilateral agencies. Apart from UNEP, with its main offices in Nairobi, all UN bodies have had headquarters located in the North. In addition, dominant states have maintained far larger and more professionally qualified delegations at the UN than subordinate states. An aristocracy of five states has held the arbitrary privilege of permanent membership and veto power in the UN's apex organ, the Security Council. The more inclusive UN General Assembly works on the principle of one state one vote, albeit regardless of the country's population. As a result China and Vanuatu formally speaking have equal voice, even though the former counts over 6,000 times more inhabitants than the latter. The past three decades have seen innumerable proposals for more democratically legitimate forms and formulas of representation at the UN, but none of these ideas has got beyond a commission report.

The WTO has likewise operated on the basis of one vote per member state. However, all parties understand that the core global trade negotiations occur between the USA and the EU. Indeed, nearly a third of WTO member governments have lacked the resources to maintain a permanent delegation in Geneva to monitor and intervene in day-to-day operations of the institution. Meanwhile most states of the South and the East have had no representation whatsoever in decision-taking at the OECD, even though many of the organization's recommendations and agreements have global implications.

The hierarchy of states has if anything been more blatant in governance institutions for global finance. At the IMF, governments of the G7 countries currently control 45 per cent of votes on the Executive Board, while 44 states in Africa between them hold less than 5 per cent (IMF, 2003a: 143–6). Several decades of cogent critiques of weighted voting arrangements in multilateral financial institutions have thus far brought no significant reform (Buira, 2003). Moreover, convention has had it that a West European is always Managing Director of the IMF, while a citizen of the USA is always President of the World Bank, where a similarly skewed allocation of votes has prevailed. Matters have improved somewhat at the BIS, where over 30 states of the South and the East have in recent years become members. The BIS has also lately opened representative offices in Hong Kong and Mexico City. However, the main BIS operations remain centred in Basle, and the BIS staff – like that of other global governance agencies – continues to come overwhelmingly from the North. Meanwhile, the IASB has developed global accounting standards with no voice from the South, even though these rules have some of their greatest (and relatively most costly) impacts in those countries.

Structural inequality of countries in the governance of globalization has also extended to civil society activities. On the whole, the strongest citizen groups working on global issues have been based in North America and Western Europe. Of course, many civil society associations in Africa, Asia, the Caribbean, Eastern Europe, Latin America and the Pacific have made notable contributions to the politics of globalization. However, even the best-resourced civil society actors in the South have usually not matched North-based academic, business, labour, NGO, professional and religious bodies. Northern elements have also generally held dominant positions in transworld civil society organizations like the ICFTU and the WWF. In consequence, Southern civil society associations have often adopted Northern agendas and activities, also when the issues concerned are not the highest priorities for the Southern 'partners'. In this respect, harsher critics have dismissed so-called 'global civil society' as a neocolonial affair.

Across regulatory agencies and civil society alike, it is clear that the inequality of countries has profoundly violated democratic principles in contemporary governance of globalization. People rightly protest when some regions inside a country are marginalized in the governance of a national society. Likewise, it cannot be democratically acceptable that most of humanity is subordinated in the regulation of transplanetary affairs simply because people happen to live on one plot of the earth's surface rather than another.

Class inequality

Next to hierarchies among states, class inequalities of the sort described in Chapter 10 have placed other major structural impediments in the way of democratic governance of global relations. That is, certain socioeconomic circles (ranging across the South as well as the North) have held arbitrary entrenched advantages over others in the regulation of global communications, ecology, finance, health, migration, money, trade and violence. It is democratically indefensible when financiers, industrialists, professionals, and people with inherited wealth have more chances to shape the governance of globalization than the majority of their fellow citizens.

Some commentators, normally of a neoliberalist persuasion, have championed the purportedly democratizing effects of global 'free' markets. In this conception, rule by the people is greatly advanced through the growth of consumer and shareholder choice. Here citizens vote with their pocketbooks and savings (rather than their ballots) for producers (rather than governors) that provide the highest returns (rather than the greatest human betterment) in a global market (rather than a territorial state). In this reconstruction of democracy, sovereignty is purportedly relocated from the state authority to the market player. As the cliché would have it, 'the customer is king'. Whereas state-based democracy focuses on citizen rights and responsibilities to maximize social justice, this market-based democracy concentrates on product quality and rates of return to maximize collective human happiness. Even the state is 'sold' to the public as an entertainment commodity through lotteries, game-show elections, war performances, and other mass media spectacles.

To be sure, consumer and shareholder power are ways to express collective will to positive ends. For example, citizens acting through consumer boycotts and ethical investment campaigns put considerable pressure for change on the *apartheid* regime in South Africa. Yet even such well-intentioned politics have a strong class bias. After all, people need assets in order to make choices and demand accountability through market transactions. Only a minority of the world's population has significant opportunities to own shares. The main shareholders with substantial clout have been large investment trusts, pension funds and insurance companies who usually have little contact with the everyday lives of the general population. Meanwhile consumer movements (usually poorly resourced) face major challenges to mobilize large publics in political campaigns. As a result, would-be market democracy invariably translates into disproportionate power for propertied classes.

Class dominance in contemporary globalization has also extended to formal regulatory regimes. Governance agencies have often been more concerned about business interests and investor confidence than other sides of public opinion. Indeed, many states have acted to reduce the capacities of organized labour to promote worker interests in contemporary globalization. Likewise, the WTO process has included companies more than consumers. Multilateral financial institutions have generally handled global debt problems in ways that protect creditors more than poor people. ICANN rules have arguably given higher priority to securing Internet revenues for investors than to expanding Internet access for ordinary people.

In these circumstances, some critics have denounced current regulation of global affairs as 'corporate rule', where 'rule by the people' has become rule by *business*people. As noted in Chapter 5, relatively small numbers of large transborder enterprises have come to dominate most sectors of today's global economy. This concentration of resources and power can, if unchecked, readily undermine democracy. Certainly, public-sector regulation has constrained transborder companies to some extent: mainly through local and country governments; and occasionally also through certain macro-regional and transworld measures. In addition, CSR schemes have imposed some self-restraints on global business. Certain large corporations have also undergone significant decentralization, adopting 'federal' structures in which lower levels of management have acquired greater autonomy from the executive board (Handy, 1992). However, it is questionable whether such external and internal constraints on corporate power have been sufficiently strong to ensure that global firms respect the general will, particularly in those parts of the world where states and civil societies are weak.

Class hierarchies are also reflected and reinforced in the day-to-day operations of governance institutions. In countries of the North and the South alike, large majorities of elected officeholders and leading bureaucrats emanate from advantaged classes, who also dominate global and regional civil services. This managerial class moves in fairly closed social networks, attending the same exclusive schools and universities, joining the same professional associations and recreational clubs, etc. People of means also have greater opportunities to learn English as the predominant language of regulating globalization. Even the offices of the agencies that govern transplanetary relations are normally located in neighbourhoods more frequented by privileged socioeconomic circles.

Civil society activity in respect of globalization, too, has disproportionately involved university-educated, computer-literate, propertied persons. Élite circles have generally dominated those elements of global civil society (such as business forums and think tanks) that have the largest resources and the highest access to governance circles. Many NGOs, too, have drawn most of their personnel and members from élite quarters. Indeed, NGO jobs can be highly coveted in poor countries, where a small privileged layer of the population has often obtained the largest share of NGO funds. Meanwhile humanity's underclasses like fisherfolk, peasants, low-paid workers, and slum dwellers have generally lacked the funds, language fluency (or translation facilities), and organizational capacities required for effective participation in global civil society. For example, costs of travel mean that peasant organizers from Brazil and India rarely meet face to face. On the few occasions that they do, long chains of translation are required from Portuguese to Spanish to English and finally to the local Indian language – and then back again (Oliveira, 2004). In short, although many contemporary civil society associations talk of involving 'the base', 'the grassroots', 'popular organizations' and 'local communities', actual opportunities for underclasses to participate in these activities have often been severely limited.

Cultural inequality

Structural inequalities in the governance of global relations go beyond country and class to arbitrarily imposed hierarchies of culture as well. Regulatory frameworks for global issues have operated overwhelmingly on western-modern lines. The rules of the game have conformed to the norms of the dominant civilization, including its dictates of secularist, anthropocentrist, instrumentalist, techno-scientist rationalism. The trimmings have also shown a decidedly western character, with office blocks, business suits and briefcases. Non-western, non-modern ways of being and believing have had little say over the agenda and little play in the policy processes of governing globalization. Regulators working within the predominant modernist paradigm have generally neither understood nor made time for other worldviews.

Thus, for example, across the world indigenous peoples have been relegated to the margins of global politics. Aboriginals have normally had minimal if any role in making regulations for the global companies and the global ecological developments that affect their homelands. Although indigenous peoples have since the 1970s gained some hearing before certain UN commissions, they have never had a vote in the organization. Meanwhile their own 'multilateral institutions' like the ICC and the UNPO have remained powerless next to the likes of the G8 and the World Bank.

Likewise, established governance channels have offered followers of non-western religions little opportunity to argue the case for, say, a global economy run on Islamic principles, or global conflict resolution pursued on Sikh lines, or global ecological governance developed on Buddhist tenets. Modern bureaucratism in the regulation of globalization has left little room for spirituality and appeals to transcendent forces, even from Christians and Jews. Adherents of many faiths have held positions in the governance of global affairs, but always on the implicit if not explicit understanding that they do not invoke their religious beliefs at the office.

Cultural issues surrounding language have also created significant hierarchies in the regulation of globalization. The dominance of western languages, particularly English, has severely disadvantaged the large majority of humanity that does not speak this language. For example, many trade negotiators from Francophone Africa have struggled to follow – let alone intervene in – the English-based WTO process. Moreover, it is often hard for ideas and principles that are not easily translated into English to get a hearing in global forums.

Cultural hierarchies have also marked much civil society activity on globalization. Groups like the Muslim Brothers in Egypt and the Buddhist-inspired Spiritual Education Movement in Thailand are exceptions that demonstrate the rule. Indigenous peoples have also had only marginal involvement in civil society activities concerning global issues. Their own associations like the Assembly of First Nations in Canada or the Coordination of Indigenous Peoples Organizations of Brazil (COIAB) have put little emphasis on questions of globalization. Other civil society groups have rarely consulted aboriginals. Even the Office of the General Secretary of UNPO in The Hague is located far from any aboriginal homeland and as of 1995 included only one staff person from the indigenous groups that the agency purported to represent.

In short, then, current governance of globalization involves widespread cultural subordinations. Many people who feel that the growth of transplanetary connections threatens values that are precious to them look for ways to express their concerns and protect their way of life. Yet existing governance arrangements for global relations have provided severely limited possibilities for cultural pluralism and intercultural negotiation. In frustration with unresponsive legal-institutional arrangements, people in subordinated cultural circles can be driven to direct their politics into irregular channels and, in some cases, into violence.

Gender inequality

Further hierarchies of involvement in the governance of globalization have prevailed on gender lines. The marginalization of women can start early, when girls in many parts of the world suffer unequal access to essential services like education and health care, thereby compromising their ability to become full citizens in adult life. On the whole, regulation of global affairs has followed a more masculine agenda. Issues of relatively greater concern to women such as reproductive health or the care economy have struggled to gain attention next to matters like arms control and intellectual property rights.

The masculine shape of the agenda is probably closely interlinked with male predominance in policymaking positions. Across the world, women have figured little in the upper ranks of the state or in the leadership of regional and global governance agencies. For example, in 2002 at the IMF 54 women constituted 15 per cent of managerial staff, while 645 women constituted 85 per cent of support staff (IMF, 2003a: 89). Such inequalities in personnel are significant. A critical mass of women leaders could encourage greater gender justice, even if the individual women involved were not outspokenly feminist.

Gender inequalities have also extended to civil society activism on global issues. Large numbers of women have participated in citizen initiatives concerning globalization, particularly in the ranks of NGOs and social movements. In exceptional cases, like the NGO sector in Canada, broad gender equality has also prevailed in the leadership of civil society work on globalization. However, more often than not men have held the reins in this sphere as well. For example, women have on the whole exercised quite limited influence in business forums, labour organizations, religious bodies and research institutes that address global issues. Across all of civil society, men have figured disproportionately on the boards, executives, delegations and professional staff of organizations, while women have provided the bulk of administrative support. Gender subordination has meant that, structurally, women have had less access and influence in civil society engagement of globalization issues than men with an otherwise similar social profile.

Other inequalities

As discussed in Chapter 10, social inequality in contemporary globalization has extended beyond stratifications of country, class, culture and gender to include in addition hierarchies of age, (dis)ability, race, sexual orientation, and urban/rural location. Subordinations along these various lines have also been reflected in, and sustained by, the governance of globalization, thereby undermining its democratic credentials.

Much of the problem has lain in getting these inequalities discussed at all in the regulatory sphere. For example, aside from rare events like the 2001 UN-sponsored World Conference against Racism, discriminations based on colour have almost never got a hearing in governance of globalization.

Likewise, UNICEF is one of very few (and poorly resourced) places in suprastate governance that has focused on young people. No global agency at all has existed specifically to consider problems of the elderly, disabled people, or sexual minorities in the way that the ILO has (whatever its other defects) highlighted labour issues.

People subordinated by age, race, rural residence or sexuality have also tended to face extra difficulties to access the institutions that govern globalization. For example, it took 57 years (until May 2002) before the first teenagers got to address the UN General Assembly (Schäfer, 2005). Another event striking for its rarity was an initiative in 1998 by the 2B1 Foundation to give young people aged 10–16 from across the world an opportunity to design a digital global civilization through a Junior Summit (2B1, 2004). The main governance institutions for transplanetary problems are all located in big cities that many poor rural people cannot reach. In addition, the officials who regulate global affairs have predominantly urban backgrounds and are to that extent not well equipped to understand rural issues. Meanwhile people of colour have been severely underrepresented in the civil and military services that have governed global politics.

Civil society, too, has tended to reproduce more than resist these social inequalities. Important global civil society initiatives have promoted the interests of the disabled, rural people and sexual minorities; however, these activities have tended to operate at the margins. The relative invisibility of people of colour in citizen campaigns on globalization has been striking, even in countries with multiracial populations like Brazil, Canada and France (cf. Martinez, 2000). Moreover, certain civil society groups like neo-Nazis have been unabashedly racist. With regard to age, civil society engagement of globalization has on the whole had disproportionate inputs and leadership from middle-aged persons. Indeed, veteran civil society professionals have frequently regarded young people mainly as a source of numbers and/or low-paid and voluntary labour, rather than as serious colleagues and potentially equal contributors. Likewise, very few civil society associations have taken specific steps to incorporate the views of children and the elderly into their work on globalization.

In sum, various structures of dominance – by country, class, culture, gender, race, age, (dis)ability and more – have deprived most of the world's people of adequate opportunities to know about, participate in, and exercise control over the governance of global relations. Together these structural inequalities have produced far more dominance than democracy. Arbitrary social hierarchies have also often compromised democracy within and through civil society; thus when civil society has given voice in governance of globalization to 'the people', some parts of the demos have tended to speak louder than others.

Globalization and (un)democracy in summary

Citizen ignorance

- school and university curricula have generally prepared young people poorly for global citizenship
- mass media coverage of globalization and its governance has generally been wanting in both quantity and quality
- civil society efforts at public education on global issues, while laudable, have remained modest overall
- although many agencies concerned with the regulation of globalization have become more transparent about their activities, much of this governance is still obscured from the public

Institutional failings (on local, national, regional and global scales)

- governance agencies have rarely put questions of global policy to public referenda
- issues of globalization and its governance have usually figured only marginally in elections to representative offices
- local, national and regional parliaments have exercised limited oversight over the governance of globalization, while transworld agencies have lacked a legislative arm of any kind
- judiciary processes for public accountability in the governance of globalization have been sorely underdeveloped, particularly in relation to global institutions
- civil society associations have made modest contributions to public participation in and public accountability of governance agencies concerned with globalization, but the citizen groups themselves have often suffered shortfalls in their internal democratic practices

Structural inequalities (relating to countries, classes, cultures, genders and more)

- dominant social circles have had a disproportionate say in determining agenda priorities in the governance of globalization
- people from subordinate groups have tended to be systematically marginalized in policy decision-taking related to global affairs
- although some civil society initiatives have concertedly resisted structural hierarchies in the governance of globalization, on the whole these activities have tended to reproduce the inequalities of society at large

Conclusion

Taking in sum the educational shortcomings, institutional failings and structural subordinations surveyed above and reviewed in the summary box, contemporary globalization has shown very weak democratic credentials. Emergent polycentric governance of global affairs has had low levels of participation from and accountability to a knowledgeable public. The demos has on the whole been uninformed and uninvolved when it comes to regulating questions such as global climate change, global financial crises, global militarization, or global tourism. Claude Ake and others have had ample reason to link globalization as it has unfolded so far with 'a politics of disempowerment' (1999: 182). Whereas democracy normally entails majority rule with minority rights, governance of today's more global world has sooner come down to minority rule without majority rights.

Thus the regulation of growing transplanetary connectivity has been singularly lacking in democratic legitimacy. Authority is legitimate when a governed people acknowledge that their rulers have a right to rule over them. Legitimacy can be derived from a number of sources besides democracy, including charismatic leadership, technical expertise, and moral justice. However, the shortfalls in democratic legitimacy with regard to governance of contemporary globalization are so great that no amount of charisma, efficiency and morality can compensate.

As a result, the regulation of global relations has to date rested more on coercion than on democratic consent. Much of this coercion has been repressive, in terms of violations of human rights, withholding of resources (aid, loans, etc.), and armed intervention. Other coercion has taken softer and quieter forms, particularly as people have been bought off their democratic deprivation the consumerism discussed in Chapter 5.

However, democratic deficits in contemporary globalization have not been wholly met with passivity and resignation. On the contrary, resistance to disenfranchisement in the governance of global affairs has grown in recent years. Much so-called 'anti-globalization' activity has been driven by anger at the unavailability of democratic politics through official governance mechanisms. It remains to be seen whether (as is explored further in Chapter 12) current discontent will be contained with mild reforms to policy processes, or whether the resistance will spur a deeper reinvention of democracy in global politics.

Either way, the key point to stress at the present juncture is that global spaces are not inherently undemocratic. Many of the initiatives mentioned in this chapter indicate that globalization and democratization can be complementary. The future reinvigoration of democracy demands not a reversal of transplanetary connectivity, but a concerted search for new concepts and practices that can make 'rule by the people' work in postterritorialist, poststatist, postnationalist politics.

Chapter 12

(Re)constructing Future Globalizations

Main points of this chapter
General policy strategy
Enhancing human security
Enhancing social equality
Enhancing democracy
Towards implementation
Conclusion

Main points of this chapter

- a policy strategy that combines ambitious reformism with cautious transformism offers the most promising way forward in respect of contemporary globalization
- various specific initiatives (ranging from personal lifestyle changes to global public policies) can improve the outcomes of globalization in regard to human security, social equality and democracy
- current circumstances pose both opportunities and obstacles for implementation of these measures

In compiling a normative assessment of contemporary globalization, the preceding three chapters have consistently advanced a twofold general argument. First, globalization has to date had mixed consequences for human security, social equality and democracy – including some significant negative repercussions. Second, the downsides have resulted not from transplanetary connectivity as such, but from the policy orientations (mainly neoliberalist) that have prevailed over recent decades in respect of growing global relations.

The second of these theses implies that changes in policy approaches to globalization (in particular reorientations away from neoliberalism) could produce greater security, equality and democracy. So political choices are important. It is not the case, as some commentators once suggested, that There Is No Alternative (TINA) to liberalization, deregulation, privatization, and fiscal conservatism as the policy framework to guide increased transplanetary connectivity. Rather, in the motto of many critical globalization activists, other worlds are possible. Yes, as discussed in Chapter 4, powerful structural forces have propelled contemporary accelerated globalization: turns in capitalist production; the state and emergent polycentric governance; national and nonterritorial identities; and rationalist knowledge. But this does not mean that actors have no scope to shape, and reshape, those structural impulses and thereby to influence the course of globalization. On the contrary, agency matters (Bleiker, 2000). It is possible to make use of globalization as well as to be used by it. More strongly, today's policymakers, as well as citizens at large, arguably have ethical responsibilities to handle a more global world to better effect.

Yet what, more specifically, should those different (non-neoliberalist) policy courses be? How can one optimally, as James Mittelman has put it, 'rewrite the script of globalization' (1999: 15)? It is one thing to diagnose ills and quite another to prescribe suitable treatments. Moreover, it is one thing to advance attractive proposals and quite another to get them implemented. These concerns of policy formulation and political action are the subject of this final chapter.

In elaborating strategy for more secure, more equitable and more democratic future globalizations, the first section below distinguishes several possible general policy courses that could be taken and then identifies and justifies the broad approach adopted here. This strategy can be characterized as a blend of ambitious reformism and cautious transformism. Subsequent sections of the chapter then describe various concrete measures that could be taken with this general orientation in order to steer globalization towards greater human security, social equality and democracy. The final section of the chapter considers the main challenges that face the implementation of ambitious reformism/cautious transformism in globalization politics today.

Although this discussion promotes one kind of broad policy approach, the chapter title deliberately refers to 'globalizations' in the plural. In other words, central to the alternative orientation advocated here is an avoidance of past tendencies to impose a single universalist blueprint on globalization, of whatever liberalist, social-democratic, socialist, eco-centrist, theist or other colour. A veritable *Post*-Washington Consensus should not be a consensus in the sense of establishing one uniform policy framework for all; rather, a more open future would encourage different constituencies to pursue diverse and autonomously formulated policies towards globalization.

General policy strategy

Before considering specific policy steps to enhance human security, social equality and democracy in future globalizations, it is as well to consider the overall policy framework in which those concrete proposals might be couched. There is otherwise a danger that particular policy initiatives are pursued without a strategic vision that sets main priorities and long-term objectives. The following paragraphs first survey a spectrum of possible general policy orientations toward globalization. A combination of ambitious reformism and cautious transformism is then identified and justified as a preferable broad strategy. The scene is thereby set for the discussion in later sections of particular policy measures and political challenges for their implementation.

Broad options

As noted in Chapter 1, four main policy approaches toward globalization can be distinguished, namely, neoliberalism, rejectionism, reformism and transformism. To be sure, this fourfold typology is overly neat. Each of the categories encompasses a spectrum ranging from mild to uncompromising variants. Moreover, the dividing lines between the four stylized models can blur in practice. The simplified schema is employed here for analytical convenience rather than to provide precise pigeonholes into which every policy and each commentator on globalization can be unambiguously slotted. The broad distinction between neoliberalism, rejectionism, reformism and transformism is a useful way to stress that very different types of policy courses can be pursued *vis-à-vis* globalization.

To recapitulate, neoliberalist approaches have prescribed four central policy pillars for the practice of globalization: liberalization of cross-border transactions; deregulation of market dynamics; privatization of both asset ownership and social service provision; and tight limits on public spending. In a word, neoliberalists have advocated market-led globalization with a minimal role for public policy. In a neoliberalist strategy, governance agencies create an enabling environment for global market forces and then let the private sector deliver the social good with (according to theory) maximum efficiency.

In contrast to *laissez-faire*, rejectionist strategies towards globalization seek to reverse the trend and rebuild society without transplanetary connectivity on the basis of self-sufficient local and country units. For rejectionists, globalization is incorrigible. From this perspective a more global world invariably entails cultural imperialism, dictatorship, ecological catastrophe, poverty and war. Hence the only way to handle globalization is to block it.

Like rejectionist strategies, reformist programmes oppose the neoliberalist market-led orientation to globalization. However, instead of dismissing globalization altogether, reformist approaches advocate policy interventions by public agencies to enhance the fruits and limit the harms of transplanetary relations. In part, such regulatory measures are pursued through state and substate laws and institutions, as in past social-democratic politics. In addition, however, reformism when applied to contemporary large-scale globalization also puts major store by suprastate mechanisms of macro-regional and global public policy.

Transformist strategies share with reformist perspectives a conviction that globalization can be reshaped in more positive directions than the neoliberalist course that has dominated over the past quarter-century. However, whereas reformists seek to make existing social structures produce better outcomes, transformists seek better outcomes through a change of social structures. Thus reformists would use public policy measures to achieve greater human security, social equality and democracy *through* capitalism, but transformists would *transcend* capitalism to realize those goals. Similarly, reformists aim to work within the logics of polycentric governance, established patterns of identity construction, and rationalist knowledge to improve the results of globalization, while transformists aim to construct altogether new modes of regulation, identity politics, and epistemology.

The difference between these four broad policy orientations can be illustrated with reference to any substantive global issue. In relation to global ecology, for example, neoliberalists suggest that 'free market environmentalism' with 'eco-preneurship' by 'enviro-capitalists' can solve problems such as climate change and biodiversity loss (Anderson and Leal, 1991, 1997). In contrast, rejectionists argue that large-scale transplanetary connectivity is inherently disastrous for ecological integrity, so that globalization must be replaced with localization if human and other life on earth is to survive (Hines, 2000; Monbiot, 2003). Meanwhile, reformists maintain that public policies (including in particular global laws and institutions) can rescue the planet from ozone depletion, deforestation, and the like (Young, 1996; Benedick, 1998). From a more deeply critical perspective, transformists affirm that environmental destruction is intrinsic to the logic of capital accumulation and anthropocentric techno-scientific rationalism. Hence these radicals advocate a fundamental reconstruction of production and knowledge structures – for example, in line with Thomas Berry's 'earth spirituality' or Vandana Shiva's 'earth democracy' – in order to achieve a viable global ecology.

The four types of strategy also take fundamentally different approaches to global finance. For neoliberalists, unhampered transplanetary market flows of savings and investments greatly enhance economic growth for all. On the neoliberalist account, periodic instability and crises are an unavoidable and comparatively small price to pay for these gains. For rejectionists, however, global finance entails an unacceptable loss of sovereignty and exploitation by multinational corporations that can only be averted with a turn to closed national financial markets and/or the creation of autonomous local monies (Bond and Bullard, 1999; Community Currencies, 2005). For reformists, transplanetary finance requires a fully fledged global regulatory apparatus, including a transworld central bank, in order to avoid oligopoly, limit instability, avert crisis, achieve fair distribution of benefits, and assure democratic control (Eatwell and Taylor, 2000). For transformists, modern capitalist finance itself is a deeply flawed system of domination that requires deconstruction and transcendence (Goede, 2001; Robotti, 2003).

With regard to digital development, neoliberalists have held that global market competition will bring advanced information and communications technologies to all. Such a vision has underlain, for example, several WTO agreements on telecoms and IT as well as the G8-sponsored DOT Force. In contrast, all-out rejectionists have in Luddite fashion refused to engage with electronic mass media and the Internet as corrupting technologies that undercut autonomy, community and morality. More optimistically, reformists have argued that public policy interventions from substate, state and suprastate authorities can counter digital divides and ensure that the global information infrastructure reaches and benefits all (Kahin and Nesson, 1997). Meanwhile transformists have urged people to exploit the opportunities that digital technologies offer to create new and better modes of production, governance, identity politics, and knowledge.

And so one could continue to distinguish contending policy strategies towards global migration flows, global health problems, global military operations, and other issues. Having said that, it is important not to reify the fourfold distinction between neoliberalism, rejectionism, reformism and transformism. In practice, policy commentators and policy measures often blend several of these four tendencies. For example, the 'Augmented Washington Consensus' initiatives described in Chapter 1 have added modest reformist elements to the neoliberalist formula. The Vatican has advocated reformist policies like debt relief for poor countries, while at the same time transformist voices in the Roman Catholic Church have championed liberation theology. A number of labour unions and NGOs have straddled rejectionism, reformism and transformism in their approaches to globalization: sometimes urging protectionism; sometimes promoting suprastate regulation; sometimes advocating social revolution.

These complexities acknowledged, policymakers and citizens at large still face a basic choice in their attitude towards globalization between: (a) supporting prevailing neoliberalist orthodoxy; (b) rejecting globality in all forms; (c) pursuing a reformist programme of proactive public policy initiatives; or (d) adopting a transformist strategy of deeper structural change. Drawing on the account of causal dynamics in Chapters 4–8, the assessment of normative challenges in Chapters 9–11, and the author's own political proclivities, this book suggests that a strategy that couples ambitious reformism with cautious transformism offers the most hopeful forward orientation for globalization in the early twenty-first century.

Against neoliberalism

In combining inspirations from reformism and transformism, the strategy pursued here opts against neoliberalism. On the one hand, this decision flows logically from the critiques of liberalist and political realist explanations in Chapter 4. In other words, theoretical positions inform policy choices. In addition, the strategic orientation adopted here is empirically grounded. That is, the evidence of recent globalization does not suggest that neoliberalist policies – even with recent injections of post-Washington Consensus reforms – can maximize human security, social equality and democracy.

Neoliberalist policies have three main conceptual shortcomings. First, they fail to address the deeper social forces that are at work in globalization. Neoliberalist discourse is generally couched in loose and superficial talk of 'technological innovation', 'market forces', 'international competition' and 'economic growth'. These accounts ignore the more fundamental issue of capitalism. Yet policies toward globalization that neglect the central role of surplus accumulation and associated tendencies of exploitation cannot hope to achieve poverty eradication, decent work conditions, environmental sustainability, cultural self-determination, and peace.

Second, and related to the irreparable oversight regarding capitalism, neoliberalist policies are inherently incapable of generating maximal good from globalization because they downplay or outright ignore issues of structural inequality. Arbitrary and unjust hierarchies of class, country, faith, gender, race and other social categories cannot be significantly corrected unless combating these inequalities is made a foremost policy priority. This neoliberalism singularly fails to do, merely promising that the benefits of global markets will eventually 'trickle down' to the poor and the weak. Indeed, neoliberalists often argue that public policies to reduce inequality will 'distort' markets and reduce productivity. Yet some of the most prosperous parts of the world like Scandinavia also manifest the lowest social inequalities as a result of proactive public policies.

A third intrinsic conceptual flaw in neoliberalist policies towards globalization is their materialist orientation. The economism of neoliberalism ignores the importance of identity, solidarity, faith, spirituality, aesthetics and more on the ideational sides of human security, equality and democracy. Although the delivery of adequate material welfare is essential to put globalization on a durable course, the provision of physical comforts on its own does not guarantee human dignity and the realization of human potentials.

These conceptual shortfalls of neoliberalism have fed practical failings. Although marketist policies towards globalization have often (though not always) promoted economic efficiency, they have also – as earlier chapters have extensively shown – done considerable harm. Global 'free markets' have frequently perpetuated or deepened ecological degradation, destitution, labour abuses, xenophobia, cultural destruction, class and country hierarchies, oligopoly, democratic deficits, and other violences.

In these circumstances, neoliberalist discourse has sometimes appeared to be an ideology of the powerful that obscures – and in this way helps to sustain – sufferings, especially of the vulnerable. Indeed, is it accidental that neoliberalist accounts of globalization have mainly emanated from dominant social circles and countries? This observation is not meant to suggest that proponents of neoliberalism have held a conscious objective to harm large parts of humanity. On the contrary, many committed neoliberalists have in all sincerity believed that their prescriptions advance the construction of a good society. Yet, however laudable the intentions of individual neoliberalists might be, this approach to globalization has in practice mostly served the interests of the privileged and all too often undermined the position of the weak.

A redirection of globalization away from neoliberalist policies is therefore desirable. It is also possible. The position is not, as Francis Fukuyama claimed at the dawn of the post-Cold War world, one of 'the end of history', where no alternatives to neoliberalist orthodoxy are viable (Fukuyama, 1992). On the contrary, substantial possibilities exist to develop visions, policy tools and political constituencies for different courses of globalization.

Against rejectionism

That alternative course cannot and should not be one of rejectionist de-globalization. As with neoliberalism, the failings of this policy strategy are both conceptual and empirical. Rejectionist calls to undo globalization and establish sovereign local and national orders are neither workable nor desirable.

In terms of misconceptions, rejectionists have tended to romanticize the unglobalized past. After all, territorialist times also knew much – and in some cases more – poverty, arbitrary social hierarchies, authoritarian governance, warfare, ecological damage, and cultural destruction. Also contrary to rejectionist assumptions, as noted earlier in Chapter 2, the local has not in practice always offered a cosy alternative to purportedly faceless globality.

Moreover, proponents of rejectionist policies tend to forget the benefits of globalization that would be lost if transworld links were cut. As earlier chapters have indicated, transplanetary connectivity has encouraged many positive developments in regard to material welfare. Also contrary to many rejectionist claims, and as shown in Chapters 2 and 7, globalization has sometimes helped to reinvigorate rather than undermine cultural heritages. In addition, against another main rejectionist premise, globalization has often promoted increased rather than decreased ecological awareness, albeit in a context of greater environmental degradation.

In any case, rejectionism is an impracticable policy strategy. As stressed in Chapter 4, the forces behind the current growth of transplanetary and supraterritorial connectivity are too strong to eliminate the trend. The notion that global capitalism in extractive, manufacturing, information, communications, biotechnology, nanotechnology and care industries could be switched off seems outside the realm of the possible in contemporary political economy. Likewise, it appears fanciful to think that all regulatory apparatuses beyond the state could be dissolved, that all identity impulses beyond the nation could be denied, and that all knowledge could be purged of global consciousness. Great as the harms of neoliberalist globalization may often have been, rejectionist pleas for de-globalization are an ostrich reaction that fails to address the challenges in a workable fashion. It is a non-starter to think that countries and localities of the twenty-first century can cocoon themselves from global communications, global finance, global governance and the like and thereby make globalization go away.

Certainly, alternative policies towards globalization could strive to enhance local and national initiatives regarding the ways that different people in different contexts handle transplanetary issues. Indeed, such devolutionary steps might substantially advance a democratization of globalization. However, this strategy involves globalization through localization (recalling from Chapter 2 that the two are not inherently contradictory), rather than a misguided attempt to eliminate transworld connectivity. Nor can most local and country programmes to steer globalization be successful in isolation, in the absence of coordination with other local and national moves elsewhere across the planet. Rejectionist strivings to retrieve some kind of Westphalian sovereignty are foredoomed to failure.

Even if rejectionist policies were viable, would they be desirable? It is quite understandable that people who have felt besieged under neoliberalist globalization might defensively pursue territorialist refuge in a localism of cultural, ecological and economic protectionism. Yet all too often rejectionist sentiments have involved inward-looking parochialism. Moreover, anger and frustration about harms of neoliberalist globalization have injected some strains of rejectionism with violences of exclusionary nationalism, racism, and religious fundamentalism. Against this negativism, reformist and transformist strategies offer possibilities for positive globalizations on other than neoliberalist lines.

For ambitious reformism

Whereas neoliberalist strategies of globalization are undesirable, and rejectionist programmes are in addition impracticable, reformist policies are both more attractive and more feasible. This broadly social-democratic approach to globalization rests on a firm understanding of the material forces behind the process, coupled with a determination to exploit proactive policy interventions to shape capitalist production and emergent polycentric governance to positive ends. On the negative side, however, reformism tends to underestimate the power of structural inequalities, to be elitist, and to neglect ideational aspects of globalization. Hence this book urges the adoption of an ambitious reformism that seeks the maximum possible gains from globally oriented social democracy and then looks to transformist inspirations to make up for shortcomings in this approach.

As a major plus, reformist strategies towards globalization reject neoliberalism's blind faith in markets and recognize that *laissez-faire* can generate harm as well as good. Indeed, reformists go beyond talk of 'market competition' to call 'global capitalism' by its name. To alleviate sufferings and increase opportunities under global accumulation, reformists advocate the use of democratically determined public policies. For example, to improve human security under globalization, reformists have called for binding environmental regulations, enforceable labour standards, quality public health services, and effective arms controls. To combat social inequality, reformists have argued for measures such as redistributive taxes, abolition of unsustainable poor country debts, and concerted efforts to increase female literacy. To reduce democratic deficits in globalization, reformists have urged steps such as popular referenda, maximum transparency of official decision-making, and enhanced civil society consultation in policymaking processes.

Also to their credit, reformist strategies towards increased transplanetary connectivity recognize that – against obsolete rejectionist fixations on local and national sovereignty – at least some of this corrective public policy needs to operate through suprastate laws and institutions. For instance, many reformists regard social democracy through macro-regional apparatuses as an important means to harness globalization to humane ends. Regionalism moreover allows policies on global issues to be adapted for the particular priorities and cultures of different areas of the planet. In addition, reformists see the necessity of achieving a substantial expansion of transworld governance if progressive public policy is to be effective under more globalized conditions. Ambitious reformists therefore promote the construction of bodies like a global environmental organization, a global central bank, a global competition authority, and additional – and stronger – global courts. At the same time, reformists are acutely aware of the need to improve the democratic credentials of macro-regional and global governance.

Reformism not only has these attractions in principle, but its prescriptions are also viable in practice. It is technically quite possible to formulate effective policies for publicly controlled globalization and to devise workable institutional mechanisms to administer these measures. Neoliberalists are only too ready to dismiss attempts to harness global markets as unfeasible, and certainly the technical challenges facing effective global environmental agreements, global taxes and the like should not be underestimated. However, political will also opens a way. After all, concerted efforts backed by substantial resources have succeeded in attaining countless other technical breakthroughs in globalization: from nuclear weapons and the Internet to the CLS and the TRIPS agreement. Similar levels of commitment could yield major advances in effective global social democracy.

Indeed, the political environment for reformist policies towards globalization has become more auspicious in recent years. Growing constituencies – including among some élite circles – have backed at least milder versions of reformism. For example, the directors of the WEF have cautioned that 'the globalized economy must not become synonymous with "free market on the rampage"' (Schwab and Smadja, 1996). Unadulterated neoliberalism persists in some quarters, but considerable support has grown for the view – here expressed by the head of UNDP – that 'globalization is too important to be left as unmanaged as it is at present' (HDR, 1999: v). Putting this point more metaphorically, a UNICEF official has declared that globalization is a bumpy road full of potholes, so cars need to be equipped with good shock absorbers (Vandemoortele, 2000).

Some analysts have suggested that the recent rise of reformism in globalization politics marks a recurrence of what the economic sociologist Karl Polanyi called a 'double movement' (Polanyi, 1944). In this purported systemic rhythm of market society, a movement of *laissez-faire* gives way to a countermovement of resistance and regulation, as citizens and their governments react against the undesirable social and environmental consequences of untrammelled market capitalism. Writing in the 1940s, before the accelerated globalization of the past half-century, Polanyi described the double movement in relation to territorial capitalism. Today a new generation of Polanyian arguments have suggested that a civilizing countermovement against neoliberalism could be underway in global capitalism (Mendell and Salée, 1991: xv–xvii; Gill, 1995b; Block, 2003; Silver and Arrighi, 2003).

Such optimistic diagnoses of triumphant resistance to *laissez-faire* warrant some caution, however. Yes, ultra-liberalism of the 1980s and early 1990s thankfully did not sweep away all concerns with social justice, social rights, social responsibility, and social regulation. Yes, there has been greater plurality of visions and more public debate about globalization since the late 1990s, after the monochrome neoliberalist politics of the preceding fifteen years. Yet progress on reformist paths has been limited and slow. After all, élite circles have issued public urgings for more economically, socially and environmentally responsible globalization as far back as the late 1980s. Since then an endless stream of UN meetings and reports, IMF and World Bank initiatives, G8 and WEF schemes, and CSR programmes have all promised a more humane globalization. But how much concrete advance of reformism has actually been booked between the time that UNICEF called for 'adjustment with a human face' in 1987 and the advocacy by an ILO-sponsored commission of 'a fair globalization' in 2004 (Cornia *et al.*, 1987–8; WCSDG, 2004)?

Reflecting on this disappointing history, some would-be reformist talk looks more like rhetoric to defuse opposition to neoliberalism than a substantial alteration of the policy framework. These politics – in the vein of an 'Augmented Washington Consensus' – amount to 'neoliberalism with knobs on' rather than full-scale reformism, where the governance of globalization would be based on principles of redistribution, rights and regulation. Thus, for example, widespread discussion of a 'new global financial architecture' in the wake of the crises in Asia, Russia and Latin America in the late 1990s produced few concrete results. Even the seemingly promising Financing for Development process, pursued through the UN since 1997, has run aground in minor gestures. Likewise, the Doha cycle of multilateral trade negotiations was launched in late 2001 as a 'Development Round', but the talks have so far done little to re-regulate global commerce in favour of the poor.

Indeed, neoliberalists have on various occasions captured and tamed reformist discourse. Thus, for example, international financial institutions have repackaged 'poverty eradication' in lamer terms of 'poverty reduction'. In neoliberalist hands, the struggle for 'transparency' has become largely a campaign against corruption. Rather than 'mobilization' of 'civil society', neoliberalism with knobs on has yielded 'consultation' of 'NGOs'. As one activist has despaired, 'global managers adopt a language that takes the mantle of the critics and takes energy out of their movement' (Barr, 2002).

Instead of these attenuations, the policy strategy advocated here insists on an ambitious reformism that does not stop at social safety nets, environmental impact statements, and corporate citizenship, but in addition undertakes far-reaching public regulation and progressive redistribution of resources. 'Thin' reformists only invoke proactive public policy to prevent or clean up major market damage. In contrast, 'thick' reformists reject the neoliberalist emphasis on market-led globalization and shift the initiative to public policy management. In ambitious reformism state, substate and suprastate laws and institutions take firm hold of the steering wheel and harness forces of globalization to explicit and democratically determined public measures. Ambitious reformism looks beyond band-aids to full treatment. Fingers in holes do not salvage a structurally flawed dyke. When facing a wide chasm (of security, equality and democracy problems) it is unwise to take a small step.

But do even ambitious reformists take sufficiently large leaps in their efforts to reshape globalization? Laudable though their intentions may be, social democrats often fail to tackle structural inequalities as vigorously as a fully egalitarian strategy would require. Ambitious reformists give ample attention to policies of income redistribution, as well as improved access to resources and services for underprivileged circles. However, social democrats look for the best possible deal within capitalism, a mode of production whose inherent logic inclines toward inequality. Radical socialists therefore criticize reformists for failing to pursue more egalitarian post-capitalist solutions.

Indeed, it is perhaps telling that reformist politics tend to be elitist, according little role in policymaking to social movements of the oppressed themselves. Under social-democratic strategies of 'steering' globalization, it is progressive circles of the global managerial class that design the driving mechanism and occupy the driving seat. The 'democracy' in global social democracy tends not to extend beyond the limited mechanisms of popularly elected representative institutions and professional civil society bodies.

In addition to dangers of elitism and excessive moderation in combating structural inequalities, reformist strategies towards globalization tend, like neoliberalism, to suffer from materialism. Thus social democratic policies generally give little attention to ideational aspects of human security, to cultural and psychological aspects of social inequality, and to the role of identity politics and knowledge power in building or blocking democracy. Indeed, with culturally blind self-regard many advocates of global social democracy fail to appreciate that this policy strategy has derived largely from specific contexts in Western Europe and North America. Reformist controls of transplanetary capitalism are generally conceived on an assumption that the Northern welfare state provides a universal formula, when global public policy arguably needs to emanate from extended intercultural dialogue among diverse visions.

These important shortcomings acknowledged, ambitious reformism retains considerable potential for generating more positive future globalizations. Much can be gained from proactive public regulation of global capitalism, including concerted interventions to bring a more equitable distribution of benefits and harms. To be sure, the reform measures described in the next sections would not – even if completely implemented – yield immediate or total security, equality and democracy. However, these steps offer the prospect of substantially improved results of transplanetary relations within a generation.

For cautious transformism

The pitfalls of reformism – including its more ambitious variants – can be partly reduced through engagement with transformist strategies that seek through globalization to reconstruct the primary structures of social life. Already in the preceding paragraphs, insights from these more radical programmes have helped to identify key limitations to reformist approaches. In addition to providing critique, transformist visions – or at least some of them – can also inspire positive concrete changes in the ways that global relations are practised. That said, exuberant enthusiasts tend to overestimate current possibilities to achieve full-scale revolutions to post-capitalist, post-bureaucratic, post-national, post-rationalist globalizations.

In terms of positive contributions of transformist orientations, socialist inspirations regarding the mode of production can help to place the focus of globalization politics on achieving equality, as opposed to merely reducing inequality. Attaining a good is more than avoiding a bad: ensuring equivalent life chances for all (as transformist socialism advocates) entails more than eliminating gross inequities (as reformist social democracy urges). Thus notions such as post-capitalist solidarity economics with alternative models of work and consumption merit a serious hearing and concerted efforts at elaboration and implementation.

Likewise, anarchist visions of alternative non-bureaucratic governance merit serious attention in the contemplation of more progressive governance of global relations. The promotion of decentralized, small-scale, non-hierarchical, non-professionalized decision-taking on transplanetary matters could enhance the possibilities for all people to debate and shape their global futures. As such, anarchist inspirations could make major contributions to a democratization of globalization. This orientation, too, could help to lift the sights of global politics to higher aspirations than competition, efficiency, and growth alone.

In respect of identity, postmodernist inspirations could encourage moves towards more constructive dynamics of being and belonging than traditional forms of both communitarianism (with its tendencies towards violent othering) and cosmopolitanism (with its tendencies towards cultural imperialism). Against communitarianism, alternative modes of identity construction could refuse binary us–them oppositions and reject the accompanying politics of exclusion, instead recognizing and celebrating the multifaceted hybrid character of the self and its plurality of overlapping group affiliations. Against traditional cosmopolitanism, postmodernist identity politics could deny the universality of any one mode of being and instead base global solidarity on a respect of difference and mutually enhancing intercultural interchange. By breaking down artificial divisions and exaggerated oppositions between identities, a postmodernist approach would also undermine hierarchy and inequality in social relations.

With regard to knowledge, too, postmodernist critiques could help to further the trend toward more reflexive rationality and at the same time create more space in globalization for a plurality of epistemologies. Although rationalist knowledge has borne significant fruits, its underlying drive for human control of nature and society has also generated profound tensions with ecological integrity and democracy. Postmodernist promotion of more open, plural and variable knowledges could help to improve cultural and ecological security as well as to combat authoritarian impositions of one mode of knowledge over others.

Many of the preceding comments are highly general and thereby point up one of the principal reasons for advocating a *cautious* transformism, namely, the generally underdeveloped formulation of these more radical alternatives to neoliberalist globalization. For their part, global socialists have not delineated specific contours of a post-capitalist mode of production; nor have they indicated exactly how this structure would yield more human security, social equality and democracy. Likewise, global anarchists and global postmodernists have not offered very precise accounts of post-bureaucratic governance and post-rationalist knowledge. In short, these transformist approaches have provided much more detail about what they oppose in other strategies of globalization than about what they support as alternative futures. The critiques are immensely helpful in revealing the limitations of globalization-as-it-is, but protest needs to be matched by proposal in order to realize globalization-as-it-could-be. Indeed, if insufficiently grounded in clearly formulated visions and carefully evaluated tactics, experiments in transformist social practices could unleash new violences, possibly producing even greater harms than those that currently prevail.

Yet even if they were fully formulated, transformist strategies toward globalization seem non-starters for the time being. As indicated in Chapter 1, global socialism, anarchism and postmodernism at present only find favour on the fringes of politics, with almost no following in powerful quarters. On the contrary, as seen in Chapters 5–8, contemporary globalization has to date deepened rather than reduced the forces of capitalism, bureaucratism, communitarianism and rationalism. To be sure, radical critiques can inspire individuals to attempt to practise alternative globalizations through their personal life's choices. However, the current balance of wider social forces is such that it would be rash to expect full-scale reconfigurations of primary social structures in the short or medium term. Transformism is a political strategy for the long run.

Hence, given the various considerations discussed above, the broad policy approach to globalization suggested here lies in a grey area where reformism waxes into transformism. On the one hand, this politics places great faith in the capacities of public policy – including in particular an expansion of suprastate regulatory schemes – to improve the human consequences of contemporary globalization. On the other hand, the perspective recognizes that capitalism in respect of production, bureaucratism in respect of governance, conventional communitarianism and cosmopolitanism in respect of identity, and rationalism in respect of knowledge all have certain inherent limitations when it comes to furthering human security, social equality and democracy. Vigorous pursuit of reformist policies coupled with vigorous exploration of transformist possibilities seems the best way forward in a more global world. As noted later in this chapter, implementation of such a strategy faces major political hurdles, but with concerted efforts its realization lies within the realm of the possible.

Enhancing human security

Between laying out general strategy and evaluating challenges of implementation lies the identification of specific proposals that could translate a vision of ambitious reformism coupled with cautious transformism into contemporary political practice. The next sections review various steps that could be pursued in the short and medium term to give this agenda effect. Indeed, as seen in preceding chapters, ruling élites have over the past decade already taken some modest steps in reformist directions.

The first set of proposals addresses the concerns about human security discussed in Chapter 9. The dozen points below could reduce the previously identified harms in respect of military violence, crime, ecological degradation, health problems, poverty, financial instability, unemployment, labour exploitation, cultural damage, and social fragmentation. In line with ambitious reformism, the proposals give particular emphasis to the development of global public policies through transworld institutions. That said, these suprastate initiatives are not treated as a project of global government, but within a context of polycentric governance where states and substate authorities retain a major role. Capacity for effective regulation of global relations needs to be developed across multi-scalar governance, rather than in transworld institutions alone.

1 Human rights

Perhaps the most far-reaching progressive global public policy initiative would be legally to subordinate all transplanetary governance to human rights standards. Within democratic states, all national legislation normally must conform to an overarching bill of rights or some similar instrument. However, to date human rights have not similarly reigned supreme over global regulation. Thus it has not been possible legally to judge the acceptability or otherwise of global governance against the standards of, say, the two global covenants on human rights signed in 1966 and in force since 1976.

This pair of covenants – one on civil and political rights, the other on cultural, economic and social rights – could be raised to the status of a legally binding and enforced transplanetary bill of rights. Perhaps suitable amendments of the existing principles might be necessary to obtain the agreement of all states. Once in place, citizens would have a powerful formal mechanism with which to require that suprastate policies *vis-à-vis* globalization did not undermine human security – and on the contrary guaranteed at least minimum living standards. On this basis challenges could be brought against, for example, IMF-sponsored macroeconomic reforms or WTO rulings when such global governance measures violated basic rights.

A step of this kind seems achievable, given the significant advances that the global human rights movement has already made since the 1940s. The past decade has witnessed notable advances in establishing the International Criminal Court with binding jurisdiction and judgments. A larger and longer concerted campaign could place a bill of rights at the core of global governance as a whole.

2 Arms control

As seen in Chapters 6 and 9, the growth of polycentric governance in the context of globalization has included some development of transgovernmental, macro-regional and global regimes to limit the spread and use of weapons. However, regulation to restrict the militarization of transplanetary spaces could be considerably widened and upgraded. For example, policies could be developed to ban not only nuclear proliferation and chemical weapons, but also antiballistic missiles (ABMs). Such a measure would prevent the spread of supraterritorial counter-weapons of the sort pursued by the US Government in its Strategic Defense Initiative (SDI) proposal of the 1980s and anti-missile tests of recent years. Apart from weapons of mass destruction (WMD), regulation could also place far more effective controls on cross-border trade in conventional arms.

In time these different mechanisms, together with the IAEA and the OPCW, could be linked under an umbrella global arms control authority. States would thereby cede some competence over the military field to suprastate governance, as they have already done to one degree or another in every other policy area. Yet, as on other questions, it would be a case of a global agency supplementing rather than supplanting state governance.

3 Conflict management

Other public policy mechanisms could increase protection against armed violence when it looms or has already begun. For example, United Nations peacekeeping operations could be enhanced with full-scale early-warning mechanisms that link governments and civil society watchdogs to a conflict prevention division of the Secretariat. UN contingents could then intercede in trouble spots sooner and with better intelligence about local circumstances, thereby averting a conflagration or at least reducing its damage.

Serious consideration could also be given to establishing a formal regime of 'peace building' or even 'peace enforcement' (Daniel and Hayes, 1995). Already in ad hoc cases like Cambodia and East Timor, UN-sanctioned military operations have gone beyond a traditional peacekeeping role to intervene proactively in ongoing wars and insurgencies. However, officially sanctioned permanent procedures for so-called 'second-generation' peacekeeping would speed up reaction times and lend greater legitimacy to such operations. All manner of genocides and other humanitarian disasters might be lessened or prevented as a result.

Peacekeeping and peace enforcement efforts could be bolstered with the creation of permanent and specifically trained regional and global military units. For fifty years multilateral armed contingents have been formed on an ad hoc basis, often at a cost of precious time and extra political difficulties that detract from their effectiveness. It would be far more efficient if bodies like the UN and the African Union had their own troops available, although great care would be required to ensure that such forces were publicly accountable.

4 Ecological security

To improve environmental conditions under increasingly globalized circumstances, suprastate mechanisms to reduce ecological degradation could go well beyond the existing measures described in Chapters 6 and 9. For instance, the polluter-pays principle could be applied not only to greenhouse gases under the Climate Convention and Kyoto Protocol, but also to sulphur dioxide emissions, tropical wood consumption, pesticide use, air travel, and more. Various financial incentives administered through local, national, regional and global programmes could be employed to encourage the development and use of renewable energy sources. Consumption of non-renewable energy could be priced with attention to its environmental damage. Global trade laws would need to incorporate ecological clauses to counter commercial disincentives to the pursuit of important environmental legislation.

In the private sector, meanwhile, companies could go beyond hijacking the slogan of 'sustainable development' and make it a veritable core of their business practices (Heerings and Zeldenrust, 1995; Greer and Bruno, 1996; Welford, 1997). Indeed, codes of conduct for global corporations could include specific and enforceable environmental targets instead of broad declarations of immeasurable and unmonitored aspirations. However, CSR schemes should be supplements to rather than (as many corporate executives have regarded them) substitutes for public policies on ecological sustainability.

Indeed, public transplanetary regulation of environmental problems warrants a substantial upgrade with the creation of a Global Environmental Organization (GEO) in place of a small and relatively marginalized body like UNEP. A GEO would monitor and coordinate efforts that are currently dispersed across several hundred multilateral environmental agreements and associated commissions. A global environmental agency would also need to work on a par with – rather than be subordinated to – other transworld bodies, particularly those covering finance and trade. The framework of global governance would then encourage careful negotiations between goals of productivity and sustainability, as against existing institutional arrangements, which tend to enthrone economic efficiency above all other policy objectives.

The promotion of ecological integrity is also an area where personal initiative can play a considerable role even when decisive public policy is absent. Relevant steps might encompass recycling, limiting numbers of offspring, using public transport rather than private motorcars, making 'green' consumer choices in purchases of food and other household goods, and reducing consumption generally. Of course public policies that promote such measures have more effect than individual choices in isolation, but that fact is no reason to persist with avoidable personal contributions to environmental damage.

5 Health treatment

Global public health has received even less attention in contemporary policy-making than the other areas of human security discussed so far; hence proposals for the future build on a smaller and more fragile base of suprastate regulation. One major advance in this area would be to undertake a substantial expansion of publicly funded research into illnesses and debilitations whose treatment does not promise major commercial windfalls and therefore tends to get neglected by private business. In the absence of such official interventions, cold remedies for wealthy hypochondriacs will continue to attract more scientific attention than prospective cures for malaria and tuberculosis.

Once treatments are available, global public policy measures could help to ensure that all sufferers obtain access to the relief. 'Market forces' and existing intellectual property rules give priority to the profits of several pharmaceutical companies over the health of hundreds of millions of poor people. States by themselves cannot take effective steps to control the global firms in question, which often price medications well beyond the incomes of most of humanity. And veritable access is required, as opposed to bureaucratic labyrinths such as the 2003 WTO agreement, which has to date delivered no noteworthy practical relief to AIDS patients in poor countries.

6 Socially sensitive economic restructuring

The growth of global production, finance and trade requires economic adjustments, including some that can be highly disruptive and damaging. However, the social costs need not be as heavy as those that have often accompanied neoliberalist policies. Approaches to economic restructuring under globalizing capitalism could therefore be reoriented so that issues like the adequate provision of education, employment, health, and shelter gain greater priority.

To this end policy aims could be more ambitious than mildly reformist initiatives like the MDGs at the UN, the PRSPs at the Bretton Woods institutions, and NEPAD at the G8. The mindset of 'safety nets' against the worst deprivations wants replacement with an agenda of 'social justice' that offers everyone maximal opportunities to pursue a good life. Relevant measures to this more ambitious end fall mainly in the next section on enhancing social equality under globalization.

In addition, in procedural terms, poverty eradication could be more successfully achieved if the formulation and execution of policies of macroeconomic restructuring fully integrated relevant expertise from socially geared bodies with that of economically adept institutions. Among global agencies, then, UNDP and UNICEF would collaborate closely with the IMF and the World Bank. At the same time, suprastate bodies that deal with structural adjustment could work more closely with social departments of national and local governments, as well as with trade unions, faith-based social service providers, and socially oriented NGOs.

7 Debt relief

Another major policy step towards poverty eradication would be better management of global debt problems. More could be done, building on the initiatives described in Chapter 9, to combat the social harms of transworld debts in much of the South. Relief could cover more borrowings, on more generous terms, and at a faster rate than has been witnessed to date under the HIPC. Where repayment difficulties are chronic, as in the case of many of the poorest countries, global debts could be cancelled, as has already occurred on several occasions. Moreover, the monies released through debt relief could be earmarked for increased social spending. This principle has already governed the HIPC programme and several cancellations of bilateral debts. Better debt monitoring mechanisms could ensure that future borrowings do not repeat the deplorable scenario of the past thirty years.

In cases where governments of so-called 'middle-income countries' default on debt repayment, smoother and more predictable rescheduling processes could be developed. In this regard proposals for a Sovereign Debt Restructuring Mechanism (SDRM) could be resuscitated to handle crises of the sort that have in recent years afflicted Argentina, Brazil and Turkey. The SDRM would involve a global bankruptcy court that operated on US Chapter XI-like lines to work out the debt crises of borrower states, as an advance on ad hoc IMF-led emergency rescues. The US Treasury and other major creditors regrettably sidelined the SDRM in 2002, in favour of reliance on national courts in whose jurisdiction the debt contracts were signed. However, these judges generally lack the expertise and the democratic legitimacy to deal with foreign debtor states (Sgard, 2004).

8 Financial regulation

Other more ambitious measures to reconstruct the so-called 'global financial architecture' could also be pursued. Public-sector regulation can harness supraterritorial financial markets considerably more than neoliberalists have tended to suggest. Just as 'rocket scientists' in the commercial sector have developed ever more sophisticated financial instruments, so 'high-flier' regulators could devise ever more sophisticated supervisory mechanisms if the requisite political weight were put behind the efforts.

One fairly modest move, already pursued by some governments since the Asia crisis, is a more nuanced approach to capital controls. Even many mainstream economists now agree that liberalization of cross-border capital flows should be timed and sequenced more carefully (Griffith-Jones, 1998). Indeed, in some cases bars on capital transfers between countries (especially short-term credits) could serve positive purposes for economic and social development. More selective regulatory measures, too, could protect vulnerable markets from speculative runs by global investors. For example, governments could impose a special exchange rate on equity investments from abroad or prohibit domestic borrowing by nonresidents (Williamson, 1999).

More ambitiously, states could collectively introduce a tax on foreign-exchange transactions as a way to reduce speculation and volatility in that enormous market. This proposal is generally known as the Tobin tax, named after the economist James Tobin who first formulated the idea in 1971. A fractional charge on foreign-exchange dealings would encourage greater stability by eliminating many of the marginal profits that attract currency speculators. Supporters of liberalized global finance have long rejected the technical feasibility of a Tobin tax, but the CLS and other concerted efforts could arguably overcome these challenges if the political will were present. Since 1999 several parliaments (including those of Belgium, Canada and Germany) have urged further development of a currency transactions tax, but most financial regulators have remained resistant. (For more on the Tobin tax, see Eichengreen *et al.*, 1995; Haq *et al.*, 1996; Schmidt, 1999; Patomaki, 2001.)

More generally, global monetary and financial regulation could be consolidated in a transplanetary financial authority. Such a body could be created either by upgrading the IMF or by forming a new institution that fused and superseded the IMF and the BIS (Gunter, 1996; Eatwell, 2000; Girvan, 2000). Whereas current IMF resources amount to only a small fraction of the annual value of trade between countries, a global central bank would have sufficient means at its disposal to provide emergency support in any crisis of cross-border finance.

This transworld institution could also administer a distinct global currency that filled the roles now covered by transplanetary national denominations like the US dollar and the Japanese yen. Possibly the SDR could be upgraded into the sort of money that John Maynard Keynes envisioned in the early 1940s under the name of the 'bancor'. Alternatively, some other supraterritorial currency could be devised, for example, with reference to the value of a basket of the most traded commodities in global markets (Lietaer, 1996). In any case a single transworld denomination of this kind could remove many of the instabilities that the foreign exchange markets generate at present. The introduction of a non-national global currency could also help to redress the arbitrary inequalities that are bolstered when the denominations of already powerful states take pride of place as transplanetary monies.

9 Job creation

As indicated in Chapter 9, global capitalism has posed major challenges to employment prospects. An expansion of job support initiatives from public-sector agencies could help to address this problem. For example, education and training programmes can be reoriented in order better to equip workers with the sorts of perspectives and skills (such as global thinking and computer literacy) that are central to labour in supraterritorial capitalism. In addition, fiscal incentives could be devised that encourage employers to retain and retrain staff as companies restructure in the face of globalization. More ambitiously, multilateral agencies could embark on job-creating global public works projects, for example, to supply underprivileged parts of the planet with full telecommunications services or to undertake programmes of environmental restoration.

In addition, more transformist inspirations could prompt policymakers and citizens at large to think more critically about the nature of work in a more global world. For example, public policies could discourage the expansion of sectors such as call centres that often exploit low-skilled workers and vulnerable consumers alike. In addition, government and corporate policies could increase job opportunities by reducing overwork among people in jobs, thereby bettering their quality of life and at the same time creating new positions. Needless to say, such a measure could only succeed if wages were set at levels that made decreased working hours possible.

10 Labour standards

Other policy reorientations to improve the security of people in work are also available. For example, the ILO could acquire greater capacities to monitor and enforce compliance with its core conventions, say, with compulsory dispute hearings of the kind that the WTO provides in regard to trade. Moves could also be started toward the establishment of a global regime of minimum wages, whose levels might for the time being be weighted in relation to the per capita income of a country.

Further protection of labour conditions could be pursued outside the ILO. For example, a chapter on workers' rights could be included in the WTO as well as all regional trade accords. In addition, security in the workplace could be a prominent feature of an independently monitored and fully enforced code of conduct for global companies. Such a regime of rigorous social auditing could perhaps be created with a further upgrade of the OECD Guidelines for Multinational Enterprises.

Meanwhile workers themselves could improve their terms and conditions in global capitalism by nurturing transplanetary solidarities beyond the modest levels noted in Chapter 7. As Charles Tilly has argued, 'chauvinistic and protectionist responses will not defend labor's effective rights . . . workers have to invent new strategies at the scale of international capital' (1995: 20–1). A promising turn in this regard has seen the conclusion of several collective bargaining agreements between a global company and a global trade secretariat (rather than a national union). The first such accord was reached in 1988 between Danone and the International Union of Food, Agricultural, Hotel, Restaurant, Catering, Tobacco and Allied Workers' Associations (IUF). Other agreements followed in the 1990s involving the hotel chain ACCOR, the energy concern Statoil, and the furniture maker IKEA together with, respectively, the IUF, the International Chemical, Energy and Mining Workers, and the International Federation of Building and Wood Workers (Justice, 1999: 7).

11 Cultural diversity

Various legal and institutional reforms could also bolster cultural security, that is, safety and confidence in identities and accompanying frameworks of meaning. For example, school curricula could do more to expose young people to multiple histories and civilizations. States could do more (on the lines described in Chapter 7) to accord formal recognition to minority cultures. Macro-regional and transworld agencies could develop more sites like the EU Committee of the Regions where micro-nations have a voice. Suprastate economic governance in particular could be reformed in the direction of greater cultural sensitivity.

More generally, institutions as well as individuals could nurture cultural security in a globalizing world by developing what might be called an 'interculturalist' approach to identity politics. Adopting this stance, encounters between people with different identities and knowledges would be conducted in a spirit of dialogue rather than confrontation. Reigning principles would be mutual recognition, respect, responsibility and (when tensions rise) restraint (Scholte, 1996: 595–600; 1999: 66–9, 80–3). Intercultural reciprocity contrasts fundamentally with the 'us–them' framework of communitarianism, an approach that has tended to denigrate, exclude and suppress 'otherness'. In intercultural cosmopolitanism no one would impose their life-world as a universal model. In the words of a Buddhist reformer, 'We do not want to have one value standard as the measure of others; each culture has its own intrinsic values that need not be measured against others' (Hutanuwatr, 2002). In such a spirit 6,500 people from different faiths met in a Parliament of the World's Religions at Chicago in 1993 to affirm a common global ethic without erasing each other's identity (Küng and Kuschel, 1993). Such initiatives demonstrate that it is possible to have human solidarity through cultural difference.

12 Ethical investment

All of the preceding policy proposals could in different ways promote another umbrella goal of human security in a more global world: namely, social cohesion. A further practicable reformist measure to this end is so-called ethical investment, where savings are utilized in ways that avoid social ills (e.g., the arms trade) and preferably also positively advance social goods (e.g., fair trade programmes). A host of ethical investment schemes have already become available, but both their number and their standards could be scaled up considerably. Individual savers can further this cause with their personal investment decisions. In addition, the movement can gain all the more impetus as and when large institutional players like trade union pension funds demand that their investments meet high ethical standards.

Enhancing social equality

In addition to countering human security problems, other initiatives in the spirit of ambitious reformism and cautious transformism can go some way to reduce the social inequalities under globalization that were discussed in Chapter 10. Indeed, a number of the measures to enhance human security discussed above can simultaneously work to alleviate the inequities that result from arbitrary social hierarchies. In regard to class, for example, measures to eradicate poverty, improve employment conditions, and increase social cohesion can at the same time lessen inequalities in life chances between various socioeconomic groups. As for the stratification of countries, steps to create socially sustainable structural adjustment, to remove excessive debt burdens, and to stabilize financial markets can simultaneously narrow gaps between the North and the South. Alternative identity politics can reduce cultural hierarchies while promoting cultural security. The following pages set out further proposals that specifically target problems of social inequality.

1 Suprastate anti-monopoly mechanisms

Measures to counter centralizing tendencies in global capitalism (identified in Chapter 5) could work against various social inequalities. After all, market concentration has allowed investors and managers – who generally already hold considerable wealth and power advantages over other classes – to accumulate undue levels of additional surplus. Winners of the global oligopoly game have also been disproportionately white, male, urban and based in the North.

Several anti-monopoly mechanisms could be developed in respect of global capital. In macro-regional governance, for instance, other institutions could follow the example of the EU in establishing a regime of competition rules. A rigorous global anti-monopoly framework could also be developed, building on existing modest initiatives such as the UN Restrictive Practices Code and the OECD Committee on Competition Law and Policy. These efforts could bring the creation of a Global Competition Office linked to the WTO (Fortin, 1992: 86–8) or a self-standing global anti-trust authority.

2 Changes to global intellectual property rules

As noted in Chapter 10, existing suprastate rules governing intellectual property disproportionately favour those in positions of advantage. Regimes such as TRIPS could be amended so that predatory capitalists cannot claim ownership of ideas, tools and techniques from marginalized groups (like poor people in the South) who created them but are unaware of the principle and workings of intellectual property. Likewise, IPRs could be altered to prevent the commodification by powerful corporate interests of traditional goods (medicines, plants, etc.) that were previously freely available to the poor.

In other respects global intellectual property rules could be relaxed to favour the South. After all, significant aspects of early industrialization in the North were based on the exploitation of innovations from abroad, without the intervention of global laws regarding patents, trademarks, designs and copyrights. The application of stringent transplanetary intellectual property rights in effect denies poorer countries significant opportunities that were available in a previous era to today's North. Alternative intellectual property regimes could establish a more equitable balance between protections for innovators and opportunities for producers. One modest initiative in this direction is the Creative Commons project that seeks to replace the absolute 'all rights reserved' of traditional copyright with a conditional 'some rights reserved' principle (Creative Commons, 2005).

3 Global redistributive taxation

A third set of measures that could counter inequality in globalization relate to transworld taxes. Various schemes for global taxes have circulated since the 1970s (Carlsson *et al.*, 1995: 217–21; Wachtel, 2000). Much as progressive taxation through states has worked against class and other arbitrary hierarchies within countries, so transplanetary taxation through transworld institutions could reduce inequities between classes and countries as they are generated through global capitalism. In addition, the revenues gained from global taxes could help to fund a number of programmes to enhance human security, as covered in the preceding section. All of the taxes described below are progressive: that is, they would apply mainly to the more wealthy sections of humanity that are most able to pay them.

One especially appealing proposal for a global levy is the aforementioned Tobin tax on foreign-exchange transactions. Given the huge volume of this business, even a very low rate of this charge would yield substantial revenues that could be used to improve the life opportunities of disadvantaged circles, especially in poor countries, with improved education, health care, etc. As wholesale foreign-exchange dealings mainly involve the richest circles, a Tobin tax could achieve poverty alleviation through wealth alleviation.

Suprastate taxation of global corporations would be another measure to help achieve a more equitable distribution of the gains of transplanetary capitalism. The absence of transworld taxation of profits has allowed globally operating companies to manipulate state tax frameworks to their advantage, for example, through transfer pricing and offshore arrangements. Global taxation of corporate profits could close such loopholes and ensure that big capital contributes its due share to public funds. Another suprastate corporate tax to fund global public goods could levy a fee on cross-border mergers and acquisitions.

Other possible global taxes include a 'bit tax' on data sent through the Internet. Such a charge could generate more revenue than total world ODA (HDR, 1999: 66). Meanwhile a levy of $100 on each patent registered with the World Intellectual Property Organization (WIPO) could have raised $350 million in 1998 (HDR, 1999: 74). Further transplanetary taxes could apply to use of the so-called 'global commons', such as the deep seabed, the electromagnetic spectrum, flight paths, sea lanes, and ocean fishing areas. Further global taxes have been suggested in respect of cross-border arms sales and transboundary pollution.

The administration of transplanetary taxes could be overseen through relevant existing global institutions (e.g., the BIS for a Tobin tax or the ITU for a bit tax). Alternatively, a single global revenue service could be created for this purpose. In either case the development of transplanetary taxes would make issues concerning the democratization of globalization all the more urgent. Indeed, transworld taxation could easily fail to advance social equality if global governance remained captured by privileged circles owing to the severe democratic deficits laid out in Chapter 11.

4 Abolition of offshore finance

Another significant step to create more equal opportunities in globalization would be to dismantle offshore finance centres. Efforts through the OECD since 2000 to censure tax havens for lack of transparency and poor cooperation with overseas tax authorities have been welcome; yet so far they have had limited effect. Moreover, the OECD initiative has failed to address the core ethical objection to offshore finance: namely, that these facilities allow people with the greatest means to be free riders in a world replete with need and inequality. True, offshore tax arrangements have generated some revenue for the host governments, including in some poor countries. However, these public funds have in most cases done little to eliminate underprivilege among the local populations. As for employment, although offshore finance centres have created some work, these jobs could also exist if the same deposits were placed in onshore accounts. Tellingly, no one has articulated a convincing economic or social justification for offshore finance centres. They should and could be eliminated through global rules governing taxation.

5 North–South redistribution through global economic regimes

A number of other reforms could reduce the hierarchies between countries that have been reflected in, and substantially sustained by, global economic regimes. To begin with, several steps could be taken to improve the North–South balance in global economic decision taking. For example, votes in the Bretton Woods institutions could be redistributed away from the currently prevailing quota formula that has so heavily favoured major states (Buira, 2003). In addition, the BIS and the OECD could further expand their membership to encompass governments of poor as well as rich countries. Meanwhile the central organs of the UN (where the South has greater representation and voting strength) could upgrade their involvement in global economic governance with the creation of an Economic Security Council in place of the existing rather limp Economic and Social Council (Carlsson *et al.*, 1995: 153–62).

Other reforms of globalization could aim to reduce North–South hierarchies in particular sectors of the economy. In the area of global communications, for example, many of the recommendations of the UNESCO-sponsored MacBride Commission, published in 1980, remain relevant for the twenty-first century (UNESCO, 1980; Golding and Harris, 1997). To highlight one specific proposal, more resources could be dedicated to the development of organizations like the Caribbean News Agency and the Inter Press Service that advance Southern perspectives in global journalism (Musa, 1997).

In respect of global money, the IMF could distribute substantial new allocations of SDRs largely if not exclusively to the South. This so-called 'SDR-aid link' could provide poor countries with more foreign exchange reserves and (if the cumulative SDR allocations were sufficiently large) could decrease the dominance in the world economy of North-based currencies. In another step to bolster the position of the South in global monetary affairs, poor states could be accorded greater resources to build up their central banks, making them less dependent in monetary and financial policy on suprastate agencies like the Bretton Woods institutions.

In the area of global credit, since commercial markets largely lock out poor countries, multilateral development banks could provide increased loans to the South on concessionary terms. In particular, more long-term low-interest credits of the kind supplied through the International Development Association (an arm of the World Bank) could be made available to the poorest countries. In addition, expanded micro-credit schemes could channel more global finance to low-income circles (especially women) in the South (Holcombe, 1995; Johnson and Rogaly, 1997).

Various other reforms could improve North–South distribution in respect of global trade. For instance, suprastate initiatives could accomplish much more than the previously mentioned GSP and ACP arrangements have done to reduce trade barriers for the South to markets of the North. In particular the abolition of agricultural subsidies in the North is long overdue. Scope also exists for a large expansion of alternative trade schemes of the kind described in Chapter 10. Meanwhile the WTO could develop commodity regimes that would enhance export earnings for poor countries of key primary products, for example, with guaranteed minimum prices.

6 Gender sensitivity

Much could be done to advance equality between men and women in global relations simply by raising awareness of gender issues. Official, corporate and civil society agencies often contribute to gender inequality in good part because they are blind to social constructions of sex roles. To counter this tendency the United Nations Secretariat has over the past decade promoted so-called 'gender mainstreaming', whereby the assessment of implications for women and men is made integral to the design, implementation, monitoring and evaluation of any policy action. Gender assessments could also be introduced in transworld agencies like the BIS and the WTO that have hitherto lacked such mechanisms. In addition, the development activities of multilateral agencies could extend recent steps specifically to target female poverty. Structural adjustment packages sponsored by suprastate bodies could be reconstructed with greater regard to the gendered impacts of these programmes. Global labour standards could give more direct and systematic attention to promoting equal opportunities for women and men in the workplace. Care work as discussed in Chapter 5 could receive greater policy recognition and attention. Labour protection measures with special relevance to women could be developed, for example, in relation to the global sex trade and migrant domestic workers. At the same time greater resources could be dedicated to the promotion of women's human rights through CEDAW and other suprastate mechanisms. Collectively, such steps could bring gender concerns to the heart of global public policy.

7 Women in global leadership

Gender inequalities could be further redressed in globalization with the appointment of more women to executive positions in suprastate governance agencies, transworld companies, and global civil society associations. On the whole women tend to have greater awareness of and sympathy toward gender justice issues. Even where certain women executives lack these sensitivities, they can still by their example demonstrate the possibilities and accomplishments of female leadership in global organizations.

8 Attention to race, urban/rural and age hierarchies

Along with reforms that address class, country and gender inequalities, further measures could be taken to counter subordinations in globalization of people of colour, rural populations, children and the elderly. Several existing initiatives in these areas by UN agencies and various civil society associations were mentioned in Chapter 10. However, just as problems of race, urban/rural divides and age have been less studied in relation to globalization than those of class, North/South divides and gender, so too fewer specific proposals for corrective action have emerged. More attention could be given to assessing and redressing these generally less highlighted forms of stratification in transplanetary spaces. The principle of policy mainstreaming could be applied to these hierarchies as well as those of gender.

Taking the above eight broad suggestions together, it is clear that global public policies and other measures in the vein of ambitious reformism mixed with cautious transformism could make substantial inroads into the inequalities that have developed in globalization to date. True, many socialists have concluded that the tensions between capitalism and distributive justice run so deep that only a full-scale transformation of the mode of production can remove arbitrary hierarchies from social relations. Yet, even if this argument is accepted in principle, it remains possible and desirable to pursue reforms that lessen social inequalities within capitalism, especially if acceptable and feasible post-capitalist alternatives are not immediately in sight.

Enhancing democracy

In keeping with the threefold conception of normative politics pursued in Part III of this book, improvements in globalization need to address questions of democracy together with those of human security and social equality. Indeed, some of the measures mentioned in the preceding two sections could also promote greater democracy in global relations. In particular, as stressed in Chapter 11, social equality and democracy are inextricably interlinked, so that suggested policies to reduce arbitrary hierarchies at the same time could increase opportunities for subordinated people to participate in global politics. Likewise, with respect to human security, policies to eradicate poverty, improve employment conditions, and deepen social cohesion also create circumstances in which people are better able actively to involve themselves in processes of collective self-determination.

The present section considers further measures that directly address the educational, institutional and structural problems with democracy in contemporary globalization that were identified in Chapter 11. Some of the proposals focus on changes to suprastate institutions, but others suggest initiatives involving substate and state mechanisms. In this way local and national democracy are seen to be part of global democracy. Notions that state and local governments have no role in the democratization of globalization would be decidedly misplaced.

1 Subsidiarity

Not only do state and substate governments have an important place in global democracy, but their role in governing transplanetary relations could wherever possible be enhanced relative to suprastate institutions. Yes, for reasons elaborated in Chapter 6, significant elements of macro-regional and transworld regulation are indispensable for effective governance of a more global world. Moreover, as the following paragraphs indicate, there are multiple ways to bring substantially greater democracy to suprastate governance. That said, the default position for more democratic regulation of globalization would be, following the principle of subsidiarity, wherever possible to devolve legislation and its implementation to the smallest and nearest sphere, where individual citizens (especially those with limited means) usually have their greatest opportunities for direct involvement in policy processes.

In particular, public participation and public accountability in the governance of global flows could be considerably enhanced with further devolution to substate authorities. Wherever possible, at least part of the formulation and execution of policies relating to global concerns could involve local government and local civil societies. Provincial, district and municipal bodies are often best placed to gauge and reflect the local pulse on global problems as these issues affect specific people in specific contexts. Substate authorities could on suitable occasions use public hearings or referenda to consult constituents on matters concerning global relations as they impact upon that locality. In this vein villages and districts in Thailand convened Civic Forums in the late 1990s to deliberate the use of a Social Investment Fund sponsored by the World Bank in the wake of the Asia financial crisis.

Of course, to reiterate a caution emphasized in earlier chapters, local politics are not 'naturally' democratic. The local is not inherently more genuine and generous than other arenas. Devolution is therefore not a magic formula for democratic globalization. Moreover, as global relations expand further, people may increasingly refashion the local in supraterritorial terms, for example, around websites and transworld conferences. These qualifications made, substate governments and local civil societies could still play a much greater role in governing transplanetary connections than has generally occurred to date.

2 Public education

As emphasized in the previous chapter, 'rule by the people' cannot prevail in the governance of globalization if most people are largely ignorant of what the trend involves and the rules and regulatory institutions that relate to transplanetary issues. Thus another key step towards more democratic future globalizations would be to upgrade public awareness of the subject. This rise in consciousness could be achieved through curricular reforms in schools and universities, through improved mass media coverage of global problems and their governance, and through enhanced public education efforts by regulatory agencies and civil society associations.

Public education about globalization and its governance could promote either more modest or more radical democratization. More reformist pedagogy would alert citizens to institutional aspects of governing globalization and the ways that the regulatory bodies in question have and have not operated democratically. More transformist approaches to public education would put the spotlight on structural inequalities in globalization and the ways that governance processes either reinforce or counter those obstacles to democracy. The aim of radical pedagogy would be to give people, especially the oppressed, knowledge that advances their struggles against social injustice. In these cases learning about globalization is part of a larger strategy of public mobilization for progressive change.

Public education about globalization needs to be designed for diverse audiences, including marginalized circles in particular. Textbook learning in the classroom best suits more academically inclined citizens, who tend to be drawn disproportionately from socially privileged classes. Yet public education must also address those people, often in subordinated positions, who would gain greater insight into global affairs from other methods of learning, such as informal discussion groups, rallies and artistic performances. Moreover, in order to have greater democratic effect, educational materials on global affairs need to be available in local languages.

3 Transparency

Public education on globalization and its governance is greatly facilitated to the extent that the regulatory processes in question are visible to citizens. Hence a third step to promote greater democracy in globalization would be to improve the transparency of relevant policymaking processes. As noted in Chapter 11, a number of institutions involved in governing globalization have already taken notable steps to open their proceedings to public scrutiny, but much more can still be done. The regulatory agencies concerned could disclose more documents, produce more publications, issue more press releases, and maintain more extensive websites. In addition, the governance institutions in question could make greater efforts to present materials in ways that are more accessible to the lay citizen: for example, with non-technical terminology, translation into local languages, and user-friendly websites. The resulting greater transparency could make it easier for interested citizens to determine what decisions regulatory bodies have taken, from among what options, and on what grounds. People could then be better equipped to judge whether a given substate, state, suprastate or private governance organization was acting competently, ethically, and in their interest.

4 Electoral politics

Further democratization of globalization could be achieved through a reinvigoration of electoral processes. Campaigns for local, national and regional assemblies could give more attention to global issues *inter alia* through election rallies, candidate debates, and the platforms of political parties. Voters could thereby become more aware of global questions, and the selection of governors could – far more than at present – test public views on, for instance, the way that a regulatory institution is responding to global ecological problems or global economic developments.

Democracy could also be furthered with increased use of public referenda on major questions of governing globalization. In this way the electorate – rather than a cabinet, legislature or court – would have the final say on a state's accession to key multilateral institutions and agreements. To be sure, effective democracy through referenda presupposes a competent electorate following improved public education and greater transparency on global matters.

5 Nonterritorial constituencies

In order more effectively to reflect the full range of public sentiments in the contemporary more global world, legislative institutions could be refashioned to include nonterritorial as well as territorial representatives. As elaborated in Chapter 7, people have in the context of intensified globalization increasingly acquired identities and associated social bonds that are not based on territorial location and state-centred nationality. Yet few current governance frameworks include a formal recognition of nonterritorial interests connected with age, caste, class, diaspora, disability, faith, gender, race or sexual orientation.

Various mechanisms could be put in place to ensure that nonterritorial voices are guaranteed the representation that territorially based constituencies have generally denied them. For example, certain seats in legislative arms on the various tiers of polycentric governance could be specifically designated for business executives, communities of belief, disabled persons, farmers, sexual minorities, women, workers, etc. Such a principle has already operated in the national congress of Indonesia. In suprastate governance each of the main global and regional institutions could, alongside its existing chamber of state delegates, acquire a permanent civic assembly with seats allocated to nonterritorial constituencies. Such a mix of territorial and nonterritorial chambers would better reflect the realities of contemporary identity politics.

6 Parliamentary oversight

Another set of steps towards greater democracy in the regulation of transplanetary affairs would upgrade the monitoring and control of policies on globalization by representative assemblies. For instance, national congresses could exercise far closer scrutiny over the ratification and implementation of treaties concerning global matters. State legislatures could also perform much more rigorous oversight of their government's involvement in transstate networks and suprastate agencies. Parliamentary examination of private governance mechanisms could enhance the public transparency and accountability of those instruments. In all of these ways state legislatures could place greater democratic checks on the unelected technocrats who have held most of the initiative in governing global affairs to date.

In line with earlier urgings for devolution, representative bodies in substate governance could also more thoroughly review policies on globalization, for example, by examining the local impacts of suprastate policies. A positive development in this direction has seen many municipal assemblies monitor the local application of Agenda 21, the manifesto that resulted from the Earth Summit of 1992. In addition, district and provincial assemblies could exercise greater democratic control over, for example, arrangements made by substate governments in regard to global companies or global credits.

In addition to upgrading national and local processes, legislative oversight of the governance of global issues could be enhanced with the creation of more interparliamentary instruments. Transstate networks of legislators of the kind that have already emerged for environmental issues through the GLOBE network could also be developed in regard to transplanetary aspects of culture, employment, finance, health, and trade. In addition, interparliamentary bodies could be constructed to scrutinize each major global governance institution, not just the World Bank as at present.

Alternatively, these legislative networks could be formally integrated as parliamentary organs within the transworld bodies. In this case each member state would – as already occurs in the Parliamentary Assembly of the Council of Europe – designate several of its sitting national legislators to participate in a global congress for the FAO, the IMF, the WTO, etc. These indirectly elected bodies would meet at regular intervals to review the policies of the global agency concerned.

In the longer term one could perhaps move to the construction of directly elected transworld parliaments. However, for reasons indicated in Chapter 11, such a step looks for the time being to remain impracticable and in some senses also undesirable. On the other hand, directly elected representative assemblies could be introduced to additional regional governance frameworks like ASEAN, MERCOSUR and SADC as these bodies reach a greater degree of institutional development.

7 Judicial processes

In addition to legislative oversight, another avenue for increased public accountability in the governance of globalization is through judicial reviews of policy decisions and their consequences. Individually and through civil society associations, citizens could make greater use of relevant courts, inspectorates and ombudspersons to obtain redress for errors and omissions committed by policymakers in regard to global issues. In addition, new accountability instruments could be created where they are currently not available (for example, an external evaluation office for the WTO).

Within state and substate government, citizens could use judicial processes to press for a national or local authority's compliance with the global conventions or plans of action that it has endorsed. In addition, state and substate courts or other policy evaluation mechanisms could be accessed to demand compensation for harms caused by flawed national and local policies towards global flows of one kind or another. Similarly, citizens could make more use of state and substate courts to sue global organizations for damages caused within the jurisdiction of those judicial bodies. Particular attention could be given to enhancing access for marginalized people to judiciary mechanisms. In this way global bodies such as UNHCR, Citibank or Greenpeace would face greater grassroots accountability.

Where global courts are not in prospect to adjudicate on the actions and inactions of suprastate agencies, efforts can focus on improving other means for public evaluation of their programmes and projects. UN bodies, the BIS and the OECD could acquire the sorts of mechanisms (like external policy evaluations and ombudspersons) that have been introduced at the Bretton Woods institutions since the mid-1990s. Meanwhile the IMF and World Bank inspectorates could increase the range and frequency of their policy assessments. Both the existing and prospective accountability processes could take more evidence directly from affected citizens, particularly through relevant civil society associations that involve subordinated groups, as opposed to relying solely on submissions from technocratic 'experts' in official circles. To encourage their autonomy, policy auditors of suprastate agencies could be appointed by, and responsible to, an outside body and not (as sometimes currently happens) the institution whose policy is being reviewed. The results of these evaluations would normally be released to the public with an invitation for reactions, and the agency concerned would follow up each assessment report with a published and carefully monitored action plan to address any well-founded criticisms and recommendations.

8 Public control of private governance

The preceding proposals have mainly focused on public governance bodies; however, the democratization of globalization also needs to encompass the private regulatory mechanisms discussed in Chapter 6. On the one hand, greater democratic participation and accountability could be developed in relation to bodies such as the IASB and ICANN by integrating procedures of public consultation and public evaluation into their policy processes. Increased relations with parliamentary bodies and civil society associations would be ways to achieve this end.

That said, fuller democratization demands the eventual abolition of the regulation of global affairs through private bodies. Governance agencies for public affairs that are formally appointed by and responsible to private interests fundamentally contradict democratic principles. CSR schemes and the like might be justified as transitional stopgaps in situations where public global governance is at present absent or underdeveloped. However, they are not long-term substitutes for public institutions.

9 Civil society development

Several earlier proposals have already mentioned the potentials of civil society contributions to the democratization of globalization. Indeed, a larger quantity and higher quality of civil society engagement of transplanetary issues could greatly enhance public education, public debate, public participation, public transparency and public accountability in the governance of global affairs. In addition, reformist and transformist initiatives by citizen groups (e.g., to promote debt cancellation or changes in intellectual property laws) could help to reduce the social inequalities that have so often frustrated democracy in respect of transworld problems (Scholte, 2004b: ch 3).

Major increases of resources would be necessary in order more fully to realize the democratizing potentials of civil society activities on global issues. Partly these greater means could be obtained from larger memberships that paid larger subscriptions. In addition, institutional sponsors like philanthropic foundations could increase their support of civil society programmes that address global affairs. Governments could amend statutes where existing laws inhibit the operations of civil society organizations. For instance, legal changes could introduce tax-exempt status for these associations where it is currently absent. For the rest, civil society bodies working on global issues could sometimes coordinate their efforts more carefully and share information more generously with each other. In some cases competition between organizations for funds, members, and the moral high ground has undermined civil society capacities to influence policy.

Civil society bodies could also upgrade their democratization of globalization through internal organizational improvements. For example, many of these citizen groups could give more attention to their self-education on global affairs, so that they would be better equipped to educate the wider public. Civil society associations could also take proactive steps to enhance the participation in their activities of subordinated social circles, thereby countering the tendency in much of civil society to reproduce the hierarchies of wider society. In addition, civil society groups could take greater care to nurture their own public transparency and accountability (Scholte, 2004b: ch 5).

Meanwhile governance agencies (substate, state and suprastate alike) could improve their mechanisms for engagement with citizen groups on global issues. For instance, regulatory bodies could appoint more specialist civil society liaison officers, and other staff could be given better training and greater incentives to develop links with civil society interlocutors. In-country representatives of suprastate agencies could meet on a regular basis with local citizen organizations. In these consultations officials could give particular attention to reaching marginalized constituencies. For the rest, governing authorities could do more to involve civil society associations in official conferences and to involve themselves in civil society events.

In sum, a number of eminently feasible measures are available to bring greater public participation and public accountability to the regulation of transplanetary affairs. Global democracy is therefore not an oxymoron. Overall, the above nine proposals have a mainly reformist thrust, albeit that they consistently urge proactive steps to involve structurally disadvantaged people. In addition, a more thorough democratization of globalization could be achieved if the above initiatives were combined with the proposals in the preceding section for progressive redistribution of world resources and the suggestions discussed in relation to cultural security for alternative identity politics.

Towards implementation

It is relatively easy to compile wish lists. It is something else to get wishes fulfilled. The past decades have seen the production of countless glossy reports with attractive proposals for more humane courses of globalization. Some suggestions (like the target ODA for OECD member states of 0.7 per cent of GDP) have been repeated for decades without effect. Such stalemates have encouraged cynicism in some quarters about the prospects for substantive policy change on matters of global order. The present discussion would therefore be incomplete – and could seem facilely utopian – if it did not consider the challenges of moving from the drawing board to concrete actions. This chapter is not the place to develop detailed plans to guide particular campaigns for specific policy alterations. However, it is important to identify the general circumstances that both favour and hinder the implementation of projects to reconstruct globalization on ambitiously reformist and cautiously transformist lines.

Auspicious circumstances

A number of current conditions favour a shift to more humane globalizations than the currently prevailing neoliberalist orientations. To begin with, the technical means are available as never before to pursue effective global public policies for reformist change and to activate global social movements for transformist change. Innovations in information and communications technologies have made possible unprecedented degrees of transplanetary policy coordination. Transworld governance institutions and global civil society organizations have developed further than ever. No doubt additional advances in these areas are necessary in order fully to realize the sorts of future globalizations proposed in this chapter. However, wide-ranging and deeply influential global public policies and global citizen movements are no longer social science fiction.

As well as technical conditions, various political circumstances also favour new directions in globalization. For one thing, people have generally become far more aware of, and concerned about, global problems. True, as repeatedly urged in the last two chapters, far more public education is needed on globalization and its governance. Yet it is easy to forget how much more globally conscious policymakers and citizens at large have already become in the past half-century. To this extent people today are on the whole markedly more receptive to notions of global regulation than previous generations.

Also auspicious for the implementation of alternative future globalizations is the growth of cosmopolitan attachments that was described in Chapter 7. Although most people continue to identify their community and their destiny heavily in terms of countries and localities, nonterritorial transworld identities (including transplanetary humanity) now also attract notable support in many quarters. As a result, citizens are today more inclined to see their interests on a wide range of issues served at least partly through global public policies.

Politics in the early twenty-first century furthermore favours redirections of globalization owing to the growth of alter-globalization sentiments. Significant proportions of citizens are expressing dissatisfaction with prevailing neoliberalist policies and showing themselves to be receptive to different approaches. For example, the Jubilee 2000 Coalition mobilized millions of people across more than 60 countries in favour of increased debt relief for the South (Collins *et al.*, 2001). The global Making Poverty History campaign does similarly at present. Likewise, the World Social Forum process (including its regional, national and local offshoots) has proved far larger and more sustained than even its most optimistic proponents imagined at the outset in 2001.

Finally, circumstances are auspicious for new courses of globalization inasmuch as ruling élites have gained incentives to support change. Many (though far from all) governance leaders, corporate executives, mainstream journalists, and orthodox academics have acknowledged that reforms to globalization are needed if the social structures that underpin their power (like capitalism and rationalism) are to remain sustainable. Even the biggest winners of neoliberalist globalization have felt some discomforts of ecological insecurity, financial instability and ambiguous identities. Even the greatest ideologues of neoliberalism have noted vocal and sometimes also violent opposition to their cause. Hence recent politics have witnessed the previously noted retreats from ultra-liberalism. Dominant circles aim to keep change to a minimum, of course, and to neutralize dissent with limited concessions. However, proponents of more far-reaching redirections of globalization can exploit this receptiveness to reform among ruling élites to push the agenda beyond 'Washington Plus' to fully fledged global public policies.

Challenges

Not everything is hopeful in the politics of alter-globalizations, though. For one thing, advocates of major change must not underestimate the continuing force of neoliberalist policy frameworks. 'Free market' approaches retain very powerful backing: from commercial quarters, including big capital in particular; from official quarters, including economic and financial policy-makers in particular; and from knowledge-producing quarters, including mainstream mass media and social scientists in particular. Although many public pronouncements from these élites have in recent years conveyed a rhetoric of reform, internal discourses within ruling circles have moved far less. The challenge to deconstruct neoliberalist orthodoxy remains daunting. Support for *laissez-faire*, market-led globalization has deep material and ideational roots. Materially, neoliberalist approaches to globalization have created wealthy, privileged and powerful winners. Ideologically, many proponents of neoliberalism have supported this policy orientation with well-meaning conviction and in some cases evangelical fervour. To date few leading beneficiaries of neoliberalist globalization have followed the examples of the financier George Soros and the economist Joseph Stiglitz in turning to vigorous critique of the approach (Soros, 1998; Stiglitz, 2002).

A second and related major obstacle that stands in the way of alter-globalization politics are the strong monopoly tendencies that have developed in capitalism under neoliberalist policies of the past decades. The main corporate players in contemporary globalization have become very big and very strong. True, outside observers can overestimate the power of global capital. Large transworld companies are not monolithic actors with omnipotent executives at the helm. However, big capital can normally marshal far greater material and ideological resources than the proponents of change. Movements for alternative globalizations therefore need to be conducted in ways that do not provoke concentrated capital to wield its greater power to block the campaigns.

A third big challenge for proponents of redirected globalization is the current concentration of governance power in the US government, coupled with the unreceptiveness of successive US administrations towards the development of full-scale global public policies. The problem is partly structural: the Washington-based state has far more influence than is democratically healthy, both within its own territorial jurisdiction and across the wider world. The problem is also partly national: as noted in Chapter 4, the political culture of US ruling circles has certain qualities (e.g. messianism, manichaeism, and militarism) that tend to make these élites disinclined to engage fully in multilateralism. Although these difficulties have been particularly pronounced during the current presidency of George W. Bush, they have figured to significant degrees in all US administrations, of both

Democrat and Republican parties, across the past half-century of intense globalization.

A fourth major challenge to the implementation of alternative globalizations – the continuing pull of the sovereignty principle – resides both in the USA, where it has been particularly strong, and across the rest of the planet. The proposals for change laid out in this chapter involve considerably increased authority for both substate and suprastate agencies. Moves toward polycentric governance have already progressed considerably, as indicated in Chapter 6. A large expansion of global public policy on the lines described above would extend this trend further and make old notions of sovereignty even more impracticable than they have already become. Still, myths of Westphalian-style sovereignty continue to have widespread currency and attraction. Many people still insist that unilateral, supreme, comprehensive and absolute authority (usually placed in a nation-state) does – or can and should – prevail. These circles need to be persuaded that post-statist governance is not only inevitable in a more global world, but potentially more liberating as well. Contrary to their hopes, continued invocation of Westphalian ideas of sovereignty actually hinders rather than enhances the possibilities of collective self-determination in respect of transplanetary issues.

Fifth, successful implementation of far-reaching global public policies faces the challenge of building sufficient institutional capacity. A turn from neoliberalism to global social democracy requires that public governance bodies obtain considerably increased means to regulate effectively. In some cases the agencies need a larger bulk of resources: more staff, more funds, more equipment, more offices, more data, and so on. In other cases the organizations need to deploy existing resources differently to acquire new capacities. Suprastate institutions in particular lack enough means at present to execute a programme of ambitiously reforming and cautiously transforming globalization. However, proposals for large increases in resources to regional and transworld authorities are likely to face considerable resistance. Even the IMF, while promoting a neoliberalist agenda, has endured a succession of long and hard struggles since the late 1970s to obtain increased quotas, especially from the US Congress. In addition, the various suprastate organizations need vastly to improve their capacities of coordination with each other, in place of the debilitating turf battles and other rivalries that have often hampered global governance to date. Meanwhile, state and substate tiers of governance need to acquire sufficient means to coordinate policy successfully with suprastate bodies. If transplanetary public policies are to be made appropriate to the particular conditions of different countries and districts, then state and substate agencies need to be equipped to achieve that global-local fit. Likewise, representative organs in state and local governments must acquire the capacities to exercise informed democratic checks of the sort recommended earlier on macro-regional and transworld authorities. In short, the struggle to change globalization involves struggles to supply the institutional means to effect that change.

Still another, sixth, major challenge for efforts to redirect globalization on more humane tracks is to mobilize larger publics behind these proposals. Although Jubilee 2000, the WSF and a range of consumer boycotts have impressively demonstrated the possibilities of 'people power' in the politics of globalization, effective public pressure for global change has to date been the exception rather than the rule. Much more needs to be done – through both general public education on globalization and specific campaigns for specific proposals – to build constituencies for a transworld anti-monopoly mechanism, a transplanetary central bank, redistributive global taxes, and alternative identity politics. Different, more progressive courses of globalization cannot be imposed from above. Neoliberalists have usually pursued their agenda with top-down politics, an approach that has generally proved untenable in the long run. Advocates of change must not repeat this mistake.

Finally, implementation of alternative, more humane globalizations must avoid the neoliberalist error of cultural imperialism by constructing fundamentally different kinds of identity politics. This is much easier said than done. Built up over centuries, the immense hubris of western modernism readily stands in the way of veritable intercultural communication and negotiation over the course of globalization. The very proposals outlined in this chapter have a heavily west-centric character. Good intentions notwithstanding, this package of ambitious reformism and cautious transformism could easily become yet another form of neo-colonial imperialism. Thus, rather than being a fixed set of political objectives, the suggestions made here would better be offered up for intercultural deliberations that would no doubt refashion the policies in ways that could attract wider support. The outcome could be something of a global social contract, where parties from different sectors and cultures reach a transplanetary condominium that is politically sustainable.

Conclusion

In a word, this chapter has argued that alternative globalizations are possible, albeit also difficult to achieve. The harms of intensified globality experienced over the past half-century are not integral to transplanetary connectivity as such. As summarized in the box below, many initiatives could steer globalizations toward greater human security, social equality and democracy.

Towards more humane globalizations

Enhancing human security

- subordinate all global governance to human rights standards
- improve regimes for transworld arms control
- upgrade suprastate mechanisms of conflict management
- enhance global rules and regulatory institutions for environmental protection
- develop proactive global public policies on health
- highlight the social dimensions of global economic restructuring
- provide better management of global debts, including cancellation where the burdens are unsustainable
- expand suprastate regulation of global finance
- increase public policies for job creation while also rethinking the nature of work
- intensify suprastate promotion of labour standards
- raise the priority of cultural security and develop ethics of interculturalism to further it
- promote ethical investment practices

Enhancing social equality

- develop suprastate mechanisms to counter monopoly tendencies in global capitalism
- amend global intellectual property rules in favour of subordinated countries and classes
- introduce progressive global taxes
- abolish offshore finance arrangements
- pursue North–South redistribution through changes to global economic regimes
- integrate gender justice concerns into all governance of globalization
- appoint more women to global leadership positions
- increase attention to race, urban/rural, age and other discriminations in global relations

Enhancing democracy

- adopt subsidiarity as a default principle for governing globalization
- improve public education on global affairs
- further raise transparency in the governance of global relations
- reinvigorate electoral politics to give more attention to global concerns
- provide better representation of nonterritorial constituencies in legislative assemblies
- increase parliamentary scrutiny of policies on globalization
- enhance the role of courts, inspectorates and ombudspersons in governing globalization

→

→

- heighten public control of private governance mechanisms that touch public interest and eventually abolish them
- upgrade the involvement of civil society associations in the governance of global relations

Exploiting the possibilities
- enabling technological and organizational developments
- greater public awareness of global problems
- larger transworld solidarities among people
- unprecedented levels of popular mobilization on globalization issues
- increased receptiveness among élites to reform policies on globalization

Addressing the challenges
- continuing substantial force of neoliberalism
- large power of big capital
- resistance of the dominant US state to global public policy
- persistent attachments to myths of (Westphalian) sovereignty
- underdeveloped institutional capacities to formulate and implement global public policies
- limited popular constituencies for far-reaching policy innovations
- inexperience with ethics of interculturalism, particularly among western modernists

Admittedly this chapter has provided only a sketch of more humane redirections of globalization. Further research (some of it already being undertaken by others) is needed to work out the details of the various proposals, to assess more precisely the technicalities of implementation, and to calculate more exactly the likely impacts of the measures. In addition, further political analysis (some of it already ongoing) is needed to determine the most effective ways of overcoming resistance against and building momentum for alternative trajectories of globalization.

However, these detailed investigations go beyond the scope of the present book. This chapter has sought to lay the ground for such work by establishing the key point that major change of globalization is available and desirable. The concern should not be that people are powerless in the face of neoliberalist policies; rather, our disquiet should be that we have not done more to exploit the substantial potentials to chart more progressive courses of globalization.

Conclusion

To boil a dozen chapters down to half a dozen sentences, this critical introduction to globalization has advanced the following replies to the core questions that were set out in its introduction:

1. In terms of definition, the term globalization reveals most about social relations when it is understood as the spread of transplanetary (and in contemporary times also increasingly supraterritorial) connections between people.
2. In terms of chronology, accelerated and intense growth of transplanetary and supraterritorial connectivity has mainly occurred over the past fifty years.
3. In terms of causation, globalization can be explained in terms of a world-systemic dynamic in which the expansion of transplanetary and supraterritorial spaces has interrelated with certain turns in capitalist production, bureaucratic governance, identity politics, and rationalist knowledge.
4. In terms of social continuity and change, the past half-century of heightened globalization has involved important reconfigurations of geography, economy, polity, identity and knowledge, albeit that territoriality, older forms of capital, the state, the nation, and modern rationality still figure crucially in contemporary life.
5. In terms of normative concerns, recent speedy growth of global relations has, next to some important benefits, also significantly undermined human security, social equality and democracy.
6. In terms of policy responses, a politics that combines ambitiously reformist and cautiously transformist measures can substantially reduce potential harms and greatly increase potential gains of heightened transplanetary connectivity in the twenty-first century.

These general conclusions have important implications for social analysis. Contemporary globalization has rendered methodological territorialism obsolete. It is no longer possible to comprehend geography in terms of territorial spaces alone. Significant aspects of social relations now transcend territorial arenas. A post-territorialist conception of social geography goes hand in hand with post-territorialist understandings of culture, ecology, economics, politics and psychology. The major growth of transplanetary and supraterritorial connectivity over the past fifty years requires that social researchers henceforth pose their questions and develop their answers in a different kind of spatial frame. In addition, researchers can – as attempted in this book – use studies of globalization as an occasion to transcend disciplinary divides and to reformulate general models of social explanation.

This book's account of globalization also has significant implications for political practice. Heightened levels of transplanetary connectivity have rendered statist policy and nationalist citizenship of an earlier era obsolete. Today every substantive issue-area – be it health, leisure, migration or warfare – needs to be addressed through multi-scalar governance that includes a notable transworld dimension. Correspondingly, to achieve a good society in this more global world, the polity needs to be reconstructed in a post-territorialist fashion, where citizen rights and responsibilities acquire suprastate as well as state-bound qualities.

As seen in Chapters 6 and 7, some moves towards polycentric governance and multidimensional citizenship have already transpired. However, it may be hoped that books such as this one can help political consciousness and practices to catch up with larger historical trends. Indeed, as stressed throughout, this critical introduction has aimed to empower as well as enlighten. The more people understand globalization, the more they can realize their potentials to shape it in their preferred directions. This book opened with a concerned citizen's frustrations that 'we don't know what globalization is, but we have to act!' Hopefully the book now closes leaving the reader with greater comprehension and greater capacity for informed and effective action.

Bibliography

2B1 (2004) Website of the 2B1 Foundation, www.2b1.org, accessed on 22 October.

Abegglen, J. C. (1994) *Sea Change: Pacific Asia as the New World Industrial Center*. New York: Free Press.

Abrahams, D. (2004) *Regulating Corporations: A Resource Guide*. Geneva: United Nations Research Institute for Social Development.

Abramson, J. B. *et al.* (1988) *The Electronic Commonwealth: The Impact of New Media Technologies on Democratic Politics*. New York: Basic Books.

Abu-Lughod, J. L. (1989) *Before European Hegemony: The World System A.D. 1250–1350*. New York: Oxford University Press.

Abu-Lughod, L. (1989) 'Bedouins, Cassettes and Technologies of Public Culture', *Middle East Report*, no. 159 (July–August), pp. 7–11.

Adam, B. D. (1987) *The Rise of a Gay and Lesbian Movement*. Boston, MA: Twayne.

Adam, B. D. *et al.* (eds) (1999) *The Global Emergence of Gay and Lesbian Politics: National Imprints of a Worldwide Movement*. Philadelphia: Temple University Press.

ADB (1999) *Cooperation with Civil Society Organizations: Policy and Guidelines*. Abidjan: African Development Bank, October.

Adler, E. (2003) 'Constructivism and International Relations', in W. Carlsnaes *et al.* (eds), *Handbook of International Relations*. London: Sage, pp. 95–118.

Aghion, P. and J. G. Williamson (1998) *Growth, Inequality and Globalization*. Cambridge: Cambridge University Press.

Agnew, J. (1998) *Geopolitics: Re-visioning World Politics*. London: Routledge.

Ahvenainen, J. (1981) *The Far Eastern Telegraphs: the History of Telegraphic Communications between the Far East, Europe and America before the First World War*. Helsinki: Suomalainen Tiedeakatemia.

AI-LGBT (2005) Website of the Amnesty International Lesbian, Gay, Bisexual and Transgender Network, www.ai-lgbt.org, accessed on 18 January.

Ake, C. (1999) 'Globalization, Multilateralism and the Shrinking Democratic Space', in M. G. Schechter (ed.), *Future Multilateralism: The Political and Social Framework*. Tokyo: United Nations University Press, pp. 179–95.

Akehurst, M. (1972–3) 'Jurisdiction in International Law', *British Yearbook of International Law*, vol. 46, pp. 145–257.

Alber, J. and G. Standing (eds) (2000) 'Social Dumping, Catch-up or Convergence? Europe in a Comparative Global Context', *Journal of European Social Policy*, vol. 10, no. 2 (May), pp. 99–119.

Albert, M. and L. Hilkermeier (eds) (2004) *Observing World Politics: Niklas Luhmann and International Relations*. London: Routledge.

Albrow, M. (1996) *The Global Age: State and Society Beyond Modernity*. Cambridge: Polity Press.

Aldecoa, F. and M. Keating (eds) (1999) *Paradiplomacy in Action: The Foreign Relations of Subnational Governments*. London: Frank Cass.

Alexander, T. (1996) *Unravelling Global Apartheid: An Overview of World Politics*. Cambridge: Polity Press.

Altman, D. (2001) *Global Sex*. Chicago: University of Chicago Press.

Amin, A. (ed.) (1994) *Post-Fordism: A Reader*. Oxford: Blackwell.

Amin, A. (1997) 'Placing Globalization', *Theory, Culture and Society*, vol. 14, no. 2 (May), pp. 123–38.

Amin, S. (1996) 'The Challenge of Globalization', *Review of International Political Economy*, vol. 3, no. 2 (Summer), pp. 216–59.

Amin, S. (1997) *Capitalism in the Age of Globalization*. London: Zed.
Anaya, S.J. (1996) *Indigenous Peoples in International Law*. New York: Oxford University Press.
Anderson, B. (1992) *Long-Distance Nationalism: World Capitalism and the Rise of Identity Politics*. Amsterdam: Centre for Asian Studies Amsterdam.
Anderson, B. (2000) *Doing the Dirty Work: The Global Politics of Domestic Labour*. London: Zed.
Anderson, J. (1996) 'The Shifting Stage of Politics: New Medieval and Postmodern Territorialities?', *Environment and Planning D: Society and Space*, vol. 14, no. 2 (April), pp. 133–53.
Anderson, M. (1989) *Policing the World: Interpol and the Politics of International Police Co-operation*. Oxford: Clarendon.
Anderson, T. L. and D. R. Leal (1991) *Free Market Environmentalism*. Oxford: Westview.
Anderson, T. L. and D. R. Leal (1997) *Enviro-Capitalists: Doing Good While Doing Well*. Lanham, MD: Rowman & Littlefield.
Anderson, W. T. (1990) *Reality Isn't What It Used To Be: Theatrical Politics, Ready-to-Wear Religion, Global Myths, Primitive Chic, and Other Wonders of the Postmodern World*. San Francisco: Harper & Row.
Andriof, J. and M. McIntosh (eds) (2001) *Perspectives on Corporate Citizenship*. Sheffield: Greenleaf.
Anheier, H. *et al.* (eds) (2001) *Global Civil Society 2001*. Oxford: Oxford University Press.
Aniol, W. (2002) *Paradoksy globalizacji* ['Paradoxes of Globalization']. Warsaw: Aspra.
Antrobus, P. (2004) *The Global Women's Movement: Origins, Issues and Strategies*. London: Zed.
AP (1999a) 'Indonesians Living in Poverty Reach 130 Million', Associated Press newswire, 15 January.
AP (1999b) 'World Bank Estimates 200 Million "Newly Poor" ', Associated Press newswire, 3 June.
Appadurai, A. (1990) 'Disjuncture and Difference in the Global Cultural Economy', *Public Culture*, vol. 2, no. 3 (Spring), pp. 1–24.
Appadurai, A. (1996) *Modernity at Large: Cultural Dimensions of Globalization*. Minneapolis, MN: University of Minnesota Press.
Appiah, K. A. and H. L. Gates (eds) (1997) *The Dictionary of Global Culture*. New York: Knopf.
Araghi, F. A. (1995) 'Global Depeasantization, 1945–1990', *The Sociological Quarterly*, vol. 36, no. 2 (Spring), pp. 337–68.
Archer, M. (1990) 'Foreword', in M. Albrow and E. King (eds), *Globalization, Knowledge and Society: Readings from International Sociology*. London: Sage, pp. 1–2.
Archibugi, D. (ed.) (2003) *Debating Cosmopolitics*. London: Verso.
Archibugi, D. *et al.* (eds) (1998) *Re-imagining Political Community: Studies in Cosmopolitan Democracy*. Cambridge: Polity Press.
Arituwa, P. (2003) Author's interview with the head of the Human Rights and Governance Department, Uganda Joint Christian Council, Kampala, August.
Armijo, L.E. (ed.) (1999) *Financial Globalization and Democracy in Emerging Markets*. Basingstoke: Palgrave Macmillan.
Aronowitz, S. and W. DiFazio (1994) *The Jobless Future: Sci-Tech and the Dogma of Work*. Minneapolis, MN: University of Minnesota Press.
Aslanbeigui, N. *et al.* (eds) (1994) *Women in the Age of Economic Transformation. Gender Impact of Reforms in Post-Socialist and Developing Countries*. London: Routledge.
Augé, M. (1992) *Non-Places: Introduction to an Anthropology of Supermodernity*. London: Verso, 1995.
Augé, M. (1994) *An Anthropology for Contemporaneous Worlds*. Stanford, CA: Stanford University Press, 1999.
Aviat, A. and N. Coeurdacier (2004) 'The Geography of Trade in Goods and Assets'. Paper for the CESifo Venice Summer Institute Workshop on Dissecting Globalization, 21–22 July.

Axford, B. (1995) *The Global System: Economics, Politics and Culture.* Cambridge: Polity Press.

Bacchetta, M. *et al.* (1998) *Electronic Commerce and the Role of the WTO.* Geneva: World Trade Organization.

Badie, B. (1995) *La fin des territories. Essai sur le désordre international et sur l'utilité social du respect.* Paris: Fayard.

Baer, J. B. and O. G. Saxon (1949) *Commodity Exchanges and Futures Trading.* New York: Harper & Brothers.

Baker, D. *et al.* (eds) (1998) *Globalization and Progressive Economic Policy.* Cambridge: Cambridge University Press.

Balaam, D. N. and M. V. Veseth (2001) *Introduction to International Political Economy.* Upper Saddle River, NJ: Prentice-Hall, 2nd edn.

Balanyá, B. *et al.* (2000) *Europe Inc.: Regional and Global Restructuring and the Rise of Corporate Power.* London: Pluto.

Baldwin, R. E. and P. Martin (1999) 'Two Waves of Globalization: Superficial Similarities, Fundamental Differences', in H. Siebert (ed.), *Globalization and Labor.* Tübingen: Mohr Siebeck, pp. 3–58.

Balleroni, E. (1995) 'Women To Be Given Priority', *Politiken Summit*, 8 March, p. 7.

Bamyeh, M. (2000) *The Ends of Globalization.* Minneapolis: University of Minnesota Press.

Bandow, D. and I. Vásquez (eds) (1994) *Perpetuating Poverty: The World Bank, the IMF, and the Developing World.* Washington, DC: Cato Institute.

Barber, B. R. (1996) *Jihad vs. McWorld.* New York: Ballantine.

Barker, D. and J. Mander (n.d.) *Invisible Government – the World Trade Organization: Global Government for the New Millennium?* San Francisco: International Forum on Globalization.

Barlow, M. and T. Clarke (2001) *Global Showdown: How the New Activists Are Fighting Global Corporate Rule.* Toronto: Stoddart.

Barnet, R. J. and J. Cavanagh (1994) *Global Dreams: Imperial Corporations and the New World Order.* New York: Simon & Schuster.

Barnett, M. (2005) 'Social Constructivism', in J. Baylis and S. Smith (eds), *The Globalization of World Politics: An Introduction to International Relations.* Oxford: Oxford University Press, 3rd edn, pp. 251–70.

Barnett, T. and A. Whiteside (2002) *AIDS in the Twenty-First Century: Disease and Globalization.* Basingstoke: Palgrave Macmillan.

Barr, G. (2002) President of the Canadian Council for International Co-operation, in discussion with the author, Ottawa, 2 May.

Bartlett, C. A. and S. Ghoshal (1998) *Managing Across Borders: The Transnational Solution.* London: Random House Business Books, 2nd edn.

Basch, L. G. *et al.* (1994) *Nations Unbound: Transnational Projects, Postcolonial Predicaments, and Deterritorialized Nation-States.* Langhorne, PA: Gordon & Breach.

Bastian, J.-P. *et al.* (eds) (2001) *La globalisation du réligieux.* Paris: Harmattan.

Bauman, Z. (1998) *Globalization: The Human Consequences.* Cambridge: Polity Press

Baylis, J. and S. Smith (eds) (2005) *The Globalization of World Politics: An Introduction to International Relations.* Oxford: Oxford University Press, 3rd edn.

Bayne, N. (2000) *Hanging in There: The G7 and G8 Summit in Maturity and Renewal.* Aldershot: Ashgate.

Beales, A. C. F. (1931) *The History of Peace: A Short Account of the Organised Movements for International Peace.* London: Bell.

Beck, U. (1986) *Risk Society: Towards a New Modernity.* London: Sage, 1992.

Beck, U. (1988) *Ecological Politics in an Age of Risk.* Cambridge: Polity Press, 1995.

Beck, U. (1994) 'The Reinvention of Politics: Towards a Theory of Reflexive Modernization', in U. Beck *et al.*, *Reflexive Modernization: Politics, Tradition and Aesthetics in the Modern Social Order.* Cambridge: Polity Press, pp. 1–55.

Beck, U. (1997) *The Reinvention of Politics: Rethinking Modernity in the Global Social Order.* Cambridge: Polity Press.

Beck, U. (1999) *World Risk Society*. Cambridge: Polity Press.

Beetham, D. (1997) 'Market Economy and Democratic Polity', *Democratization*, vol. 4, no. 1 (Spring), pp. 76–93.

Bell, D. (1973) *The Coming of Post-Industrial Society*. London: Heinemann.

Bellamy Foster, J. (1994) 'Waste Away', *Dollars & Sense*, no. 195 (September–October), p. 7.

Bello, W. (2004) *Deglobalization: Ideas for a New World Economy*. London: Zed, 2nd edn.

Bello, W. *et al.* (1994) *Dark Victory: The United States, Structural Adjustment, and Global Poverty*. London: Pluto.

Bendell, J. (2004) *Barricades and Boardrooms: A Contemporary History of the Corporate Accountability Movement*. Geneva: United Nations Research Institute for Social Development, Technology, Business and Society Programme Paper No. 13.

Benedick, R. E. (1998) *Ozone Diplomacy: New Directions in Safeguarding the Planet*. Cambridge, MA: Harvard University Press, rev'd edn.

Beneria, L. and S. Feldman (eds) (1992) *Unequal Burden: Economic Crises, Persistent Poverty, and Women's Work*. Boulder, CO: Westview.

Bennett, A. (1999) 'Hip Hop am Main: The Localization of Rap Music and Hip Hop Culture', *Media, Culture & Society*, vol. 21, no. 1 (January), pp. 77–91.

Bentham, J. (1789) *An Introduction to the Principles of Morals and Legislation*. London: Hafner, 1948.

Berdal, M. and M. Serrano (eds) (2002) *Transnational Organized Crime and International Security: Business as Usual?* Boulder, CO: Rienner.

Berger, J. *et al.* (1998–9) 'The Threat of Globalism', *Race & Class*, vol. 40, nos 2/3 (October–March).

Berger, P. (ed.) (1999) *The Desecularization of the World: Resurgent Religion and World Politics*. Washington, DC: Eerdmans.

Berger, P. L. and S. P. Huntington (eds) (2002) *Many Globalizations: Cultural Diversity in the Contemporary World*. Oxford: Oxford University Press.

Bergsten, C. F. (1996) 'Globalizing Free Trade', *Foreign Affairs*, vol. 75, no. 3 (May/June), pp. 105–20.

Berkovitch, N. (1999) *From Motherhood to Citizenship: Women's Rights and International Organizations*. Baltimore, MD: Johns Hopkins University Press.

Bernal, M. (1987) *Black Athena: The Afroasiatic Roots of Classical Civilization*. London: Free Association Books.

Berry, A. (2002) 'Globalization, Liberalization and Inequality: An Analysis with Focus on Data Problems'. Paper presented at the UNRISD Conference on Improving Knowledge of Social Development in International Organizations, Nyon, 30 May.

Beyer, P. (1994) *Religion and Globalization*. London: Sage.

Beynon, J. and D. Dunkerley (eds) (2000) *Globalization: The Reader*. London: Athlone.

Bhagwati, J. N. (ed.) (1977) *The New International Economic Order: The North–South Debate*. Cambridge, MA: MIT Press.

Bhagwati, J. N. (2004) *In Defense of Globalization*. New York: Oxford University Press.

Bhalla, S. S. (2002) *Imagine There's No Country: Poverty, Inequality, and Growth in the Era of Globalization*. Washington, DC: Institute for International Economics.

Biel, R. (2000) *The New Imperialism: Crisis and Contradictions in North–South Relations*. London: Zed.

Biermann, F. (2000) 'The Case for a World Environment Organization', *Environment*, vol. 42 (November), pp. 22–31.

Biersteker, T. J. and C. Weber (eds) (1996) *State Sovereignty as Social Construct*. Cambridge: Cambridge University Press.

Bircham, E. and J. Charlton (eds) (2001) *Anti-Capitalism: A Guide to the Movement*. London: Bookmarks.

BIS (1996) *International Banking and Financial Market Developments*. Basle: Bank for International Settlements.

BIS (1997) *Core Principles for Effective Banking Supervision*. Basle: Bank for International Settlements.

BIS (1998) *68th Annual Report*. Basle: Bank for International Settlements.

BIS (2000a) 'Quarterly Review: International Banking and Financial Market Developments', June.

BIS (2000b) *70th Annual Report*. Basle: Bank for International Settlements.

BIS (2001a) 'Central Bank Survey of Foreign Exchange and Derivatives Market Activity in April 2001: Preliminary Global Data', Bank for International Settlements press release, 9 October.

BIS (2001b) *Quarterly Review, December 2001*. Basle: Bank for International Settlements.

BIS (2001c) *71st Annual Report*. Basle: Bank for International Settlements.

BIS (2004) *OTC Derivatives Market Activity in the Second Half of 2003*. Basle: Bank for International Settlements Monetary and Economic Department.

Blaney, D. and N. Inayatullah (1994) 'Prelude to a Conversation of Cultures in International Society? Todorov and Nandy on the Possibility of Dialogue', *Alternatives*, vol. 19, no. 1 (Winter), pp. 23–51.

Bleeke, J. and D. Ernst (eds) (1993) *Collaborating to Compete: Using Strategic Alliances and Acquisitions in the Global Marketplace*. New York: John Wiley.

Bleiker, R. (2000) *Popular Dissent, Human Agency and Global Politics*. Cambridge: Cambridge University Press.

Blinder, A. S. (1999) 'Eight Steps to a New Financial Order', *Foreign Affairs*, vol. 78, no. 5 (September–October), pp. 50–63.

Block, F. (2003) 'Karl Polanyi and the Writing of *The Great Transformation*', *Theory & Society*, vol. 32, no. 3, pp. 1–32.

Blustein, P. (2001) *The Chastening: Inside the Crisis that Rocked the Global Financial System and Humbled the IMF*. Washington, DC: Public Affairs.

Boden, D. (1990) 'Reinventing the Global Village: Communication and the Revolutions of 1989', in A. Giddens (ed.), *Human Societies: An Introductory Reader in Sociology*. Cambridge: Polity Press, 1992, pp. 327–31.

Bolger, A. (2004) 'FT500: Insurance', *Financial Times*, 27 May, p. 7.

Boli, J. (2006) 'World Polity Theory', in R. Robertson and J. A. Scholte (eds), *Encyclopaedia of Globalization*. London: Routledge.

Boli, J. and G. M. Thomas (1999) *Constructing World Culture: International Nongovernmental Organizations since 1875*. Stanford, CA: Stanford University Press.

Bond, P. and N. Bullard (1999) *Their Reform and Ours: The Balance of Forces and Economic Analysis that Inform a New Global Financial Architecture*. Bangkok: Chulalongkorn University Press.

Booth, K. (ed.) (1991) *New Thinking about Strategy and International Security*. London: HarperCollins.

Booth, K. and T. Dunne (eds) (2002) *Worlds in Collision: Terror and the Future of Global Order*. Basingstoke: Palgrave Macmillan.

Bordo, M. D. *et al.* (1999) 'Is Globalization Today Really Different than Globalization a Hundred Years Ago?', in S. M. Collins and R. Z. Lawrence (eds), *Brookings Trade Forum 1999*. Washington, DC: Brookings Institution Press.

Born, G. B. (1996) *International Civil Litigation in United States Courts: Commentary and Materials*. London: Kluwer Law International, 3rd edn.

Born, K. E. (1977) *International Banking in the 19th and 20th Centuries*. Leamington Spa: Berg.

Boughton, J. (2001) *Silent Revolution: The International Monetary Fund 1979–89*. Washington, DC: International Monetary Fund.

Bouma, J. J. *et al.* (eds) (2001) *Sustainable Banking: The Greening of Finance*. Sheffield: Greenleaf/Deloitte and Touche.

Bourdieu, P. (1998) *Acts of Resistance: Against the New Myths of Our Time*. Cambridge: Polity.

Bové, J. and F. Dufour (2001) *The World Is Not for Sale: Farmers against Junk Food*. London: Verso.

Bowles, P. and B. Wagman (1997) 'Globalization and the Welfare State: Four Hypotheses and Some Empirical Evidence', *Eastern Economic Journal*, vol. 23, no. 3, pp. 317–36.

Boyer, R. and D. Drache (eds) (1996) *States against Markets: The Limits of Globalization.* London: Routledge.
Boyle, E. H. (2002) *Female Genital Cutting: Cultural Conflict in the Global Community.* Baltimore, MD: Johns Hopkins University Press.
Bradford, S. and R. Z. Lawrence (2004) *Has Globalization Gone Far Enough? The Costs of Fragmented Markets.* Washington, DC: Institute for International Economics.
Brand, U. *et al.* (2000) *Global Governance. Alternative zur neoliberalen Globalisierung?* Münster: Westfälisches Dampfboot.
Bratton, W. W. *et al.* (eds) (1996) *International Regulatory Competition and Coordination: Perspectives on Economic Regulation in Europe and the United States.* Oxford: Clarendon.
Braudel, F. (1958) 'History and the Social Sciences: The *Longue Durée*', in *On History*. London: Weidenfeld & Nicolson, 1980, pp. 25–54.
Braudel, F. (1979a) *Civilization and Capitalism 15th–18th Century. Volume II: The Wheels of Commerce.* London: Collins, 1983.
Braudel, F. (1979b) *Civilization and Capitalism 15th–18th Century. Volume III: The Perspective of the World.* London: Collins, 1984.
Brayton, S. (2002) 'Outsourcing War: Mercenaries and the Privatization of Peacekeeping', *Journal of International Affairs*, vol. 55, no. 2 (Spring), pp. 303–29.
Brecher, J. and T. Costello (1994) *Global Village or Global Pillage: Economic Reconstruction from the Bottom Up.* Boston, MA: South End Press.
Breidenbach, J. and I. Zukrigl (1998) *Tanz der Kulturen. Kulturelle Identität in einer globalisierten Welt.* Munich: Kunstmann.
Brenner, N. (1998) 'Global Cities, Glocal States: Global City Formation and State Territorial Restructuring in Contemporary Europe', *Review of International Political Economy*, vol. 5, no. 1 (Spring), pp. 1–37.
Brenner, N. (1999) 'Beyond State-Centrism? Space, Territoriality, and Geographical Scale in Globalization Studies', *Theory and Society*, vol. 28, no. 1 (February), pp. 39–78.
Brenner, N. *et al.* (eds) (2003) *State/Space: A Reader.* Oxford: Blackwell.
Breslin, S. (2000) 'Decentralisation, Globalisation and China's Partial Re-engagement with the Global Economy', *New Political Economy*, vol. 5, no. 2 (July), pp. 205–26.
Breslin, S. and G. D. Hook (eds) (2002) *Microregionalism and World Order.* Basingstoke: Palgrave Macmillan.
Breslin, S. *et al.* (eds) (2002) *New Regionalisms in the Global Political Economy: Theories and Cases.* London: Routledge.
Bretherton, C. and J. Vogler (1999) *The European Union as a Global Actor.* London: Routledge.
Breton, G. and M. Lambert (eds) (2003) *Universities and Globalization: Private Linkages, Public Trust.* Paris: United Nations Educational, Scientific and Cultural Organization.
Broad, R. (ed.) (2002) *Global Backlash: Citizen Initiatives for a Just World Economy.* Lanham, MD: Rowman & Littlefield.
Brock, L. (1993) 'Im Umbruch der Weltpolitik', *Leviathan*, vol. 21, no. 2, pp. 163–73.
Bromley, S. (1999) 'Marxism and Globalisation', in A. Gamble *et al.* (eds), *Marxism and Social Science.* Basingstoke: Palgrave Macmillan, pp. 280–301.
Brotton, J. (1999) 'Terrestrial Globalism: Mapping the Globe in Early Modern Europe', in D. Cosgrove (ed.), *Mappings.* London: Reaktion Books, pp. 71–89.
Brown, C. (2001) 'Cosmopolitanism, World Citizenship and Global Civil Society', *Critical Review of International Social and Political Philosophy*, vol. 3, no. 1 (Summer), pp. 7–27.
Brown, D. M. and E. H. Fry (eds) (1993) *States and Provinces in the International Economy.* Berkeley, CA: Institute of Governmental Studies Press, University of California.
Brown, L. D. *et al.* (2001) 'Civil Society Legitimacy: A Discussion Guide', in Brown (ed.), *Practice-Research Engagement and Civil Society in a Globalizing World.* Cambridge, MA: Hauser Center for Nonprofit Organizations, Harvard University.
Brown, N. (1990) *New Strategy through Space.* Leicester: Leicester University Press.

Brown, R. (1995) 'Globalization and the End of the National Project', in J. Macmillan and A. Linklater (eds), *Boundaries in Question: New Directions in International Relations*. London: Pinter, pp. 54–68.

Brown, T. (1999) 'World Financial Crisis Not Over – UNICEF's Bellamy', Reuters despatch of 29 April.

Brühl, T. *et al.* (eds) (2001) *Die Privatisierung der Weltpolitik. Entstaatlichung und Kommerzialisierung im Globalisierungsprozeß*. Bonn: Dietz.

Brundtland, G. H. (2000) Address to the Annual Conference of the Academic Council of the United Nations System, Oslo, 17 June.

Bryan, L. and D. Farrell (1996) *Market Unbound: Unleashing Global Capitalism*. New York: John Wiley.

Bryant, C. G. A. and D. Jary (eds) (1991) *Giddens' Theory of Structuration: A Critical Appreciation*. London: Routledge.

Bryant, R. C. (1999) 'Standards and Prudential Oversight for an Integrating World Financial System'. Paper for a meeting of the Tokyo Club Foundation for Global Studies and the Royal Institute of International Affairs.

Bryant, R. C. (2000) *Turbulent Waters: Cross-Border Finance in the 21st Century*. Washington, DC: Brookings Institution.

Brysk, A. (2000) *From Tribal Village to Global Village: Indian Rights and International Relations in Latin America*. Stanford, CA: Stanford University Press.

Bryson, J. R. and P. W. Daniels (eds) (1998) *Service Industries in the Global Economy*, 2 vols. Cheltenham: Elgar.

Brzezinski, Z. (1993) *Out of Control: Global Turmoil on the Eve of the Twenty-First Century*. New York: Charles Scribner's Sons.

BT (2000) *Variety and Values: a Sustainable Response to Globalisation?* London: British Telecommunications Corporate Reputation & Social Policy Unit.

Buchanan, P.J. (1998) *The Great Betrayal: How American Sovereignty and Social Justice Are Being Sacrificed to the Gods of the Global Economy*. Boston, MA: Little, Brown.

Budge, I. (1996) *The New Challenge of Direct Democracy*. Cambridge: Polity Press.

Budhoo, D. L. (1990) *Enough Is Enough*. New York: Apex.

Buell, F. (1994) *National Culture and the New Global System*. Baltimore: Johns Hopkins University Press.

Buira, A. (ed.) (2003) *Challenges to the World Bank and IMF: Developing Country Perspectives*. London: Anthem.

Bull, H. (1977) *The Anarchical Society: A Study of Order in World Politics*. Basingstoke: Palgrave Macmillan.

Bunch, C. and N. Reilly (1994) *Demanding Accountability: the Global Campaign and Vienna Tribunal for Women's Human Rights*. New York: Center for Women's Global Leadership and the United Nations Development Fund for Women.

Burbach, R. and K. Danaher (eds) (2000) *Globalize This! The Battle against the World Trade Organization and Corporate Rule*. Monroe, ME: Common Courage Press.

Burbach, R. and W. I. Robinson (1999) 'The Fin de Siècle Debate: Globalization as Epochal Shift', *Science and Society*, vol. 63, no.1 (Spring), pp. 10–39.

Burbach, R. *et al.* (1997) *Globalization and its Discontents: The Rise of Postmodern Socialisms*. London: Pluto.

Burchill, S. *et al.* (2005) *Theories of International Relations*. Basingstoke: Palgrave Macmillan, 3rd edn.

Burki, S. J. and G. Perry (1998) *Beyond the Washington Consensus: Institutions Matter*. Washington, DC: World Bank.

Burnham, P. (1997) 'Globalisation: States, Markets and Class Relations', *Historical Materialism*, vol. 1, no. 1, pp. 150–60.

Burtless, G. *et al.* (1998) *Globaphobia: Confronting Fears about Open Trade*. Washington, DC: Brookings Institution.

Burton, J.W. (1972) *World Society*. Cambridge: Cambridge University Press.

Cable, V. (1994) *The World's New Fissures: Identities in Crisis.* London: Demos.

Cable, V. (1995) 'The Diminished Nation-State: A Study in the Loss of Economic Power', *Daedalus*, vol. 124, no. 2 (Spring), pp. 23–54.

Cable, V. (1999) *Globalization and Global Governance.* London: Pinter.

Cairncross, F. (1997) *The Death of Distance: How the Communications Revolution Will Change Our Lives.* London: Orion Business.

Calvocoressi, P. (1987) *A Time for Peace: Pacifism, Internationalism and Protest Forces in the Reduction of War.* London: Hutchinson.

Cameron, R. and V. I. Bovykin (eds) (1991) *International Banking 1870–1914.* New York: Oxford University Press.

Cameron, A. and R. Palan (2004) *The Imagined Economies of Globalization.* London: Sage.

Camilleri, J. A. and J. Falk (1992) *The End of Sovereignty? The Politics of a Shrinking and Fragmenting World.* Aldershot: Elgar.

Camilleri, J. A. *et al.* (eds) (1995) *The State in Transition: Reimagining Political Space.* Boulder, CO: Rienner.

Campbell, D. (1998) *Writing Security: United States Foreign Policy and the Politics of Identity.* Manchester: Manchester University Press, rev'd edn.

Campbell, D. and M. Dillon (eds) (1993) *The Political Subject of Violence.* Manchester: Manchester University Press.

Campbell, T. (1987) *The Earliest Printed Maps 1472–1500.* London: British Library.

CapGemini (2004) *World Wealth Report 2004*, online at: www.us.capgemini.com/DownloadLibrary/files/FSI_WorldWealthReport2004.pdf – accessed on 28 October.

Cardenas, S. (2003) 'Emerging Global Actors: The United Nations and National Human Rights Institutions', *Global Governance*, vol. 9, no. 1 (January–March), pp. 23–42.

Cardoso, F. H. (1996) 'La globalización y et nuevo orden mundial', *Boletín editorial de el Colegio de Mexico*, No. 68.

Carlsson, I. *et al.* (1995) *Our Global Neighbourhood.* Oxford: Oxford University Press.

Carneiro, S. (2002) Executive Coordinator of Geledes – Black Woman's Institute, interviewed by the author in Porto Alegre, Brazil, 1 February.

Carnoy, M. *et al.* (1993) *The New Global Economy in the Information Age.* University Park, PA: Pennsylvania State University Press.

Carothers, T. (2000) 'Struggling with Semi-Authoritarians', in P. Burnell (ed.), *Democracy Assistance: International Co-operation for Democratization*, London: Frank Cass, pp. 210–26.

Carter, A. (2001) *The Political Theory of Global Citizenship.* London: Routledge.

Castells, M. (1989) *The Informational City: Information Technology, Economic Restructuring, and the Urban-Regional Process.* Oxford: Blackwell.

Castells, M. (1996–7) *The Information Age: Economy, Society and Culture.* Oxford: Blackwell.

Castells, M. (2001) *The Internet Galaxy: Reflections on the Internet, Business, and Society.* Oxford: Oxford University Press.

Castles, S. (2000) *Ethnicity and Globalization: From Migrant Worker to Transnational Citizen.* London: Sage.

Castles, S. and A. Davidson (2000) *Citizenship and Migration: Globalization and the Politics of Belonging.* Basingstoke: Palgrave Macmillan.

Castles, S. and M.J. Miller (1998) *The Age of Migration: International Population Movements in the Modern World.* Basingstoke: Palgrave Macmillan, 2nd edn.

Cerny, P. G. (1990) *The Changing Architecture of Politics: Structure, Agency and the Future of the State.* London: Sage.

Cerny, P. G. (1993) 'Plurilateralism: Structural Differentiation and Functional Conflict in the Post-Cold War World Order', *Millennium*, vol. 22, no.1 (Spring), pp. 27–51.

Cerny, P. G. (1996) 'Globalization and Other Stories: the Search for a New Paradigm for International Relations', *International Journal*, vol. 51, no. 4 (Autumn), pp. 617–37.

Cerny, P. G. (1997) 'Paradoxes of the Competition State: The Dynamics of Political Globalization', *Government and Opposition*, vol. 32, no. 2 (Spring), pp. 251–74.

Cervinski, G. (2004) Member of the National Council of the Movement of Dam-Affected People, in discussion with the author in Brasilia, 20 November.

CFGS (2001) *Rethinking Governance: An Inventory of Ideas to Enhance Participation, Transparency and Accountability*. Victoria, BC: University of Victoria Centre for Global Studies.

Chambers, S. and W. Kymlicka (eds) (2002) *Alternative Conceptions of Civil Society*. Princeton, NJ: Princeton University Press.

Chandler, A. D. (1986) 'The Evolution of Modern Global Competition', in M. E. Porter (ed.), *Competition in Global Industries*. Boston, MA: Harvard Business School Press, pp. 405–48.

Chase-Dunn, C. K. (1989) *Global Formation: Structures of the World Economy*. Oxford: Blackwell.

Cheah, P. and B. Robbins (eds) (1998) *Cosmopolitics: Thinking and Feeling beyond the Nation*. Minneapolis, MN: University of Minnesota Press.

Chesnaid, F. (1994) *La mondialisation du capital*. Paris: Syros.

Chesnais, F. *et al.* (eds) (2000) *European Integration and Global Corporate Strategies*. London: Routledge.

Childers, E. (1994) 'United Nations Reform: Relevance of the Southern Perspective'. Geneva: International NGO Network on Global Governance and Democratization of International Relations, Topical Papers 3.

CHIPS (2005) Website of the Clearing House Interbank Payment System www.chips.org, accessed on 24 January.

Chomsky, N. (1998) *Profits over People: Neoliberalism and the Global Order*. New York: West Group.

Chopra, J. and T. G. Weiss (1992) 'Sovereignty Is No Longer Sacrosanct: Codifying Humanitarian Intervention', *Ethics and International Affairs*, vol. 6, pp. 95–117.

Chossudovsky, M. (1997) *The Globalisation of Poverty: Impacts of IMF and World Bank Reforms*. London: Zed.

Chowdhry, G. and S. Nair (eds) (2002) *Power, Postcolonialism, and International Relations: Reading Race, Gender, and Class*. London: Routledge.

CHS (2003) *Human Security Now: Protecting and Empowering People*. New York: Commission on Human Security. Also online at www.humansecurity-chs.org.

CI (2005) Website of Consumers International: www.consumersinternational. org, accessed on 3 February.

CIA (2004) Website of the Computer Industry Almanac, www.c-i-a.com/, press release of 3 September, accessed on 28 October.

Cipolla, C. M. (1956) *Money, Prices, and Civilization in the Mediterranean World: Fifth to Seventeenth Century*. Princeton, NJ: Princeton University Press.

CIPR (2002) *Integrating Intellectual Property Rights and Development Policy*. London: Commission on Intellectual Property Rights, UK Department for International Development.

Clapp, J. (1998) 'The Privatization of Global Environmental Governance: ISO 14000 and the Developing World', *Global Governance*, vol. 4, no. 3 (July–September), pp. 295–316.

Clapp, J. (2002) 'What the Pollution Havens Debate Overlooks', *Global Environmental Politics*, vol. 2, no. 2 (May), pp. 11–19.

Clark, I. (1997) *Globalization and Fragmentation: International Relations in the Twentieth Century*. Oxford: Oxford University Press.

Clark, I. (1999) *Globalization and International Relations Theory*. Oxford: Oxford University Press.

Clark, J. D. (2001) 'Ethical Globalization: the Dilemmas and Challenges of Internationalizing Civil Society', in M. Edwards and J. Gaventa (eds), *Global Citizen Action*. Boulder, CO: Rienner, pp. 17–28.

Clark, J. D. (ed.) (2003) *Globalizing Civic Engagement: Civil Society and Transnational Action*. London: Earthscan.

Clayton, M. and A. Williams (eds) (2000) *The Ideal of Equality*. Basingstoke: Palgrave Macmillan.

Clift, B. (2003) *French Socialism in a Global Era*. London: Continuum.

CLS (2004) 'CLS Bank Settles New Record Value', press release of 15 December, posted on the website of the Continuous Linked Settlement Bank, www.cls-group.com/news, accessed on 21 January 2005.

Cockburn, A. and J. St. Clair (2000) *Five Days that Shook the World: Seattle and Beyond*. London: Verso.

Cohen, B. J. (1977) *Organizing the World's Money: The Political Economy of International Monetary Relations*. Basingstoke: Palgrave Macmillan, 1978.

Cohen, E. S. (2001) 'Globalization and the Boundaries of the State: A Framework for Analyzing the Changing Practice of Sovereignty', *Governance*, vol. 14, no. 1 (January), pp. 75–97.

Cohen, J. L. and A. Arato (1992) *Civil Society and Political Theory*. Cambridge, MA: MIT Press.

Cohen, R. (1997) *Global Diasporas: An Introduction*. London: UCL Press.

Cohen, R. and S.M. Rai (eds) (2000) *Global Social Movements*. London: Athlone Press.

Cohen, S. and J. Zysman (1987) *Manufacturing Matters: The Myth of the Post-Industrial Economy*. New York: Basic Books.

Cohn, T. H. (2002) *Governing Global Trade: International Institutions in Conflict and Convergence*. Aldershot: Ashgate.

Coker, C. (2001) *Humane Warfare*. London: Routledge.

Coleman, W. D. and G. R. D. Underhill (eds) (1998) *Regionalism and Global Economic Integration: Europe, Asia and the Americas*. London: Routledge.

Collins, C. J. L. *et al.* (2001) 'Jubilee 2000: Citizen Action across the North–South Divide', in M. Edwards and J. Gaventa (eds), *Global Citizen Action*. Boulder, CO: Rienner, pp. 135–48.

Commoner, B. (1971) *The Closing Circle: Confronting the Environmental Crisis*. London: Cape, 1972.

Community Currencies (2005) Website www.ratical.org/many_worlds/cc/, accessed on 22 February.

Connolly, W. E. (1991) 'Democracy and Territoriality', *Millennium*, vol. 20, no. 3 (December), pp. 463–84.

Connolly, W. E. (1995) *The Ethos of Pluralization*. Minneapolis: University of Minnesota Press.

Connor, W. (1994) *Ethnonationalism: The Quest for Understanding*. Princeton, NJ: Princeton University Press.

Coote, B. (1996) *The Trade Trap: Poverty and the Global Commodity Markets*. Oxford: Oxfam, 2nd edn.

Cornia, G. A. *et al.* (1987–8) *Adjustment with a Human Face*, 2 vols. Oxford: Clarendon.

Cornia, G. A. (ed.) (2004) *Inequality, Growth, and Poverty in an Era of Liberalization and Globalization*. Oxford: Oxford University Press.

Correa, C. M. (2000) *Intellectual Property Rights, the WTO and Developing Countries: The TRIPS Agreement and Policy Options*. London/Penang: Zed/Third World Network.

Cox, K. R. (ed.) (1997) *Spaces of Globalization: Reasserting the Power of the Local*. New York: Guilford.

Cox, R. W. (1987) *Production, Power, and World Order: Social Forces in the Making of History*. New York: Columbia University Press.

Cox. R. W. (1997) 'An Alternative Approach to Multilateralism for the Twenty-First Century', *Global Governance*, vol. 3, no. 1 (January–April), pp. 103–16.

Coyle, D. (2000) *Governing the World Economy*. Cambridge: Polity.

Craig, W. L. *et al.* (1998) *International Chamber of Commerce Arbitration*. Dobbs Ferry, NY: Oceana Publications, 3rd edn.

Cram, L. *et al.* (eds) (1999) *Developments in the European Union*. Basingstoke: Palgrave Macmillan.

Creative Commons (2005) Website www.creativecommons.org, accessed on 9 March.

Crosby, A. (1972) *The Columbian Exchange: Biological and Cultural Consequences of 1492*. Westport, CT: Greenwood.

Cross, M. and R. Moore (eds) (2002) *Globalization and the New City*. New York: Palgrave.

Cruickshank, M. (1992) *The Gay and Lesbian Liberation Movement*. London: Routledge.

CSGR (2005) CSGR Globalisation Index, available on the website of the Centre for the Study of Globalisation and Regionalization, www.csgr.org, accessed on 16 February.

Curtin, P. D. (1969) *The Atlantic Slave Trade: A Census*. Madison, WI: University of Wisconsin Press.

Cutler, A. C. *et al.* (eds) (1999) *Private Authority in International Affairs*. Albany, NY: State University of New York Press.

Cvetkovich, A. and D. Kellner (eds) (1997) *Articulating the Global and the Local: Globalization and Cultural Studies*. Boulder, CO: Westview.

Czempiel, E. -O. and J. N. Rosenau (eds) (1989) *Global Changes and Theoretical Challenges*. Lexington, MA: Lexington Books.

Dai, X. (2003) 'A New Mode of Governance? Transnationalisation of European Regions and Cities in the Information Age', *Telematics and Informatics*, vol. 20, no. 3 (__), pp. 193–215.

Dalla Costa, M. and G. F. Dalla Costa (eds) (1993) *Paying the Price: Women and the Politics of International Economic Strategy*. London: Zed.

Danaher, K. and J. Marks (2003) *Insurrection: The Citizen Challenge to Corporate Power*. London: Routledge.

Daniel, D. C. and B. C. Hayes (eds) (1995) *Beyond Traditional Peacekeeping*. Basingstoke: Palgrave Macmillan.

Daston, L. (1999) 'The Moralised Objectivities of Science', in W. Carl and L. Daston (eds), *Wahrheit und Geschichte*. Göttingen: Vandenhoeck and Ruprecht.

Dawson, M. C. (1999) 'Globalization, the Racial Divide, and a New Citizenship', in R. D. Torres *et al.* (eds), *Race, Identity, and Citizenship: A Reader*. Oxford: Blackwell, pp. 373–85.

De Cecco, M. (1974) *Money and Empire: The International Gold Standard, 1890–1914*. Oxford: Blackwell.

Deacon, B. (1997) *Global Social Policy: International Organizations and the Future of Welfare*. London: Sage.

Deacon, B. *et al.* (2003) *Global Social Governance: Themes and Prospects*. Helsinki: Globalism and Social Policy Programme.

Deardorff, A. (2003) 'What Might Globalization's Critics Believe?' *World Economy*, vol. 26, no. 5 (May), pp. 639–58.

Delanty, G. (2000) *Citizenship in a Global Age: Society, Culture, Politics*. Buckingham: Open University Press.

Demac, D. A. (ed.) (1986) *Tracing New Orbits: Cooperation and Competition in Global Satellite Development*. New York: Columbia University Press.

Denters, E. (1996) *Law and Policy of IMF Conditionality*. Dordrecht: Kluwer.

Desmarais, A. A. (2002) 'The Vía Campesina: Consolidating an International Peasant and Farm Movement', *Journal of Peasant Studies*, vol. 29, no. 2 (January), pp. 91–124.

Devall, B. and G. Sessions (1985) *Deep Ecology: Living as if Nature Mattered*. Salt Lake City: Smith.

Devine, J. (1996) *NGOs: Changing Fashion or Fashioning Change?* Bath: Centre for Development Studies, University of Bath.

Dezalay, Y. and B. G. Garth (1996) *Dealing in Virtue: International Commercial Arbitration and the Construction of a Transnational Legal Order*. Chicago: University of Chicago Press.

DFID (1997) *Eliminating World Poverty: A Challenge for the 21st Century. White Paper on International Development*. London: The Stationery Office/Cm 3789.

Dhonte, P. and I. Kapur (1997) *Toward a Market Economy: Structures of Governance*. Washington, DC: IMF Working Paper 97/11.

Diamond, L. and M. F. Plattner (eds) (1996) *The Global Resurgence of Democracy*. Baltimore: Johns Hopkins University Press, 2nd edn.

Dicken, P. (2003) *Global Shift: Transforming the World Economy*. London: Sage, 4th edn.

Dirlif, A. (1997) *Postcolonial Aura: Third World Criticism in the Age of Global Capitalism*. Boulder, CO: Westview.

Doggart, C. (1993) *Tax Havens and Their Uses*, London: Economist Intelligence Unit.

Dollar, D. and A. Kraay (2000) *Growth is Good for the Poor*. Washington, DC: World Bank.

Doremus, P. N. *et al.* (1998) *The Myth of the Global Corporation.* Princeton, NJ: Princeton University Press.

Douglas, I. (1996) 'The Myth of Globali[z]ation: A Poststructural Reading of Speed and Reflexivity in the Governance of Late Modernity'. Paper presented at the 38th Annual Convention of the International Studies Association, San Diego, April.

Dower, N. (2003) *An Introduction to Global Citizenship.* Edinburgh: Edinburgh University Press.

Dower, N. and J. Williams (eds) (2002) *Global Citizenship: A Critical Reader.* Edinburgh: Edinburgh University Press.

Dowmunt, T. (ed.) (1993) *Channels of Resistance: Global Television and Local Empowerment.* London: BFI/Channel 4.

Drache, D. (ed.) (2001) *The Market or the Public Domain? Global Governance and the Assymmetry of Power.* London: Routledge.

Drache, D. and M. Froese (2003) *The Great Global Poverty Debate: Balancing Private Interests and Public Good at the* WTO. Toronto: Robarts Centre for Canadian Studies, York University.

Drainville, A. C. (1998) 'The Fetishism of Global Civil Society: Global Governance, Transnational Urbanism and Sustainable Capitalism in the World Economy', in M. P. Smith and L. E. Guarnizo (eds), *Transnationalism from Below.* New Brunswick, NJ: Transaction, pp. 35–63.

Drori, G. S. (forthcoming) 'United Nations' Dedications: A World Culture in the Making?' *International Sociology.*

Drori, G. S. *et al.* (2003) *Science in the Modern World Polity: Institutionalization and Globalization.* Stanford, CA: Stanford University Press.

Drucker, P. F. (1989) *The New Realities.* London: Butterworth.

Drucker, P. F. (1993) *Post-Capitalist Society.* Oxford: Butterworth-Heinemann.

Dryzek, J. S. (1999) 'Transnational Democracy', *Journal of Political Philosophy*, vol. 7, no. 1 (March), pp. 30–51.

Dubey, M. (1996) *An Unequal Treaty: World Trading Order after GATT.* New Delhi: New Age International.

Duchacek, I. D. *et al.* (eds) (1988) *Perforated Sovereignties and International Relations: Trans-Sovereign Contacts of Subnational Governments.* Westport, CT: Greenwood.

Duggan, P. and H. Dashner (eds) (1994) *Women's Lives in the New Global Economy.* Amsterdam: International Institute for Research and Education.

Dunn, J. (ed.) (1995) *Contemporary Crisis of the Nation State?* Oxford: Blackwell.

Dunne, T. and N. J. Wheeler (eds) (1999) *Human Rights in Global Politics.* Cambridge: Cambridge University Press.

Dunning, J. H. (1993) *The Globalization of Business: The Challenge of the 1990s.* London, Routledge.

Dunning, J. H. (1997) 'The Advent of Alliance Capitalism', in J. H. Dunning and K. A. Hamdani (eds), *The New Globalism and Developing Countries.* Tokyo: United Nations University Press, pp. 12–50.

Durbin, A. and C. Welch (2002) 'The Environmental Movement and Global Finance', in J. A. Scholte with A. Schnabel (eds), *Civil Society and Global Finance.* London: Routledge, pp. 213–27.

Dyer-Witheford, N. (1999) *Cyber-Marx: Cycles and Circuits of Struggle in High-Technology Capitalism.* Chicago: University of Illinois Press.

Eade, J. (ed.) (1997) *Living the Global City: Globalization as a Local Process.* London: Routledge.

Eatwell, J. (2000) 'From Cooperation to Coordination to Control?' *New Political Economy*, vol. 4, no. 3 (November), pp. 410–15.

Eatwell, J. and L. Taylor (2000) *Global Finance at Risk: The Case for International Regulation.* Cambridge: Polity.

Eckersley, R. (1992) *Environmentalism and Political Theory: Toward an Ecocentric Approach.* London: University College London Press.

Edwards, M. (2000) *NGO Rights and Responsibilities: A New Deal for Global Governance*. London: Foreign Policy Centre.

Edwards, M. (2004) *Future Positive: International Co-operation in the 21st Century*. London: Earthscan, rev. edn.

Edwards, M. and J. Gaventa (eds) (2001) *Global Citizen Action*. Boulder, CO: Rienner.

Ehrenreich, B. and A. R. Hochschild (eds) (2002) *Global Woman: Nannies, Maids, and Sex Workers in the New Economy*. New York: Metropolitan Books.

Eichengreen, B. *et al.* (1995) 'Two Cases for Sand in the Wheels of International Finance', *Economic Journal*, vol. 105, no. 428 (January), pp. 162–72.

Eichengreen, B. (1999) *Toward a New International Financial Architecture: A Practical Post-Asia Agenda*. Washington, DC: Institute for International Economics.

Einhorn, B. (1993) *Cinderella Goes to Market: Citizenship, Gender and Women's Movements in East Central Europe*. London: Verso.

Eisenstein, Z. R. (1998) *Global Obscenities: Patriarchy, Capitalism, and the Lure of Cyberfantasy*. New York: New York University Press.

EIU (1957) *A History of the London Metal Exchange*. London: Economist Intelligence Unit.

Ekholm, K. and J. Friedman (1985) 'Towards a Global Anthropology', *Critique of Anthropology*, vol. 5, no. 1, pp. 97–119.

Elden, S. (2005) 'Missing the Point: Globalization, Deterritorialization and the Space of the World', *Transactions of the Institute of British Geographers*, vol. 30, no. 1, pp. 8–19.

Elliott, L. and G. Cheeseman (eds.) (2004) *Forces for Good: Cosmopolitan Militaries in the Twenty-First Century*. Manchester: Manchester University Press.

Elson, D. and R. Pearson (1981) 'Nimble Fingers Make Cheap Workers: An Analysis of Women's Employment in Third World Export Manufacturing', *Feminist Review*, no. 7 (Spring), pp. 87–107.

Embong, A. R. (2000) 'Globalization and Transnational Class Relations: Some Problems of Conceptualization', *Third World Quarterly*, vol. 21, no. 6, pp. 989–1000.

Emerson, R. (1960) *From Empire to Nation: the Rise to Self-Assertion of Asian and African Peoples*. Cambridge, MA: Harvard University Press, 1962.

Epstein, B. (2001) 'Anarchism and the Anti-Globalization Movement', *Monthly Review*, vol. 53, no. 4, (September), pp.1–14.

Erie, S. P. (2004) *Globalizing L.A.: Trade, Infrastructure, and Regional Development*. Stanford, CA: Stanford University Press.

Eschle, C. and B. Maiguashca (2005) *Critical Theories, International Relations and 'the Anti-Globalisation Movement': The Politics of Global Resistance*. London: Routledge.

Escorcia, G. (1999) Anecdote related to the author by the Director of Global Thinkers, Mexico City, 8 June.

Esping-Andersen, G. (1990) *The Three Worlds of Welfare Capitalism*. Cambridge: Polity Press.

Esping-Andersen, G. (1994) *After the Golden Age: The Future of the Welfare State in the New Global Order*. Geneva: UNRISD Occasional Paper 7, World Summit for Social Development.

Esping-Andersen, G. (ed.) (1996) *Welfare States in Transition: National Adaptations in Global Economies*. London: Sage.

Esposito, J. (ed.) (1990) *The Iranian Revolution: Its Global Impact*. Miami, FL: Florida International University Press.

EST (1997) 'The Economist Survey of Telecommunications', *The Economist*, vol. 344, no. 8034 (13 September).

ETC (2004) *Down on the Farm: The Impact of Nano-Scale Technologies on Food and Agriculture*. Ottawa: ETC Group , online at: www.etcgroup.org.

EU (1998) *The Impact of Globalization on Statistics. Summary, Conclusion, Recommendations*. Brussels: European Commission, Globalization Reflection Group, 29 May.

Euroclear (2005) Website of Euroclear, www.euroclear.com, accessed on 3 February.

Europarl (2004) Website of the European Parliament, www.europarl.eu.int, accessed on 2 November.

Evans, P. (1997) 'The Eclipse of the State? Reflections on Stateness in an Era of Globalization', *World Politics*, vol. 50, no. 1 (October), pp. 62–87.

Everard, J. (1999) *Virtual States: Globalization, Inequality and the Internet*. London: Routledge.

Falk, R. A. (1992) *Explorations at the Edge of Time: The Prospects for World Order*. Philadelphia: Temple University Press.

Falk, R. A. (1993) 'Global Apartheid', *Third World Resurgence*, no. 37 (November), pp. 15–16.

Falk, R. A. (1995) *On Humane Governance: Toward a New Global Politics*. Cambridge: Polity Press.

Falk, R. A. (1999) *Predatory Globalization: a Critique*. Cambridge: Policy Press.

FAO (1998) *The State of Food and Agriculture 1998*. Rome: Food and Agriculture Organization.

FATF (2004) 'Basic Facts about Money Laundering', online at: www1.oecd.org/fatf/Mlaundering_en.htm, accessed on 21 January.

Fawcett, L. and A. Hurrell (eds) (1995) *Regionalism in World Politics: Regional Organization and International Order*. Oxford: Oxford University Press.

Featherstone, M. (ed.) (1990) *Global Culture: Nationalism, Globalization and Modernity*. London: Sage.

Featherstone, M. (1991) *Consumer Culture and Postmodernism*. London: Sage.

Featherstone, M. *et al.* (eds) (2002) 'Special Issue on Cosmopolis', *Theory, Culture and Society*, vol. 19, no. 1–2 (February–April).

Febvre, L. and L. J. Martin (1958) *The Coming of the Book: The Impact of Printing 1450–1800*. London: Verso, 1984.

Fennema, M. (1982) *International Networks of Banks and Industry*. The Hague: Nijhoff.

Ferrer, A. (1997) *Hechos y ficciones de la globalización* ['Facts and Fictions of Globalization']. Buenos Aires: Fondo de Cultura Economica.

Findlay, T. (1995) 'Armed Conflict Prevention, Management and Resolution', in *SIPRI Yearbook 1995*. Oxford: Oxford University Press, pp. 37–82.

Fine, R. (2003) 'Taking the "Ism" out of Cosmopolitanism: An Essay in Reconstruction', *European Journal of Social Theory*, vol. 6, no. 4 (November), pp. 451–70.

Fisher, W. F. and T. Ponniah (eds) (2003) *Another World is Possible: Popular Alternatives to Globalization at the World Social Forum*. London: Zed.

Fitzgerald, F. (2000) *Way Out There in the Blue: Reagan, Star Wars and the End of the Cold War*. New York: Simon & Schuster.

Flora, C. B. (1990) 'Rural Peoples in a Global Economy', *Rural Sociology*, vol. 55, no. 2 (Spring), pp. 157–77.

Florini, A. M. (ed.) (2000) *The Third Force: The Rise of Transnational Civil Society*. Tokyo/Washington, DC: Japan Center for International Exchange/Carnegie Endowment for International Peace.

Fontana, M. (2003) *Modeling the Effects of Trade on Women at Work and at Home: A Comparative Perspective*. Washington, DC: International Food Policy Research Institute, Macroeconomics Division, Discussion Paper No. 110, March.

Fortin, C. (1992) 'The United Nations and Development in the 1990s', in P. Streeten *et al.*, *International Governance*. Brighton: University of Sussex, pp. 69–95.

Fortune (1995) 'The Merger Mania Continues', *Fortune*, vol. 132 (25 December), pp. 33–40.

Foster, J. W. with A. Anand (eds) (1999) *Whose World Is It Anyway? Civil Society, the United Nations and the Multilateral Future*. Ottawa: United Nations Association in Canada.

Foster, R. J. (1991) 'Making National Cultures in the Global Ecumene', *Annual Review of Anthropology*, vol. 20, pp. 235–60.

Foucault, M. (1966) *The Order of Things*. London: Tavistock, 1970.

Fowler, A. (1994) 'Capacity Building and NGOs: A Case of Strengthening Ladles for the Global Soup Kitchen?' *Institutional Development*, vol. 1, no. 1, pp. 18-25.

Fox, J. A. and L. D. Brown (eds) (1998) *The Struggle for Accountability: The World Bank, NGOs and Grassroots Movements*. Cambridge, MA: MIT Press.

FPIF (2002) 'Globalization and Militarization', *Foreign Policy in Focus*, 5 February, online at: www.fpif.org/briefs/vol7/v7nlmilglob.html.

Franda, M. (2001) *Governing the Internet: The Emergence of an International Regime*. Boulder, CO: Rienner.

Frankel, J. A. (ed.) (1998) *The Regionalization of the World Economy*. Chicago: University of Chicago Press.

Frederick, H. (1993) 'Computer Networks and the Emergence of Global Civil Society', in L. Harasim (ed.), *Global Networks: Computers and International Communication*. Cambridge, MA: MIT Press, pp. 283–95.

French, H. (2000) *Vanishing Borders: Protecting the Planet in the Age of Globalization*. Washington, DC: Worldwatch Institute.

Friedman, J. (1994) *Cultural Identity and Global Process*. London: Sage.

Friedrichs, J. (2001) 'The Meaning of New Medievalism', *European Journal of International Relations*, vol. 7, no. 4 (December), pp. 475–502.

Fry, E. H. (1995) 'The Vincibility of Modern Nation-States: Challenges from the International and Subnational Arenas'. Paper presented to the 36th Annual Convention of the International Studies Association, Chicago, 21–25 February.

Fry, E. H. (1998) *The Expanding Role of State and Local Governments in U.S. Foreign Affairs*. New York: Council on Foreign Relations Press.

Fry, E. H. (2006) 'Substate Governance', in R. Robertson and J. A. Scholte (eds), *The Encyclopedia of Globalization*. London: Routledge.

FSF (1999) Website of the Financial Stability Forum: http://www.fsforum.org.

FT500 (1997) 'The FT500 Survey', *Financial Times Supplement*, 24 January.

Fuentes, A. and B. Ehrenreich (1983) *Women in the Global Factory*. Boston, MA: South End.

Fukuyama, F. (1992) *The End of History and the Last Man*. London: Hamish Hamilton.

Funk, N. and M. Mueller (eds) (1993) *Gender Politics and Post-Communism: Reflections from Eastern Europe and the Former Soviet Union*. New York: Routledge.

Fustukian, S. *et al.* (2002) 'Workers' Health and Safety in a Globalising World', in K. Lee *et al.* (eds), *Health Policy in a Globalising World*. Cambridge: Cambridge University Press, pp. 208–28.

G8 (2004) Websites of the G8 Information Centre, http://www.g8.utoronto.ca, and G8 Online, http://www.g8online.org, accessed on 10 January.

GACGC (1995) *World in Transition: the Threat to Soils. 1994 Annual Report*. Bonn: Economica [German Advisory Council on Global Change].

Galizia, M. (1993) Personal communication to the author from Michele Galizia of the University of Berne, July.

Gamble, A. (1994) *The Free Economy and the Strong State: The Politics of Thatcherism*. Basingstoke: Palgrave Macmillan.

Gamble, A. (2001) 'Neo-Liberalism', *Capital and Class*, vol. 75 (Autumn), pp. 127–34.

Gamble, A. and A. Payne (eds) (1996) *Regionalism and World Order*. Basingstoke: Palgrave Macmillan.

Gamble, C. (1994) *Timewalkers: The Prehistory of Global Civilization*. Cambridge, MA: Harvard University Press.

Garret, L. (1994) *The Coming Plague: Newly Emerging Diseases in a World Out of Balance*. New York: Farrar, Straus & Giroux.

Garrett, G. (1998) *Partisan Politics in the Global Economy*. Cambridge: Cambridge University Press.

Garrett, G. (2001) 'Globalization and Government Spending around the World', *Studies in Comparative International Development*, vol. 35, no. 4 (Winter), pp. 3–29.

Gates, B. (1995) *The Road Ahead*. London: Viking.

Gaventa, J. (1999) 'Learning across Boundaries: Strengthening Participation in North and South'. Paper presented at the Third International NGO Conference, University of Birmingham, 10–13 January.

Gay, P. (1966) *The Enlightenment: An Interpretation*. New York: Knopf.

Gelber, H. G. (1997) *Sovereignty through Interdependence.* London: Kluwer Law International.

Gelernter, D. H. (1995) *1939: The Lost World of the Fair.* New York: Free Press.

George, S. and F. Sabelli (1994) *Faith and Credit: the World Bank's Secular Empire.* Boulder, CO: Westview.

Gereffi, G. and M. Korzeniewicz (eds) (1994) *Commodity Chains and Global Capitalism.* Westport, CN: Praeger.

Germain, R. (ed.) (1999) *Globalization and Its Critics: Perspectives from Political Economy.* Basingstoke: Palgrave Macmillan.

Germain, R. D. and M. Kenny (eds) (2005) *The Idea of Global Civil Society: Politics and Ethics in a Globalizing Era.* London: Routledge.

Geyer, M. and C. Bright (1995) 'World History in a Global Age', *American Historical Review*, vol. 100, no. 4 (October), pp. 1034–60.

Geyer, R. (1998) 'Globalisation and the (Non-) Defence of the Welfare State', *West European Politics*, vol. 21, no. 3 (July), pp. 77–102.

Geyer, R. *et al.* (eds) (2000) *Globalization, Europeanization, and the End of Scandinavian Social Democracy?* Basingstoke: Palgrave Macmillan.

Ghai, D. (1994) 'Structural Adjustment, Global Integration and Social Democracy', in R. Prendergast and F. Stewart (eds), *Market Forces and World Development.* New York: St. Martin's, pp. 15–44.

Ghai, D. (ed.) (1991) *The IMF and the South: The Social Impact of Adjustment.* London: Zed.

Giddens, A. (1984) *The Constitution of Society: Outline of the Theory of Structuration.* Cambridge: Polity.

Giddens, A. (1990) *The Consequences of Modernity.* Cambridge: Polity.

Giddens, A. (1991) *Modernity and Self-Identity: Self and Society in the Late Modern Age.* Cambridge: Polity Press.

Giddens, A. (1994) 'Living in a Post-Traditional Society', in U. Beck *et al.*, *Reflexive Modernization: Politics, Tradition and Aesthetics in the Modern Social Order.* Cambridge: Polity Press, pp. 56–109.

Giddens, A. (1996) 'On Globalization', excerpts from a keynote address at the UNRISD Conference on Globalization and Citizenship, 1 December 1996, online at: www.unrisd.org (under 'viewpoints').

Giddens, A. (1998) *The Third Way: the Renewal of Social Democracy.* Cambridge: Polity Press.

Giddens, A. (2002) *Runaway World: How Globalisation is Reshaping our Lives.* London: Profile, 2nd edn.

Gilbert, A. (1999) *Must Global Politics Constrain Democracy? Great-Power Realism, Democratic Peace, and Democratic Internationalism.* Princeton, NJ: Princeton University Press.

Gilbert, E. and E. Helleiner (eds) (1999) *Nation-States and Money: The Past, Present and Future of National Currencies.* London: Routledge.

Gill, S. (ed.) (1993) *Gramsci, Historical Materialism and International Relations.* Cambridge: Cambridge University Press.

Gill, S. (1995a) 'Globalisation, Market Civilisation, and Disciplinary Neoliberalism', *Millennium*, vol. 24, no. 3 (Winter), pp. 399–423.

Gill, S. (1995b) 'Theorizing the Interregnum: The Double Movement and Global Politics in the 1990s', in B. Hettne (ed.), *International Political Economy: Understanding Global Disorder.* London: Zed, pp. 65–99.

Gill, S. (1996) 'Globalization, Democratization, and the Politics of Indifference', in J. H. Mittelman (ed.), *Globalization: Critical Reflections* Boulder: Rienner, pp. 205–28.

Gill, S. (ed.) (1997) *Globalization, Democratization and Multilateralism.* London: Macmillan/United Nations University Press.

Gills, B. (ed.) (1997) 'Special Issue: Globalisation and the Politics of Resistance', *New Political Economy*, vol. 2, no. 1 (March).

Gills, B. *et al.* (eds) (1993) *Low Intensity Democracy: Political Power in the New World Order.* London: Pluto.

Gilpin, R. (2001) *Global Political Economy: Understanding the International Economic Order*. Princeton, NJ: Princeton University Press.
Gilroy, B. M. (1993) *Networking in Multinational Enterprises: The Importance of Strategic Alliances*. Columbia: University of South Carolina Press.
Gilson, J. (2002) *Asia Meets Europe*. Cheltenham: Elgar.
Girvan, N. (2000) 'A Perspective from the South', *New Political Economy*, vol. 4, no. 3 (November), pp. 415–19.
Giulianotti, R. (1999) *Football: A Sociology of the Global Game*. Cambridge: Polity.
Glasius, M. *et al.* (eds) (2002) *Global Civil Society 2002*. Oxford: Oxford University Press.
Glick Schiller, N. and G. E. Fouron (1999) 'Terrains of Blood and Nation: Haitian Transnational Social Fields', *Ethnic and Racial Studies*, vol. 22, no. 2 (March), pp. 340–66.
Glick Schiller, N. and G. E. Fouron (2001) *Georges Woke Up Laughing: Long-Distance Nationalism and the Search for Home*. Durham, NC: Duke University Press.
Global Compendium (2005) Online resource of the Globalization and Autonomy Project, www.strange.mcmaster.ca/home_en.html, accessed on 23 January.
Global Reach (2004a) 'Global Internet Statistics (by Language)', online at: www.glreach.com/globstats/, accessed on 22 October.
Global Reach (2004b) 'Worldwide eCommerce Growth', online at: www.glreach.com/eng/ed/art/2004.ecommerce.php3, accessed on 22 October.
Goede, M. de (2001) 'Discourses of Scientific Finance and the Failure of Long-Term Capital Management', *New Political Economy*, vol. 6, no. 2 (July), pp. 149–70.
Goldin, I. *et al.* (1993) *Trade Liberalisation: Global Economic Implications*. Paris: OECD/World Bank.
Golding, P. and P. Harris (eds) (1997) *Beyond Cultural Imperialism: Globalization, Communication and the New International Order*. London: Sage.
Golshani, M. (ed.) (2004) *Can Science Dispense with Religion?* Tehran: Institute for Humanities and Cultural Studies, 3rd edn.
Gómez, J. (2000) *Politica e democracia em tempos de globalizaçao* ['Politics and Democracy in the Time of Globalization']. Petrópolis: Editora Vozes.
Goodman, D. S. G. and G. Segal (eds) (1994) *China Deconstructs: Politics, Trade and Regionalism*. London: Routledge.
Goodman, J. (2000) 'Stopping a Juggernaut: The Anti-MAI Campaign', in J. Goodman and P. Ranald (eds), *Stopping the Juggernaut*. Annandale, NSW: Pluto Press, pp. 33–52.
Google (2005) Website of Google Web Search: www.google.com, accessed on 4 May.
Gorbachev Foundation (2003) *Facets of Globalization: Difficult Issues of Contemporary Development*. Moscow: Alpina [in Russian with summary in English].
Gore, C. (2000) 'The Rise and Fall of the Washington Consensus as a Paradigm for Developing Countries', *World Development*, vol. 28, no. 5 (May), pp. 789–804.
Gorz, A. (1988) *Critique of Economic Reason*. London: Verso, 1989.
Gottman, J. (1973) *The Significance of Territory*. Charlottesville: University Press of Virginia.
Gowan, P. (1999) *The Global Gamble: Washington's Faustian Bid for World Dominance*. London: Verso.
Graeber, D. (2002) 'The New Anarchists', *New Left Review*, vol. 13 (January–February), pp. 61–73.
Gray, J. (1998) *False Dawn: The Delusions of Global Capitalism*. London: Granta.
Gray, J. (2001) 'The Era of Globalisation Is Over', *New Statesman*, vol. 30, issue 4556, 24 September, pp. 25–7.
Graz, J.C. (2003) 'How Powerful Are Transnational Elite Clubs? The Social Myth of the World Economic Forum', *New Political Economy*, vol. 8, no. 3 (November), pp. 321–40.
Greer, J. and K. Bruno (1996) *Greenwash: The Reality behind Corporate Environmentalism*. Penang: Third World Network.
Gregory, D. and J. Urry (eds) (1985) *Social Relations and Spatial Structures*. Basingstoke: Palgrave Macmillan.

Greider, W. (1997) *One World, Ready or Not: The Manic Logic of Global Capitalism*. London: Allen Lane.

Griffith-Jones, S. (1998) *Global Capital Flows: Should They Be Regulated?* New York: St Martin's.

Group of Lisbon (1994) *Limits to Competition*, Cambridge, MA: MIT Press, 1995.

Grzybowski, C. (2004) Director of the Brazilian Institute of Social and Economic Analysis (IBASE), in discussion with the author, Rio de Janeiro, 17 November.

Guéhenno, J.-M. (1995) *The End of the Nation-State*. Minneapolis: University of Minnesota Press.

Guidry, J. A. *et al.* (2000) *Globalization and Social Movements: Culture, Power, and the Transnational Public Sphere*. Ann Arbor, MI: University of Michigan Press.

Gunaratna, R. (2002) *Inside Al Qaeda: Global Network of Terror*. New York: Columbia University Press.

Gunter, B. G. (1996) 'Reforming the International Monetary System towards a World Central Bank: A Summary of Proposals and Fallacies', in J. M. Griesgraber and B.G. Gunter (eds), *The World's Monetary System: Toward Stability and Sustainability in the Twenty-First Century*. London: Pluto, pp. 115–35.

Gurr, T. R. (1994) 'Peoples against States: Ethnopolitical Conflict and the Changing World System', *International Studies Quarterly*, vol. 38, no. 3 (September), pp. 347–77.

Gurr, T. R. (2000) 'Ethnic Warfare on the Wane', *Foreign Affairs*, vol. 79, no. 3 (May–June), pp. 52–64.

Haas, P. M. (1992) 'Introduction: Epistemic Communities and International Policy Coordination', *International Organization*, vol. 46, no. 1 (Winter), pp. 1–35.

Haas, P.M. *et al.* (eds) (1993) *Institutions for the Earth: Sources of Effective International Environmental Protection*. Cambridge, MA: MIT Press.

Habermas, J. (1998) *The Postnational Constellation*. Cambridge: Polity Press, 2001.

HABITAT (2003) *The Challenge of Slums: Global Report on Human Settlements 2003*. London: Earthscan/United Nations Human Settlements Programme.

Hajnal, P. I. (1999) *The G7/G8 System: Evolution, Role and Documentation*. Aldershot: Ashgate.

Hajnal, P. I. (2002) 'Oxfam International', in P. I. Hajnal (ed.), *Civil Society in the Information Age*. Aldershot: Ashgate, pp. 57–66.

Haley, M. A. (1999) 'Emerging Market Makers: The Power of Institutional Investors', in L. E. Armijo (ed.), *Financial Globalization and Democracy in Emerging Markets*. Basingstoke: Palgrave Macmillan, pp. 74–90.

Halifax Initiative (2004) *Who's Minding the Store? Legislator Oversight of the Bretton Woods Institutions*. Ottawa: Halifax Initiative, online at: www.halifaxinitiative.org, accessed on 31 October.

Hall, R. B and T. J. Biersteker (eds) (2003) *The Emergence of Private Authority in Global Governance*. Cambridge: Cambridge University Press.

Halperin, M. H. and D. J. Scheffer (1992) *Self-Determination in the New World Order*. Washington, DC: Carnegie Endowment for International Peace.

Hamelink, C. J. (1983) *Cultural Autonomy in Global Communications*. New York: Longmans.

Hampton, M. (1996) *The Offshore Interface: Tax Havens in the Global Economy*. Basingstoke: Macmillan.

Hampton, M. P. and J. P. Abbott (eds) (1999) *Offshore Finance Centres and Tax Havens: The Rise of Global Capital*. Basingstoke: Palgrave Macmillan.

Hanawat, B. A. and M. Kobialka (eds) (2000) *Medieval Practices of Space*. Minneapolis: University of Minnesota Press.

Hancock, D. (1995) *Citizens of the World: London Merchants and the Integration of the British Atlantic Community, 1735–1785*. Cambridge: Cambridge University Press.

Handley, S. (ed.) (2001) *The Links Effect: A Good Practice Guide to Transnational Partnerships and Twinning of Local Authorities*. London: Local Government International Bureau.

Handy, C. (1992) 'Balancing Corporate Power: a New Federalist Paper', *Harvard Business Review*, vol. 70, no. 6 (November–December), pp. 59–72.

Hannerz, U. (1987) 'The World in Creolisation', *Africa*, vol. 57, pp. 546–59.
Hannerz, U. (1992) *Cultural Complexity: Studies in the Social Organization of Meaning*. New York: Columbia University Press.
Hannerz, U. (1996) *Transnational Connections: Culture, People, Places*. London: Routledge.
Haq, M. ul *et al.* (eds) (1996) *The Tobin Tax: Coping with Financial Volatility*. New York: Oxford University Press.
Harcourt, W. (ed.) (1999) *Women @ Internet: Creating New Cultures in Cyberspace*. London: Zed.
Harding, S. (1998) *Is Science Multicultural? Postcolonialisms, Feminisms, and Epistemologies*. Bloomington, IN: Indiana University Press.
Hardt, M. and A. Negri (2000) *Empire*. Cambridge, MA: Harvard University Press.
Harris, J. (1998–9) 'Globalisation and the Transformation of Capitalism', *Race & Class*, vol. 40, no. 2/3 (October–March), pp. 21–35.
Harrod, J. (1992) *Labour and Third World Debt*. Brussels: International Federation of Chemical, Energy and General Workers' Unions.
Harrod, J. and R. O'Brien (eds) (2002) *Global Unions? Theory and Strategy of Organised Labour in the Global Political Economy*. London: Routledge.
Harvey, D. (1989) *The Condition of Postmodernity: An Enquiry into the Conditions of Cultural Change*. Oxford: Blackwell.
Harvey, D. (1993) 'From Space to Place and Back Again: Reflections on the Condition of Postmodernity', in J. Bird *et al.* (eds), *Mapping the Futures: Local Cultures, Global Change*. London: Routledge, pp. 3–29.
Harvey, D. (2000) *Spaces of Hope*. Edinburgh: Edinburgh University Press.
Harvey, R. (1995) *The Return of the Strong: The Drift to Global Disorder*. Basingstoke: Palgrave Macmillan.
Haufler, V. (2001) *The Public Role for the Private Sector: Industry Self-Regulation in a Global Economy*. Washington, DC: Carnegie Endowment for International Peace.
Hawkesworth, M. (2003) 'Global Containment: The Production of Feminist Invisibility and the Vanishing Horizon of Justice', in M. B. Steger (ed.), *Rethinking Globalism*. Lanham, MD: Rowman & Littlefield, pp. 51–65.
Hawthorne, N. (1851) *The House of the Seven Gables: A Romance*. Edinburgh: Paterson, 1883.
HDR (1991) *Human Development Report 1991*. New York: Oxford University Press.
HDR (1994) *Human Development Report 1994*. New York: Oxford University Press.
HDR (1995) *Human Development Report 1995*. New York: Oxford University Press.
HDR (1996) *Human Development Report 1996*. New York: Oxford University Press.
HDR (1997) *Human Development Report 1997*. New York: Oxford University Press.
HDR (1999) *Human Development Report 1999*. New York: Oxford University Press.
HDR (2003) *Human Development Report 2003*. New York: Oxford University Press.
Heater, D. (2002) *World Citizenship: Cosmopolitan Thinking and its Opponents*. London: Continuum.
Hedetoft, U. and M. Hjort (eds) (2002) *The Postnational Self: Belonging and Identity*. Minneapolis: University of Minnesota Press.
Heerings, H. and I. Zeldenrust (1995) *Elusive Saviours: Transnational Corporations and Sustainable Development*. Utrecht: International Books.
Heidegger, M. (1950) 'The Thing', in *Poetry, Language, Thought*. New York: Harper & Row, 1971, pp. 165–82.
Heidel, W. A. (1937) *The Frame of the Ancient Greek Maps, With a Discussion of the Discovery of the Sphericity of the Earth*. New York: American Geographical Society, Research Series No. 20.
Heinrichsohn, E. (2000) *World State, World Citizenship: How a New Consciousness Can Save the World from Self-Destruction*. New York: Fouque.
Held, D. (1995a) *Democracy and the Global Order: From the Modern State to Cosmopolitan Governance*. Cambridge: Polity Press.
Held, D. (1995b) 'Democracy and the New International Order', in D. Archibugi and D. Held (eds), *Cosmopolitan Democracy: An Agenda for a New World Order*. Cambridge: Polity Press, pp. 96–120.

Held, D. (2004) *Global Covenant: The Social Democratic Alternative to the Washington Consensus*. Cambridge: Polity Press.

Held, D. and A. McGrew (1993) 'Globalization and the Liberal Democratic State', *Government and Opposition*, vol. 28, no. 2 (Spring), pp. 261–85.

Held, D. and A. McGrew (eds) (2002) *Governing Globalization: Power, Authority and Global Governance*. Cambridge: Polity.

Held, D. and A. McGrew (2003) *The Global Transformations Reader: An Introduction to the Globalization Debate*. Cambridge: Polity Press.

Held, D. and M. Koenig-Archibugi (eds) (2003) *Taming Globalization: Frontiers of Governance*. Cambridge: Polity.

Held, D. *et al.* (1999) *Global Transformations: Politics, Economics and Culture*. Cambridge: Polity.

Helleiner, E. (1994) *States and the Reemergence of Global Finance: From Bretton Woods to the 1990s*. Ithaca, NY: Cornell University Press.

Helleiner, E. (1998) 'Electronic Money: a Challenge to the Sovereign State?' *Journal of International Affairs*, vol. 51, no. 2 (Spring), pp. 387–410.

Helleiner, E. (1999) 'Sovereignty, Territoriality, and the Globalization of Finance', in D. A. Smith *et al.* (eds), *States and Sovereignty in the Global Economy*. London: Routledge, pp. 138–57.

Helliwell, J. F. (1998) *How Much Do National Borders Matter?* Washington, DC: Brookings Institution.

Helliwell, J. F. (2000) *Globalization: Myths, Facts and Consequences*. Toronto: C.D. Howe Institute.

Henderson, D. (1999) *The MAI Affair: A Story and its Lessons*. London: Royal Institute of International Affairs.

Herbst, J. and A. Olukoshi (1994) 'Nigeria: Economic and Political Reforms at Cross Purposes', in S. Haggard and S. B. Webb (eds), *Voting for Reform: Democracy, Political Liberalization, and Economic Adjustment*. New York: Oxford University Press, pp. 453–502.

Herman, B. (2002) 'Civil Society and the Financing for Development Initiative at the United Nations', in J. A. Scholte with A. Schnabel (eds), *Civil Society and Global Finance*. London: Routledge, pp. 162–77.

Herman, E. S. and R. W. McChesney (1997) *The Global Media: The New Missionaries of Corporate Capitalism*. London: Cassell.

Hermet, G. *et al.* (2005) *La gouvernance. Un concept et ses applications*. Paris: Karthala.

Herod, A. *et al.* (eds) (1998) *An Unruly World? Globalization, Governance and Geography*. London: Routledge.

Hertz, N. (2001) *The Silent Takeover: Global Capitalism and the Death of Democracy*. London: Heinemann.

Hettne, B. (1994) 'The Regional Factor in the Formation of a New World Order', in Y. Sakamoto (ed.), *Global Transformation: Challenges to the State System*. Tokyo: United Nations University Press, pp. 134–66.

Hettne, B. *et al.* (eds) (1999) *Globalism and the New Regionalism*. Basingstoke: Palgrave Macmillan.

Hettne, B. *et al.* (eds) (2000) *The New Regionalism and the Future of Security and Development*. Basingstoke: Palgrave Macmillan.

Hettne, B. *et al.* (eds) (2001) *Comparing Regionalisms: Implications for Global Development*. Basingstoke: Palgrave Macmillan.

Hewison, K. (1999) *Localism in Thailand: A Study of Globalisation and its Discontents*. Coventry: ESRC/University of Warwick Centre for the Study of Globalisation and Regionalisation, Working Paper No. 39/99.

Heyzer, N. *et al.* (eds) (1994) *The Trade in Domestic Workers: Causes, Mechanisms and Consequences of International Migration*. London: Zed.

Higgott, R. A. (2000) 'Contested Globalization: The Changing Context and Normative Challenges', *Review of International Studies*, vol. 26, no. 5 (December), pp. 131–53.

Higgott, R. A. and A. Payne (eds) (2000) *The New Political Economy of Globalization*. Cheltenham: Elgar.
Hilferding, R. (1910) *Finance Capital: A Study of the Latest Phase of Capitalist Development*. London: Routledge, 1981.
Hill, K. A. and J. E. Hughes (1998) *Cyberpolitics: Citizen Activism in the Age of the Internet*. Lanham, MD: Rowman & Littlefield.
Hines, C. (2000) *Localization: A Global Manifesto*. London: Earthscan.
Hinsley, F. H. (1963) *Power and the Pursuit of Peace: Theory and Practice in the History of Relations between States*. Cambridge: Cambridge University Press.
Hironaka, A. (2004) *Neverending Wars: Weak States, the International Community, and the Perpetuation of Civil War*. Cambridge, MA: Harvard University Press.
Hirst, P. and G. Thompson (1996) 'Globalisation: Ten Frequently Asked Questions and Some Surprising Answers', *Soundings*, vol. 4 (Autumn), pp. 47–66.
Hirst, P. and G. Thompson (1999) *Globalization in Question: The International Economy and the Possibilities of Governance*. Cambridge: Polity, 2nd edn.
Hix, S. (1999) *The Political System of the European Union*. Basingstoke: Palgrave Macmillan.
Hochschild, A. R. (2000) 'Global Care Chains and Emotional Surplus Value', in W. Hutton and A. Giddens (eds), *On the Edge: Living with Global Capitalism*. London: Cape, pp. 130–46.
Hocking, B. (1993) *Localizing Foreign Policy: Non-Central Governments and Multilayered Diplomacy*. Basingstoke: Palgrave Macmillan.
Hodges, M. *et al.* (eds) (1999) *The G8's Role in the New Millennium*. Aldershot: Ashgate.
Hoekman, B. M. and M. M. Kostecki (1995) *The Political Economy of the World Trading System: From GATT to WTO*. Oxford: Oxford University Press.
Hoeven, R. van der (2002) personal communication to the author, Nyon, 30 May.
Holcombe, S. H. (1995) *Managing to Empower: The Grameen Bank's Experience of Poverty Alleviation*. London: Zed.
Holden, B. (ed.) (2000) *Global Democracy: Key Debates*. London: Routledge.
Holm, H. H. and G. Sørensen (1995) 'International Relations Theory in a World of Variation', in *Whose World Order? Uneven Globalization and the End of the Cold War*. Boulder, CO: Westview, pp. 187–206.
Holstein W. J. *et al.* (1990) 'The Stateless Corporation', *Business Week*, 14 May, pp. 52–9.
Holthoon, F. van and M. van der Linden (eds) (1988) *Internationalism in the Labour Movement 1830–1940*. Leiden: Brill.
HomeNet (1999) 'Using the ILO Convention on Home Work'. Leeds: HomeNet International (homenet@gn.apc.org).
Honeygold, D. (1989) *International Financial Markets*. Cambridge: Woodhead-Faulkner.
Hoogvelt, A. (2001) *Globalisation and the Postcolonial World: The New Political Economy of Development*. Basingstoke: Palgrave Macmillan, 2nd edn.
Hook, G. and I. Kearns (eds) (1999) *Subregionalism and World Order*. Basingstoke: Palgrave Macmillan.
Hopkins, D. *et al.* (eds) (2001) *Religions/Globalizations: Theories and Cases*. Durham, NC: Duke University Press.
Hopkins, M. (1999) *The Planetary Bargain: Corporate Social Responsibility Comes of Age*. Basingstoke: Palgrave Macmillan.
Horsman, M. and A. Marshall (1994) *After the Nation-State: Citizens, Tribalism and the New World Disorder*. London: HarperCollins.
Hout, W. and J. Grugel (eds) (1999) *Regionalism across the North/South Divide: State Strategies and Globalization*. London: Routledge.
Houtart, F. and F. Polet (2001) *The Other Davos: The Globalization of Resistance to the World Economic System*. London: Zed.
Hovden, E. and E. Keene (eds) (2002) *The Globalization of Liberalism*. Basingstoke: Palgrave Macmillan.
Hudson, Y. (ed.) (1999) *Globalism and the Obsolescence of the State*. Lewiston, NY: Mellen Press.

Hughes, C.W. (2005) 'Japan, East Asian Regionalization and Selective Resistance to Globalization: Regional Divisions of Labour and Financial Cooperation', in R. Stubbs and G. R. D. Underhill (eds), *Political Economy and the Changing Global Order*. Oxford: Oxford University Press, 3rd edn.

Hume, D. (1741–2) *Essays: Moral, Political and Literary*. London: Grant Richards, 1903.

Humphreys, D. (1996) *Forest Politics: The Evolution of International Cooperation*. London: Earthscan.

Humphreys, D. (2003) 'Life Protective or Carcinogenic Challenge? Global Forests Governance Under Advanced Capitalism', *Global Environmental Politics*, vol. 3, no. 2 (May), pp. 40–56.

Huntington, S. P. (1991) *The Third Wave: Democratization in the Late Twentieth Century*. Norman: University of Oklahoma Press.

Huntington, S. P. (1993) 'The Clash of Civilizations?' *Foreign Affairs*, vol. 72, no. 3 (Summer), pp. 22–49.

Huntington, S. P. (1996) *The Clash of Civilizations and the Remaking of World Order*. New York: Simon & Schuster.

Hurrell, A. and N. Woods (eds) (1999) *Inequality, Globalization, and World Politics*. Oxford: Oxford University Press.

Hutanuwatr, P. (2002) Director of Wongsanit Ashram, in conversation with the author in Bangkok, 13 June.

Hutchings, K. and R. Dannreuther (eds) (1999) *Cosmopolitan Citizenship*. Basingstoke: Palgrave Macmillan.

Huth, A. (1937) *La radiodiffusion. Puissance mondiale* ['Radio Broadcasts: World Power']. Paris: Gallimard.

Hutton, W. (1996) *The State We're In*, rev. edn. London: Vintage.

Ianni, O. (1992) *A sociedade global*. Rio de Janeiro: Civilização Brasileira.

Ianni, O. (1996) *A era do globalismo*. Rio de Janeiro: Civilização Brasileira.

ICAO (1998) *Annual Civil Aviation Report 1997*. Montreal: International Civil Aviation Organisation.

ICAO (2003) Website of the International Civil Aviation Organization: www.icao.org, accessed on 24 August.

ICFTU (1998) 'Globalisation on Trial'. Statement of the International Confederation of Free Trade Unions to the Annual Meetings of the IMF and World Bank.

ICI (2004) *2004 Mutual Fund Fact Book*. Washington, DC: Investment Company Institute.

ICI (2005) 'Trends in Mutual Fund Investing December 2004', Investment Company Institute press release, 28 January, available at www.ici.org, accessed on 1 February 2005.

ICLEI (2003) Website of the International Council for Local Environmental Initiatives: http://www.iclei.org, accessed on 14 December.

IDEA (1997) *Voter Turnout from 1945 to 1997: A Global Report*. Stockholm: Institute for Democracy and Electoral Assistance.

IFAT (2004) Website of the International Fair Trade Association, www.ifat.org, accessed on 22 October.

IFC (1996) *Emerging Stock Markets Factbook 1996*. Washington, DC: International Finance Corporation.

ILGA (2005) Website of the International Lesbian and Gay Association: www.ilga.org, accessed on 18 January.

ILO (1995) *World Employment 1995*. Geneva: International Labour Organization.

ILO (1998) *Labour and Social Issues Relating to Export Processing Zones*. Geneva: International Labour Organization.

ILO (2003) *Employment and Social Policy in Respect of Export Processing Zones (EPZs)*. Geneva: International Labour Organization Committee on Employment and Social Policy, 286th session, GB.286/ESP/3.

Imber, M. F. (1989) *The USA, ILO, UNESCO and IAEA: Politicization and Withdrawal in the Specialized Agencies*. Basingstoke: Palgrave Macmillan.

IMF (1993) *International Financial Statistics Yearbook*. Washington, DC: International Monetary Fund.

IMF (1996) *Annual Report 1996*. Washington, DC: International Montary Fund.

IMF (2001) *International Capital Markets: Developments, Prospects, and Key Policy Issues*. Washington, DC: International Monetary Fund.

IMF (2003a) *Annual Report 2003: Making the Global Economy Work for All*. Washington, DC: International Monetary Fund.

IMF (2003b) 'Guide for IMF Staff Relations with Civil Society Organizations', 10 October, available at www.imf.org/external/np/cso/eng/2003/101003. htm.

IMF (2003c) Website of the International Monetary Fund: www.imf.org/external/np/ins/english/about.htm, accessed on 15 December.

IMF (2004) 'IMF Members' Quotas and Voting Power, and IMF Board of Governors', 9 April, online at: www.imf.org/external/np/sec/memdir/ members.htm.

Inayatullah, S. and I. Milojevic (1999) 'Exclusion and Communication in the Information Era: From Silences to Global Conversations', in W. Harcourt (ed.), *Women @ Internet: Creating New Cultures in Cyberspace*. London: Zed, pp. 76–90.

Inoguchi, T. (2001) *Global Change: A Japanese Perspective*. Basingstoke: Palgrave Macmillan.

INTELSAT (2005) Website of the International Telecommunications Satellite Organization, www.intelsat.com, accessed on 4 May.

Internet (2004) Website of Internet World Stats: www.internetworldstats.com, accessed on 22 October.

IPCC (1995) IPCC *Second Assessment. Climate Change 1995*. Geneva: World Meteorological Organization/United Nations Environment Programme.

IPPPH (2004) Website of the Initiative on Public–Private Partnerships for Health: www.ippph.org, accessed on 31 August.

ISC (2005) Website of the Internet Software Consortium, www.isc.org, accessed on 4 May.

ISMA (1995) *Annual Report 1994*. Zürich: International Securities Market Association.

ITU (2004) Website of the International Telecommunication Union, www.itu.int/wsis, accessed on 3 April.

ITWF (2004) Website of the International Transport Workers Federation, www.itf.org.uk, accessed on 3 April.

Iyer, P. (2000) *The Global Soul: Jet Lag, Shopping Malls, and the Search for Home*. New York: Knopf.

Jackson, J. H. (1998) *The World Trade Organisation*. London: Cassell.

Jacob, C. (1999) 'Mapping in the Mind: The Earth from Ancient Alexandria', in D. Cosgrove (ed.), *Mappings*. London: Reaktion Books, pp. 24–49.

James, H. (1996) *International Monetary Cooperation since Bretton Woods*. New York: Oxford University Press.

James, H. (2001) *The End of Globalization: Lessons from the Great Depression*. Cambridge, MA: Harvard University Press.

Jameson, F. (1991) *Postmodernism, Or, The Cultural Logic of Late Capitalism*. London: Verso.

Jameson, F. and M. Miyoshi (eds) (1998) *The Cultures of Globalization*. Durham, NC: Duke University Press.

Jarvis, A. P. and A. J. Paolini (1995) 'Locating the State', in J. A. Camilleri *et al.* (eds), *The State in Transition: Reimagining Political Space*. Boulder, CO: Rienner, pp. 3–19.

Jenkins, R. *et al.* (eds) (2002) *Corporate Responsibility and Labour Rights: Codes of Conduct in the Global Economy*. London: Earthscan.

Jessop, B. (1993) 'Towards a Schumpeterian Workfare State? Preliminary Remarks on Post-Fordist Political Economy', *Studies in Political Economy*, vol. 40 (Spring), pp. 7–39

Jessop, B. (1994) 'Changing Forms and Functions of the State in an Era of Globalization and Regionalization', in R. Delorme and K. Dopfer (eds), *The Political Economy of Diversity: Evolutionary Perspectives on Economic Order and Disorder*. Aldershot: Elgar, pp. 102–25.

Joekes, S. and A. Weston (1994) *Women and the New Trade Agenda*. New York: UNIFEM.

John, J. and A. Chenoy (eds) (1996) *Labour, Environment and Globalisation: Social Clause in Multilateral Trade Agreements: A Southern Response*. New Delhi: Centre for Education and Communication.

Johnson, J. and G. Laxer (2003) 'Solidarity in the Age of Globalization: Lessons from the Anti-MAI and Zapatista Struggles', *Theory and Society*, vol. 32, pp. 39–91.

Johnson, S. (1998) *Black Globalism: the International Politics of a Non-State Nation*. Aldershot: Ashgate.

Johnson, S. and B. Rogaly (1997) *Microfinance and Poverty Reduction*. Oxford: Oxfam/ACTIONAID.

Jolly, R. (1995) Remarks by the Acting Director of UNICEF at the World Summit for Social Development, Copenhagen, 5–12 March.

Jones, A. (1994) 'Wired World: Communications Technology, Governance and the Democratic Uprising', in E. A. Comor (ed.), *The Global Political Economy of Communication: Hegemony, Telecommunication and the Information Economy*. Basingstoke: Palgrave Macmillan, pp. 145–64.

Jones, C. (1999) *Global Justice: Defending Cosmopolitanism*. Oxford: Oxford University Press.

Jones, G. (1993) 'Multinational Banking Strategies', in H. Cox *et al.* (eds), *The Growth of Global Business*. London: Routledge, pp. 38–61.

Jones, G. (1996) 'Transnational Corporations – A Historical Perspective', in UNCTAD, *Transnational Corporations and World Development*. London: International Thomson Business Press, pp. 3–26.

Jones, S. G. (ed.) (1994) *CyberSociety: Computer-Mediated Communication and Community*. London: Sage.

Jordan, B. (1995) 'Globalizing Trade Unions', *Multinational Monitor*, vol. 16 (June), pp. 26–8.

Jørgensen, K. E. and B. Rosamond (2002) 'Europe: Laboratory for a Global Polity?' in M. Ougaard and R. Higgott (eds), *Towards a Global Polity*. London: Routledge, pp. 189–206.

Joyner, D. (2004) 'Restructuring the Multilateral Export Control Regime System', *Journal of Conflict and Security Law*, vol. 9 (Summer), pp. 181–211.

Juergensmeyer, M. (1993) *The New Cold War? Religious Nationalism Confronts the Secular State*. Berkeley: University of California Press.

Justice, D. W. (1999) 'The New Codes of Conduct and the Social Partners'. Geneva: International Labour Organization.

Kahler, M. and D. A. Lake (eds) (2003) *Governance in a Global Economy: Political Authority in Transition*. Princeton, NJ: Princeton University Press.

Kahin, B. and C. Nesson (eds) (1997) *Borders in Cyberspace: Information Policy and the Global Information Infrastructure*. Cambridge, MA: MIT Press.

Kaiser, R. (2005) 'Sub-State Governments in International Arenas: Paradiplomacy and Multi-Level Governance in Europe and North America', in G. Lachapelle and S. Paquin (eds), *Mastering Globalization: New Sub-States' Governance and Strategies*. London: Routledge, pp. 90–103.

Kaldor, M. (1999) *New and Old Wars: Organised Violence in a Global Era*. Cambridge: Polity.

Kaldor, M. (2003) *Global Civil Society: An Answer to War*. Cambridge: Polity.

Kaldor, M. *et al.* (2000) 'Seattle: December '99?' *Millennium: Journal of International Studies*, vol. 29, no. 1, pp. 103–40.

Kamel, R. (1990) *The Global Factory: Analysis and Action for a New Economic Era*. Philadelphia: American Friends Service Committee.

Kaneko, M. (1999) *Han Gurouburizumu: Shijou Kaiku no Senryakuteki Shikou* ['Anti-Globalism: Strategic Thinking on Market Reforms']. Tokyo: Iwanami Shoten.

Kang, N.-H. and K. Sakai (2000) *International Strategic Alliances: Their Role in Industrial Globalization*. Paris: OECD, STI Working Papers 2000/5.

Kaplan, R.D. (2000) *The Coming Anarchy: Shattering the Dreams of the Post Cold War*. New York: Random House.

Kapstein, E. B. (1991–2) ' "We Are Us": the Myth of the Multinational', *The National Interest*, vol. 26 (Winter), pp. 55–62.

Kapstein, E. B. (1994) *Governing the Global Economy: International Finance and the State*. Cambridge, MA: Harvard University Press.

Kapstein, E. B. (1996) 'Workers and the World Economy', *Foreign Affairs*, vol. 75, no. 3 (May–June), pp. 16–37.

Karatnycky, A. (1999) 'The 1998 Freedom House Survey: the Decline of Illiberal Democracy', *Journal of Democracy*, vol. 10, no. 1 (January), pp. 112–25.

Katz, P. L. (1988) *The Information Society: An International Perspective*. New York: Praeger.

Kaul, I. *et al.* (eds) (1999) *Global Public Goods: International Cooperation in the 21st Century*. New York: Oxford University Press.

Kaul, I. *et al.* (eds) (2003) *Providing Public Goods: Managing Globalization*. New York: Oxford University Press.

Kautsky, K. (1914) 'Ultra-Imperialism', *New Left Review*, No. 59 (January–February 1970), pp. 41–6.

Keane, J. (2003) *Global Civil Society?* Cambridge: Cambridge University Press.

Kearney/FP (2001) 'Measuring Globalization', *Foreign Policy*, No. 122 (January–February), pp. 56–65.

Kearney/FP (2002) 'Globalization's Last Hurrah?' *Foreign Policy*, No. 128 (January–February), pp. 38–51.

Kearney/FP (2003) 'Measuring Globalization: Who's Up, Who's Down', *Foreign Policy*, No. 134 (January–February), pp. 60–72.

Kearney/FP (2004) 'Economic Reversals, Forward Momentum', *Foreign Policy*, No. 141 (March–April), pp. 54–69.

Keating, M. (1999) 'Regions and International Affairs: Motives, Opportunities and Strategies', in F. Aldecoa and M. Keating (eds), *Paradiplomacy in Action: The Foreign Relations of Subnational Governments*. London: Cass, pp. 1–16.

Keating, M. (2001) *Nations against the State: The New Politics of Nationalism in Quebec, Catalonia and Scotland*. Basingstoke: Palgrave Macmillan.

Keck, M. and K. Sikkink (1998) *Activists beyond Borders: Transnational Advocacy Networks in International Politics*. Ithaca, NY: Cornell University Press.

Kempadoo, K. and J. Doezema (eds) (1998) *Global Sex Workers: Rights, Resistance, and Redefinition*. London: Routledge.

Kennedy, P. and C. J. Danks (eds) (2001) *Globalization and National Identities: Crisis or Opportunity?* Basingstoke: Palgrave Macmillan.

Kennedy, P. M. (1987) *The Rise and Fall of the Great Powers: Economic Change and Military Conflict from 1500 to 2000*. New York: Random House.

Keohane, R. O. (1998) 'International Institutions: Can Interdependence Work?' *Foreign Policy*, No. 110 (Spring), pp. 82–96.

Keohane, R. O. (2001) 'Governance in a Partially Globalized World', *American Political Science Review*, vol. 95, no. 1 (March), pp. 1–13.

Keohane, R. O. and L. L. Martin (1995) 'The Promise of Institutionalist Theory', *International Security*, vol. 20, no. 1 (Summer), pp. 39–51.

Keohane, R. O. and J. S. Nye (1977) *Power and Interdependence: World Politics in Transition*. Boston, MA: Little, Brown.

Keohane, R. O. and J. S. Nye (2000) 'Globalization: What's New? What's Not? (And So What?)' *Foreign Policy*, no. 118 (Spring), pp. 104–19.

Kepel, G. (1991) *The Revenge of God: the Resurgence of Islam, Christianity and Judaism in the Modern World*. Cambridge: Polity Press, 1994.

Kerr, I. M. (1984) A History of the Eurobond Market: the First 21 Years. London: Euromoney.

Kessler, C. S. (2000) 'Globalization: Another False Universalism?' *Third World Quarterly*, vol. 21, no. 6, pp. 931–42.

Khagram, S. (2000) 'Toward Democratic Governance for Sustainable Development: Transnational Civil Society Organizing around Big Dams', in A. M. Florini (ed.), *The Third Force: The Rise of Transnational Civil Society*. Tokyo/Washington, DC: Japan Center for International Exchange/Carnegie Endowment for International Peace, pp. 83–114.

Khagram, S. *et al.* (eds) (2002) *Restructuring World Politics: Transnational Social Movements, Networks, and Norms*. Minneapolis: University of Minnesota Press.

Khan, L. A. (1996) *The Extinction of Nation-States: A World without Borders*. The Hague: Kluwer Law International.

Khor, M. (1995) Address to the International Forum on Globalization, New York City, November.

Khor, M. (2001) *Globalization and the South*. Penang, Malaysia: Third World Network.

Kidder, T. and M. McGinn (1995) 'In the Wake of NAFTA: Transnational Workers' Networks', *Social Policy*, vol. 25, no. 4 (Summer), pp. 14–21.

Kidron, M. and R. Segal (1995) *The State of the World Atlas*, 5th edn. London: Penguin.

Kilminster, R. (1997) 'Globalization as an Emergent Concept', in A. Scott (ed.), *The Limits of Globalization: Cases and Arguments*. London: Routledge, pp. 257–83.

Kim, S. S. 'Chinese Perspectives on World Order', in D. Jacobsen (ed.), *Old Nations, New World: Conceptions of World Order*. Boulder, CO: Westview, pp. 37–74.

King, A. and B. Schneider (1991) *The First Global Revolution: A Report by the Council of the Club of Rome*. New York: Pantheon.

King, A. D. (2000) 'Cities: Contradictory Utopias', in J. Nederveen Pieterse (ed.), *Global Futures: Shaping Globalization*. London: Sage, pp. 224–41.

King, A. D. (ed.) (1991) *Culture, Globalization and the World-System: Contemporary Conditions for the Representation of Identity*. Basingstoke: Palgrave Macmillan.

King, R. *et al.* (2000) *Sunset Lives: British Retirement Migration to the Mediterranean*. Oxford: Berg.

Kingsnorth, P. (2003) *One No, Many Yeses: A Journey to the Heart of the Global Resistance Movement*. London: Free Press.

Kirton, J. J. *et al.* (eds) (2001) *Guiding Global Order: G8 Governance in the Twenty-First Century*. Aldershot: Ashgate.

Kitchin, R. (1998) 'Towards Geographies of Cyberspace', *Progress in Human Geography*, vol. 22, no. 3, pp. 385–406.

Kitchin, R. and M. Dodge (2002) 'The Emerging Geographies of Cyberspace', in R. J. Johnston *et al.* (eds), *Geographies of Global Change: Remapping the World*. Oxford: Blackwell, pp. 340–54.

Klein, N. (2000) *No Logo: Taking Aim at the Brand Bullies*. London: Flamingo.

Klein, N. (2002) *Fences and Windows: Dispatches from the Front Lines of the Globalization Debate*. Toronto: Vintage Canada.

Knill, C. and D. Lehmkuhl (2002) 'Private Actors and the State: Internationalization and Changing Patterns of Governance', *Governance: An International Journal of Public Policy*, vol. 15, no. 1 (January), pp. 41–64.

Kobrin, S. J. (1998a) 'Back to the Future: Neomedievalism and the Post Modern Digital World Economy', *Journal of International Affairs*, vol. 51, no. 2 (Spring), pp. 361–86.

Kobrin, S. J. (1998b) 'The MAI and the Clash of Globalizations', *Foreign Policy*, no. 112 (Autumn), pp. 97–109.

Koch, C. (2003) *The Day the World Said NO to War: 02/15*. Edinburgh: AK Distribution.

Korten, D. C. (1995) *When Corporations Rule the World*. West Hartford, CT: Kumarian Press.

Kotkin, J. (1992) *Tribes: How Race, Religion, and Identity Determine Success in the New Global Economy*. New York: Random House.

Kraidy, M. M. (1999) 'The Global, the Local, and the Hybrid: A Native Ethnography of Glocalization', *Critical Studies in Mass Communication*, vol. 16, no. 4 (December), pp. 456–76.

Krasner, S. D. (1993) 'Economic Interdependence and Independent Statehood', in R. H. Jackson and A. James (eds), *States in a Changing World: A Contemporary Analysis*. Oxford: Clarendon, pp. 301–21.

Krasner, S. D. (1994) 'International Political Economy: Abiding Discord', *Review of International Political Economy*, vol. 1, no. 1 (Spring), pp. 13–19.

Krasner, S. D. (1999) *Sovereignty: Organized Hypocrisy*. Princeton, NJ: Princeton University Press.

Krasner, S. D. (2001) 'Abiding Sovereignty', *International Political Science Review*, vol. 22, no. 3 (July), pp. 229–52.

Krasner, S. D. (ed.) (2003) *Problematic Sovereignty: Contested Rules and Political Possibilities*. New York: Columbia University Press.

Krause, K. and M. C. Williams (eds) (1997) *Critical Security Studies: Concepts and Cases*. London: UCL Press.

Kroebner, A. L. (1945) 'The Ancient Greek *Oikoumenê* as an Historic Culture Aggregate', *Journal of the Royal Anthropological Institute of Great Britain and Ireland*, vol. 75, pp. 9–20.

Krueger, A. O. (ed.) (1998) *The WTO as an International Organization*. Chicago: University of Chicago Press.

Krugman, P. (2000) *The Return of Depression Economics*. London: Penguin, rev'd edn.

Ku, C. (2001) *Global Governance and the Changing Face of International Law*. New Haven, CN: ACUNS Reports & Papers, No. 2.

Kuhn, S. E. (1995) 'Winning Strategies for the Next Ten Years', *Fortune*, vol. 132, no. 25 (25 December), pp. 44–50.

Küng, H. (1990) *Global Responsibility: In Search of a New World Ethic*. London: SCM, 1991.

Küng, H. and K.-J. Kuschel (eds) (1993) *A Global Ethic: The Declaration of the Parliament of the World's Religions*. London: SCM.

Kurzer, P. (1993) *Business and Banking: Political Change and Economic Integration in Western Europe*. Ithaca, NY: Cornell University Press.

Kwon, H. (2000) 'Globalisation, Unemployment and Policy Responses in Korea: Repositioning the State?' Paper to the Globalism and Social Policy Programme seminar, New Delhi, November.

Kymlicka, W. (2001) *Contemporary Political Philosophy*. Oxford: Oxford University Press, 2nd edn.

Lacarrieu, M. and L. Raggio (1997) 'Citizenship within the Globalization Context: an Analysis of Trends within Mercosur', *The Mankind Quarterly*, vol. 37, no. 3 (Spring), pp. 263–81.

Lang, T. and C. Hines (1993) *The New Protectionism: Protecting the Future against Free Trade*. London: Earthscan.

Langmore, J. *et al.* (2002) 'Global Social Policy Forum: The Future of Finance for Development', *Global Social Policy*, vol. 2, no. 2 (August), pp. 131–9.

Lapidoth, R. (1992) 'Sovereignty in Transition', *Journal of International Affairs*, vol. 45, no. 2 (Winter), pp. 325–46.

Lash, S. (1990) *Sociology of Postmodernism*. London: Routledge.

Lash, S. and J. Urry (1994) *Economies of Signs and Space*. London: Sage.

Latinobarómetro (2004) *Summary Report Latinobarómetro 2004: A Decade of Measurements*. Santiago: Corporación Latinobarómetro.

Leanne, S. (1994) 'African-American Initiatives against Minority Rule in South Africa: A Politicized Diaspora in World Politics'. Doctoral dissertation, University of Oxford.

Lechner, F. J. and J. Boli (eds) (2000) *The Globalization Reader*. Oxford: Blackwell.

Leclerc, G. (2000) *La mondialisation culturelle. Les civilisations à l'épreuve*. Paris: Presses Universitaires de France.

Lee, E. (1996) *The Labour Movement and the Internet: The New Internationalism*. London: Pluto.

Lee, E. (1997a) 'Globalisation and Labour Standards: A Review of the Issues', *International Labour Review*, vol. 136, no. 2 (Summer), pp. 173–190.

Lee, E. (1997b) *The Labour Movement and the Internet: The New Internationalism*. London: Pluto.

Lee, H.K. (1999) 'Globalization and the Emerging Welfare State – The Experience of South Korea', *International Journal of Social Welfare*, vol. 8, no. 1, pp. 23–37.

Lee, K. (ed.) (2003) *Health Impacts of Globalization: Towards Global Governance*. Basingstoke: Palgrave Macmillan.

Lee, K. *et al.* (eds) (2002) *Health Policy in a Globalising World*. Cambridge: Cambridge University Press.

Lefebvre, H. (1974) *The Production of Space*. Oxford: Blackwell, 1991.

LeHeron, R. (1993) *Globalized Agriculture: Political Choice*. Oxford: Pergamon.

Lehmkuhl, D. (2003) 'Resolving Transnational Disputes: Commercial Arbitration and the Multiple Providers of Governance Services'. Paper for the 2003 ECPR Joint Sessions, Edinburgh, 28 March–2 April.

Lekhi, R. (2000) 'The Politics of African America On-Line', *Democratization*, vol. 7, no. 1 (Spring), pp. 76–101.

Lenin, V. I. (1917) *Imperialism, the Highest Stage of Capitalism*. New York: International Publishers, 1939.

Levich, R. M. *et al.* (eds) (2002) *Ratings, Rating Agencies and the Global Financial System*. Norwell, MA: Kluwer Academic.

Levitt, T. (1983) 'The Globalization of Markets', *Harvard Business Review*, vol. 61, no. 3 (May–June), pp. 92–102.

Lewis, W. A. (1978) *The Evolution of the International Economic Order*. Princeton, NJ: Princeton University Press.

Lietaer, B. (1996) 'Global Currency Proposals', in J. M. Griesgraber and B. G. Gunter (eds), *The World's Monetary System: Toward Stability and Sustainability in the Twenty-First Century*. London: Pluto, pp. 94–114.

Lim, L. (1990) 'Women's Work in Export Factories: the Politics of Cause', in I. Tinker (ed.), *Persistent Inequalities: Women and World Development*. Oxford: Oxford University Press, pp. 101–19.

Lindert, P. H. and J. G. Williamson (2001) 'Does Globalization Make the World More Unequal?' NBER Working Paper Series No. 8228.

Ling, L. H. M. (2000) 'Globalization and the Spectre of Fu Manchu: White Man's Burden as Dark Irony', in J.-S. Fritz and M. Lensu (eds), *Value Pluralism, Normative Theory and International Relations*. Basingstoke: Palgrave Macmillan, pp. 132–59.

Linklater, A. (1998) *The Transformation of Political Community: Ethical Foundations of the Post-Westphalian Era*. Cambridge: Polity Press.

Linklater, A. (2002) 'Cosmopolitan Citizenship', in E. F. Isin and B. S. Turner (eds), *Handbook of Citizenship Studies*. London: Sage, pp. 317–32.

Lipschutz, R. D. (1992) 'Reconstructing World Politics: The Emergence of Global Civil Society', *Millennium*, vol. 21, no. 3 (Winter), pp. 389–420.

Lipschutz, R. D. with J. Mayer (1996) *Global Civil Society and Global Environmental Governance*. Albany, NY: State University of New York Press.

Litfin, K. T. (ed.) (1998) *The Greening of Sovereignty in World Politics*. Cambridge, MA: MIT Press.

Llambi, L. (1994) 'Comparative Advantages and Disadvantages in Latin American Nontraditional Fruit and Vegetable Exports', in P. McMichael (ed.), *The Global Restructuring of Agro-Food Systems*. Ithaca, NY: Cornell University Press, pp. 190–213.

Lloyd, J. (1998) ' "Digital Age" Skirts Rural America's Sparsely Populated Areas, Especially in the West, Are Missing High-Tech Infrastructure Vital to 21st-Century Economy', *Christian Science Monitor*, 31 December.

Loader, B. D. (ed.) (1998) *Cyberspace Divide: Equality, Agency and Policy in the Information Society*. London: Routledge.

LoC (1999), Website of the Library of Congress, http://lcweb.loc.gov/catalog/, accessed on 6 December.

LoC (2005) Website of the Library of Congress, http://catalog.loc.gov/, accessed on 7 February.

Lockwood, B. (2004) 'How Robust Is the Kearney/Foreign Policy Globalisation Index?' *The World Economy*, vol. 27, no. 4 (April), pp. 507–24.

Lorwin, L. L. (1953) *The International Labor Movement: History, Policies, Outlook*. New York: Harper & Brothers.

Lovelock, J. E. (1979) *Gaia: A New Look at Life on Earth*. Oxford: Oxford University Press.

Lovelock, J. E. (1972) 'Gaia as Seen through the Atmosphere', *Atmospheric Environment*, vol. 6, issue 8 (August), pp. 579–80.

Low, M. (1997) 'Representation Unbound: Globalization and Democracy', in K. R. Cox (ed.), *Spaces of Globalization: Reasserting the Power of the Local.* New York: Guilford, pp. 240–80.

Lowenfeld, A. F. (2002) *International Litigation and Arbitration.* St. Paul, MN: West Group, 2nd edn.

Luce, C.B. (1943) Speech to the House of Representatives, *Congressional Record*, vol. 89, 9 February.

Luhmann, N. (1982) 'The World Society as a Social System', *International Journal of General Systems*, vol. 8, pp. 131–8.

Luke, T. W. (1995) 'New World Order or Neo-World Orders: Power, Politics and Ideology in Informationalizing Glocalities', in M. Featherstone *et al., Global Modernities.* London: Sage, pp. 91–107.

MacAloon, J. J. (1981) *This Great Symbol: Pierre de Coubertin and the Origins of the Modern Olympic Games.* Chicago: University of Chicago Press.

Mackenzie, D. (1990) *Inventing Accuracy: A Historical Sociology of Nuclear Missile Guidance.* Cambridge, MA: MIT Press.

Mackinlay, J. (2002) *Globalisation and Insurgency.* Oxford: Oxford University Press, Adelphi Paper 352.

Maclean, J. (1999) 'Philosophical Roots of Globalization: Philosophical Routes to Globalization', in R. Germain (ed.), *Globalization and its Critics: Perspectives from Political Economy.* Basingstoke: Palgrave Macmillan, pp. 3–66.

Madden, P. (1992) *Raw Deal: Trade and the World's Poor.* London: Christian Aid.

Magdoff, H. (1992) 'Globalization – to What End?', in R. Miliband and L. Panitch (eds), *Socialist Register 1992.* London: Merlin, pp. 44–75.

Maghroori, R. and B. Ramberg (eds) (1982) *Globalism versus Realism: International Relations' Third Debate.* Boulder, CO: Westview.

Maguire, K. (2000) 'A Tobacco Giant and Its Global Reach', *Guardian*, 31 January.

Main, J. (1989) 'How To Go Global – and Why', *Fortune*, vol. 120, no. 5 (28 August), pp. 54–8.

Manalansan, M. (1997) 'In the Shadows of Stonewall: Examining Gay Transnational Politics and the Diasporic Dilemma', in L. Lowe and D. Lloyd (eds), *The Politics of Culture in the Shadow of Capital.* Durham, NC: Duke University Press, pp. 485–505.

Mandaville, P. G. (2001) *Transnational Muslim Politics: Reimagining the Umma.* London: Routledge.

Mandel, R. (2002) *Armies without States: The Privatization of Security.* Boulder, CO: Rienner.

Mandell, L. (1990) *The Credit Card Industry: A History.* Boston: Twayne.

Mander, J. and E. Goldsmith (eds) (1996) *The Case against the Global Economy and the Turn to the Local.* San Francisco: Sierra Club Books.

Mani, M. and D. Wheeler (1998) 'In Search of Pollution Havens? Dirty Industry in the World Economy, 1960 to 1995', *Journal of Environment and Development*, vol. 7, no. 3 (September), pp. 215–47.

Mann, M. (1986) *The Sources of Social Power. Vol. I: A History of Power from the Beginning to A.D. 1760.* Cambridge: Cambridge University Press.

Mann, M. (1988) *States, War and Capitalism: Studies in Political Sociology.* Oxford: Blackwell.

Mann, M. (1997) 'Has Globalization Ended the Rise and Rise of the Nation-State?', *Review of International Political Economy*, vol. 4, no. 3 (Autumn), pp. 472–96.

Mansfield, E. D. and H. V. Milner (eds) (1997) *The Political Economy of Regionalism.* New York: Columbia University Press.

Marchand, M. H. and A. S. Runyan (eds) (2000) *Gender and Global Restructuring: Sightings, Sites and Resistances.* London: Routledge.

Marglin, S. A. (1988) *Lessons of the Golden Age of Capitalism.* Helsinki: World Institute for Development Economics Research.

Mariana (2002) Activist with the Homeless Workers Movement (MTST), interviewed by the author in Rio de Janeiro on 28 January.

Marks, G. *et al.* (1996) *Governance in the European Union*. London: Sage.

Marrison, A. (ed.) (1998) *Free Trade and Its Reception 1815–1960*. London: Routledge.

Marshall, D. D. (1996) 'Understanding Late-Twentieth-Century Capitalism: Reassessing the Globalization Theme', *Government and Opposition*, vol. 31, no. 2 (Spring), pp. 193–215.

Martib, B. (2000) *New Leaf or Fig Leaf: The Challenge of the New Washington Consensus*. London: Bretton Woods Project and Public Services International.

Martin, H.-P. and H. Schumann (1996) *The Global Trap: Globalization and the Assault on Prosperity and Democracy*. London: Zed, 1997.

Martinez, E. (2000) 'Where Was the Color in Seattle? Looking for Reasons Why the Great Battle was so White?' *ColorLines*, vol. 3, no. 1 (Spring), available online at www.arc.org/C_Lines/CLArchive/story3_1_02.html, accessed on 1 February 2005.

Marty, M. E. and R. S. Appleby (eds) (1991) *Fundamentalisms Observed*. Chicago: University of Chicago Press.

Marx, K. (1857–8) *Grundrisse: Foundations of the Critique of Political Economy*. Harmondsworth: Penguin, 1973.

Marx, K. (1867) *Capital, Volume I*. London: Lawrence & Wishart, 1970.

Marx, K. and F. Engels (1848) *Manifesto of the Communist Party*. Moscow: Progress, 1977.

Maskus, K. E. (2000) *Intellectual Property Rights in the Global Economy*. Washington, DC: Institute for International Economics.

Massey, D. (1994) *Space, Place and Gender*. Cambridge: Polity.

MasterCard (2003) Website of MasterCard, www.mastercard.com, accessed on 18 July and 23 August.

Mattelart, A. (1989) *Advertising International: The Privatisation of Public Space*. London: Routledge, 1991.

Mattli, W. (2001) 'Private Justice in a Global Economy: From Litigation to Arbitration', *International Organization*, vol. 55, no. 4 (Autumn), pp. 919–48.

Mawle, A. (1997) 'Women, Environment and the United Nations', in F. Dodds (ed.), *The Way Forward: Beyond Agenda 21*. London: Earthscan, pp. 146–57.

Mayall, J. (ed.) (1996) *The New Interventionism 1991–1994*. Cambridge: Cambridge University Press.

Mayobre, E. (ed.) (1999) *G-24: The Developing Countries in the International Financial System*. Boulder, CO: Rienner.

Mazlish, B. and R. Buultjens (eds) (1993) *Conceptualizing Global History*. Boulder, CO: Westview.

Mazrui, A. A. (1994) 'Global Apartheid: Structural and Overt', *Alternatives*, vol. 19, no. 2 (Spring), pp. 185–7.

McChesney, R. W. (1997) 'The Global Media Giants: The Nine Firms that Dominate the World', *Extra*, November/December, online at: www.fair.org/extra/9711/gmg.html, accessed on 1 February 2005.

McChesney, R. W. *et al.* (eds) (1998) *Capitalism and the Information Age: The Political Economy of the Global Communication Revolution*. New York: Monthly Review Press.

McCormick, J. (1989) *Reclaiming Paradise: The Global Environmental Movement*. Bloomington, IN: Indiana University Press.

McCulloch, N. *et al.* (2001) *Trade Liberalization and Poverty: A Handbook*. London: CEPR/DFID.

McDowell, L. and G. Court (1994) 'Gender Divisions of Labour in the Post-Fordist Economy: The Maintenance of Occupational Sex Segregation in the Financial Services Sector', *Environment and Planning A*, vol. 26, no. 9 (September), pp. 1397–418.

McGrew, A. (1997a) 'Globalization and Territorial Democracy: An Introduction', in A. McGrew (ed.), *The Transformation of Democracy? Globalization and Territorial Democracy*. Cambridge: Polity Press, pp. 1–24.

McGrew, A. (ed.) (1997b) *The Transformation of Democracy? Globalization and Territorial Democracy*. Cambridge: Polity Press.

McGrew, A. (2006) 'Democracy', in R. Robertson and J. A. Scholte (eds), *Encyclopedia of Globalization*. London: Routledge.

McKelvey, M. *et al.* (eds) (2004) *The Economic Dynamics of Modern Biotechnology*. Cheltenham: Elgar.

McKenzie, R. B. and D. R. Lee (1991) *Quicksilver Capitalism: How the Rapid Movement of Wealth Has Changed the World*. New York: Free Press.

McLuhan, M. and Q. Fiore (1968) *War and Peace in the Global Village*. New York: McGraw-Hill.

McMichael, P. (1993) 'World Food System Restructuring under a GATT Regime', *Political Geography*, vol. 12, no. 3 (May), pp. 198–214.

McMichael, P. (1996a) *Development and Social Change: A Global Perspective*. Thousand Oaks, CA: Pine Forge Press.

McMichael, P. (1996b) 'Globalization: Myths and Realities', *Rural Sociology*, vol. 61, no. 1 (Spring), pp. 25–55.

McMichael, P. (ed.) (1994) *The Global Restructuring of Agro-Food Systems*. Ithaca, NY: Cornell University Press.

McNeill, W. H. (1963) *The Rise of the West: A History of the Human Community*. Chicago: University of Chicago Press.

McNeill, W. H. (1976) *Plagues and Peoples*. Oxford: Blackwell.

McNeill, W. H. (1986) *Polyethnicity and National Unity in World History*. Toronto: University of Toronto Press.

McQuaig, L. (1999) *The Cult of Impotence*. Toronto: Penguin.

Meadows, D. H. *et al.* (1992) *Beyond the Limits: A Global Collapse or a Sustainable Future*. London: Earthscan.

Mehta, M. (2006) 'Nanotechnology', in R. Robertson and J. A. Scholte (eds), *Encyclopedia of Globalization*. London: Routledge.

Mekata, M. (2000) 'Building Partnerships toward a Common Goal: Experiences of the International Campaign to Ban Landmines', in A. M. Florini (ed.), *The Third Force: The Rise of Transnational Civil Society*. Tokyo/Washington, DC: Japan Center for International Exchange/Carnegie Endowment for International Peace, pp. 143–76.

Mendell, M. and D. Salée (eds) (1991) *The Legacy of Karl Polanyi: Market, State and Society at the End of the Twentieth Century*. Basingstoke: Palgrave Macmillan.

Mendonsa, E. (2001) *Continuity and Change in a West African Society: Globalization's Impact on the Sisala of Ghana*. Durham, NC: Carolina Academic Press.

Merle, M. (1974) *Sociologie des relations internationales*. Paris: Dalloz.

Mertes, T. (ed.) (2004) *A Movement of Movements: Is Another World Really Possible?* London: Verso.

Meyer, B. and P. Geschiere (eds) (1998) 'Globalisation and Identity: Dialectics of Flows and Closures', *Development and Change*, vol. 29, no. 4 (October), pp. 601–928.

Meyer, J. *et al.* (1997) 'World Society and the Nation-State', *American Journal of Sociology*, vol. 103, no. 1, pp. 144–81.

Mhone, G. and O. Edigheji (eds) (2003) *Governance in the New South Africa: The Challenges of Globalisation*. Lansdowne: University of Cape Town Press.

Michelmann, H. J. and P. Soldatos (eds) (1990) *Federalism and International Relations: The Role of Subnational Units*. Oxford: Clarendon.

Michie, J. (ed.) (2003) *The Handbook of Globalisation*. Cheltenham: Elgar.

Mies, M. (1998) *Patriarchy and Accumulation on a World Scale: Women in the International Division of Labour*. London: Zed, 2nd edn.

Milanovic, B. (1999) 'True World Income Distribution, 1988 and 1993: First Calculation Based on Household Surveys Alone', World Bank Policy Research Working Papers No. 2244, November.

Milanovic, B. (2005) *Worlds Apart: Measuring Global and International Inequality*. Princeton, NJ: Princeton University Press.

Miles, E. L. *et al.* (2002) *Environmental Regime Effectiveness: Confronting Theory with Evidence*. Cambridge, MA: MIT Press.

Miller, M. (1991) *Debt and the Environment: Converging Crises*. New York: United Nations.

Miller, M. *et al.* (2004) 'World Finance and the US "New Economy": Welfare Efficiency and Moral Hazard'. Draft paper, October.

Minear, L. and T. G. Weiss (1995) *Mercy under Fire: War and the Global Humanitarian Community*. Boulder, CO: Westview.

Mingkwan, Suwan and Tern Tarat (2002) Fisherfolk in Ubon Ratchathani Province, Thailand, in discussion with the author in Mae Mun Man Yuan village on 16 June.

Mishra, R. (1999) *Globalization and the Welfare State*. Cheltenham: Elgar.

MIT (2004) Website of the Unwiring the World Project: http://www.media.mit.edu/unwired/assumptions.html, accessed on 22 October.

Mittelman, J. H. (1999) *The Future of Globalization*. Bangi: Penerbit Universiti Kebangsaan Malaysia.

Mittelman, J. H. (2000) *The Globalization Syndrome: Transformation and Resistance*. Princeton, NJ: Princeton University Press.

Mittelman, J. H. (2002) 'Globalization: An Ascendant Paradigm?', *International Studies Perspectives*, vol. 3, no. 1 (February), pp. 1–14.

Mittelman, J. H. and R. Johnston (1999) 'The Globalization of Organized Crime, the Courtesan State, and the Corruption of Civil Society', *Global Governance*, vol. 5, no. 1 (January–March), pp. 103–26.

Mittelman, J. H. and N. Othman (eds) (2001) *Capturing Globalization*. London: Routledge.

Mlinar, Z. (ed.) (1992) *Globalization and Territorial Identities*. Aldershot: Avebury.

Moghadam, V. M. (ed.) (1993) *Democratic Reform and the Position of Women in Transitional Economies*. Oxford: Clarendon.

Mohanty, C. T. (2003) *Feminism without Borders: Decolonizing Theory, Practicing Solidarity*. Bloomington, IN: Indiana University Press.

Monbiot, G. (2003) *The Age of Consent: A Manifesto for a New World Order*. London: Flamingo.

Moon, G. (1995) *Free Trade: What's in it for Women?* Fitzroy (Australia): Community Aid Abroad.

Morrison, B. (ed.) (2003) *Transnational Democracy: A Critical Consideration of Sites and Sources*. Aldershot: Ashgate.

Morrissey, O. and I. Filatotchev (2000) 'Globalisation and Trade: The Implications for Exports from Marginalised Economies', *Journal of Development Studies*, vol. 37, no. 2 (December), pp. 1–12.

Mosco, V. (1988) 'Introduction: Information in the Pay-Per Society' in Mosco and J. Wasko (eds), *The Political Economy of Information*. Madison: University of Wisconsin Press, pp. 3–26.

Mosler, D. and R. Catley (2000) *Global America: Imposing Liberalism on a Recalcitrant World*. Westport, CT: Praeger.

Mosse, G. L. (1985) *Nationalism and Sexuality: Respectability and Abnormal Sexuality in Modern Europe*. New York: Fertig.

Mowlana, H. (1997) *Global Information and World Communication: New Frontiers in International Relations*. London: Sage, 2nd edn.

MPA (2004) Website of the Maritime and Port Authority of Singapore, www.mpa.gov.sg, accessed on 8 February.

Münch, R. (2001) *Nation and Citizenship in the Global Age: From National to Transnational Ties and Identities*. Basingstoke: Palgrave Macmillan.

Munck, R. (2002) *Globalisation and Labour: The New Great Transformation*. London: Zed.

Munck, R. and P. Waterman (eds) (1999) *Labour Worldwide in the Era of Globalization: Alternative Union Models in the New World Order*. Basingstoke: Palgrave Macmillan.

Murphy, C. N. (1994) *International Organization and Industrial Change: Global Governance since 1850*. Cambridge: Polity Press.

Musa, M. (1997) 'From Optimism to Reality: an Overview of Third World News Agencies', in P. Golding and P. Harris (eds), *Beyond Cultural Imperialism: Globalization, Communication and the New International Order*. London: Sage, pp. 117–46.

Muzaffar, C. (1993) *Human Rights and the New World Order*. Penang: Just World Trust.
MWD (2003) *Merriam-Webster Dictionary*, www.m-w.com/cgi-bin/dictionary, accessed on 16 September.
My Vuong, T. (1999) 'World Wide Net: Vietnamese Using High Tech to Stay in Touch with Culture', *San Jose Mercury News*, 20 February.
Myers, N. (1993) *Ultimate Security: the Environmental Basis of Political Stability*. New York: Norton.
Myers, N. (1996) 'Problems of the Next Century'. Paper for UNED-UK seminar, Green College, Oxford, 24 June.
Myers, N. (ed.) (1985) *The Gaia Atlas of Planet Management*. London: Pan.
Myhre, D. (1994) 'The Politics of Globalization in Rural Mexico: Campesino Initiatives to Restructure the Agricultural Credit System', in P. McMichael (ed.), *The Global Restructuring of Agro-Food Systems*. Ithaca, NY: Cornell University Press, pp. 145–69.
Naess, A. (1976) *Ecology, Community and Lifestyle*. Cambridge: Cambridge University Press, 1989.
Nahavandian, M. (2004) Director of the National Globalization Studies Programme of Iran, in discussions with the author, Tehran, 23 and 25 December.
Naisbitt, J. (1994) *Global Paradox: The Bigger the World Economy, the More Powerful Its Smallest Players*. London: Brealey.
Naples, N. and M. Desai (eds) (2002) *Women's Activism and Globalization*. London: Routledge.
Naughton, J. (2001) 'Contested Space: The Internet and Global Civil Society', in H. Anheier *et al.* (eds), *Global Civil Society 2001*. Oxford: Oxford University Press, pp. 147–68.
Nayyar, D. (ed.) (2002) *Governing Globalization: Issues and Institutions*. Oxford: Oxford University Press.
Neal, L. (1985) 'Integration of International Capital Markets: Quantitative Evidence from the Eighteenth to Twentieth Centuries', *Journal of Economic History*, vol. 45, no. 2 (June), pp. 219–26.
Nederveen Pieterse, J. (1995) 'Globalization as Hybridization', in M. Featherstone *et al.* (eds), *Global Modernities*. London: Sage, pp. 45–68.
Nederveen Pieterse, J. (ed.) (2000) *Global Futures: Shaping Globalization*. London: Sage.
Nederveen Pieterse, J. (2004) *Globalization and Culture: Global Mélange*. Lanham, MD: Rowman & Littlefield.
Neef, D. (1998) *The Knowledge Economy*. Boston, MA: Butterworth-Heinemann.
Negroponte, N. (1995) *Being Digital*. London: Hodder & Stoughton.
Nescafé (2003) Website of Nescafé, www.nescafe.com/main_nest.asp, accessed on 14 July.
Neufeld, M. J. (1995) *The Rocket and the Reich: Peenemunde and the Coming of the Ballistic Missile Era*. Cambridge, MA: Harvard University Press.
Neumayer, E. (2001) *Greening Trade and Investment: Environmental Protection Without Protectionism*. London: Earthscan.
Newell, P. (2000) *Climate for Change: Non-State Actors and the Global Politics of the Greenhouse*. Cambridge: Cambridge University Press.
Newell, P. and J. Whalley (1999) 'Towards a World Environment Organisation?' *IDS Bulletin*, vol. 30, no. 3 (July), pp. 16–24.
NIC (2001) *The Global Infectious Disease Threat and its Implications for the United States*. Washington, DC: National Intelligence Council, NIC 99-17D.
Nicholson, M. (1999) 'How Novel Is Globalisation?' in M. Shaw (ed.), *Politics and Globalisation: Knowledge, Ethics and Agency*. London: Routledge, pp. 23–34.
Niebuhr, R. (1932) *Moral Man and Immoral Society: A Study in Ethics and Politics*. New York: Scribner.
Norberg-Hodge, H. (1999a) 'Bringing the Economy Back Home: Towards a Culture of Place', *The Ecologist*, vol. 29, no. 3 (May/June), pp. 215–18.
Norberg-Hodge, H. (1999b) 'The March of the Monoculture', *The Ecologist*, vol. 29, no. 3 (May–June), pp.194–7.

Norris, P. (2001) *Digital Divide: Civic Engagement, Information Poverty, and the Internet Worldwide*. Cambridge: Cambridge University Press.

Notes from Nowhere (2003) *We Are Everywhere: The Irresistible Rise of Global Antic Capitalism*. London: Verso.

Nussbaum, M. C. *et al*. (1996) *For Love of Country*. Boston, MA: Beacon Books.

Nye, J. S. (1990) *Bound to Lead: The Changing Nature of American Power*. New York: Basic Books.

Nye, J. S. and J. D. Donahue (eds) (2000) *Governance in a Globalizing World*. Washington, DC: Brookings Institution.

Ó Tuathail, G. (1996) *Critical Geopolitics: The Politics of Writing Global Space*. London: Routledge.

Ó Tuathail, G. (1998) 'Political Geography III: Dealing with Deterritorialization', *Progress in Human Geography*, vol. 22, no. 1 (March), pp. 81–93.

Ó Tuathail, G. (2000) 'Borderless Worlds? Problematising Discourses of Deterritorialisation', *Geopolitics*, vol. 4, no. 2 (Autumn), pp. 139–54.

O'Brien, R. (1992) *Global Financial Integration: The End of Geography*. London: Pinter.

O'Brien, R. (2000) 'The Agency of Labour in a Changing Global Order', in R. Stubbs and G. R. D. Underhill (eds), *Political Economy and the Changing Global Order*. Oxford: Oxford University Press, pp. 38–47.

O'Brien, R. *et al*. (2000) *Contesting Global Governance: Multilateral Economic Institutions and Global Social Movements*. Cambridge: Cambridge University Press.

O'Byrne, D. J. (2003) *The Dimensions of Global Citizenship: Political Identity beyond the Nation-State*. London: Frank Cass.

O'Rourke, K. (2002) 'Globalization and Inequality: Historical Trends', in World Bank, *Annual Bank Conference on Development Economics 2001/2002*. New York: Oxford University Press, pp. 39–67.

O'Rourke, K. H. and J. G. Williamson (1999) *Globalization and History: The Evolution of a Nineteenth-Century Atlantic Economy*. Cambridge, MA: MIT Press.

OECD (1996a) *Financial Market Trends 63*. Paris: Organisation for Economic Cooperation and Development, February.

OECD (1996b) *International Capital Market Statistics 1950–1995*. Paris: Organisation for Economic Cooperation and Development.

OECD (2001) *Bridging the Digital Divide: Issues and Policies in the OECD Countries*. Paris: OECD Committee for Information, Computers and Communication Policy.

OECD (2004) *OECD in Figures 2004: Statistics on the Member Countries*. Paris: Organisation for Economic Cooperation and Development.

OED (1989) *The Oxford English Dictionary*. Oxford: Clarendon, 2nd edn.

Ohmae, K. (1990) *The Borderless World: Power and Strategy in the Interlinked Economy*. New York: HarperCollins.

Ohmae, K. (1995) 'Putting Global Logic First', *Harvard Business Review*, vol. 73, no. 1 (January–February), pp. 119–25.

Olesen, T. (2002) 'Long Distance Zapatismo: Globalization and the Construction of Solidarity'. PhD dissertation, University of Aarhus.

Oliveira, J. J. de (2004) National council member of the Movement of Dam-Affected People (MAB), in discussion with the author, Brasilia, 20 November.

Oloka-Onyango, J. (1999) 'Comprehensive Examination of Thematic Relating to the Elimination of Racial Discrimination. Globalization in the Context of Increasing Incidence of Racism, Racial Discrimination and Xenophobia'. Working paper for ECOSOC, Commission on Human Rights, Sub-Commission on Prevention of Discriminations and Protection of Minorities, in accordance with Sub-Commission Decision 1998/104.

Onuf, N. G. (1991) 'Sovereignty: Outline of a Conceptual History', *Alternatives*, vol. 16, no. 4 (Fall), pp. 425–46.

Ooms, G. (2004) Remarks by the General Director of Médecins sans Frontières, Belgium to a conference on 'Power and Responsibility: The Changing Role of Non State Actors', Brussels, 1 December.

OPCW (2004) Website of the Organization for the Prohibition of Chemical Weapons, http://www.opcw.nl/, accessed on 13 January.

Ortega y Gasser, J. (1930) *The Revolt of the Masses*. London: Allen & Unwin, 1961.

Osiander, A. (2001) 'Sovereignty, International Relations, and the Westphalian Myth', *International Organization*, vol. 55, no. 2 (Spring), pp. 251–87.

Ougaard, M. (2004) *Political Globalization: State, Power and Social Forces*. Basingstoke: Palgrave Macmillan.

Paasi, A. (2003) 'Territory', in J. Agnew *et al.* (eds), *A Companion to Political Geography*. Oxford: Blackwell, pp. 109–22.

Paehlke, R. C. (2003) *Democracy's Dilemma: Environment, Social Equity, and the Global Economy*. Cambridge, MA: MIT Press.

Palan, R. (1998) 'Trying to Have Your Cake and Eating It: How and Why the State System Has Created Offshore', *International Studies Quarterly*, vol. 42, no. 4 (December), pp. 625–44.

Palan, R. (2003) *The Offshore World: Sovereign Markets, Virtual Places, and Nomad Millionaires*. Ithaca, NY: Cornell University Press.

Panitch, L. (1996) 'Rethinking the Role of the State', in J. H. Mittelman (ed.), *Globalization: Critical Reflections*. Boulder, CO: Rienner, pp. 83–113.

Parlamento Centroamericano (2004) Website of the Central American Parliament, www.parlacen.org.gt/, accessed on 2 November.

Parreñas, R. S. (2001) *Servants of Globalization: Women Migration and Domestic Work*. Stanford, CA: Stanford University Press.

Patel, S. *et al.* (2001) 'Squatting on the Global Highway: Community Exchanges for Urban Transformation', in M. Edwards and J. Gaventa (eds), *Global Citizen Action*. Boulder, CO: Rienner, pp. 231–45.

Patomaki, H. (2001) *Democratising Globalisation: The Leverage of the Tobin Tax*. London: Zed

Patomaki, H. and T. Teivainen (2004) *A Possible World: Democratic Transformation of Global Institutions*. London: Zed Books.

Pauly, L. W. (1997) *Who Elected the Bankers? Surveillance and Control in the World Economy*. Ithaca, NY: Cornell University Press.

Pearson, R. (1998) ' "Nimble Fingers" Revisited: Reflections on Women and Third World Industrialisation in the Late Twentieth Century', in C. Jackson and R. Pearson (eds), *Feminist Visions of Development: Gender Analysis and Policy*. London: Routledge, pp. 171–88.

Pease, B. and K. Pringle (eds) (2001) *A Man's World? Changing Men's Practices in a Globalized World*. London: Zed.

Peccei, A. (1969) *The Chasm Ahead*. Basingstoke: Palgrave Macmillan.

Pendergrast, M. (1993) *For God, Country and Coca-Cola: The Unauthorized History of the Great American Soft Drink and the Company that Makes It*. London: Weidenfeld & Nicolson.

Pennycook, A. (1994) *The Cultural Politics of English as an International Language*. Harlow: Longman.

PEOPLink (2004) Website of PEOPLink: www.peoplink.org, accessed on 22 October.

Peters, R. (1979) *Islam and Colonialism: The Doctrine of Jihad in Modern History*. The Hague: Mouton.

Peterson, V. S. (1992) 'Transgressing Boundaries: Theories of Knowledge, Gender, and International Relations', *Millennium*, vol. 21, no. 2 (Summer), pp. 183–206.

Peterson, V. S. (2003) *A Critical Rewriting of Global Political Economy: Integrating Reproductive, Productive, and Virtual Economies*. London: Routledge.

Peterson, V. S. and A. S. Runyan (1999) *Global Gender Issues*. Boulder, CO: Westview, 2nd edn.

Petras, J. (1993) 'Cultural Imperialism in the Late 20th Century', *Journal of Contemporary Asia*, vol. 23, no. 2, pp. 139–48.

Petras, J. and H. Veltmeyer (2001) *Globalization Unmasked: Imperialism in the 21st Century*. London: Zed.

Pettman, J. J. (1996) 'An International Political Economy of Sex?' in E. Kofman and G. Youngs (eds), *Globalization: Theory and Practice*. London: Pinter, pp. 191–208.

Pettman, J. J. (1997) 'Body Politics: International Sex Tourism', *Third World Quarterly*, vol. 18, no. 1, pp. 93–108.

Pettman, R. (2005) 'Anti-Globalisation Discourses in Asia', in C. Eschle and B. Maiguashca (eds), *Critical Theories, International Relations and 'the Anti-Globalisation Movement'*. London: Routledge, pp. 77–86.

Pianta, M. (2001) 'Parallel Summits of Global Civil Society', in H. Anheier *et al.* (eds), *Global Civil Society 2001*. Oxford: Oxford University Press, pp. 169–94.

Picciotto, S. (2001) 'Democratizing Globalism', in D. Drache (ed.), *The Market or the Public Domain? Global Governance and the Assymmetry of Power*. London: Routledge, pp. 335–59.

Piening, C. (1997) *Global Europe: The European Union in World Affairs*. Boulder, CO: Rienner.

Pierre, J. (ed.) (2000) *Debating Governance: Authority, Steering, and Democracy*. Oxford: Oxford University Press.

Pietilä, H. and J. Vickers (1996) *Making Women Matter: The Role of the United Nations* London: Zed, 3rd edition.

Pigman, G. A. (2002) 'A Multifunctional Case Study for Teaching International Political Economy: The World Economic Forum as Shar-pei or Wolf in Sheep's Clothing?', *International Studies Perspectives*, vol. 3, no. 3 (August), pp. 291–309.

Pijl, K. van der (1989) 'The International Level', in T. B. Bottomore (ed.), *The Capitalist Class: An International Study*. New York: Harvester Wheatsheaf, pp. 237–66.

Pijl, K. van der (1998) *Transnational Classes and International Relations*. London: Routledge.

Piot, C. (1999) *Remotely Global: Village Modernity in West Africa*. Chicago: University of Chicago Press.

Pirages, D. (2006) 'Disease', in R. Robertson and J. A. Scholte (eds), *Encyclopedia of Globalization*. London: Routledge

Ploman, E. W. (1984) *Space, Earth and Communication*. Westport, CT: Quorum.

Poewe, K. (ed.) (1994) *Charismatic Christianity as a Global Culture*. Columbia, SC: University of South Carolina Press.

Pogge, T. W. (2002) *World Poverty and Human Rights: Cosmopolitan Responsibilities and Reforms*. Cambridge: Polity Press.

Pogue, Z. (2001) 'A Look at the First Transatlantic Telesurgery', accessed at www.stanford.edu/~zpogue/telemedicine/first.htm.

Poissant, L. (2004) Remarks at joint seminar of the Robarts Centre, York University and the Canada Research Chair on Globalization, Citizenship and Democracy, University of Quebec at Montreal, Montreal, 14 May.

Poku, N. K. and A. Whiteside (eds) (2002) 'Special Issue: Global Health and Governance: HIV/AIDS', *Third World Quarterly*, vol. 23, no. 2 (April).

Polanyi, K. (1944) *The Great Transformation*. Boston, MA: Beacon Press, 1957.

Poovey, M. (1998) *A History of the Modern Fact: Problems of Knowledge in the Sciences of Wealth and Society*. Chicago: University of Chicago Press.

Porta, D. *et al.* (eds) (1999) *Social Movements in a Globalizing World*. New York: St. Martin's.

Porter, G. and J. W. Brown (1996) *Global Environmental Politics*. Boulder, CO: Westview, 2nd edn.

Porter, G. *et al.* (2000) *Global Environmental Politics*. Boulder, CO: Westview, 3rd edn.

Porter, M. E. (1990) *The Competitive Advantage of Nations*. Basingstoke: Palgrave Macmillan.

Porter, M. E. (ed.) (1986) *Competition in Global Industries*. Boston, MA: Harvard Business School Press.

Porter, T. (1993) *States, Markets and Regimes in Global Finance*. Basingstoke: Palgrave Macmillan.

Porter, T. (2005) *Globalization and Finance*. Cambridge: Polity.

Porter, T. and W. Coleman (2002) 'Transformations in the Private Governance of Global Finance', Paper presented at the International Studies Association Annual Convention, New Orleans, March.

Portes, R. and H. Rey (1999) 'The Determinants of Cross-Border Equity Flows', *NBER Working Paper 7336*.

Poulin, L. (2004) 'Cellular Telephony and Its Impact on Globalization on the African Continent', *Center for Global Studies Bulletin* (Fall), pp. 5–6

Prakash, A. and J. A. Hart (eds) (1999) *Globalization and Governance*. London: Routledge.

Pretzlik, C. (2004) 'FT500: Banking', *Financial Times*, 27 May, p. 7.

Price, R. (1998) 'Reversing the Gun Sights: Transnational Civil Society Targets Land Mines', *International Organization*, vol. 52, no. 3 (Summer), pp. 613–44.

Princen, T. and M. Finger (1994) *Environmental NGOs in World Politics: Linking the Local and the Global*. London: Routledge.

Pritchett, L. (1997) 'Divergence, Big Time', *Journal of Economic Perspectives*, vol. 11, no. 3 (Summer), pp. 3–17.

PTT (1951) *Verslag van het Staatsbedrijf de Posterijen, Telegrafie en Telefonie over het jaar 1950*. The Hague: Staatsdrukkerij.

Pucik, V. *et al.* (eds) (1992) *Globalizing Management: Creating and Leading the Competitive Organization*. New York: John Wiley.

Purdy, D. (1997) 'Social Policy', in M. J. Arts and N. Lee (eds), *The Economics of the European Union*. Oxford: Oxford University Press, 2nd edn, pp. 267–91.

Raghavan, C. *et al.* (1996) 'Globalisation or Development', *Third World Resurgence*, no. 74 (October), pp. 11–34.

Rai, S. M. (2004) 'Gendering Global Governance', *International Feminist Journal of Politics*, vol. 6, no. 4 (December), pp. 579–601.

Rajora, R. (2001) 'Gyandoot: Responsive Governance and Equitable Development through Community Network'. Unpublished paper.

Rajput, P. and H. L. Swarup (eds) (1994) *Women and Globalisation: Reflections, Options and Strategies*. New Delhi: Ashish.

Ralston Saul, J. (2004) 'The End of Globalism', *Harper's Magazine* (February).

Ravenhill, J. F. (2001) *APEC and the Construction of Pacific Rim Regionalism*. Cambridge: Cambridge University Press.

Raymond, E. S. (1999) *The Cathedral and the Bazaar: Musings on Linux and Open Source by an Accidental Revolutionary*. Cambridge: O'Reilly.

Reed, D. (ed.) (1996) *Structural Adjustment, the Environment and Sustainable Development*. London: Earthscan.

Reich, M. R. (ed.) (2002) *Public–Private Partnerships for Public Health*. Cambridge, MA: Harvard University Press.

Reinicke, W. H. (1998) *Global Public Policy: Governing without Government?* Washington, DC: Brookings Institution.

Reinicke, W. H. (1999–2000) 'The Other World Wide Web: Global Public Policy Networks', *Foreign Policy*, no. 117 (Winter), pp. 44–57.

Reiser, O. L. and B. Davies (1944) *Planetary Democracy: An Introduction to Scientific Humanism*. New York: Creative Age Press.

Rex, J. (1998) 'Transnational Migrant Communities and the Modern Nation-State', in R. Axtmann (ed.), *Globalization and Europe: Theoretical and Empirical Investigations*. London: Pinter, pp. 59–76.

Rhedding-Jones, J. (2002) 'English Elsewhere: Glocalization, Assessment and Ethics', *Journal of Curriculum Studies*, vol. 34, no. 4 (July), pp. 383–404.

Rheingold, H. (1993) *The Virtual Community: Homesteading on the Electronic Frontier*. Reading, MA: Addison-Wesley.

Rhodes, C. (ed.) (1996) *The European Union in the World Community*. Boulder, CO: Rienner.

Rhodes, M. (1996), 'Globalization and West European Welfare States: A Critical Review of Recent Debates', *Journal of European Social Policy*, vol. 6, no. 4, pp. 305–27.

Rhodes, R. A. W. (1997) *Understanding Governance: Policy Networks, Governance Reflexivity and Accountability*. Buckingham: Open University Press.

Rich, B. (1994) *Mortgaging the Earth: The World Bank, Environmental Impoverishment and the Crisis of Development*. London: Earthscan.

Richardson, J. (ed.) (1996) *European Union: Power and Policy-Making*. London: Routledge.

Richmond, A. H. (1994) *Global Apartheid: Refugees, Racism and the New World Order*. Toronto: Oxford University Press.

Richter, J. (2001) *Holding Corporations Accountable: Corporate Conduct, International Codes, and Citizen Action*. London: Zed.

Rieger, E. and S. Leibfried (2003) *Limits to Globalization: Welfare States and the World Economy*. Cambridge: Polity.

Riezman, R. *et al.* (2004) 'Metrics Capturing the Degree to which Individual Economies Are Globalized'. Paper for the CESifo Venice Summer Institute Workshop on Dissecting Globalization, 21–22 July.

Rifkin, I. (2003) *Spiritual Perspectives on Globalization: Making Sense of Economic and Cutural Upheaval*. Woodstock, VT: Skylight Paths.

Rifkin, J. (1995) *The End of Work: The Decline of the Global Labor Force and the Dawn of the Post-Market Era*. New York: Putnam.

Rifkin, J. (1998) *The Biotech Century: How Genetic Commerce Will Change the World*. London: Phoenix.

Risse, T. (2000) Remarks to the Annual Conference of the Academic Council on the United Nations System, Oslo, 18 June.

Ritzer, G. (1995) *Expressing America: A Critique of the Global Credit Card Society*. Thousand Oaks, CA: Pine Forge Press.

Ritzer, G. (1996) *The McDonaldization of Society: An Investigation into the Changing Character of Contemporary Social Life*. Thousand Oaks, CA: Pine Forge Press, rev'd edn.

Rivera, M. *et al.* (1995) *DAWN's Perspectives on Social Development*. Santo Domingo: Center for Feminist Research and Action.

Robbins, B. (1999) *Feeling Global: Internationalism in Distress*. New York: New York University Press.

Roberts, R. (ed.) (1994) *Offshore Financial Centres*. Cheltenham: Elgar.

Roberts, S. M. (1995) 'Small Place, Big Money: The Cayman Islands and the International Financial System', *Economic Geography*, vol. 71, no. 3 (July), pp. 237–56.

Robertson, R. (1983) 'Interpreting Globality', in *World Realities and International Studies Today*. Glenside, PA: Pennsylvania Council on International Education, pp. 7–20.

Robertson, R. (1992) *Globalization: Social Theory and Global Culture*. London: Sage.

Robertson, R. (1995) 'Globalization: Time-Space and Homogeneity-Heterogeneity', in M. Featherstone *et al.* (eds), *Global Modernities*. London: Sage, pp. 25–44.

Robertson, R. (2001) 'Globality', in N. J. Smelser and P. B. Baltes (eds), *International Encyclopedia of the Social and Behavioral Sciences*. Oxford: Elsevier/Pergamon, pp. 6254–8.

Robertson, R. and J. Chirico (1985) 'Humanity, Globalization, and Worldwide Religious Resurgence: A Theoretical Exploration', *Sociological Analysis*, vol. 46, no. 3, pp. 219–42.

Robertson, R. and W. R. Garrett (eds) (1991) *Religion and Global Order*. New York: Paragon House.

Robertson, R. and J. A. Scholte (eds) (2006) *Enclyclopedia of Globalization*. London: Routledge.

Robertson, R. and K. White (eds) (2002) *Globalization*. London: Routledge, 6 volumes.

Robins, K. and F. Webster (1988) 'Cybernetic Capitalism, Technology, Everyday Life', in V. Mosco and J. Wasko (eds), *The Political Economy of Information*. Madison: University of Wisconsin Press, pp. 44–75.

Robinson, W. I. (1996a) 'Globalisation: Nine Theses on Our Epoch', *Race & Class*, vol. 38, no. 2 (October–December), pp. 13–31.

Robinson, W. I. (1996b) *Promoting Polyarchy: Globalization, US Intervention and Hegemony*. Cambridge: Cambridge University Press.

Robinson, W.I. and J. Harris (2000) 'Toward a Global Ruling Class? Globalization and the Transnational Capitalist Class', *Science and Society*, vol 64, no. 1 (Spring), pp. 11–54.

Robotti, P. (2003) 'The Political Economy of Hedge Fund Regulation', PhD dissertation, University of Warwick.

Rodrik, D. (1998) 'Why Do More Open Economies Have Bigger Governments?', *Journal of Political Economy*, vol. 106, no. 5 (October), pp. 997–1032.

Rodrik, D. (2001) *The Global Governance of Trade as if Development Really Mattered*. New York: United Nations Development Programme.

Rohwer, J. (1992) 'China: The Titan Stirs', *The Economist*, vol. 325, no. 7787 (28 November), Supplement.

Ronit, K. and V. Schneider (eds) (2000) *Private Organizations in Global Politics*. London: Routledge.

Rosamond, B. (2000) *Theories of European Integration*. Basingstoke: Palgrave Macmillan.

Rosecrance, R. (1995) 'The Obsolescence of Territory', *New Perspectives Quarterly*, vol. 12, no. 1, pp. 44–50.

Rosenau, J. N. (1980) *The Study of Global Interdependence: Essays on the Transnationalization of World Affairs*. London: Pinter.

Rosenau, J. N. (1990) *Turbulence in World Politics: A Theory of Change and Continuity*. Princeton, MJ: Princeton University Press.

Rosenau, J. N. (1997) *Along the Domestic-Foreign Frontier: Exploring Governance in a Turbulent World*. Cambridge: Cambridge University Press.

Rosenau, J. N. (2003) *Distant Proximities: Dynamics beyond Globalization*. Princeton, NJ: Princeton University Press.

Rosenau, J. N. and E.-O. Czempiel (eds) (1992) *Governance without Government: Order and Change in World Politics*. Cambridge: Cambridge University Press.

Rosenberg, J. (2001) *The Follies of Globalization Theory: Polemical Essays*. London: Verso.

Rosenberg, J. (2005) 'Globalization Theory – A Post Mortem', *International Politics*, vol. 42, no. 1 (Spring), pp. 2–74.

Rowbotham, S. and S. Linkogle (2001) *Women Resist Globalization: Mobilizing for Livelihoods and Rights*. London: Zed.

Rozendaal, G. van (2002) *Trade Unions and Global Governance: The Quest of Trade Unions for a Social Clause*. London: Continuum.

Rubenstein, C. (1991) 'The Flying Silver Message Stick: Update 1985–86 on Long Songs Collected 1971–74', *Sarawak Museum Journal*, vol. 42, No. 63 (new series), pp. 61–157.

Rudra, N. (2002) 'Globalization and the Decline of the Welfare State in Less-Developed Countries', *International Organization*, vol. 56, no. 2 (Spring), pp. 411–45.

Ruggie, J. G. (1993) 'Territoriality and Beyond: Problematizing Modernity in International Relations', *International Organization*, vol. 47, no. 1 (Winter), pp. 139–74.

Ruggie, J. G. (1998) *Constructing the World Polity: Essays in International Institutionalization*. London: Routledge.

Rugman, A. (2001) *The End of Globalization*. London: Random House Business Books.

Rugman, A. M. and A. Verbeke (1990) *Global Corporate Strategy and Trade Policy*. London: Routledge.

Ruigrok, W. and R. van Tulder (1995) *The Logic of International Restructuring: the Management of Dependencies in Rival Industrial Complexes*. London: Routledge.

Rüland, J. *et al.* (eds) (2002) *Asia-Pacific Economic Cooperation (APEC): The First Decade*. London: Routledge Curzon.

Rüland, J. *et al.* (eds) (forthcoming) *Interregionalism in a Globalized World*.

Runyan, A. S. (1996) 'The Places of Women in Trading Places: Gendered Global/Regional Regimes and Inter-nationalized Feminist Resistance', in E. Kofman and G. Youngs (eds), *Globalization: Theory and Practice*. London: Pinter, pp. 238–52.

Rupert, M. (2000) *Ideologies of Globalization: Contending Visions of a New World Order*. London: Routledge.

Rupert, M. and H. Smith (eds) (2002) *Historical Materialism and Globalization*. London: Routledge.

Ruse, M. and D. Castle (eds) (2002) *Genetically Modified Foods: Debating Biotechnology*. Amherst, NY: Prometheus Books.

Sack, R. (1986) *Human Territoriality: Its Theory and History.* Cambridge: Cambridge University Press.

Said, E. W. (1978) *Orientalism*. New York: Random House.

Sakamoto, Y. (1997) *Sotaika no Jidai* ['The Age of Relativization']. Tokyo: Iwanami Shinso.

Salamon, L. M. (1994) 'The Rise of the Nonprofit Sector', *Foreign Affairs*, vol. 73, no. 4 (July–August), pp. 109–22.

Salcedo, R. (2003) 'When the Global Meets the Local at the Mall', *American Behavioral Scientist*, vol. 46, no. 8 (April), pp. 1084–103.

Salter, L. (1999) 'The Standards Regime for Communication and Information Technologies', in A. C. Cutler *et al.* (eds), *Private Authority in International Affairs*. Albany, NY: State University of New York Press, pp. 97–127.

Sampson, G. P. (ed.) (2001) *The Role of the WTO in Global Governance*. Tokyo: United Nations University Press.

Sandbrook, R. (ed.) (2003) *Civilizing Globalization*. Albany, NY: State University of New York Press.

Sander, H. (1996) 'Multilateralism, Regionalism and Globalisation: The Challenges to the World Trading System', in H. Sander and A. Inotai (eds), *World Trade after the Uruguay Round: Prospects and Policy Options for the Twenty-First Century*. London: Routledge, pp. 17–36.

SAPRI (2004) Website of the Structural Adjustment Policy Review Initiative, www.worldbank.org/research/sapri/, accessed on 19 January.

SAPRIN (2004) Website of the Structural Adjustment Policy Review International Network: www.saprin.org/, accessed on 19 January.

Sassen, S. (1997) *Losing Control? Sovereignty in an Age of Globalization*. New York: Columbia University Press.

Sassen, S. (2001) *The Global City: New York, London, Tokyo*. Princeton, NJ: Princeton University Press, 2nd edn.

Sassen, S. (ed.) (2002) *Global Networks, Linked Cities*. London: Routledge.

Saunders, J. (1989) *Across Frontiers: International Support for the Miners' Strike of 1984–85*. London: Canary.

Sauvant, K. P. and H. Hasenpflug (eds) (1977) *The New International Economic Order: Confrontation or Cooperation between North and South?* Boulder, CO: Westview.

Schäfer, W. (2005) 'The Uneven Globality of Children', *Journal of Social History*, vol. 38, no. 4 (Summer).

Schäfer, W. *et al.* (2003) 'The New Global History: Toward a Narrative for Pangaea Two', *Erwägen Wissen Ethik*, vol. 14, no. 1, pp. 75–135.

Schechter, M. G. (ed.) (1999a) *Future Multilateralism: The Political and Social Framework*. Tokyo: United Nations University Press.

Schechter, M. G. (ed.) (1999b) *Innovation in Multilateralism*. Tokyo: United Nations University Press.

Schiller, D. (1999) *Digital Capitalism: Networking the Global Market System*. Cambridge, MA: MIT Press.

Schiller, H. I. (1991) 'Not Yet the Post-Imperialist Era', *Critical Studies in Mass Communication*, vol. 8, no. 1 (March), pp. 13–28.

Schiller, H. I. and A. R. Schiller (1988) 'Libraries, Public Access to Information, and Commerce', in V. Mosco and J. Wasko (eds), *The Political Economy of Information*. Madison: University of Wisconsin Press, pp. 146–66.

Schmidt, R. (1999) *A Feasible Foreign Exchange Transaction Tax*. Ottawa: North–South Institute.

Schmidt, V. A. (1995) 'The New World Order, Incorporated: The Rise of Business and the Decline of the Nation-State', *Daedalus*, vol. 124, no. 2 (Spring), pp. 75–106.

Scholte, J. A. (1993) *International Relations of Social Change*. Buckingham: Open University Press.

Scholte, J. A. (1995) 'The International Construction of Indonesian Nationhood, 1930–1950', in H. Antlöv and S. Tønnesson (eds), *Imperial Policy and Southeast Asian Nationalism 1930–1957*. London: Curzon, pp. 191–226.

Scholte, J. A. (1996) 'The Geography of Collective Identities in a Globalizing World', *Review of International Political Economy*, vol. 3, no. 4 (Winter), pp. 565–607.

Scholte, J. A. (1997) 'Global Capitalism and the State', *International Affairs*, vol. 73, no. 3 (July), pp. 427–52.

Scholte, J. A. (1999) 'Security and Community in a Globalizing World: African Experiences', in C. Thomas and P. Wilkin (eds), *Globalization, Human Security, and the African Experience*. Boulder, CO: Rienner, pp. 59–84.

Scholte, J. A. (2000) 'Global Civil Society', in N. Woods (ed.), *The Political Economy of Globalization*. Basingstoke: Palgrave Macmillan, pp. 173–201.

Scholte, J. A. (2001) 'The Globalization of World Politics', in J. Baylis and S. Smith (eds), *The Globalization of World Politics: An Introduction to International Relations*. Oxford: Oxford University Press, 2nd edn, pp. 13–32.

Scholte, J. A. (2002a) 'Civil Society and Governance in the Global Polity', in M. Ougaard and R. Higgott (eds), *Towards a Global Polity*. London: Routledge, pp. 145–65.

Scholte, J. A. (2002b) *Civil Society Voices and the International Monetary Fund*. Ottawa: North–South Institute.

Scholte, J. A. (2002c) 'Governing Global Finance', in D. Held and A. McGrew (eds), *Governing Globalization: Power, Authority and Global Governance*. Cambridge: Polity, pp. 189–208.

Scholte, J. A. (2003) *The Sources of Neoliberal Globalisation*. Geneva: United Nations Research Institute for Social Development (UNRISD), online at: www.unrisd.org.

Scholte, J. A. (2004a) 'Civil Society and Democratically Accountable Global Governance', *Government and Opposition*, vol. 39, no. 2 (Spring), pp. 211–33.

Scholte, J. A. (2004b) *Democratizing the Global Economy? The Role of Civil Society*. Coventry: Centre for the Study of Globalization and Regionalization, online at: www.csgr.org/research/publications.

Scholte, J. A. (2004c) 'Globalisation Studies Past and Future: A Dialogue of Diversity', *Globalizations*, vol. 1, no. 1 (September), pp. 102–10.

Scholte, J. A. (2004d) 'The WTO and Civil Society', in B. Hocking and S. McGuire (eds), *Trade Politics: International, Domestic and Regional Perspectives*. London: Routledge, 2nd edn, pp. 146–61.

Schreiter, R. J. (1997) *The New Catholicity: Theology between the Global and the Local*. Maryknoll, NY: Orbis Books.

Schrijver, N. J. (1997) *Sovereignty over Natural Resources: Balancing Rights and Duties*. Cambridge: Cambridge University Press.

Schulz, M. *et al.* (eds) (2001) *Regionalization in a Globalizing World: A Comparative Perspective on Forms, Actors and Processes*. London: Zed.

Schwab, K. and C. Smadja (1996) 'Start Taking the Backlash against Globalization Seriously', *International Herald Tribune*, 2 February.

Scott, H. S. and P. A. Wellons (2000) *International Finance: Transactions, Policy and Regulation*. New York: Foundation Press.

Segal, G. (1994) *China Changes Shape: Regionalism and Foreign Policy*. London: International Institute of Strategic Studies.

Segerstrom, P. (2003) 'Naomi Klein and the Anti-Globalization Movement', in M. Lundahl (ed.), *Globalization and Its Enemies*. Stockholm: EFI Economic Research Institute, Stockholm School of Economics, pp. ___.

Sen, J. *et al.* (eds) (2004) *World Social Forum: Challenging Empires*. New Delhi: Viveka Foundation.

Seoane, J. and E. Taddei (eds) (2001) *Resistencias mundiales (De Seattle a Porto Alegre)* ['Global Resistance (From Seattle to Porto Alegre)']. Buenos Aires: Consejo Latinamericano de Ciencias Sociales.

Sgard, J. (2004) *IMF in Theory: Sovereign Debts, Judicialisation and Multilateralism*. Paris: Centre d'Etudes Prospectives et d'Informations Internationales, Working Paper 2004-21, December.

Shakespeare, W. (1595–6) *A Midsummer Night's Dream* (ed. H. F. Brooks). London: Methuen, 1979.

Shapiro, C. and H. R. Varian (1999) *Information Rules: A Strategic Guide to the Network Economy*. Boston, MA: Harvard Business School Press.

Shapiro, M. J. (1994) 'Moral Geographies and the Ethics of Post-Sovereignty', *Public Culture*, vol. 6, no. 3 (Spring), pp. 479–502.

Shapiro, M. J. and H. R. Alker (1996) *Challenging Boundaries: Global Flows, Territorial Identities*. Minneapolis: University of Minnesota Press.

Shaw, M. (1994) *Global Society and International Relations: Sociological Concepts and Political Perspectives*. Cambridge: Polity Press.

Shaw, M. (1997) 'The State of Globalization: Toward a Theory of State Transformation', *Review of International Political Economy*, vol. 4, no. 3 (Autumn), pp. 497–513.

Shaw, M. (2000) *Theory of the Global State: Globality as Unfinished Revolution*. Cambridge: Cambridge University Press.

Shaw, M. (ed.) (1984) *War, State and Society*. Basingstoke: Palgrave Macmillan.

Shaw, M. (ed.) (1999) *Politics and Globalisation: Knowledge, Ethics and Agency*. London: Routledge.

Shaw, T. M. (2004) 'The Commonwealth(s) and Global Governance', *Global Governance*, vol. 10, no. 4 (October–December), pp. 499–516.

Shearer, D. (1998) 'Outsourcing War', *Foreign Policy*, no. 112 (Fall), pp. 68–81.

Shelley, L. I. (1995) 'Transnational Organized Crime: an Imminent Threat to the Nation-State?', *Journal of International Affairs*, vol. 48, no. 2 (Winter), pp. 463–89.

Shin, D. C. (1994) 'On the Third Wave of Democratization: A Synthesis and Evaluation of Recent Research and Theory', *World Politics*, vol. 47, no. 1 (October), pp. 135–70.

Shiva, V. (1997) *Biopiracy: the Plunder of Nature and Knowledge*. Boston, MA: South End Press.

Short, J. R. (2001) *Global Dimensions: Space, Place and the Contemporary World*. London: Reaktion Books.

Shuman, M. H. (2000) *Going Local: Creating Self-Reliant Communities in a Global Age*. New York: Routledge.

Signs (2001) 'Globalization and Gender', *Signs: Journal of Women in Culture and Society*, vol. 26, no. 4 (Summer).

Silver, B. (2003) *Forces of Labour: Workers Movements and Globalisation since 1870*. Cambridge: Cambridge University Press.

Silver, B. J. and G. Arrighi (2003) 'Polanyi's "Double Movement": The *Belle Époques* of British and U.S. Hegemony Compared', *Politics & Society*, vol. 31, no. 2, pp. 325–55.

Simai, M. (1995) 'The Politics and Economics of Global Employment' in M. Simai (ed.), *Global Employment: an International Investigation into the Future of Work, Volume 1*. London: Zed, pp. 3–29.

Simmons, P. J. and C. de Jonge Oudraat (eds) (2001) *Managing Global Issues: Lessons Learned*. Washington, DC: Carnegie Endowment for International Peace.

Simonson, K. (2006) 'World Economic Forum', in R. Robertson and J. A. Scholte (eds), *Encyclopedia of Globalization*. London: Routledge.

Simpson, J. (1988) *Behind Iranian Lines*. London: Fontana, 1989.

Sinclair, T. J. (2005) *The New Masters of Capital: American Bond Rating Agencies and the Global Economy*. Ithaca, NY: Cornell University Press.

Singer, H. W. (1995) 'An Historical Perspective', in M. ul Haq *et al.* (eds), *The UN and the Bretton Woods Institutions: New Challenges for the Twenty-First Century*. Basingstoke: Palgrave Macmillan, pp. 17–25.

Singer, P. (1972) 'Famine, Affluence and Morality', *Philosophy and Public Affairs*, vol. 1, no. 2 (Spring), pp. 229–43.

Singer, P. (2002) *One World: The Ethics of Globalization*. New Haven, CT: Yale University Press.

Singer, P. W. (2003) *Corporate Warriors: The Rise of the Privatized Military Industry*. Ithaca, NY: Cornell University Press.

Sklair, L. (1995) *Sociology of the Global System*. Hemel Hempstead: Harvester Wheatsheaf, 2nd edn.

Sklair, L. (2001) *The Transnational Capitalist Class*. Oxford: Blackwell.

Skrobanek, S. *et al.* (1997) *The Traffic in Women: Human Realities of the International Sex Trade*. London: Zed.

Slaughter, A.-M. (2000) 'Government Networks: The Heart of the Liberal Democratic Order', in G.H. Fox and B.R. Roth (eds), *Democratic Governance and International Law*. Cambridge: Cambridge University Press, pp. 199–235.

Slaughter, A.-M. (2004) *A New World Order*. Princeton, NJ: Princeton University Press.

Smart, B. (1999) *Facing Modernity: Ambivalence, Reflexivity and Morality*. London: Sage.

Smillie, I. (1999) 'At Sea in a Sieve? Trends and Issues in the Relationship between Northern NGOs and Northern Governments', in I. Smillie and H. Helmich (eds), *Stakeholders: Government–NGO Partnerships for International Development*. London: Earthscan.

Smith, A. (1776) *The Wealth of Nations*. Harmondsworth: Penguin, 1970.

Smith, A. D. (1990a) 'The Supersession of Nationalism?', *International Journal of Comparative Sociology*, vol. 31, no. 1–2 (January–April), pp. 1–31.

Smith, A. D. (1990b) 'Towards a Global Culture?' in M. Featherstone (ed.), *Global Culture: Nationalism, Globalization and Modernity*. London: Sage, pp. 171–91.

Smith, A. D. (1995) *Nations and Nationalism in a Global Era*. Cambridge: Polity Press.

Smith, J. and H. Johnston (eds) (2002) *Globalization and Resistance: Transnational Dimensions of Social Movements*. Lanham, MD: Rowman & Littlefield.

Smith, J. *et al.* (eds) (1997) *Transnational Social Movements and Global Politics: Solidarity beyond the State*. Syracuse, NY: Syracuse University Press.

Smith, M. P. and L. E. Guarnizo (eds) (1998) *Transnationalism from Below*. New Brunswick, NJ: Transaction.

Smouts, M.-C. (1999) 'Multilateralism from Below: A Prerequisite for Global Governance', in M. G. Schechter (ed.), *Future Multilateralism: the Political and Social Framework*. Tokyo: United Nations University Press, pp. 292–311.

Smythe, E. (2000) 'State Authority and Investment Security: Non-State Actors and the Negotiation of the Multilateral Agreement on Investment at the OECD', in R. A. Higgott *et al.* (eds), *Nonstate Actors and Authority in the Global System*. London: Routledge, pp. 74–90.

Snell-Hornby, M. (2000) 'Communicating in the Global Village: On Language, Translation and Cultural Identity', in C. Schäffner (ed.), *Translation in the Global Village*. Clevedon: Multilingual Matters, pp. 11–28.

Södersten, B. (2004) (ed.) *Globalization and the Welfare State*. Basingstoke: Palgrave Macmillan.

Sopa, V. (2002) Peasant activist in North East Thailand, interviewed by the author in Bangkok on 10 June.

Sørensen, G. (1999) 'Sovereignty: Change and Continuity in a Fundamental Institution', *Political Studies*, vol. 47, no. 3, pp. 590–604.

Sørensen, G. (2004) *The Transformation of the State: Beyond the Myth of Retreat*. Basingstoke: Palgrave Macmillan.

Soroos, M. J. (1986) *Beyond Sovereignty: The Challenge of Global Policy*. Columbia, SC: University of South Carolina Press.

Soros, G. (1998) *The Crisis of Global Capitalism: Open Society Endangered*. London: Little, Brown.

South Centre (1997) *The TRIPS Agreement: A Guide for the South*. Geneva: South Centre.

Sparr, P. (ed.) (1994) *Mortgaging Women's Lives: Feminist Critiques of Structural Adjustment*. London: Zed.

Spero, J. E. (1990) *The Politics of International Economic Relations*, 4th edn. London: Unwin Hyman.

Speth, J. G. (1996) 'Global Inequality: 358 Billionaires vs. 2.3 Billion People', *New Perspectives Quarterly*, vol. 13, no. 4 (Fall), pp. 32–3.

Speth, J. G. (2001) Remarks to the Annual Conference of the Academic Council on the United Nations System, Puebla.

Spruyt, H. (1994) *The Sovereign State and its Competitors: An Analysis of Systems Change*. Princeton, NJ: Princeton University Press.

Spybey, T. (1996) *Globalization and World Society*. Cambridge: Polity Press.

Stalker, P. (2000) *Workers without Frontiers: The Impact of Globalization on International Migration*. Boulder, CO: Rienner.

Standing, G. (1999) *Global Labour Flexibility: Seeking Redistributive Justice*. Basingstoke: Palgrave Macmillan.

Starr, A. (2000) *Naming the Enemy: Anti-Corporatist Movements Confront Globalization*. London: Zed.

Starr, A. (2003) 'Anti-Racism in the North American Anti-Globalization Movement', in L. Panitch and C. Leys (eds), *Socialist Register*. London: Merlin, pp. 265–80.

Starr, A. (2005) *Global Revolt: A Guide to the Movement against Globalization*. London: Zed.

Staveren, I. van (2002) 'Global Finance and Gender', in J. A. Scholte with A. Schnabel (eds), *Civil Society and Global Finance*. London: Routledge, pp. 228–46.

St-Denis, J. (2002) International Cooperation Officer of the Unions Central of Quebec (CSQ), interviewed by the author in Montreal, 1 May.

Steenbergen, B. van (ed.) (1994) *The Condition of Citizenship*. London: Sage.

Steger, M. B. (ed.) (2004) *Rethinking Globalism*. Lanham, MD: Rowman & Littlefield.

Steger, M. B. (2005) *Globalism: Market Ideology Meets Terrorism*. Lanham, MD: Rowman & Littlefield, 2nd edn.

Steinmo, S. (1994) 'The End of Redistribution? International Pressures and Domestic Tax Policy Choices', *Challenge* (November–December), pp. 9–17.

Stern, P. C. *et al.* (eds) (1992) *Global Environmental Change: Understanding the Human Dimensions*. Washington, DC: National Academy Press.

Stewart, F. and A. Berry (2000) 'Globalization, Liberalization and Inequality: Real Causes, Expectations, and Experience', *Challenge*, vol. 43, no. 1 (January–February), pp. 44–92.

Stienstra, D. (1994) *Women's Movements and International Organizations*. Basingstoke: Palgrave Macmillan.

Stiglitz, J. (1998) *More Instruments and Broader Goals: Moving toward the Post-Washington Consensus*. Helsinki: United Nations World Institute for Development Economics Research Annual Lectures, 7 January.

Stiglitz, J. (2002) *Globalization and Its Discontents*. New York: Norton.

Stokhof, W. and P. van der Velde (eds) (1999) *ASEM: The Asia–Europe Meeting. A Window of Opportunity*. London: Kegan Paul.

Stone, D. (2004) 'Transfer Agents and Global Networks in the "Transnationalisation" of Policy', *Journal of European Public Policy*, vol. 11, no. 3, pp. 545–66.

Stopford, J. M. and S. Strange (1991) *Rival States, Rival Firms: Competition for World Market Shares*. Cambridge: Cambridge University Press.

Storey, D. (2001) *Territory: The Claiming of Space*. Harlow: Prentice Hall.

Strange, S. (1986) *Casino Capitalism*. Oxford: Blackwell.

Strange, S. (1994) *States and Markets*. London: Pinter, 2nd edn.

Strange, S. (1996) *The Retreat of the State: the Diffusion of Power in the World Economy*. Cambridge: Cambridge University Press.

Strange, S. (1998) *Mad Money*. Manchester: Manchester University Press.

Strassoldo, R. (1992) 'Globalism and Localism: Theoretical Reflections and Some Evidence', in Z. Mlinar (ed.), *Globalization and Territorial Identities*. Aldershot: Avebury.

Stryker, R. (1998) 'Globalization and the Welfare State', *International Journal of Sociology and Social Policy*, vol. 18, no. 2/3/4, pp. 1–49.

Suárez Aguilar, E. (1999) personal communication to the author, Mexico City, June.
Suganami, H. (1978) 'A Note on the Origin of the Word "International" ', *British Journal of International Studies*, vol. 4, no. 3 (October), pp. 226–32.
Sulak Sivaraksa (1999) *Global Healing: Essays and Interviews on Structural Violence, Social Development and Spiritual Transformation*. Bangkok: Sathirakoses-Nagapradipa Foundation.
Sullivan, S. (1997) *From War to Wealth: Fifty Years of Innovation*. Paris: Organisation for Economic Cooperation and Development.
Sutcliffe, B. (1998) 'Freedom to Move in the Age of Globalization', in D. Baker *et al.* (eds), *Globalization and Progressive Economic Policy*. Cambridge: Cambridge University Press, pp. 325–36.
Sutcliffe, B. (2002) *A More or Less Unequal World? World Income Distribution in the 20th Century*. Bilbao, Spain: Universidad del Pais Vasco, Hegoa, Working Paper No. 31.
Sutcliffe, B. and A. Glyn (2003) 'Measures of Globalisation and Their Misinterpretation', in J. Michie (ed.), *The Handbook of Globalisation*. Cheltenham: Elgar, pp. 61–78.
Swank, D. (1998) 'Funding the Welfare State: Globalization and the Taxation of Business in Advanced Market Economies', *Political Studies*, vol. 46, no. 4 (September), pp. 671–92.
Swank, D. (2002) *Global Capital, Political Institutions, and Policy Change in Developed Welfare States*. Cambridge: Cambridge University Press.
Sweezy, P. and H. Magdoff (1985) 'The Strange Recovery of 1983–1984', *Monthly Review*, vol. 37, no. 5 (October), pp. 1–11.
SWIFT (2005) Website of the Society for Worldwide Interbank Financial Telecommunications, http://www.swift.com, accessed on 24 January.
Tabb, W.K. (2001) *The Amoral Elephant: Globalization and the Struggle for Social Justice in the Twenty-First Century*. New York: Monthly Review Press.
Tanner, S. (1997) 'Healing the Sky to Survive Globalization: a Gender Analogy', in T. Schrecker (ed.), *Surviving Globalism: The Social and Environmental Challenges*. Basingstoke: Palgrave Macmillan, pp. 141–57.
Tanzi, V. (1996) 'Globalization, Tax Competition and the Future of Tax Systems', *IMF Working Paper Series*, WP/96/141.
Tanzi, V. (2000) *Globalization, Technological Developments, and the Work of Fiscal Termites*. Washington, DC: International Monetary Fund.
Taylor, K. (ed.) (1975) *Henri Saint-Simon (1760–1825): Selected Writings on Science, Industry and Social Organisation*. London: Croom Helm.
Taylor, P. J. (2000) 'Izations of the World: Americanization, Modernization and Globalization', in C. Hay and D. Marsh (eds), *Demystifying Globalization*. Basingstoke: Palgrave Macmillan, pp. 49–70.
Taylor, P. J. *et al.* (1996) 'On the Nation-State, the Global, and Social Science', *Environment and Planning A*, vol. 28, no. 11 (November), pp. 1917–95.
Taylor, R. (2004) *Creating a Better World: Interpreting Global Civil Society*. Bloomfield, CT: Kumarian.
Taylor, T. (1997) *Global Pop: World Music, World Markets*. London: Routledge.
Taylor, W. C. and A. M. Weber (1996) *Going Global: Four Entrepreneurs Map the New World Marketplace*. New York: Viking.
Tchistiakov, G. (2002) Priest in the Russian Orthodox Church, interviewed by the author in Moscow, 14 January.
TCO (2001) Website of the Transnational Corporations Observatory, www.transnationale.org, accessed on 29 October.
Teeple, G. (1995) *Globalization and the Decline of Social Reform*. Atlantic Highlands, NJ: Humanities Press.
Teitelbaum, B. (2001) personal communication to the author, Brisbane, Australia, 2–4 October.
Teivanen, T. (2002) 'The World Social Forum and Global Democratisation: Learning from Porto Alegre', *Third World Quarterly*, vol. 23, no. 4 (August), pp. 621–32.
Teschke, B. (2003) *The Myth of 1648: Class, Geopolitics, and the Making of Modern International Relations*. London: Verso.

Thomas, C. and P. Wilkin (eds) (1997) *Globalization and the South*. Basingstoke: Palgrave Macmillan.
Thomas, C. and P. Wilkin (eds) (1999) *Globalization, Human Security, and the African Experience*. Boulder, CO: Rienner.
Thomas, D. (1999) Presentation by David Thomas of Saatchi & Saatchi to the Global Forum on Poverty Eradication, Council of Europe, Strasbourg, 15 October.
Thompson, D. (1999) 'Democratic Theory and Global Society', *Journal of Political Philosophy*, vol. 7, no. 2 (June), pp. 111–25.
Thomson, J. E. and S. D. Krasner (1989) 'Global Transactions and the Consolidation of Sovereignty', in E.-O. Czempiel and J. N. Rosenau (eds), *Global Changes and Theoretical Challenges*. Lexington, MA: Lexington Books, pp. 195–220.
Thorne, C. (1992) 'American Political Culture and the End of the Cold War', *Journal of American Studies*, vol. 26, no. 3, pp. 303–30.
Thrift, N. (1996) *Spatial Formations*. London: Sage.
Tilly, C. (1990) *Coercion, Capital, and European States, AD 990–1990*. Oxford: Blackwell.
Tilly, C. (1995) 'Globalization Threatens Labor's Rights', *International Labor and Working Class History*, no. 47 (Spring), pp. 1–23.
Time Warner (2004) *TimeWarner 2003 Annual Report*. New York: Time Warner, Inc.
Tober, D. (1993) 'One World – One Vision for Business', in S. Bushrui *et al.* (eds), *Transition to a Global Society*. Oxford: Oneworld, pp. 98–107.
Toffler, A. (1980) *The Third Wave*. London: Collins.
Toffler, A. and H. Toffler (1994) *Creating a New Civilization: The Politics of the Third Wave*. Atlanta: Turner.
Tomlinson, J. (1991) *Cultural Imperialism: A Critical Introduction*. London: Pinter.
Tomlinson, J. (1995) 'Homogenisation and Globalisation', *History of European Ideas*, vol. 20, nos 4–6 (February), pp. 891–7.
Tomlinson, J. (1999) *Globalization and Culture*. Chicago: University of Chicago Press.
Torpey, J. C. (2000) *The Invention of the Passport: Surveillance, Citizenship, and the State*. Cambridge: Cambridge University Press.
Toynbee, A. (1948) *Civilisation on Trial*. Oxford: Oxford University Press.
Treadgold, A. (1993) 'Cross-Border Retailing in Europe: Present Status and Future Prospects', in H. Cox *et al.* (eds), *The Growth of Global Business*. London: Routledge, pp. 119–35.
Trogrlic, J. F. (2001) National Secretary of the French Democratic Labour Confederation (CFDT), interviewed by the author in Paris on 10 December.
Turgot, A. R. J. (1750) 'A Philosophical Review of the Successive Advances of the Human Mind', in R. L. Meek (ed.), *Turgot on Progress, Sociology and Economics*. Cambridge: Cambridge University Press, 1973, pp. 41–59.
Udall, L. (1998) 'The World Bank and Public Accountability: Has Anything Changed?', in J. A. Fox and L. D. Brown (eds), *The Struggle for Accountability: The World Bank, NGOs and Grassroots Movements*. Cambridge, MA: MIT Press, pp. 391–436
UGI (1999) *Money across Frontiers: The Explosion of Global Finance*. Cheltenham: Understanding Global Issues 99/3.
UIA (1998) *Yearbook of International Organizations 1998/99, Vol. 1*. Munich: Saur/Union of International Associations.
UIA (2001) *Yearbook of International Organizations 2001/2002, Volume 5*. Munich: Saur/Union of International Associations.
ul Haq, M. *et al.* (eds) (1995) *The UN and the Bretton Woods Institutions: New Challenges for the Twenty-First Century*. Basingstoke: Palgrave Macmillan.
UMU (2003) Comment to the author from a student at Uganda Martyrs University, Nkozi, 3 September.
UN (1997) *World Economic and Social Survey 1997*. New York: United Nations.
UN (2000) *Millennium Declaration*. New York: United Nations.
UN (2002) *International Migration Report*. New York: United Nations Department of Economic and Social Affairs, online at: www.un.org/esa/population/publications.

UNCTAD (1994) *World Investment Report 1994*. Geneva: United Nations Conference on Trade and Development.

UNCTAD (1995) *Trade and Development Report 1995*. Geneva: United Nations.

UNCTAD (1996) *The TRIPS Agreement and Developing Countries*. Geneva: United Nations Conference on Trade and Development.

UNCTAD (2000) *Least Developed Countries 1999 Report*. Geneva: United Nations Conference on Trade and Development.

UNCTAD (2001) *World Investment Report 2001: Promoting Linkages*. Geneva: United Nations.

UNCTAD (2002) *World Investment Report 2002 (Overview)*. Geneva: United Nations.

UNCTAD (2003) *Least Developed Countries 2002 Report*. Geneva: United Nations Conference on Trade and Development.

UNCTAD (2004) *World Investment Report 2004: The Shift towards Services*. Geneva: United Nations.

UNDP (1998) *National Human Development Report 1998: The Russian Federation*. Moscow: United Nations Development Programme.

UNDP (2002) 'UNDP and Civil Society Organizations: A Policy Note on Engagement', available at www.undp.org/mainundp/propoor/civil.htm.

UNESCO (1980) *Many Voices, One World*. Paris: International Commission for the Study of Communication Problems, UNESCO.

UNESCO (1987) *Women and Media Decision-Making: The Invisible Barriers*. Paris: United Nations Educational, Scientific and Cultural Organisation.

UNESCO (1989) *World Communication Report*. Paris: United Nations Educational, Scientific and Cultural Organization.

UNESCO (1999) *Statistical Yearbook 1999*. Paris: United Nations Educational, Scientific and Cultural Organization.

UNESCO (2000) *Education for All Year 2000 Assessment: Statistical Document*. Paris: UNESCO Institute for Statistics.

UNHCR (1999) *1998 Global Report*. Geneva: United Nations High Commissioner for Refugees.

UNICEF (1991) *The State of the World's Children 1991*. Oxford: Oxford University Press.

UNICEF (1998) *The State of the World's Children 1998*. Oxford: Oxford University Press.

UNICEF (2003a) *Official Summary: The State of the World's Children 2004*. New York: United Nations Children's Fund.

UNICEF (2003b) *The State of the World's Children 2004: Girls, Education and Development*. New York: United Nations Children's Fund.

UNIFEM (2004) *UNIFEM Annual Report 2003/2004*. New York: United Nations Development Fund for Women.

UNPO (1995) *The First Three Years 1991–1994*. The Hague: Unrepresented Nations and Peoples Organization. See also http://www.unpo.org.

Urry, J. (2002) *The Tourist Gaze*. London: Sage, 2nd edn.

Urry, J. (2003) *Global Complexity*. Cambridge: Polity.

Utting, P. (2006) 'Corporate Social Responsibility', in R. Robertson and J.A. Scholte (eds), *Encyclopaedia of Globalization*. London: Routledge.

Vandemoortele, J. (2000) Remark of the Chief of Policy Analysis, UNICEF at a meeting of the Council of Europe attended by the author, 23 June.

Vandenberg, A. (ed.) (2000) *Citizenship and Democracy in a Global Era*. Basingstoke: Palgrave Macmillan.

Velea, G. (1996) 'Foreigners in Germany (III)', *Nine O'Clock* [Bucharest], No. 1118 (8–10 March), p. 3.

Vertovec, S. and R. Cohen (eds.) (2002) *Conceiving Cosmopolitanism: Theory, Context, and Practice*, Oxford and New York: Oxford University Press.

Vickers, J. (1991) *Women and the World Economic Crisis*. London: Zed.

Victor, D. G. (2004) *The Collapse of the Kyoto Protocol and the Struggle to Slow Global Warming*. Princeton, NJ: Princeton University Press, rev'd edn.

Visa (2003) Website of Visa Corporation, www.visa.com, accessed on 23 August.

Vivarelli, M. (2004) 'Globalization, Skills and Within-Country Inequality in Developing Countries', in E. Lee and M. Vivarelli (eds), *Understanding Globalization, Employment, and Poverty Reduction*. Basingstoke: Palgrave Macmillan, pp. 211–46.

Wachtel, H. (2000) 'The Mosaic of Global Taxes', in J. Nederveen Pieterse (ed.), *Global Futures: Shaping Globalization*. London: Sage, pp. 99–114.

Wade, R. (1996) 'Globalization and Its Limits: Reports of the Death of the National Economy Are Greatly Exaggerated', in S. Berger and R. Dore (eds), *National Diversity and Global Capitalism*. Ithaca, NY: Cornell University Press, pp. 60–88.

Wade, R. (2002) Remarks to the conference on 'Globalization and Inequality', Centre for the Study of Globalisation and Regionalisation, University of Warwick, 15 March.

Wade, R. H. (2004) 'Is Globalization Reducing Poverty and Inequality?' *World Development*, vol. 32, no. 4 (April), pp. 567–89.

Walker, R. B. J. (1991) 'On the Spatiotemporal Conditions of Democratic Practice', *Alternatives*, vol. 16, no. 2 (Spring), pp. 243–62.

Walker, R .B. J. (1995) 'International Relations and the Concept of the Political', in K. Booth and S. Smith (eds), *International Relations Theory*. Cambridge: Polity Press, pp. 306–27.

Wallace, H. (1996) 'Politics and Policy in the EU: The Challenge of Governance', in H. Wallace and W. Wallace (eds), *Policy-Making in the European Union*. Oxford: Oxford University Press, 3rd edn, pp. 3–36.

Wallace, H. and W. Wallace (eds) (2000) *Policy-Making in the European Union*. Oxford: Oxford University Press, 4th edn.

Wallensteen, P. and M. Sollenberg (2000) 'Armed Conflict 1989–1999', *Journal of Peace Research*, vol. 37, no. 5 (September), pp. 635–49.

Wallerstein, I. (1974) *The Modern World-System, 1: Capitalist Agriculture and the Origins of the European World-Economy in the Sixteenth Century*. New York: Academic Press.

Wallerstein, I. (1979) *The Capitalist World-Economy*. Cambridge: Cambridge University Press.

Wallerstein, I. (1986) 'Societal Development, or Development of the World-System?', *International Sociology*, vol. 1 (March), pp. 3–17.

Wallerstein, I. (1991) *Unthinking Social Science: The Limits of Nineteenth-Century Paradigms*. Cambridge: Polity Press.

Walton, J. and D. Seddon (1994) *Free Markets and Food Riots: The Politics of Global Adjustment*. Oxford: Blackwell.

Wambedde, Z. (2003) staff member of Mental Health Uganda, in conversation with the author, Mbale, 1 September.

Wang Ning (ed.) (2002) *Quanqiuhua yu wenhua. Xifang yu Zhongguo* ['Globalization and Culture: West and China']. Beijing: Peking University Press.

Wapner, P. (1996) *Environmental Activism and World Civic Politics*. New York: State University of New York Press.

Warkentin, C. (2001) *Reshaping World Politics: NGOs, the Internet, and Global Civil Society*. Lanham, MD: Rowman & Littlefield.

Warnier, J.-P. (2003) *La mondialisation de la culture* ['The Globalization of Culture']. Paris: Editions la Découverte.

Warren, K. J. (ed.) (1996) *Ecological Feminist Philosophies*. Bloomington, IN: Indiana University Press.

Warschauer, M. (2002) *Technology and Social Inclusion: Rethinking the Digital Divide*. Cambridge, MA: MIT Press.

Waterman, P. (1998) *Globalization, Social Movements and the New Internationalisms*. London: Mansell.

Waters, M. (1995) *Globalization*. London: Routledge.

Waters, M. (2001) *Globalization*. London: Routledge, 2nd edn.

Watson, J. L. (2000) 'China's Big Mac Attack', *Foreign Affairs*, vol. 79, no. 3 (May–June), pp. 120–34.

Watts, S. (1997) *Epidemics and History: Disease, Power and Imperialism.* New Haven, CT: Yale University Press.

WCSDG (2004) *A Fair Globalization: Creating Opportunities for All.* Geneva: International Labour Organization, World Commission on the Social Dimension of Globalization.

Weber, E. J. (1977) *Peasants into Frenchmen: The Modernization of Rural France 1870–1914.* London: Chatto & Windus.

Webster (1961) *Webster's Third New International Dictionary of the English Language Unabridged.* Springfield, MA: Merriam.

Webster, D. (1984) 'Direct Broadcast Satellites: Proximity, Sovereignty and National Identity', *Foreign Affairs*, vol. 62, no. 5 (Summer), pp. 1161–74.

Weiss, L. (1998) *The Myth of the Powerless State: Governing the Economy in a Global Era.* Cambridge: Polity.

Weiss, L. (ed.) (2003) *States in the Global Economy: Bringing Domestic Institutions Back In.* Cambridge: Cambridge University Press.

Weiss, T. G. and L. Gordenker (eds) (1996) *NGOs, the UN, and Global Governance.* Boulder, CO: Rienner.

Weiss, T. G. *et al.* (1994) *The United Nations and Changing World Politics.* Boulder, CO: Westview.

Welford, R. (1997) *Hijacking Environmentalism: Corporate Responses to Sustainable Development.* London: Earthscan.

Wells, C. (1987) *The UN, UNESCO and the Politics of Knowledge.* Basingstoke: Palgrave Macmillan.

Wells, H. G. (1938) *World Brain.* London: Methuen.

Went, R. (1996) *Grenzen aan de globalisering?* ['Limits to Globalization?'] Amsterdam: Het Spinhuis.

Went, R. (2000) *Globalization: Neoliberal Challenge, Radical Responses.* London: Pluto.

Whalley, J. (1996) 'Developing Countries and System Strengthening in the Uruguay Round', in W. Martin and L. A. Winters (eds), *The Uruguay Round and the Developing Countries.* Cambridge: Cambridge University Press, pp. 409–34.

Whatmore, S. (1994) 'Global Agro-Food Complexes and the Refashioning of Rural Europe', in A. Amin and N. Thrift (eds), *Globalization, Institutions, and Regional Development in Europe.* Oxford: Oxford University Press, pp. 46–67.

WHC (2004) Website of the World Heritage Convention, www.whc.unesco.org, accessed on 31 August.

Wheeler, N. J. (2000) *Saving Strangers: Humanitarian Intervention in International Society.* Oxford: Oxford University Press.

Whitfield, P. (1994) *The Image of the World: 20 Centuries of World Maps.* London: British Library.

WHO (2001) 'Special Theme: Globalization', *Bulletin of the World Health Organization*, vol. 79, no. 9, pp. 802–4, 827–93.

Wichterich, C. (2000) *The Globalized Woman: Reports from a Future of Inequality.* London: Zed.

Wiener, J. (1999) *Globalization and the Harmonization of Law.* London: Pinter.

Wilde, R. (2001) 'From Danzig to East Timor and Beyond: The Role of International Territorial Administration', *American Journal of International Law*, vol. 95, no. 3 (July), pp. 583–606.

Willetts, P. (ed.) (1996) *'Conscience of the World': The Influence of Non-Governmental Organisations in the UN System.* Washington, DC: Brookings Institution.

Williams, G. (2001) 'Megalomedia: The Voice of Globalization', *New Internationalist*, No. 333 (April), available at www.newint.org/, accessed on 1 February 2005.

Williams, M. (1996) 'Rethinking Sovereignty', in E. Kofman and G. Youngs (eds) *Globalization: Theory and Practice.* London: Pinter, pp. 109–22.

Williams, P. (1994) 'Transnational Criminal Organisations and International Security', *Survival*, vol. 36, no. 1 (Spring), pp. 96–113.

Williams, P. (2000) Remarks to the Annual Conference of the Academic Council on the United Nations System, Oslo, 18 June.

Williamson, J. (1990) 'What Washington Means by Policy Reform', in J. Williamson (ed.), *Latin American Adjustment: How Much Has Happened?* Washington, DC: Institute for International Economics, pp. 7–20.

Williamson, J. (1997) 'The Washington Consensus Reassessed', in L. Emmerij (ed.), *Economic and Social Development into the XXI Century*. Washington, DC: Inter-American Development Bank, pp. 48–61.

Williamson, J. (1999) Lecture at University of Warwick by John Williamson, Chief Economist, South Asia Region, the World Bank, 3 February.

Willkie, W. L. (1943) *One World*. London: Cassell.

Wills, J.E. (2001) *1688: A Global History*. New York: Norton.

Wilmer, F. (1993) *The Indigenous Voice in World Politics: Since Time Immemorial*. London: Sage.

Wilson, E. O. (ed.) (1988) *Biodiversity*. Washington, DC: National Academy Press.

Winslow, A. (ed.) (1995) *Women, Politics, and the United Nations*. Westport, CT: Greenwood.

Wirtz, J. J. and J. A. Larsen (eds) (2001) *Rocket's Red Glare: Missile Defenses and the Future of World Politics*. Boulder, CO: Westview.

Wood, A. (1994) *North–South Trade, Employment and Inequality: Changing Fortunes in a Skill-Driven World*. Oxford: Clarendon.

Wood, D. (2005) *Governing Global Banking: The Basel Committee and the Politics of Financial Globalisation*. Aldershot: Ashgate.

Wood, S. *et al.* (2003) *The Social and Economic Challenges of Nanotechnology*. Swindon: Economic and Social Research Council.

Woolf, V. (1938) *Three Guineas*. London: Hogarth.

World Bank (1992) *Export Processing Zones*. Washington, DC: World Bank Industry and Development Division.

World Bank (1994) *World Debt Tables 1994–95: External Finance for Developing Countries. Volume 1*. Washington, DC: World Bank.

World Bank (1996) *Annual Report 1996*. Washington, DC: World Bank.

World Bank (1997) *World Development Report 1997: the State in a Changing World*. New York: Oxford University Press.

World Bank (2000) *Consultations with Civil Society Organizations: General Guidelines for World Bank Staff*. Washington, DC: World Bank, NGO and Civil Society Unit.

World Bank (2001) *World Development Report 2000/2001: Attacking Poverty*. New York: Oxford University Press.

World Bank (2002) *World Development Report 2002: Building Institutions for Markets*. New York: Oxford University Press.

World Bank (2004) *World Development Report 2004: Making Services Work for Poor People*. New York: Oxford University Press.

World Bank (2005) *World Development Report 2005: A Better Investment Climate for Everyone*. New York: Oxford University Press.

Wriston, W. B. (1992) *The Twilight of Sovereignty: How the Information Revolution Is Transforming Our World*. New York: Charles Scribner's Sons.

WTO-1 (1991) *Current Travel and Tourism Indicators*. Madrid: World Tourism Organization.

WTO-1 (2002) Website of the World Tourism Organization, www.world-tourism.org/market_research/facts&figures/menu.htm.

WTO-2 (1996a) *Annual Report 1996, Volume I*. Geneva: World Trade Organization.

WTO-2 (1996b) 'Ruggiero Calls for Trading System to be Kept in Line with Globalization Process'. World Trade Organization press release, 22 February.

WTO-2 (2002) *Annual Report 2002*. Geneva: World Trade Organization.

WTTC (2005) Website of the World Travel & Tourism Council, http://www.wttc.org/, accessed on 3 February.

Wurm, S. A. (ed.) (1996) *Atlas of the World's Languages in Danger of Disappearing*. Paris: United Nations Educational, Scientific and Cultural Organisation.

Yeates, N. (1999), 'Social Politics and Policy in an Era of Globalization: Critical Reflections', *Social Policy & Administration*, vol. 33, no. 4 (December), pp. 372–93.

Yeates, N. (2001) *Globalization and Social Policy*. London: Sage.

Yeates, N. (2004) 'Global Care Chains: Critical Reflections and Lines of Enquiry', *International Feminist Journal of Politics*, vol. 6, no. 3 (September), pp. 369–91.

Young, O. R. *et al.* (eds) (1996) *Global Environmental Change and International Governance*. Hanover, NH: University Press of New England.

Young, P. (1991) *Person to Person: The International Impact of the Telephone*. Cambridge: Granta.

Yuen, E. *et al.* (eds) (2001) *The Battle of Seattle: The New Challenge to Capitalist Globalization*. New York: Soft Skull.

Zadek, S. (2001) *The Civil Corporation: The New Economy of Corporate Citizenship*. London: Earthscan.

Zadek, S. *et al.* (eds) (1997) *Building Corporate Account Ability: Emerging Practices in Social and Ethical Accounting, Auditing and Reporting*. London: Earthscan.

Zakaria, F. (1997) 'The Rise of Illiberal Democracy', *Foreign Affairs*, vol. 76, no. 6 (November/December), pp. 22–43.

Zarate, J. C. (1998) 'The Emergence of a New Dog of War: Private International Security Companies, International Law, and the New World Disorder', *Stanford Journal of International Law*, vol. 34, no. 1 (Winter), pp. 75–162.

Zevin, R. (1992) 'Are Financial Markets More Open? If So, Why and with What Effects?' in T. Banuri and J.B. Schor (eds), *Financial Openness and National Autonomy: Opportunities and Constraints*. Oxford: Clarendon, pp. 43–83.

Zolo, D. (1997) *Cosmopolis: Prospects for World Government*. Cambridge: Polity.

Zubiri, A. U. (1999) 'The International Relations of Basque Nationalism and the First Basque Autonomous Government (1890–1939)', in F. Aldecoa and M. Keating (eds), *Paradiplomacy in Action: The Foreign Relations of Subnational Governments*. London: Frank Cass, pp. 170–84.

Zumthor, P. (1993) *La mesure du monde. Représentation de l'espace au Moyen Age* ['The Scale of the World: Representation of Space in the Middle Ages']. Paris: Seuil.

Zysman, J. (1996) 'The Myth of a "Global" Economy: Enduring National Foundations and Emerging Regional Realities', *New Political Economy*, vol. 1, no. 2 (June), pp. 157–84.

Index

accountability, 35, 43, 349, 353–4, 361, 363, 365–7, 369–71, 380–1, 398, 410, 413–17
accounting, 137, 145, 183, 216, 252, 296
  see also global accounting
acid rain, 30, 72, 75, 100, 114
advertising, 68–9, 80, 92, 94, 163, 165, 178, 271
aeroplane, 20
aesthetics, 5, 150, 256–7, 273–4, 387
African National Congress, 232
African Union, 236, 282, 398
age, xviii, 6–7, 14–15, 18, 46, 73, 83, 116, 149, 197, 220, 225–6, 232, 239, 252, 278, 305, 316–17, 319, 340, 342–3, 345, 351, 378–9, 409, 413, 421
  see also children, elderly, youth
agent-structure problem, 21, 47, 83, 122–3, 157, 269, 383
aid, *see* official development assistance
AIDS, 31, 72–3, 91, 209, 219, 225, 250, 279–80, 288–9, 331, 399
air travel, 20, 41, 43, 62, 64, 68 69, 71, 76, 79, 82, 93, 95, 98, 100, 104, 107–8, 117–18, 125, 142, 144, 164, 177, 180, 182, 199, 204, 209, 216, 219, 235, 238, 245–6, 252, 268, 270, 272–3, 280, 283–4, 286, 311, 323, 336, 398, 406
Al Qaida, 71
alter-globalization, 41, 219, 382–423
alternative trade schemes, 220, 332, 404, 408
American Telephone & Telegraph Company (AT&T), *see* AT&T
Americanization, 16, 26, 32, 53, 58, 80, 245, 250, 306
Amnesty International, 215, 243, 250, 259
anarchism, 38, 45, 154, 259, 394–5
Andean pact, 207
Andorra, government of, 203
Antarctica, 211
anti-globalization movement, 40–1, 54, 56, 219, 221, 247, 250, 311, 381
anti-trust policy, 42–3, 183, 210, 390, 405, 421–2
apartheid, 35, 194, 206, 234, 243, 247, 249, 343–4, 374
  see also global apartheid
arbitration, 215–16
Argentina, government of, 203
arms control, 72, 219, 282–3, 312, 378, 390, 397, 422
Asia–Europe Meetings (ASEM), 207
Asian financial crisis, 198, 209, 211, 292–4, 329, 333, 343, 392, 401, 411
Asian Monetary Fund, 209
Asia-Pacific Economic Cooperation (APEC), 77, 207
Association of South East Asian Nations (ASEAN), 207, 363, 414
asylum seekers, 68, 105, 200, 219
AT&T, 92, 102
atomic capital, *see* nanotechnology
Australia, government of 197, 205
Austria, government of 205
Austro-Hungarian Empire, 228
automated teller machine (ATM), 69, 74, 109

Baha'ism, 225, 244
balance of power, 124, 126
Bank for International Settlements (BIS), 99–100, 209, 211, 213, 223, 259, 295, 306, 360, 367–8, 373, 401, 406–8, 415
banking, 62, 69–70, 74, 76, 82, 86, 95–6, 110–13, 117, 142, 161, 167–9, 181, 199, 216, 252, 294–5, 299, 302, 323, 329, 333, 375
Basque country, 203, 228, 233, 238
Belgium, government of, 203, 234
Bhutan, government of, 145
bilateral investment treaties (BITs), 142, 324
biodiversity, 31, 62, 72, 80, 114, 117, 189, 211, 221, 241, 262, 287, 306, 385
biological diversity, *see* biodiversity
biological weapons, 212, 282

biotechnology, 4, 159–60, 162, 173–4, 183–4, 280, 287, 328, 389
Black Sea Economic Cooperation, 363
Bolivia, government of, 192
bonds, 62, 70, 96, 111–12, 117, 142, 145, 166–8, 294
bond-rating agencies, 216, 329, 333
books, 67, 271
brain-drain, 105, 298
Brazil, government of, 195, 201, 204, 228, 238
Bretton Woods, 99, 108–9, 144, 146, 209, 296, 333
BRICS (Brazil, Russia, India, China, South Africa), 31
Britain, government of, 127, 142, 178, 195, 220, 231, 234, 239, 331
BSE, 31, 72, 288
Buddhism, 41, 58, 71, 87, 244, 260–1, 307, 377, 404
bureaucracy/bureaucratism, 28–9, 58, 132–3, 150, 154, 259, 275, 353, 370, 377, 393–5, 399, 424
Burkina Faso, government of, 192
Burma, government of, 206, 212
business associations, 225, 300, 367, 373, 376, 378

Cable News Network (CNN), 16, 104, 230
Canada, government of, 203–4, 234
canals, 93
capital controls, 16, 38, 40, 56, 142, 401
capitalism, 2–4, 6, 8, 15–16, 21, 23–5, 28–9, 31–2, 38, 42–7, 58, 66–7, 88–90, 99, 119, 121–2, 124, 128–30, 132–7, 139–41, 145–7, 151–3, 156, 159–84, 193, 208, 226, 229–32, 245, 247–8, 257, 259, 275, 286, 297–9, 301–2, 310, 313–15, 319–23, 325, 336–7, 339–40, 345–6, 383–4, 386–8, 390–5, 399, 402–3, 405–6, 409–10, 418, 422–4
  definition, 137
  see also commercial capitalism, communication capitalism, concentration of capital, consumer capitalism, finance capitalism, industrial capitalism, information capitalism, late capitalism, post-capitalism
care capital, 149, 159–60, 162, 175–6, 184, 302, 389
CARE International, 217
Cedel/Clearstream, 112
Central American Parliament, 363
chaebols, 230
chemical weapons, 212, 282, 397
children, 35, 68, 97, 108, 175–6, 212, 240, 245, 271, 289–91, 302, 317, 320, 338, 340, 342–4, 346, 356, 379, 409
China, government of, 127, 139, 178, 191, 195, 205, 207, 212, 232, 236, 238, 287, 373
chlorofluorocarbons (CFCs), 279
Christianity, 26, 41, 45, 48, 87–8, 97, 215, 236, 244–5, 259–61, 307, 340, 377, 386
citizenship, 37, 67, 134, 147, 187, 224, 228, 237, 239, 243–4, 246, 253–5, 309, 356, 380, 425
civil society, 7, 17, 25, 35, 37, 40, 44, 58, 71, 77, 86, 97, 106, 117, 125, 128, 150, 185, 188, 214–15, 218–21, 225, 246, 264, 285, 334, 339, 344, 348, 351–3, 355, 358–9, 361, 367–71, 373–80, 390, 392–3, 397, 408–9, 411, 414–16, 423
  definition, 218
  see also global civil society
civil wars, 30, 282–3
'clash of civilizations' thesis, 26, 245
class, xviii, 5–6, 14, 17, 19, 26, 32, 34, 36, 40, 45–6, 48, 65, 73, 79, 82–4, 89, 99, 101, 116, 119, 124, 126, 128–30, 132, 135–7, 139, 147, 149, 154, 164, 184, 189, 193, 198–9, 220, 224–6, 228, 239, 241, 252–3, 258, 278, 305, 308, 316, 318–25, 330, 334–5, 340, 342, 344–6, 351, 354, 371, 374–6, 378–80, 387–8, 404–6, 409, 413, 422
  definition, 246
  see also global class
Clearing House Interbank Payments System (CHIPS), 110–12
climate change, 31, 62, 72, 75, 90, 100, 113–14, 119, 191, 209, 211, 219, 221–2, 241, 262, 280–1, 287, 372, 381, 384, 398
Coca-Cola, 73, 94, 164–5
Codex Alimentarius Commission, 216
Cold War, 35, 102, 115, 245, 283
colonialism, 16, 58, 63, 94–5, 98, 132, 142–3, 148, 151, 188, 191, 227,

236, 239, 246, 252, 260, 300, 320, 333–4, 345, 421
see also decolonization
Columbian exchange, 89
commercial capitalism, 161, 176, 229, 302
commodification, 138–9, 153, 161–77, 184, 273
definition, 161, 229
commodity agreements, 94
commodity exchanges, 93–4, 108
commodity markets, 408
Commonwealth, 209, 239
communications capitalism, 159–60, 170–3, 176–7, 181, 184, 389
communism, 99, 115, 149, 164, 195, 352–3
communitarianism, 27–9, 244, 253–4, 275, 309, 394–5, 403
community, 79, 190, 253
competition policy, *see* anti-trust policy
competition state, 25
complexity theory, 122
computers, 20, 30, 67, 83, 92, 94, 103, 108, 118, 162, 170–2, 182–3, 189, 199, 219, 252, 263, 266–7, 271–3, 280, 283, 286, 294–5, 297, 309, 311, 327, 342, 376, 402
see also e-commerce, e-mail, Internet, World Wide Web
concentration of capital, 177, 182–4, 388, 405, 419, 422
see also anti-trust policy
Concert of Europe, 242
Confucianism, 26, 58, 261
constructivism, 3, 21, 121–3, 125, 131–2, 135–6, 154
consumer capitalism, 159–60, 162–5, 173, 175, 177, 181, 184, 264, 302
consumer movement, 129, 164, 218, 289, 304, 325, 334, 374–5, 421
consumerism, 4, 24, 26, 80, 108, 116, 161–4, 250, 264, 286, 305, 381, 399
Continuous Linked Settlements (CLS), 110, 112, 391, 401
corporate alliances, 4, 71, 105, 160, 178–80
corporate citizenship, *see* corporate social responsibility
corporate social responsibility (CSR), 164, 215, 286, 304, 310, 375, 391–2, 398, 415
corporatism, 139, 196
cosmocracy, 187
cosmopolitan democracy, 37
cosmopolitanism, 56, 187, 191, 212, 220, 224, 226, 229, 240–2, 244, 394–5, 404, 418
Costa Rica, government of, 196
Council of Europe, 207, 236, 363, 414
courts, 7, 75, 194, 201, 210, 212, 216, 353, 366–7, 369, 371, 390, 400, 412, 414–15, 422
Creative Commons, 405
credit cards, 64, 69, 74, 76, 95, 100, 108–9, 183, 189, 328
crime, 6, 30, 71–2, 105, 189, 193, 200, 203–4, 212, 218, 280–1, 284–5, 289, 308, 311–12, 396
criminal networks, 71
Cuba, government of, 145
culture, 6, 16, 19, 28–9, 42, 46, 55, 66, 79, 83, 126, 128, 130, 135, 154, 209, 219, 236–7, 240, 253, 263, 265, 280, 284, 306, 311, 318, 345, 349, 351, 353, 364, 371, 376–7, 379–80, 387–90, 393–4, 396, 403–4, 414, 417, 422, 424
effects of globalization on, 14, 18, 26, 32, 40, 56–9, 80–1, 207, 230, 235, 245, 260, 305–6, 314, 384, 388
see also interculturalism
cyberspace, 68, 77, 138, 144, 216, 247, 267, 307, 327, 342
Czechoslovakia government of, 192

dams, 72, 114, 221, 305
data, *see* statistics
debt, 31, 95–6, 137, 168–70, 219, 286, 288–9, 292, 294, 296, 313, 333, 343, 359, 369, 375, 390, 400, 404, 416, 418, 422
decentralization, *see* devolution
decolonization, 16, 33, 139, 192, 195, 225, 231, 334
see also colonialism
deep ecology, *see* ecocentrism
deforestation, 72, 114, 221, 235, 286, 364, 385, 398
de-globalization, 37, 41, 43, 56, 297, 388–9
demergers, 181–2

democracy, xv, xvii, xviii, 6–8, 29–30, 35–8, 42–4, 47, 56–7, 67, 84, 124, 129, 147, 154, 184, 201, 217–18, 220, 223, 254, 278, 309, 318, 348–83, 385–90, 392–5, 400, 406–7, 410–17, 420–2, 424
  definition, 349
Denmark, government of, 194, 197
deregulation, 38–40, 56
derivatives, 70, 74, 110, 112–13, 117, 161, 165–9, 189, 216, 294, 296, 299, 329, 364
desertification, 72, 115
deterritorialization, 17, 77, 110, 187, 225, 237, 248, 268
development cooperation, 204, 218, 243
devolution, 203, 222, 234, 364–5, 389, 410–11, 413
diasporas, 5, 77, 81, 92, 148–9, 153, 204, 226–7, 237–9, 250, 254, 283, 285, 413
digital divide, 36, 219, 327–8, 330, 386
(dis)abled persons, 7, 35, 79, 116, 130, 175, 189, 220, 226, 239, 251–2, 305, 316–17, 319–20, 340, 342, 344–6, 351, 354, 378–9, 413
disciplines (academic), xiv, xvii, xviii, 27, 47, 51, 62, 66, 125, 262, 269–70, 272, 274–5, 425
diseases, 61, 72, 75, 88–9, 91, 98, 114, 116, 145, 150, 174, 200, 203, 217, 222, 242–3, 280–1, 288, 313, 315, 328, 357
domestic work, 68, 73, 105, 134, 149, 175–6, 237, 246, 336–8, 378, 409
double movement, 391

EASDAQ, 70
East African Community (EAC), 77, 363
Eastern Orthodoxy, 26, 241, 260
ecocentrism, 41, 154, 256–9, 261–2, 274, 383
ecology, xvii, 6, 29–30, 33, 40, 42–3, 56–7, 60, 62, 64, 67, 71–2, 76–7, 107, 116, 119, 123, 128, 132–3, 144, 150, 152, 154, 174, 190, 193, 200, 204–5, 208, 210–11, 215, 221, 241, 261–2, 265, 280–1, 283, 285–8, 289, 296, 304–5, 311–12, 317, 319, 342, 349, 365, 384, 387–90, 392, 394, 396, 398–9, 402, 414, 418, 422, 424
  see also environmental movements, global ecology, sustainable development
education, 57, 116, 150, 163, 188, 229, 231, 246, 270–1, 293, 297, 321–4, 335–6, 338–9, 343–4, 351, 353–7, 359, 361, 371, 375, 378, 380, 399, 402–3, 406, 410–13, 416, 418, 421–2
efficiency, xvii, 6, 29, 31, 38–42, 266, 294, 303, 307, 313, 319, 343, 349, 371, 384, 387, 394, 399
elderly, 68, 175, 317, 319, 340, 342, 344, 346, 379, 409
elections, 7, 36, 213, 231–2, 350–3, 361–4, 370–1, 374, 380, 390, 412–13, 422
electronic commerce (e-commerce), 17, 68, 108, 165, 177, 210
electronic mail (e-mail), 35, 68, 90, 103, 200, 251, 268
El Salvador, government of, 192
emerging market financial crises, 169
empire, 187
employment/unemployment, 6, 32, 42, 246, 248, 281, 293–4, 296–300, 308, 313, 315, 319, 324, 335–7, 339, 342, 396, 399, 402, 404, 407, 410, 414, 422
  see also labour conditions
'end of history' thesis, 32, 275, 388
English language, 14, 26, 48, 50, 73, 80, 246, 271–2, 274, 305, 327, 361, 375–6
Enlightenment, 32, 89–90, 151–2, 260, 265, 307, 314
environment, *see* ecology
environmental movements, 30, 97, 113, 129, 194, 215, 218, 221, 241, 262, 325, 334, 339, 364
epistemology, 27, 258–66, 274, 307–8, 385, 394
equality, xv, 6–8, 29, 33–5, 47, 56, 82, 84, 87, 119, 126, 128, 130, 132, 135, 154, 160, 184, 195, 278, 316–51, 371–9, 382–3, 385, 387–8, 390, 392–5, 400, 404–11, 421–2, 424
  definition of, 317
equity, *see* justice
Eritrea, government of, 192
Esperanto, 73, 100–1, 271
ethical investment, 374, 404, 422
Ethiopia, government of, 192

euro, xiii, 62, 69, 109–10, 208, 232, 252
eurobonds, *see* bonds
Euroclear, 112, 167
European Social Charter, 303–4
European Social Forum, 77, 365
European Union (EU), 37, 40, 69, 71, 143, 167, 181, 190, 197, 203, 205, 207–8, 231–2, 236–7, 239, 243, 298, 303–4, 332, 338, 352, 363, 366, 370, 373, 403, 405
  see also Maastricht Treaty
export processing zones (EPZs), 33, 107, 117, 143, 178, 297–8, 336

fascism, 38, 263
facsimile, 64, 67, 92, 102–3, 260, 268, 271, 323
faith, *see* religion
family planning, *see* reproduction
feminism, 3, 33, 99, 121–5, 133–6, 149, 154, 240, 261–3, 309, 345, 378
fibre-optic cables, 102, 119
film, 67, 73, 80, 172–3, 251, 271, 273
finance, 4, 6, 61
finance capitalism, 4, 6, 24, 34, 61, 159–61, 165–70, 173, 176–7, 181, 184, 294, 299, 302
  see also banking, derivatives, foreign exchange, global finance, insurance, securities markets
Financial Action Task Force (FATF), 285
Financial Stability Forum (FSF), 295
Financing for Development (FfD), *see* United Nations Financing for Development
fisheries, 72
Flanders, government of, 203
flexibilization, 301–2, 304, 309, 314, 325, 336
food, 14, 31, 34, 69, 73, 79, 81, 89, 163, 174, 216, 238, 262, 265, 273, 288, 324, 337–8, 341–2
Food and Agriculture Organization (FAO), 414
food security, 34, 94, 116, 150, 241, 291, 293, 340, 342–3
Fordism, 24, 301, 314
foreign direct investment (FDI), xiii, 16, 19, 31, 55, 61, 105–6, 117–18, 143, 166, 183, 193, 211, 297–8, 323, 328
foreign exchange, xiii, 16, 31, 38, 43, 56, 69, 74, 95, 109–10, 112, 117, 139, 142, 165–8, 189, 210, 220, 266, 286, 294, 299, 332, 401, 406, 408
forests, *see* deforestation
Forest Stewardship Council, 215, 364
foundations, 71, 194, 216, 218, 220, 289, 307, 370, 416
Four Motors, 205–6
France, government of, 127, 195, 205, 231
Francophonie, 238–9
Free Papua Organization (OPM), 235
Free Trade Area of the Americas (FTAA), 207
Fretilin (Revolutionary Front of an Independent East Timor), 232
Friends of the Earth, 223
fundamentalism, *see* religious revivalism

Gaia hypothesis, 116, 262
gender, xviii, 3, 5–6, 14, 15, 19, 26, 33–4, 36, 43, 46, 48, 73, 82–3, 99, 101, 116, 128, 130, 133–7, 147–9, 154, 184, 189, 219–21, 224–6, 239–410, 252–4, 263, 278, 305, 316–20, 334–40, 342, 344–6, 351, 354, 371, 377–80, 387, 405, 408–9, 413, 422
  definition, 248
  see also patriarchy, women
General Agreement on Tariffs and Trade (GATT), 99–100, 143, 145, 206, 215, 331
Generalized System of Preferences (GSP), 303, 332, 408
generation, *see* age
genetically modified (GM), 31, 69, 72, 173–4, 279, 286, 328
genetic capitalism, *see* biotechnology
genocide, 212, 243, 281, 398
geography, xiv, 22, 59–60, 63–4, 66–8, 76, 78, 82, 121, 131, 136, 147, 156, 225, 231, 255, 258, 267–8, 280, 308, 345, 351, 424
  see also space
Germany, government of, 194, 205, 228, 231
global, *see* globality, globalization
global accounting, 137–8, 153, 179, 373
global *apartheid*, 29, 34, 340
global care chains, 176
global central bank, 43, 223, 386, 401
global citizenship, *see* citizenship
global city, 76–7, 119, 204

global civil society, 18, 35, 41–3, 74, 118–19, 142, 145, 149, 171, 194, 206, 218–22, 238, 246, 259, 289, 310, 339, 351–2, 369, 374, 376, 379, 409, 417
see also civil society
global class, 240, 246–8, 254, 393
see also class
global commodity chains, 68
global commons, 211
global communications, xiv, 4, 14, 18, 24, 31, 33–4, 36, 41, 51, 61, 67, 69, 71, 73, 77, 81–2, 88, 90–2, 98, 101–4, 130,133, 139, 164–5, 186, 202, 208–9, 216, 230, 238, 245, 249, 258, 262, 265, 268, 270, 282, 284, 286, 289, 327, 330, 336–8, 340–2, 346, 350, 354, 360, 362, 374, 389, 407
Global Compact, *see* UN Global Compact
global companies, 17, 18, 33–4, 36, 39, 43, 70, 79, 88–90, 97–8, 105, 107, 111, 113, 117, 119, 138, 140, 142, 160, 162, 168, 171–4, 176–7, 178–81, 183, 186, 189, 193–4, 198–9, 203, 205–6, 209, 213, 215, 220, 230, 246, 259, 284–5, 289, 294, 297–8, 300, 302, 309, 313–14, 328, 331, 341–3, 354, 357, 360, 375–6, 385, 398–9, 403, 406, 409, 414, 419
global competition, 23, 31–2, 183, 196–7, 209, 288, 293, 302–3, 308, 324, 329, 342, 346, 386, 394
global conferences, 51, 68, 73, 98, 116, 219, 248, 251, 307, 339, 357, 368, 370, 378, 411, 414
global consciousness, 18, 58, 73–5, 89–90, 99–101, 116, 118, 130, 152, 202, 208, 256, 267, 312, 389, 402, 418, 423
global corporations, *see* global companies
global ecology, xiv, 24, 31, 36, 51, 72, 74–5, 77, 87, 90–1, 100, 113–15, 118, 186, 189–90, 198, 202, 207, 212, 230, 235, 241, 244, 257–8, 262, 266, 270, 284–5, 287, 311–12, 354, 356, 362, 364–5, 374, 376–7, 385, 390, 412
see also ecology
global factory, 33, 68
see also export processing zone, global production
global finance, 14, 24, 31, 33–4, 36, 61, 62, 69–71, 74, 76–7, 86, 89–91, 95–6, 99, 110–13, 118, 134, 139–40, 142, 146, 149, 166, 168–9, 174, 177, 186, 189, 191, 193, 202, 206, 209, 214, 216, 220, 222–3, 238, 245–6, 257–8, 284–6, 292, 294–6, 313, 323, 329, 332–3, 336–7, 340–1, 346, 354, 357, 360, 362, 372–4, 381, 385–6, 389, 399, 401, 408, 414, 422
see also finance
global governance, 18, 30, 33–5, 38, 43–4, 71, 74, 88, 98–101, 106, 125, 128,141–2, 144–5, 171, 175, 185–6, 188, 190–1, 198, 200, 209–14, 218–23, 229–30, 232, 241, 246, 248–9, 259, 285, 287, 289, 293, 303, 306–7, 310, 312, 320, 325, 333, 339, 343–4, 346, 355–6, 360, 362, 365–6, 368, 372, 378, 385, 389, 396–9, 403, 413–15, 417–18, 420–2
global health, *see* health
global law, *see* law
global markets, xiv, 14, 23, 25, 32–4, 40, 51, 64, 69, 74, 91, 93–4, 107–8, 125, 138, 143, 153, 161–2, 165, 181–3, 198, 214, 230, 238, 258, 265–6, 273, 282, 288, 291, 298, 312, 336, 341–2, 374, 387, 390, 402
global mass media, *see* mass media
global money, 62, 69, 74, 89, 95–6, 100, 108–10, 119, 127, 139, 160, 189, 191, 198, 209, 241, 328, 346, 354, 374, 401–2, 408
see also money
global organizations, 31, 34, 61, 70–1, 74, 81, 91, 96–8, 99, 105–6, 134, 138, 171, 179, 202, 238, 241, 245, 258, 284–5, 312, 341–2, 346
global production, xiv, 64, 68–9, 74, 91, 97, 100–1, 107, 113, 118, 125, 143, 164, 177, 179, 193, 198, 216, 258, 268, 300, 304, 336, 341, 399
global products, 77, 80, 90, 94, 108, 115, 118, 138–9, 143, 160–1, 164–5, 241, 323, 328, 340
global public goods, 243–4, 310, 382–43, 406
global public policy, 106, 393, 396, 399, 409, 417–20, 422–3

Global Reporting Initiative (GRI), 215, 364, 367
global socialism, *see* socialism
global social movements, 26, 34, 45, 58, 320, 325, 339, 344, 346, 417
  see also social movements
global sourcing, 68, 74, 153
global trade regime, 33, 210, 219, 303, 313, 331, 356, 398
  see also World Trade Organization
global travel, xiv, 34, 55, 61, 68–9, 88, 92–3, 104–5, 116–18, 130, 139, 151, 202, 208, 265, 341
  see also migration
global village, 73, 116, 241
global warming, *see* climate change
globalism, xvii, 17–18, 47, 49–50, 75–8, 85, 208, 251, 348
globality, 28, 51, 60, 64–5, 67–75, 118–19, 356
globalization, xiii, 355, 395
  causation, xvii, 2, 4, 8, 15, 20–2, 121–54, 424
  definition, xv, xvii, 1–3, 8, 15–17, 46, 49–84, 424
  and social change (general), 2, 4–7, 22–9, 149, 156–8
  history of, xiv, xv, xvii, 2–3, 8, 15, 46, 85–120, 424
  indexes, 55, 87, 101
  politics of, xviii, 1–2, 45, 50, 67, 82–4
  policies towards, 6–8, 14, 37–46, 53, 121–2, 125, 153–4, 196, 289, 362, 382, 424
  scale, xiv, 15, 17–19, 46, 54
  terminology, 14, 50–2, 60, 64–5, 141
  theory of, xv, xviii, 3, 20, 22
  unevenness of, 18, 50, 81–2
glocalization, 26, 80
gold standard, 95–6, 109
governance, xv, 6–8, 19, 21–2, 24–5, 28–9, 35, 37, 39, 42, 56, 60, 66, 76, 90, 121–2, 131, 136, 140–9, 152–4, 156–7, 185–224, 226, 228–9, 254, 256, 258, 274–5, 280, 308, 347–52, 355–62, 364, 366–8, 370–7, 379–81, 383, 385–6, 389, 392, 394–6, 410–11, 414, 416, 420, 422, 424–5
  definition of, 140–1, 214
  see also global governance
greenhouse effect, *see* climate change
Greenpeace, 113, 415
Group of Seven/Eight (G7/8), 192, 200, 208, 223, 289, 295, 300, 326, 330, 360, 368, 372–3, 376, 386, 391, 400
Group of 10 (G10), 201, 372
Group of 20 (G20), 201, 223, 372
Group of 24 (G24), 201, 223, 372
Group of 30 (G30), 295
Group of 77 (G77), 201, 249, 382
Gulf Cooperation Council (GCC), 207, 363

Haiti, government of, 237
harmonization, *see* standardization
health, xiii, 6, 14, 72, 74–5, 144, 163, 175, 188, 195–7, 200, 202, 209, 216, 229–30, 265, 281, 288–9, 293, 296, 301–3, 312–13, 317, 321, 323–4, 335, 338, 343–4, 354–6, 362, 374, 378, 386, 390, 396, 399, 406, 414, 422, 425
hedge funds, 112, 169, 189, 220, 292
hegemony, 121, 124, 127, 130, 133, 135, 146, 372
heterogenization, 26, 32, 47, 80–1
high modernity, 265–6
Hinduism, 26, 41, 45, 244–5, 259–61, 307
History, 66
HIV, *see* AIDS
Hollywood, 16, 80, 250, 328, 338
homogenization/homogeneity, 26, 47, 50, 57–8, 75, 80–1, 235, 240, 281, 306
homosexuality, *see* sexuality
Human Development Report, 44, 325, 330, 336
humanity, 5, 73, 89, 99, 146, 151, 212, 220, 226, 239–40, 246, 252, 254, 321, 418
human rights, 34, 40, 57, 62, 72, 116, 125, 144–5, 190, 193, 200, 204, 208–9, 212, 215, 218–19, 224, 236, 240–6, 325, 334, 339, 342–3, 346, 352, 366–7, 381, 396–7, 409, 422
human security, *see* security
humanitarian intervention, 212, 242
humanitarian relief, 6, 31, 97, 100, 217–18, 242, 244, 280, 282, 289, 310, 342, 357, 369
hybridity/hybridization, 5–7, 26, 32, 81, 136, 147, 149, 156, 224–7, 252–5, 263, 273–4, 305, 315, 394

hypercapitalism, 4, 7, 24, 29, 136, 139, 147, 160, 175, 177, 184

Iceland, government of, 231
idealism (methodological), 20–1, 47, 121, 131–3, 146, 269
identity, xv, 2, 4–8, 19, 21–2, 25–8, 29, 32, 42, 44–5, 56, 60, 76, 81, 101, 116, 121–2, 127, 130–3, 136, 140, 145–9, 152–4, 156–7, 224–56, 258, 274–5, 280–1, 296, 304–6, 308–9, 314, 318, 383, 385–7, 389, 393–4, 403–4, 413, 417–18, 421, 424
immigration, *see* migration
imperialism, 16, 26, 32–3, 58–9, 81, 98–9, 133–6, 139, 148, 151–2, 154, 247, 325–6, 334, 384, 394, 421
India, government of, 164, 203, 205, 232
indigenous peoples, 26, 45, 56, 73, 79–81, 89, 130, 133, 154, 205, 215, 233–5, 248, 253, 261, 280, 305–7, 310, 331, 344, 364, 376–7
individualism (methodological), *see* agent-structure problem
Indonesia, government of, 228, 232, 413
industrial capitalism, 23, 34, 147, 159–61, 165, 170, 173, 176, 184, 229
inequality, *see* equality
information age/economy, 14, 23, 35, 162, 170, 272
information capitalism, 4, 159–60, 170–3, 176–7, 181, 184, 302, 389
Institute of International Finance (IIF), 219, 223
insurance business, 70, 74, 110, 112–13, 145, 161, 166, 168, 181–2, 200, 375
intellectual property, 73, 143–4, 175, 200, 210, 222, 331, 378, 399, 405–6, 416, 422
interculturalism/interculturality, xiv, 26, 44, 253, 263, 265, 273, 377, 393–4, 403–4, 421–3
international, 14, 51, 55–6, 61, 65–6, 78–9, 82, 148, 228, 234
  relationship to global, 2, 356–7
  terminology, 15
International Accounting Standards Board (IASB), 145, 216, 223, 296, 360, 367, 373, 415
International Air Transport Association (IATA), 216
International Association of Insurance Supervisors (IAIS), 145, 295
International Atomic Energy Agency (IAEA), 36, 212, 282, 397
International Chamber of Commerce (ICC), 216, 246
International Civil Aviation Organization (ICAO), 144
International Confederation of Free Trade Unions (ICFTU), 44, 219–20, 247, 373
International Council for Local Environmental Initiatives (ICLEI), 204
International Court of Justice (ICJ), 73, 367
International Criminal Court (ICC), 73, 212, 243, 397
International Criminal Police Organization (Interpol), 73, 99, 285
International Federation of Accountants (IFAC), 145, 216, 296
International Labour Organization (ILO), 44, 212, 293, 303, 324, 339, 379, 391, 402–3
International Lesbian and Gay Association (ILGA), 251
International Monetary Fund (IMF), 18, 33–4, 39, 69, 71, 99–100, 109, 111, 141–2, 145, 197, 209–11, 213, 219, 223, 230, 246, 292–3, 295–6, 306, 324, 332–3, 355, 360, 362–3, 365–7, 373, 378, 391, 396, 400–1, 408, 414–15, 420
International Organization for Standardization (ISO), 99, 144, 216
International Organization of Employers (IOE), 39
International Organization of Securities Commissions (IOSCO), 145, 205, 295, 306
International Red Cross and Red Crescent Movement, 97
International Securities Market Association (ISMA), 144, 223, 295
International Telecommunications Satellite Organization (INTELSAT), 102
International Telecommunication Union (ITU), 98, 144, 216, 330, 338, 406

International Union of Local Authorities, 204
internationalization, 3, 16–17, 19, 47, 49, 54–6, 59, 84–6
Internet, 17, 36, 41, 64, 67–8, 77, 79, 81–2, 103, 108, 117, 119, 134, 139, 142, 145, 171–2, 177, 183, 189, 191, 198, 209, 219, 222, 235, 238, 247–51, 271–2, 285, 305–6, 323, 327–8, 332, 337, 354, 358, 360–1, 368, 375, 386, 391, 406
Internet Corporation for Assigned Names and Numbers (ICANN), 144, 216, 360, 366, 368, 375, 415
interregionalism, 207
intra-firm trade, 68, 107, 118, 179, 189
Inuit Circumpolar Conference (ICC), 235, 376
Iran, government of, 194
Irish Republican Army (IRA), 71
Islam, 13, 26, 41, 45, 58, 88, 97, 194, 236, 244–5, 260–1, 307, 317, 377
Israel, government of, 260

Japan, government of, 127, 148, 192, 205, 207, 209
Judaism, 26, 41, 48, 237–8, 244–5, 260–1, 307, 340, 377
justice, xvii, 14, 29, 33, 36, 42, 57, 67, 83, 217, 219–20, 316, 345, 374, 391, 400, 409, 411

Kazakstan, government of, 231
knowledge, 2–6, 8, 19, 21–2, 28, 32, 42, 44–7, 60, 67, 80, 119, 121–2, 125, 130, 132–4, 136, 140, 145–6, 149–52, 154, 156–7, 244, 256–75, 280–1, 306–8, 314, 318, 383, 385–6, 389, 393–5, 403, 424
knowledge society, 23
Kyoto Protocol, 212

labour, 38, 68
labour conditions, 32, 42–3, 72, 80, 129, 139, 212–13, 215, 219, 246, 280–1, 284, 288, 296, 300–4, 308, 311, 314, 318, 339, 344, 387–8, 390, 394, 396, 402–3, 409, 422
  see also employment, flexibilization
labour movements, 45, 71, 97, 99–100, 116, 129, 178, 195, 215, 218–20, 235, 240, 246–8, 300–1, 304, 319–20, 324–5, 346, 352, 358, 364, 367, 373, 375, 378, 386, 400, 403–4
land-mines, 282
languages, 80, 125, 130–1, 148, 188–9, 229, 231, 234, 238, 269, 306, 320, 361, 376–7, 412
late modernity, 266
law, 72, 74–5, 78–80, 90, 98–9, 106, 125, 129, 134, 143–5, 150–1, 153, 175, 189, 201–2, 209, 213, 229, 234–5, 248, 351, 370, 377, 385, 405, 416
League of Arab States, 206, 236
League of Nations, 99–100
Lebanon, government of, 192, 234
legislatures, *see* parliaments
legitimacy, 381
liberalism, 3, 7, 35, 38, 121–6, 128–30, 133–6, 153, 263, 348, 350–5, 387
liberalization, 3, 16, 19, 25, 38–40, 49, 56–7, 59, 84–6, 141–3, 146, 153, 172, 183, 196, 210, 291–2, 294, 298–9, 313, 318, 323–4, 329–33, 343, 357, 382, 384, 401
literacy, 290–1, 342, 390, 402
literature, 66, 116, 225, 250, 263
local government *see* substate governance
localism, 20, 41–2, 47, 58, 78–9, 108, 220, 262, 356, 364, 410–12, 414–16, 418, 420
locality/localization, 79, 190, 235, 257, 309, 372, 384–5, 388–9
  see also substate governance
London Club, 333
London Interbank Offered Rate (LIBOR), 70
Long Term Capital Management (LTCM), 169, 279, 292, 294

Maastricht Treaty, 205, 232, 236, 304
  see also European Union
macro-region(alism), *see* regionalization
Malaysia, government of, 232
maps, 63, 88, 100, 151, 268
Marrakech Agreement, 210
Marxism, 3, 21, 23, 121–5, 128–30, 134–7, 154, 179, 191, 344
mass media, 7, 26, 34–5, 39, 45, 58, 62, 74, 81, 94, 99, 144, 164–5, 173, 178, 181–2, 189, 193, 219, 230, 232, 235, 242, 246, 250, 264, 271, 273, 279, 281, 284–5, 305–6, 311, 328, 330, 338, 341–2, 344, 351–3, 355–9, 361–2, 369, 374, 380, 386, 411, 419
  see also radio, television

materialism (methodological), 21, 47, 121, 125, 130, 133, 146, 269, 387, 393
McDonald's, 16, 80, 82, 94, 165, 198–9
men's movement, 248
mercenaries, 217
MERCOSUR (Southern Common Market), 207, 304, 368, 414
mergers and acquisitions (M&A), 160, 172, 177, 180–4, 298–9
methodology, 5, 27, 55, 59, 65–7, 121, 157, 229, 256–7, 269–72, 274, 318, 424
methodological territorialism, 76, 86,
Mexico, government of, 238
micro-credit schemes, 70, 337, 408
micro-nations, 5, 76, 199, 226–8, 233–5, 239, 254, 283
Microsoft, 298
migration, 14, 19, 34, 38, 40, 55, 64, 68, 70, 74, 89, 92, 105, 118, 127, 134, 145, 162, 176, 191, 200, 208, 230, 237–8, 251–2, 263, 280, 288, 303, 305, 313, 342, 354, 374, 386, 409, 425
militarism, 28, 284
military/militarization, xiii, xiv, 35, 71, 74–5, 77, 98, 115, 127, 130, 142, 146, 173, 190–1, 199–200, 206, 209, 211, 217, 227, 242, 249, 263, 265, 283, 304, 312, 351–2, 360, 379, 381, 386, 396–8, 419
millennium bug (Y2K), 279, 311
Millennium Development Goals (MDGs), 293, 400
missiles, 30, 64, 71, 93, 98, 100, 115, 279, 283, 397
mobile telephones, *see* telephone
modernity, xiv, 15–16, 28–9, 47, 58–9, 81, 84, 86, 88, 121, 124–6, 132, 150–1, 154, 244, 257, 260, 264–6, 376, 421, 423
  see also high modernity, late modernity, postmodernity
money, 76, 88, 137, 191, 232–3, 268
  see also global money
money laundering, 30, 211, 285
Mormons, 245
Multilateral Agreement on Investment (MAI), 142, 221, 303
multilateralism, xiii, 37, 187, 207, 218, 376, 419
multinational corporations, *see* global companies
music, 73, 81, 116, 161, 165, 173, 183, 225, 242, 250–1, 263, 265, 273, 328, 369
Muslims, *see* Islam

nanotechnology, 159–60, 162, 173–5, 280, 328, 389
NASDAQ, 70, 172
national identity, *see* nationhood
nationalism, 18, 20–1, 28, 30, 41–3, 130, 134, 136, 140, 147–9, 152–3, 156, 189, 224–6, 228–30, 233, 237, 239–40, 244, 245, 253, 280, 305, 308–10, 315, 334, 381, 393, 421
  definition, 225
nationhood, xiv, xviii, 5, 8, 26, 56, 65–6, 73, 101, 132, 147–8, 156, 226–7, 229, 231–9, 241, 245, 252–4, 255, 257, 262, 305, 350–1, 354, 389, 413, 424
  definition, 227
  see also micro-nations, region-nation, state-nation, transworld nation
neocolonialism, 374
neo-Gramscianism, 129
neoliberalism, 3, 7–8, 37–45, 47, 56–7, 59, 83, 120, 124–5, 141, 185, 188, 194, 197, 210, 214, 217, 221, 232, 259, 288–90, 292, 294, 296, 299–300, 304, 308, 310, 314–15, 318–21, 323–5, 327, 329–30, 332, 338–9, 342–3, 345–6, 352, 357, 382–93, 395, 399 ,401, 417–21, 423
  definition, 38
neo-nazism, 370, 379
Netherlands, government of, 197
networks, 23, 45, 63, 71, 77, 162, 170, 187, 222
New International Economic Order (NIEO), 332
'new mediævalism' thesis, 187
New Partnership for Africa's Development (NEPAD), 293, 330, 400
New World Information and Communications Order (NWICO), 232, 330
New Zealand, government of, 195
newly industrializing countries (NICs), 31, 291, 296, 298, 303, 313, 327, 341
Nigeria, government of, 234

nomads, 234
nongovernmental organizations (NGOs), 35, 71, 113, 170, 194, 196, 215, 218, 220–1, 248, 259, 282, 310, 314, 332, 334, 342, 346, 352, 358, 367, 369, 373, 376, 378, 386, 392, 400
  see also civil society
Non-Aligned Movement (NAM), 249
North American Free Trade Agreement (NAFTA), 235, 247, 304
North Atlantic Treaty Organization (NATO), 199, 207, 284, 326, 363
North–South gaps/relations, 33–4, 36, 48, 82, 119, 137, 164, 176, 248, 316–17, 319–20, 324–35, 340, 346, 372, 374, 404–5, 407–8, 422
nuclear weapons, xiii, 115, 200, 212, 242, 282–3, 372, 391, 397

official development assistance (ODA), 31, 208, 293, 329–30, 332–3, 346, 381, 406, 417
offshore arrangements, 4, 62, 70, 76, 95, 100, 110, 112, 138, 142, 160, 177–8, 184, 189, 211, 302, 323–4, 329, 346, 406–7, 422
Ogoni movement, 234
oligopoly, *see* concentration of capital
Olympic Games, 93, 100, 165, 230, 284
ontology, 5, 27, 55, 256–7, 267–9, 274
opinion polls, 361–2
Organization for Security and Cooperation in Europe (OSCE), 207, 282, 363
Organization for Economic Cooperation and Development (OECD), 39, 106, 142–44, 146, 192, 200, 209, 211, 215, 221, 282, 285, 295, 304, 306, 324, 326, 331, 333, 360, 367–8, 373, 403, 405, 407, 415, 417
Organization of African Unity (OAU), *see* African Union
Organization of American States (OAS), 206, 363
Organization of the Islamic Conference, 245
Organization of Petroleum Exporting Countries (OPEC), 332
Ottoman Empire, 236
outer-space, 72–3, 100, 106, 116
Oxfam, 217, 219, 358
ozone depletion, 30, 62, 72, 75, 90, 113, 189, 211, 241, 287, 385

Pan-Africanism, 149, 236, 249
Pan-Asianism, 236
Pan-Turkism, 236
parliaments, 7, 43–4, 200, 205, 351, 361–6, 368–71, 380, 393, 401, 404, 412–15, 422
passports, 93, 239
patriarchy, 128, 134–5, 248, 335
  see also gender
peace, 6, 14, 29, 30, 38, 56, 281–4, 289, 308, 312, 317, 349, 387
peace movements, 97, 116, 129, 218–19, 242, 376
peacekeeping operations, 71, 115, 212, 280, 282, 397–8
peasantry, 1, 23, 33–4, 42, 45, 71, 79, 239, 246–7, 341, 343–4, 376
peasant movements, 129, 218
  see also Vía Campesina
personal computer (PC), *see* computer
Philippines, government of the, 231, 234
pilgrims, 68, 74, 93, 245
plurilateralism, 187
political parties, 45, 218, 230, 351–3, 363, 370, 412
political realism, 3, 21, 121–30, 133–6, 145, 345, 387
pollution, 262, 286, 288, 312, 406
polycentrism, 4–5, 7, 29, 136, 141, 147, 156, 185–7, 202, 213, 217–18, 222, 229, 300, 348, 350–1, 354–6, 381, 383, 385, 389, 396–7, 413, 420, 425
population, 72, 87, 220, 287, 290, 298, 399
Portugal, government of, 238
positivism, 21
postal services, 67, 74, 90
post-capitalism, 23–4, 28, 159–60, 173, 183, 410
post-colonialism, 21, 132–4
post-Fordism, *see* flexibilization
post-industrial society, 23, 162, 170
postmodernism, 3, 5, 14, 21, 28–30, 38, 58, 121–5, 132–6, 154, 253, 256–9, 262–6, 271, 273–4, 308, 314, 345, 394–5
postmodernity, 47
poststructuralism, *see* postmodernism

poverty, 6, 56, 150, 174, 218, 281, 284, 289–94, 296, 305, 308, 311, 313, 317, 319, 325, 336, 341, 359, 375, 384, 387–8, 392, 396, 399–400, 404–6, 408, 410
  definition of, 290
Poverty Reduction Strategy Papers (PRSPs), 197, 368, 400
press agencies, 91
private governance, 4, 25, 128, 141–2, 145, 185–6, 188, 214–18, 222–3, 295, 304, 348, 354–6, 360, 362, 364–5, 367–8, 370, 372, 412–13, 415, 423
privatization, 38, 40, 56, 143, 172, 217, 232, 299, 323, 338, 357, 362, 382, 384
production, xv, 4, 8, 19, 21–4, 28, 60, 66, 76, 119, 122, 127, 131, 136–41, 147, 149, 152–3, 156–84, 224, 226, 254, 256, 258, 274–5, 280, 383, 385–6, 389, 392, 394–5, 406, 424
property, 141, 301, 303, 375–6

Quebec, government of, 203–5, 228

race, xviii, 6, 14, 19, 26, 34, 42, 46, 73, 80, 82–3, 97, 99, 101, 116, 119, 126, 130, 135, 137, 147–9, 154, 184, 189, 219–20, 224–6, 229, 236, 239–41, 249–50, 253–4, 278, 305, 309, 316–20, 340–6, 351, 355, 364, 371, 378–9, 387, 405, 409, 413, 422
racism, 30, 133, 212, 249, 341–3, 378–9, 389
radio, 35, 67, 79, 91–2, 100–1, 104, 117, 165, 189, 268, 273, 283, 305–6, 328, 341, 356, 358–9
radioactive fallout, 72, 75, 114
railways, 62, 68, 76, 93, 96, 104, 107, 172, 176, 268
rationalism, 4–5, 7, 8, 16, 21, 27–9, 38, 45, 58, 84, 86, 119, 122, 132–6, 142, 146, 151–4, 156, 244, 256–9, 261–6, 272, 274–5, 280, 307, 314, 345, 376, 383, 385, 393–5, 418, 424
  definition, 150
realism, *see* political realism
referenda, *see* elections
reflexivity, 5, 7, 28–9, 136, 154, 170, 256, 258, 264–6, 272, 274, 307–8, 314, 394
reformism (in policy orientation toward globalization), 3, 7–8, 38, 41–7, 259, 278, 290, 310, 383–7, 389–93, 396, 400, 404, 406, 411, 416–17, 419–21, 424
refugees, 68, 74, 105, 200, 209, 222
region-nation, 5, 226–8, 236–7, 239, 254
regionalism/regionalization, 24, 37, 39, 43, 56, 77, 78, 82, 95, 111, 125, 128, 141–3, 145–6, 185–6, 188, 190, 200, 202, 204–9, 214, 222, 224, 226, 232, 235, 243, 246, 251, 282, 298, 303, 324, 356, 362–4, 366, 368, 370, 372, 375, 378, 385, 390, 397, 403, 405, 410, 412–14, 418, 420–1
  relationship to globalization, 208–9
regulation, *see* governance
rejectionism (in policy orientation towards globalization), 3, 7, 37, 41–3, 45, 47, 230, 259–60, 278, 290, 297, 384–6, 388–90
religion, xviii, 5, 15, 26, 45, 57, 65, 73, 79–80, 87, 99, 101, 108, 116, 128, 130, 132, 147–9, 151, 163, 188–9, 191, 193, 218, 220, 224–6, 228, 239–40, 244–6, 257, 259–61, 305, 340, 346, 354, 358, 364, 367, 373, 377–8, 387, 389, 400, 404, 413
religious revivalism, 5, 18, 27, 30, 41, 43, 81, 97, 199, 219, 230, 244–5, 254, 256–64, 274, 283, 305, 307, 309, 312, 345
reproduction, 134, 175, 220, 248, 336, 344, 378
reterritorialization, 76–7
risk society, 28, 31, 279, 295, 311
rockets, *see* missiles
Royal Dutch/Shell, 354
rural areas, 14, 19, 34–5, 341, 344
  see also urban/rural divide
Rushdie affair, 260
Russia, government of, 200, 205, 212, 231

Saami, 205, 233, 235
San Marino, government of, 203
SARS, xiii, 31, 72, 279, 288, 311
satellites, 30, 64, 67, 71, 77, 81, 102–4, 170–1, 189, 199, 232, 238, 242, 245, 250, 283, 286, 306, 357
Saudi Arabia, government of, 232
Save the Children, 217

schools, *see* education
science, 32, 80, 132, 150–1, 153, 174, 244, 257–9, 261, 263–6, 307–8
secularism, 150–1, 153–4, 258–62, 264, 307–8, 376
securities markets, 31, 70, 74, 96, 110–13, 116, 142, 152, 161, 165–9, 172, 200, 266, 294, 296, 299, 323, 329, 364
security, xv, xvii, xviii, 6–8, 29–32, 47, 56, 84, 220, 263, 278–315, 348, 351, 357, 382–3, 385, 387, 390, 393, 395–404, 406, 410, 421–2, 424
semiconductors, 170, 182
sex trade, 30, 68, 175–6, 252, 337–8, 409
sexuality, xviii, 26, 45, 73, 79, 81, 83, 116, 126, 130, 134, 147, 149, 188–9, 220, 225–6, 239, 240, 250, 252, 254, 280, 316–17, 320, 345, 354, 378–9, 413
Shack/Slum Dwellers International, 220, 248
shipping, 62, 68, 76, 96, 104, 107, 142, 177, 286, 302, 406
Sikhism, 237–8, 244, 307, 377
slave trade, 89, 90, 236
Slovenia, government of, 231
social cohesion, 6, 281, 284, 296, 301, 308–10, 314, 318, 396, 404, 410
  see also community
social democracy, 42–4, 46, 383–4, 391–4, 420
  see also reformism
social justice, *see* justice
socialism, 38, 41, 45, 139, 149, 176, 195, 259, 300, 322–4, 334, 383, 392–3, 395, 409
social movements, xiv, 116, 218, 262, 320, 324, 334, 378, 393
  see also global social movements
Society for Worldwide Interbank Financial Telecommunications (SWIFT), 110–12
Somalia, government of, 192, 343
South, *see* North–South relations
South Africa, government of, 194, 201, 205–6, 249, 343, 374
Southern African Development Community (SADC), 414
Southern Common Market, *see* MERCOSUR
South Korea, government of, 196, 198, 201, 207
sovereignty, 18, 24–5, 126, 188–92, 210, 212–13, 222, 228, 233, 254, 308, 350–1, 374, 385, 388–9, 390, 420, 423
Soviet Union, 148, 192, 241
space, 16–17, 59–61, 63–6, 75, 77, 82, 84, 118, 140, 145, 147, 152, 185, 224–5, 251, 256, 258, 265, 267–9, 274, 307, 424
  see also geography
Spain, government of, 194, 234
Special Drawing Rights (SDRs), 69, 95, 109, 402, 408
special economic zone, *see* export processing zones
species extinction, *see* biodiversity
speed, 268, 273
sport, 62, 64, 73, 100, 103, 116, 163, 230, 232, 239, 251, 273
standardization, 72, 82, 99, 125, 144, 153, 208, 232, 330
state, xiv, 4–5, 8, 14, 18–19, 21, 24–5, 32, 35–9, 42, 45, 55–7, 63, 65–68, 77–8, 87, 101, 105, 124, 126–30, 132–6, 138, 141–5, 148, 152–4, 177–8, 180, 185–6, 188–203, 205–7, 212–15, 217–19, 221–2, 224–6, 228–9, 231–4, 239, 243, 251, 257, 262, 301, 305, 310, 312, 314, 320, 323–4, 330, 334, 338, 343, 345–6, 348, 350–4, 356, 360, 362, 365–8, 370–5, 378, 383–4, 386, 389, 392, 396–7, 399, 401, 403, 406, 410, 412–16, 419–20, 424–5
  see also competition state, sovereignty, statism, welfare state, workfare state
state-nation, 5, 224, 226, 228–9, 231–4, 239, 252–5, 305, 308, 354
statism, 4–5, 28, 47, 78, 136, 139–41, 147, 156, 185, 187–92, 202–3, 213–14, 218, 222, 228–9, 234, 237, 280, 300, 305, 308, 310, 315, 330, 347, 351, 353–4, 356, 381, 420, 425
  definition of, 186
statistics, xiv, 20, 86–7, 145, 175, 229, 295, 318–9, 321, 335, 340
stock markets, *see* securities markets
strategic alliance, *see* corporate alliances
stress, 269, 301, 336

structural adjustment programmes, 30–1, 33, 195, 197, 199, 211, 220, 250, 270, 286, 289, 293, 299, 303, 324, 362, 400, 404, 408
structuralism, (methodological), *see* agent-structure problem
subsidiarity, 37, 213, 410–11, 422
substate governance, 4, 18, 25, 71, 78–9, 128, 140–2, 185–6, 188, 202–6, 208, 213, 218, 222, 224, 231, 234, 348, 354–5, 360, 364–5, 370, 375, 384, 386, 392, 396, 410–16, 420
suprastate governance, 4–5, 25, 140–1, 185–6, 202, 205, 213–14, 218, 231, 234, 282, 295, 312, 324, 334, 338–9, 348, 352, 354–6, 360, 362, 365–7, 379, 385–6, 390, 392, 395–400, 408–10, 412–16, 420
supraterritoriality, 3, 17 , 20, 36, 50, 59–62, 64–70, 73, 75–8, 84, 86, 90–1, 95, 97, 101, 103, 105–9, 111–14, 116, 118, 120, 144, 147–9, 153, 156, 161, 166, 170–1, 180, 185–7, 189–91, 198–9, 202–3, 219, 225–6, 229–30, 234, 239–40, 247, 251, 253, 262, 268–9, 305, 353, 401, 424
sustainable development, 44, 204, 261–2
Sweden, government of, 194
Switzerland, government of, 205, 362

taxation, 39, 43, 68, 137–9, 144, 177–9, 189, 193, 195–7, 211, 285, 287, 291, 323–4, 329, 390, 401, 406–7, 416, 421–2
technology, 2, 17, 21, 23, 30–1, 35–6, 119, 121, 124–6, 129–30, 132–3, 135–7, 164, 171–2, 183, 191, 208, 258–9, 264–6, 271–2, 274, 283, 286, 306, 312, 314, 331, 341–2, 386–7, 417, 423
telecommunications, 62, 74, 90, 94, 103, 118, 125, 142, 144, 170, 172–3, 177–8, 181–2, 193, 204, 219, 230, 272, 286, 289, 330, 341–2, 386, 402
  see also facsimile, Internet, telegraph, telephone
telegraph, 67, 91, 95, 100–1
telephone, 35, 55, 61–2, 67, 70, 79, 82, 86, 91–2, 100–3, 108, 112, 117, 119, 139, 162, 170–2, 189, 200, 235, 238, 242, 251–2, 260, 268, 280, 283, 302, 327, 341
television, 35–6, 62, 64, 67, 79, 81, 92, 103–4, 108, 116–18, 145, 165, 170–1, 230, 232, 238, 245, 250–2, 267–8, 271, 273, 306, 309, 328, 356–7, 359
territorialism, 8, 60, 63, 65–7, 75–6, 78, 86, 91, 109, 131–40, 147–8, 151–3, 176, 185–6, 188–9, 191–4, 203, 208, 225, 227–8, 231, 240, 243–4, 251, 267–8, 280, 283, 305–6, 308, 310, 315, 326, 344, 346, 350, 381, 388–9, 391, 424–5
  see also methodological territorialism
territoriality, 61, 62, 84, 95–6, 225, 229, 233, 237, 239, 254, 257, 263, 268, 282, 300, 308, 320, 325, 348, 351, 353, 366, 413, 422, 424
  (continuing importance of), 3, 50, 64, 76–7, 156, 192, 226
terrorism, 30, 71, 115, 199, 280, 284, 311–12, 370
think tanks, 39, 150, 218, 259, 307, 376, 378
Third World, *see* North–South relations
time, 61–2, 257, 267–9, 274, 340
Tobin tax, 44, 401, 406
tourism, 68, 74, 93, 100, 104, 118, 145, 163–5, 205, 230, 235, 251, 264, 272, 305, 364, 381
toxic waste, 76, 286
trade, 19, 30–1, 33, 38, 55–7, 61, 72–3, 76, 88–90, 107–8, 117–18, 142–4, 146, 171, 173, 179, 182, 189, 200, 208–9, 214, 216, 221, 230, 285–7, 289, 291, 294, 299, 313, 318, 323, 328–30, 332, 336, 343, 360, 362, 373–4, 377, 392, 399, 401–2, 408, 414
  see also alternative trade schemes, intra-firm trade
Trade-Related Aspects of Intellectual Property Rights (TRIPS), 144, 331, 391, 405
  see also intellectual property
trade unions, *see* labour movement
transfer pricing, 38, 179, 406
transformism (as policy orientation towards globalization), 3, 7–8, 38, 41, 44–7, 259, 278, 290, 383–7, 389–90, 393, 395–6, 402, 404, 409, 411, 416–17, 420–1, 424

transgovernmental relations, *see* transstate relations
translation, 125, 376, 412
transnational corporations, *see* global companies
transnational relations, 65
transparency, 35, 40, 295, 349, 359–61, 365, 370, 380, 390, 392, 412–13, 416, 422
transstate relations, 193, 199–202, 222–3, 231, 233, 354, 356, 360, 368, 397, 413–14
  definition of, 200
transworld nation, *see* diasporas
traveller's cheques, 95, 100
Tunisia, government of, 196
Turkey, government of, 239

Uganda, government of, 195, 203
unemployment, *see* employment
United Nations (UN), 37, 39, 44, 68, 71, 73, 99–100, 106, 115, 144–6, 148, 208–9, 212–13, 219–21, 229, 235, 243, 246, 248, 282, 287, 293, 296, 300, 330, 333, 338–9, 343, 352, 356, 360, 362–3, 367–8, 370, 372–3, 376, 378–9, 391, 397–8, 400, 407–9, 415
United Nations Centre on Human Settlements (HABITAT), 205
United Nations Children's Fund (UNICEF), 289, 343–4, 379, 391, 400
United Nations Commission on Human Rights, 212
United Nations Commission for Sustainable Development, 211, 368
United Nations Conference on Trade and Development (UNCTAD), 291, 333, 339
United Nations Development Fund for Women (UNIFEM), 339
United Nations Development Programme (UNDP), 44, 209, 221, 287, 290, 333, 391, 400
United Nations Educational, Scientific and Cultural Organization (UNESCO), 71, 73, 330–1, 407
United Nations Environment Programme (UNEP), 201, 221, 287, 372, 398
United Nations Financing for Development, 333, 392
United Nations Food and Agriculture Organization (FAO), 221
United Nations Fund for Population Activities (UNFPA), 289
United Nations Global Compact, 215, 304
United Nations High Commissioner for Refugees (UNHCR), 217, 415
United States of America (USA), government of, 38, 40, 71, 73, 98, 109, 115, 127–8, 133, 135, 142, 145–6, 148, 152, 191, 194–5, 197, 205–6, 210, 212, 239, 249, 283, 286, 331, 343, 365, 372–3, 400, 419–20, 423
Universal Postal Union (UPU), 98
universal time coordination (UTC), 99
universalization, 3, 16, 49, 57–9, 81, 84–6, 281, 353
Unrepresented Nations and Peoples Organization (UNPO), 235, 376–7
urban areas, 19, 30, 34, 58, 60, 76, 164, 204–5, 341, 346
urban–rural divide, xviii, 6, 14, 48, 82, 119, 184, 278, 316–17, 319–20, 340–1, 344–5, 351, 378–9, 405, 409, 422
Uruguay Round, 247, 291, 331, 346, 362, 365
  see also Marrakech Agreement
US dollar, 62, 69, 76, 95, 111, 402

value added tax (VAT), 324
Vanuatu, government of, 373
Vía Campesina, 45, 71, 247, 344
video conference, 67, 102
Vietnam, government of, 195, 232

Wallonia, government of, 203
war, 6, 30, 71, 126, 134, 148, 150, 180, 193, 198–9, 201, 217, 222, 229–30, 242, 280–5, 311–12, 344, 351, 374, 381, 384, 388, 425
  see also world wars
Washington Consensus, xiii, 38, 40, 146, 383, 386–7, 392, 418
websites, *see* World Wide Web
welfare state, 25, 33, 38, 194–8, 222, 300, 393
western/westernization, 3, 16, 25, 49, 58–9, 81, 84–6, 88, 154, 244–5, 306, 309, 353, 364, 376–7, 421, 423

Western European Union (WEU), 363
Westphalian system, 25, 188–93, 198–9, 201–3, 213, 222, 350–1, 389, 420, 423
women, 7, 30, 33–4, 42, 45, 80, 82, 97, 99, 108, 119, 128, 130, 133, 136, 149, 175, 196, 239, 262, 302–3, 305, 310, 317, 319, 334–9, 344, 346, 354, 359, 377–8, 390, 408–9, 413, 422
women's movements, 129, 218–19, 221, 230, 240, 248, 254, 325, 339, 346
work, *see* employment
workfare state, 25
working conditions, *see* labour conditions
world (concept of), 64, 257
World Bank, 18, 31, 33–5, 39, 70, 99–100, 110–11, 141, 197, 205, 209, 211, 213, 219–21, 246, 286, 290, 292–3, 296, 306, 318, 321, 331, 339, 355, 360, 362, 365, 367, 373, 376, 391, 400, 408, 411, 414–15
World Confederation of Labour (WCL), 247
World Conservation Union (IUCN), 221
World Economic Forum (WEF), 14, 39, 220, 246–7, 325, 391
world fairs, 92–3, 100, 232
World Federation of Stock Exchanges, 216
World Gender Organization, 339
World Health Organization (WHO), 72, 145, 190, 215, 217, 289, 343, 363
World Intellectual Property Organization (WIPO), 144, 406
world literature, 116
World Meteorological Organization (WMO), 221
World Organization of United Cities and Local Governments, 204
world music, 116
world records, 116
World Resources Institute (WRI), 221
world services, 92, 104
World Social Forum (WSF), 14, 44, 219, 357, 365, 369, 418, 421
world society theory, 64, 125
world-system theory, 19, 129, 270, 345
World Tourism Organization (WTO), 216
World Trade Organization (WTO), xiii, 1, 18, 36, 71, 106, 143–4, 146, 172, 206, 208–11, 213, 215, 219, 221, 247, 288–9, 295, 298, 300, 303, 324, 330–1, 333, 343, 346, 360, 363, 365–8, 373, 375, 377, 386, 392, 396, 399, 402–3, 405, 408, 414
  see also Marrakech Agreement, Uruguay Round
World Vision International, 217
world wars, 90–1, 94, 96, 98, 115, 148, 195, 212, 236, 247
World Wide Fund for Nature (WWF), 113, 221, 241, 373
World Wide Web, 171, 230, 238, 245, 271, 356, 358, 360, 411–12

youth, 45, 116, 149, 164, 218, 237, 239–40, 250, 254, 305, 342, 345–6, 379
Yugoslavia government of, 192

Zapatistas, 45, 235
Zone of Peace and Cooperation of the South Atlantic, 207
Zoroastrianism, 87